NANOETHICS ∎

BICENTENNIAL
1807
⊛WILEY
2007
BICENTENNIAL

THE WILEY BICENTENNIAL—KNOWLEDGE FOR GENERATIONS

*E*ach generation has its unique needs and aspirations. When Charles Wiley first opened his small printing shop in lower Manhattan in 1807, it was a generation of boundless potential searching for an identity. And we were there, helping to define a new American literary tradition. Over half a century later, in the midst of the Second Industrial Revolution, it was a generation focused on building the future. Once again, we were there, supplying the critical scientific, technical, and engineering knowledge that helped frame the world. Throughout the 20th Century, and into the new millennium, nations began to reach out beyond their own borders and a new international community was born. Wiley was there, expanding its operations around the world to enable a global exchange of ideas, opinions, and know-how.

For 200 years, Wiley has been an integral part of each generation's journey, enabling the flow of information and understanding necessary to meet their needs and fulfill their aspirations. Today, bold new technologies are changing the way we live and learn. Wiley will be there, providing you the must-have knowledge you need to imagine new worlds, new possibilities, and new opportunities.

Generations come and go, but you can always count on Wiley to provide you the knowledge you need, when and where you need it!

WILLIAM J. PESCE
PRESIDENT AND CHIEF EXECUTIVE OFFICER

PETER BOOTH WILEY
CHAIRMAN OF THE BOARD

NANOETHICS
THE ETHICAL AND SOCIAL IMPLICATIONS OF NANOTECHNOLOGY

EDITED BY

Fritz Allhoff
Western Michigan University
The Nanoethics Group

Patrick Lin
Dartmouth College
The Nanoethics Group

James Moor
Dartmouth College

John Weckert
Charles Sturt University
Western Michigan University

WILEY-INTERSCIENCE
A JOHN WILEY & SON, INC., PUBLICATION

This material is based upon work supported by the U.S. National Science Foundation under Grant No. 0620694 and 0621021. Any opinions, findings, and conclusions or recommendations expressed in this material are those of the authors and do not necessarily reflect the views of the National Science Foundation.

For general information on our other products and services or for technical support, please contact our Customer Care Department within the United States at (800) 762-2974, outside the United States at (317) 572-3993 or fax (317) 572-4002.

Wiley also publishes its books in a variety of electronic formats. Some content that appears in print may not be available in electronic formats. For more information about Wiley products, visit our Web site at www.wiley.com.

Library of Congress Cataloging-in-Publication Data

Nanoethics : The Ethical and Social Implications of Nanotechnology /
Fritz Allhoff ... [et al.].
   p. cm.
 Includes index.
 ISBN 978-0-470-08416-8 (cloth) – ISBN 978-0-470-08417-5 (pbk.)
 1. Nanotechnology–Social aspects.   2. Nanotechnology–Moral and ethical
aspects.   I. Allhoff, Fritz.
 T174.7.N373199 2005
 620'.5—dc22   2007006005

10 9 8 7 6 5 4 3 2 1

To our families and to our many possible futures

CONTENTS

FOREWORD: ETHICAL CHOICES IN NANOTECHNOLOGY
DEVELOPMENT   xi
Mihail C. Roco

PREFACE   xv

CONTRIBUTORS   xvii

PART I   INTRODUCTION: THE NANOTECHNOLOGY DEBATE   1

1 NANOSCIENCE AND NANOETHICS: DEFINING THE
DISCIPLINES   3
Patrick Lin and Fritz Allhoff

2 WHY THE FUTURE DOESN'T NEED US   17
Bill Joy

3 ON THE NATIONAL AGENDA: U.S. CONGRESSIONAL
TESTIMONY ON THE SOCIETAL IMPLICATIONS OF
NANOTECHNOLOGY   40
Ray Kurzweil

PART II   BACKGROUND: NANOTECHNOLOGY IN CONTEXT   55
John Weckert

4 NANOTECH'S PROMISE: OVERCOMING HUMANITY'S
MORE PRESSING CHALLENGES   57
Christine Peterson and Jacob Heller

5 DEBATING NANOTECHNOLOGIES   71
Richard A. L. Jones

6 IN THE BEGINNING: THE U.S. NATIONAL
NANOTECHNOLOGY INITIATIVE   80
Neal Lane and Thomas Kalil

PART III   ISSUES: PREPARING FOR THE NEXT REVOLUTION   89
John Weckert

7 THE NANOTECHNOLOGY R(EVOLUTION)   91
Charles Tahan

**8 TECHNOLOGY REVOLUTIONS AND THE PROBLEM
OF PREDICTION**   101
Nick Bostrom

**9 COMPLEXITY AND UNCERTAINTY: A PRUDENTIAL
APPROACH TO NANOTECHNOLOGY**   119
Jean-Pierre Dupuy

10 THE PRECAUTIONARY PRINCIPLE IN NANOTECHNOLOGY   133
John Weckert and James Moor

PART IV   ISSUES: HEALTH AND ENVIRONMENT   147
James Moor

11 NANOTECHNOLOGY AND RISK: WHAT ARE THE ISSUES?   149
Anne Ingeborg Myhr and Roy Ambli Dalmo

**12 PERSONAL CHOICE IN THE COMING ERA
OF NANOMEDICINE**   161
Robert A. Freitas, Jr.

13 ARE WE PLAYING GOD WITH NANOENHANCEMENT?   173
Ted Peters

**14 ANTICIPATING THE ETHICAL AND POLITICAL
CHALLENGES OF HUMAN NANOTECHNOLOGIES**   185
David H. Guston, John Parsi, and Justin Tosi

PART V   ISSUES: DEMOCRACY AND POLICY   199
James Moor

**15 GLOBAL TECHNOLOGY REGULATION AND POTENTIALLY
APOCALYPTIC TECHNOLOGICAL THREATS**   201
James J. Hughes

16 DELIBERATIVE DEMOCRACY AND NANOTECHNOLOGY   215
Colin Farrelly

17 **RHETORIC OF "STAKEHOLDING"** 225
David M. Berube

18 **RULES OF ENGAGEMENT: DEMOCRACY AND DIALOGUE IN CREATING NANOTECHNOLOGY FUTURES** 241
Jack Stilgoe and James Wilsdon

PART VI ISSUES: BROADER SOCIETAL IMPACT 251
John Weckert

19 **NANOTECHNOLOGY AND PRIVACY: INSTRUCTIVE CASE OF RFID** 253
Jeroen van den Hoven

20 **NANOTECHNOLOGY AND THE MILITARY** 267
Daniel Moore

21 **CAN NANOSCIENCE BE A CATALYST FOR EDUCATIONAL REFORM?** 277
Patricia Schank, Joseph Krajcik, and Molly Yunker

22 **IMPACT OF NANOTECHNOLOGIES ON DEVELOPING COUNTRIES** 291
Joachim Schummer

PART VII ISSUES: THE DISTANT FUTURE? 309
Fritz Allhoff

23 **CHALLENGES AND PITFALLS OF EXPONENTIAL MANUFACTURING** 311
Mike Treder and Chris Phoenix

24 **NANOETHICS AND THE HIGH FRONTIER** 323
Tihamer Toth-Fejel and Christopher Dodsworth

25 **ETHICS FOR ARTIFICIAL INTELLECTS** 339
J. Storrs Hall

26 **NANOTECHNOLOGY AND LIFE EXTENSION** 353
Sebastian Sethe

INDEX 367

FOREWORD ▐

Ethical Choices in Nanotechnology Development

Mihail C. Roco

Nanotechnology products are reaching the market with an annual growth rate of over 25 percent, stimulated by a worldwide research investment in 2006 exceeding $10 billion. Both promises and concerns about the societal implications of this new technology are being voiced with increasing frequency. The concerns must be answered to the satisfaction of both the public and experts. Without an attention to ethics, it would not be possible to ensure efficient and harmonious development, to cooperate between people and organizations, to make the best investment choices, to prevent harm to other people, and to diminish undesirable socioeconomic implications.

In a general sense, of course, these concerns are very old. Science and technology have been at the core of human endeavor for as long as we have *been* human. Indeed, human potential and technological development are coevolving, and quality of life has increased tremendously with technological advancements. However, since antiquity, it has been a perception that technological developments are not friendly to human nature—maybe because of its transforming changes. When the Greek god Prometheus taught humans to use fire and other tools, he also told them that this will bring an *"an eternity of torture."*

As old as these concerns are, however, they seem to have particular resonance when it comes to nanotechnology—not least because nanotechnology allows us to work at the very foundation of matter, the first level of organization for both living and man-made systems. At this scale all fundamental structures, properties, and functions of materials and devices are established. This is the lowest scale for transforming capabilities (manufacturing) for practical uses.

Nanotechnology creates a broad technological platform for many fields of application. The potential benefits are large, and so are the potential unexpected consequences. We already know that nanoparticles may penetrate and accumulate in human tissue, designed molecules may self-assemble into artificial tissues, active nanosystems may evolve in time, nanostructured implants may affect the heart and mind, hybrid systems may interface with biological systems, and systematic control of DNA with nanotechnology tools may fundamentally alter genetics. For these and other reasons, societal and in particular the multifaceted ethical aspects need to be fully considered from the beginning to realize the most equitable results among people, organizations, and countries.

The immediate ethical concerns from the first generation of nanoproducts are environmental, health, and safety effects. However, we should also consider issues that may arise farther in the future, such as implications that nanotechnology might have on information access, privacy, welfare, and human dignity. Also, we need to invest in long-term societal needs for basic resources (such as water, energy, and food) and maintaining a clean, shared environment. Responding and interacting with the public and civil organizations on all these aspects may be the ultimate test for the successful introduction of nanotechnology. After all, political leaders, not academic leaders, will ultimately craft the laws governing nanotechnology's future, though this is not to say that the latter should not inform the former.

Ethical concerns in the development of nanotechnology should be a priority in *governance*. The governance of nanotechnology needs to be transformative, responsible (including professional ethics), visionary, and inclusive. All indications are that the future needs us. Novel, converging technologies are key drivers for change in industry, medicine, and society and such changes require specific policies and governance. One should consider long-term anticipatory scenarios and multistakeholder engagement. Until very recently, broad nanoscale investigations such as understanding biological systems, connecting the brain and mind, and simulating and controlling large nanosystems have been beyond the reach of human action. Now a variety of new discoveries and tools allow scientists, engineers, doctors, philosophers, and economists to study and even to transform those systems. Such transformations are expected to fundamentally affect human progress. As science and technology advance, new ethical issues are raised. The approach for risk governance suggested by the International Risk Governance Council (www.irgc.org) considers two reference frameworks for nanotechnology: one for passive nanostructures and a second for active nanoscale devices and systems. Ethical issues are relevant to both frameworks, and their relevance only increases over time. This volume is a step in that direction.

There is a *dilemma of choices* in the complex societal system where nanotechnology and social interactions develop. First, beyond a few very simple principles, the rules of ethical behavior are not universally accepted. They are functions of group interests, ideologies, and religions. Also, this is a decision to be made not necessarily by scientists using a systematic approach, but by elected leaders and civil and many other organizations tasked to make decisions about governance in a complex, evolving society. Should we give priority to societal benefits or else to individual rights? For example, it would be unethical to limit the development of basic needs of a large cross section of population for the interest of smaller groups. However, it is unethical to affect others without consent. Democratic principles for equal opportunity, access to information, knowledge, and development are other challenges. Experts, the public, and others need information and must participate in order to make best choices. Progress in the long term cannot be derailed even if the road is not straight. Progress is faster with proper vision and choices guided by moral values, transformative goals, collective benefits, and professional ethics.

The promise of nanotechnology, however, will not be realized by simply supporting research. Just as nanotechnology is changing how we think about unity of matter at the nanoscale and manufacturing, it is also changing how we think about the management of the research enterprise. Quite simply, it is changing some of our long-held and often-cherished methods of governing science and engineering. The ideas advanced in this volume may help foster new approaches.

Nanotechnology is entering new science and engineering challenges such as building nanomachines and nanosystems, designing new molecules, developing nanobiotechnology and nanobiomedicine, agricultural products, energy conversion, and environment. All trends for published papers, patents, and worldwide investments experience exponential growth, with potential inflexion points in several years. We have to make deliberate choices for future developments. Ethical aspects are increasing in relative importance, and their upstream consideration may be a key for the successful and sustained application of nanotechnology.

This volume includes essays from an outstanding group of distinguished contributors in key aspects of "nanoethics," from large intellectual strokes on major trends made by Ray Kurzweil and Bill Joy to basic concepts on complexity and precautionary principle, health and environmental concerns, democracy and policy, society, economics and equity, and visionary ideas. This is a rich material and not surprisingly with many opinions. The reader is exposed to the basic definitions on ethics, research issues, philosophical dimensions, and economical and political implications of this emerging field. The entire collection of contributions stimulates thinking about what is specific for nanotechnology and why ethics is important in the context of the new technology development. It provides intellectual and practical guidance on addressing ethical concerns and what research is needed and what directions may take. This is a timely publication that is prepared to become a reference in the field of societal dimensions of nanotechnology.

PREFACE

In the last several months and as recently as this morning, nanotechnology has made the news in such a way that immediately triggers ethical and social questions—or "nanoethics" questions. For instance, invisibility cloaks that can hide objects or people seem to raise serious privacy and national security issues. "Bionic hornets" that are designed to track and hunt down military insurgents resurrect worries about another arms race and misuse by terrorists.

Granted, it may take years to perfect such fantastic innovations—though it is not too early to begin thinking through their implications—but nanoethics is also highly relevant today. For instance, nanotechnology has already made its way into ordinary products, from clothing to sports equipment to cosmetics and much more, raising concerns about both consumer and manufacturing worker health risks. The environment and animals are similarly at potential risk from such products as a "nanotechnology washing machine" that releases over 100 quadrillion silver ions into the water to better sanitize clothes.

Nanoethics, then, poses such broad questions as: Are companies morally required to address or otherwise mitigate these risks before such products reach the marketplace? How will our expectations or conception of privacy change in the face of virtually invisible surveillance devices? If we can embed ever-shrinking devices into our bodies to enhance physical and mental performance, what are the implications for personal identity as well as society at large?

But it is far from being all bad news with nanotechnology. Billed as the "Next Industrial Revolution," it is predicted to provide profound benefits to the world, such as cleaner air and water, affordable energy, more effective medical treatments, much greater computing power, and more—benefits that perhaps will ultimately overshadow any harms (though that does not relieve us of the obligation to prevent such harms).

However, nanoethics even has a role in these positive areas in asking, for instance: What is our moral obligation to help developing countries with these advances? How might radical medical advances change our notion of disease as well as the doctor–patient relationship? If nanotechnology might help extend our life span by 20, 50, 100, or even 1000 years and more, as some predict, is cheating death to that extent necessarily a "good" thing, and how disruptive would that be to society, for example, with respect to overpopulation and pensions?

This anthology was conceived to help spark a thoughtful discussion on the full range of issues in nanoethics, which we found missing in the literary marketplace. It is not enough to focus on just near-term questions, such as related to regulation and risks with respect to the environment, health, and safety; nanoethics is far richer than that, as the reader might already see from just the preceding discussion. In this volume, we also tackle other important and far-reaching issues, from the need for educational reform to the ethics of nano-enabled space exploration and everything in between.

Further, we designed this anthology to be accessible to a broad audience with little familiarity with either nanotechnology or ethics, particularly since it is the general public who may be the largest beneficiary—or victim—of nanotechnology, and so the everyday person needs to understand its possible impact. At the same time, this collection of essays is valuable for students as well as industry stakeholders, policymakers, and others to better understand the issues and debate.

Finally, we need to thank many individuals for enabling us to create such an ambitious volume, the first of its kind. Our contributors truly represent the "A-list" in nanotechnology and nanoethics, hailing from leading universities such as Oxford, Cambridge, Stanford, Berkeley, Dartmouth, and other top organizations. We are indebted to the editors and staff at Wiley, who include Amy Byers, Darla Henderson, Becky Amos, Lisa Van Horn, and others. Special thanks are also owed to those who have supported our efforts and provided guidance: Jeff Dean, Priscilla Regan, Alison Niedbalski, Burleigh Wilkins, Brenna Robertson, and undoubtedly others. And we thank the U.S. National Science Foundation for providing support for our investigations, under Grant numbers 0620694 (to Western Michigan University) and 0621021 (to Dartmouth College).

Most of all, we thank you—the reader—for your interest in nanotechnology and its ethics. By engaging the issues as early as possible, we can together clear a responsible path for emerging sciences, such as nanotechnology, to help humanity realize its great potential.

FRITZ ALLHOFF
PATRICK LIN
JAMES MOOR
JOHN WECKERT

Kalamazoo, Michigan
Hanover, New Hampshire
March 2007

CONTRIBUTORS

EDITORS

Fritz Allhoff, Ph.D., is an assistant professor of philosophy at Western Michigan University. He is the cofounder of The Nanoethics Group (www.nanoethics.org), a nonpartisan organization that explores social, ethical, and legal questions pertaining to nanotechnology. Fritz recently held fellowships at both the American Medical Association's Institute for Ethics for bioethics research and The Australian National University for nanoethics research. He is the author or editor of several books in philosophy and ethics, including two nanoethics anthologies and a nanoethics monograph to date. Finally, he is the principal investigator on a recent award from the National Science Foundation to investigate ethical issues pertaining to nanotechnology and human enhancement.

Patrick Lin, Ph.D., is the director and cofounder of The Nanoethics Group (www.nanoethics.org), a nonpartisan and independent organization focused on the social and ethical impact of emerging technologies, especially nanotechnology. He is also a postdoctoral associate at Dartmouth College and an adjunct faculty member at Western Michigan University. Patrick is currently working on several books as well as a project funded by the National Science Foundation to study the ethics of human enhancement and nanotechnology. He earned his B.A. from the University of California at Berkeley and his M.A. and Ph.D. from the University of California at Santa Barbara.

James Moor is a professor of philosophy at Dartmouth College and is an adjunct professor with The Centre for Applied Philosophy and Public Ethics (CAPPE) at the Australian National University. His publications include work on computer ethics, nanoethics, philosophy of artificial intelligence, philosophy of mind, philosophy of science, and logic. He is editor-in-chief of the journal *Minds and Machines* and associate editor of the journal *Nanoethics*. He is the president of the International Society for Ethics and Information Technology (INSEIT) and has received the American Computing Machinery SIGCAS Making a Difference Award and the American Philosophical Association Barwise Prize.

John Weckert is a professorial fellow at the Centre for Applied Philosophy and Public Ethics, a center funded by the Australian Research Council based at Charles Sturt University, the University of Melbourne, and the Australian National University. He has published widely on the ethics of information and communication technology and is the founding editor-in-chief of the journal *Nanoethics: Ethics for Technologies that Converge at the Nanoscale*.

CHAPTER AUTHORS

David M. Berube has been a principal or coprincipal investigator on four National Science Foundation societal and ethical grants totaling nearly $4 million. He has published dozens of articles in argumentation and in nanoscience and technology risk and policy studies. He has written two books, including *Nanohype: Beyond the Nanotechnology Buzz* (2006). He has degrees in psychology, biology, and communication, and he is a full professor in the University of South Carolina graduate school, a member of the NanoCenter, and the government and industrial coordinator in the *nano*Science and Technology Studies program. He teaches graduate courses in risk communication, arguments in science and technology, and technical film.

Nick Bostrom is director of the Future of Humanity Institute at Oxford University. His wide research interests include the foundations of probability theory, scientific methodology, ethics, and global catastrophic risk. He is a leading thinker on the ethics of human enhancement and on the consequences of anticipated future technologies such as nanotechnology and artificial intelligence. He has published more than 100 articles in journals such as *Nature, Journal of Philosophy, Mind*, and *Ethics*, and he is the author or editor of three books. His writings have been translated into more than 15 different languages.

Roy Ambli Dalmo is currently a researcher funded by the European Union project IMAQUANIM (Improved Immunity of Aquacultured Animals) at the Department of Marine Biotechnology at the University of Tromsø, Norway. He is also coordinating projects on safety aspects of DNA vaccines (with A. I. Myhr) and the development of targeting nanoparticle-based vaccines on fish.

Christopher Dodsworth earned a Ph.D. in philosophy at the University of Michigan in Ann Arbor, with primary interests in metaethics (especially questions concerning the nature and origin of the normativity of moral obligations) and in nearly all areas of philosophy of religion. With also a B.S. and an M.S. in electrical engineering, he is working as a research scientist for General Dynamics Advanced Information Systems.

Jean-Pierre Dupuy is professor of social and political philosophy at École Polytechnique, Paris. He also holds a number of appointments at Stanford University, including full professor in the French and political science departments, researcher at the Center for the Study of Language and Information (CSLI), Science-Technology-Society Program affiliate, and a fellow of the Symbolic Systems Forum. He is also a member of Académie Française des Technologies. In addition to several books in French, his latest ones are *The Mechanization of the Mind— On the Origins of Cognitive Science* (Princeton University Press, 2000) and *Self-Deception and Paradoxes of Rationality* (CSLI Publications, Stanford University, 1998).

Colin Farrelly is assistant professor in the Department of Political Science (cross appointed with the Department of Philosophy) at the University of Waterloo in Canada.

Colin is a political philosopher, and his published articles include papers on genetic intervention, ideal theory, historical materialism, and freedom of expression. He is the author of *An Introduction to Contemporary Political Theory* (Sage Publications, 2004). He was most recently a research fellow at the Centre for the Study of Social Justice at Oxford University where he worked on a book on genetics and justice.

Robert A. Freitas, Jr. J.D., published the first detailed technical design study of a medical nanorobot ever in a peer-reviewed mainstream biomedical journal and is the author of *Nanomedicine* (www.nanomedicine.com), the first book-length technical discussion of the medical applications of nanotechnology and medical nanorobotics. Volume I was published in October 1999 by Landes Bioscience while Freitas was a research fellow at the Institute for Molecular Manufacturing (IMM) in Palo Alto, California. Freitas published Volume IIA in October 2003 while serving as a research scientist at Zyvex Corp., a nanotechnology company in Richardson, Texas, during 2000–2004. Freitas (www.rfreitas.com) is now completing Volumes IIB and III as senior research fellow at IMM, and in 2006 founded the Nanofactory Collaboration (www.MolecularAssembler.com/Nanofactory).

David H. Guston is professor of political science and associate director of the Consortium for Science, Policy and Outcomes at Arizona State University. He is also director of the Center for Nanotechnology in Society at ASU, a National Science Foundation–designated Nano-scale Science and Engineering Center. Guston's *Between Politics and Science* (Cambridge University Press, 2000) won the 2002 Don K. Price Prize from the American Political Science Association for best book in science and technology policy. He is the North American editor of the journal *Science and Public Policy*. Guston holds a B.A. from Yale and a Ph.D. from MIT and performed postdoctoral training at Harvard. He is a fellow of the American Association for the Advancement of Science.

J. Storrs Hall, Ph.D., is a research fellow at the Institute of Molecular Manufacturing as well as an independent scientist and author. His most recent book is *Nanofuture: What's Next for Nanotechnology* (Prometheus, 2005). He is currently writing a book about artificial intelligence and machine ethics. He was the founding chief scientist of Nanorex, Inc. His research background includes artificial intelligence, compilers, microprocessor design, massively parallel processor design, computer-aided design software, and automated multilevel design. His inventions include swarm robotic systems, self-bootstrapping automated manufacturing systems, adiabatic logic, and agoric operating systems.

Jacob Heller is a policy associate for the Foresight Nanotech Institute. A Truman Scholar, he received his B.A. in politics and economics from Pitzer College. Jacob is the founder and director of A Computer in Every Home, an organization that provides free computers and technical education to needy students.

James J. Hughes, Ph.D. teaches health policy at Trinity College in Hartford, Connecticut. Hughes also serves as the executive director of the World Transhumanist Association (transhumanism.org) and its affiliated Institute for Ethics and Emerging

Technologies (ieet.org). Hughes produces the weekly syndicated public affairs talk show *Changesurfer Radio* and is the author of *Citizen Cyborg: Why Democratic Societies Must Respond to the Redesigned Human of the Future.* He is a fellow of the World Academy of Arts and Sciences.

Richard A. L. Jones is professor of physics at the University of Sheffield. His first degree and Ph.D. in physics both come from Cambridge University. Following postdoctoral work at Cornell University, he was a lecturer at the University of Cambridge's Cavendish Laboratory, before moving to Sheffield in 1998. He is an experimental physicist whose research focuses on the properties of macromolecules near interfaces and the exploitation of these to make functional devices. In addition to his experimental program in nanoscale science, he also comments extensively on the social and economic implications of nanotechnology. In 2006 he was elected a fellow of the Royal Society.

Bill Joy is a partner at Kleiner Perkins Caufield & Byers where he does green technology venture investing. He was a cofounder and chief scientist of Sun Microsystems. While a graduate student at the University of California at Berkeley, he designed and implemented the Berkeley version of UNIX and its pioneering support for the Internet protocols. Author of more than 40 patents, Bill is a member of the National Academy of Engineering and a fellow of the American Academy of Arts and Sciences.

Thomas Kalil is special assistant to the chancellor for science and technology at the University of California at Berkeley, was deputy assistant to the president for technology and economic policy, and deputy director of the National Economic Council during the Clinton administration.

Joseph Krajcik, a professor of science education in the School of Education at the University of Michigan, works with science teachers to bring about sustained change by creating classroom environments in which students use learning technologies to find solutions to important intellectual questions that subsume important learning goals. He has authored and coauthored more than 100 manuscripts and makes frequent presentations on his research as well presentations that translate research findings into classroom practice. He received a Ph.D. in science education from the University of Iowa and, before that, taught high-school chemistry for seven years.

Ray Kurzweil, as one of the leading inventors of our time, has been called the "rightful heir to Thomas Edison" by the media and "the best at predicting the future of artificial intelligence" by Bill Gates. He invented the first print-to-speech reading machine, the first CCD flat-bed scanner, and many other breakthroughs. He received the National Medal of Technology from President Clinton, was inducted into the Inventor's Hall of Fame, has 13 honorary doctorates, and received awards from three U.S. presidents. Ray is also the author of four national best-sellers, including *The Singularity is Near.* For more information, visit www.kurzweilAI.net.

Neal Lane is a Malcolm Gillis University professor, senior fellow of the James A. Baker III Institute for Public Policy, and member of the Department of Physics and

Astronomy at Rice University. He was director of the National Science Foundation from 1993 to 1998 and science advisor to President Clinton beginning in 1998.

Daniel Moore holds a Ph.D. in materials science and engineering from Georgia Tech, with a research focus on nanoscale materials synthesis and design. He received a B.A. in physics and mathematics from the University of Chicago. At Georgia Tech, Daniel served on the institute's honor committee and received numerous fellowships, including the MacArthur Foundation's Sam Nunn Security Program fellowship. With a minor in international affairs, his fellowship research focused on the use of nanotechnology in international affairs, both in military use and in solving issues in the developing world.

Anne Ingeborg Myhr is employed as a senior scientist at The Norwegian Institute of Gene Ecology in Tromsø, Norway. She has an M.A. in biotechnology from NTNU, Trondheim, and a Ph.D. from the University of Tromsø. The title of her Ph.D. thesis was "Precaution, Context and Sustainability. A Study of How Ethical Values May Be Involved in Risk Governance of GMOs." Myhr's present research engagements are within the use of DNA vaccines (experimental and theoretical work), elaboration of philosophical perspectives on genetically modified organisms (GMOs), and capacity building in risk assessment and management of GMO use and release in the third world. She has also been involved in the Norwegian Research Council's foresight processes on nanotechnology and is a member of the National Committee for Research Ethics in Science and Technology.

John Parsi graduated from Arizona State University with a B.S. in political science and a B.A. in sociology in May of 2002. After graduation, John accepted a position as assistant director of the documentary film company Quattro Terzi in Milan, Italy. In spring of 2004, John returned to Arizona State to pursue a Ph.D. in political science, receiving his M.A. in May 2006. John began his work for the Center for Nanotechnology in Society in the fall of 2005. His work spans the major political and philosophical questions concerning contemporary society within both the political and scientific realms. John's major projects regard the exploration of the political and philosophical issues of human enhancement, media representations of marginalized groups, and theoretical framing of the global social justice movement. Within the sphere of human enhancement, John is working on the need for anticipatory governance when examining the political and ethical dimensions of advancing technology.

Ted Peters is professor of systematic theology at Pacific Lutheran Theological Seminary and the Graduate Theological Union in Berkeley, California. He coedits *Theology and Science*, published by the Center for Theology and the Natural Sciences. He is author of *Playing God? Genetic Determinism and Human Freedom* (Routledge, rev. ed., 2003); *Science, Theology, and Ethics* (Ashgate, 2003); and *Anticipating Omega* (Vandenhoeck & Ruprecht, 2006). He is coauthor of *Can You Believe in God and Evolution?* (Abingdon, 2006) and coeditor of *Bridging Science and Religion* (Fortress, 2003). He currently serves on the Scientific and Medical Accountability Standards Committee of the California Institute for Regenerative Medicine.

Christine Peterson is founder and vice president of Foresight Nanotechnology Institute, the leading nanotechnology public interest group, educating the public, researchers, and policymakers on nanotechnology and policy issues. She directs the Foresight Institute Feynman prizes, Foresight conferences on molecular nanotechnology, and Foresight Vision Weekends. She serves on the advisory board of the International Council on Nanotechnology, the editorial advisory board of NASA's *Nanotech Briefs*, and California's Blue Ribbon Task Force on Nanotechnology. She is coauthor of *Unbounding the Future: the Nanotechnology Revolution* (1991). An interest in high-technology intellectual property issues led her to coin the term "open-source software."

Chris Phoenix, director of research of the Center for Responsible Nanotechnology, has studied nanotechnology and molecular manufacturing for more than 18 years. He obtained his B.S. in symbolic systems and M.S. in computer science from Stanford University in 1991. From 1991 to 1997, he worked as an embedded software engineer at Electronics for Imaging. In 1997, he left the software field to concentrate on dyslexia correction and research. Since 2000, he has focused on studying and writing about molecular manufacturing. Chris is a published author in nanotechnology and nanomedical research, and he maintains close contacts with many leading researchers in the field.

Mihail C. Roco is senior advisor for nanotechnology at the National Science Foundation and a key architect of the National Nanotechnology Initiative. Under his chairmanship, the NNI budget has increased about 10-fold to $1.3 billion in 2006. Prior to joining the National Science Foundation, he was professor of mechanical engineering. Roco is credited with 13 inventions and has authored/coauthored over 200 scientific and engineering articles as well as 12 books and manuals. He is the editor-in-chief of the *Journal of Nanoparticle Research*. Roco is a correspondent member of the Swiss Academy of Engineering Sciences, a fellow of the ASME, a fellow of the AIChE, and a fellow of the Institute of Physics. He was named engineer of the year in the United States in 1999 and 2004 by the National Society of Professional Engineers and NSF and a top technology leader of 2004 by Scientific American.

Patricia Schank, a computer scientist in the Center for Technology in Learning at SRI International, works with experts and practitioners in science education to develop innovative learning technology. As the principal investigator for NanoSense, she leads the development of nanoscience curricula for high school and workshops to advance nanoscience education. She has also led the development of software to help students create representations of chemical phenomena, simulation-based assessments to measure complex science learning, and an online community to support teacher professional development. She has an M.S. in computer science and a Ph.D. in education from the University of California at Berkeley.

Joachim Schummer is currently the Heisenberg Fellow at the University of Darmstadt, Germany, and adjunct professor at the University of South Carolina, to study philosophical, societal, and ethical dimensions of nanotechnologies, on which he has published a dozen papers and edited four special issues and three volumes:

Discovering the Nanoscale (IOS Press 2004, with Davis Baird and Alfred Nordmann), *Nanotechnology Challenges* (World Scientific, 2006, with Davis Baird), and *Nanotechnologien im Kontext* (AKA, 2006, with Alfred Nordmann and Astrid Schwarz). He serves on several international boards, including the UNESCO expert group on nanotechnology and ethics. He is also the editor-in-chief of *HYLE: International Journal for Philosophy of Chemistry* (since 1995).

Sebastian Sethe holds the position of researcher at the Sheffield Institute for Biotechnological Law and Ethics, United Kingdom. He has a Ph.D. in life extension innovation management as well as an M.A. in biotechnological law and ethics. He is a coeditor on two major anthologies on the science and ethics of life extension. Sebastian is also coauthor on a number of "hard science" review papers in biomedicine and cytology. He has served in the past as a director for the not-for-profit organization Immortality Institute (www.ImmInst.org), a leading international grass-roots forum for discussions and knowledge exchange on the scientific conquest of death.

Jack Stilgoe joined Demos as a researcher in January 2005. He works on a range of science and innovation projects. Previously, he was a research fellow in the Science and Technology Studies Department at University College, London, where he looked at debates between scientists and the public about the possible health risks of mobile phones. He has a degree in economics, an M.Sc. in science policy, and a Ph.D. in the sociology of science. He has recently published papers in the journals *Science and Public Policy* and *Public Understanding of Science*.

Charles Tahan is a National Science Foundation Distinguished International Postdoctoral Research Fellow, located at the Cavendish Laboratory of the University of Cambridge (United Kingdom) with extended visits to the Centre for Quantum Computer Technology (Australia) and the University of Tokyo (Japan). His research focuses on the intersection of quantum physics, nanotechnology, and information theory, including quantum electronics and optics, quantum many-body physics in mesoscopic systems, and quantum information-processing devices. While in the Physics Department of the University of Wisconsin-Madison, he worked with professors in sociology, public affairs, history of science, and engineering to codevelop and teach a course on nanotechnology and its societal implications.

Justin Tosi is a political science Ph.D. student at Arizona State University. He holds a B.A. in politics and philosophy from the University of Virginia.

Tihamer Toth-Fejel is a research engineer at General Dynamics. He is also on the scientific advisory board for Nanorex and on the steering committee of the Nanomanufacturing Technical Group (Society of Manufacturing Engineers). He has been involved with and published in nanotechnology for over two decades, ever since nanotechnology pioneer Eric Drexler off-handedly solved an intractable problem in Toth-Fejel's master's thesis when they were both graduate students. Tihamer's recent projects include two design studies for the NASA Institute for Advanced Concepts: one for a Kinematic Cellular Automata type of self-replicating system and another for a molecular nanocube approach to nanofactories. He received his B.S. in electrical engineering from Lehigh University and his M.S. in electrical engineering from the University of Notre Dame.

Mike Treder is a professional writer, speaker, and activist with a background in media and communications. In 2002, he cofounded the Center for Responsible Nanotechnology (CRN), a nonprofit research and advocacy organization. CRN's goal is the creation and implementation of wise, comprehensive, and balanced plans for global management of molecular manufacturing. As an accomplished presenter on the societal implications of emerging technologies, Mike has addressed conferences and groups in the United States, Canada, Great Britain, Spain, Germany, Italy, Switzerland, Australia, New Zealand, and Brazil.

Jeroen van den Hoven is full professor of ethics at Delft University of Technology, The Netherlands. He is editor-in-chief of the journal *Ethics and Information Technology*. An edited volume on information technology and moral philosophy (with John Weckert) is appearing in 2007 with Cambridge University Press. Van den Hoven is also member of Advisory Group for IT of the European Commission.

James Wilsdon is head of science and innovation at Demos. He advises a wide range of organizations on science policy, emerging technologies, democracy, and sustainability, and his recent publications include *See-through Science: Why Public Engagement Needs to Move Upstream* (with Rebecca Willis, Demos, 2004); *Masters of the Universe: Science, Politics and the New Space Race* (with Melissa Mean, Demos, 2004); *The Adaptive State: Strategies for Personalising the Public Realm* (edited with Tom Bentley, Demos, 2003); and *Digital Futures: Living in a Networked World* (Earthscan, 2001). He is an honorary research fellow at Lancaster University and an associate director of Forum for the Future.

Molly Yunker, a doctoral student in science education in the School of Education at the University of Michigan, works with students to help them develop a deeper conceptual understanding of various science topics, including nanoscience and earth science concepts. Molly received a B.S. and M.S. in geological sciences from Case Western Reserve University, where her work focused on experimental studies of interdiffusion of metals at high temperatures and high pressures.

PART I

INTRODUCTION: THE NANOTECHNOLOGY DEBATE

NANOSCIENCE AND NANOETHICS: DEFINING THE DISCIPLINES

Patrick Lin and Fritz Allhoff

Nanoethics, or the study of nanotechnology's ethical and social implications, is an emerging but controversial field. Outside of the industry and academia, most people are first introduced to nanotechnology through fictional works that posit scenarios—which scientists largely reject—of self-replicating "nanobots" running amok like a pandemic virus (Crichton, 2002). In the mainstream media, we are beginning to hear more reports about the risks nanotechnology poses on the environment, health, and safety, with conflicting reports from within the industry.

But within the nanotechnology industry, there is a strange schizophrenia afoot. We have heard about the wonderful things that nanotechnology might enable—not just today's mundane products, such as better sports equipment or cosmetics, but the truly fantastic applications. Our imagination seems to be our only limit, as scientists and other experts predict such innovations as toxin-eating nanobots, exoskeletons that enable us to leap walls in a single bound, affordable space travel for everyone, nanofactories that can make anything we want, and even near immortality.

Yet nearly in the same breath many advocates continue to deny or to ignore that nanotechnology will cause any significant disruptions or raise any serious ethical questions that we have to worry about—dismissively labeling these as "hype" (e.g., The Nanotech Schism, 2004). But how is this possible? How can such a brave new science, one that is so full of potential that it has been called the "Next Industrial Revolution" by governments and scientists, not also impact our relationships, society, environment, economy, or even global politics in profound ways (e.g., National Science and Technology Council, 2000)?

Let's take a step back and consider *any* given technology we have created: gunpowder, the printing press, the camera, the automobile, nuclear power, the computer, Prozac, Viagra, the mobile phone, the Internet. Undoubtedly, these have brought us much good, but each has also changed society in important, fundamental ways and caused new problems, such as increased pollution, urban sprawl, cybercrimes, privacy concerns, intellectual property concerns, drug dependencies, new cases of sexually transmitted diseases, other unintended health problems, mutually assured destruction, and much more. The point here is not that we would have been better off without these inventions. Rather, we should come to terms that our creations can have unintended or unforeseen consequences.

Many of the social problems associated with the aforementioned technologies might have been anticipated and mitigated with some forethought. This is a lesson not lost on policymakers and scientists today, for instance, in having spent millions of dollars to study the ethical implications of decoding the human genome, such as privacy and genetic discrimination concerns. The same lesson, however, apparently was lost on the commercial biotechnology industry, which recently discovered that by ignoring its ethical and social issues—specifically, the possible harm from genetically modified foods on human health and the environment—they invited a public backlash that crippled progress and sent corporate stocks plummeting.

To be sure, no one expects ethicists, scientists, policymakers, and other experts to anticipate and address all possible scenarios. It is a plain fact of the human condition that we do not and cannot know everything. We do not fault Thomas Edison, for instance, for the copyright-violating devices that his phonograph would inspire, or Henry Ford for the agonizing commutes we endure daily, or Bill Gates for the email "spam" we receive.

And when we try to make predictions about technology, we are often wrong. Consider the following infamous predictions: "This 'telephone' has too many shortcomings to be seriously considered as a means of communication. The device is inherently of no value to us" (Western Union, 1876); "Who the hell wants to hear actors talk?" (H. M. Warner, Warner Brothers, 1927); "I think there is a world market for maybe five computers" (Thomas Watson, chairman of IBM, 1943); "With over 50 foreign cars already on sale here, the Japanese auto industry isn't likely to carve out a big slice of the U.S. market" (*BusinessWeek*, August 2, 1968); and "There is no reason anyone would want a computer in their home" (Ken Olson, founder of Digital Equipment Corp., 1977).

Clearly, it is easy to be too conservative or short-sighted in estimating the future impact of technology. The dangers associated with technology can likewise be underestimated, for instance, as was the case with asbestos, lead paint, and the pesticide DDT. But this is not just a failing of our distant past. In 2006 alone, a study has suggested that mobile phones, after all our years of using them, can cause brain tumors and infertility (Hardell et al., 2006). Another study showed that computer manufacturing workers, after decades on the job, are at a much greater risk of death from cancer and other illnesses (Clapp, 2006). In the same year, the U.S. Environmental Protection Agency (EPA) concluded that a key chemical (PFOA) used to make Teflon—the ubiquitous material used for the last

50 years in nonstick cookware, carpeting, clothing, food packaging, and thousands of other products and traces of which can be found in the blood of nearly everyone in the United States and other developed nations—is a carcinogen (EPA, 2006).

At the other end of the spectrum, some predictions also overestimate the role of technology, as was the case with robotic maids, flying cars, meal-in-a-pill, and the death of privacy, for instance. So it is no surprise that the impact of nanotechnology should be both understated and overhyped, and in either case, we can trust that it will have consequences that we have not even considered or imagined. However, not being certain about the future does not relieve us of any moral obligation to investigate the issues we can anticipate as being reasonable possibilities or relevant. From the rapid pace of new technologies entering our lives, we can now appreciate that such technologies will have societal implications, for better or worse. Learning from history, we also now understand that we have a responsibility to consider these scenarios in advance to mitigate any harms, if not also to maximize benefits.

Discourse into the ethical and social dimensions of nanotechnology—so-called nanoethics—is therefore critical to guide the development of nanotechnology. This anthology provides a broad introduction to nanoethics, with contributions by some of the most respected names in the field.

1. WHAT IS NANOTECHNOLOGY?*

First, we need to be clear on what nanotechnology is before we can appreciate the ethical and social questions that arise therein. Nanotechnology is a new category of technology that involves the precise manipulation of materials at the molecular level or a scale of roughly 1 to 100 nanometers—with a nanometer equaling one-billionth of a meter—in ways that exploit novel properties that emerge at that scale. How small exactly is a billionth of a meter? As one journalist had put it, "If a nanometer were somehow magnified to appear as long as the nose on your face, then a red blood cell would appear the size of the Empire State Building, a human hair would be about two or three miles wide, one of your fingers would span the continental United States, and a normal person would be about as tall as six or seven planet Earths piled atop one another" (Keiper, 2003, p. 18).

Working at the nanoscale, it turns out that ordinary materials can have extraordinary properties about which we are still learning. At the nanoscale, quantum physics begins to play a key role in the behavior of materials, and the large surface-to-volume ratio of elements means that they are much more reactive. So, for instance, things that are brittle at the ordinary scale may possess superstrength at the nanoscale, and things that do not normally conduct electricity now might at the nanoscale, among other surprising changes to physical and chemical properties.

As a specific example of how properties change with scale, aluminum is used ubiquitously to make harmless soda cans, but in fine powder form, it can explode

---

* Much of the next four sections is reprinted from Allhoff and Lin (2006) with permission of *International Journal of Applied Philosophy*.

violently when in contact with air. But it is not only about the size: By precisely manipulating common elements at the nanoscale, scientists can fashion new materials. For example, carbon atoms bound together in a relatively loose configuration may create coal or graphite found in pencils; in a tighter configuration, carbon makes diamonds; and in an even more precise configuration, it creates carbon nanotubes, one of the strongest materials known, estimated to be up to 100 times stronger than steel at one-sixth the weight.

Given these new properties, nanotechnology is predicted to enable such things as smaller, faster processing chips that enable computers to be imbedded in our clothing or even in our bodies; medical advances for dramatically less invasive surgeries and more targeted drug delivery; lighter, stronger materials that make transportation safer and energy efficient (e.g., enabling us to travel farther into space); new military capabilities such as energy weapons and lighter armor; and countless other innovations. Some even predict that nanotechnology will extend our life span by hundreds of years or more by enabling cellular repair, which might slow, halt, or reverse the aging process (Freitas, 2004). And because nanotechnology may enable us to manipulate individual atoms—the very building blocks of nature—some have predicted that we will be able to create virtually anything we want in the future (Drexler, 1986, pp. 14, 58–63).

Today, however, research is still continuing on the basic science, so we are years and possibly decades away from most of the fantastic nanotechnology products that have been predicted, if they ever come to fruition at all. Nevertheless, companies are beginning to productize more of their research to create commercially viable applications based on nanomaterials. These nanotechnology products are quickly entering the marketplace today, from stain-resistant pants to scratch-resistant paint to better sports equipment to more effective cosmetics and sunblock.

In fact, Procter & Gamble, as one example of a leading consumer goods company, announced in 2006 that it is looking to incorporate nanotechnology into its products (O'Donnell, 2006). Other notable companies made similar statements recently as well, such as BASF's plan to invest US$221 million in nanotechnology research and development over just the next three years (James, 2006).

2. IS NANOTECHNOLOGY A DISTINCT DISCIPLINE?

Before we investigate the myriad issues in nanoethics as covered in this anthology, we must first address a persistent meta controversy surrounding the status of nanotechnology itself, which casts questions about the legitimacy of nanoethics as its own discipline.

Despite massive spending in nanotechnology by corporations and countries—the U.S. government alone is expected to invest over US$1.2 billion in 2007 through its National Nanotechnology Initiative (NNI)—there is still a debate over whether "nanotechnology" is an independent or new science, so unique from other fields that it should require or deserve its own category or moniker. Some have complained that nanotechnology is *not* distinct from other sciences—or at least its boundaries might be somewhat hazy—and therefore its ethics must be equally ill-defined. Others argue further that nanoethics is not an interesting or distinct field because it does not raise any new questions that are not already considered by, say, bioethics or computer ethics. In the remaining part of this introduction, we will argue that nanoethics should be afforded legitimacy, and we will also set some context for the essays that follow in this anthology.

At first glance, this controversy seems strange, given that so much is being invested in nanotechnology worldwide. If nanotechnology were not a distinct science, then why does it command so much attention and money? Many people, however, believe nanotechnology to be merely a convergence or amalgamation of several existing disciplines, such as chemistry, biology, physics, material science, engineering, information technology, and so on; claims like this have at least some truth.

As an example of biology inspiring engineering, scientists are creating artificial noses with nanosized sensors which can accurately "sniff" out smells that are otherwise imperceptible to humans (Nanomix, 2006). Similar work has been done to create artificial compound eyes (Jeong, 2006), borrowing from nature's design of insect eyes, as well as artificial skin (Maheshwari and Saraf, 2006) using nanomaterials to mimic the sensitivity of touch. And entire research centers have been created to explore this rich field, including Georgia Institute of Technology's Center for Biologically Inspired Designs (CBID) and the University of California at Berkeley's Center for Interdisciplinary Bio-Inspiration in Education and Research (CIBER).

But does drawing from other scientific areas preclude nanotechnology from being a field in its own right? Consider the similar and ongoing debate in philosophy of science whether chemistry, biology, and other established sciences can be reduced to simply physics. One line of thought is that these other fields operate the way they do given the laws of physics that govern how atoms, molecules, and their dependent structures interact with each other and the world. But no matter which side of the debate we take here, no one on either side actually suggests that chemistry and biology, for example, do not constitute their own disciplines; so it would be inconsistent to insist that nanotechnology—even if it substantially borrows from other fields—cannot be meaningfully discussed or investigated as a field of its own. As with these other scientific fields, nanotechnology seems to bring something unique to the discussion that merits recognition as its own field; in other words, it is greater than the sum of its parts. At the least, it appears to be the first to integrate otherwise-distinct fields into this one area.

Another source of the controversy about nanotechnology's ontological status comes from various opinions on when the field was first created. Many point to Richard Feynman in 1959 as the founding father of nanotechnology, others to Norio Taniguchi in 1974, and sill others to K. Eric Drexler in 1986. But as the following statement from physicist Richard A.L. Jones (2006, p. 995) indicates, a growing sentiment in the field points to a much more recent, and unlikely, person:

> Perhaps a better candidate to be considered nanotechnology's father figure is President Clinton, whose support of the USA's National Nanotechnology Initiative converted overnight many industrious physicists, chemists and materials scientists into nanotechnologists. In this cynical (though popular) view, the idea of nanotechnology did not emerge naturally from its parent disciplines, but was imposed on the scientific community from outside.

So depending on whom one speaks to, nanotechnology might have been first established anywhere from 1959 to 2000. And if former U.S. President Bill Clinton can plausibly claim the title "father of nanotechnology," then it is no wonder that many scientists and other experts regard nanotechnology as merely a political construct or a marketing buzzword invented to resuscitate old disciplines that appear to be losing ground, particularly in the United States, where the decline of science graduates has been well documented.

3. WHAT IS THE STATUS OF NANO*ETHICS*?

Whether or not nanotechnology is a fabricated area of study and indistinct from other scientific fields, which is not a question we intend or need to answer here, we can already now understand some of the controversy surrounding the status of nanoethics: If nanotechnology is just a fancy term for a range of other fields, then ethical and social questions arising from nanotechnology would seem to be the same kind of questions already raised in these other fields.

Indeed, one critic, Sören Holm (2005), asks:

> It is difficult to specify exactly what could make an area of technology so special that it needs its own ethics, but a minimal requirement must be that it either raises ethical issues that are not raised by other kinds of technologies, or that it raises ethical issues of a different (*i.e.*, larger) magnitude than other technologies. Is this the case for nanotechnology?

Philip Ball (2003), science writer *for Nature*, elaborates on this point:

> Questions about safety, equity, military involvement and openness are ones that pertain to many other areas of science and technology [and not just nanotechnology]. It would be a grave and possibly dangerous distortion if nanotechnology were to come to be seen as a discipline that raises unprecedented ethical and moral issues. In this respect, I think it genuinely does differ from some aspects of biotechnological research, which broach entirely new moral questions.

These are fair and forgivable concerns, and current research in nanoethics might even support this position. For instance, in shrinking down devices, nanotechnology is expected to create a new class of surveillance devices that are virtually invisible and undetectable, thereby raising privacy questions; however, according to critics, these questions do not appear to be new but simply an extension of the current debate about privacy. Nanotechnology is also predicted to play a critical role in developing human-enhancing technologies, such as cybernetic body parts or an exoskeleton that gives us superhuman strength or infrared vision; however, society has already been discussing the ethics of such technologies with respect to biotechnology and cognitive sciences. In the more distant future, some people envision nanotechnology's role in extending the human life span to the point of near immortality; but the question of whether we want or should live longer or forever—as well as its political, economic, and social impacts—does not seem dependent on nanotechnology per se.

On the other hand, some issues are emerging that appear unique to nanotechnology, namely the new environmental, health, and safety (EHS) risks arising from nanomaterials. For instance, research studies suggest that some nanoparticles are directly harmful to animals, and because they can be taken up by cells, they might enter our food chain to unknown effects on human health (Clithrani et al., 2006). Other research asks whether carbon nanotubes will be the next asbestos, since both have the same whiskerlike shape that makes it so difficult to purge from our lungs if inhaled (Gogotsi, 2003). And the flip side of creating superstrong materials such as carbon nanotubes is their fate at the end of a product life-cycle: Will these materials persist indefinitely in our landfills, as is the case with Styrofoam or nuclear waste (Colvin and Wiesner, 2002)?

One new ethical issue is perhaps not enough to legitimize the independence of nanoethics. And in fact, we could perhaps reduce even this apparently unique issue to belong to another discipline, such as engineering or environmental ethics that questions the wisdom of creating products that do not decompose. But there are other good reasons for believing that nanoethics deserves our attention, especially if we believe that nanotechnology itself is a distinct field.

First, nanoethics also commands a significant amount of attention and money, though far less than the amount poured into nanotechnology. In the United States, the NNI currently sets aside approximately $43 million for the "identification and quantification of the broad implications of nanotechnology for society, including social, economic, workforce, educational, ethical, and legal implications." [1] So it would certainly be strange that there would be so much invested by various government agencies, universities, publishers, and other organizations globally if nanoethics were not important as its own field. Of course, there is a possibility that all these organizations and scholars have been fooled because nanotechnology and its ethics allegedly do not exist, but that appears more unlikely than correctly and reasonably identifying nanotechnology as a meaningful area of its own. And at any rate, the point is perhaps already moot given that nanoethics and nanotechnology have taken a life of their own.

Second, it is unclear why we should accept the litmus test that, to be counted as a new discipline in its own right, nanoethics must raise either new or larger ethical issues than already raised by previous technologies. Looking again at chemistry, for example, whether or not we can properly categorize it as a subset of physics (because chemistry arguably does not raise new questions that cannot be answered by physics), there is no existential dilemma about its status as a legitimate category; no one is proposing to do away with the name or reorganize the university chemistry laboratory under the physics department. Therefore, it is unclear why such a dilemma would exist with nanoethics, even if nanoethics can be wholly contained within another field or set of fields.

Third, to the extent that nanotechnology is a convergence of many disciplines in the first place, it should be no surprise that nanoethics is a convergence of many ethical areas as well. So even if a new area of ethics requires raising new or larger issues, that standard may no longer apply with the discovery or creation of nanotechnology. Rather, nanotechnology might uniquely draw from other disciplines like no other discipline before it.

Rather than an argument that nanotechnology is not a distinct discipline because it does not truly break new ground, nanotechnology seems to represent a new pinnacle in our understanding about the world. We are finally able to integrate our learning from a wide range of fields (e.g., physics, chemistry, biology, engineering, and others) to create profoundly useful applications which can be categorized under the moniker of nanotechnology. So just as, for example, architecture can be regarded as a convergence of aesthetic design and engineering, so too can nanotechnology and nanoethics be rightfully acknowledged even if they are a convergence of other fields. Again, the whole of nanotechnology is arguably greater than the sum of its parts because of the new synergies or interplay between the various parts.

Fourth, nanoethics *does* seem to raise new ethical issues insofar as it adds a new dimension, or "flavor," to current ethical debates. For instance, though privacy may be a relatively old debate, the possibility of creating near-invisible and undetectable devices did not meaningfully exist prior to nanotechnology, so nanotechnology brings a new urgency and reality to the issue of privacy. Further, nanotechnology may help shift the privacy debate in an entirely new direction: Whereas worries about unauthorized or unwanted surveillance have traditionally focused on a few agencies, notably governmental organizations, the possibility of cheap, ubiquitous tracking devices "decentralizes" surveillance and changes the terms of the debate.

Nanotechnology likewise is putting a new spotlight and elevating other ethical issues, such as related to human enhancement or longevity. Even something as apparently tangential as the ethics of space exploration and settlements—or space ethics—now overlaps with nanoethics because only with nanotechnology does the possibility of extended space flights and terraforming (i.e., the ability to create a hospitable atmosphere and environment on another planet or moon) become plausible.

Finally, it is not even clear that the question of whether nanotechnology and nanoethics are disciplines in their own right has any real consequence to our discussion here. That is, even if we agree that both are not distinct disciplines, it does not follow that nanoscientists and nanoethicists should stop conducting their work, nor does it follow that the massive levels of funding for both nanotechnology and its social impact should be diminished. Rather, it seems that, even if nanotechnology and nanoethics were each comprised of overlapping, established areas in science and philosophy, they nonetheless are comprised of *something*. Furthermore, it is this constitution that legitimizes the disciplines, not their entitlement to necessarily proprietary issues which continue to exist even if the associative terms of nanotechnology and nanoethics are successfully challenged.

In other words, the debate seems to be more semantic than substantive; this debate is not an obstacle to intelligently discussing either nanotechnology or nanoethics. Even if we agree that both borrow substantially from other areas and therefore should not be considered as distinct disciplines in their own right, we can nevertheless stipulate that we mean nanotechnology to be simply short-hand or abbreviations of some longer and unwieldy (yet technically accurate) descriptors such as, for instance, the development, characterization, and functionalization of materials based on nanoscale research in chemistry, physics, biology, engineering, materials science, and so on. And perhaps nanoethics means something like the ethical, social, environmental, medical, political, economic, legal issues, and so on, arising from nanotechnology (as defined by the preceding) or however we want to precisely define these terms. Regardless, the point is that these terms can be stipulated as is linguistically useful to capture actual investigation in the world; the conceptual independence of those investigations does not deprecate the enterprise.

4. ISSUES IN NANOETHICS

If nanoethics is a distinct discipline—or even if it is not, but we still understand what the term describes—then what are its issues? Again, controversy surrounds even this question. If we are conservative and only acknowledge those issues that will likely or possibly arise from current lines of research in nanotechnology—which is primarily focused on the discovery and applications of new nanomaterials—then nanoethics certainly covers some of the issues mentioned above: EHS impacts, privacy, human enhancement, as well as global security (since the military is a major driver of nanotechnology research to such a degree that some fear a new arms race) (Lawlor, 2005). Other relevant issues may include research ethics (if some research seems to dangerous to publish or pursue), intellectual property (if today's patent-grab and processes stifle innovation), and humanitarianism (why we are not doing more to solve poverty, hunger, energy, clean water, and other problems through nanotechnology).

But more imaginative people, such as Drexler, postulate a more advanced form of nanotechnology in our future—sometimes called "molecular manufacturing" —by which we can position individual molecules with exact precision. The difference between how we create nanomaterials today (e.g., carbon nanotubes) with precisely positioned molecules and molecular manufacturing is the difference between engineering and chemistry. Carbon nanotubes rely on bulk chemical processes and reactions at high temperatures to create the desired configuration of carbon atoms, which is similar in principle to the usual chemistry experiments in which various elements and compounds are thrown together in bulk and shaken up to predictably create a batch of new compounds.[2] In contrast, molecular manufacturing is envisioned to be more like a construction job, grabbing single atoms and deliberately attaching them to others to form the desired structure. This high degree of precision, without messy chemical reactions, would in theory enable us to create practically any possible object.

This line of thought is instantiated by a detailed speculative design for a "nanofactory" that might be a portable or desktop device—a black box of sorts—that can create virtually any object we want, from cakes to computers. To oversimplify things, raw materials, say dirt and water, might go in one end, and a raw steak or perhaps an unmanned fighter jet might come out the other. While this may sound like science fiction, the theory behind it seems sound: If we can precisely manipulate molecules and physical objects are only made up of molecules, then why wouldn't we be able create any physical object we want?

If this still sounds far-fetched, consider the similarities with today's 3-D printers that can print out plastic or ceramic objects one thin layer at a time. No longer limited to producing only manufacturing prototypes and machine parts, 3-D printers recently broke new ground in printing out fully functional and fashionable footwear, among an expanding and impressive array of print-on-demand products (Engineering & Management Services, 2006). The nanofactory operates by the same concept, except with much more precision and a mix of different materials.

So if advance nanotechnology is in our possible future, then it raises truly unique and serious questions; following the litmus test considered earlier, it may strongly support nanoethics as a legitimate discipline. Molecular manufacturing appears to have the potential to wreak havoc on our economic system where millions might lose their jobs overnight in the manufacturing and other industries and perhaps eliminating the need for global trade. If people and terrorists can easily create weapons with personal nanofactories, that may threaten global security and the lives of millions or billions of others. Some of the more fantastic issues are also related to advanced forms of nanotechnology, if not directly to molecular manufacturing, such as longevity or immortality, space settlements, and artificial intelligence.

However, because these issues are tied to advanced forms of nanotechnology—the plausibility or likelihood of which is contentious among mainstream scientists—critics may believe that it is inappropriate or premature to consider such issues now. But we do not need to resolve that question here in order to take seriously the ethical and social issues advanced nanotechnology might raise. Even if advanced nanotechnology is a remote possibility, its scenarios appear so disruptive that they merit consideration. A simple cost–benefit analysis might justify spending $5 million over the next decade to study and perhaps mitigate a scenario that has a 1 percent possibility of causing $1 billion of economic disruption, which has an expected negative utility or value of $10 million. (These figures are purely hypothetical but appear to be in a plausible range.)

As an analogy, if decoding the human genome had just a small likelihood of, say, leading to employment or insurance discrimination based on a person's genetic predisposition, we would then still expect that scenario to be important enough to warrant an investigation; in fact, such ethics research has been ongoing in the last decade. Or more abstractly, if a political course had even a bare possibility to leading to a devastating war, costing the lives of millions, it seems that we are morally obligated to seriously consider that possibility, no matter how remote.

With nanotechnology, so much is still unknown that scientists are really not in a position to accurately forecast what is likely or not and by when. Some believe molecular manufacturing is inevitable; others disagree. But again, if history is any guide, most of our mid- and long-term predictions about technology will be overly optimistic or pessimistic. Many things we have today were once believed to be impossible or impractical—such as gas streetlights, residential electricity, telephones, highways, radio, airplanes, rockets, and even today's ubiquitous personal computer—so perhaps the prudent course is to treat most of these possibilities as reasonable until proven otherwise.

Even near-term challenges in technology—such as how to shrink the smallest computer processor even further—seem difficult if not intractable to us *right now*, but somehow we find a way to sustain Moore's law, which posits a doubling of processing power every 18 months and which some predict will soon fail to hold (Zhirnov et al., 2003). Technology is moving rapidly indeed and may be limited now only by our imagination, so it is not implausible to think any technical challenges associated with molecular manufacturing might be eventually solved.

Indeed, scientists have recently announced creating a blueprint, and then a working prototype, of an "invisibility cloak" —essentially a heavy blanket created with nanomaterials that can bend, instead of reflect or diffuse, light and other electromagnetic waves around the object cloaked, just as water might flow around a rock in the middle of a stream (Pendry et al., 2006). (This, too, seems to give rise to ethical issues associated only with nanotechnology, namely privacy and security, if we are still interested in identifying unique issues.) But as late as 2006, such innovations would have been thought as merely science fiction, consigned to fantasy worlds such as Harry Potter's. Again, throughout history and even now, ideas that have been dismissed as unworkable somehow become reality, despite their technical challenges, so it is not irrational to treat molecular manufacturing, space settlements, and so on as a real possibility absent compelling evidence to the contrary.

Furthermore, no matter how speculative some of these scenarios seem to be, they provide a useful platform to test our moral principles as at least "thought experiments," which is a commonly accepted practice in ethics. For instance, no one thinks that anyone would plausibly be kidnapped and surgically connected to a famous violinist—the premature detachment of whom would lead to the violinist's death—but this hypothetical example isolates and tests out intuitions in Judith Jarvis Thomson's discussion about the moral permissibility of abortion (Thomson, 1971).

Also, few actually question the wisdom of sending spiders into outer space on the grounds that spiders do not exist and may never exist in space (unless we introduce them into space); yet this sort of experiment is useful to study the relationship between gravity and a spider's ability to orient itself and spin webs by isolating gravity as a variable. As it applies to nanotechnology, even if cybernetic people never exist, the possibility of human enhancement provides a platform, or thought experiment, to explore intuitions related to human dignity, personal identity, and other concepts.

Given all this controversy, it should also be no surprise that the questions in nanoethics seem ill-defined as compared to, say, ethical questions in decoding the human genome, as some critics have pointed out (Harris, 2006). Nanotechnology itself is fractured into different approaches or visions, each of which raises it own questions, so, until there is a consensus on what nanotechnology is and will be, it will be difficult to gain a consensus on a plausible set of issues for nanoethics. Moreover, the overlap of nanotechnology with other disciplines—and the overlap of nanoethics with bioethics and other areas—contributes to this challenge.

5. NANOTECHNOLOGY: A MAELSTROM OF ETHICAL AND SOCIAL ISSUES

That said, it is still important to look at both near-term and speculative issues in nanoethics for reasons previously stated. This anthology will present some of the most exciting ethical debates emerging from developments in nanotechnology and by some of the most prominent names in the field.

In Part I, in addition to this introduction, we start the debate in nanoethics with an infamous article by Bill Joy, co-founder of Sun Microsystems, which takes a dystopian view about our future in a technology-dominated world. A counterpoint to this worry is provided by the U.S. Congressional testimony of acclaimed technology inventor Ray Kurzweil, who has been called the "rightful heir to Thomas Edison" by the media, about the implications of nanotechnology on ethics and society.

In Part II, we set some context for the issues with background about where nanotechnology is predicted to help society and individuals the most; how nanotechnology recently exploded onto the national and global scene with the U.S. NNI; and what the controversy or debate is surrounding nanotechnology itself in more detail.

Part III addresses one of the most immediate or near-term issue in nanotechnology: ethical considerations in research and preparing for the new era of nanotechnology. On the frontlines of nanotechnology, scientists play a pivotal role—even if reluctant or unintentional—in how their creations impact the world. We start here with a look at the history of technological revolutions in order to glean any lessons, and we also take a closer look at the role of government and science in driving the nanotechnology revolution. We continue with discussions about the role of complexity, uncertainty, and the so-called precautionary principle (the prudential guideline in science) in nanotechnology research.

In Part IV, we look at the next area of concern as nanotechnology research is applied to the real world: its impact on the environment and health. Nanotechnology is predicted to have broad benefits in the field of medicine; this part examines how our concept of medicine might then change as well as the ethical issues surrounding the use of nanotechnology for purposes other than therapy, such as for human enhancement. We also examine the impact of nanotechnology on the environment and nature.

In Part V, because there is much concern today about regulating nanotechnology's apparent risks to the EHS, our discussion naturally transitions to issues in regulation and public policy. Returning to Chapter 2, we look at alternatives to relinquishment as ways to deal with apocalyptic technological threats. This leads into a broader discussion about guiding nanotechnology in the framework of a democracy. And we take a critical look at current initiatives worldwide to engage the public and other stakeholders in the development of nanotechnology.

Part VI investigates specific policy issues in nanotechnology and society. As a top concern, we can anticipate privacy issues in nanotechnology by looking at a related debate with radio frequency identification (RFID) devices. Nanotechnology is also expected to profoundly increase military capabilities, thereby raising associated ethical issues. Of course, for countries such as the United States, much of the innovation in nanotechnology—including military superiority—may occur in other global regions, given the well-covered decline in science education in the United States, so we also explore educational reform specific to nanotechnology. With an eye still on global affairs, we consider the impact and potential of nanotechnology for developing countries.

Finally, in Part VII, we consider more temporally distant and theoretically speculative issues. Again, molecular manufacturing would seem to lead to massive disruption if it becomes a reality. We also consider the ethics of space exploration, artificial intelligence, and life extension—in which nanotechnology is expected to play an essential role.

This collection certainly does not address every relevant issue in nanoethics, but it gives a sense of the depth and diversity of ethical and social issues in nanotechnology and provides a starting point for further discussions and investigations. The chapters also do not necessarily reflect the viewpoints of the editors or publisher, but only of their authors, whom we thank for their generous contributions. As nanoethics gains momentum, we hope to see more industry experts, academics, and the broader public engaged in this critical field—helping to guide science and humanity to a better future.

NOTES

1. See the U.S. National Nanotechnology Initiative website. http://www. nano.gov/html/society/home_society.html, accessed November 13, 2006.
2. Other methods also exist to create carbon nanotubes, e.g., using high-pressure gas or electricity or lasers, but they do not change the point here that existing methods are radically different and less precise than molecular manufacturing.

REFERENCES

Allhoff, F. and Lin, P. 2006. What's so special about nanotechnology and nanoethics? *International Journal of Applied Philosophy*, 2 (2): 179–190.

Ball, P. 2003. *Nanotechnology in the Firing Line.* Nanotechweb.org, December 23, 2003.

Chithrani, B. D., Ghazani, A. A., and Chan, W. C. W. 2006. Determining the size and shape dependence of gold nanoparticle uptake into mammalian cells. *Nano Letters* 6 (4): 662–668.

Clapp, R. W. 2006. Mortality among US employees of a large computer manufacturing company: 1969–2001. *Environmental Health* 5 (30): 1–32.

Colvin, V., and Wiesner, M. 2002. Environmental implications of nanotechnology: Progress in developing fundamental science as a basis for assessment. Keynote presentation delivered at the US EPA's Nanotechnology and the Environment: Applications and Implications STAR Review Progress Workshop, Arlington, VA, August 28, 2002.

Crichton, M. 2002. *Prey.* New York: HarperCollins.

Drexler, K. E. 1986. *Engines of Creation.* New York: Anchor Books.

Engineering & Management Services (EMS). 2006. *On the Job: 3D Printing Gives Footwear Company a Leg Up on Competition.* Engineering & Manufacturing Services, February 10, 2006.

Freitas, R. A., Jr. 2004. Nanomedicine. In S. Sethe (Ed.), *The Scientific Conquest of Death: Essays on Infinite Lifespans*, Buenos Aires: Libros En Red, 2004, pp. 77–92.

Gogotsi, Y. 2003. How safe are nanotubes and other nanofilaments? *Material Research Innovations*, 7 (4): 192–194.

Hardell, L., Carlberg, M., and Mild, K. H. 2006. Pooled analysis of two case-control studies on use of cellular and cordless telephones and the risk of malignant brain tumours diagnosed in 1997–2003. *International Archives of Occupational and Environmental Health* 79 (8): 630–639.

Harris, R. 2006. Nanotechnology: More than just a buzzword? Paper presented at the University of California, Santa Barbara, Center for Nanotechnology and Society, May 4, 2006.

Holm, S. 2005. *Does Nanotechnology Require a New 'Nanoethics'?*, London: Cardiff Centre for Ethics, Law & Society, August 2005.

James, K. 2006. BASF sets aside $221 million for Nano R&D, opens Asian center. *Small Times*, March 20, 2006, p. 26.

Jeong, K.-H., Kim, J., and Lee, L. P. 2006. Biologically inspired artificial compound eyes. *Science* 312 (5773): 557–561.

Jones, R. A. L. 2006. Hollow centre. *Nature*, 440 (7087): 995.

Keiper, A. 2003. The nanotechnology revolution. *The New Atlantis* Summer (2): 19.

Lawlor, M. 2005. Small matters. *Signal Magazine/AFCEA*, p. 47.

Maheshwari, V., and Saraf, R. F. 2006. High-resolution thin-film device to sense texture by touch. *Science* 312 (5779): 1501–1504.

Nanomix 2006. Nanomix and UC Berkeley announce E-nose detection collaboration. Press release, March 16, 2006.

National Science and Technology Council. 2000. *National Nanotechnology Initiative: Leading to the Next Industrial Revolution*. National Science and Technology Council's Committee on Technology, February 2000.

O'Donnell, K. 2006. Procter & Gamble eyes nanotech. *MarketWatch*, January 25, 2006, p. 57.

Pendry, J. B., Schurig, D., and Smith, D. R. 2006. Controlling electromagnetic fields. *Science Express*, May 25, 2006.

The nanotech schism. 2004. *The New Atlantis*, Winter (4): 101–103.

Thomson, J. J. 1971. A defense of abortion. *Philosophy and Public Affairs* 1 (1): 47–66.

U. S. Environmental Protection Agency (EPA). 2006. EPA seeking PFOA reductions. Press release, January 25, 2006.

Zhirnov, V., Cavin, R., Hutchby, J., and Bourianoff, G. 2003. Limits to binary logic switch scaling—A Gedanken model. *Proceedings of the IEEE* 91 (11): 1934–1939.

2

WHY THE FUTURE DOESN'T NEED US*

Bill Joy

From the moment I became involved in the creation of new technologies, their ethical dimensions have concerned me, but it was only in the autumn of 1998 that I became anxiously aware of how great are the dangers facing us in the twenty-first century. I can date the onset of my unease to the day I met Ray Kurzweil, the deservedly famous inventor of the first reading machine for the blind and many other amazing things.

Ray and I were both speakers at George Gilder's Telecosm conference, and I encountered him by chance in the bar of the hotel after both our sessions were over. I was sitting with John Searle, a Berkeley philosopher who studies consciousness. While we were talking, Ray approached and a conversation began, the subject of which haunts me to this day.

I had missed Ray's talk and the subsequent panel that Ray and John had been on, and they now picked right up where they'd left off, with Ray saying that the rate of improvement of technology was going to accelerate and that we were going to become robots or fuse with robots or something like that, and John countering that this couldn't happen because the robots couldn't be conscious.

While I had heard such talk before, I had always felt sentient robots were in the realm of science fiction. But now, from someone I respected, I was hearing a strong argument

* "Why the Future Doesn't Need Us" © April 4, 2000 by Bill Joy. This chapter originally appeared in *Wired* magazine. Reprinted by permission of the author.

Nanoethics: The Ethical and Social Implications of Nanotechnology. Edited by Allhoff, Lin, Moor, Weckert that they were a near-term possibility. I was taken aback, especially given Ray's proven ability to imagine and create the future. I already knew that new technologies like genetic engineering and nanotechnology were giving us the power to remake the world, but a realistic and imminent scenario for intelligent robots surprised me.

It's easy to get jaded about such breakthroughs. We hear in the news almost every day of some kind of technological or scientific advance. Yet this was no ordinary prediction. In the hotel bar, Ray gave me a partial preprint of his then-forthcoming book *The Age of Spiritual Machines,* which outlined a utopia he foresaw—one in which humans gained near immortality by becoming one with robotic technology. On reading it, my sense of unease only intensified; I felt sure he had to be understating the dangers, understating the probability of a bad outcome along this path.

I found myself most troubled by a passage quoted by Kurzweil (1998) detailing a *dys*topian scenario:[1]

The New Luddite Challenge

First let us postulate that the computer scientists succeed in developing intelligent machines that can do all things better than human beings can do them. In that case presumably all work will be done by vast, highly organized systems of machines and no human effort will be necessary. Either of two cases might occur. The machines might be permitted to make all of their own decisions without human oversight, or else human control over the machines might be retained.

If the machines are permitted to make all their own decisions, we can't make any conjectures as to the results, because it is impossible to guess how such machines might behave. We only point out that the fate of the human race would be at the mercy of the machines. It might be argued that the human race would never be foolish enough to hand over all the power to the machines. But we are suggesting neither that the human race would voluntarily turn power over to the machines nor that the machines would willfully seize power. What we do suggest is that the human race might easily permit itself to drift into a position of such dependence on the machines that it would have no practical choice but to accept all of the machines' decisions. As society and the problems that face it become more and more complex and machines become more and more intelligent, people will let machines make more of their decisions for them, simply because machine-made decisions will bring better results than man-made ones. Eventually a stage may be reached at which the decisions necessary to keep the system running will be so complex that human beings will be incapable of making them intelligently. At that stage the machines will be in effective control. People won't be able to just turn the machines off, because they will be so dependent on them that turning them off would amount to suicide.

On the other hand it is possible that human control over the machines may be retained. In that case the average man may have control over certain private machines of his own, such as his car or his personal computer, but control over large systems of machines will be in the hands of a tiny elite—just as it is today, but with two differences. Due to improved techniques the elite will have greater control over the masses; and because human work will no longer be necessary the masses will be superfluous, a useless burden on the system. If the elite is ruthless they may simply decide to exterminate the mass of humanity. If they are humane they may use propaganda or other psychological or biological techniques to reduce the birth rate until the mass of humanity becomes extinct, leaving the world to the elite. Or, if the elite consists of soft-hearted liberals, they may decide to play the role of good shepherds to the rest of the human race. They will see to it that everyone's physical needs are satisfied, that all children are raised under psychologically hygienic conditions, that everyone has a wholesome hobby to keep him busy, and that anyone who may become dissatisfied undergoes "treatment" to cure his "problem." Of course, life will be so purposeless that people will have to be biologically or psychologically engineered either to remove their need for the power process or make them "sublimate" their drive for power into some harmless hobby. These engineered human beings may be happy in such a society, but they will most certainly not be free. They will have been reduced to the status of domestic animals.

In the book, you don't discover until you turn the page that the author of this passage is Theodore Kaczynski—the Unabomber. I am no apologist for Kaczynski. His bombs killed three people during a 17-year terror campaign and wounded many others. One of his bombs gravely injured my friend David Gelernter, one of the most brilliant and visionary computer scientists of our time. Like many of my colleagues, I felt that I could easily have been the Unabomber's next target.

Kaczynski's actions were murderous and, in my view, criminally insane. He is clearly a Luddite, but simply saying this does not dismiss his argument; as difficult as it is for me to acknowledge, I saw some merit in the reasoning in this single passage. I felt compelled to confront it.

Kaczynski's dystopian vision describes unintended consequences, a well-known problem with the design and use of technology, and one that is clearly related to Murphy's law: Anything that can go wrong, will. (Actually, this is Finagle's law, which in itself shows that Finagle was right.) Our overuse of antibiotics has led to what may be the biggest such problem so far: the emergence of antibiotic-resistant and much more dangerous bacteria. Similar things happened when attempts to eliminate malarial mosquitoes using DDT caused them to acquire DDT resistance; malarial parasites likewise acquired multi-drug-resistant genes (Garrett, 1994, pp. 47–52, 414, 419, 452).

The cause of many such surprises seems clear: The systems involved are complex, involving interaction among and feedback between many parts. Any changes to such a system will cascade in ways that are difficult to predict; this is especially true when human actions are involved.

I started showing friends the Kaczynski quote from *The Age of Spiritual Machines;* I would hand them Kurzweil's book, let them read the quote, and then watch their reaction as they discovered who had written it. At around the same time, I found Hans Moravec's book *Robot: Mere Machine to Transcendent Mind.* Moravec is one of the leaders in robotics research and was a founder of the world's largest robotics research program, at Carnegie Mellon University. *Robot* gave me more material to try out on my friends material surprisingly supportive of Kaczynski's argument. For example (Moravec, 1998):

The Short Run (Early 2000s)

Biological species almost never survive encounters with superior competitors. Ten million years ago, South and North America were separated by a sunken Panama isthmus. South America, like Australia today, was populated by marsupial mammals, including pouched equivalents of rats, deers, and tigers. When the isthmus connecting North and South America rose, it took only a few thousand years for the northern placental species, with slightly more effective metabolisms and reproductive and nervous systems, to displace and eliminate almost all the southern marsupials.

In a completely free marketplace, superior robots would surely affect humans as North American placentals affected South American marsupials (and as humans have affected countless species). Robotic industries would compete vigorously among themselves for matter, energy, and space, incidentally driving their price beyond human reach. Unable to afford the necessities of life, biological humans would be squeezed out of existence.

There is probably some breathing room, because we do not live in a completely free marketplace. Government coerces nonmarket behavior, especially by collecting taxes. Judiciously applied, governmental coercion could support human populations in high style on the fruits of robot labor, perhaps for a long while.

A textbook dystopia—and Moravec is just getting wound up. He goes on to discuss how our main job in the twenty-first century will be "ensuring continued cooperation from the robot industries" by passing laws decreeing that they be "nice" [2] and to describe how seriously dangerous a human can be "once transformed into an unbounded superintelligent robot." Moravec's view is that the robots will eventually succeed us—that humans clearly face extinction.

I decided it was time to talk to my friend Danny Hillis. Danny became famous as the cofounder of Thinking Machines Corporation, which built a very powerful parallel supercomputer. Despite my current job title of chief scientist at Sun Microsystems, I am more a computer architect than a scientist, and I respect Danny's knowledge of the information and physical sciences more than that of any other single person I know. Danny is also a highly regarded futurist who thinks long term—four years ago he started the Long Now Foundation, which is building a clock designed to last 10,000 years, in an attempt to draw attention to the pitifully short attention span of our society.

So I flew to Los Angeles for the express purpose of having dinner with Danny and his wife, Pati. I went through my now-familiar routine, trotting out the ideas and passages that I found so disturbing. Danny's answer—directed specifically at Kurzweil's scenario of humans merging with robots—came swiftly and quite surprised me. He said, simply, that the changes would come gradually and that we would get used to them.

But I guess I wasn't totally surprised. I had seen a quote from Danny in Kurzweil's (1998) book in which he said, "I'm as fond of my body as anyone, but if I can be 200 with a body of silicon, I'll take it." It seemed that he was at peace with this process and its attendant risks, while I was not.

While talking and thinking about Kurzweil, Kaczynski, and Moravec, I suddenly remembered a novel I had read almost 20 years ago—*The White Plague* (1982), by Frank Herbert—in which a molecular biologist is driven insane by the senseless murder of his family. To seek revenge he constructs and disseminates a new and highly contagious plague that kills widely but selectively. (We're lucky Kaczynski was a mathematician, not a molecular biologist.) I was also reminded of the Borg of *Star Trek,* a hive of partly biological, partly robotic creatures with a strong destructive streak. Borg-like disasters are a staple of science fiction, so why hadn't I been more concerned about such robotic dystopias earlier? Why weren't other people more concerned about these nightmarish scenarios?

Part of the answer certainly lies in our attitude toward the new—in our bias toward instant familiarity and unquestioning acceptance. Accustomed to living with almost routine scientific breakthroughs, we have yet to come to terms with the fact that the most compelling twenty-first-century technologies—robotics, genetic engineering, and nanotechnology—pose a different threat than the technologies that have come before. Specifically, robots, engineered organisms, and nanobots share a dangerous amplifying factor: They can self-replicate. A bomb is blown up only once—but one bot can become many and quickly get out of control.

Much of my work over the past 25 years has been on computer networking, where the sending and receiving of messages create the opportunity for out-of-control replication. But while replication in a computer or a computer network can be a nuisance, at worst it disables a machine or takes down a network or network service. Uncontrolled self-replication in these newer technologies runs a much greater risk: substantial damage in the physical world.

Each of these technologies also offers untold promise: The vision of near immortality that Kurzweil sees in his robot dreams drives us forward; genetic engineering may soon provide treatments, if not outright cures, for most diseases; and nanotechnology and nanomedicine can address yet more ills. Together they could significantly extend our average life span and improve the quality of our lives. Yet, with each of these technologies, a sequence of small, individually sensible advances leads to an accumulation of great power and, concomitantly, great danger.

What was different in the twentieth century? Certainly, the technologies underlying the weapons of mass destruction (WMDs)—nuclear, biological, and chemical (NBC)—were powerful and the weapons an enormous threat. But building nuclear weapons required, at least for a time, access to both rare—indeed, effectively unavailable—raw materials and highly protected information; biological and chemical weapons programs also tended to require large-scale activities.

The twenty-first-century technologies—genetics, nanotechnology, and robotics (GNR)—are so powerful that they can spawn whole new classes of accidents and abuses. Most dangerously, for the first time, these accidents and abuses are widely within the reach of individuals or small groups. They will not require large facilities or rare raw materials. Knowledge alone will enable the use of them.

Thus we have the possibility not just of WMDs but of knowledge-enabled mass destruction (KMD), this destructiveness hugely amplified by the power of self-replication.

I think it is no exaggeration to say we are on the cusp of the further perfection of extreme evil, an evil whose possibility spreads well beyond that which WMDs bequeathed to the nation-states, on to a surprising and terrible empowerment of extreme individuals.

Nothing about the way I got involved with computers suggested to me that I was going to be facing these kinds of issues.

My life has been driven by a deep need to ask questions and find answers. When I was 3, I was already reading, so my father took me to the elementary school, where I sat on the principal's lap and read him a story. I started school early, later skipped a grade, and escaped into books—I was incredibly motivated to learn. I asked lots of questions, often driving adults to distraction.

As a teenager I was very interested in science and technology. I wanted to be a ham radio operator but didn't have the money to buy the equipment. Ham radio was the Internet of its time: very addictive and quite solitary. Money issues aside, my mother put her foot down—I was not to be a ham; I was antisocial enough already.

I may not have had many close friends, but I was awash in ideas. By high school, I had discovered the great science fiction writers. I remember especially Heinlein's *Have Spacesuit Will Travel* (1958) and Asimov's *I, Robot* (1950), with its three laws of robotics. I was enchanted by the descriptions of space travel and wanted to have a telescope to look at the stars; since I had no money to buy or make one, I checked books on telescope making out of the library and read about making them instead. I soared in my imagination.

Thursday nights my parents went bowling, and we kids stayed home alone. It was the night of Gene Roddenberry's original *Star Trek,* and the program made a big impression on me. I came to accept its notion that humans had a future in space, Western style, with big heroes and adventures. Roddenberry's vision of the centuries to come was one with strong moral values, embodied in codes like the prime directive: to not interfere in the development of less technologically advanced civilizations. This had an incredible appeal to me; ethical humans, not robots, dominated this future, and I took Roddenberry's dream as part of my own.

I excelled in mathematics in high school, and when I went to the University of Michigan as an undergraduate engineering student, I took the advanced curriculum of the mathematics majors. Solving math problems was an exciting challenge, but when I discovered computers, I found something much more interesting: a machine into which you could put a program that attempted to solve a problem, after which the machine quickly checked the solution. The computer had a clear notion of correct and incorrect, true and false. Were my ideas correct? The machine could tell me. This was very seductive.

I was lucky enough to get a job programming early supercomputers and discovered the amazing power of large machines to numerically simulate advanced designs. When I went to graduate school at the University of California at Berkeley in the mid-1970s, I started staying up late, often all night, inventing new worlds inside the machines; solving problems; writing the code that argued so strongly to be written.

In *The Agony and the Ecstasy,* Irving Stone's (1961) biographical novel of Michelangelo, Stone described vividly how Michelangelo released the statues from the stone, "breaking the marble spell," carving from the images in his mind.[3] In my most ecstatic moments, the software in the computer emerged in the same way. Once I had imagined it in my mind I felt that it was already there in the machine, waiting to be released. Staying up all night seemed a small price to pay to free it—to give the ideas concrete form.

After a few years at Berkeley I started to send out some of the software I had written—an instructional Pascal system, Unix utilities, and a text editor called vi (which is still, to my surprise, widely used more than 20 years later)—to others who had similar small PDP-11 and VAX minicomputers. These adventures in software eventually turned into the Berkeley version of the Unix operating system, which became a personal "success disaster" —so many people wanted it that I never finished my PhD. Instead I got a job working for DARPA putting Berkeley Unix on the Internet and fixing it to be reliable and to run large research applications well. This was all great fun and very rewarding. And, frankly, I saw no robots here or anywhere near.

Still, by the early 1980s, I was drowning. The Unix releases were very successful, and my little project of one soon had money and some staff, but the problem at Berkeley was always office space rather than money—there wasn't room for the help the project needed, so when the other founders of Sun Microsystems showed up I jumped at the chance to join them. At Sun, the long hours continued into the early days of workstations and personal computers, and I have enjoyed participating in the creation of advanced microprocessor technologies and Internet technologies such as Java and Jini.

From all this, I trust it is clear that I am not a Luddite. I have always, rather, had a strong belief in the value of the scientific search for truth and in the ability of great engineering to bring material progress. The Industrial Revolution has immeasurably improved everyone's life over the last couple hundred years, and I always expected my career to involve the building of worthwhile solutions to real problems, one problem at a time.

I have not been disappointed. My work has had more impact than I had ever hoped for and has been more widely used than I could have reasonably expected. I have spent the last 20 years still trying to figure out how to make computers as reliable as I want them to be (they are not nearly there yet) and how to make them simple to use (a goal that has met with even less relative success). Despite some progress, the problems that remain seem even more daunting.

But while I was aware of the moral dilemmas surrounding technology's consequences in fields like weapons research, I did not expect that I would confront such issues in my own field, or at least not so soon.

Perhaps it is always hard to see the bigger impact while you are in the vortex of a change. Failing to understand the consequences of our inventions while we are in the rapture of discovery and innovation seems to be a common fault of scientists and technologists; we have long been driven by the overarching desire to know that is the nature of science's quest, not stopping to notice that the progress to newer and more powerful technologies can take on a life of its own.

I have long realized that the big advances in information technology come not from the work of computer scientists, computer architects, or electrical engineers but from that of physical scientists. The physicists Stephen Wolfram and Brosl Hasslacher introduced me, in the early 1980s, to chaos theory and nonlinear systems. In the 1990s, I learned about complex systems from conversations with Danny Hillis, the biologist Stuart Kauffman, the Nobel laureate physicist Murray Gell-Mann, and others. Most recently, Hasslacher and the electrical engineer and device physicist Mark Reed have been giving me insight into the incredible possibilities of molecular electronics.

In my own work, as codesigner of three microprocessor architectures—SPARC, picoJava, and MAJC—and as the designer of several implementations thereof, I've been afforded a deep and first-hand acquaintance with Moore's law. For decades, Moore's law has correctly predicted the exponential rate of improvement of semiconductor technology. Until last year I believed that the rate of advances predicted by Moore's law might continue only until roughly 2010, when some physical limits would begin to be reached. It was not obvious to me that a new technology would arrive in time to keep performance advancing smoothly.

But because of the recent rapid and radical progress in molecular electronics—where individual atoms and molecules replace lithographically drawn transistors—and related nanoscale technologies, we should be able to meet or exceed the Moore's law rate of progress for another 30 years. By 2030, we are likely to be able to build machines, in quantity, a million times as powerful as the personal computers of today—sufficient to implement the dreams of Kurzweil and Moravec.

As this enormous computing power is combined with the manipulative advances of the physical sciences and the new, deep understandings in genetics, enormous transformative power is being unleashed. These combinations open up the opportunity to completely redesign the world, for better or worse: The replicating and evolving processes that have been confined to the natural world are about to become realms of human endeavor.

In designing software and microprocessors, I have never had the feeling that I was designing an intelligent machine. The software and hardware are so fragile and the capabilities of the machine to "think" so clearly absent that, even as a possibility, this has always seemed very far in the future.

But now, with the prospect of human-level computing power in about 30 years, a new idea suggests itself: that I may be working to create tools which will enable the construction of the technology that may replace our species. How do I feel about this? Very uncomfortable. Having struggled my entire career to build reliable software systems, it seems to me more than likely that this future will not work out as well as some people may imagine. My personal experience suggests we tend to overestimate our design abilities.

Given the incredible power of these new technologies, shouldn't we be asking how we can best coexist with them? And if our own extinction is a likely, or even possible, outcome of our technological development, shouldn't we proceed with great caution?

The dream of robotics is, first, that intelligent machines can do our work for us, allowing us lives of leisure, restoring us to Eden. Yet in his history of such ideas, *Darwin Among the Machines*, George Dyson (1997) warns: "In the game of life and evolution there are three players at the table: human beings, nature, and machines. I am firmly on the side of nature. But nature, I suspect, is on the side of the machines." As we have seen, Moravec agrees, believing we may well not survive the encounter with the superior robot species.

How soon could such an intelligent robot be built? The coming advances in computing power seem to make it possible by 2030. And once an intelligent robot exists, it is only a small step to a robot species—to an intelligent robot that can make evolved copies of itself.

A second dream of robotics is that we will gradually replace ourselves with our robotic technology, achieving near immortality by downloading our consciousnesses; it is this process that Danny Hillis thinks we will gradually get used to and that Ray Kurzweil elegantly details in *The Age of Spiritual Machines*.

But if we are downloaded into our technology, what are the chances that we will thereafter be ourselves or even human? It seems to me far more likely that a robotic existence would not be like a human one in any sense that we understand, that the robots would in no sense be our children, that on this path our humanity may well be lost.

Genetic engineering promises to revolutionize agriculture by increasing crop yields while reducing the use of pesticides; to create tens of thousands of novel species of bacteria, plants, viruses, and animals; to replace reproduction, or supplement it, with cloning; to create cures for many diseases, increasing our life span and our quality of life; and much, much more. We now know with certainty that these profound changes in the biological sciences are imminent and will challenge all our notions of what life is.

Technologies such as human cloning have in particular raised our awareness of the profound ethical and moral issues we face. If, for example, we were to reengineer ourselves into several separate and unequal species using the power of genetic engineering, then we would threaten the notion of equality that is the very cornerstone of our democracy.

Given the incredible power of genetic engineering, it's no surprise that there are significant safety issues in its use. My friend Amory Lovins recently cowrote, along with Hunter Lovins (2000), an editorial that provides an ecological view of some of these dangers. Among their concerns is that "the new botany aligns the development of plants with their economic, not evolutionary, success." Amory's long career has been focused on energy and resource efficiency by taking a whole-system view of human-made systems; such a whole-system view often finds simple, smart solutions to otherwise seemingly difficult problems, and is usefully applied here as well.

After reading the Lovins' editorial, I saw an op-ed by Gregg Easterbrook in *The New York Times* (November 19, 1999) about genetically engineered crops under the headline "Food for the Future: Someday, rice will have built-in vitamin A. Unless the Luddites win."

Are Amory and Hunter Lovins Luddites? Certainly not. I believe we all would agree that golden rice, with its built-in vitamin A, is probably a good thing if developed with proper care and respect for the likely dangers in moving genes across species boundaries.

Awareness of the dangers inherent in genetic engineering is beginning to grow, as reflected in the Lovins' editorial. The general public is aware of, and uneasy about, genetically modified foods and seems to be rejecting the notion that such foods should be permitted to be unlabeled.

But genetic engineering technology is already very far along. As the Lovins note, the U.S. Department of Agriculture (USDA) has already approved about 50 genetically engineered crops for unlimited release; more than half of the world's soybeans and a third of its corn now contain genes spliced in from other forms of life.

While there are many important issues here, my own major concern with genetic engineering is narrower: that it gives the power—whether militarily, accidentally, or in a deliberate terrorist act—to create a "white plague".

The many wonders of nanotechnology were first imagined by the Nobel laureate physicist Richard Feynman (1960) in a speech he gave in 1959, subsequently published under the title "There's Plenty of Room at the Bottom." The book that made a big impression on me, in the mid-1980s, was Eric Drexler's (1986) *Engines of Creation,* in which he described beautifully how manipulation of matter at the atomic level could create a utopian future of abundance, where just about everything could be made cheaply and almost any imaginable disease or physical problem could be solved using nanotechnology and artificial intelligences.

A subsequent book, *Unbounding the Future: The Nanotechnology Revolution,* which Drexler (1993) cowrote, imagines some of the changes that might take place in a world where we had molecular-level "assemblers." Assemblers could make possible incredibly low cost solar power, cures for cancer and the common cold by augmentation of the human immune system, essentially complete cleanup of the environment, incredibly inexpensive pocket supercomputers (in fact, any product would be manufacturable by assemblers at a cost no greater than that of wood), spaceflight more accessible than transoceanic travel today, and restoration of extinct species.

I remember feeling good about nanotechnology after reading *Engines of Creation.* As a technologist, it gave me a sense of calm; that is, nanotechnology showed us that incredible progress was possible and indeed perhaps inevitable. If nanotechnology was our future, then I didn't feel pressed to solve so many problems in the present. I would get to Drexler's utopian future in due time; I might as well enjoy life more in the here and now. It didn't make sense, given his vision, to stay up all night, all the time.

Drexler's vision also led to a lot of good fun. I would occasionally get to describe the wonders of nanotechnology to others who had not heard of it. After teasing them with all the things Drexler described I would give a homework assignment of my own: "Use nanotechnology to create a vampire; for extra credit create an antidote."

With these wonders came clear dangers, of which I was acutely aware. As I said at a nanotechnology conference (Joy, 1989, p. 269), "We can't simply do our science and not worry about these ethical issues" But my subsequent conversations with physicists convinced me that nanotechnology might not even work—or, at least, it wouldn't work anytime soon. Shortly thereafter I moved to Colorado, to a skunk works I had set up, and the focus of my work shifted to software for the Internet, specifically on ideas that became Java and Jini.

Then, last summer, Brosl Hasslacher told me that nanoscale molecular electronics was now practical. This was *new* news, at least to me, and I think to many people, and it radically changed my opinion about nanotechnology. It sent me back to *Engines of Creation.* Rereading Drexler's work after more than 10 years, I was dismayed to realize how little I had remembered of its lengthy section called "Dangers and Hopes," including a discussion of how nanotechnologies can become "engines of destruction."

Indeed, in my rereading of this cautionary material today, I am struck by how naive some of Drexler's safeguard proposals seem and how much greater I judge the dangers to be now than even he seemed to then. (Having anticipated and described many technical and political problems with nanotechnology, Drexler started the Foresight Institute in the late 1980s "to help prepare society for anticipated advanced technologies" —most important, nanotechnology.)

The enabling breakthrough to assemblers seems quite likely within the next 20 years. Molecular electronics—the new subfield of nanotechnology where individual molecules are circuit elements—should mature quickly and become enormously lucrative within this decade, causing a large incremental investment in all nanotechnologies.

Unfortunately, as with nuclear technology, it is far easier to create destructive uses for nanotechnology than constructive ones. Nanotechnology has clear military and terrorist uses, and you need not be suicidal to release a massively destructive nanotechnological device—such devices can be built to be selectively destructive, affecting, for example, only a certain geographical area or a group of people who are genetically distinct.

An immediate consequence of the Faustian bargain in obtaining the great power of nanotechnology is that we run a grave risk—the risk that we might destroy the biosphere on which all life depends.

As Drexler (1986, p. 172) explained:

"Plants" with "leaves" no more efficient than today's solar cells could out-compete real plants, crowding the biosphere with an inedible foliage. Tough omnivorous "bacteria" could out-compete real bacteria: They could spread like blowing pollen, replicate swiftly, and reduce the biosphere to dust in a matter of days. Dangerous replicators could easily be too tough, small, and rapidly spreading to stop—at least if we make no preparation. We have trouble enough controlling viruses and fruit flies.

Among the cognoscenti of nanotechnology, this threat has become known as the "gray goo problem." Though masses of uncontrolled replicators need not be gray or gooey, the term "gray goo" emphasizes that replicators able to obliterate life might be less inspiring than a single species of crabgrass. They might be superior in an evolutionary sense, but this need not make them valuable.

The gray goo threat makes one thing perfectly clear: We cannot afford certain kinds of accidents with replicating assemblers.

Gray goo would surely be a depressing ending to our human adventure on Earth, far worse than mere fire or ice, and one that could stem from a simple laboratory accident.[4] Oops.

It is most of all the power of destructive self-replication in GNR that should give us pause. Self-replication is the modus operandi of genetic engineering, which uses the machinery of the cell to replicate its designs, and the prime danger underlying gray goo in nanotechnology. Stories of run-amok robots like the Borg, replicating or mutating to escape from the ethical constraints imposed on them by their creators, are well established in our science fiction books and movies. It is even possible that self-replication may be more fundamental than we thought and hence harder—or even impossible—to control. A recent article by Stuart Kauffman 1996 in *Nature* titled

"Self-Replication: Even Peptides Do It" discusses the discovery that a 32-amino-acid peptide can "autocatalyze its own synthesis." We don't know how widespread this ability is, but Kauffman (p. 496) notes that it may hint at "a route to self-reproducing molecular systems on a basis far wider than Watson-Crick base-pairing."

In truth, we have had in hand for years clear warnings of the dangers inherent in widespread knowledge of GNR technologies—of the possibility of knowledge alone enabling mass destruction. But these warnings haven't been widely publicized; the public discussions have been clearly inadequate. There is no profit in publicizing the dangers.

The NBC technologies used in twentieth-century weapons of mass destruction were and are largely military, developed in government laboratories. In sharp contrast, the twenty-first-century GNR technologies have clear commercial uses and are being developed almost exclusively by corporate enterprises. In this age of triumphant commercialism, technology—with science as its handmaiden—is delivering a series of almost magical inventions that are the most phenomenally lucrative ever seen. We are aggressively pursuing the promises of these new technologies within the now-unchallenged system of global capitalism and its manifold financial incentives and competitive pressures. In *Pale Blue Dot,* a book describing his vision of the human future in space, Carl Sagan (1994) writes:

> This is the first moment in the history of our planet when any species, by its own voluntary actions, has become a danger to itself—as well as to vast numbers of others.
>
> It might be a familiar progression, transpiring on many worlds—a planet, newly formed, placidly revolves around its star; life slowly forms; a kaleidoscopic procession of creatures evolves; intelligence emerges which, at least up to a point, confers enormous survival value; and then technology is invented. It dawns on them that there are such things as laws of Nature, that these laws can be revealed by experiment, and that knowledge of these laws can be made both to save and to take lives, both on unprecedented scales. Science, they recognize, grants immense powers. In a flash, they create world-altering contrivances. Some planetary civilizations see their way through, place limits on what may and what must not be done, and safely pass through the time of perils. Others, not so lucky or so prudent, perish.

I am only now realizing how deep his insight was and how sorely I miss, and will miss, his voice. For all its eloquence, Sagan's contribution was not least that of simple common sense—an attribute that, along with humility, many of the leading advocates of the twenty-first-century technologies seem to lack.

I remember from my childhood that my grandmother was strongly against the overuse of antibiotics. She had worked since before World War I as a nurse and had a commonsense attitude that taking antibiotics, unless they were absolutely necessary, was bad for you.

It is not that she was an enemy of progress. She saw much progress in an almost 70-year nursing career; my grandfather, a diabetic, benefited greatly from the improved treatments that became available in his lifetime. But she, like many levelheaded people, would probably think it greatly arrogant for us, now, to be designing a robotic "replacement species" when we obviously have so much trouble making relatively simple things work and so much trouble managing—or even understanding—ourselves.

I realize now that she had an awareness of the nature of the order of life and of the necessity of living with and respecting that order. With this respect comes a necessary humility that we, with our early-twenty-first-century chutzpah, lack at our peril. The commonsense view, grounded in this respect, is often right, in advance of the scientific evidence. The clear fragility and inefficiencies of the human-made systems we have built should give us all pause; the fragility of the systems I have worked on certainly humbles me.

We should have learned a lesson from the making of the first atomic bomb and the resulting arms race. We didn't do well then, and the parallels to our current situation are troubling.

The effort to build the first atomic bomb was led by the brilliant physicist J. Robert Oppenheimer. Oppenheimer was not naturally interested in politics but became painfully aware of what he perceived as the grave threat to Western civilization from the Third Reich, a threat surely grave because of the possibility that Hitler might obtain nuclear weapons. Energized by this concern, he brought his strong intellect, passion for physics, and charismatic leadership skills to Los Alamos and led a rapid and successful effort by an incredible collection of great minds to quickly invent the bomb.

What is striking is how this effort continued so naturally after the initial impetus was removed. In a meeting shortly after V-E Day with some physicists who felt that perhaps the effort should stop, Oppenheimer argued to continue. His stated reason seems a bit strange: not because of the fear of large casualties from an invasion of Japan, but because the United Nations, which was soon to be formed, should have foreknowledge of atomic weapons. A more likely reason the project continued is the momentum that had built up—the first atomic test, Trinity, was nearly at hand.

We know that in preparing this first atomic test the physicists proceeded despite a large number of possible dangers. They were initially worried, based on a calculation by Edward Teller, that an atomic explosion might set fire to the atmosphere. A revised calculation reduced the danger of destroying the world to a three-in-a-million chance. (Teller says he was later able to dismiss the prospect of atmospheric ignition entirely.) Oppenheimer, though, was sufficiently concerned about the result of Trinity that he arranged for a possible evacuation of the southwest part of the state of New Mexico. And, of course, there was the clear danger of starting a nuclear arms race.

Within a month of that first, successful test, two atomic bombs destroyed Hiroshima and Nagasaki. Some scientists had suggested that the bomb simply be demonstrated, rather than dropped on Japanese cities—saying that this would greatly improve the chances for arms control after the war—but to no avail. With the tragedy of Pearl Harbor still fresh in Americans' minds, it would have been very difficult for President Truman to order a demonstration of the weapons rather than use them as he did—the desire to quickly end the war and save the lives that would have been lost in any invasion of Japan was very strong. Yet the overriding truth was probably very simple: As the physicist Freeman Dyson later said, "The reason that it was dropped was just that nobody had the courage or the foresight to say no."

It's important to realize how shocked the physicists were in the aftermath of the bombing of Hiroshima, on August 6, 1945. They describe a series of waves of emotion:

first, a sense of fulfillment that the bomb worked, then horror at all the people that had been killed, and then a convincing feeling that on no account should another bomb be dropped. Yet of course another bomb was dropped, on Nagasaki, only three days after the bombing of Hiroshima.

In November 1945, three months after the atomic bombings, Oppenheimer stood firmly behind the scientific attitude, saying, "It is not possible to be a scientist unless you believe that the knowledge of the world, and the power which this gives, is a thing which is of intrinsic value to humanity, and that you are using it to help in the spread of knowledge and are willing to take the consequences."

Oppenheimer went on to work, with others, on the Acheson-Lilienthal report, which, as Richard Rhodes says in his recent book *Visions of Technology,* "found a way to prevent a clandestine nuclear arms race without resorting to armed world government" (Rhodes, 2000); their suggestion was a form of relinquishment of nuclear weapons work by nation-states to an international agency.

This proposal led to the Baruch Plan, which was submitted to the United Nations in June 1946 but never adopted (perhaps because, as Rhodes suggests, Bernard Baruch had "insisted on burdening the plan with conventional sanctions," thereby inevitably dooming it, even though it would "almost certainly have been rejected by Stalinist Russia anyway" Rhodes, 2000). Other efforts to promote sensible steps toward internationalizing nuclear power to prevent an arms race ran afoul either of U.S. politics and internal distrust or distrust by the Soviets. The opportunity to avoid the arms race was lost and very quickly.

Two years later, in 1948, Oppenheimer seemed to have reached another stage in his thinking, saying, "In some sort of crude sense which no vulgarity, no humor, no overstatement can quite extinguish, the physicists have known sin; and this is a knowledge they cannot lose."

In 1949, the Soviets exploded an atom bomb. By 1955, both the United States and the Soviet Union had tested hydrogen bombs suitable for delivery by aircraft. And so the nuclear arms race began.

Nearly 20 years ago, in the documentary *The Day After Trinity,* Freeman Dyson summarized the scientific attitudes that brought us to the nuclear precipice:

"I have felt it myself. The glitter of nuclear weapons. It is irresistible if you come to them as a scientist. To feel it's there in your hands, to release this energy that fuels the stars, to let it do your bidding. To perform these miracles, to lift a million tons of rock into the sky. It is something that gives people an illusion of illimitable power, and it is, in some ways, responsible for all our troubles—this, what you might call technical arrogance, that overcomes people when they see what they can do with their minds" (Else, 1981).

Now, as then, we are creators of new technologies and stars of the imagined future, driven—this time by great financial rewards and global competition—despite the clear dangers, hardly evaluating what it may be like to try to live in a world that is the realistic outcome of what we are creating and imagining.

In 1947, *The Bulletin of the Atomic Scientists* began putting a doomsday clock on its cover. For more than 50 years, it has shown an estimate of the relative nuclear danger we have faced, reflecting the changing international conditions. The hands on the clock have moved 15 times and today, standing at 9 minutes to midnight, reflect continuing and real danger from nuclear weapons. The recent addition of India and Pakistan to the list of nuclear powers has increased the threat of failure of the nonproliferation goal, and this danger was reflected by moving the hands closer to midnight in 1998.

In our time, how much danger do we face, not just from nuclear weapons, but from all of these technologies? How high are the extinction risks?

The philosopher John Leslie has studied this question and concluded that the risk of human extinction is at least 30 percent,[5] while Ray Kurzweil believes we have "a better than even chance of making it through," with the caveat that he has "always been accused of being an optimist." Not only are these estimates not encouraging, but they do not include the probability of many horrid outcomes that lie short of extinction.

Faced with such assessments, some serious people are already suggesting that we simply move beyond Earth as quickly as possible. We would colonize the galaxy using von Neumann probes, which hop from star system to star system, replicating as they go. This step will almost certainly be necessary 5 billion years from now (or sooner if our solar system is disastrously impacted by the impending collision of our galaxy with the Andromeda galaxy within the next 3 billion years), but if we take Kurzweil and Moravec at their word, it might be necessary by the middle of this century.

What are the moral implications here? If we must move beyond Earth this quickly in order for the species to survive, who accepts the responsibility for the fate of those (most of us, after all) who are left behind? And even if we scatter to the stars, isn't it likely that we may take our problems with us or find, later, that they have followed us? The fate of our species on Earth and our fate in the galaxy seem inextricably linked.

Another idea is to erect a series of shields to defend against each of the dangerous technologies. The Strategic Defense Initiative, proposed by the Reagan administration, was an attempt to design such a shield against the threat of a nuclear attack from the Soviet Union. But as Arthur C. Clarke (1998, p. 526), who was privy to discussions about the project, observed: "Though it might be possible, at vast expense, to construct local defense systems that would 'only' let through a few percent of ballistic missiles, the much touted idea of a national umbrella was nonsense. Luis Alvarez, perhaps the greatest experimental physicist of this century, remarked to me that the advocates of such schemes were 'very bright guys with no common sense.'"

Clarke continued: "Looking into my often cloudy crystal ball, I suspect that a total defense might indeed be possible in a century or so. But the technology involved would produce, as a by-product, weapons so terrible that no one would bother with anything as primitive as ballistic missiles."

In *Engines of Creation*, Eric Drexler (1986) proposed that we build an active nanotechnological shield—a form of immune system for the biosphere—to defend against dangerous replicators of all kinds that might escape from laboratories or otherwise be maliciously created. But the shield he proposed would itself be extremely dangerous—nothing could prevent it from developing autoimmune problems and attacking the biosphere itself.[6]

Similar difficulties apply to the construction of shields against robotics and genetic engineering. These technologies are too powerful to be shielded against in the time frame of interest; even if it were possible to implement defensive shields, the side effects of their development would be at least as dangerous as the technologies we are trying to protect against.

These possibilities are all thus either undesirable or unachievable or both. The only realistic alternative I see is relinquishment: to limit development of the technologies that are too dangerous by limiting our pursuit of certain kinds of knowledge.

Yes, I know, knowledge is good, as is the search for new truths. We have been seeking knowledge since ancient times. Aristotle opened his *Metaphysics* with the simple statement: "All men by nature desire to know." We have, as a bedrock value in our society, long agreed on the value of open access to information and recognize the problems that arise with attempts to restrict access to and development of knowledge. In recent times, we have come to revere scientific knowledge.

But despite the strong historical precedents, if open access to and unlimited development of knowledge henceforth puts us all in clear danger of extinction, then common sense demands that we reexamine even these basic, long-held beliefs.

It was Nietzsche who warned us, at the end of the nineteenth century, not only that God is dead but that "faith in science, which after all exists undeniably, cannot owe its origin to a calculus of utility; it must have originated *in spite of* the fact that the disutility and dangerousness of the 'will to truth,' of 'truth at any price' is proved to it constantly." It is this further danger that we now fully face—the consequences of our truth-seeking. The truth that science seeks can certainly be considered a dangerous substitute for God if it is likely to lead to our extinction.

If we could agree, as a species, what we wanted, where we were headed, and why, then we would make our future much less dangerous—we might understand what we can and should relinquish. Otherwise, we can easily imagine an arms race developing over GNR technologies, as it did with the NBC technologies in the twentieth century. This is perhaps the greatest risk, for once such a race begins, it's very hard to end it. This time—unlike during the Manhattan Project—we aren't in a war, facing an implacable enemy that is threatening our civilization; we are driven, instead, by our habits, our desires, our economic system, and our competitive need to know.

I believe that we all wish our course could be determined by our collective values, ethics, and morals. If we had gained more collective wisdom over the past few thousand years, then a dialogue to this end would be more practical, and the incredible powers we are about to unleash would not be nearly so troubling.

One would think we might be driven to such a dialogue by our instinct for self-preservation. Individuals clearly have this desire, yet as a species our behavior seems to be not in our favor. In dealing with the nuclear threat, we often spoke dishonestly to ourselves and to each other, thereby greatly increasing the risks. Whether this was politically motivated, or because we chose not to think ahead, or because when faced with such grave threats we acted irrationally out of fear, I do not know, but it does not bode well.

The new Pandora's boxes of genetics, nanotechnology, and robotics are almost open, yet we seem hardly to have noticed. Ideas can't be put back in a box; unlike uranium or plutonium, they don't need to be mined and refined, and they can be freely copied. Once they are out, they are out. Churchill remarked, in a famous left-handed compliment, that the American people and their leaders "invariably do the right thing, after they have examined every other alternative." In this case, however, we must act more presciently, as to do the right thing only at last may be to lose the chance to do it at all.

As Thoreau (1854) said, "We do not ride on the railroad; it rides upon us," and this is what we must fight in our time. The question is, indeed, Which is to be master? Will we survive our technologies?

We are being propelled into this new century with no plan, no control, no brakes. Have we already gone too far down the path to alter course? I don't believe so, but we aren't trying yet, and the last chance to assert control—the fail-safe point—is rapidly approaching. We have our first pet robots as well as commercially available genetic engineering techniques, and our nanoscale techniques are advancing rapidly. While the development of these technologies proceeds through a number of steps, it isn't necessarily the case—as happened in the Manhattan Project and the Trinity test—that the last step in proving a technology is large and hard. The breakthrough to wild self-replication in robotics, genetic engineering, or nanotechnology could come suddenly, reprising the surprise we felt when we learned of the cloning of a mammal.

And yet I believe we do have a strong and solid basis for hope. Our attempts to deal with WMDs in the last century provide a shining example of relinquishment for us to consider: the unilateral U.S. abandonment, without preconditions, of the development of biological weapons. This relinquishment stemmed from the realization that while it would take an enormous effort to create these terrible weapons, they could from then on easily be duplicated and fall into the hands of rogue nations or terrorist groups.

The clear conclusion was that we would create additional threats to ourselves by pursuing these weapons and that we would be more secure if we did not pursue them. We have embodied our relinquishment of biological and chemical weapons in the 1972 Biological Weapons Convention (BWC) and the 1993 Chemical Weapons Convention (CWC) (Meselson, 1999).

As for the continuing sizable threat from nuclear weapons, which we have lived with now for more than 50 years, the U.S. Senate's recent rejection of the Comprehensive Test Ban Treaty makes it clear relinquishing nuclear weapons will not be politically easy. But we have a unique opportunity, with the end of the Cold War, to avert a multipolar arms race. Building on the BWC and CWC relinquishments, successful abolition of nuclear weapons could help us build toward a habit of relinquishing dangerous technologies. [Actually, by getting rid of all but 100 nuclear weapons worldwide—roughly the total destructive power of World War II and a considerably easier task—we could eliminate this extinction threat (Doty, 1999)].

Verifying relinquishment will be a difficult problem but not an unsolvable one. We are fortunate to have already done a lot of relevant work in the context of the BWC and other treaties. Our major task will be to apply this to technologies that are naturally much more commercial than military. The substantial need here is for transparency, as difficulty of verification is directly proportional to the difficulty of distinguishing relinquished from legitimate activities.

I frankly believe that the situation in 1945 was simpler than the one we now face: The nuclear technologies were reasonably separable into commercial and military uses and monitoring was aided by the nature of atomic tests and the ease with which radioactivity could be measured. Research on military applications could be performed at national laboratories such as Los Alamos, with the results kept secret as long as possible.

The GNR technologies do not divide clearly into commercial and military uses; given their potential in the market, it's hard to imagine pursuing them only in national laboratories. With their widespread commercial pursuit, enforcing relinquishment will require a verification regimen similar to that for biological weapons, but on an unprecedented scale. This, inevitably, will raise tensions between our individual privacy and desire for proprietary information and the need for verification to protect us all. We will undoubtedly encounter strong resistance to this loss of privacy and freedom of action.

Verifying the relinquishment of certain GNR technologies will have to occur in cyberspace as well as at physical facilities. The critical issue will be to make the necessary transparency acceptable in a world of proprietary information, presumably by providing new forms of protection for intellectual property.

Verifying compliance will also require that scientists and engineers adopt a strong code of ethical conduct, resembling the Hippocratic oath, and that they have the courage to whistleblow as necessary, even at high personal cost. This would answer the call—50 years after Hiroshima—by the Nobel laureate Hans Bethe, one of the most senior of the surviving members of the Manhattan Project, that all scientists "cease and desist from work creating, developing, improving, and manufacturing nuclear weapons and other weapons of potential mass destruction" (Bethe, 1995)[7] In the twenty-first century, this requires vigilance and personal responsibility by those who would work on both NBC and GNR technologies to avoid implementing WMDs and knowledge-enabled mass destruction.

Thoreau (1854) also said that we will be "rich in proportion to the number of things which we can afford to let alone." We each seek to be happy, but it would seem worthwhile to question whether we need to take such a high risk of total destruction to gain yet more knowledge and yet more things; common sense says that there is a limit to our material needs—and that certain knowledge is too dangerous and is best forgone.

Neither should we pursue near immortality without considering the costs, without considering the commensurate increase in the risk of extinction. Immortality, while perhaps the original, is certainly not the only possible utopian dream.

I recently had the good fortune to meet the distinguished author and scholar Jacques Attali (1992), whose book *Lignes d'horizons* (*Millennium,* in the English translation) helped inspire the Java and Jini approach to the coming age of pervasive computing, as previously described in this magazine. In his new book *Fraternités*, Attali (2000) describes how our dreams of utopia have changed over time:

> At the dawn of societies, men saw their passage on Earth as nothing more than a
> labyrinth of pain, at the end of which stood a door leading, via their death, to the
> company of gods and to *Eternity.* With the Hebrews and then the Greeks, some
> men dared free themselves from theological demands and dream of an ideal City

where *Liberty* would flourish. Others, noting the evolution of the market society, understood that the liberty of some would entail the alienation of others, and they sought *Equality*.

Jacques helped me understand how these three different utopian goals exist in tension in our society today. He goes on to describe a fourth utopia, *Fraternity*, whose foundation is altruism. Fraternity alone associates individual happiness with the happiness of others, affording the promise of self-sustainment.

This crystallized for me my problem with Kurzweil's dream. A technological approach to Eternity—near immortality through robotics—may not be the most desirable utopia, and its pursuit brings clear dangers. Maybe we should rethink our utopian choices.

Where can we look for a new ethical basis to set our course? I have found the ideas in the book *Ethics for the New Millennium* (2001), by the Dalai Lama, to be very helpful. As is perhaps well known but little heeded, the Dalai Lama argues that the most important thing is for us to conduct our lives with love and compassion for others and that our societies need to develop a stronger notion of universal responsibility and of our interdependency; he proposes a standard of positive ethical conduct for individuals and societies that seems consonant with Attali's Fraternity utopia.

The Dalai Lama further argues that we must understand what it is that makes people happy and acknowledge the strong evidence that neither material progress nor the pursuit of the power of knowledge is the key—that there are limits to what science and the scientific pursuit alone can do.

Our Western notion of happiness seems to come from the Greeks, who defined it as "the exercise of vital powers along lines of excellence in a life affording them scope" (Hamilton, 1942, p. 35).

Clearly, we need to find meaningful challenges and sufficient scope in our lives if we are to be happy in whatever is to come. But I believe we must find alternative outlets for our creative forces, beyond the culture of perpetual economic growth; this growth has largely been a blessing for several hundred years, but it has not brought us unalloyed happiness, and we must now choose between the pursuit of unrestricted and undirected growth through science and technology and the clear accompanying dangers.

It is now more than a year since my first encounter with Ray Kurzweil and John Searle. I see around me cause for hope in the voices for caution and relinquishment and in those people I have discovered who are as concerned as I am about our current predicament. I feel, too, a deepened sense of personal responsibility—not for the work I have already done, but for the work that I might yet do, at the confluence of the sciences.

But many other people who know about the dangers still seem strangely silent. When pressed, they trot out the "this is nothing new" riposte—as if awareness of what could happen is response enough. They tell me that there are universities filled with bioethicists who study this stuff all day long. They say that all this has been written about before and by experts. They complain that my worries and arguments are already old hat.

I don't know where these people hide their fear. As an architect of complex systems I enter this arena as a generalist. But should this diminish my concerns? I am aware of how much has been written about, talked about, and lectured about so authoritatively. But does this mean it has reached people? Does this mean we can discount the dangers before us?

Knowing is not a rationale for not acting. Can we doubt that knowledge has become a weapon we wield against ourselves?

The experiences of the atomic scientists clearly show the need to take personal responsibility, the danger that things will move too fast, and the way in which a process can take on a life of its own. We can, as they did, create insurmountable problems in almost no time flat. We must do more thinking up front if we are not to be similarly surprised and shocked by the consequences of our inventions.

My continuing professional work is on improving the reliability of software. Software is a tool, and as a toolbuilder I must struggle with the uses to which the tools I make are put. I have always believed that making software more reliable, given its many uses, will make the world a safer and better place; if I were to come to believe the opposite, then I would be morally obligated to stop this work. I can now imagine such a day may come.

This all leaves me not angry but at least a bit melancholic. Henceforth, for me, progress will be somewhat bittersweet.

Do you remember the beautiful penultimate scene in *Manhattan* where Woody Allen is lying on his couch and talking into a tape recorder? He is writing a short story about people who are creating unnecessary, neurotic problems for themselves because it keeps them from dealing with more unsolvable, terrifying problems about the universe.

He leads himself to the question, "Why is life worth living?" and to consider what makes it worthwhile for him: Groucho Marx, Willie Mays, the second movement of the Jupiter Symphony, Louis Armstrong's recording of "Potato Head Blues," Swedish movies, Flaubert's *Sentimental Education*, Marlon Brando, Frank Sinatra, the apples and pears by Cézanne, the crabs at Sam Wo's, and, finally, the showstopper: his love Tracy's face.

Each of us has our precious things, and as we care for them we locate the essence of our humanity. In the end, it is because of our great capacity for caring that I remain optimistic we will confront the dangerous issues now before us.

My immediate hope is to participate in a much larger discussion of the issues raised here, with people from many different backgrounds, in settings not predisposed to fear or favor technology for its own sake.

As a start, I have twice raised many of these issues at events sponsored by the Aspen Institute and have separately proposed that the American Academy of Arts and Sciences take them up as an extension of its work with the Pugwash Conferences. (These have been held since 1957 to discuss arms control, especially of nuclear weapons, and to formulate workable policies.)

It's unfortunate that the Pugwash meetings started only well after the nuclear genie was out of the bottle—roughly 15 years too late. We are also getting a belated start on seriously addressing the issues around twenty-first-century technologies—the prevention of knowledge-enabled mass destruction—and further delay seems unacceptable.

So I'm still searching; there are many more things to learn. Whether we are to succeed or fail, to survive or fall victim to these technologies, is not yet decided. I'm up late again—it's almost 6 am. I'm trying to imagine some better answers, to break the spell and free them from the stone.

NOTES

1. This passage is from Kaczynski's Unabomber Manifesto, which was published jointly, under duress, by *The New York Times* and *The Washington Post* to attempt to bring his campaign of terror to an end. I agree with David Gelernter (1997, p. 120), who said about their decision:

   > It was a tough call for the newspapers. To say yes would be giving in to terrorism, and for all they knew he was lying anyway. On the other hand, to say yes might stop the killing. There was also a chance that someone would read the tract and get a hunch about the author; and that is exactly what happened. The suspect's brother read it, and it rang a bell.
   >
   > I would have told them not to publish. I'm glad they didn't ask me. I guess.

2. Isaac Asimov described what became the most famous view of ethical rules for robot behavior in his book *I, Robot* in 1950 in his three laws of robotics: 1. A robot may not injure a human being, or, through inaction, allow a human being to come to harm. 2. A robot must obey the orders given it by human beings, except where such orders would conflict with the first law. 3. A robot must protect its own existence, as long as such protection does not conflict with the first or second law.

3. Michelangelo wrote a sonnet that begins:

   > Non ha l' ottimo artista alcun concetto
   >   Ch' un marmo solo in sè non circonscriva
   >   Col suo soverchio; e solo a quello arriva
   >   La man che ubbidisce all' intelleto.

   Stone (1961, p. 6) translates this as:

   > The best of artists hath no thought to show
   >   which the rough stone in its superfluous shell
   >   doth not include; to break the marble spell
   >   is all the hand that serves the brain can do.

   Stone (p. 144) describes the process: "He was not working from his drawings or clay models; they had all been put away. He was carving from the images in his mind. His eyes and hands knew where every line, curve, mass must emerge, and at what depth in the heart of the stone to create the low relief."

4. In his 1963 novel *Cat's Cradle*, Kurt Vonnegutt imagined a gray-goo-like accident where a form of ice called ice-nine, which becomes solid at a much higher temperature, freezes the oceans.

5. This estimate is in Leslie's book *The End of the World: The Science and Ethics of Human Extinction*, where he notes that the probability of extinction is

substantially higher if we accept Brandon Carter's doomsday argument, which is, briefly, that "we ought to have some reluctance to believe that we are very exceptionally early, for instance in the earliest 0.001 percent, among all humans who will ever have lived. This would be some reason for thinking that humankind will not survive for many more centuries, let alone colonize the galaxy. Carter's doomsday argument doesn't generate any risk estimates just by itself. It is an argument for *revising* the estimates which we generate when we consider various possible dangers" Routledge, 1996, p. 145).

6. As David Forrest suggests in his paper "Regulating Nanotechnology Development" (available at www.foresight.org/NanoRev/Forrest1989.html), "If we used strict liability as an alternative to regulation it would be impossible for any developer to internalize the cost of the risk (destruction of the biosphere), so theoretically the activity of developing nanotechnology should never be undertaken." Forrest's analysis leaves us with only government regulation to protect us—not a comforting thought."

7. See also Hans Bethe's 1997 letter to President Clinton, at www.fas.org/bethecr. htm.

REFERENCES

Asimov, I. 1950. *I, Robot*. New York: Bantam Books.

Attali, J. 1992. *Millennium: Winners and Losers in the Coming Order*. Williston, VT: Three Rivers Press.

Attali, J. 2000. *Fraternités*. Paris: Le Livre de Poche.

Bethe, H. 1995. Appeal to scientists to cease work on nuclear weapons. Public statement by Hans Bethe on August 6, 1995. http://www.wagingpeace.org/articles/00000/1995_bethe-appeal-scientists.htm

Clarke, A. C. 1998. Presidents, experts, and asteroids. *Science,* June 5. Reprinted as Science and society. In *Greetings, Carbon-Based Bipeds! Collected Essays, 1934–1998*. New York St. Martin's Press, 1999.

Dalai Lama. 2001. *Ethics for the New Millennium*. New York: Penguin Putnam.

Doty, P. 1999. The forgotten menace: Nuclear weapons stockpiles still represent the biggest threat to civilization. *Nature* 402: 583.

Drexler, E. 1986. *Engines of Creation: The Coming Era of Nanotechnology*. New York: Anchor Books.

Drexler, E. 1993. *Unbounding the Future: The Nanotech Revolution*. New York: Quill Press.

Dyson, G. 1997. *Darwin Among the Machines: The Evolution of Global Intelligence*. New York: Perseus Books.

Else, J. 1981. *The Day After Trinity: J. Robert Oppenheimer and The Atomic Bomb*. Available at www.pyramiddirect.com.

Feynman, R. 1960. There's plenty of room at the bottom. *Engineering & Science*. February 1960. Pasadena, CA: Caltech.

Garrett, L. 1994. *The Coming Plague: Newly Emerging Diseases in a World Out of Balance*. New York: Penguin.

Gelenter, D. 1997. *Drawing Life: Surviving the Unabomber*. New York: Free Press.

Hamilton, E. 1942. *The Greek Way.* New York: W. W. Norton.

Heinlein, R.A. 1958. *Have Spacesuit, Will Travel.* New York: Charles Scribners.

Herbert, F. 1982. *The White Plague.* New York: Putnam Adult Series.

Joy, W. 1989. The future of computation. In B. C. Crandall and Lewis, J. (Eds.), *Nanotechnology: Research and Perspectives.* Cambridge, MA: MIT Press. See also www.foresight. org/Conferences/MNT01/Nano1.html.

Kauffman, S. 1996. Self-replication: Even peptides do It. *Nature* 382, August 8; see www.santafe. edu/sfi/People/kauffman/sak-peptides.html.

Kurzweil, R. 1998. *The Age of Spiritual Machine: When Computers Exceed Human Intelligence.* New York: Viking Press.

Leslie, J. 1996. *The End of the World: The Science and Ethics of Human Extinction.* New York: Routledge.

Lovins, A. and Lovins, H. 2000. A tale of two botanies. *Wired*, March 2000, Issue 8: 04.

Meselson, Matthew. "The Problem of Biological Weapons." Presentation to the 1,818th Stated Meeting of the American Academy of Arts and Sciences, January 13, 1999. (minerva.amacad.org/archive/bulletin4.htm)

Moravec, H. 1998. *Robot: Mere Machine to Transcendental Mind.* New York: Oxford University Press.

Rhodes, R. 2000. *Visions of Technology: A Century of Vital Debate about Machine Systems and the Human World.* New York: Simon & Schuster.

Sagan, C. 1994. *Pale Blue Dot: A Vision of the Human Future in Space.* Colorado Springs, CO: Ballantine Books.

Stone, I. 1961. *The Agony and the Ecstasy.* New York: Doubleday.

Thoreau, H. 1854. *Walden.* Boston: Ticknor and Fields.

Vonnegutt, K. 1963. *Cat's Cradle.* New York: Bantam Doubleday.

3

ON THE NATIONAL AGENDA: U.S. CONGRESSIONAL TESTIMONY ON THE SOCIETAL IMPLICATIONS OF NANOTECHNOLOGY*

Ray Kurzweil

FULL VERBAL TESTIMONY

Chairman Boehlert, distinguished members of the U.S. House of Representatives Committee on Science, and other distinguished guests, I appreciate this opportunity to respond to your questions and concerns on the vital issue of the societal implications of nanotechnology. Our rapidly growing ability to manipulate matter and energy at ever smaller scales promises to transform virtually every sector of society, including health and medicine, manufacturing, electronics and computers, energy, travel, and defense. There will be increasing overlap between nanotechnology and other technologies of increasing influence, such as biotechnology and artificial intelligence. As with any other technological transformation, we will be faced with deeply intertwined promise and peril.

In my brief verbal remarks, I only have time to summarize my conclusions on this complex subject, and I am providing the committee with an expanded written response that attempts to explain the reasoning behind my views.

* This chapter represents Ray Kurzweil's testimony presented April 9, 2003, at the Committee on Science, U.S. House of Representatives, hearing to examine the societal implications of nanotechnology and consider H.R. 766, The Nanotechnology Research and Development Act of 2003. A complete version of this chapter was originally published as Ray Kurzweil, "Testimony of Ray Kurzweil on the Societal Implications of Nanotechnology," www.kurzweilAI.net. Reprinted with permission.

Eric Drexler's 1986 thesis developed the concept of building molecule-scale devices using molecular assemblers that would precisely guide chemical reactions. Without going through the history of the controversy surrounding feasibility, it is fair to say that the consensus today is that nanoassembly is indeed feasible, although the most dramatic capabilities are still a couple of decades away.

The concept of nanotechnology today has been expanded to include essentially any technology where the key features are measured in a modest number of nanometers (under 100 by some definitions). By this standard, contemporary electronics has already passed this threshold.

For the past two decades, I have studied technology trends, along with a team of researchers who have assisted me in gathering critical measures of technology in different areas, and I have been developing mathematical models of how technology evolves. Several conclusions from this study have a direct bearing on the issues before this hearing. Technologies, particularly those related to information, develop at an exponential pace, generally doubling in capability and price–performance every year. This observation includes the power of computation, communication (both wired and wireless), DNA sequencing, brain scanning, brain reverse engineering, and the size and scope of human knowledge in general. Of particular relevance to this hearing, the size of technology is itself inexorably shrinking. According to my models, both electronic and mechanical technologies are shrinking at a rate of 5.6 per linear dimension per decade. At this rate, most of technology will be "nanotechnology" by the 2020s.

The golden age of nanotechnology is, therefore, a couple of decades away. This era will bring us the ability to essentially convert software, that is, information, directly into physical products. We will be able to produce virtually any product for pennies per pound. Computers will have greater computational capacity than the human brain, and we will be completing the reverse engineering of the human brain to reveal the software design of human intelligence. We are already placing devices with narrow intelligence in our bodies for diagnostic and therapeutic purposes. With the advent of nanotechnology, we will be able to keep our bodies and brains in a healthy, optimal state indefinitely. We will have technologies to reverse environmental pollution. Nanotechnology and related advanced technologies of the 2020s will bring us the opportunity to overcome age-old problems, including pollution, poverty, disease, and aging.

We hear increasingly strident voices that object to the intermingling of the so-called natural world with the products of our technology. The increasing intimacy of our human lives with our technology is not a new story, and I would remind the committee that, had it not been for the technological advances of the past two centuries, most of us here today would not be here. Human life expectancy was 37 years in 1800. Most humans at that time lived lives dominated by poverty, intense labor, disease, and misfortune. We are immeasurably better off as a result of technology, but there is still a lot of suffering in the world to overcome. We have a moral imperative, therefore, to continue the pursuit of knowledge and of advanced technologies that can continue to overcome human affliction.

There is also an economic imperative to continue. Nanotechnology is not a single field of study that we can simply relinquish, as suggested by Bill Joy's essay, "Why the Future Doesn't Need Us" (Chapter 2). Nanotechnology is advancing on hundreds of fronts and is an extremely diverse activity. We cannot relinquish its pursuit without essentially relinquishing all of technology, which would require a Brave New World totalitarian scenario, which is inconsistent with the values of our society.

Technology has always been a double-edged sword, and that is certainly true of nanotechnology. The same technology that promises to advance human health and wealth also has the potential for destructive applications. We can see that duality today in biotechnology. The same techniques that could save millions of lives from cancer and disease may also empower a bioterrorist to create a bioengineered pathogen.

A lot of attention has been paid to the problem of self-replicating nanotechnology entities that could essentially form a nonbiological cancer that would threaten the planet. I discuss in my written testimony steps we can take now and in the future to ameliorate these dangers. However, the primary point I would like to make is that we will have no choice but to confront the challenge of guiding nanotechnology in a constructive direction. Any broad attempt to relinquish nanotechnology will only push it underground, which would interfere with the benefits while actually making the dangers worse.

As a test case, we can take a small measure of comfort from how we have dealt with one recent technological challenge. There exists today a new form of fully nonbiological self-replicating entity that didn't exist just a few decades ago: the computer virus. When this form of destructive intruder first appeared, strong concerns were voiced that, as they became more sophisticated, software pathogens had the potential to destroy the computer network medium they live in. Yet the "immune system" that has evolved in response to this challenge has been largely effective. Although destructive self-replicating software entities do cause damage from time to time, the injury is but a small fraction of the benefit we receive from the computers and communication links that harbor them. No one would suggest we do away with computers, local area networks, and the Internet because of software viruses.

One might counter that computer viruses do not have the lethal potential of biological viruses or of destructive nanotechnology. This is not always the case: We rely on software to monitor patients in critical care units, to fly and land airplanes, to guide intelligent weapons in our current campaign in Iraq, and other "mission-critical" tasks. To the extent that this is true, however, this observation only strengthens my argument. The fact that computer viruses are not usually deadly to humans only means that more people are willing to create and release them. It also means that our response to the danger is that much less intense. Conversely, when it comes to self-replicating entities that are potentially lethal on a large scale, our response on all levels will be vastly more serious, as we have seen since 9/11.

I would describe our response to software pathogens as effective and successful. Although they remain (and always will remain) a concern, the danger remains at a nuisance level. Keep in mind that this success is in an industry in which there is no regulation and no certification for practitioners. This largely unregulated industry is also enormously productive. One could argue that it has contributed more to our technological and economic progress than any other enterprise in human history.

Some of the concerns that have been raised, such as Bill Joy's article, are effective because they paint a picture of future dangers as if they were released on today's unprepared world. The reality is that the sophistication and power of our defensive technologies and knowledge will grow along with the dangers.

The challenge most immediately in front of us is not self-replicating nanotechnology, but rather self-replicating biotechnology. The next two decades will be the golden age of biotechnology, whereas the comparable era for nanotechnology will follow in the 2020s and beyond. We are now in the early stages of a transforming technology based on the intersection of biology and information science. We are learning the "software" methods of life and disease processes. By reprogramming the information processes that lead to and encourage disease and aging, we will have the ability to overcome these afflictions. However, the same knowledge can also empower a terrorist to create a bioengineered pathogen.

As we compare the success we have had in controlling engineered software viruses to the coming challenge of controlling engineered biological viruses, we are struck with one salient difference. As I noted, the software industry is almost completely unregulated. The same is obviously not the case for biotechnology. A bioterrorist does not need to put his "innovations" through the FDA (Food and Drug Administration). However, we do require the scientists developing the defensive technologies to follow the existing regulations, which slow down the innovation process at every step. Moreover, it is impossible, under existing regulations and ethical standards, to test defenses to bioterrorist agents on humans. There is already extensive discussion to modify these regulations to allow for animal models and simulations to replace infeasible human trials. This will be necessary, but I believe we will need to go beyond these steps to accelerate the development of vitally needed defensive technologies.

With the Human Genome Project, 3 to 5 percent of the budgets were devoted to the ethical, legal, and social implications (ELSIs) of the technology. A similar commitment for nanotechnology would be appropriate and constructive.

Near-term applications of nanotechnology are far more limited in their benefits as well as more benign in their potential dangers. These include developments in the materials area involving the addition of particles with multi-nanometer features to plastics, textiles, and other products. These have perhaps the greatest potential in the area of pharmaceutical development by allowing new strategies for highly targeted drugs that perform their intended function and reach the appropriate tissues while minimizing side effects. This development is not qualitatively different than what we have been doing for decades in that many new materials involve constituent particles that are novel and of a similar physical scale. The emerging nanoparticle technology provides more precise control, but the idea of introducing new nonbiological materials into the environment is hardly a new phenomenon. We cannot say a priori that all nanoengineered particles are safe, nor would it be appropriate to deem them necessarily unsafe. Environmental tests thus far have not shown reasons for undue concern, and it is my view that existing regulations on the safety of foods, drugs, and other materials in the environment are sufficient to deal with these near-term applications.

The voices that are expressing concern about nanotechnology are the same voices that have expressed undue levels of concern about genetically modified organisms (GMOs). As with nanoparticles, GMOs are neither inherently safe nor unsafe, and reasonable levels of regulation for safety are appropriate. However, none of the dire warnings about GMOs have come to pass. Already, African nations, such as Zambia and Zimbabwe, have rejected vitally needed food aid under pressure from European antiGMO activists. The reflexive antitechnology stance that has been reflected in the GMO controversy will not be helpful in balancing the benefits and risks of nanoparticle technology.

In summary, I believe that existing regulatory mechanisms are sufficient to handle near-term applications of nanotechnology. As for the long term, we need to appreciate that a myriad of nanoscale technologies are inevitable. The current examinations and dialogues on achieving the promise while ameliorating the peril are appropriate and will deserve sharply increased attention as we get closer to realizing these revolutionary technologies.

ABRIDGED WRITTEN TESTIMONY

I am pleased to provide a more detailed written response to the issues raised by the committee. In this written portion of my response, I address the following issues:

- A small sample of examples of true nanotechnology: a few of the implications of nanotechnology two to three decades from now.
- The deeply intertwined promise and peril of nanotechnology and related advanced technologies: Technology is inherently a doubled-edged sword, and we will need to adopt strategies to encourage the benefits while ameliorating the risks. Relinquishing broad areas of technology, as has been proposed, is not feasible and attempts to do so will only drive technology development underground, which will exacerbate the dangers.

A Small Sample of Examples of True Nanotechnology

Ubiquitous nanotechnology is two to three decades away. A prime example of its application will be to deploy billions of "nanobots" : small robots the size of human blood cells that can travel inside the human bloodstream. This notion is not as futuristic as it may sound in that there have already been successful animal experiments using this concept. There are already four major conferences on "BioMEMSs" (biological micro-electronic mechanical systems) covering devices in the human bloodstream.

Consider several examples of nanobot technology, which, based on miniaturization and cost reduction trends, will be feasible within 30 years. In addition to scanning the human brain to facilitate human brain reverse engineering, these nanobots will be able to perform a broad variety of diagnostic and therapeutic functions inside the bloodstream and human body. Robert Freitas, for example, has designed robotic replacements for human blood cells that perform hundreds or thousands of times more effectively than their biological counterparts. With Freitas's "respirocytes" (robotic red blood cells), you could do an Olympic sprint for 15 minutes without taking a breath. His robotic macrophages will be far more effective than our white blood cells at combating pathogens. His DNA repair robot would be able to repair DNA transcription errors and even implement needed DNA changes. Although Freitas's conceptual designs are two or three decades away, there has already been substantial progress on bloodstream-based devices. For example, one scientist has cured type I diabetes in rats with a nanoengineered device that incorporates pancreatic islet cells. The device has 7-nanometer pores that let insulin out but block the antibodies which destroy these cells. There are many innovative projects of this type already under way.

Clearly, nanobot technology has profound military applications, and any expectation that such uses will be "relinquished" are highly unrealistic. Already, the DOD (Department of Defense) is developing "smart dust," which are tiny robots the size of insects or even smaller. Although not quite nanotechnology, millions of these devices can be dropped into enemy territory to provide highly detailed surveillance. The potential application for even smaller, nanotechnology-based devices is even greater. Want to find Saddam Hussein or Osama bin Laden? Need to locate hidden weapons of mass destruction? Billions of essentially invisible spies could monitor every square inch of enemy territory, identify every person and every weapon, and even carry out missions to destroy enemy targets. The only way for an enemy to counteract such a force is, of course, with their own nanotechnology. The point is that nanotechnology-based weapons will obsolete weapons of larger size.

In addition, nanobots will also be able to expand our experiences and our capabilities. Nanobot technology will provide fully immersive, totally convincing virtual reality in the following way. The nanobots take up positions in close physical proximity to every interneuronal connection coming from all of our senses (e.g., eyes, ears, skin). We already have the technology for electronic devices to communicate with neurons in both directions that requires no direct physical contact with the neurons. For example, scientists at the Max Planck Institute have developed "neuron transistors" that can detect the firing of a nearby neuron or, alternatively, can cause a nearby neuron to fire or suppress it from firing. This amounts to two-way communication between neurons and the electronic-based neuron transistors. The institute scientists demonstrated their invention by controlling the movement of a living leech from their computer. Again, the primary aspects of nanobot-based virtual reality that are not yet feasible are size and cost.

When we want to experience real reality, the nanobots just stay in position (in the capillaries) and do nothing. If we want to enter virtual reality, they suppress all of the inputs coming from the real senses and replace them with the signals that would be appropriate for the virtual environment. You (i.e., your brain) could decide to cause your muscles and limbs to move as you normally would, but the nanobots again intercept these interneuronal signals, suppress your real limbs from moving, and instead cause your virtual limbs to move and provide the appropriate movement and reorientation in the virtual environment.

The Web will provide a panoply of virtual environments to explore. Some will be re-creations of real places, others will be fanciful environments that have no "real" counterpart. Some indeed would be impossible in the physical world (perhaps, because they violate the laws of physics). We will be able to "go" to these virtual environments by ourselves, or we will meet other people there, both real people and simulated people. Of course, ultimately there won't be a clear distinction between the two.

By 2030, going to a website will mean entering a full-immersion virtual-reality environment. In addition to encompassing all of the senses, these shared environments can include emotional overlays as the nanobots will be capable of triggering the neurological correlates of emotions, sexual pleasure, and other derivatives of our sensory experience and mental reactions.

In the same way that people today beam their lives from webcams in their bedrooms, "experience beamers" circa 2030 will beam their entire flow of sensory experiences and, if so desired, their emotions and other secondary reactions. We'll be able to plug in (by going to the appropriate website) and experience other people's lives as in the plot concept of *Being John Malkovich*. Particularly interesting experiences can be archived and relived at any time.

We won't need to wait until 2030 to experience shared virtual-reality environments, at least for the visual and auditory senses. Full-immersion visual–auditory environments will be available by the end of this decade, with images written directly onto our retinas by our eyeglasses and contact lenses. All of the electronics for the computation, image reconstruction, and very high bandwidth wireless connection to the Internet will be embedded in our glasses and woven into our clothing, so computers as distinct objects will disappear.

In my view, the most significant implication of the development of nanotechnology and related advanced technologies of the twenty-first century will be the merger of biological and nonbiological intelligence. First, it is important to point out that, well before the end of the twenty-first century, thinking on nonbiological substrates will dominate. Biological thinking is stuck at 1026 calculations per second (for all biological human brains), and that figure will not appreciably change, even with bioengineering changes to our genome. Nonbiological intelligence, on the other hand, is growing at a double-exponential rate and will vastly exceed biological intelligence well before the middle of this century. However, in my view, this nonbiological intelligence should still be considered human as it is fully derivative of the human–machine civilization. The merger of these two worlds of intelligence is not merely a merger of biological and nonbiological thinking mediums but more importantly one of method and organization of thinking.

One of the key ways in which the two worlds can interact will be through nanobots. Nanobot technology will be able to expand our minds in virtually any imaginable way. Our brains today are relatively fixed in design. Although we do add patterns of interneuronal connections and neurotransmitter concentrations as a normal part of the learning process, the current overall capacity of the human brain is highly constrained, restricted to a mere hundred trillion connections. Brain implants based on massively distributed intelligent nanobots will ultimately expand our memories a trillion fold, and otherwise vastly improve all of our sensory, pattern recognition, and cognitive abilities. Since the nanobots are communicating with each other over a wireless local area network, they can create any set of new neural connections, can break existing connections (by suppressing neural firing), can create new hybrid biological–nonbiological networks, as well as add vast new nonbiological networks.

Using nanobots as brain extenders is a significant improvement over the idea of surgically installed neural implants, which are beginning to be used today (e.g., ventral posterior nucleus, subthalamic nucleus, and ventral lateral thalamus neural implants to counteract Parkinson's disease and tremors from other neurological disorders, cochlear implants, and others). Nanobots will be introduced without surgery, essentially just by injecting or even swallowing them. They can all be directed to leave, so the process is easily reversible. They are programmable, in that they can provide virtual reality one minute and a variety of brain extensions the next. They can change their configuration and clearly can alter their software. Perhaps most importantly, they are massively distributed and therefore can take up billions or trillions of positions throughout the brain, whereas a surgically introduced neural implant can only be placed in one or at most a few locations.

Deeply Intertwined Promise and Peril of Nanotechnology and Related Advanced Technologies

Technology has always been a double-edged sword, bringing us longer and healthier life spans, freedom from physical and mental drudgery, and many new creative possibilities on the one hand while introducing new and salient dangers on the other. Technology empowers both our creative and destructive natures. Stalin's tanks and Hitler's trains used technology. We still live today with sufficient nuclear weapons (not all of which appear to be well accounted for) to end all mammalian life on the planet. Bioengineering is in the early stages of enormous strides in reversing disease and aging processes. However, the means and knowledge will soon exist in a routine college bioengineering lab (and already exists in more sophisticated labs) to create unfriendly pathogens more dangerous than nuclear weapons. As technology accelerates toward the full realization of biotechnology, nanotechnology, and "strong" AI (artificial intelligence at human levels and beyond), we will see the same intertwined potentials: a feast of creativity resulting from human intelligence expanded manyfold combined with many grave new dangers.

Consider unrestrained nanobot replication. Nanobot technology requires billions or trillions of such intelligent devices to be useful. The most cost-effective way to scale up to such levels is through self-replication, essentially the same approach used in the biological world. And in the same way that biological self-replication gone awry (i.e., cancer) results in biological destruction, a defect in the mechanism curtailing nanobot self-replication would endanger all physical entities, biological or otherwise. I address below steps we can take to address this grave risk, but we cannot have complete assurance in any strategy that we devise today.

Other primary concerns include "who is controlling the nanobots?" and "who are the nanobots talking to?" Organizations (e.g., governments, extremist groups) or just a clever individual could put trillions of undetectable nanobots in the water or food supply of an individual or of an entire population. These "spy" nanobots could then monitor, influence, and even control our thoughts and actions. In addition to introducing physical spy nanobots, existing nanobots could be influenced through software viruses and other software "hacking" techniques. When there is software running in our brains, issues of privacy and security will take on a new urgency.

My own expectation is that the creative and constructive applications of this technology will dominate, as I believe they do today. However, I believe we need to invest more heavily in developing specific defensive technologies. As I address further below, we are at this stage today for biotechnology and will reach the stage where we need to directly implement defensive technologies for nanotechnology during the late teen years of this century.

If we imagine describing the dangers that exist today to people who lived a couple of hundred years ago, they would think it mad to take such risks. On the other hand, how many people in the year 2000 would really want to go back to the short, brutish, disease-filled, poverty-stricken, disaster-prone lives that 99 percent of the human race struggled through a couple of centuries ago? We may romanticize the past, but up until fairly recently, most of humanity lived extremely fragile lives where one all-too-common misfortune could spell disaster. Substantial portions of our species still live in this precarious way, which is at least one reason to continue technological progress and the economic enhancement that accompanies it.

People often go through three stages in examining the impact of future technology: awe and wonderment at its potential to overcome age-old problems; then a sense of dread at a new set of grave dangers that accompany these new technologies; followed, finally and hopefully, by the realization that the only viable and responsible path is to set a careful course that can realize the promise while managing the peril.

This congressional hearing was party inspired by Bill Joy's cover story for *Wired* magazine, "Why The Future Doesn't Need Us" (Chapter 2). Bill Joy, cofounder of Sun Microsystems and principal developer of the Java programming language, has recently taken up a personal mission to warn us of the impending dangers from the emergence of self-replicating technologies in the fields of genetics, nanotechnology, and robotics, which he aggregates under the label GNR. Although his warnings are not entirely new, they have attracted considerable attention because of Joy's credibility as one of our leading technologists. It is reminiscent of the attention that George Soros, the currency arbitrager and arch capitalist, received when he made vaguely critical comments about the excesses of unrestrained capitalism.

Joy's concerns include genetically altered designer pathogens, followed by self-replicating entities created through nanotechnology. And if we manage to survive these first two perils, we will encounter robots whose intelligence will rival and ultimately exceed our own. Such robots may make great assistants, but who's to say that we can count on them to remain reliably friendly to mere humans?

Although I am often cast as the technology optimist who counters Joy's pessimism, I do share his concerns regarding self-replicating technologies; indeed, I played a role in bringing these dangers to Bill's attention. In many of the dialogues and forums in which I have participated on this subject, I end up defending Joy's position with regard to the feasibility of these technologies and scenarios when they come under attack by commentators who I believe are being quite shortsighted in their skepticism. Even so, I do find fault with Joy's prescription: halting the advance of technology and the pursuit of knowledge in broad fields such as nanotechnology.

In his essay (Chapter 2), Bill Joy eloquently describes the plagues of centuries past and how new self-replicating technologies, such as mutant bioengineered pathogens and "nanobots" run amok, may bring back long-forgotten pestilence. Indeed these are real dangers. It is also the case, which Joy acknowledges, that it has been technological advances, such as antibiotics and improved sanitation, which have freed us from the prevalence of such plagues. Suffering in the world continues and demands our steadfast attention. Should we tell the millions of people afflicted with cancer and other devastating conditions that we are canceling the development of all bioengineered treatments because there is a risk that these same technologies may someday be used for malevolent purposes? Having asked the rhetorical question, I realize that there is a movement to do exactly that, but I think most people would agree that such broad-based relinquishment is not the answer.

The continued opportunity to alleviate human distress is one important motivation for continuing technological advancement. Also compelling are the already apparent economic gains I discussed above that will continue to hasten in the decades ahead. The continued acceleration of many intertwined technologies are roads paved with gold (I use the plural here because technology is clearly not a single path). In a competitive environment, it is an economic imperative to go down these roads. Relinquishing technological advancement would be economic suicide for individuals, companies, and nations.

Relinquishment Issue

This brings us to the issue of relinquishment, which is Bill Joy's most controversial recommendation and personal commitment. I do feel that relinquishment at the right level is part of a responsible and constructive response to these genuine perils. The issue, however, is exactly this: At what level are we to relinquish technology?

Ted Kaczynski would have us renounce all of it. This, in my view, is neither desirable nor feasible, and the futility of such a position is only underscored by the senselessness of Kaczynski's deplorable tactics. There are other voices, less reckless than Kaczynski's, who are nonetheless arguing for broad-based relinquishment of technology. Bill McKibben (McKibben, 2000), the environmentalist who was one of the first to warn against global warming, takes the position that "environmentalists must now grapple squarely with the idea of a world that has enough wealth and enough technological capability, and should not pursue more." In my view, this position ignores the extensive suffering that remains in the human world, which we will be in a position to alleviate through continued technological progress.

Another level would be to forego certain fields—nanotechnology, for example—that might be regarded as too dangerous. But such sweeping strokes of relinquishment are equally untenable. As I pointed out above, nanotechnology is simply the inevitable end result of the persistent trend toward miniaturization that pervades all of technology. It is far from a single centralized effort, but is being pursued by a myriad of projects with many diverse goals.

One observer wrote:

A further reason why industrial society cannot be reformed... is that modern technology is a unified system in which all parts are dependent on one another. You can't get rid of the "bad" parts of technology and retain only the "good" parts. Take modern medicine, for example. Progress in medical science depends on progress in chemistry, physics, biology, computer science and other fields. Advanced medical treatments require expensive, high-tech equipment that can be made available only by a technologically progressive, economically rich society. Clearly you can't have much progress in medicine without the whole technological system and everything that goes with it.

The observer I am quoting is, again, Ted Kaczynski (Kaczynski, 1995). Although one will properly resist Kaczynski as an authority, I believe he is correct on the deeply entangled nature of the benefits and risks. However, Kaczynski and I clearly part company on our overall assessment on the relative balance between the two. Bill Joy and I have dialogued on this issue both publicly and privately, and we both believe that technology will and should progress and that we need to be actively concerned with the dark side. If Bill and I disagree, it's on the granularity of relinquishment that is both feasible and desirable.

Abandonment of broad areas of technology will only push them underground where development would continue unimpeded by ethics and regulation. In such a situation, it would be the less stable, less responsible practitioners (e.g., terrorists) who would have all the expertise.

I do think that relinquishment at the right level needs to be part of our ethical response to the dangers of twenty-first-century technologies. One constructive example of this is the proposed ethical guideline by the Foresight Institute, founded by nanotechnology pioneer Eric Drexler, that nanotechnologists agree to relinquish the development of physical entities that can self-replicate in a natural environment. Another is a ban on self-replicating physical entities that contain their own codes for self-replication. In what nanotechnologist Ralph Merkle calls the "broadcast architecture," such entities would have to obtain such codes from a centralized secure server, which would guard against undesirable replication. I discuss these guidelines further below.

The broadcast architecture is impossible in the biological world, which represents at least one way in which nanotechnology can be made safer than biotechnology. In other ways, nanotech is potentially more dangerous because nanobots can be physically stronger than protein-based entities and more intelligent. It will eventually be possible to combine the two by having nanotechnology provide the codes within biological entities (replacing DNA), in which case biological entities can use the much safer broadcast architecture. I comment further on the strengths and weaknesses of the broadcast architecture below.

As responsible technologies, our ethics should include such "fine-grained" relinquishment, among other professional ethical guidelines. Other protections will need to include oversight by regulatory bodies, the development of technology-specific "immune" responses, as well as computer-assisted surveillance by law enforcement organizations. Many people are not aware that our intelligence agencies already use advanced technologies such as automated word spotting to monitor a substantial flow of telephone conversations. As we go forward, balancing our cherished rights of privacy with our need to be protected from the malicious use of powerful twenty-first-century technologies will be one of many profound challenges. This is one reason that such issues as an encryption "trap door" (in which law enforcement authorities would have access to otherwise secure information) and the FBI "Carnivore" email-snooping system have been controversial, although these controversies have abated since September 11, 2001.

As a test case, we can take a small measure of comfort from how we have dealt with one recent technological challenge. There exists today a new form of fully nonbiological self-replicating entity that didn't exist just a few decades ago: the computer virus. When this form of destructive intruder first appeared, strong concerns were voiced that, as they became more sophisticated, software pathogens had the potential to destroy the computer network medium they live in. Yet the "immune system" that has evolved in response to this challenge has been largely effective. Although destructive self-replicating software entities do cause damage from time to time, the injury is but a small fraction of the benefit we receive from the computers and communication links that harbor them. No one would suggest we do away with computers, local area networks, and the Internet because of software viruses.

One might counter that computer viruses do not have the lethal potential of biological viruses or of destructive nanotechnology. This is not always the case; we rely on software to monitor patients in critical care units, to fly and land airplanes, to guide intelligent weapons in our current campaign in Iraq, and other "mission-critical" tasks. To the extent that this is true, however, this observation only strengthens my argument. The fact that computer viruses are not usually deadly to humans only means that more people are willing to create and release them. It also means that our response to the danger is that much less intense. Conversely, when it comes to self-replicating entities that are potentially lethal on a large scale, our response on all levels will be vastly more serious, as we have seen since 9/11.

I would describe our response to software pathogens as effective and successful. Although they remain (and always will remain) a concern, the danger remains at a nuisance level. Keep in mind that this success is in an industry in which there is no regulation and no certification for practitioners. This largely unregulated industry is also enormously productive. One could argue that it has contributed more to our technological and economic progress than any other enterprise in human history. I discuss the issue of regulation further below.

Development of Defensive Technologies and the Impact of Regulation

Joy's treatise (Chapter 2) is effective because he paints a picture of future dangers as if they were released on today's unprepared world. The reality is that the sophistication and power of our defensive technologies and knowledge will grow along with the dangers. When we have "gray goo" (unrestrained nanobot replication), we will also have "blue goo" ("police" nanobots that combat the "bad" nanobots). The story of the twenty-first-century has not yet been written, so we cannot say with assurance that we will successfully avoid all misuse. But the surest way to prevent the development of the defensive technologies would be to relinquish the pursuit of knowledge in broad areas. We have been able to largely control harmful software virus replication because the requisite knowledge is widely available to responsible practitioners. Attempts to restrict this knowledge would have created a far less stable situation. Responses to new challenges would have been far slower, and it is likely that the balance would have shifted toward the more destructive applications (e.g., software viruses).

The challenge most immediately in front of us is not self-replicating nanotechnology but rather self-replicating biotechnology. The next two decades will be the golden age of biotechnology, whereas the comparable era for nanotechnology will follow in the 2020s and beyond. We are now in the early stages of a transforming technology based on the intersection of biology and information science. We are learning the "software" methods of life and disease processes. By reprogramming the information processes that lead to and encourage disease and aging, we will have the ability to overcome these afflictions. However, the same knowledge can also empower a terrorist to create a bioengineered pathogen.

As we compare the success we have had in controlling engineered software viruses to the coming challenge of controlling engineered biological viruses, we are struck with one salient difference. As I noted above, the software industry is almost completely unregulated. The same is obviously not the case for biotechnology. A bioterrorist does not need to put his "innovations" through the FDA. However, we do require the scientists developing the defensive technologies to follow the existing regulations, which slow down the innovation process at every step. Moreover, it is impossible, under existing regulations and ethical standards, to test defenses to bioterrorist agents. There is already extensive discussion to modify these regulations to allow for animal models and simulations to replace infeasible human trials. This will be necessary, but I believe we will need to go beyond these steps to accelerate the development of vitally needed defensive technologies.

For reasons I have articulated above, stopping these technologies is not feasible, and pursuit of such broad forms of relinquishment will only distract us from the vital task in front of us. In terms of public policy, the task at hand is to rapidly develop the defensive steps needed, which include ethical standards, legal standards, and defensive technologies. It is quite clearly a race. As I noted, in the software field, the defensive technologies have remained a step ahead of the offensive ones. With the extensive regulation in the medical field slowing down innovation at each stage, we cannot have the same confidence with regard to the abuse of biotechnology.

In the current environment, when one person dies in gene therapy trials, there are congressional investigations and all gene therapy research comes to a temporary halt. There is a legitimate need to make biomedical research as safe as possible, but our balancing of risks is completely off. The millions of people who desperately need the advances to be made available by gene therapy and other breakthrough biotechnology advances appear to carry little political weight against a handful of well-publicized casualties from the inevitable risks of progress.

This equation will become even more stark when we consider the emerging dangers of bioengineered pathogens. What is needed is a change in public attitude in terms of tolerance for needed risk.

Hastening defensive technologies is absolutely vital to our security. We need to streamline regulatory procedures to achieve this. However, we also need to greatly increase our investment explicitly in the defensive technologies. In the biotechnology field, this means the rapid development of antiviral medications. We will not have time to develop specific countermeasures for each new challenge that comes along. We are close to developing more generalized antiviral technologies, and these need to be accelerated.

I have addressed here the issue of biotechnology because that is the threshold and challenge that we now face. The comparable situation will exist for nanotechnology once replication of nanoengineered entities has been achieved. As that threshold comes closer, we will then need to invest specifically in the development of defensive technologies, including the creation of a nanotechnology-based immune system. Bill Joy and other observers have pointed out that such an immune system would itself be a danger because of the potential of "autoimmune" reactions (i.e., the immune system using its powers to attack the world it is supposed to be defending).

However, this observation is not a compelling reason to avoid the creation of an immune system. No one would argue that humans would be better off without an immune system because of the possibility of autoimmune diseases. Although the immune system can itself be a danger, humans would not last more than a few weeks (barring extraordinary efforts at isolation) without one. The development of a technological immune system for nanotechnology will happen even without explicit efforts to create one. We have effectively done this with regard to software viruses. We created a software virus immune system not through a formal grand design project but rather through our incremental responses to each new challenge. We can expect the same thing will happen as challenges from nanotechnology based dangers emerge. The point for public policy will be to specifically invest in these defensive technologies.

It is premature today to develop specific defensive nanotechnologies since we can only have a general idea of what we are trying to defend against. It would be similar to the engineering world creating defenses against software viruses before the first one had been created. However, there is already fruitful dialogue and discussion on anticipating this issue, and significantly expanded investment in these efforts is to be encouraged.

As I mentioned above, the Foresight Institute (2001), for example, has devised a set of ethical standards and strategies for assuring the development of safe nanotechnology. These guidelines include:

- "Artificial replicators must not be capable of replication in a natural, uncontrolled environment."
- "Evolution within the context of a self-replicating manufacturing system is discouraged."
- "MNT (molecular nanotechnology) designs should specifically limit proliferation and provide traceability of any replicating systems."
- "Distribution of molecular manufacturing development capability should be restricted whenever possible, to responsible actors that have agreed to the guidelines. No such restriction need apply to end products of the development process."

Other strategies that the Foresight Institute has proposed include:

- Replication should require materials not found in the natural environment.
- Manufacturing (replication) should be separated from the functionality of end products. Manufacturing devices can create end products but cannot replicate themselves, and end products should have no replication capabilities.
- Replication should require replication codes that are encrypted and time limited. The broadcast architecture mentioned earlier is an example of this recommendation.

These guidelines and strategies are likely to be effective with regard to preventing accidental release of dangerous self-replicating nanotechnology entities. The situation with regard to intentional design and release of such entities is more complex and more challenging. We can anticipate approaches that would have the potential to defeat each of these layers of protections by a sufficiently determined and destructive opponent.

Take, for example, the broadcast architecture. When properly designed, each entity is unable to replicate without first obtaining replication codes. These codes are not passed on from one replication generation to the next. However, a modification to such a design could bypass the destruction of the replication codes and thereby pass them on to the next generation. To overcome that possibility, it has been recommended that the memory for the replication codes be limited to only a subset of the full replication code so that there is insufficient memory to pass the codes along. However, this guideline could be defeated by expanding the size of the replication code memory to incorporate the entire code. Another protection that has been suggested is to encrypt the codes and to build in protections such as time expiration limitations in the decryption systems. However, we can see the ease with which protections against unauthorized replications of intellectual property such as music files have been defeated. Once replication codes and protective layers are stripped away, the information can be replicated without these restrictions.

My point is not that protection is impossible. Rather, we need to realize that any level of protection will only work to a certain level of sophistication. The "meta" lesson here is that we will need to continue to advance the defensive technologies and keep them one or more steps ahead of the destructive technologies. We have seen analogies to this in many areas, including technologies for national defense, as well as our largely successful efforts to combat software viruses, that I alluded to above.

What we can do today with regard to the critical challenge of self-replication in nanotechnology is to continue the type of effective study that the Foresight Institute has initiated. With the Human Genome Project, 3 to 5 percent of the budgets were devoted to the ELSIs of the technology. A similar commitment for nanotechnology would be appropriate and constructive.

Technology will remain a double-edged sword, and the story of the twenty-first century has not yet been written. It represents vast power to be used for all humankind's purposes. We have no choice but to work hard to apply these quickening technologies to advance our human values, despite what often appears to be a lack of consensus on what those values should be.

REFERENCES

Drexler, E. 1986. *Engines of Creation: The Coming Era of Nanotechnology*. New York: Anchor Books.

Foresight Institute. 2001. *Foresight Guidelines on Molecular Technology*. http://www.foresight.org/guidelines/current.html

Kaczynski, T. 1995. *Unabomber Manifesto*. http://www.kurzweilai.net/meme/frame.html?main=/articles/art0182.html

McKibben, B. 2000. How much is enough? The environmental movement as a pivot point in human history. Lecture at the Harvard Seminar on Environmental Values, October 18, 2000. http://www.ecoethics.net/hsev/newscience/mckibben.htm

PART II

BACKGROUND: NANOTECHNOLOGY IN CONTEXT

John Weckert

Following the brief look at nanotechnology and its issues in Part I, it would be helpful at this point to provide some context or background discussion to support our further investigations into nanoethics.

First, we want to be clear that nanotechnology is expected to deliver profound, immeasurable benefits—which may very well outweigh many of the possible problems arising from nanotechnology. An ongoing danger for ethicists working in ethics applied to some field such as nanotechnology is that of becoming, or of being perceived to be, overly focused on only the negative. They always seem to be concerned about dangers or problems of the technology, which is understandable since this is primarily where ethical and social issues lie.

So in Chapter 4, Foresight Nanotech Institute's Christine Peterson and Jacob Heller discuss a number of areas in which nanotechnology can make a substantial contribution to humanity: global energy needs, clean and abundant water, health, the environment, powerful information technology, and the development of space. Further, these potential benefits suggest that there may be ethical problems not just in causing harm from the uses of technology but also in not fixing problems when the technology could do so. While, in general, it is thought that the duty to avoid doing harm is stronger than the duty to do good, it does not follow that there is not a duty to do good.

In Chapter 5, University of Sheffield physicist Richard Jones continues the line of discussion started in the introduction of examining some of the disputes and tensions

Nanoethics: The Ethical and Social Implications of Nanotechnology. Edited by Allhoff, Lin, Moor, Weckert
Copyright © 2007 John Wiley & Sons, Inc.

within nanotechnology itself. The most obvious of these is the argument about what is often called "molecular manufacturing," which is the view attributed to K. Eric Drexler. Opponents of this view, represented most famously by Nobel laureate Richard Smalley, doubt that Drexler's vision is possible or at least that it is unlikely to become a reality in the foreseeable future.

Both sides to the molecular manufacturing debate believe that the benefits of nanotechnology will be great, but they emphasize different benefits. In the molecular manufacturing camp, the focus is on a world of inexpensive abundance—a world in which just about anything will be able to be manufactured cleanly, cheaply, and in any desired amount. In the opposing camp, the benefits are seen more as arising out of developments continuous with other sciences and enhancements of current technologies and products: stronger and lighter materials, smaller and more powerful computers, better drug delivery, and so on. This is the mainstream view, and developments here are at least partly market driven. The background provided by Jones is necessary in order to understand much of the current discussion, particularly the more popular views, surrounding nanotechnology. (We return to molecular manufacturing in Part VII.)

Chapter 6 helps explain what it means to say that nanotechnology is "market driven." In our more idealistic moments, we like to think that scientific researchers follow their research wherever it may lead in order to further knowledge, whatever that knowledge might be. This is at best a partial truth. In general, scientists work in areas for which funding is available, and this funding tends to be made available in those areas where the private corporation or the public funding body believes that there will be some tangible benefit in the not-too-distant future. Society, through corporations that require profits for their shareholders and through government funding bodies sensitive to their electorates (in democratic countries), has an important role in deciding what research will be undertaken. Neal Lane and Thomas Kalil, who were top advisors to U.S. President Clinton in creating the National Nanotechnology Initiative (NNI), illustrate this well in their discussion of the NNI, as just one example of a country that is making nanotechnology a priority funding area for research. A larger percentage of nanotechnology projects are funded, not because they are necessarily of a higher standard than other projects, but because governments want to encourage this field. There is a standard joke, and not just in the United States, that "nanotechnology" is Greek for "funding."

4

NANOTECH'S PROMISE: OVERCOMING HUMANITY'S MOST PRESSING CHALLENGES*

Christine Peterson and Jacob Heller

Properly evaluating nanoethics requires that we look at nanotechnology from all sides. Many of the chapters in this volume focus on the possible negative consequences of nanotechnology: It could cause problems for the environment or health, widen economic disparities, increase surveillance, or create dangerous weapons. Understanding the potential downsides of nanotechnology is of enormous value, since it is vital for managing and mitigating them. But it would be a mistake to miss the forest for a few ugly trees—to judge nanotechnology only by its risks. Humanity still struggles with problems of resource scarcity, disease, pollution, and other technology-related constraints.

The promise of nanotechnology is that, if properly applied, it may offer better solutions for some of the most intractable and longstanding challenges faced by humanity. When considering ethical implications of the technology, it is important that we do not ignore the repercussions of forgoing the potential benefits of nanotechnology. The wise and ethical development of nanotechnology can relieve much needless poverty, pain, and death; this fact must be weighed along with nanotechnology's potential downsides in order to have a balanced ethical understanding of nanotechnology.

* The authors are grateful to Bryan Bruns, Robert A. Freitas, Jr., Steve Gillett, Miki Litmanovitz, Ralph C. Merkle, and Norm Wu for their helpful comments on previous drafts.

Nanoethics: The Ethical and Social Implications of Nanotechnology. Edited by Allhoff, Lin, Moor, Weckert
Copyright © 2007 John Wiley & Sons, Inc.

Foresight Nanotech Institute, founded in 1986, was the first organization to study nanotechnology policy issues. Its mission is to minimize nanotechnology's downsides and maximize its benefits. To promote discussion on strategies to minimize the potential dangers associated with advanced nanotechnology, Foresight has promoted discussion of risks and strategies for addressing them. In one initiative, Foresight collaborated with organizations and individuals in the nanotechnology community to formulate the Foresight Guidelines for Responsible Nanotechnology Development (Jacobstein, 2006).

To help understand how best to realize nanotechnology's benefits, Foresight is now focusing on six major challenges faced by humanity that can be addressed with nanotechnology: (1) meeting global energy needs with clean solutions, (2) providing abundant clean water globally, (3) increasing health and longevity of human life, (4) healing and preserving the environment, (5) making powerful information technology available everywhere, and (6) enabling the development of space (Foresight Nanotech Institute, 2005). This chapter will discuss the positive uses and implications of nanotechnology in the context of these challenges, in both short-term and long-term applications. Short-term nanotechnology is on the very close horizon (3 to 5 years), where the technology is already being researched and the remaining hurdles are product development and commercialization. Long-term nanotechnology products have less clear time frames, but the technologies discussed are widely believed to be technologically feasible. Some long-term nanotechnology applications may arrive as soon as 5 to 10 years from now, while others may not appear for decades.

This chapter gives special attention to ways that nanotechnology can help the billions of people who still live in poverty, since it is for these people that nanotechnology can make the most dramatic contribution. Unfortunately, just because a technology has the opportunity to serve the neediest does not mean that it will. Previous technologies with similar possibilities have not always lived up to their full promise of improving the lives of the impoverished, in part because they were not coupled with the needed economic and political conditions. For example, advocates of biotechnology argued that it would be used to increase crop yields in Africa, create a vaccine for malaria, and provide inexpensive AIDS treatments. However, because existing market incentives were insufficient for corporations to invest in such solutions and because there was no political will to provide incentives to develop these solutions, the promises of biotechnology remain unfulfilled.

Fortunately, the direction of nanotechnology is not predetermined; as a technological revolution in its infancy, it can still be guided to increase the chances that it will live up to its promise. However, unless those who advocate the beneficial use of nanotechnology make their voices heard, market forces and political concerns alone—not the urgent requirements of those most in need—will prevail in shaping the direction of nanotechnology. Ensuring that beneficial nanotechnologies are developed and used appropriately will therefore require the resolute participation of concerned citizens, nonprofits, government, and industry. It is of extreme importance that these groups work together to ensure that nanotechnology takes on these pressing challenges.

MEETING GLOBAL ENERGY NEEDS WITH CLEAN SOLUTIONS

Challenges

Today's patterns of energy use are not environmentally sustainable, yet our energy needs are increasing with time. The global energy challenge facing us today is to find ways to expand access to energy while mitigating harm to the environment. Nanotechnology will open the door to both producing sustainable energy and expanding energy availability for those who cannot afford it today.

The reliance on hydrocarbon fuels underlies our energy woes. There is increasing consensus that over the coming decades, and certainly by the end of this century, it is essential to shift away from our current dependence on nonrenewable hydrocarbon fuels. Hydrocarbon fuel use accounts for the majority of human-created greenhouse gases, which significantly contribute to climate change. Anthropogenic climate change is already taking effect and could have disastrous environmental consequences. A U.S. National Aeronautics and Space Administration (NASA) study found that Earth's temperature has risen since 1975; 2005 ties 1998 as the hottest years on record for the last century (Hansen et al., 2006). Climate change may decrease crop yield globally, spread tropical diseases such as malaria, and expand desertification (Intergovernmental Panel on Climate Change, 2001). Clearly, we cannot continue rapid growth in hydrocarbon-based energy production and must find some way to reduce climate disruption to avert widespread and irreversible environmental damage.

However, stopping all growth in energy usage is not necessarily the best option—or even a feasible option—since without increased use of energy by the world's poorest people, their prospects for economic advancement are dim. Electricity provides light as well as convenient energy for a host of applications in homes and businesses, expanding possibilities for economic development and employment. Today, around 1.6 billion people cannot afford access to electric power [International Energy Agency (IEA), 2002]. If current technological and economic trends persist through 2030, 1.4 billion, or 18 percent of the world's population, will still have no access to electricity (IEA, 2002).

Nanotechnology Solutions

Nanotechnology could enable a variety of solutions that will help fill our energy needs without putting undue strain on the environment. In the short term, nanotechnology could aid in the production of clean energy as well as its transmission and conservation through much more precise and efficient applications. In the long term, productive nanosystems—the capability to manufacture with atomic precision (Drexler, 1986)—have the potential to enable an extremely efficient use of energy resources.

One of the most exciting possible short-term applications of nanotechnology comes from increasing the energy output of low-cost photovoltaic (solar) cells. Earth receives far more energy from the sun in a day than we use in an entire year, yet we are only capable of capturing and using a tiny fraction of that energy. Due to its current high cost and low efficiency, solar energy provides only 0.1 percent of the world's energy today.

A study by the U.S. Department of Energy (DOE, 2005) concluded that one of the most important steps to getting cheap and efficient solar energy is the use of nanotechnology.

A recent study found that quantum dots, specialized nanocrystals that exhibit unique physical properties because of their size, can be manipulated to emit more than three times the electrons per photon absorbed compared to current solar panel technology (Ellingson et al., 2005). Applications of nanoscale technology currently in research and development include other approaches to increasing the efficiency of solar cells, using lower cost materials, and allowing flexible installation on rooftops, walls, and other locations. As we develop better solar cells with nanotechnology, it will become possible to begin replacing hydrocarbon fuel technology with solar energy. This energy can become cheap and efficient enough to be used in remote locations, which would help meet the energy needs of the poor. In the long term, we might even be able to perform artificial photosynthesis using nanotechnology-enabled innovations to store energy from the sun in chemical bonds the same way plants do, making energy even more transportable while resolving the intermittency problem inherent in solar energy.

Hydrogen fuel cell technology represents another clean and efficient alternative to hydrocarbon fuels where nanotechnology could make a significant contribution. Fuel cells work by separating the electron from the proton in hydrogen to use the electron to power an electric circuit, and its only byproducts are heat and water. Already, nanotechnology companies and labs are working on myriad applications to make fuel cell technology a reality. One company has designed a nanostructured hydrocarbon polymer electrolyte membrane, the key part of a fuel cell, which produces less heat and water, works with greater speed, and is cheaper than conventional fuel cells (Wu, 2005). Researchers using carbon nanotubes spaced 1 nanometer apart have built structures to store hydrogen efficiently, a notoriously hard task, so that it can be regularly used in cars. Finally, nanotechnology can make clean hydrogen production possible. Today, hydrogen production requires energy, which usually means burning hydrocarbon fuels—negating the environmental benefits of hydrogen. Experiments underway are using nanowires to create a photovoltaic cell that can power the production of hydrogen using only the power of the sun.

Nanotechnology will not only make energy collection more productive, but also make its transmission easier. Currently, between 7 and 10 percent of energy is lost in transmission between the power plant and its final destination due to resistance in the wires. Technology currently under development based on carbon nanotubes, which are over 10 times more conductive than the copper wires used today, would allow electrons to flow down wires as easily as photons of light through optic cables (McCarthy, 2006). Using this new technology, electricity could travel over 1000 miles with hardly any loss of power. Energy could also be transmitted from power plants to remote and impoverished locations, expanding the reach of energy to those who cannot access it today.

Nanotechnology inventions are also helping electronic devices become more mobile by supplying a constant source of energy. Konarka Technologies, a U.S. company, uses nanotechnology to create flexible plastic solar cells that are more powerful than most inflexible semiconductor cells. Its plastic solar cells are being used in products as diverse as handbags and military tents to aid in powering cell phones and electronic equipment. As these technologies progress, it will become increasingly unnecessary to "plug into the wall," making technology more portable and usable. This will enable those in remote and impoverished areas to use electronic devices without access to electric power.

In the long term, the application of nanotechnology, including the advent of productive nanosystems, will greatly reduce the power requirements of manufacturing processes. With today's technology, we often burn fuel, losing a lot of its potential energy to heat (Gillett, 2002). With tomorrow's nanotechnology, we may well be able to construct matter by ordering and manipulating molecules, combining them as a fuel cell does rather than burning, greatly conserving energy. Manufacturing using productive nanosystems offers one of our brightest hopes for maintaining a high level of productive output without overtaxing our environment.

PROVIDING ABUNDANT CLEAN WATER GLOBALLY

Challenges

In the developed world, we have come to expect clean, abundant, and low-cost drinking water. For millions in the developing world, clean water is in short supply. The problem is multifaceted, having political, economic, and natural causes. Although no technology can be a panacea for the world water shortage, nanotechnology can make significant contributions.

The world is facing a water crisis that is worsening with time. Water use has almost doubled over the last 50 years and will likely double again in the next 20 years. Still, 1.1 billion people do not have sufficient drinking water and 2.4 billion people do not have sanitary water [World Health Organization (WHO), 2000]. Around 6000 people, most under the age of five, die every day from water-borne illness (World Water Assessment Programme, 2003). If current trends continue, at least one in four people would live in countries affected by chronic or recurring shortages of freshwater by 2050 (Gardner-Outlaw and Engelman, 1997).

Clean water access is necessary for the world's poor to advance economically. Water is essential for agriculture, which many of the global poor depend on for their income and food, and is also a key raw material for many industries. A workforce that is afflicted by chronic water shortages often has less capacity for productive labor, due to either illnesses or the time required to find and transport water to the home.

Developed countries also face difficult water issues. Providing clean drinking water is especially challenging in arid areas, such as Tucson, Arizona, where water is limited and sometimes must be transported over long distances. Populations will continue to rise, and global climate change will continue to worsen water scarcity; the ability to sanitize, desalinate, and transport water will become important tasks that could be aided by nanotechnology.

Nanotechnology Solutions

Nanotechnology can offer many advances that can help supply abundant clean water to everyone in the world, especially the poor. Nanotechnology could enable better methods of purifying, filtering, and desalinating water, while also providing inexpensive ways to detect toxins and bacteria.

Nanotechnology that is currently being researched could, in the relatively short term, make enormous contributions to decentralized water purification and desalination. Nanotechnology filtration systems will have pores only a few water molecules in size that would screen out almost all pollutants, toxins, salts, minerals, bacteria, and viruses. With atomically precise water filters, we could have ultrapure filtered water no matter how contaminated the original water source (Pergamit, 2006). Researchers at the Lawrence Livermore National Laboratories were able to create a water desalinization and demineralization system based on carbon nanotubes. The system, which was only the size of a coin, filtered water with extreme efficiency and required 75 percent less energy than normal water purifiers (Holt et al., 2006). Being less energy intensive, technologies like this could be more affordable for those in impoverished areas, making water purification decentralized and accessible to the world's poor.

Nanotechnology can also aid in the detection of toxins in water, which would help water cleanup and contaminant removal. A nanotechnology lab-on-a-chip that uses genetically modified bacteria was developed to detect specific toxins in water by researchers at Tel Aviv University in Israel (Popovtzer et al., 2006). The detector they developed is able to identify toxins within 10 minutes, is cheap to produce, and is easily portable.

In the long term, nanotechnology could make our water technology work more like biological water purification systems. Nanomachines could be designed to work like kidneys, selectively choosing which materials they will keep in the water and which they will discard. In this way, they could "seek and destroy" molecules unsafe for consumption. If made cheap enough, they could be utilized in water sources used by poor people, making inexpensive and decentralized water purification a reality.

INCREASING THE HEALTH AND LONGEVITY OF HUMAN LIFE

Challenges

Due to advances in medicine and the biosciences, humans are living much longer and healthier lives. However, disease still tragically claims the lives of tens of millions globally every year. The health challenge is to overcome technological and cost barriers to make treatments available to everyone who needs them. Although much of this work will continue to be done in the field of biotechnology, nanotechnology can significantly contribute to alleviate global health problems.

Over the last 20 years, 30 new infectious diseases have been discovered, including HIV/AIDS, Ebola, and SARS, while other diseases such as dysentery and malaria still kill millions in the developing world every year. Infectious diseases account for at least 30 percent of deaths each year worldwide. AIDS alone has infected 65 million and claimed the lives of 25 million people (Joint UN Programme, 2006). Cancer is another leading world killer, accounting for 12 percent of deaths every year. In 2002 alone, there were 10.9 million new cancer cases and 6.7 million cancer-related deaths, and these rates are predicted to increase by 50 percent over the next 20 years (Parkin et al., 2005; WHO, 2003).

Disease takes its toll not only on human life but also on the economies of the extreme poor. Diseases endemic to impoverished areas of the world, including tropical diseases, HIV/AIDS, tuberculosis, and malaria, prevent people from entering the workforce and engaging in society. As leading development economist Jeffrey Sachs (2004) put it, "societies burdened by large numbers of sick and dying individuals cannot escape poverty." Clearly, there is a lot that must be done to address these seemingly intractable biomedical problems.

Nanotechnology Solutions

Nanotechnology has a lot to offer in the fight against disease. Many exciting nanoscience breakthroughs are laying the groundwork for advanced disease detection systems and treatments as well as enhancing our understanding of diseases. More exciting are the possible long-term nanotechnology medical innovations, many of which could involve nanosystems that can reorder matter at the molecular level.

Much of the current nanotechnology research is focused on cancer. Nanotechnology devices now being researched will aid in the detection and destruction of cancerous cells. According to the U.S. Department of Health and Human Services (HHS, 2004) Cancer Nanotech Plan, cancer research currently underway seeks to pinpoint the molecular signatures of cancer so that it can be discovered and managed at its earliest stages and will likely be developed soon. HHS expects that before 2015 there will be devices small enough to enter the body and deliver localized treatments directly to cancer cells, which will enhance the efficacy of cancer treatment while reducing its side effects. Current research along those lines is already underway, including research on gold particles heated by laser that can be used to destroy tumor cells (Richardson et al., 2006). Based in part on these encouraging results, the U.S. National Cancer Institute has set itself a new goal: "to eliminate suffering and death due to cancer by 2015 (von Eschenbach, 2004)."

Nanotechnology research has also been conducted on diseases that disproportionately impact the developing world, including HIV/AIDS. The disease is notoriously hard to fight since our immune system cannot recognize it because the virus constantly mutates. However, HIV/AIDS always binds to cells using the same protein structures, and studies have been able to use nanoparticles as decoys for those proteins, diverting the virus from cells (Nolting et al., 2003).

Nanotechnology can also be used to detect specific sequences of genes. Research has used carbon nanotubes that selectively bind to DNA to detect gene sequences, such as those that could trigger genetic disorders or are contained in deadly bacteria. One research team has found that specialized carbon nanotubes will glow different colors when bound to specific strands of DNA, a method that can be used to identify as many as 50 different DNA sequences at a time (Jeng et al., 2006).

In the long term, nanotechnology could enable the "comprehensive monitoring, control, construction, repair, defense, and improvement of all human biological systems, working from the molecular level, using engineered nanodevices and nanostructures" (Freitas, 1999). Automated molecularly precise nanosystems could be able to use genetic markers to detect and destroy viruses and bacteria (Freitas, 2005), which would essentially eliminate the threat of infectious diseases (de Grey, 2005). Technology based on similar concepts could also be used to reorder molecules and repair the effects of aging, extending the length and enhancing the quality of human life.

HEALING AND PRESERVING THE ENVIRONMENT

Challenges

As our population continues to expand, we will put increasing demands on our natural environment. The environmental challenge is to find a way to live in a sustainable manner while still providing for the needs of our growing population. Policy innovations and conservation will be helpful but may not be enough.

Our environment is degrading daily. The global impacts of anthropogenic global warming discussed above are only now beginning to be felt and will likely prove destructive in the years to come. Pollutants decrease the quality of life for millions globally. Our forests are being lost at an alarming rate, while 27 percent of our coral reefs is already destroyed and two-thirds more is projected to be lost by 2050 (Wilkinson, 2000).

Making matters worse, pressures on our environment will continue to mount with time. The United Nations (UN, 2004) estimates that the world population will expand to over 9 billion people by 2050. Providing for the needs of 3 billion more people will require more food, energy, transport, and space, all of which strain the environment. Efforts to drastically cut consumption in the developed world are unlikely to be successful, since many are unwilling to make dramatic lifestyle changes. Technological solutions that make it possible to more effectively and efficiently meet our needs while reducing or eliminating environmental impacts would significantly contribute to our well-being.

Nanotechnology Solutions

Nanotechnology holds the possibility for relieving many of the man-made pressures placed on our environment. First, it can make conservation easier by providing lightweight materials and less polluting technologies in the short term and by enabling "zero-waste" production in the long term. Second, nanotechnology can help detect pollutants, aiding in the protection of human health and the environment. Third, it can aid in environmental cleanup by neutralizing and removing pollutants, bringing the environment back to a healthier state.

Already, nanotechnology is enabling lightweight and strong materials that will greatly reduce our energy needs. Lighter materials in cars and trucks would reduce our energy usage and therefore produce less environmental pollution. Nanotechnology inventions would likely reduce energy requirements and their associated pollutants in other ways as well: Nanotechnology-based lighting could reduce energy consumption by 10 percent in the United States, reducing carbon emissions by 200 million tons per year (Masciangioli and Zhang, 2003).

In the long term, nanotechnology production could almost completely eliminate pollutant byproducts associated with present-day manufacturing. The productive nanosystems of advanced nanotechnology could construct at the molecular level using a nanoscale assembly line bringing molecules together with atomic precision, and keeping any byproducts under complete control for reuse (Drexler, 1992).

Nanotechnology could greatly aid in pollutant detection. Contamination detection is needed for informing us of the extent and severity of pollution in a specific area, measuring effects of remediation, and enforcement of environmental laws. Already, some semiconductor-based single-walled carbon nanotubes have been used as highly sensitive electrically based sensors that can detect miniscule amounts of toxic gases in the air. In the future, such sensors could be connected to a global network, allowing us to have an exact understanding of where pollutants are at all times.

Nanotechnology will also be employed to remedy environmental harm. Today, research is being conducted to efficiently filter water and remove pollutants from contaminated soil. In the long term, molecular nanomachine systems will be able to work with molecular-level precision to find and neutralize pollutants. For example, nanomachine systems could be designed to consume and process oil to efficiently clean up oil spills, selectively remove heavy metals and toxic chemicals from water and soil, or remove carbon dioxide from the atmosphere to help reduce greenhouse gas pollution.

MAKING POWERFUL INFORMATION TECHNOLOGY AVAILABLE EVERYWHERE

Challenges

Due to great advances in telecommunication and information technology, we are able to connect to powerful networks for transmitting and processing information, giving us instant access to endless knowledge and allowing us to communicate globally. Yet, many in the developing world have never even seen a computer. Only 13 percent of the world's population has Internet access; only 2.6 percent of Africa's population is online (International Telecommunications Union, 2006). Furthermore, we are constrained by the limits of our present computing power, which, although fast, is still incapable of performing important calculations at sufficient speeds. The challenge of information and communication technology is to bring the power of global networks and powerful computing to every corner of the globe.

Communications technology is understood to be vital to economic growth, since it helps both to connect producers to markets and educate workers. Efforts in Bangladesh that introduced cell phones to rural villages invigorated economies there, pulling thousands out of poverty. With cell phones, farmers have earned more for their products and have paid less for their supplies, yields have increased because of timely weather and pest information, and health care has improved (Power to the People, 2006). However, in many parts of the world, the technological and financial barriers to bringing phone and Internet access are still too high with current technology.

With better communications networks and faster and more portable computing, we will have the ability to connect more people to worldwide networks. Enhanced global communication could also promote greater cross-cultural understanding and opportunities for cooperation and could ensure that critical information is immediately disseminated to all concerned, helping us react better to sudden important events such as natural disasters.

Nanotechnology Solutions

Nanotechnology can make great additions to the field of electronics, enabling the world of pervasive computing—a world where computers are always available and connected to the network. In the short term, nanotechnology will make computers faster and more portable. In the long term, major new advances for computing and communications may become available.

Nanotechnology inventions are making computers smaller, faster, more portable, and more usable. The next step is delivering the power of a laptop (or better) in the palm of one's hand. Reducing the size of electronic components will undoubtedly employ nanotechnology techniques; nanotechnology is already being researched that could help shrink the size of memory storage, transistors, microprocessors, and wiring, and many information storage technology improvements already operate at the nanoscale. As computers get smaller, cheaper, and more portable, the possibility of using them in poor and rural areas becomes increasingly feasible.

In the long term, nanotechnology should facilitate the use of quantum computing. Quantum computing utilizes the unique quantum properties of molecules to greatly outperform present-day computing. While processors today use bits (0s and 1s) to do computations, quantum processors could use quantum bits, encoded in the quantum states of particles such as electrons and photons. These particles can be in more than one state at once, so they can process many more computations than today's processors. According to the Los Alamos National Laboratories (2004), 100 quantum particles can do the work of millions of today's best computers. Although quantum computing may not debut this decade, it is certainly on the technological horizon (Brooks, 2002). With quantum computing, the ability to do more computation and to store more information at your fingertips, seemingly instantaneously, would become a reality. Such computing power would also enable a host of applications, including the discovery of drugs and vaccines using only computer simulations—a feat that requires networks of millions of computers today.

ENABLING THE DEVELOPMENT OF SPACE

Challenges

Satellites already play a vital role in communications, environmental monitoring, and scientific research but are still limited by the high cost of launching rockets into orbit. If costs can be reduced and technological capabilities improved, then space offers an abundance of raw materials, energy, and even potential living space that, if well utilized, could greatly enhance the human condition. Current technology is prohibitively expensive and inefficient, but with nanotechnology, space exploration and development will become much more achievable.

The National Space Society (2006), the U.S. leading space advocacy group, highlights four reasons to develop space: survival, growth, prosperity, and curiosity. Developing space could help guarantee human and animal survival by relieving pressures on our biosphere while diversifying the location of human habitation; we can avoid becoming extinct from a single global catastrophe, such as the asteroid or comet impact that killed off the dinosaurs. Space exploration also allows us to reach new frontiers and to expand our living spaces. It brings with it the promise of prosperity, since harvesting space resources can bring an abundance of raw materials and energy. Finally, we may be able to discover many new insights into our origins, physics, and the natural universe by the exploration of space.

Our exploration of space is limited by a number of cost and technological barriers. Simply getting into orbit around Earth requires an enormous investment in fuels and technology. Traveling to planets in our solar system is extremely difficult. The possibility of creating large factories or colonies that would orbit Earth is currently denied to us because of their difficulty and expense, since they must be constructed in space—with each piece being brought up in shuttles in separate payloads—or constructed from asteroidal resources that would require much processing in space.

Nanotechnology Solutions

The promise that nanotechnology holds for space is enormous. NASA has been one of the strongest proponents of developing nanotechnology, seeing its potential contribution to space exploration as multifaceted and profound. Although many applications of nanotechnology to space exploration are long term and may seem on the verge of science fiction, their scientific underpinnings are well founded. Others promise more immediate benefits.

Some nanotechnology space applications have already been discussed in this chapter. Better photovoltaic cells could power spacecraft and satellites, providing a constant source of energy. New, stronger, and lighter materials will enable spacecraft to travel further with less energy requirements. In the longer term, productive nanosystems will make the construction of strong, lightweight spacecraft easy and possible on a mass scale.

Millions of dollars are going into researching other space applications of nanotechnology. Shorter term applications include better life support systems and radiation-shielding technologies for astronauts (David, 2004). Nanotechnology is also helping us study space: A carbon nanotube-based X-ray diffraction spectrometer which can fit in the palm of one's hand has already been created and may be used as early as 2010 to study rocks and soil on Mars.

Nanotechnology could also be used to repair spacecraft in flight. One danger of space travel is space debris, which can poke holes into vessels. Even the tiniest holes could spell disaster for a satellite or crewed spaceship. One technology now under research is intended to repair spacecraft similar to the way skin repairs itself when damaged and has been shown to work in simulated spacelike conditions (Knight, 2006).

Other nanotechnology space applications include the space elevator. The goal of a space elevator is to replace costly and difficult rocket propulsion with an elevator-like structure that could carry payloads and humans into space. Such an invention would not only make space travel easier by facilitating its most difficult step—escaping Earth's gravity—but would also make development of space settlements feasible using Earth-built parts, without the need to mine asteroids. However, the cable that supports the space elevator needs to be exceedingly strong and light, an impossible feat with the materials available today. Nanotechnology materials, such as carbon nanotubes, are already being researched for use in space elevators. LiftPort Group, a private U.S. company, has an ambitious plan to build a space elevator by 2018 with carbon nanotubes. It has already done preliminary tests with a mile-long cable that was extremely strong but only 5 centimeters wide and about as thick as six sheets of paper (Groshong, 2006).

CONCLUSION

Nanotechnology's potential benefits are varied, diverse, and important. The applications of nanotechnology will range from purifying water to aiding in space exploration. The possibilities extend far beyond what's written here; although the Foresight challenges represent some of the most pressing challenges that nanotechnology can address, they are far from an exhaustive list of the possible beneficial applications of nanotechnology.

We have a choice on how nanotechnology will unfold. If we passively let market forces, geopolitical agendas, and military competition alone determine the direction of nanotechnology, it is unlikely that nanotechnology will fulfill its greatest potential in a timely fashion; instead of applications that could save millions in the developing world from disease, nanotechnology could be focused only on more luxurious consumer goods and powerful nanoweapons. As participants in democratic systems, we have the power to require that government research and development funding go toward meeting these important challenges, that publicly funded inventions which could alleviate emergencies in the developing world are not locked up for decades by expensive patents, and that humanity as a whole benefits from the nanotechnology revolution. As private citizens, we have the capability to shape nanotechnology's future through nongovernment initiatives, such as developing guidelines for the safe and ethical implementation of nanotechnology or offering incentives for the most important research. Since nanotechnology is just now beginning, we have the ability—and the ethical duty—to ensure that nanotechnology is used most beneficially.

REFERENCES

Brooks, M. 2002. Quantum computing making tremendous progress. *New Scientist*. Available: http://www.newscientist.com/article.ns?id=dn3114.

David, L. 2004. *Nanotechnology: Scientists pin big hopes on a small scale. Space.com*. Available: http://www.space.com/businesstechnology/technology/nanotech_space_041222.html.

de Grey, A. 2005. *Developing biomedical tools to repair molecular and cellular damage.* Foresight Nanotech Institute. Available: http://foresight.org/challenges/health002.html.

Department of Energy (DOE). 2005. *Basic research needs for solar energy utilization.* U.S. Department of Energy, Office of Science. Available: http://www.sc.doe.gov/bes/reports/files/SEU_rpt.pdf.

Drexler, K. E. 1986. *Engines of Creation.* New York: Anchor Books.

Drexler, K. E. 1992. *Nanosystems: Molecular Machinery, Manufacturing, and Computation.* New York: Wiley.

Ellingson, R. J., Beard, M. C., Johnson, J. C., Yu, P., Micic, O. I., Nozik, A. J., Shabaev, A., and Efros, A. L. 2005. Highly efficient multiple exciton generation in colloidal PbSe and PbS quantum dots. *Nano Letters* 5: 865–871.

Foresight Nanotech Institute. 2005. Foresight nanotechnology challenges. Available: http://foresight.org/challenges/index.html.

Freitas, R. A. Jr. 1999. Nanomedicine, *Volume I:* Basic Capabilities. Austin, TX: Landes Bioscience.

Freitas, R. A. Jr. 2005. Microbivores: Artificial mechanical phagocytes using digest and discharge protocol. *Journal of Evolution and Technology* 14: 1–52. Available: http://jetpress.org/volume14/freitas.pdf.

Gardner-Outlaw, T., and Engelman, R. 1997. *Sustaining Water, Easing Scarcity: A Second Update.* Washington DC: Population Action International.

Gillett, S. 2002. Nanotechnology: Clean energy and resources for the future. White Paper for the Foresight Nanotech Institute. Available: http://www.foresight.org/impact/whitepaper_illos_rev3.PDF.

Groshong, K. 2006. Space-elevator tether climbs a mile high. *New Scientist.* Available: http://www.newscientistspace.com/article.ns?id=dn8725.

Hansen, J., Ruedy, R., Sato, M., and Lo, K. 2006. Global temperature trends: 2005 Summation. U.S. National Aeronautics and Space Administration (NASA) Goddard Institute for Space Studies. Available: http://data.giss.nasa.gov/gistemp/2005/.

Health and Human Services (HHS). 2004. Cancer nanotechnology plan. Available: http://nano.cancer.gov/about_alliance/cancer_nanotechnology_plan.pdf.

Holt, J. K., Park, H. G., Wang, Y., Stadermann, M., Artyukhin, A. B., Grigoropoulos, C. P., Noy, S., and Bakajin, O. 2006. Fast mass transport through sub-2-nanometer carbon nanotubes. *Science* 312: 1034–1037.

International Energy Agency (IEA). 2002. *World Energy Outlook*, 2nd ed. Paris: OECD/IEA. Available: http://www.iea.org/Textbase/nppdf/free/2000/weo2002.pdf.

International Telecommunications Union (ITU). 2006. World Telecommunication/ICT development report. Executive summary. Available: http://www.itu.int/ITU-D/ict/publications/wtdr_06/material/WTDR2006_Sum_e.pdf.

Intergovernmental Panel on Climate Change (IPCC). 2001. *Climate Change 2001: Working Group II: Impacts, Adaptation and Vulnerability.* Geneva: IPCC. Available: http://www.grida.no/climate/ipcc_tar/wg2/005.htm.

Jacobstein, N. 2006. *Foresight Guidelines for Responsible Nanotechnology Development Version 6.* Available: http://www.foresight.org/guidelines/current.html.

Jeng, E. S., Moll, A. E., Roy, A. C., Gastala, J. B., and Strano, M. S. 2006. Detection of DNA hybridization using the near-infrared band-gap fluorescence of single-walled carbon nanotubes. *Nano Letters* 6 (3): 371–375.

Joint UN Programme on HIV/AIDS (UNAIDS). 2006. *Report on the global AIDS epidemic.* Geneva: UNAIDS.

Knight, W. 2006. Spacecraft skin "heals" itself. *New Scientist.* Available: http://www. newscientistspace.com/article.ns?id=dn8623.

Los Alamos National Laboratories. 2004. Quantum computation: A revolutionary nanotechnology. Available: http://www.lanl.gov/mst/nano/computing.html.

McCarthy, V. 2006. Glowing future for nano in energy to be explored at nanotech 2006 in Boston. National Science and Technology Institute. Available: http://www.nsti.org/news/ item.html?id=49.

Masciangioli, T., and Zhang, W. X. 2003. Environmental technologies at the nanoscale. *Environmental Science & Technology* 37: 102A–108A.

National Space Society (NSS). 2006. NSS statement of philosophy. Available: http://www.nss.org/about/philosophy.html, accessed June 26, 2006.

Nolting, B., Yu, J., Gang-yu, L., Cho, S., Kauzlarich, S., and Gervay-Hague, J. 2003. Synthesis of gold glyconanoparticles and biological evaluation of recombinant Gp120 interactions. *Langmuir* 19 (16): 6465–6473.

Parkin, M. D., Bray, F., Ferlay, J., and Pisani, P. 2005. Global cancer statistics, 2002. *CA: A Cancer Journal for Clinicians* 55: 74–108.

Pergamit, G. 2006. Water and nanotechnology experts Q&A: Gayle Pergamit. *Foresight Nanotech Update* 56: 5–7.

Popovtzer, R., Neufeld, T., Ron, E. Z., Rishpon, J., and Shacham-Diamand, Y. 2006. Electrochemical "lab-on-a-chip" for toxicity detection in water. *Technical Proceedings of the 2006 NSTI Nanotechnology Conference and Trade Show* 2: 205–208.

Power to the people. 2006. The Economist. Available: http://www.economist.com/science/ displaystory.cfm?story_id=5571572.

Richardson, H. H., Hickman, Z. N., Govorov, A. O., Thomas, A. C., Zhang, W., and Kordesch, M. E. 2006. Thermooptical properties of gold nanoparticles embedded in ice: Characterization of heat generation and melting. *Nano Letters* 6 (4): 783–788.

Sachs, J. D. 2004. Health in the developing world. *Bulletin of the World Health Organization* 82: 947–952.

United Nations Population Division. 2004. World Population Prospects: The 2004 Revision Population Database. Available: http://esa.un.org/unpp/.

von Eschenbach, A. C. 2004. End of suffering, death from cancer by 2015. *USA Today*, January 21, 2004, p. A15.

Wilkinson, C. 2000. *Status of Coral Reefs of the World: 2000.* Cape Ferguson, Australia: Australian Institute of Marine Science.

World Health Organization (WHO)/UNICEF. 2000. *Global Water Supply and Sanitation Assessment 2000 Report.* Geneva: WHO.

World Health Organization (WHO). 2003. *World Cancer Report.* Washington DC: IARC Press.

World Water Assessment Programme (WWAP). 2003. *Water for People, Water for Life.* Barcelona: UNESCO and Berghahn Books.

Wu, N. 2005. VC view: Nano power!. Extreme nano. Available: http://www.extremenano.com/ article/VC+View+Nano+Power/157689_1.aspx.

5

DEBATING NANOTECHNOLOGIES*

Richard A. L. Jones

Nanotechnology has become associated with some very far-reaching claims. Its more enthusiastic adherents believe that it will be utterly transformational in its effects on the economy and society, making material goods of all sorts so abundant as to be essentially free, restoring the environment to a pristine condition, and revolutionizing medicine to the point where death can be abolished. Nanotechnology has been embraced by governments all over the world as a source of new wealth, with the potential to take the place of information technology as a driver for rapid economic growth (Amato, 1999). Breathless extrapolations of a new, trillion-dollar nanotechnology industry arising from nowhere are commonplace.

These optimistic visions have led to new funding being lavished on scientists working on nanotechnology, with the total amount being spent a subject for competition between governments across the developed world.[1] Meanwhile, in fast developing countries like India and China, substantial investments are being made in nanotechnology, with the expectation that this will allow these countries to not merely catch up with Western countries but surpass their achievements in some areas (Hassan, 2005). As an antidote to all this optimism, nongovernmental organisations (NGOs) and environmental

* I would like to thank many colleagues whose insights have sharpened my understanding of this subject, in particular Stephen Wood, Alison Geldart, James Wilsdon, Jack Stilgoe, Phil Macnaghten, Brian Wynne, Rob Doubleday, Matthew Kearnes, and Richard Wilson.

groups have begun to mobilize against what they see as another example of excessive scientific technological hubris (ETC Group, 2003),[2] which falls clearly in the tradition of nuclear energy and genetic modification, as a technology which promised great things but delivered, in their view, more environmental degradation and social injustice.

And yet, despite this superficial agreement on the transformational power of nanotechnology, whether for good or bad, there are profound disagreements not just about what the technology can deliver but about what it actually is. The most radical visions originate from the writings of K. Eric Drexler (1986), who wrote an influential and widely read book, *Engines of Creation*. This popularized the term *nanotechnology*, developing the idea that mechanical engineering principles could be applied on a molecular scale to create nanomachines which could build up any desired material or artefact with ultimate precision atom by atom. It is this vision of nanotechnology, subsequently developed in more technical writings by Drexler (1992), that has entered popular culture through films and science fiction books, perhaps most notably in Neal Stephenson's novel *The Diamond Age* 1995. It is in this form that nanotechnology has become part of what one might call the belief package of the transhumanist movement, together with an anticipation of technologies for the enhancement of human capabilities, the radical extension of human life spans, and a confidence in the possibility of developing strong artificial intelligence.

The credibility of Drexler's visions of nanotechnology in the mainstream scientific community has not been helped either by this association with speculative fiction or indeed with what many regard as a fringe, quasi-religious movement with strong cultish aspects. In a falling out which has become personally vituperative, leading scientific establishment figures, notably the Nobel laureate Richard Smalley, have publicly ridiculed the Drexlerian project of shrinking mechanical engineering to molecular dimensions (Drexler and Smalley, 2003). Drexler has retaliated by claiming the mantle of the iconic American physicist Richard Feynman (1992), whose 1959 lecture "There's Plenty of Room at the Bottom" has become one of the foundational myths of nanotechnology.[3] Drexler's (2004) argument is that mainstream nanoscience has appropriated the rhetoric of Feynman's vision while rejecting its substance.

It is certainly true that what is dominating the scientific research agenda is not any single vision but instead a rather heterogeneous collection of technologies whose common factor is simply a question of scale. These evolutionary nanotechnologies[4] typically involve the shrinking down of existing technologies, notably in information technology, to smaller and smaller scales. Some of the products of these developments are already in the shops. The very small, high-density hard-disk drives that are now found not just in computers but also in consumer electronics like MP3 players and digital video recorders rely on the ability to create nanoscale multilayer structures which have entirely new physical properties like giant magnetoresistance. Not yet escaped from the laboratory are new technologies like molecular electronics, in which individual molecules play the role of electronic components. Formidable obstacles remain before these technologies can be integrated to form practical devices that can be commercialised, but the promise is yet another dramatic increase in computing power. Another area which may in the future permit the continuation of the exponential growth of computing power that we have come to expect is the successful implementation of quantum computing, perhaps using the precise control of the interactions between electrons and photons that is made possible in quantum dot and quantum well structures.

While it is natural to focus on ways by which the capabilities and power of modern information technology may be enhanced by evolutionary nanotechnologies, one should not neglect developments whereby computing and communications devices whose raw performance is no greater, or even less, than devices which are available today but at very small cost become possible. Developments in plastic electronics promise a world of disposable electronics and computers produced by technologies like printing at a cost so low that even the cheapest artefact might carry significant computing power. It is this kind of development that underpins the idea of ambient computing and the universal, intelligent artefact.

Another area in which evolutionary nanotechnologies are expected by some to have significant impacts is in medicine and health care (European Science Foundation, 2005). Substantial emphasis is being placed now on the idea of targeted drug delivery. This is particularly relevant for anticancer therapeutics, which are typically highly toxic molecules; the idea, then, is to wrap these molecules up in a nanoscale delivery device which keeps the molecules isolated until a trigger at the target releases them. Another area of rapid development is in the field of diagnostic devices, where the detection of large numbers of biochemical markers at the single-molecule level and the fast and cheap sequencing of DNA are in prospect.

A number of products which boast of their nanotechnological antecedents are already on shop shelves. There are two very well publicised examples. The active ingredient in some sunscreens consists of titanium dioxide crystals whose sizes are in the nanoscale range. In this size range, the crystals, and thus the sunscreen, are transparent to visible light, rather than having the intense white characteristic of the larger titanium dioxide crystals familiar in white emulsion paint. Another widely reported application of nanotechnology is in fabric treatments, which by coating textile fibers with molecular size layers give them properties such as stain resistance. These applications, although mundane, result from the principle that matter when divided on this very fine scale can have different properties from bulk matter. However, it has to be said that these kinds of products represent the further development of trends in materials science, colloid science, and polymer science that have been in train for many years. This kind of incremental nanotechnology, then, does involve new and innovative science, but it isn't different in character to other applications of materials science that may not have the *nano-* label. To this extent, the decision to refer to these applications as nanotechnology involves marketing as much as science. But what we will see in the future is more and more of this kind of application making its way to the marketplace, offering real, if not revolutionary, advances over the products that have gone before. It seems likely that these developments won't be introduced in a single "nanotechnology industry" ; rather these innovations will find their way into the products of all kinds of existing industries, often in rather an unobtrusive way.

The idea of a radical nanotechnology, along the lines mapped out by Drexler and his followers, has thus been marginalized on two fronts. Those interested in developing the immediate business applications of nanotechnology have concentrated on the incremental developments that are close to bringing products to market now and are keen to downplay the radical visions because they detract from the immediate business credibility of their short-term offerings. Meanwhile the nanoscience community is energetically pursuing a different evolutionary agenda. Is it possible that both scientists and the nanobusiness community are too eagerly dismissing Drexler's ideas—could there be, after all, something in the idea of a radical nanotechnology?

One aspect of Drexler's argument is important and undoubtedly correct. We know that a radical nanotechnology, with sophisticated nanoscale machines operating on the molecular scale, can exist because cell biology is full of such machines. But Drexler goes further. He argues that if nature can make effective nanomachines from soft and floppy materials, with the essentially random design processes of evolution, then the products of a synthetic nanotechnology, using the strongest materials and the insights of engineering, will be very much more effective. Another view is that this underestimates the way in which biological nanotechnology exploits and is optimized for the peculiar features of the nanoscale world (Whitesides, 2001). To take just one example of a highly efficient biological nanomachine, adenosine triphosphate (ATP) synthase is a remarkable rotary motor which life forms as different as bacteria and elephants all use to synthesize the energy storage molecular ATP. The efficiency with which it converts energy from one form to another is very close to 100 percent, a remarkable result when one considers that most human-engineered energy conversion devices, such as steam turbines and gas engines, struggle to exceed 50 percent efficiency. This is one example, then, of a biological nanomachine that is close to optimal. The reason for this is that biology uses design principles very different from those we learn about in human-scale engineering that exploit the special features of the nanoworld (Jones, 2004). There's no reason in principle why we could not develop a radical nanotechnology that uses the same design principles as biology, but the result would look very different to the miniaturized cogs and gears of the Drexlerian vision. In this view, radical nanotechnologies will be possible, but they will owe more to biology than to conventional engineering.

It isn't yet clear what form a biology-inspired radical nanotechnology might take, nor what impacts it might have. One could take an approach that seeks inspiration from biological design principles but uses entirely synthetic materials to execute them. This would be a truly biomimetic nanotechnology (Jones, 2005). Alternatively, one could use existing components of biological origin, such as biological molecular motors, and reassemble them in wholly or partially synthetic contexts (Ball, 2002). The latter approach, which could be called *biokleptic nanotechnology*,[5] has the advantage that it exploits the effectiveness of evolution in perfecting very efficient nanoscale machines as well as the technological base of the biotechnology industry and seems very likely to deliver rapid results. A development that is closely related, though usually not directly associated with nanotechnology, is the idea of synthetic biology (Benner and Sismour, 2005). In one realisation of this, an existing, already very simple, microorganism is further simplified by removal of genes coding for all but the most essential functions (Hutchison et al., 1999). The resulting minimally complex organism is then used as a vehicle into which desired functions can be incorporated (Phoenix and Drexler, 2004).[6]

Discussion of the possible impacts of nanotechnology, both positive and negative, has shown signs of becoming polarized along the same lines as the technical discussion.

The followers of Drexler promise on the one hand a world of abundance of all material needs and an end to disease and death. But they've also introduced perhaps the most persistent and gripping notion—the idea that artificial, self-replicating nanoscale robots would escape our control and reproduce indefinitely, consuming all the world's resources, and rendering existing life extinct. The idea of this plague of "gray goo" has become firmly embedded in our cultural consciousness, despite some indications of regret from Drexler, who has more lately emphasized the idea that self-replication is neither a desirable nor a necessary feature of a nanoscale robot [Nanotechnology Research Coordination Group (NRCG), 2005]. The reaction of nanoscientists and business people to the idea of gray goo has been open ridicule. Actually, it is worth taking the idea seriously enough to give it a critical examination. Implicit in the notion of gray goo is the assumption that we will be able to engineer what is effectively a new form of life that is more fit, in a Darwinian sense, and better able to prosper in Earth's environment than existing life forms. On the other hand, the argument that biology at the cell level is already close to optimal for the environment of Earth means that the idea that synthetic nanorobots will have an effortless superiority over natural life forms is much more difficult to sustain.

Meanwhile, mainstream nanobusiness and nanoscience have concentrated on one very short term danger, the possibility that new nanoparticles may be more toxic than their macroscale analogues and precursors. This fear is very far from groundless; since one of the major selling points of nanoparticles is that their properties may be different from the analogous matter in a less finely divided state, it isn't at all unreasonable to worry that toxicity may be another property that depends on size (NRCR, 2005). But it could be noted that there is something odd about the way the debate has become so focused on this one issue, driven by an unlikely alliance of convenience among nanobusiness, nanoscience, government, and the environmental movement, all of whom have different reasons for finding it a convenient focus. For the environmental movement, it fits a well-established narrative of reckless corporate interests releasing toxic agents into the environment without due care and attention. For nanoscientists, it's a very contained problem which suggests a well-defined research agenda (and the need for more funding). By tinkering with regulatory frameworks, governments can be seen to be doing something, and nanobusinesses can demonstrate their responsibility by their active participation in the process.

The dominance of nanoparticle toxicity in the debate is a vivid illustration of a danger that a number of researchers have drawn attention to—the tendency for all debates on the impact of science on society to end up exclusively focused on risk assessment. This is nicely put by Wilsdon and Wills (2004): "in the 'risk society' perhaps the biggest risk is that we never get around to talking about anything else." Nanotechnology—even in its evolutionary form—presents us with plenty of very serious things to talk about that go well beyond simple issues of risk (Whitesides, 2005). How will privacy and civil liberties survive in a world in which every artefact, no matter how cheap, includes a networked computer? How will medical ethics deal with a blurring of the line between the human and the machine and the line between remedying illness and enhancing human capabilities? The question is how a public debate can move away from risk assessment to these much richer questions.

This question is perhaps particularly pointed in the United Kingdom, where, partly as a result of an unfortunate series of misadventures at the interface between science and government in the 1980s and 1990s, erosion of trust in the authority of science led to the widespread rejection in the marketplace of the products of the nascent agricultural biotechnology industry (Jasanoff, 2005). This has brought about a renewed urgency to the idea of public engagement with science. In this context, it is almost inevitable that the emerging debate about nanotechnology or nanotechnologies has been framed in terms of nanotechnology becoming "the next GM" (genetic modification). Indeed, this comparison has been explicitly invited by campaigning NGOs, while scientists and representatives of a very proscience government have similarly seen the debate about genetic modification as a warning of what might go wrong with a debate about nanotechnology.

One common response to perceived problems in the public acceptability of a new technology, from the side of its proponents, has been to assume that if the public were properly educated about the technology, its advantages, and its risks, acceptance would necessarily follow. In an influential critique (Wynne, 1995), this position has been labeled the "deficit model" of public understanding of science, and it is argued that it should be replaced by a much more reflexive model of public engagement with science. This should be seen as part of an explicit agenda of democratizing science, in which public engagement with science is regarded as a two-way process in which research priorities and potential technological trajectories are set with explicit reference to public values (Wilsdon et al., 2005). In this view, debates about nanotechnologies should be considered neither as vehicles for garnering public support for a technology whose trajectory is conceptualized in a rigidly deterministic way nor as mechanisms for putting the brakes on progress (Kearnes et al., 2006). Rather, it presupposes a way of conceptualizing the future development path of technologies that resembles a garden of forking paths, rather than the linear roadmaps that are so prominent a feature of technology prediction.

There is, however, an argument that new technologies like nanotechnology are potentially so dehumanizing and existentially dangerous that we should consciously relinquish them (Joy, 2000). Bill McKibben 2003, for example, makes this case very eloquently in his book *Enough*. A key part of this argument consists of a rejection of the values of the transhumanists, who consciously seek to transcend humanity through technology. An even stronger attack on transhumanist values in this context is made by Schummer (2004). Notwithstanding one's position on transhumanism, there is a basic premise in McKibben's thesis which is open to criticism. While the technology we currently have may well be considered to be "enough" by a relatively prosperous inhabitant of a developed country, this is very much less clear if one takes a global view. Mankind currently depends for its very existence at current population levels on technology. To take just one example, our agriculture depends on the artificial fixation of nitrogen, which is made possible by the energy we derive from fossil fuels (Smil, 2000). And yet the shortcomings of our existing technologies are quite obvious, from the eutrophication that excessive use of synthetic fertilizers causes to the prospect of global climate change as a result of our dependence on fossil fuels.

Thus, one can easily make the argument that new technologies, including nanotechnologies, are urgently required to allow the world to make a transition to a state in which a large but stable population of the world can have decent standards of living on a sustainable basis. It has been argued that nanotechnology could play an important role in this, for example by delivering cheap solar cells and the infrastructure for a hydrogen economy together with cheap ways of providing clean water (Salamanca-Buentello et al., 2005). On the other hand, there is a debate to be had about the political and commercial structures that would be required to ensure that the technology bring benefits to the poor as well as the rich (Meridian Institute, 2005).

It is clear, then, that there is no single "nanotechnology debate," nor is there even any agreement on what is being debated; there has been a fundamental lack of clarity even about what nanotechnology is, or even if it is a single thing at all. What is interesting is that the contested notion of nanotechnology has nucleated a discussion centered on a range of concerns about technology in general and applied molecular science in particular. Some of these debates are not at all new. Questions of toxicology, environmental impact, and the management of risk and the perception of risk are familiar ones, and these debates play along lines made familiar by previous debates about nuclear energy, agricultural biotechnology, and the products of the chemical industry. Questions about the role of technology in wealth creation and the associated questions about intellectual property and the relationship between new technology and development and sustainability are no less important for being not entirely novel. What, perhaps, provides freshness to these issues is the sense that they are being played out in the midst of significant change in the culture of science, in which old linear models in which "pure" and "applied" science are separate and sequential are replaced by a move to "mode II" knowledge production (Gibbons et al., 1994), in which knowledge is generated in a fundamentally interdisciplinary fashion, explicitly in the context of application, and often with the close involvement of commercial actors at all stages of the process.

More novel is the way the nanotechnology debate has focused the different assumptions held by different interest groups about the role of technology in visions of the future. What radical environmentalists and transhumanists have in common is a highly deterministic view of how technology unfolds together with a strongly normative attitude to this evolution. It is this attitude that leads, in the case of radical environmentalists, to the conviction that the progress of technology must be stopped dead to preserve human values or, for the transhumanists, to the conviction that pressing ahead with the development of powerful technologies is a moral obligation. Taking a less deterministic view, however, permits one to envisage a wide variety of possible trajectories for technology development and in this way find a place for a more pluralistic vision in which there is a role for democratic values in determining the way the future is shaped.

NOTES

1. For a good, U.S.-centered narrative of the development of the idea of nanotechnology in government and science policy, see Berube 2006.
2. A report from Greenpeace (Arnall, 2003) was considerably more nuanced.
3. The claim that this lecture did play a foundational role in nanotechnology is critically examined by Toumey (2005).

4. A three-fold classification of nanotechnology, into incremental nanotechnology, evolutionary nanotechnology, and radical nanotechnology, was introduced by Wood et al. 2003. The usage of the plural "nanotechnologies," emphasizing the variety and heterogenous nature of the technologies so described, was popularized by a report commissioned by the U.K. government from the Royal Society and Royal Academy of Engineering, Royal Society/Royal Academy of Engineering (2004).

5. I believe this word was coined by N. Seeman.

6. For a view on the ethical issues of synthetic biology from a prominent worker in the field, see Church 2005.

REFERENCES

Amato, I. 1999. *Nanotechnology: Shaping the World Atom by Atom*, Washington, D.C.: National Science and Technology Council.

Arnall, A. H. 2003. *Future Technologies, Today's Choices*, London: Greenpeace Environmental Trust.

Ball, P. 2002. Tutorial: Natural strategies for the molecular engineer. *Nanotechnology* 13: 15–28.

Benner S. A., and Sismour, A. M. 2005. Synthetic biology. *Nature Reviews Genetics* 6: 533–543.

Berube, D. 2006. *Nano-hype: The Truth Behind the Nanotechnology Buzz*, Amherst, NY: Prometheus Books.

Church, G. 2005. Let us go out and safely multiply. *Nature* 438: 423.

Drexler, K. E. 1986. *Engines of Creation*, New York: Anchor Press/Doubleday.

Drexler, K. E. 1992. *Nanosystems: Molecular Machinery, Manufacturing, and Computation*. New York: Wiley.

Drexler, K. E. 2004. Nanotechnology: From Feynman to funding. *Bulletin of Science, Technology and Society* 24(1): 21–27.

Drexler, K. E. and Smalley, R. 2003. Nanotechnology: Drexler and Smalley make the case for and against "molecular assemblers." *Chemical and Engineering News* 81(48): 37–42.

ETC Group 2003. The Big Down—Atomtech: Technologies converging at the nanoscale. Available: www.etcgroup.org.

European Science Foundation 2005. *ESF Forward Look on Nanomedicine*. Strasbourg Cedex, France: ESF.

Feynman, R. 1992. There's plenty of room at the bottom. *Journal of Microelectromechanical Systems* 1(1): 60–66.

Gibbons, M., et al. 1994. *The New Production of Knowledge*. London: Sage.

Hassan, M. H. A. 2005. Small things and big changes in the developing world. *Science* 309: 65–66.

Hutchison, C. A. et al. 1999. Global transposon mutagenesis and a minimal mycoplasma genome. *Science* 286: 2165–2169

Jasanoff, S. 2005. *Designs on Nature*, Princeton, NJ: Princeton University Press.

Jones, R. A. L. 2004. *Soft Machines: Nanotechnology and Life*, Oxford: Oxford University Press.

Jones, R. A. L. 2005. Biomimetic nanotechnology with synthetic macromolecules. *Journal of Polymer Science Part B-Polymer Physics* 43: 3367–3368

Joy, B. 2000. Why the future doesn't need us. *Wired* 8: 04.

Kearnes, M., Macnaghten, P., and Wilsdon, J. 2006. *Governing at the Nanoscale*, London: Demos.

McKibben, B. 2003. *Enough: Genetic Engineering and the end of Human Nature.* London: Bloomsbury.

Meridian Institute. 2005. *Nanotechnology and the Poor: Opportunities and Risks.*

Nanotechnology Research Co-ordination Group. 2005. Characterising the potential risks posed by engineered nanoparticles: A first UK government research report. Her Majesty's Government. Available: http://www.defra.gov.uk/environment/nanotech/research/pdf/nanoparticles-riskreport.pdf.

Phoenix, C., and Drexler, E. 2004. Safe exponential manufacturing. *Nanotechnology* 15: 869–872.

Royal Society/Royal Academy of Engineering. 2004. *Nanoscience and Nanotechnologies: Opportunities and Uncertainties.* London: Royal Society.

Salamanca-Buentello, F., Persad, D. L., Court, E. B., Martin, D. K., Daar, A. S., and Singer, P. A. 2005. Nanotechnology and the developing world. *PloS Medicine* 2 (4): 300–303.

Schummer, J. 2004. Societal and ethical implications of nanotechnology: Meanings, interest groups, and social dynamics. *Techne* 8 (2): 56–87.

Smil, V. 2000. *Feeding the Earth*, Cambridge, MA: MIT Press.

Stephenson, N. 1995. *The Diamond Age*, New York: Doubleday.

Toumey, C. 2005. Apostolic succession: does nanotechnology descend from Richard Feynman's 1959 talk? *Engineering and Science* 68 (1): 16–23.

Whitesides, G. M. 2001. The once and future nanomachine. *Scientific American* 285: 78–83.

Whitesides, G. M. 2005. Nanoscience, nanotechnology, and chemistry. *Small* 1 (2): 172–179.

Wilsdon, J., and Willis, R. 2004. *See Through Science: Why Public Engagement Needs to Move Upstream*, London: Demos.

Wilsdon, J., Wynne, B., and Stilgoe, J. 2005. *The Public Value of Science*, London: Demos.

Wood, S., Jones, R., and Geldart, A. 2003. *The Social and Economic Challenges of Nanotechnology*, Swindon, United Kingdom: Economic and Social Research Council.

Wynne, B. 1995. The public understanding of science. In S. Jasanoff, G. E. Markle, J. C. Peterson, and T. Pinch, (eds.), *Handbook of Science and Technology Studies* Thousand Oaks, CA: Sage.

6

IN THE BEGINNING: THE U.S. NATIONAL NANOTECHNOLOGY INITIATIVE*

Neal Lane and Thomas Kalil

The United States, which made a major early commitment to nanotechnology in 2000, has been the world's research leader, but as the promise of nanotechnology has grown, the government commitment has flattened. We are concerned that lukewarm support for nanoscale science and engineering (S&E) puts U.S. technological leadership at risk and might prevent the country from realizing the full potential of nanotechnology.

President Clinton unveiled the National Nanotechnology Initiative (NNI) in a major science policy address at Caltech on January 21, 2000. His fiscal year (FY) 2001 budget proposed almost doubling the federal funding for nanoscale S&E from $270 million in FY2000 to $495 million in FY2001. The president's speech triggered a wave of primarily positive media coverage of nanotechnology and eventually led to increased investment in nanoscience and nanotechnology by universities, states, venture-backed start-ups, Global 1000 companies, and foreign governments. As two of the primary White House advocates for the NNI, we are delighted by the progress that has been made to date by researchers and entrepreneurs. We believe that this progress justifies continued increases in federal investment in nanoscale S&E, particularly as part of a larger effort to reverse the cuts in funding in the physical sciences and engineering.

* This chapter is reprinted with permission from *Issues in Science and Technology*, Lane, N. and Kalil, T., "The National Nanotechnology Initiative: Present at Creation," Summer 2005, pp. 49–54. Copyright © 2005 by the University of Texas at Dallas, Richardson, Texas.

Although President Clinton did much to increase public awareness of nanotechnology, the concept can be traced to Richard Feynman's brilliant 1959 lecture "There's Plenty of Room at the Bottom." He urged his audience to consider the possibility that we could eventually "arrange the atoms the way we want; the very atoms, all the way down!" (Feynman, 1960). Feynman's vision began to seem less fanciful in 1985, when IBM researchers developed the scanning tunneling microscope. Four years later, IBM researchers used the microscope to "write" the letters for IBM with 35 individual xenon atoms. In the 1980s and 1990s, researchers also began to synthesize and characterize nanostructures, such as buckminsterfullerene, carbon nanotubes, quantum dots, and nanowires, with novel and useful properties.

Federal agencies began to launch programs in nanoscale S&E, such as the Defense Advanced Research Project Agency's ULTRA Electronics Program. Beginning in 1996, federal program officers at the National Science Foundation (NSF) and other agencies began to meet and share information on their respective efforts in nanoscale S&E. By 1998, one of us testified before Congress that "If I were asked for an area of S&E that will most likely produce the breakthroughs of tomorrow, I would point to nanoscale science and engineering" (Lane, 1998).

Our efforts to develop a formal interagency initiative in nanoscale S&E began in earnest in the fall of 1998. An interagency working group, cochaired by Thomas Kalil and the NSF's Mike Roco, was created under the auspices of the National Science and Technology Council. In January 1999, a workshop led by Paul Alivisatos (University of California at Berkeley), Stan Williams (Hewlett Packard), and Mike Roco helped develop a detailed research agenda.

Beginning in 1999, we and other members of the administration began an active campaign to have the NNI included as one of the president's initiatives in the FY2000 budget. We told the science agencies that if they proposed increases in funding for nanoscale S&E above the budget "guidance" they had received from the Office of Management and Budget (OMB), we would fight for those increases. We began to educate other senior White House staffers about the long-term promise of nanotechnology and worked with the research community to identify a series of ambitious but plausible grand challenges (e.g., storing the Library of Congress in a device the size of a sugar cube or detecting cancerous tumors before they are visible to the human eye) that would be easy to communicate to the public. We worked closely with OMB professional staff to develop a rationale for increased investment.

Advocates made a number of arguments on behalf of the NNI which we believe are still valid today. First, nanoscale S&E has the potential to be as important as previous general-purpose technologies, such as the steam engine, the transistor, and the Internet. At a size of 1 to 100 nanometers, materials, structures, and devices exhibit new and often useful physical, electrical, mechanical, optical, and magnetic properties. Second, expanded funding for nanotechnology can help revitalize the physical sciences and engineering because it builds on disciplines such as condensed-matter physics, materials science, chemistry, and engineering. Third, the NNI will help attract and prepare the next generation of scientists, engineers, and entrepreneurs. Because roughly two-thirds of the funding for the NNI flows to university researchers, it directly supports undergraduates, graduates, and postdocs. Fourth, it is clear that realizing the potential of nanotechnology will require supporting long-term, high-risk research that is beyond the time horizons of corporations, which are understandably focused on nearer term research and product development. As President Clinton noted in his Caltech speech, "Some of these [nanotechnology] research goals will take 20 or more years to achieve. But that is why ... there is such a critical role for the federal government" (Clinton, 2000). Finally, a 1998 technology evaluation concluded that global leadership in nanotechnology was up for grabs. We hoped that the NNI would allow the United States to strengthen its position in this critical technology.

The close alliance between the National Economic Council and the Office of Science and Technology Policy (OSTP; particularly with the support of OSTP's Duncan Moore and Kelly Kirkpatrick) proved to be quite effective. The President's Council of Advisors on Science and Technology (PCAST) reviewed the NNI proposal and, based on the report of a panel of experts, chaired by then President of MIT Chuck Vest and such distinguished scientists as the late Rick Smalley, joined in recommending the initiative to the president. In the late fall of 1999, President Clinton decided to include the NNI as one of his key budget initiatives for FY2001, making it the centerpiece of a much broader research initiative to address the growing imbalance in federal funding for biomedical research and the physical sciences and engineering. In a December 1999 budget meeting, when the NNI was being considered, the president expressed enthusiasm for what he playfully called "my tiny little initiative." He even kept a reference to nanotechnology in his 2000 State of the Union address against the recommendations of his speechwriters, who were interested in making his speech shorter. He proposed a nearly $3 billion increase for his 21st Century Research Fund, including an additional $1 billion for university research and an NSF request that was nearly double the largest dollar increase the agency had ever seen. Targeted initiatives such as the NNI helped capture the imagination of the president and his senior advisors, making the potential benefits of increasing overall funding for research much more tangible. The initiatives benefited not only targeted areas such as information technology and nanotechnology but also a broad range of S&E disciplines.

The NNI included nanotechnology research funding in five categories: fundamental research, grand challenges, centers and networks, research infrastructure, and societal implications and workforce education and training. The original list of grand challenges, which echoed some of Richard Feynman's 1959 predictions, included nanostructured materials by design; nanoelectronics, photonics, and magnetics; therapeutics and diagnostics; and other challenges related to the environment, energy, space technology, manufacturing, and instrumentation.

Of course, the NNI was never intended as a vehicle to fund all research at the nanometer scale. Indeed, many disciplines, such as chemistry, condensed-matter physics, and AMO (atomic, molecular, and optical) physics, focus on intrinsically nanoscale phenomena. Rather, the NNI emphasizes fundamental new properties and functions of materials, devices, and systems because of their small size; novel phenomena and properties that are nonscalable outside the nanometer domain; the ability to control and manipulate matter at the nanometer scale; and integration along length scales.

There was very little opposition to the NNI, although Sun Microsystems cofounder Bill Joy warned in a widely read article ("Why the Future Doesn't Need Us," *Wired*, April 2000) that the confluence of genetics, nanotechnology, and robotics presented society with a dilemma. Unlike nuclear weapons, which require the resources of a nation state to develop, genetics, nanotechnology, and robotics will be driven by private enterprise and will therefore be low cost and widely available. Joy argued that "an immediate consequence of the Faustian bargain in obtaining the great power of nanotechnology is that we run a grave risk—the risk that we might destroy the biosphere on which all life depends (Chapter 2)." Although most scientists disagreed with Joy's specific scenarios, such as superhuman artificial intelligence with its own agenda and self-replicating assemblers, there is no question that the destructive power available to small groups is increasing over time. Joy's article underscored the importance of considering the unintended consequences of technological advances, and the discussions motivated by Joy's article have continued to this day.

With support from industry, the research community, and even former House Speaker Newt Gingrich, the Clinton administration was able to persuade Congress to provide $422 million in funding for nanoscale S&E. By the fall of 2000, the NNI was officially launched, and a National Nanotechnology Coordination Office was created to help encourage information sharing and collaboration across the federal government.

PROGRESS SINCE 2000

In the more than six years since the birth of the NNI, considerable progress has been made. Funding has continued to increase, to over $1.3 billion in FY2006. There are now 13 agencies with funding and another 12 agencies that participate in the interagency discussions, although 90 percent of the budget goes to NSF, the Department of Defense, the Department of Energy (DOE), and the National Institutes of Health (NIH). As many as 50 centers and user facilities will be in operation in 2006, such as Nanoscale Science and Engineering Centers and the DOE's Nanoscale Science Research Centers. Congress has passed, and President Bush has signed, the 21st Century Nanotechnology Research and Development Act. This legislation provides multiyear authorization for the NNI, although its primary practical effect to date has been to increase the number of reviews and reporting requirements.

The NNI funding has resulted in an expansion of fundamental understanding of nanoscale phenomena and many research results with potentially revolutionary applications. In widely cited journals such as *Science*, *Nature*, and *Physical Review Letters*, the percentage of journal articles related to nanoscale S&E has increased from 1 percent in 1992 to over 5 percent by 2003. The breadth of activity is impressive. For example, researchers are developing:

- Gold nanoshells with localized heating for the targeted destruction of malignant cancer cells, an approach that involves minimal side effects
- Genetically engineered viruses that can self-assemble inorganic materials such as gallium arsenide
- Low-cost hybrid solar cells that combine inorganic "nanorods" with conducting polymers

- A scale that can detect a zeptogram, the weight of a single protein
- Quantum dots that can "slow light," opening the door to all-optical networks
- Nanoscale iron particles that can reduce the costs of cleaning up contaminated groundwater

The increased funding has also triggered broader institutional responses at leading U.S. research universities. Universities are hiring more faculty in this interdisciplinary area, investing in new buildings that are capable of housing twenty-first-century nanoscience research, and creating shared facilities for nanoscale imaging, characterization, synthesis, and fabrication. Colleges and departments are experimenting with educating truly interdisciplinary nanoscientists and engineers, with new courses, lab rotations, and two or more faculty mentors in different disciplines.

The NNI has continued to evolve over time. In response to the concerns about the potential environmental and health risks of nanomaterials, the latest NNI strategic plan identifies "responsible development of nanotechnology" as one of the four principal goals. Several agencies have stepped up their research in this area, although as we argue below, more can and should be done. The National Toxicology Program, for example, is investigating the toxicity of nanotubes, quantum dots, and titanium dioxide. The Environmental Protection Agency (EPA) is supporting research on the fate and transport of manufactured nanomaterials in the environment. The EPA and other regulatory agencies are exploring whether existing laws and regulations such as the Toxic Substances Control Act need to be modified to take into account the size-dependent properties of nanoparticles.

In addition to these federal activities, states, the private sector, start-ups, and foreign governments have also increased their investment in nanotechnology. According to Lux Research, corporations invested $3.8 billion in nanotechnology research and development in 2004. Of the 30 companies on the Dow Jones industrial index, 19 have launched nanotechnology initiatives, and 1200 nanotechnology-related start-ups have emerged, about half of them in the United States. Companies are moving beyond novelty uses of nanotechnology, such as stain-resistant pants, to begin marketing truly valuable products.

Still, as a commercial enterprise, nanotechnology is in its infancy. For example, companies are still not able to reliably purchase high-quality nanotechnology building blocks such as nanotubes, metal oxide nanoparticles, and fullerenes.

WHITHER THE NNI?

Although the NNI has made significant progress, we are concerned that federal funding for nanoscale S&E has been flat in recent years. The administration's FY2007 budget, for example, actually proposes a small decrease in funding as compared to the level of support provided by Congress in FY2006.

We believe that there is a compelling case for sustained increases in federal funding for nanoscale S&E. We believe this should be done in the context of increased investments in the physical sciences and engineering more generally, as proposed by the

Administration's American Competitiveness Initiative. First, federal agencies are still able to fund only a tiny fraction of the meritorious proposals that are submitted. In its most recent solicitation for Nanoscale Science and Engineering Centers, for example, the NSF received 48 proposals and could fund only 6. Even when an agency does fund a proposal, the size and duration of the grant are often inadequate. Second, foreign governments are continuing to aggressively ramp up their investments in nanoscale S&E. Given that international leadership in nanotechnology is up for grabs, allowing U.S. funding to stagnate while foreign governments continue to provide double-digit increases seems to us to be an incredibly risky strategy. Third, only the federal government is in a position to support the long-term, high-risk research that is beyond the time horizons of companies. Finally, researchers have demonstrated the potential of nanotechnology to make important contributions to a wide range of national goals and key economic sectors, such as health, clean energy, information technology, new materials, national and homeland security, sustainable development, manufacturing, and space exploration. Stagnant or declining budgets will make it difficult to pursue these and other opportunities. Below are just a few of the areas where new and expanded initiatives in nanoscale S&E would make a big difference.

Invest in Nanotechnology for Clean Energy. Experts believe that combating global warming may require the ability to generate 15 to 30 terawatts of carbon-free energy worldwide by 2050 (Hoffert, 2002). By comparison, today's total global energy consumption is a little less than 15 terawatts. Considering that 85 percent of our current global primary energy consumption is from fossil fuels, this is a daunting challenge. Researchers have identified a variety of ways in which nanotechnology could help solve our long-term energy challenges. These include a dramatic reduction in the cost of photovoltaics, direct photoconversion of light and water to produce hydrogen, and transformational advances in energy storage and transmission. The United States desperately needs an Apollo-type project to reduce the threat of climate change and its dependence on Middle East oil. Nanotechnology could play a key role in creating new sources of carbon-free energy that are competitive with fossil fuels.

Extend "Moore's Law" with Nanoelectronics. In the 1990s, the U.S. economy began to experience significant increases in productivity, the most important determinant of the country's long-run standard of living. Much of this increase could be traced to business investments in information and communications technologies combined with the managerial and organizational innovations needed to take advantage of the dramatically lower cost of storing, processing, and transmitting information. The semiconductor industry believes that today's technology will approach fundamental performance limits in 2020. If we want the benefits of Moore's law to continue for decades to come, increased investment is needed to explore alternatives such as quantum computing, spintronics, molecular electronics, and computing based on nanostructures such as nanowires and nanotubes.

Establish a "Pioneer Award" for Nanoscale S&E. One of the frequent complaints of scientists and engineers is that flat science budgets and proposal pressure have made the peer review process more conservative. Some scientists joke that "you have to do the experiment before you can write the grant." NIH Director Elias Zerhouni is attempting to counteract this trend by providing a Pioneer Award to support exceptional researchers interested in pursuing high-risk, high-impact research. Researchers are given $500,000 per year in direct costs for five years, which gives them the time and resources to explore innovative ideas and approaches to challenges in biomedical research. The NSF should be given the budget to launch a similar program in nanoscale S&E and possibly other areas as well.

Create Nanotechnology-Related Education and Outreach Activities that Scale. One of the explicit goals of the NNI is to excite young boys and girls about science, particularly the physical sciences and engineering. The U.S. trends are troubling, particularly when compared with emerging economic competitors in Asia. Last year, for example, 65,000 U.S. high school students participated in the local fairs used to select the finalists for the Intel Science and Engineering Fair. In China, that number was 6 million! Currently, agencies such as the NSF encourage researchers to engage in education and outreach activities to increase the number of high school and undergraduate students that pursue careers in S&E and to increase public understanding of science. These activities are worthwhile and praiseworthy, but we believe that the federal government must also experiment with interventions that have the potential to reach millions of children. We would like to see an IMAX movie that would explain the promise of nanotechnology to every middle school student in the United States or a video game about nanotechnology that is as engaging as *Halo 2* or *Everquest*.

Understand and Mitigate the Environmental and Human Health Effects of Nanomaterials. As many experts have noted, our current understanding of the environmental and human health effects of nanomaterials is limited. A failure to understand and manage these health risks could put the nanotechnology revolution on hold. Reinsurance companies such as Swiss Re have made it very clear that they do not wish to be left holding the bag if nanotechnology poses significant risks to human health. Although some research is already being done, increased funding for agencies such as the EPA, the National Institute for Occupational Safety and Health, and the National Institute for Environmental Health Sciences is clearly needed. A study by the Woodrow Wilson Center for International Scholars concluded that research on risks needs to be increased to at least $100 million per year to address current knowledge gaps in nanotechnology risk assessment. An analysis by the Wilson Center found that only $10 million of the NNI's total budget was "highly relevant" to the health and environmental risks associated with engineered nanomaterials.

Promote Nanotechnology Applications for Developing Countries. Researchers at the University of Toronto have published a list of the 10 applications of nanotechnology with the most relevance to developing countries. Examples include inexpensive systems that purify, detoxify, and desalinate water more efficiently than conventional bacterial or viral filters; clean energy; and a "lab on a chip" for research on developing country diseases. The United States should fund research collaborations between U.S. and developing country researchers to explore these applications.

Promote the Interface Between Bio and Nano. The intersection between "nano" and "bio" is an incredibly promising and fertile area. On the one hand, nanotechnology is creating powerful new tools for health care and fundamental biology. On the other hand, nature is serving as a rich source of inspiration for nanoscientists, who are challenged by the performance of biological systems such as rotary motors in the flagella of *Escherichia coli* bacteria. As Caltech's Michael Roukes observed, "The fact that the gene encodes the commonplace, mass-production of such atomically precise devices taunts us, urging us onward in our explorations!" (Roukes, 2004). Biological systems routinely assemble individual molecules into large, complex, functional structures using templated hierarchical self-assembly. The immune system develops millions of extremely similar but critically different structures (antibodies) and rapidly scans them for the desired properties. Furthermore, living systems are self-healing, self-repairing, and fault tolerant. Unfortunately, there are cultural barriers within the scientific community to research on bio-inspired materials, processes, and devices. Biologists are usually descriptive scientists who focus on understanding the components and operations of existing systems, not the creation of new systems. Although the NIH, especially the National Cancer Institute, is beginning to ramp up its activities in nanomedicine, there are many nonhealth applications of bio-inspired nanosystems. At least one federal science agency should be given the budget and the mandate to build a robust research community in this area.

Help Nanotechnology Start-ups Cross the "Valley of Death." Part of the argument for increased funding for research is that it will eventually fuel the creation of new companies, new industries, and high-wage jobs. Moving ideas from the lab to the marketplace is never easy, particularly in nanotechnology. A big gap exists between showing that a nanostructure has some novel and useful property and demonstrating high-volume, cost-effective manufacturing. Although one might argue that venture capitalists should fund this "reduction to practice," most of them are reluctant to invest in early-stage technology development. With institutional investors still counting their losses from the "dot com" era, they are urging venture capitalists to shift to later stage, less risky investments, reducing the capital available for seed investments in spin-offs from universities and national labs. We believe that the multiagency Small Business Innovation Research (SBIR) and Small Business Technology Transfer Programs should be used more aggressively to help nanotechnology start-ups cross the chasm between proof of principle and reduction to practice. The NIH has done this by increasing the duration and size of its SBIR grants for nanotechnology and allowing entrepreneurs to submit a broad range of ideas for using nanotechnology to help prevent, detect, diagnose, and treat disease. Other agencies should adopt a similar approach in applications of nanotechnology that are related to their mission.

Although the research community and companies involved in nanotechnology must be careful not to overpromise and underdeliver, the technology's long-term potential is awe inspiring. Although we will inevitably be surprised by the future course of nanotechnology, with continued investments in high-risk research many of the grand challenges that have been established will eventually be met. However, we cannot expect the United States to lead this technological revolution with policies that short change research. It is our sincere hope that we will respond to the growing challenges to U.S. scientific, technological, and economic leadership before it is too late.

REFERENCES

Clinton, W. 2000. Remarks by the President at science and technology event at Caltech, Pasadena, CA. January, 21, 2000.

Feynman, R. 1960. There's plenty of room at the bottom. *Engineering & Science.* February 1960. Pasadena, CA: Caltech.

Hoffert, M. et al. 2002. Advanced technology paths to global climate stability: energy for a greenhouse planet. *Science* 1, November 2002, vol. 298, p. 981.

Lane, N. 1998. U.S. Congressional testimony before the House Appropriations Subcommittee on VA/HUD and independent agencies. April 1, 1998.

Roukes, M. 2004. Research overview. Roukes Group at Caltech. http://www.its.caltech.edu/~nano/overview.html

PART III

ISSUES: PREPARING FOR THE NEXT REVOLUTION

John Weckert

Research ethics is often a starting point in preparing for the impact of new scientific work, commonly discussed in terms of concerns for the subjects of research or else for the researchers themselves. Will the people or animals involved be physically, psychologically, or emotionally harmed in any way? Will privacy be adversely affected? Will problems be caused to the environment? Will the researchers be in any danger?

Apart from worries about researchers working with certain nanoparticles that might be toxic, research ethics in nanotechnology also has been concerned with the broader issue of whether research into nanoscience and technology should be undertaken at all. Bill Joy was one of the first to raise the issue (Chapter 2). The thinking behind this is that technology should make the world a better place for humans and that nanotechnology might not do this. This is clearly a controversial view, not only because of its doubts about the value of nanotechnology but also because it questions whether scientists should be free to pursue scientific knowledge regardless of where those pursuits lead. The four chapters in this part consider various aspects of research as a key influencer in nanotechnology's progress and societal impact.

In Chapter 7, Charles Tahan, physicist and nanoethicist at the University of Cambridge, looks at the place of nanotechnology in the history of technology and, in particular, the history of technological revolutions. Far from nanotechnology being developed as a result of the pure research interests of scientists, he argues that the term "nanotechnology" is being used as a marketing term to help divert more funding into basic

Nanoethics: The Ethical and Social Implications of Nanotechnology. Edited by Allhoff, Lin, Moor, Weckert
Copyright © 2007 John Wiley & Sons, Inc.

scientific research, at least in the United States. Additionally, the U.S. military is driving much of the research and development and steering it in particular directions for military purposes. His discussion shows how the direction of research and development is driven by the society in which it takes place, a point continued from Chapter 6.

Arguments about whether or not nanotechnology research should be directed—or even curtailed—presuppose that it is possible to predict the outcomes of research. The military funds certain research because it predicts certain benefits from that research while others advocate a moratorium because of predicted harms. The remaining three chapters in this part all discuss the notion of prediction.

In Chapter 8, Nick Bostrom, a philosopher at Oxford University, continues with the theme of technological revolutions and examines challenges posed by attempts to predict the outcomes of these revolutions. While prediction is fraught with difficulties, some can reasonably be made with some confidence; in any case, all policy decisions involve prediction to a greater or lesser extent. The situation is further complicated, Bostrom argues, by the fact that strategic decisions regarding science and technology policy will depend not just on predictions of the scientific outcomes but also on predictions of what strategic decisions others will make.

In Chapter 9, Jean-Pierre Dupuy of École Polytechnique in Paris as well as Stanford University offers a different approach. He argues that trying to predict the outcomes of research in order to avoid possible harmful effects is inherently flawed and is based on a false metaphysics of time in which the future is not considered real. On his account of time—called "projected time" —the future is real and therefore the precautionary principle makes no sense to the extent that it proposes to change behavior in order to avoid a possible future problem. He advocates an approach that he calls "enlightened doomsaying" ; he argues that this avoids the problem encountered by the precautionary principle.

In Chapter 10, the precautionary principle is defended (though not specifically against Dupuy's criticism) by John Weckert and James Moor, coeditors of this anthology. They argue that it can be spelled out in a way that gives it force and in such a way that it does not fall prey to the many criticisms that have been charged against it, including the problem of making predictions. They illustrate their account with three different examples from nanotechnology: nanoparticles, privacy, and gray goo.

7

THE NANOTECHNOLOGY R(EVOLUTION)*

Charles Tahan

Roughly 7,000 years ago, humans began to leave their nomadic ways and form civilizations around the irrigation and cultivation of land. As a result, human society and community transformed radically. The creation of government and bureaucracy, of social classes, written language, the rule of law, the notion of the individual, standing armies, and much more, all emanated from this technological change. Dubbed the "irrigation society" by renowned management thinker Peter Drucker (1965), this first great technological revolution of humans lasted over 2,000 years.

Nowadays, the word *revolution* is used rather freely. From the "Internet revolution" to the "digital music revolution" to the "nanotechnology revolution," at what scale does an innovation become more than an innovation? In her classic work *Technological Revolutions and Financial Capital* Carlota Perez (2002) defines five technological revolutions since the end of the eighteenth century. As new technologies emerge and disseminate, they tend to follow similar economic investment cycles which Perez calls "techno-economic paradigms." However, the key realization—and what Drucker was

* The title "Nanotechnology R(evolution)" originates with a former student, Michael Markovics, in my class of spring 2005 at the University of Wisconsin-Madison: *Nanotechnology and Society* (Tahan, 2006).

The author would like to thank members of the Wisconsin Nanotechnology and Society Initiative for useful conversations and especially Greta Zenner for critical reading and editing. The author is supported by a U.S. National Science Foundation Math and Physical Sciences Distinguished International Postdoctoral Research Fellowship (Award No. DMR-0502047).

suggesting in his 1965 presidential speech to the Society of the History of Technology—is that we are living in a second great technological revolution. Beginning with the Industrial Revolution in Britain (around 1750) a person could expect to die in a world very much different from the one into which he or she was born.

A great revolution implies an increasing rate of innovation, and not just technological innovation, but also organizational and political, in many different fields. There is little doubt that the rate of innovation accelerated after 1750 (Cross and Szostak, 1995) and is still increasing. Although it is difficult to assess the evolution and longevity of such a revolution from within it, we can easily believe that as more people and more wealth come into the enterprise of innovation, more of Perez's technoeconomic paradigms will occur with increasing frequency. Nanotechnology may be one of them.

Technological revolution is always accompanied by political and social change. The two go together. The bigger the technological change, the more society must adapt to accommodate this objective reality. For example, as farmers began to accumulate wealth (that is, food) for communities, an army became necessary to protect it. Just as there are larger and smaller technological revolutions, there are larger and smaller societal changes to go along with them. In Table 7.1 we have tried to form a hierarchy of revolutions. Inevitably, revolutions are coarse grained, representing a sum of individual innovations that erupt seemingly randomly. We define four categories of revolution: great revolutions, of which there have only been two, with the present one just beginning; major revolutions or the technoeconomic paradigms of Perez, which usually last some 50 years; minor revolutions, which are finer still and are key building blocks of the major revolutions; and microrevolutions, which are largely new investment opportunities in technology that come about within the larger revolutions but also follow a cyclical pattern of investment and saturation.

Soon after World War II, governments worldwide and particularly in the United States realized that significant investment in the natural sciences could drastically affect the power and wealth of nations. Integrated electronics, the Internet, even lasers can be lumped into the age of information and telecommunications as a direct result of this investment. Much of what is today called nanotechnology naturally follows from these lines of technical pursuit and scientific inquiry. Together with the theoretical understanding of quantum physics and electrodynamics that has developed over the last century, this continuation of research has led us within reach of tremendous rewards from the manipulation and control of matter at the nanoscale. Whereas these pursuits were somewhat ignored in recent decades—significant hype and investment focusing instead on telecommunications, software and networking, and biotechnology—there is a growing realization that it is time to start pushing materials science and fundamental research again. Very recent trends in the global energy crisis and the so-called green revolution only add to this notion.

If anything, nanotechnology has become a marketing term to encompass and drive this belief that more funding is needed in the physical sciences to maintain economic, scientific, and military advantage over international competition. As evidence, roughly one-third of the budget for the National Nanotechnology Initiative (NNI) this year will go to the National Science Foundation (NSF) (Roco, 2004), which primarily supports unfettered basic research. Still, understanding how government and the military drive technological development and how nanotechnology as it stands today (and may exist

TABLE 7.1. Hierarchy of Technological Revolutions

Great revolutions (there have only been two that we know about)
    1: Irrigation society, began approximately 5000 BC and ended about 3000 BC
    2: Began with the Industrial Revolution in Britain in the eighteenth century
Major revolutions after 1750 (start date)
    Industrial Revolution (1771)
    Age of steam and railways (1829)
    Age of steel, electricity, and heavy engineering (1875)
    Age of oil, the automobile, and mass production (1908)
    Age of information and telecommunications (1971)
    Age of bioengineering (1980)?
    Second industrial revolution (1991)?
    Age of machine-phase nanotechnology (2030–2050)?
Minor revolutions (some examples)
    Personal computing
    Mobile phones
    Global networking
    Nanoparticle revolution?
Micro revolutions (some examples)
    Digital music revolution
    High-density television revolution
    Nanoparticle revolution?

in the future) may relate to prior revolutions in history has great value. Responsible encouragement of the great technological revolution in which we find ourselves is vital to human civilization.

DEFINING NANOTECHNOLOGY

Nanotechnology is a social construction. The word *nanotechnology* did not emerge as a distinct area of science but rather was introduced externally and defined by its usage in the greater societal dialogue. A primary consequence of this very public defining of the term nanotechnology is its present bipolar nature. We take a pragmatic definition of nanotechnology that combines both sides: the *reality* of the word as it is used today primarily by governments, corporations, and scientists as well as the *vision* of what the field might become (Tahan, 2007). The reality of nanotechnology—as defined mostly by government funding managers and agencies—largely encompasses ongoing research in materials science and solid-state physics. Examples include nanoparticles and quantum dots, "nano-enabled" surface coatings, transistor features that are less than 10 nanometers in scale, giant and colossal magnetoresistance (as in hard drives), spintronics, photonic band-gap structures, and more. The definition usually takes a variant like this one from the Royal Society (2004) of the United Kingdom: "Nanoscience is the study of phenomena and manipulation of materials at atomic, molecular, and macromolecular scales, where properties differ significantly from those at a larger scale." Distinct from this is the more science fiction vision of nanotechnology popularized by

Eric Drexler (1986) and in books like Neal Stephenson's (1995) *The Diamond Age*—that of atom-by-atom construction of matter and nanoscale (invisible) machines and robots, also referred to as "machine-phase nanotechnology."

The reality definition of nanotechnology is a synonym for fundamental materials and matter research, including quantum phenomena at small-length scales. The origins are clear. For the past 40 years—since the invention of the semiconductor transistor—the economic apparatus built around Moore's law has been driving material features ever smaller. Concurrently, our understanding of the basic quantum physics that governs the behavior of interacting particles (of matter and light) has been solidifying. More recently, measurement and fabrication techniques have reached a point where we can start thinking seriously about exploiting some of these novel properties that appear in the small-length regimes. As this level of control gets closer technologically, with clear opportunities in sight, the funding of these endeavors becomes more worthwhile. If nanotechnology can act as an umbrella term to drive interest and funding, so be it. The head of the NNI publicly espouses this viewpoint (Roco, 2004).

We can further separate the larger field nanotechnology, in terms of the reality and vision accompanying this emerging technology, from the recent interest in nanoparticle and quantum dot technologies. In many ways—certainly as far as environmental and human toxicity are concerned—nanotechnology can be defined much more narrowly than the above (as we have argued before; Tahan, 2007):

> Nanotechnology, at present, is nanoparticles and nanomaterials that contain nanoparticles. Nanoparticles are defined as objects or devices with at least two dimensions in the nanoscale regime (typically tens of nanometers or less) that exhibit new properties, physical, chemical, or biological, or change the properties of a bulk material, due to their size. Nanotechnology of the future will include atom-by-atom or molecule-by-molecule built active devices (Colvin, 2003).

Much of the excitement surrounding nanotechnology comes from the promise of newly gained nanoparticle synthesis techniques and a realization of their potential in many different areas. Two prominent examples are biomarkers for cancer detection (and destruction) and quantum dots in solar energy conversion devices (Scientific American 2002). Nanoparticle and nanoparticle composite technology may end up solely a minor or microrevolution separate from the broader nanotechnology field.

NANOTECHNOLOGY'S PLACE IN AN AGE OF AGES

According to Drucker (1965):

> It is not only the speed of technological change that creates a "revolution," it is its scope as well. Above all, today, as seven thousand years ago, technological developments from a great many areas are growing together to create a new human environment.

Drucker's words remain true. Nanotechnology as presently (loosely) defined will likely have several acts to play in the coming century. Certainly the utilization of nanoparticle technology has immediate promise. Much of the rest of nanotechnology in the near term can more accurately be placed within the information or biotechnology revolutions. In either case, we can find patterns. The five major revolutions that Perez outlined all follow a similar pattern. The first stage is the installation period, which has an eruption phase, when a new innovation is introduced and spreads in conflict with old products and technologies. The second is the frenzy phase, when financial capital drives the build-up of new technologies but develops tensions within the system. A turning point occurs, usually with a recession that follows the collapse of a financial bubble, and regulatory changes are made to facilitate and shape the period of development. Then follows a period of deployment, which initially has a synergy phase, when conditions are all favorable for the full flourishing of the new technology, and then the maturity phase, when signs of dwindling investment opportunities and stagnating markets appear (Perez, 2002).

Obviously there is much fluctuation in this model. Since nanotechnology as labeled takes on so many meanings, we must separate the key components. First, there is the nanoparticle/quantum dot component, and we will call this the nanoparticle revolution. Second, there is a continuation of technologies resulting in nanoscale techniques for manufacture that are being widely adopted by big industry (GE, Dupont, Intel). We can hesitantly call this a second industrial revolution (ground-up technology?). Finally, in the far distance, there is the machine-phase nanotechnology revolution, completely imaginary at this stage. Only this stage of development (promising essentially free goods) holds the potential for drastic social and political upheaval.

At the current state of development, nanotechnology simply does not represent a paradigm shift in scientists' thinking. Nanoscale investigation is an evolutionary outgrowth of a new capability to measure and fabricate at that scale. Nanotechnology must be seen in the greater trend of innovation, which, like the irrigation revolution, will likely continue well into the next millennium.

MILITARY AND TECHNOLOGICAL DEVELOPMENT

The military has long been an instigator and shaper of technological innovation. Often the high-cost buyer or buyer of last resort, the military can act both to encourage a fledgling technology and to prolong a dying one. The U.S. Department of Defense (DOD) has clearly taken an interest in nanotechnology and accounts for roughly 28 percent of all federal funding in the loosely defined field in fiscal year 2005 (Roco, 2004). One prominent example is the Institute for Soldier Nanotechnologies (Talbot, 2002) at the Massachusetts Institute of Technology (http://web.mit.edu/ISN/). Stronger and lighter materials and more explosive bombs (superthermites) are but two examples of nanotechnology's impact on future warfare.

It is widely assumed that military-born technologies spill over into civilian use for beneficial purposes. However, the military has specific objectives in its approach to technology, which might be very different from those of society at large. Historian David

Noble (1987) lays out three such objectives in his treatise on military and technology which are worth considering again in the context of nanotechnology: (1) performance (emphasis placed on meeting military objectives and what follows necessarily from them), (2) command (management techniques with decision making coming solely from the top), and (3) modern methods (a fetish for machinery that won't talk back). Noble argues that it is a misconception that the military acts only as an external input of technology. Instead, the military shapes the progress and nature of a technology or set of technologies throughout their lifetime in many cases.

One clear example of this dates back to the beginning of the United States as a nation where the military's quest for interchangeable gun parts helped spur mechanization and the Industrial Revolution in the States. Uniformity was imposed by the military contract system. "The benefits of the system, clear to the military, were not so clear to many manufacturers, given the high costs, uncertainties, and inescapable industrial conflict it engendered" (Noble, 1987). A similar example is that of *numerical control*, pioneered by the Air Force in the 1980s. Numerical control envisioned extremely precise machining based on computer and mathematical specification and extreme shortening of the chain of command from aircraft part specification to manufacture. Industry generally was not enthusiastic as the systems were very complex and not as flexible as other less demanding, though adequate, metalworking techniques. Since the military provided such a large and stable base of funding, however, industry followed the numerical control path (Noble, 1987). Industry paid the price as foreign competition became more nimble. The loss of promising alternative technologies, excessive consolidation in the metalworking industry, and slow innovation all resulted from the military's involvement.

An excellent counterexample to this phenomenon is Intel. Although the military was the initial buyer of Intel's first few-transistor circuits, its preferences did not shape Intel's future. Intel would not have survived in the rapidly changing consumer environment had its engineers been unable to make decisions. In fact, Intel has thrived on a very long chain of command. In other words, engineers very near the technology (but at the bottom of the corporate hierarchy) are entrusted with a large amount of discretion to make decisions related to technology undeniably vital to the company's future. The rate of growth in the private sector made this possible, although it is important to note that some semiconductor fabs continued at a reduced level by specializing their wares for military needs (think Fairchild Semiconductor, a founding company of Silicon Valley which has since largely left the commercial consumer electronics arena for mostly military and advanced technology contracting).

The long-term trend is an increasing shift of federal research dollars into the mission-driven agencies and away from discipline-driven research, such as in NSF, the Department of Energy's (DOE) Office of Science, and at NIST (National Institute of Standards and Technology). Apart from the National Institutes of Health (NIH), nondefense federal research and development is about the same in 2004 dollars as it was in 1980 (Duke and Dill, 2004). Basic, unfettered physical research in the United States is declining, except where it goes through the DOD mission agencies and the NNI.

In general, the military funding agencies are much stricter about how their grant money is used as compared to the NSF. Since all or most of the research money comes through the military, and they are the ones asking hard questions and threatening to pull funding, scientists at universities feel strong pressure to follow the dictated "roadmaps" instead of pursuing new physics as it is identified. Because of this, new and perhaps useful phenomena at the nanoscale—which may lay the groundwork for the next revolution 50 years hence—may be missed in this country.

LESSONS FROM THE PAST

A recent commercial by General Electric featured a "professor of nanotechnology" and a supermodel falling in love: "the perfect combination of brains and beauty" (GE, 2005) "Nanotechnologist" has become the new computer scientist, driver of the next great wealth generator. While easy to dismiss, it is important to remember that but for the abnormal obsession of a couple dozen people with the properties of semiconductors, the United States would not have led the personal computing, networking, and internet revolutions of the last half of the twentieth century. A case study is Great Britain, which irreversibly fell behind Germany and the United States because it faltered in its investment in new technologies during the age of steel, electricity, and heavy engineering (1875–1920) (Duke and Dill, 2004). Will history repeat itself in the United States?

Before World War II, U.S. universities were a joke internationally. Due to the demonstrable success of radar and the atomic bomb, the United States quickly realized that science played a key role in military victories and national power, so a large-scale investment in fundamental research began. The GI Bill supplied manpower. Through this and America's survival as a superpower after the war (and a concurrent influx of highly trained European scientists), the United States has had the good fortune to lead the last major technoeconomic revolution: the age of information and telecommunications as well as many minor ones. But as other countries catch up to America's core strengths, the U.S. leadership position is tenuous. Indeed, funding in nanotechnology in Japan and Europe is comparable to that of the United States at present (Roco, 2004; National Research Council, 2006).

If we want to lay the foundation for the next revolution, it is instructive to go back and try to understand what began in the mid-eighteenth century in England. In fact, the name Industrial Revolution is a misnomer, as innovations took place in many areas such as farm and home, in addition to manufacturing (Cross and Szostak, 1995). No one knows for sure why the Industrial Revolution began where and when it did. There are many hypotheses: Britain's institutional support of technology (world's first patent system, strong private property rights, acceptance of Jewish and other ethnic minorities); urbanization and increased life expectancy; encouragement of an empirical and utilitarian tradition (e.g., Francis Bacon's writings); consolidation of agricultural land by lords with agricultural efficiencies; increased worker migration to cities; movement of work away from the guild system (putting out system); raw material advantages; and less regulation. The list goes on. But other European countries like Germany and France, which also had better educational systems, shared many of these advances in whole or in part. The one thing other countries lacked was a transport system even remotely comparable to what England had put in place (Cross and Szostak, 1995): "Transport improvements greatly accelerated the processes of regional specialization and urbanization in England.

They also led to a dramatic increase in personal travel." This encouraged the interaction between innovators with varied backgrounds, expertise, and ideas, which is essential to the innovation process. Regionalization and localization led to mechanization.

In the present day, the United States has a mixed infrastructure in idea transportation. Although it has pioneered advancements in collaboration and interaction online, several other countries, such as South Korea and Taiwan, have superior broadband networking penetration. Residents of the United States have always enjoyed freedom to move about the country, and career success often demands it. The United States also enjoys the benefits of scale, with a large number of excellent yet independent universities and a large entrepreneurial culture (exhibited in individuals and in organizations such as top-notch private-equity entities). Presently, first-world countries like Great Britain, Australia, and Japan—although investing heavily in nanotechnology research—are struggling to match the U.S. highly efficient venture capital ecosystem. However, immigration rules since 9/11 have decreased the influx of talent from around the world, traditionally a key driver of science research. But none of this compares to the great experiment that is ongoing in the very nature of science investment in the United States.

Industrial science and technology in the United States have undergone a dramatic change in recent years, from "closed innovation" to "open innovation" (Chesbrough, 2003). In essence, the era of industrial research labs is over (Duke and Dill, 2004). Where significant basic research used to occur in the bowels of Bell Labs or Xerox PARC, industry has now focused more on development of near and more economically justifiable engineering. Extreme examples of this are companies like Intel and Cisco, which "outsource" virtually all their research. They leverage their research budgets by partnering with academia and other companies and start-ups. This is different from and in addition to what's usually called outsourcing—the farming out of actual work or jobs (in this case in research and development) to countries such as China and India (Duke and Dill, 2004): "Under Open Innovation, a company's value chain is no longer fully contained within the company, and ideas, people, and products flow across company boundaries, to and from other companies, universities, and even countries."

This business trend has left only universities and national labs to fulfill the need for basic research in the United States. From 1953 to 1996, the fraction of basic research that was performed in universities and federal labs rose from 33 to 61 percent (Duke and Dill, 2004). Is this enough to make up the difference? We simply do not yet know how this change will affect U.S. competitiveness in the future: (Duke and Dill, 2004) "The growth of biotechnology in America is largely a story of seedling ideas that came from academic scientists in research universities, funded by venture capitalists, and manned by bright graduate and postdoctoral students." Nanotechnology may prove to be the same story, or not.

There are a number of conditions that allowed the Industrial Revolution to move quickly to the United States: fast population growth; natural and artificial protection (via the Atlantic Ocean and tariffs); copying and extending prior work (of the British banking system, corporate, and insurance; manufacturing techniques, etc.); relief from bankruptcy (limited liability); legal monopoly over inventions through patent law—with strict granting of patent applications to ensure that only new and useful ideas were patented; lack of guild monopolies; vast natural resources; and receptivity to innovation. What country today has the most of these benefits? As Duke and Dill (2004) point out the United States must focus on its core strengths: innovative and fast-moving companies, talented people, and strength in basic research. With these concerns, the motivation of the NNI to pump money into fundamental research under the cover of nanotechnology seems like a very good move.

While on the surface the business trend to open innovation seems a good way to speed up business and technology growth, it is unclear what the long-term affects on the United States will be. If the majority of basic research ends up in Asia, can U.S. corporations seriously believe they will be allowed to "manage" and benefit from these new discoveries indefinitely?

CONCLUSIONS

That we are living through a great technological revolution with no end in sight is clear. What gets murky is our attempt to subclassify smaller revolutions within this larger landscape of merging innovations. The reality of nanotechnology as it stands today is the continued evolution of prior trends in information and materials science that began after World War II. That we are at a point where the exact synthesis of nanoparticles and other nanotechnologies holds great promise for medicine, energy conversion, and so on, has only fueled the belief that a renewed surge of investment is needed to harvest these potential technological breakthroughs. We have begun neither to approach the vision of nanomachines and robots that popularized the term nanotechnology nor to adequately understand the difficulty in getting there. So the great technological revolution that this may imply lies still in waiting for us to discover.

REFERENCES

Chesbrough, H. 2003. *Open Innovation: The New Imperative for Creating and Profiting From Technology*. Boston, MA: Harvard Business School Press.

Colvin, V. L. 2003. The potential environmental impact of engineered nanomaterials. *Nature Biotechnology* 21 (10): 1166–1170.

Cross, G., and Szostak, R. 1995. Origins of industrialization. Chapter 4 in *Technology and American Society: A History*. Englewood Cliffs, NJ: Prentice-Hall.

Drexler, E. 1986. *Engines of Creation: The Coming Era of Nanotechnology*. New York: Anchor Books.

Drucker, P. F. 1965. The first technological revolution and Its Lessons. Presidential address to the Society for the History of Technology, San Francisco, CA, December 29, 1965.

Duke, C., and Dill, K. 2004. The Next Technological Revolution: Will the US Lead or Fall Behind? March 22. Available: http://www.biophysics.org/pubaffairs/revolution.pdf, accessed September 27, 2006.

General Electric (GE). 2005. The Perfect Romance. Available: http://www.ge.com/stories/en/13085.html.

National Research Council. 2006. A matter of size: Triennial review of the National Nanotechnology Initiative Committee to review the National Nanotechnology Initiative. National Research Council. Available: http://www.nap.edu/catalog/11752.html.

Noble, D. F. 1987. Command performance: A perspective on military enterprise and technological change. In M. R. Smith (Ed.), *Military Enterprise and Technological Change: Perspectives on the American Experience*. Cambridge, MA: MIT Press.

Perez, C. 2002. *Technological Revolutions and Financial Capital: The Dynamics of Bubbles and Golden Ages*. Cheltenham, United Kingdom: E. Elgar.

Renn, O., and Roco, M. C. 2006. Nanotechnology and the need for risk governance. *Journal of Nanoparticle Research* 8(2).

Roco, M. C. 2004. Nanoscale science and engineering: Unifying and transforming tools. *AIChE Journal* 50(5): 890–897.

Rosenbloom, R. S., and Spencer, W. J. 1996. *Engines of Innovation*. Boston: Harvard Business School Press.

Royal Society of London. 2004. Nanoscience and nanotechnology: Opportunities and uncertainties. Document 19/04. Available: http://www.nanotec.org.uk/finalReport.htm, accessed September 27, 2006.

Scientific American. Editors. 2002. *Understanding Nanotechnology*. New York: Warner Books.

Stephenson, N. 1995. *The Diamond Age or A Young Lady's Illustrated Primer*. New York: Bantam Books.

Tahan, C. 2006. Science and Technology Studies 201: Nanotechnology and Society. Available: http://www.tahan.com/charlie/nanosociety/course201/.

Tahan, C., et al. 2006. Nanotechnology and Society: A discussion-based undergraduate course. *American Journal of Physics* 74(4): 443–448.

Tahan, C. 2007. Identifying nanotechnology in society. In M. Zelkowitz (Ed.), *Advances in Computers*. Amsterdam: Elsevier.

Talbot, D. 2002. Super soldiers. *MIT Technology Review* 105 (8): 44–50.

8

TECHNOLOGICAL REVOLUTIONS AND THE PROBLEM OF PREDICTION*

Nick Bostrom

TECHNOLOGICAL REVOLUTIONS

We might define a technological revolution as a dramatic change brought about relatively quickly by the introduction of some new technology. As this definition is rather vague, it may be instructive to complement it with a few prototypal cases:

1. Some 11,000 years ago, in the neighborhood of Mesopotamia, some of our ancestors took up agriculture, beginning the end of the hunter-gatherer era. Improved food production led to population growth, causing average nutritional status and quality of life to decline below the hunter-gatherer level. Eventually, greater population densities led to vastly accelerated cultural and technological development. Standing armies became a possibility, allowing the ancient Sumerians to embark on unprecedented territorial expansion.

2. In 1448, Johann Gutenberg invented the movable-type printing process in Europe, enabling copies of the Bible to be mass produced. Gutenberg's invention

* I am grateful to Eric Drexler, Guy Kahane, Matthew Liao, and Rebecca Roache for helpful suggestions. For a longer and more comprehensive treatment of some of these issues, see "Technological Revolutions: Ethics and Policy in the Dark," in *Nanotechnology and Society*, eds. Nigel M. de S. Cameron and M. Ellen Mitchell (Wiley), forthcoming.

became a major factor fueling the Renaissance, the Reformation, and the scientific revolution and helped give rise to mass literacy. A few hundred years later, *Mein Kampf* was mass produced using an improved version of the same technology.

3. In 1957, Soviet scientists launched Sputnik 1. In the following year, the United States created the Defense Advanced Research Projects Agency to ensure that the United States would stay ahead of its rivals in military technology. DARPA began developing a communication system that could survive nuclear bombardment by the USSR. The result, ARPANET, later became the Internet, which made available the World Wide Web, email, and other services. The long-term consequences remain to be seen.

Technological revolutions are among the most consequential things that happen to humanity, perhaps exceeded in their impact only by more gradual, nonrevolutionary technological developments. Technological change is in large part responsible for the evolution of such basic parameters of the human condition as the size of the world population, life expectancy, education levels, material standards of living, the nature of work, communication, health care, war, and the effects of human activities on the natural environment. One does not have to embrace any strong form of technological determinism or be a historical materialist to acknowledge that technological capability—through its complex interactions with individuals, institutions, cultures, and the environment—is a key determinant of the ground rules within which the game of human civilization is played out at any given point in time.

SCIENCE AND TECHNOLOGY GOVERNANCE

There has been a slow trend since World War II of intensifying endeavors to connect science and technology (S&T) policy to a broader discussion about desired social outcomes. The rise of environmentalism in the 1960s is part of this trend. The congressional Office of Technology Assessment was created to improve understanding of the societal implications of technological choices. Disease lobbies have been formed to influence the allocation of funding for medical research. Concerns about global warming have pushed increased resources into climate science and research into alternative energy sources. Some 3 percent of the budget for the Human Genome Project was set aside for studying the ethical, legal, and societal issues (ELSIs) connected to genetic information. Research into the ethical, legal, and societal issues related to nanotechnology (NELSIs) might over time outstrip that of the genetic ELSI program. The last couple of decades have also seen the establishment of a large and diverse set of grassroots organizations, think tanks, and university centers that work on technology-related issues.

There is growing apprehension that anticipated technological developments—including nanotechnology but also artificial intelligence, neurotechnology, biotechnology, and information technology—are likely to have transforming impacts on human society and perhaps on human nature itself. Some speak of an "NBIC" convergence (referring to the integration of the neurobioinformation and cognitive sciences) and explicitly link this to the prospect of human enhancement (Roco et al., 2003; Bainbridge et al., 2006).

While the spectrum of opinion represented in these discussions is quite broad, there seem to be some points of consensus, at least within the Western "mainstream" :

- Technological development will have major impacts on human society.
- These developments will create both problems and opportunities.
- "Turning back" is neither feasible nor desirable.
- There is a need for careful public examination of both the upsides and downsides of new technologies and for exploration of possible ways of limiting potential harms (including technological, regulatory, intergovernmental, educational, and community-based responses).

In addition to disagreements about the *content* of S&T policy, there are also disagreements about the *process* whereby such policy should be determined, with challenges being raised to the "official" model of the appropriate relationship between science and society, which harks back to the Enlightenment. According to the Enlightenment model, "the only scientific citizens are the scientists themselves. For science to engage in the production of properly scientific knowledge it must live in a 'free state' and in a domain apart from the rest of society. Historically, science's grip on Truth is seen as having grown progressively stronger as society's grip on science has grown progressively weaker and ever more closely circumscribed" (Elam and Bertilson, 2002; p. 133). The Enlightenment model pictures science as the goose that lays the golden egg, but only when it is protected from external interference.

This model has come under increased scrutiny since the 1960s. The notion that science is unproblematically associated with progress is no longer as widely accepted as it once was. In Europe, broad efforts are underway to change the "social contract" between science and society in order to create a larger role for public participation and deliberation in setting the priorities and limitations of S&T.

Initiatives to build more opportunities for the public to become engaged in S&T issues can be seen as an effort to rebuild public confidence and to secure science's "license to operate." But beyond such public relations goals, there are also many who argue that the S&T enterprise needs much more guidance from society in order to ensure that scientific and technological research is really directed to achieve socially beneficial outcomes. The aim is not necessarily to restrict research or to contest any particular scientific theory but to yoke the S&T behemoth to ends chosen by the people after due deliberation and debate. If S&T is such an important shaper of the modern world, it should be brought under democratic control, the thinking goes, and its workings should become more transparent to the people who have to live with the consequences.[1]

This view is reflected in a recent paper by Michael Crow and Daniel Sarewitz (2001, p. 97):

When resources are allocated for R&D [research and development] programs, the implications for complex societal transformation are not considered. The

fundamental assumption underlying the allocation process is that all societal outcomes will be positive, and that technological cause will lead directly to a desired
societal effect. The literature promoting the National Nanotechnology Initiative
expresses this view.

They continue (p. 98):

> The fact that societal outcomes are not a serious part of the framework seems to
> derive from two beliefs: (1) that the science and technology enterprise has to be
> granted autonomy to chose its own direction of advance and innovation; and (2)
> that because we cannot predict the future of science or technological innovation,
> we cannot prepare for it in advance. These are oft-articulated arguments, not straw
> men. Yet the first is contradicted by reality, and the second is irrelevant. The
> direction of science and technology is in fact dictated by an enormous number
> of constraints (only one of which is the nature of nature itself). And preparation
> for the future obviously does not require accurate prediction; rather, it requires a
> foundation of knowledge upon which to base action, a capacity to learn from expe-
> rience, close attention to what is going on in the present, and healthy and resilient
> institutions that can effectively respond or adapt to change in a timely manner.

In the remainder of this essay I want to focus on the second of these beliefs that
Crow and Sarewitz mention: the belief that, because we cannot predict the future of
innovation, we cannot prepare for it in advance.

UNPREDICTABILITY

Technological revolutions have far-reaching consequences that are difficult to predict.
This poses a challenge for technology policy. The challenge, however, is not unique to
technology policy. All major policy changes have far-reaching consequences that are
difficult to predict. There does not exist an exact science that can tells us precisely what
will happen in the long run when a government decides to abolish slavery, go to war, or
give women the right to vote.

For more modest policy changes, such as a reduction of a sales tax or the introduction
of stricter regulation on lead paint, expectations of the near-term consequences are more
tightly constrained by economic and scientific models and by parallel experience in
other countries. But social systems are complex, and even small interventions can have
large unanticipated long-term consequences. Perhaps reduced lead levels will lead to
increased intelligence in some children, and some of these might then grow up to become
more successful scientists than they would otherwise have been. Some of these scientists
might invent the future equivalent of the atomic bomb or antibiotics. Perhaps a reduced
sales tax will increase profits in one sector of the economy, some of which might be
used as campaign contributions that get a politician elected who will pass legislation
that may, in turn, have wide-ranging and unpredictable ramifications.

Even the most trivial personal decisions can have monumental consequences that
shape the fate of nations. Maybe one afternoon a thousand years ago in some Swiss

village, a young woman decided to go for a stroll to the lake. There she met a lad, and later they married and had children. Thus she became the great-grandmother of Adolf Hitler. If she had gone to the forest instead of the lake, the Holocaust and perhaps World War II would not have happened.[2]

On the other hand, the unpredictability of the future should not be exaggerated. Crow and Sarewitz (2001) appear to concede that "we cannot predict the future of science or technological innovation," but in doing so they concede too much. As Eric Drexler (2003) notes:[3]

> The future of technology is in some ways easy to predict. Computers will become faster, materials will become stronger, and medicine will cure more diseases. Nanotechnology, which works on the nanometer scale of molecules and atoms, will be a large part of this future, enabling great improvements in all these technologies.

Predictability is a matter of degree, and the degree varies radically depending on what precisely it is that we are trying to predict. Let us hence set aside the following unhelpful question:

> Is the future of science or technological innovation predictable?

A better question would be:

> How predictable are various aspects of the future of science or technological innovation?

But often, we will get more mileage out of asking:

> How much more predictable can (a certain aspect of) the future of science or technological innovations become if we devote a certain amount of resources to study it?

Or better still:

> Which particular inquiries would do most to improve our ability to predict those aspects of the future of S&T that we most need to know about in advance?

Pursuit of this question could lead us to explore many interesting avenues of research which might result in improved means of obtaining foresight about S&T developments and their policy consequences (e.g., Tetlock, 2005).

Crow and Sarewitz (2001), however, wishing to side-step the question about predictability, claim that it is "irrelevant" :

> Preparation for the future obviously does not require accurate prediction; rather, it requires a foundation of knowledge upon which to base action, a capacity to learn from experience, close attention to what is going on in the present, and healthy and resilient institutions that can effectively respond or adapt to change in a timely manner.

This answer is too quick. Each of the elements they mention as required for the preparation for the future relies in some way on accurate prediction. A capacity to learn from experience is not useful for preparing for the future unless we can correctly assume (predict) that the lessons we derive from the past will be applicable to future situations. Close attention to what is going on in the present is likewise futile unless we can assume that what is going on in the present will reveal stable trends or otherwise shed light on what is likely to happen next. It also requires prediction to figure out what kind of institutions will prove healthy, resilient, and effective in responding or adapting to future changes. Predicting the future quality and behavior of institutions that we create today is not an exact science.

It is possible, however, to reconstruct Crow and Sarewitz's (2001) argument in a way that makes more sense. Effective preparation for the future does require accurate prediction of at least certain aspects of the future. But some aspects are harder to predict than others. If we despair of predicting the future in detail, we may sensibly resort to courses of action that will do reasonably well independently of the details of how things turn out. One such course of action is to build institutional capacities that are able to respond effectively to future needs as they arise. Determining which institutional capacities will prove effective in the future does require prediction, but this is often a more feasible prediction task than predicting the details of the situations to which they will have to respond. The more the future is veiled in ignorance, the more it makes sense to focus on building general-purpose capabilities.

Recast in this way, the argument is more defensible as far as it goes. Yet its limitations become clear when we consider it within the context of S&T policy.

The tasks of S&T policy include setting priorities for the allocation of funding to research projects. It is hard to predict which lines of research will bear fruit and which will not. There are several possible ways of responding to this predicament. One is to concentrate funding on those research avenues which we can be fairly certain will bear at least some fruit. Another is to diversify the research portfolio and fund a little bit of everything. A third approach is to bet on a few research avenues that seem especially promising and accept the risk of total failure. Depending on the funders' attitude to risk and other factors, some mixture of these approaches might be optimal.[4]

But the question of predictability does not go away. Of course, it is not possible to fund a little bit of (literally) *everything*, and spreading out funding as evenly as possible among all seekers seems unlikely to be the smartest way of going about things. So how much funding should be concentrated on a few promising fields, such as nanotechnology? How tightly focused should that funding be on particular approaches, methods, and research centers? There is no simple answer. The optimal strategy will depend on just how confident the funders are in their ability to pick winners, that is, predict future advances.

The situation becomes even more complicated if we consider that some research projects might not simply fail to come to fruition but might bear poisoned fruit—produce results that we would be better off without. Certain possible weapons technologies fall into this category, but some critics of technoscience would argue that it includes a great deal else beside. Presumably, the majority's feeling that humanity ought to pursue scientific and technological research rests on the assumption that the value of the consequences of such advances is likely to be, on balance, positive. But if this assumption is true, and if it is also granted that *some* technological advances will prove detrimental, then again the question becomes whether we can be confident enough in our ability to predict in advance which particular trees will produce poisoned fruit in order to be justified in cutting them down now, or whether we should instead let them all grow, in the name of our epistemic modesty. Universal cultivation seems to require that there be just the right amount of predictability: enough so that we can expect that on balance the orchard will be beneficial to humanity and that our cultivation of it will in fact promote its growth, but not so much that we would be better off by chopping down selected trees because their growth may in the long run cause harm.

The complexity of our prediction problem increases even further when we consider that the payoff of an individual research project is not independent of what happens with other research projects. Different advances may work synergistically (as in the case of NBIC technologies) or one might preempt another and make it obsolete. When such dependencies exist, the development of an optimal research portfolio becomes more difficult. If predictability is low, we might decide to ignore such dependencies; if it is higher, on the other hand, we would be remiss not to take them into account in deciding our research priorities. The question of dependencies between potential future advances might also have to be reflected in what institutional structures we should create for the process of S&T agenda setting and implementation—for example, whether to establish a separate committee for a particular subfield. Again, the question of the degree of predictability of various aspects of the future—far from being one that can be trivially answered or sidestepped—is in fact highly difficult and central to many S&T policy issues.

From this brief discussion of predictability we can already draw several conclusions:

1. While some scientific advances and technological innovations are hard to predict with accuracy far in advance, the problem is not unique to the S&T context. Big policy decisions, small policy decisions, and trivial personal decisions all have important consequences that cannot be predicted in detail.
2. There are many aspects of scientific and technological developments that *can* be predicted.
3. all meaningful preparations for the future rely, explicitly or implicitly, on prediction.
4. the issues of the *relative* predictability of different aspects of the future and how much the predictability can be *improved* by various kinds of investment are important in thinking about how R&D programs should be structured.

A further lesson is that improvements in our ability to predict various potential S&T advances and their consequences could make a very valuable contribution to our capacity to make wise S&T policy decisions.

STRATEGIC DIMENSION

Let us now turn to consider the source of an additional level of complexity in S&T governance: strategy and politics. These impose constraints on what can be done and therefore on what it would make sense to attempt to do. As Ralph Waldo Emerson wrote:

> Web to weave, and corn to grind;
> Things are in the saddle,
> And ride mankind.

In particular, one needs to question whether mankind is really riding science and technology or whether it is the other way around.

One obvious sense in which mankind is not in the saddle is that the S&T policy decisions on this planet are not made by one unified body of rational and beneficent representatives of humanity who are trying to get us to some particular destination. Instead, there are countless agents, pursuing different and often opposing objectives, influencing various aspects of our species' S&T activities—national and regional governments, corporations, philanthropic foundations, special interest lobbies, journal editors, research councils, media organizations, consumers, voters, scientists, public intellectuals, and others. More specifically, we know two things: (1) There is no unified decision-making entity that has the power to direct or halt all research worldwide in any area and (2) many of the decision-making entities that influence S&T policies at various locations are themselves subject to influence from a variety of agents with diverging goals and agendas. Both of these facts have profound consequences for our thinking about S&T policy.

The first fact, the absence of global control of the world's S&T, makes it difficult or impossible to stop research and innovation in a particular direction even if it would be a good thing to do so. For example, even if some detailed study or public consultation concluded that a nanotechnology revolution would be detrimental to humanity, there is no clear path to preventing such a revolution from happening anyway. The government of one country might rescind public funding for research in certain areas thought likely to enable advances in nanotechnology but research would continue (albeit perhaps at a slower pace) using funding from private sources. The government might then ban all such research, whether publicly or privately funded, but other nations would almost certainly continue to push forward, and if the technology is feasible, it will eventually see the day anyway. Global bans on technological developments are very difficult to negotiate and even harder to police. The difficulties are amplified in cases where significant incentives exist for some groups for moving forward, where development can be conducted with modest resources, where concealment is possible, and where there is no salient demarcation between the hypothetically proscribed activity and legitimate research. Nanotechnology satisfies many of these conditions, so the prospect of global relinquishment appears to be close to nil, at least in lieu of dramatic advances in both surveillance technology and global governance.[5]

The infeasibility of halting certain kinds of research is a point often repeated in S&T policy discussions: "If our country does not go forward with this, someone else will and we will fall behind," or "If nanotechnology is outlawed, only outlaws will have nanotechnology" (e.g., Vandermolen, 2006) The appeal to national competitiveness seems to be one of the rhetorically most effective arguments both for increased spending on research and against regulation that would slow development.

One may compare this argument from economic competitiveness with another appealing argument for more research funding: that research is a global public good and should be supported out of love of humankind. The two arguments stand in some tension. The global public-goods argument suggests that it might be in a nation's self-interest to free-ride on other nations' S&T investment (particularly foundational research, the benefits of which are especially difficult for the producer to monopolize). If this is the case, then "national competitiveness" might actually suffer from the diversion of resources away from other sectors of society to S&T research. Yet both arguments could be true. There might be high returns for a nation to its investments in R&D and additional returns that cannot be captured domestically and instead become a positive externality benefiting other nations. In this case, both the love of humankind and the appeal to national advantage would work in tandem as reasons for increasing R&D investment.[6]

As both of these arguments illustrate, there are important consequences for S&T policy from the fact that S&T policy is not perfectly globally coordinated. But the complexity of the strategic situation increases vastly when we take into account that even within a particular country S&T decisions are not made by a single unified, perfectly rational, and perfectly beneficent agency. Policy recommendations directed to an imaginary ideal global or national decision-maker may form useful focal points for interim discussion, but ultimately they need to be transformed into recommendations addressed to some identifiable real agent. At that stage, recommendations must take into account the limitations of that agent's powers, understanding, attention, and interests. This transformation of "what should be done" in an abstract sense into sensible recommendations to an agent that can actually do things is far from straightforward.

For example, one argument that has been given for moving forward with nanotechnology research as rapidly as possible is as follows:[7]

1. The risks of advanced nanotechnology are great.
2. Reducing these risks will require a period of serious preparation.
3. Serious preparation will only begin once the prospect of advanced nanotechnology is taken seriously by broad sectors of society.
4. Broad sectors of society will only take the prospect of advanced nanotechnology seriously once there is a large research effort underway.
5. The earlier a serious research effort is initiated, the longer it will take to deliver advanced nanotechnology (because it starts from a lower level of preexisting enabling technologies).
6. Therefore, the earlier a serious research effort is initiated, the longer the period during which serious preparation will take place and the greater the reduction of the risks that will eventually have to be faced.
7. Therefore, a serious research effort should be initiated as soon as possible.

I present this argument not in order to evaluate it but to illustrate the point about strategic complexity. What naively looks like a reason for going slowly or stopping (the risks of advanced nanotechnology being great) ends up, on this line of thinking, as a reason for the opposite conclusion. Taking into account the strategic dimension can radically change one's recommendations for S&T policy.

It is interesting to consider to whom it is that this kind of argument addresses itself. The "broad sectors of society," which will supposedly begin serious preparation only after a large research effort is already underway, are presumably not the intended recipients of the message. If they were capable of and willing to understand, agree with, and act on an argument like this, then they would not need to wait for a large research effort to get underway in order to take the need for preparation seriously. The argument appears to be esoteric. There are some people who are "in the know" about the prospects of advanced nanotechnology, and these people would have a reason (so the argument goes) to direct their efforts towards accelerating the implementation of a serious nanotechnology research effort even if they thought that the risks of advanced nanotechnology outweighed the benefits.

One way the cognoscenti could do this would be by publicizing another argument for the acceleration of nanotechnology research, such as the argument that if *we* don't move forward quickly, then *somebody else*, perhaps a hostile state, will get there first—and that would be the worst possible outcome of all. Note that even this second argument addresses itself not to everybody but to a select group—in this case our compatriots, or at least the citizens of "good" states. It would not be desirable that the citizens of "bad" states urge *their* compatriots and government officials to launch a crash program for the development of advanced nanotechnology so that *they* get there first.[8]

There are actually people (perhaps not many) who think at this level of sophistication and attempt to take strategic considerations such as those above into account in deciding what they ought to do. Some of these people are well-meaning and honest and would not consent to putting forward an argument or an opinion that they did not sincerely hold to be true. Esoteric arguments do not require deception, or even active concealment, because to a significant extent audiences self-select which arguments they hear and absorb. The "nano-cognoscenti" might be the only ones who are receptive to the argument about a large research program being necessary to get broad sectors of society to take the risks seriously and start preparing. The citizens of good nations might be more likely to follow their compatriots' advice on the need to move forward with the research to avoid falling behind in a future arms race than the citizens of the bad nations who we fear might otherwise take the lead. (But how sure can we be that this is always the case?)

Predictability, or the lack thereof, again emerges as an important issue. Clearly, anticipating the responses of many different agents, how these responses will interact, and more generally how the ecology of ideas and opinions will be affected by the promulgation of one argument or another, is a daunting task—in many cases even more difficult than forecasting future developments in S&T.

BROADENING OUR DELIBERATIONS

Marie Curie (from a lecture at Vassar College, 1921) expresses an extreme version of the view that we ought to narrow the considerations taken into account:

We must not forget that when radium was discovered no one knew that it would prove useful in hospitals. The work was one of pure science. And this is a proof that scientific work must not be considered from the point of view of the direct usefulness of it. It must be done for itself, for the beauty of science, and then there is always the chance that a scientific discovery may become like the radium a benefit for humanity.

According to Curie, scientific work must be done "for itself, for the beauty of science" and with no view to its direct usefulness.

Contrast the innocence of Marie Curie's words with a well-known remark made some two and a half decades later by another distinguished physicist, Robert Oppenheimer (1947), who had spearheaded the development of the nuclear bomb:

In some sort of crude sense which no vulgarity, no humor, no overstatement can quite extinguish, the physicists have known sin; and this is a knowledge which they cannot lose.

The explosion of the first nuclear weapon in the Trinity test and the later use at Hiroshima and Nagasaki are sometimes seen as emblems of the failure of scientists to concern themselves with the societal implications of their work. In fact, many of the scientists involved in the Manhattan Project (and others, such as Linus Pauling, who declined to participate) were quite deeply concerned about societal implications. Among those agreeing to lend their skills to the project, a major motivation was the concern that Nazi Germany might otherwise get to the fission bomb first. This is an example of a strategic consideration mentioned earlier, national competitiveness. On the Marie Curie version of the Enlightenment model, neither this consideration nor scruples over how the scientific findings might later be used should be taken into account, at least not by the people doing the scientific work.

There are several general counterarguments against the view that the scope of our deliberations should be in some ways restricted.[9]

First, ignoring considerations that are evidentially relevant to potential outcomes that we care about means ignoring relevant information. Ignoring relevant information might not be rational and might impede our effectiveness in achieving our goals. The more relevant the information and the more important the goals to which it is relevant, the greater the cost of such intentional ignorance.

Second, confining deliberations within a set of fixed constraints can yield power to those who determine what these constraints should be. This power can be misused. As rhetoricians and sophisticated technocrats are well aware, the framing of an issue—which implicitly determines what kinds of consideration will be seen as being appropriate and having a bearing—often effectively determines the conclusion a deliberation will reach. In political discourse, framings are often fiercely contested. To accept a set of discourse constraints might mean buying into someone else's agenda which tilts the deliberation in favor of some predetermined position.

Third, and related to the first two arguments, one fairly likely effect of adopting a narrow framework for our deliberations of the S&T enterprise is to create a bias in favor of a certain kind of "conservatism" —conservatism not in the sense of political ideology but in the sense of a presumption in favor of business-as-usual. Scope restrictions risk ruling out radical critiques, ones that challenge the fundamental assumptions behind the common way of thinking and doing things. In the context of S&T, the effect of this would not be to perpetuate the status quo, because change in S&T is brought forth ineluctably by the intellectual advances generated by the enterprise itself. Rather, the effect could be to diminish the possibility of a *deliberate change of course*. Without recourse to radical critique, the locomotive will roll along its track, and the track might turn left or right; we might even be able to flick a switch here and there to select which branch of a bifurcation we take; but we exclude from our mental space a host of discontinuous possibilities, such as getting off the train and continuing our journey via another mode of transport.[10]

Radical critiques might challenge the metaphysical underpinnings of our worldview. They might challenge our basic values or moral norms. They might undermine our confidence in the entire S&T project. Alternatively, they might suggest that our attempts to humanize the S&T enterprise will have the opposite effect from the one intended. They might argue that one particular anticipated technological breakthrough will have consequences overshadowing all the rest and that by failing to act accordingly we are grossly misdirecting our attention and our resources. They might contend that increased public engagement and increased efforts to anticipate the societal implications will have obnoxious consequences. They might argue for relinquishment of broad areas of technological research or alternatively that everything should be put into accelerating some applications. They might suggest new ways of funding basic research that would sidestep expert panels and bureaucratic procedures. They might identify completely new ways of evaluating and measuring progress. The possibilities are myriad and impossible to specify in advance.[11]

Many radical critiques are utterly wrong, and some of them would be extremely dangerous if they became popular. Nevertheless, if we look back historically and observe how many widely held conventional wisdoms of the past are revealed as blinkered or deeply flawed by our current lights, we must surely admit that, by induction, it is likely that many of our own central beliefs, too, are deeply flawed. We need to build into our processes of individual and collective deliberation some self-correcting mechanism that enables us to question and rectify even our most deep-seated assumptions.

One way in which the scope of our deliberations can be broadened is by taking into account the kind of metalevel reflections that this essay attempts to illustrate. More specifically, one could argue that more work should be done on the normative dimensions of the S&T enterprise.

One normative dimension is ethics, and this is to some extent already part of the official programs, for example as the "E" in ELSI and NELSI and as applied ethics more generally. One might have occasional misgivings about the quality, depth, or impact of this research, but at least there is some recognition of the significance and relevance of the questions it is supposed to address.

Another normative dimension that has been given rather less attention in these programs is that of applied (normative) epistemology. This encompasses a number of important problems. One such problem is to develop better higher order epistemic principles for the conduct of scientific research. As Jaynes and Bretthorst (2003, p. 525) observed:

It appears to us that actual scientific practice is guided by instincts that have not yet been fully recognized, much less analyzed and justified. We must take into account not only the logic of science, but also the sociology of science (perhaps also its soteriology). But this is so complicated that we are not even sure whether the extremely skeptical conservatism with which new ideas are invariably received, is in the long run a beneficial stabilizing influence, or a harmful obstacle to progress.

Yet the epistemological problems go beyond the challenge of how to maximize scientific and technological advancement. As we have seen, they are also central to our thinking about the ethical and policy issues prompted by the S&T enterprise. Applied epistemology also lies at the heart of the problem of how to evaluate radical critiques of this enterprise.

There are many interesting approaches to these matters in addition to philosophical reflection and theoretical analysis. Here is a sample (Hanson, 1995; Wolfers and Zitzewitz, 2004; Leigh and Wolfers, 2006):

- Study the heuristics and biases affecting human cognition and figure our ways of applying the findings to improve our judgment.[12]
- Study the correlates of true opinion, among experts and the public, and use this information as clues to who is right in cases of disagreement and to how we might improve our own epistemic situation (Tetlock, 2005).
- Information technologies. Develop our information infrastructure in ways that will facilitate the collection, integration, and evaluation of information.
- Cognitive enhancement. Improve individual reasoning ability (e.g. concentration, memory, and mental energy) by educational, pharmaceutical, and other means.
- Study how vested interests, the mass media, and other social realities shape and bias (or facilitate) the processes' collective deliberation.
- Public deliberation. Develop procedures, formats, or rhetorical standards to improve the quality of public debate by confronting "plebiscitory" reason (Chambers, 2004).
- Subsidize and implement institutional innovations such as information markets, which have been shown to outperform expert panels in many prediction tasks.

The unifying theme is to explore how we could make ourselves smarter and wiser, both individually and as an epistemic community. The research could be slanted toward applications in S&T assessment, but it is likely to have important spill-over benefits in other areas. Such a program could be combined with more narrowly focused efforts to gather and analyze information in areas of particular concern, such as nanotechnology.

CHALLENGE OF PRAGMATIC SYNTHESIS

Finally, I want to call attention to one more "normative dimension," except that it is not really a dimension but rather the space spanned by all the other vectors. I am referring to the challenge of integrating all crucial considerations into some coherent unity that will let us determine what we have most reason to do all things considered. This might have to accommodate predictions about technology, social impacts, strategic considerations, value judgments, ethical constraints, and assorted metalevel thoughts about how all these things should fit together.

What I have in mind is not the erection of grand philosophical systems resting on foundations of indubitable first principles or the painting of "visions" or the realization of comprehensive ideological "outlooks." Rather, I am pointing to the task of attempting to think through some of the big challenges for humanity in a way that does not leave out any *crucial* consideration—by which I mean a consideration such that if it were taken into account it would overturn the conclusions we would otherwise reach about how we should direct our efforts. For example, some of the strategic considerations related to the nanotechnology initiative that I mentioned earlier might be "crucial" in that they might plausibly, if they are sound and once taken into account, rationally deliver a practical conclusion pointing in the opposite direction from the one we might otherwise believe we ought to strive toward. But not only strategic considerations but also other empirical, epistemological, axiological, and methodological considerations could be crucial in this sense.

Implicitly, we are confronting a challenge of integrating all crucial considerations every time we are attempting to make a reasoned decision about some matter which we think it is important to "get right." When our goal is very limited, we might at least sometimes succeed in meeting the challenge (albeit not usually by relying on reasoned deliberation alone). When the goal is more open ended, such as if we are attempting to decide what we have most reason to do with our own life all things considered, or if we are seeking to form an opinion on a topic such as what public policy ought to be with regard to some anticipated technological revolution, then the complexity of the synthetic challenge grows enormously. It is not clear that we ever manage to meet it in any robust sense. Instead, what answer we end up espousing might depend mostly on contingent factors such as the political inclinations of our parents, the idiosyncratic views of our thesis advisor, the current cultural climate in the place we happen to live, or the mere fact that we failed to think of some crucially relevant consideration that would have caused us to come to a very different conclusion.

What this seems to amount to is that we can have very little rational confidence that our efforts, insofar as they are aiming ultimately at important long-term goals for humanity, are not entirely wrongheaded. Our noblest and most carefully considered attempts to effect change in the world might well be pushing things further *away* from where they ought to be. Perhaps around the corner lurks some crucial consideration that we have ignored, such that if we thought of it and were able to accord it its due weight in our reasoning, it would convince us that our guiding beliefs and our struggles to date had been orthogonal or worse to the direction which would then come to appear to us as the right one. This is disconcerting.

NOTES

1. Part of this intellectual trend is the conglomeration of science and technology into "technoscience," the idea being (roughly) that science and technology are

inextricably linked and that both are socially coded, historically situated, and sustained by actor networks consisting of both human and artifacts (see, e.g., Latour, 1987). In this chapter I for the most part do not sharply separate science and technology, but it seems to me that a more nuanced treatment would have to distinguish different components of the "science and technology enterprise" (to use the term favored by Crow and Sarewitz, 2001).

2. This example is borrowed from James Lenman (2000). See also Bostrom (2006).

3. Some technology impacts are equally predictable, e.g., some new medicines will be used, will save lives, some of those people whose lives have been saved will draw state pensions, vote, etc.

4. The need to make these kinds of trade-offs, of course, is not confined to funding of the natural sciences and technology but applies to funding of the social sciences and ELSI programs too.

5. The latter proviso is not insignificant if we are thinking about longer time scales. One might also imagine that support for tough international action could increase dramatically following a big disaster such as an act of nuclear terrorism. And of course, another way in which nanotechnology research could come to a halt is as a result of a civilization-destroying global catastrophe. This proviso is also not insignificant (see Bostrom, 2002).

6. Most studies of the economic returns to R&D have not focused on the international dimension. Domestically, it appears that the social returns of R&D—although they are difficult to measure—are very high and that optimal R&D investment substantially exceeds the actual level. See, e.g., Jones and Williams (1998), and Salter and Martin (2001).

7. See Drexler (1992a, p. 242). Drexler (private communication) confirms that this reconstruction corresponds to the point he was making. Obviously, a number of implicit premises would have to be added if one wished to present the argument in the form of a deductively valid chain of reasoning. By "advanced nanotechnology" I here refer to a possible future form of radical nanotechnology, sometimes called molecular nanotechnology, or "machine-phase" nanotechnology; see also Drexler (1992b).

8. One may of course insist that the good states should develop only *defensive* nanotechnology capabilities. But offensive and defensive applications would require largely the same underlying technological advances.

9. There are also arguments in favor of various scope restrictions on our deliberations. For a discussion of some of these, see Bostrom (2007).

10. In the context of fundamental science, such a course change could be a Kuhnian paradigm shift.

11. Although not necessarily intended as "radical critiques," for a few recent examples see, for example, Joy (2000), Bostrom (2003a,b 2005), and Hanson (2003).

12. See, for example, Kahneman and Tversky (2000) and Gilovich et al. (2002). For an attempt to apply this kind of information to a technology-related issues, see Bostrom and Ord (2006).

REFERENCES

Bainbridge, W. S., and Roco, M. C. (Eds.) 2006. *Managing Nano-Bio-Info-Cogno Innovations*. Dordrecht: Springer.

Bostrom, N. 2002. Existential risks: Analyzing human extinction scenarios and related hazards. *Journal of Evolution and Technology* 9.

Bostrom, N. 2003a. Are you living in a computer simulation? *Philosophical Quarterly* 53(211): 243–255.

Bostrom, N. 2003b. Astronomical waste: The opportunity cost of delayed technological development. *Utilitas* 15(3): 308–314.

Bostrom, N. 2005. The fable of the dragon-tyrant. *Journal of Medical Ethics* 31 (5): 273–277.

Bostrom, N. 2006. Infinite ethics. Working manuscript. Available: http://www.nickbostrom.com/ethics/infinite.pdf.

Bostrom, N. 2007. Technological revolutions: Ethics and policy in the dark. In N. M. de S. Cameron (Ed.), *Nanotechnology and Society*. Hoboken, NJ: Wiley.

Bostrom, N., and Ord, T. 2006. The reversal test: Eliminating status quo bias in bioethics. *Ethics* 116(4): 656–680.

Chambers, S. 2004. Behind closed doors: Publicity, secrecy, and the quality of deliberation. *Journal of Political Philosophy* 12(4): 389–410.

Crow, M. M., and Sarewitz, D. 2001. Nanotechnology and societal transformation. In A. H. Teich, S. D. Nelson, C. McEnaney, and S. J. Lita (Eds.), *AAAS Science and Technology Policy Yearbook*. Washington, DC: American Association for the Advancement of Science, pp. 89–101.

Curie, M. 1921. Excerpt from a lecture at Vassar College, May 14, 1921. http://www.fordham.edu/nalsall/mod/curie-radium.html

Drexler, E. 2003. Nanotechnology essays: Revolutionizing the future of technology (revised 2006). *AAAS EurekAlert! InContext*, April.

Drexler, K. E. 1992a. *Engines of Creation*. Oxford: Oxford University Press.

Drexler, K. E. 1992b. *Nanosystems: Molecular Machinery, Manufacturing, and Computation*. New York: Wiley.

Elam, M., and Bertilson, M. 2002. Consuming, engaging and confronting science: The emerging dimensions of scientific citizenship. In P. Healey (Ed.), *STAGE (HPSE-CT2001–50003) Final Report*. pp. 121–158.

Gilovich, T., Griffin, D. W., and Kahneman, D. 2002. *Heuristics and Biases: The Psychology of Intuitive Judgement*. Cambridge: Cambridge University Press.

Hanson, R. 1995. Could gambling save science? Encouraging an honest consensus. *Social Epistemology* 9(1): 3–33.

Hanson, R. 2003. *Shall We Vote on Values, But Bet on Beliefs?* Available: http://hanson.gmu.edu/futarchy.pdf.

Jaynes, E. T., and Bretthorst, G. L. 2003. *Probability Theory: The Logic of Science*. Cambridge: Cambridge University Press.

Jones, C. I., and Williams, J. C. 1998. Measuring the social return to R&D. *Quarterly Journal of Economics* 113(4): 1119–1135.

Joy, B. 2000. Why the future doesn't need us. *Wired* 8.04.

Kahneman, D., and Tversky, A. 2000. *Choices, Values, and Frames*. Cambridge: Cambridge University Press.

Latour, B. 1987. *Science in Action: How to Follow Scientists and Engineers through Society*. Cambridge: Harvard University Press.

Leigh, A., and Wolfers, J. 2006. Competing approaches to forecasting elections: Economic models, opinion polling and prediction markets. *Economic Record* 82(258): 325–340.

Lenman, J. 2000. Consequentialism and cluelessness. *Philosophy and Public Affairs* 29(4): 342–370.

Oppenheimer, R. 1947. Physics in The contemporary world. Lecture at Massachusetts Institute of Technology, November 25.

Roco, M. C., and Bainbridge, W. S. 2003. *Converging Technologies for Improving Human Performance: Nanotechnology, Biotechnology, Information Technology and Cognitive Science*. Dordrecht: Kluwer Academic.

Salter, A. J., and Martin, B. R. 2001. The economic benefits of publicly funded basic research: A critical review. *Research Policy* 30(3): 509–532.

Tetlock, P. 2005. *Expert Political Judgment: How Good Is It? How Can We Know?* Princeton, NJ: Princeton University Press.

Vandermolen, T. D. 2006. Molecular nanotechnology and national security. *Air & Space Power Journal* 20(3): 96–106.

Wolfers, J., and Zitzewitz, E. 2004. Prediction markets. *Journal of Economic Perspectives* 18(2): 107–126.

9

COMPLEXITY AND UNCERTAINTY: A PRUDENTIAL APPROACH TO NANOTECHNOLOGY

Jean-Pierre Dupuy

COMPLEXITY AND SELF-ORGANIZATION

It is often asserted that the starting point of nanotechnology was the classic talk given by Feynman (1959). I submit that a major source of inspiration for the new field is to be sought in another classic lecture, the one John von Neumann gave at Caltech in 1948 on complexity and self-reproducing automata.

Turing's and Church's theses were very influential at the time, and they had been supplemented by cyberneticians Warren McCulloch and Walter Pitts' major finding on the properties of neural networks. Cybernetics' credo was then: Every behavior that is unambiguously describable in a finite number of words is computable by a network of formal neurons—a remarkable statement, as John von Neumann recognized. However, he put forward the following objection: Is it reasonable to assume as a practical matter that our most complex behaviors are describable in their totality, without ambiguity, using a finite number of words? In specific cases it is always possible: Our capacity, for example, to recognize the same triangular form in two empirical triangles displaying differences in line, size, and position can be so described. But would this be possible if it were a matter of globally characterizing our capacity for establishing "visual analogies" ? In that case, von Neumann conjectured, "it may be that the simplest way to describe a behavior is to describe the structure that generates it" (von Neumann, 1966) It is meaningless, under these circumstances, to "discover" that such a behavior can be

Nanoethics: The Ethical and Social Implications of Nanotechnology. Edited by Allhoff, Lin, Moor, Weckert
Copyright © 2007 John Wiley & Sons, Inc.

embodied in a neural network since it is not possible to define the behavior other than by describing the network itself.

Von Neumann thus posed the question of complexity, foreseeing that it would become the great question for science in the future. Complexity implied for him in this case the futility of the constructive approach of McCulloch and Pitts, which reduced a function to a structure, leaving unanswered the question of what a complex structure is capable of.

It was in the course of his work on automata theory that von Neumann was to refine this notion of complexity. Assuming a magnitude of a thermodynamical type, he conjectured that below a certain threshold it would be degenerative, meaning that the degree of organization could only decrease, but that above this threshold an increase in complexity became possible. Now this threshold of complexity, he supposed, is also the point at which the structure of an object becomes simpler than the description of its properties. Soon, von Neumann prophesied, the builder of automata would find himself as helpless before his creation as we feel ourselves to be in the presence of complex natural phenomena.[1]

At any rate, von Neumann was thus founding the so-called *bottom-up approach*. In keeping with that philosophy, the engineers of the future will not be any more the ones who devise and design a structure capable of fulfilling a function that has been assigned to them. The engineers of the future will be the ones who know they are successful when they are surprised by their own creations.

Admittedly, not all of nanotechnology falls under the category of complexity. However, the scope covered by it, especially in the case of the nano–bio–info–cogno (NBIC) convergence, is much wider and relevant than the implications of a possible Drexler-type molecular manufacturing. Even more importantly, the novel kind of uncertainty that is brought about by those new technologies is intimately linked with their being able to set off complex phenomena in the Neumannian sense.

UNCHAINING COMPLEXITY

It would be a mistake to think that, although novel, our current situation before the consequences of our technological choices is not the outcome of a long historical process. In her masterly study of the frailties of human action Hannah Arendt (1958) brought out the fundamental paradox of our time: As human powers increase through technological progress, we are less and less equipped to control the consequences of our actions. As early as 1958 she could write (pp. 230–232, my emphasis):

> The attempt to eliminate action because of its uncertainty and to save human affairs from their frailty by dealing with them as though they were or could become the planned products of human making has first of all resulted in channeling the human capacity for action, for beginning new and spontaneous processes which without men never would come into existence, into an attitude toward nature which up to the latest stage of the modern age had been one of exploring natural laws and fabricating objects out of natural material. To what extent we have begun to *act into nature*, in the literal sense of the word, is perhaps best illustrated by a recent

casual remark of a scientist who quite seriously suggested that *"basic research is when I am doing what I don't know what I am doing."* [Wernher von Braun, 1957].

This started harmlessly enough with the experiment in which men were no longer content to observe, to register, and contemplate whatever nature was willing to yield in her own appearance, but began to prescribe conditions and to provoke natural processes. What then developed into an ever-increasing skill in *unchaining elemental processes*, which, without the interference of men, would have lain dormant and perhaps never have come to pass, has finally ended in a veritable art of *"making"* nature, that is, of creating "natural" processes which without men would never exist and which earthly nature by herself seems incapable of accomplishing.

No doubt that with an incredible prescience this analysis applies perfectly well to the NBIC convergence, in particular on two scores. First, the ambition to (re-)make nature is an important dimension of the metaphysical underpinnings of the field (Dupuy, in press). Second, as explained before, it will be an inevitable temptation, not to say a task or a duty, for the nanotechnologists of the future to set off processes upon which they have no control. The sorcerer's apprentice myth must be updated: It is neither by error nor by terror that man will be dispossessed of his own creations but *by design.*

There is no need for Drexlerian self-assemblers to come into existence for this to happen. The paradigm of *complex, self-organizing systems* envisioned by von Neumann is stepping ahead at an accelerated pace, both in science and in technology. It is in the process of shoving away and replacing the old metaphors inherited from the cybernetic paradigm, like the ones that treat the mind or the genome as computer programs. Complexity has already become a catchword in biology.

In technology, new feats are being flaunted every passing week. The time has not come—and may never come—when we manufacture self-replicating machinery that mimics the self-replication of living materials. However, we are taking more and more control of living materials and their capacity for self-organization and we use them to mimic smart machinery or perform mechanical functions.

It is often the case that the philosophy implicit to a new field is given away, admittedly in a crude way, by its visionaries and ideologues. On this score it is difficult to be more explicit than Kevin Kelly (in press) when he writes: "It took us a long time to realize that the power of a technology is proportional to its inherent *out-of-controlness*, its inherent ability to surprise and be generative. In fact, unless we can worry about a technology, it is not revolutionary enough."

NEW KIND OF UNCERTAINTY AND IRRELEVANCE OF PRECAUTIONARY PRINCIPLE

Our tampering with, and setting off complex processes, in the technical, Neumannian sense of the word "complex" brings about a kind of uncertainty that is radically novel. In particular, it is completely alien to the distinctions upon which the precautionary principle rests.

The precautionary principle introduces what initially appears to be an interesting distinction between two types of risks: "known" risks and "potential" risks. It is on this distinction that the difference between prevention and precaution is made to rest: precaution would be to potential risks what prevention is to known risks.

A closer look reveals (1) that the expression "potential risk" is poorly chosen and what it designates is not a risk waiting to be realized, but a hypothetical risk, one that is only a matter of conjecture; (2) that the distinction between known risks and hypothetical risks (the term I will adopt here) corresponds to an old standby of economic thought, the distinction that John Maynard Keynes and Frank Knight independently proposed in 1921 between *risk* and *uncertainty*. A risk can in principle be quantified in terms of objective probabilities based on observable frequencies; when such quantification is not possible, one enters the realm of uncertainty.

The problem is that economic thought and the decision theory underlying it were destined to abandon this distinction as of the 1950s in the wake of the exploitation successfully performed by Leonard Savage with the introduction of the concept of subjective probability and the corresponding philosophy of choice under conditions of uncertainty: Bayesianism. In Savage's axiomatics, probabilities no longer correspond to any sort of regularity found in nature but correspond simply to the coherence displayed by a given agent's choices. In philosophical language, every uncertainty is treated as an *epistemic* uncertainty, meaning an uncertainty associated with the agent's state of knowledge. It is easy to see that the introduction of subjective probabilities erases the distinction between uncertainty and risk, between risk and the risk of risk, between precaution and prevention. If a probability is unknown, a probability distribution is assigned to it "subjectively." Uncertainty owing to lack of knowledge is brought down to the same plane as intrinsic uncertainty due to the random nature of the event under consideration. A risk economist and an insurance theorist do not see and cannot see any essential difference between prevention and precaution and, indeed, reduce the latter to the former. In truth, one observes that applications of the "precautionary principle" generally boil down to little more than a glorified version of "cost–benefit" analysis.

Against the prevailing economism, I believe it is urgent to safeguard the idea that *all is not epistemic uncertainty*. One could however argue from a philosophical standpoint that such is really the case. The fall of a die is what supplied most of our languages with the words for chance or accident. Now, the fall of a die is a physical phenomenon that is viewed today as a low-stability deterministic system, sensitive to initial conditions, and therefore unpredictable—a "*deterministic chaos*," in current parlance. But an omniscient being would be able to predict on which side the die is going to fall. Could one not then say that what is uncertain for us, but not for this mathematician-God, is uncertain only because of lack of knowledge on our part? And therefore that this uncertainty, too, is epistemic and subjective?

The correct conclusion is a different one. If a random occurrence is unpredictable for us, this is not because of a lack of knowledge that could be overcome by more extensive research; it is because only an infinite calculator could predict a future which, given our finiteness, we will forever be unable to anticipate. Our finiteness obviously cannot be placed on the same level as the state of our knowledge. The former is an unalterable aspect of the human condition, the latter a contingent fact which could at any moment be different from what it is. We are therefore right to treat the random event's uncertainty *for us* as an objective uncertainty, even though this uncertainty would vanish for an infinite observer.

Now, our situation with respect to the complex phenomena we are about to unleash is also one of objective, not epistemic, uncertainty. The novel feature this time is that we are not dealing with a random occurrence either. Neither random nor epistemically uncertain, the type of "risk" that we are confronting is a monster from the standpoint of classic distinctions. Indeed, it merits a special treatment which the precautionary principle is incapable of giving it.

We know today that what makes a complex system (e.g., a network of molecules connected by chemical reactions or a trophic system) robust is exactly what makes it exceedingly vulnerable if and when certain circumstances are met. Complexity gives those systems an extraordinary stability and a no less remarkable resilience. This is only true up to a certain point, however. Beyond certain *tipping points*, they veer over abruptly into something different that can have properties highly undesirable for people. This sudden loss of resilience gives complex systems a particularity which no engineer could transpose into an artificial system without being immediately fired from his or her job: The alarm signals go off only when it is too late. And in most cases we do not even know where these tipping points are located. Our uncertainty regarding the behavior of complex systems has thus nothing to do with a temporary insufficiency of our knowledge; it has everything to do with objective, structural properties of complex systems.

On the other hand, this uncertainty is not of the kind that is attached to random events and it is not amenable to the concept of probability. The key notion here is that of informational *incompressibility*, which is a form of *essential unpredictability*. In keeping with von Neumann's intuitions on complexity, a complex process is defined today as one for which the simplest model is the process itself. The only way to determine the future of the system is to run it: There are no shortcuts. This is a radical uncertainty: In contrast with a deterministic chaos—the source of randomness—perfect knowledge of the initial conditions would not be enough to predict the future states of the system. Its unpredictability is irremediable.

When the precautionary principle states that the "absence of certainties, given the current state of scientific and technical knowledge, must not delay the adoption of effective and proportionate preventive measures aimed at forestalling a risk of grave and irreversible damage to the environment at an economically acceptable cost," it is clear that it places itself from the outset within the framework of epistemic uncertainty. The presupposition is that *we know we are in a situation of uncertainty*. It is an axiom of epistemic logic that if I do not know p, then I know that I do not know p. Yet, as soon as we depart from this framework, we must entertain the possibility that we do not know that we do not know something. In cases where the uncertainty is such that it entails that the uncertainty itself is uncertain, it is impossible to know whether or not the conditions for the application of the precautionary principle have been met. If we apply the principle to itself, it will invalidate itself before our eyes.

Moreover, "given the current state of scientific and technical knowledge" implies that a scientific research effort could overcome the uncertainty in question, whose existence is viewed as purely contingent. It is a safe bet that a "precautionary policy" will inevitably include the edict that research efforts must be pursued—as if the gap between what is known and what needs to be known could be filled by a supplementary effort on the part of the knowing subject. But it is not uncommon to encounter cases in which *the progress of knowledge comports an increase in uncertainty* for the decision-maker, something that is inconceivable within the framework of epistemic uncertainty. Sometimes, to learn more is to discover hidden complexities that make us realize that the mastery we thought we had over phenomena was in part illusory.

TOWARD A NEW SCIENCE OF THE FUTURE

In Search of an Ethics of the Future

German philosopher Hans Jonas's (1985) fundamental work, *The Imperative of Responsibility*, cogently explains why we need a radically new ethics to rule our relation to the future in the "technological age." This "ethics of the future" [*Ethik für die Zukunft*]—meaning not a future ethics, but an ethics *for* the future, for the sake of the future, that is, the future must become the major object of our concern—starts from a philosophical aporia. Given the magnitude of the possible consequences of our technological choices, it is an absolute obligation for us to try and anticipate those consequences, assess them, and ground our choices on this assessment. Couched in philosophical parlance, this is tantamount to saying that when the stakes are high, we cannot afford not to choose consequentialism,[2] rather than a form of deontology,[3] as our guiding moral doctrine. However, the very same reasons that make consequentialism compelling, and therefore oblige us to anticipate the future, make it impossible for us to do so. Unleashing complex processes is a very perilous activity that both demands foreknowledge and prohibits it. To take just an illustration. (*The Economist*, March 2003):

> The unpredictable behaviour of nanoscale objects means that engineers will not know how to make nanomachines until they actually start building them.

Now, one of the very few unassailably universal metaethical principles is that *ought* implies *can*. There is no obligation to do that which one can not do. However, in the technological age, we do have an ardent obligation that we cannot fulfill: anticipating the future. That is the ethical aporia.

Is there a way out? Jonas's credo, which I share, is that there is no ethics without metaphysics. Only a radical change in metaphysics can allow us to escape from the ethical aporia. The major stumbling block of our current, implicit metaphysics of temporality turns out to be our conception of the *future as indeterminate*. From our belief in free will—we might act otherwise—we derive the conclusion that, the future is *not real*, in the philosophical sense: "Future contingents," that is, propositions about actions taken by a free agent in the future, For example, "John will pay back his debt tomorrow," are held to have no truth value. They are neither true nor false. If the future is not real, it is not something that we can have cognizance of. If the future is not real, it is not something that projects its shadow onto the present. Even when we know that a catastrophe is about to happen, we do not believe it: We do not believe what we know. If the future is not real, there is nothing in it that we should fear or hope for.

The derivation from free will to the unreality of the future is a sheer logical fallacy, although it would require some hard philosophical work to prove it (Dupuy, 2000b). Here I will content myself with exhibiting the sketch of an alternative metaphysics in which free will combines with a particularly hard version of the reality of the future. The idea is to *project oneself* into the future and look back at our present and evaluate it from there. This temporal *loop* between future and past I call the metaphysics of *projected time*. As we are going to see, it makes sense only if one accepts that the future is not only real but also fixed.

Critique of Scenario Approach

For the last half century, futurology has been equated with the scenario approach. If some credit is granted the foregoing, it appears that this method is no longer appropriate to tackle the kind of radical uncertainty that we are confronting.

Ever since its beginnings the scenario approach has gone to great lengths to distinguish itself from mere forecast or foresight, held to be an extension into the future of trends observed in the past. We can forecast the future state of a physical system, it is said, but not what we shall decide to do. It all started in the 1950s when French philosopher Bertrand de Jouvenel coined the term *prospective*—a substantive formed after "retrospective" —to designate a new way to relate to the future. That this new way had nothing to do with the project or the ambition of anticipating, that is, *knowing* the future, was clearly expressed by him in 1964, when he wrote: "There can be no science of the future. The future is not the realm of the 'true or false' but the realm of 'possibles.'"

There is no question that the scenario approach has helped individuals, groups, and nations to find new ways to coordinate through a jointly worked-out image of the future shared by all. However, that has been achieved in a paradoxical way. The method aimed at emphasizing the importance of the future while it denied its reality. Hence the essential question, is there a way to protect the democratic virtues of the scenario approach while jettisoning its flawed metaphysics?

From Occurring Time to Projected Time

If the future is ontologically indeterminate, shouldn't we say the same about the past? After all, there was a time when our past was the future of its own past. French philosopher André Maurois went so far as to write (Ferguson, 1997, p. 1):

> There is no privileged past.... There is an infinitude of Pasts, all equally valid.... At each and every instant of Time, however brief you suppose it, the line of events forks like the stem of a tree putting forth twin branches.

The few historians who take this line of thought seriously are those who do not shy away from writing what goes today by the name of "counterfactual history" or "virtual history." Those "What if?" historians try and put forward more or less convincing answers to such questions as: What if there had been no French Revolution? What if Hitler had invaded Britain? What if the Soviets had won the Cold War? And, of course, the Pascalian one: What if Cleopatra's nose had been different?

Among professional historians, though, widespread is the opinion that this kind of exercise is a mere "parlour game" or a "red herring."

The opposition between historians who see only historical necessity and those who are sensitive to the metaphysical postulation that things might be different from what they turned out to be can and must be transcended. The metaphysical tools exist that allow us to carry out this *Aufhebung*. We owe them to French philosopher Henri Bergson and his student Jean-Paul Sartre. The idea is that as long as human beings live, they are absolutely free, and their freedom resides entirely in their capacity to choose, that is, to invent their lives. Future-oriented counterfactual propositions such as "If I were to do this, the consequences would or might be that and I am entirely responsible for them, whatever they turn out to be" make full sense. However, as soon as "death has turned life into destiny," backward-looking counterfactual propositions such as "Had I had more time to devote to my work, I would have written the novel of the century" are completely devoid of meaning and serve as mere alibis or cheap excuses—the stuff "bad faith" is made of.

In that kind of metaphysics, counterfactual propositions are admissible only when they are future oriented. When we look back at the past, we see only necessity. There is nothing else than that which has happened, no possibility that never came to actuality. When history unfolds, then, possibilities become actual, but something strange happens to the branches that were not selected. It is not that they have become impossible: It turns out that they were never possible! As history proceeds in its course, it interjects necessity back into the past. Necessity is only retrospective.

In the framework of this metaphysics the parties to the debate about the meaning of virtual history appear to suffer from symmetrical blind spots. The "What if?" historians argue as if the possibilities that did not become actual kept existing forever in a kind of eternal limbo. The mainstream historians who refuse to ascribe any meaning to counterfactuals reason as if agents endowed with free will didn't make any difference in the way events occur.

Following Hans Jonas, my task has been to reestablish the future in its ontological status of a *real* entity. Bergsonian–Sartrean metaphysics permits exactly that: Project yourself into the future and look back from there at the present. Seen from the present the future was open, but seen from the vantage point of the future, the path that led to it appears to have been necessary. We were free to choose, to be sure, but what we chose appears to have been our destiny.

The temporal experience I am trying to describe—which I call "projected time" —is ours on a daily basis. It is facilitated, encouraged, organized, not to say imposed by numerous features of our social institutions. All around us, more or less authoritative voices are heard that proclaim what the more or less near future will be: the next day's traffic on the freeway, the result of the upcoming elections, the rates of inflation and growth for the coming year, the changing levels of greenhouse gases, and so on. The *futurists* and sundry other prognosticators know full well, as do we, that this future they announce to us as if it were written in the stars is a future of our own making. We do not rebel against what could pass for a metaphysical scandal (except, on occasion, in the voting booth). It is the coherence of this mode of coordination with regard to the future that I have endeavored to bring out.

A *sine qua non* must be respected for that coherence to be the case: a *closure condition*, as shown in the following graph. Projected time takes the form of a loop, in which past and future reciprocally determine each other:

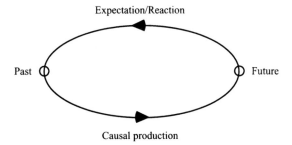

Projected time

To foretell the future in projected time, it is necessary to seek the loop's *fixed point*, where an expectation (on the part of the past with regard to the future) and a causal production (of the future by the past) coincide. The predictor, *knowing that her prediction is going to produce causal effects in the world*, must take account of this fact if she wants the future to confirm what she foretold. Traditionally, which is to say in a world dominated by religion, this is the role of the prophet, and especially that of the biblical prophet. However, I am speaking of prophecy, here, in a purely secular and technical sense. The prophet is the one who, more prosaically, seeks out the fixed point of the problem, the point where voluntarism achieves the very thing that fatality dictates. The prophecy includes itself in its own discourse; it sees itself realizing what it announces as destiny. In this sense, prophets are legion in our modern democratic societies, founded on science and technology. What is missing is the realization that this way of relating to the future, which is neither building, inventing, or creating it nor abiding by its necessity, requires a special metaphysics.

Perhaps the best way to bring out the specificity of the metaphysics of projected time is to ponder the fact that there is no such closure or looping condition as regards our "ordinary" metaphysics, in which time bifurcates into a series of successive branches, the actual world constituting one path among these. I have dubbed this metaphysics of temporality "occurring time" ; it is structured like a decision tree:

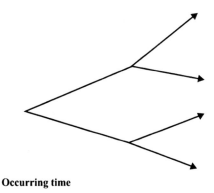

Occurring time

Obviously the scenario approach presupposes the metaphysics of occurring time. But that is also the case of the metaphysical structure of prevention. Prevention consists in taking action to ensure that an unwanted possibility is relegated to the ontological realm of nonactualized possibilities. The catastrophe, even though it does not take place, retains the status of a possibility, not in the sense that it would still be possible for it to take place, but in the sense that it will forever remain true that it could have taken place. When one announces, *in order to avert it,* that a catastrophe is coming, this announcement does not possess the status of a *prediction,* in the strict sense of the term: It does not claim to say what the future will be, but only what it would have been had one failed to take preventive measures. *There is no need for any loop to close here*: The announced future does not have to coincide with the actual future, the forecast does not have to come true, for the announced or forecast "future" is not in fact the future at all, but a possible world that is and will remain not actual.

By contrast, in projected time, the future is held to be fixed, which means that any event that is not part of the present or the future is an impossible event. It immediately follows that in projected time prudence can never take the form of prevention. Once again, prevention assumes that the undesirable event that one prevents is an unrealized possibility. The event must be possible for us to have a reason to act; but if our action is effective, it will not take place. This is unthinkable within the framework of projected time.

Such notions as "anticipatory self-defense," "preemptive attack," or "preventive war" do not make any sense in projected time. They correspond to a paradox exemplified by a classic figure from literature and philosophy, the killer judge. The killer judge "neutralizes" (murders) the criminals of whom it is "written" that they will commit a crime, but the consequence of the neutralization in question is precisely that the crime will not be committed![4] The paradox derives from the failure of the past prediction and the future event to come together in a closed loop. But, I repeat, the very idea of such a loop makes no sense in our ordinary metaphysics.

Conclusion: Exploring Set of Projected Equilibria as Substitute for Scenario Approach

The future of nanotechnology will depend on the way society is going to react to the anticipations that are being made of this future. If those anticipations are produced through the scenario method, they will be of no help in the resolution of the ethical problem. They won't restore the future in its status of a real entity of which our knowledge must be as precise as possible. I have argued that the most effective way to ascribe reality to the future is to reason in the framework of projected time. We have to explore the fixed points of the temporal loop that links the future to the past and then to the future again. Those fixed points I have called "projected equilibria."

We have called *ongoing normative assessment* the methodology that corresponds to the determination of these projected equilibria (Dupuy and Grinbaum, 2004). It is a matter of obtaining through research, public deliberation, and all other means an image of the future sufficiently optimistic to be desirable and sufficiently credible to trigger the actions that will bring about its own realization. It is easy to see that this definition can make sense only within the metaphysics of projected time, whose characteristic loop between past and future it describes precisely. Here coordination is achieved on the basis of an *image* of the future capable of ensuring a closed loop between the causal production of the future and the self-fulfilling expectation of it.

Projected time is a metaphysical construction, no less so than occurring time. The major obstacle for implementing projected time as the mode of reasoning in our minds and our institutions is that it entails the conflation of past and future, seen as determining each other. However, we are immersed in the flow of time, as the metaphor goes. Linear time is intuitively taken to represent our habitat, and the problem is to *project* the circular form of reasoning inherent in projected time onto that one-dimensional line that we call "time."

This problem justifies why we call for an *ongoing* assessment. The assessment that we are speaking about implies systems where the role of the human observer (individual or collective) is the one of observer-participant. The observer-participant, although it may seem so to him, does not analyze the system that he interacts with in terms of linear time; instead, he is constantly involved in an interplay of mutual constraints and interrelations between the system being analyzed and himself. The temporality of this relation is the circular temporality of projected time: If viewed from an external, Archimedes' point, influences go both ways, from the system to the observer and from the observer to the system. Now, if one is to transpose the observer's circular vision back into the linearly developing time, one finds that the observer cannot do all his predictive work at one and only one point in time. Circularity of relations within a complex system requires that the observer constantly revise his prediction. To make sure that the loop of interrelations between the system and himself is updated consistently and does not lead to a catastrophic elimination of any major component of either the system in question or of the observer himself, the latter must not stop addressing the question of the future at all times. No fixed-time prediction conserves its validity due to the circularity and self-referentiality of the situation.

I have said before that prevention made no sense in projected time, nor has the precautionary principle any relevance. What can take their place then? Are there projected equilibria that may protect us against a major disaster if such a denouement is in the offing? The search for an answer to that question I have called "enlightened doomsaying" (Dupuy, 2004).

From the outset it appears that this search is bound to run into an irremediable paradox. It is a matter of achieving coordination on the basis of a negative project taking the form of a fixed future that *one does not want*. One might try to transpose the above characterization of the methodology of ongoing normative assessment into the following terms: to obtain through scientific futurology and a meditation on human goals an image of the future sufficiently catastrophic to be repulsive and sufficiently credible to trigger the actions that will block its realization—but this formulation would seem to be hobbled from the outset by a prohibitive defect: self-contradiction. *If one succeeds in avoiding the undesirable future, how can one say that coordination was achieved by fixing one's sights on that same future?* The paradox is unresolved.

I will content myself here with conveying a fleeting idea of the schema on which my solution is based. Everything turns on a random occurrence—but one whose nature and structure defy the traditional categories that I discussed in the first sections of this work.

The problem is to see what type of fixed point is capable of ensuring the closure of the loop that links the future to the past in projected time. We know that the catastrophe cannot be this fixed point: The signals it would send back toward the past would trigger actions that would keep the catastrophic future from being realized. If the deterrent effect of the catastrophe worked perfectly, it would be self-obliterating. For the signals from the future to reach the past without triggering the very thing that would obliterate their source, there must subsist, inscribed in the future, an *imperfection in the closure of the loop*. I proposed above a transposition of our definition of ongoing normative assessment in order to suggest what could serve as a maxim for a rational form of doomsaying. I added that as soon as it was enunciated, this maxim collapsed into self-refutation. Now we can see how it could be amended so as to save it from this undesirable fate. The new formulation would be: to obtain an image of the future sufficiently catastrophic to be repulsive and sufficiently credible to trigger the actions that would block its realization, *barring an accident*.

One may want to quantify the likelihood of this accident. Let us say that it is an epsilon, ε, by definition weak or very weak. The foregoing explanation can then be summed up very concisely: It is because there is a likelihood ε that the deterrence will not work that it works with a likelihood $1 - ε$. What might look like a tautology (it would obviously be one in the metaphysics of occurring time) is absolutely not one here, since the preceding proposition is not true for $ε = 0$.[5] The fact that the deterrence will not work with a strictly positive likelihood ε is what allows for the inscription of the catastrophe in the future, and it is this inscription that makes the deterrence effective, *with a margin of error* ε . Note that it would be quite incorrect to say that it is the *possibility* of the error, with the likelihood ε, that saves the effectiveness of the deterrence—as if the error and the absence of error constituted two paths branching out from a fork in the road. There are no branching paths in projected time. The error is not merely possible, it is actual: It is inscribed in time, rather like a slip of the pen. In other words, the very thing that threatens us may be our salvation.

To sum up: With the NBIC convergence we are becoming capable of tampering with, and triggering off, *complex* phenomena. As a consequence we have to confront a new kind of *uncertainty*. The precautionary principle is of little help in that task.

Anticipating the consequences of our technological choices is at the same time more important and more difficult than ever. What is desperately required is a novel *science of the future*, conducive to an *ethics of the future*. In order to achieve that, we have to radically alter our metaphysics of time. The metaphysics of *projected time* provides new perspectives enabling one to ground a form of *ongoing normative assessment*. If it is a matter of avoiding a major catastrophe, this method leads to a form of *enlightened doomsaying*.

NOTES

1. On all that, see Dupuy (2000a).
2. Consequentialism as a moral doctrine has it that what counts in evaluating an action is its consequences for all individuals concerned.
3. A deontological doctrine evaluates the rightness of an action in terms of its conformity to a norm or a rule, such as the Kantian categorical imperative.

4. Here I am thinking of Voltaire's *Zadig*. The American science fiction writer Philip K. Dick produced a subtle variation on the theme in his story "Minority Report." Spielberg's movie is not up to the same standard, alas.

5. The discontinuity at $\varepsilon = 0$ suggests that something like an uncertainty principle is at work here, or rather an indeterminacy [*Unbestimmtheit*] principle. The weights ε and $1 - \varepsilon$ behave like probabilities in quantum mechanics. The fixed point must be conceived here as the *superposition* of two states, one being the accidental *and* preordained occurrence of the catastrophe, the other its nonoccurrence.

REFERENCES

Arendt, H. 1958. *Human Condition*. Chicago, IL: University of Chicago Press.

De Jouvenel, B. 1964. *L'art de la Conjecture*. Monaco: Editions du Rochere.

Dupuy, J.-P. 2000a. *The Mechanization of the Mind*. Princeton, NJ: Princeton University Press.

Dupuy, J.-P. 2000b. Philosophical foundations of a new concept of equilibrium in the social sciences: Projected equilibrium. *Philosophical Studies* **100**: 323–345.

Dupuy, J.-P. 2004. *Pour un Catastrophisme Éclairé*. Paris: Seuil.

Dupuy, J.-P. In press. *The philosophical foundations of nanoethics*. Paper presented at the NanoEthics Conference, University of South Carolina, Columbia, SC, March 2–5, 2005.

Dupuy, J.-P., and Grinbaum, A. 2004. Living with uncertainty: Toward a normative assessment of nanotechnology. *Techné*, joint issue with *Hyle*, 8 (2): 4–25.

Ferguson, N. 1997. *Virtual History*. London: Picador.

Feynman, R. 1992. There's plenty of room at the bottom. *Journal of Microelectro mechanical Systems* 1(1): 60–66.

Jonas, H. 1985. *The Imperative of Responsibility. In Search of an Ethics for the Technological Age*. Chicago, IL: University of Chicago Press.

Kelly, K. In press. Will spiritual robots replace humanity by 2100? In The Technium. Available: http://www.kk.org/thetechnium/.

von Braun, W. 1957. Interview with *New York Times*, December, 16, 1957.

von Neumann, J. 1966. *Theory of Self-Reproducing Automata*, Arthur W. Burks (Ed.). Champaign, IL: University of Illinois Press.

10

THE PRECAUTIONARY
PRINCIPLE IN
NANOTECHNOLOGY*

John Weckert and James Moor

How and why is it that I do not describe my method for remaining underwater and how long I can remain there without coming up for air? I do not wish to divulge or publish this because of the evil nature of men, who might use it for murder on the sea-bed (*Leonardo da Vinci,* quoted in White, 2000, p. 206).

Leonardo clearly thought that his discovery or invention was potentially so dangerous that it would be better if nobody else knew about it. He "played it safe" and thereby prevented its development. He was employing the precautionary principle.

The precautionary principle (PP) is thought by many to be a useful strategy for action, and an alternative to cost–benefit analysis, especially in the environmental and health areas (e.g., Ackerman and Heinzerling, 2004; UNESCO, 2005) but by many others as useless at best and dangerous at worst. A recent report extends the scope of the principle to include nanotechnology, artificial intelligence, and robotics (Arnall, 2003; see also Phoenix and Treder, 2004). In this chapter we argue that despite what is often claimed, it is a reasonable, coherent, and useful principle. We demonstrate this through examples in nanotechnology.

* This chapter was originally published as John Weckert and James Moor, "The Precautionary Principle in Nanotechnology," *International Journal of Applied Philosophy,* vol. 2, no. 2: 191–204. Reprinted with permission.

CLARIFYING PRECAUTIONARY PRINCIPLE

The general structure of the principle is this:

> If *action A* has som*e possibility P* of causing harmful *effect E,* then apply *remedy R*
> (based on Manson, 2002).

This is a generic formulation only, and each of A, P, E, and R are interpreted in various ways in different actual formulations.

Typical examples might be:

> If genetically modified (GM) crops have some possibility of harming humans or the
> environment then the development of them should be stopped;
> If the discharge into the river has some possibility of contaminating the fish, then
> the discharge should not be allowed.

1. Action A is generally some scientific research or technological or other development, for example, research into and development of genetically modified crops,
   or some activity such as discharging waste into a river.
2. Possibility P must be more than a logical possibility; it must be an empirical
   probability. There must be *some* scientific evidence that A does or can cause E,
   even if this evidence is very weak. Examples are that the GM crops cause harm
   and that the waste causes the contamination.
3. Effect E is some serious or perhaps catastrophic or irreversible harm.
4. Remedy R concerns the measures that should be taken to avoid or minimize E occurring, for example, halting or never starting the research or the
   discharge.

Some Formulations

F1. Where an activity raises threats of harm to the environment or human health,
    precautionary measures should be taken even if some cause and effect relation-
    ships are not fully established scientifically (Wingspread, 1998).

F2. In order to protect the environment, the precautionary approach should be
    widely applied by states according to their capabilities. Where there are threats
    of serious or irreversible damage, lack of full scientific certainty should not
    be used as a reason for postponing cost-effective measures to prevent environ-
    mental degradation (Principle 15 fo the 1992 Rio Declaration; cited in Manson,
    2002).

F3. Where there are significant risks of damage to the public health, we should be
    prepared to take action even when the scientific knowledge is not conclusive,
    "if the balance of likely costs and benefits justifies it" (Weed, 2003).

SOME CRITICISMS

As mentioned earlier, despite its wide acceptance and intuitive appeal, the PP is not without its strong critics.

Making Predictions

It is argued that because the PP is a risk-aversive strategy it will, or does, stifle research and development and thereby deprives humanity of many goods for at best dubious long-term benefits. More precisely, it deprives those humans living now of many benefits on the grounds that future generations will inherit a better world. Two sorts of arguments are given for this criticism. One is that future generations do not have any rights simply because existence is a prerequisite to having a right and the unconceived do not exist. The other and more common objection is that we cannot know if people in the future will be better off or not if we undertake a particular action such as halting development of some product. It is not possible, as the PP assumes, to make reasonable predictions about the future, at least with respect to developments in science and technology (Volkman, 2001; Brown, 2001). The first reason for the criticism, that future generations do not have rights, will not concern us further, because in many potential applications of the PP the interests of currently existing people will be enough, regardless of what rights, if any, future generations have. We will however return to the question of predicting.

Paradox

Another criticism is that the PP involves the same kind of problem as the "many-gods" objection to Pascal's wager (Manson, 2002); in any particular case where the PP might be applied, there is always more that one action to which it could be applied, and these actions are mutually exclusive. This is sometimes couched in terms of the PP involving a paradox. Sunstein (2005, p. 355) puts it this way: "The Precautionary Principle approaches incoherence. Because risks are on all sides of social situations, and because regulation itself increases risks of various sorts, the principle condemns the very steps that it seems to require."

Threats

A third issue concerns the causal link between the action and the effect. F1 states that the principle should be applied even if some cause-and-effect relationships are not fully established scientifically, F2 talks of lack of full scientific certainty, and F3 of scientific knowledge not being conclusive. In other words, the principle should be applied even in cases where it has not been scientifically established that harm will be caused by action A. It is enough, perhaps, if there is just a possibility of harm. This is common to all formulations and forms a central tenet of the principle. Just how to spell it out in detail is of course not so easy. There is a sense in which most cause-and-effect relationships are not fully established if by that is meant that there is no possibility that one will occur without the other. However, what seems to be meant is that the normal standards that are applied to scientific evidence can be waived if the potential dangers are great enough.

This is the most controversial aspect of the PP. Just how strong must the evidence of the causal link between A and E be? It can be quite weak if E is harmful enough, if it is catastrophic. But even in this case the mere logical possibility of a link is not enough. There must be some scientific evidence of some sort, perhaps indirect, for it. We will consider this more closely later.

These criticisms will be addressed after an examination in the next section of the PP in the context of nanotechnology.

Harm

Yet another criticism concerns the nature of the harm, but this can be disposed of more quickly. It should be noted that in the first formulation with any threat of harm the principle comes into play. This is particularly strong. The second modifies this, talking of serious or irreversible damage, something that seems, at least superficially, more plausible, but both *serious* and *irreversible* require closer examination. That some damage is serious is uncontroversial. That asbestosis is a serious health problem is unlikely to be disputed, but there is a large range of issues about which there is much disagreement. Does the destruction of the last habitat of an endangered species of butterfly (say a little, plain butterfly) constitute serious damage? The answer given would depend on the value given to the natural environment. Many would see it as serious while many others would not. But this disagreement regarding what constitutes serious damage in no way undermines the PP. As noted, in many cases there is widespread agreement that something is serious, and in a large number of cases where there is disagreement there is room for rational debate. Not all disagreement is based on mere differences in taste.

Irreversibility too poses some problems, but again problems that are not fatal to the PP. In a sense, of course, any event is irreversible given that we cannot go back and undo what has been done, but for most practical purposes many events are reversible. Suppose, for example, that I have a minor accident in my car which results in a few dents. The car is repaired by the panel beater, so for all practical purposes the damage has been reversed, even though at an atomic level parts of the car body will be very different from what they were previously. This irreversibility is trivial for most purposes and quite different from the death of someone from asbestosis, which is irreversible (barring resurrection) in a much more significant sense. Many other cases of significant irreversibility are time dependent. Destruction of a natural habitat is not necessarily irreversible if the time frame is long enough. Much of course is irreversible for practical purposes given the amount of time required for the reversal to be complete. And this is all that is necessary for irreversibility to play some useful role in the PP.

It should be noted, too, that neither formulation F1 nor F2 explicitly takes into account possible benefits. They suggest, therefore, that in many cases no benefit, regardless of how great, should be taken to outweigh the harm or damage. The second does talk of *cost-effective measures*, but F3 takes benefits explicitly into account. The PP should only be applied, it seems to suggest, if the likely costs are greater than the likely benefits.

An apparent problem here in talking about costs and benefits is that it is unclear what role the PP has. If on a cost–benefit analysis it is justified to halt some research or action, that alone is reason and the PP seems redundant. It is not redundant, of course, because application of the PP changes the relative weightings given to costs and benefits. If the PP is applied, costs have a higher weighting. Some however see this as a collapse into cost–benefit analysis with risk aversion (Sunstein, 2005, p. 363). One response to this of course is "so what"? Cost–benefit with risk aversion does seem to capture the spirit of the PP and also does not seem to really be in the spirit of cost–benefit analysis.

THREE POSSIBLE APPLICATIONS IN NANOTECHNOLOGY

The relationship between A and E seems not to be the same in all discussions of the PP even ignoring problems about the strength of the link. The most common application is like the second example above, where the action is directly related to the effect or it is feared that it is. The discharge will cause the contamination. The call by Greenpeace and Bill Joy (Joy, 2000; though he does not mention the PP explicitly) to apply the PP to nanotechnology research, however, is a little different. They want the PP applied because the research could lead to developments that might cause problems. Consider the following:

(a) *If nanotechnology research continues, then there is a possibility of self-replicating robots being developed and therefore the possibility of the gray goo problem (on the grounds that these robots might escape—they cannot be contained).* Suppose that the causal link between A, the research, and E, the self-replicating machines, is well established [it is not, e.g., the fat-and-sticky-fingers problem discussed by Smalley (2001) and Drexler (2001)]. If action A is taken, then E will almost certainly occur. But suppose too that E in itself is not the problem. If it is in some way contained or controlled, then no harmful consequences will result. Suppose now that if self-replicating machines were developed [of the type that Drexler (1986) envisaged], then they would have the ability to self-replicate indefinitely, and the gray goo problem would be the result if they were not suitably controlled. If they are suitably controlled, no harm need result. Given that in the schematic version of the PP, E is the harmful consequence to be avoided, a better way of stating the situation here is this: Action A causes state S (with some probability) and state S leads to event E (with some probability). In this example the scientific evidence of the link between A and the harm E would have to be of two kinds. The link between A and the self-replication machines, say S, would be the evidence that comes from the physical sciences. However, the link between S, those machines, and the harm E would need to be established by the social sciences, because it would concern the ability of people to keep the machines contained indefinitely. This seems to make the application of the PP to research into nanotechnology more problematic. The scientists can claim with some justification (although this requires more examination) that what they are doing in itself causes no harm. What might cause harm is the misuse of their results, carelessness, or accidents. Additionally, and this is a stronger point, curtailment of the research will very likely deprive the world of significant benefits. This is different from the waste example. In that case there are no benefits except that disposing the waste into the river may be cheaper and more convenient than discharging it in any other way.

(b) *If nanoparticles are used in products then there is a possibility that health will be damaged (we do not know of their effects).* The problem here is different from that in (a). In the gray goo case, if self-assembling robots are developed, and if they are not controlled in some way, then it is quite likely that there would be a catastrophe. There is little doubt that humans, and all life, would be endangered. In the case of nanoparticles, however, it is not known if they have harmful effects or not, but our knowledge of whether or not they have will depend on scientific evidence alone and not on predictions of human behavior.

(c) *Developments in nanoelectronics will endanger personal privacy.* This case is different again. Given what we know about threats to privacy using current technologies, we can be certain that privacy will be under much more threat with the development of nanotechnology. However, in this case the evidence is not from the physical sciences but rather is based on what we know of human behavior.

Summary of Issues Raised

The preceding three cases reveal a number of problems in talking about the PP in relation to nanotechnology. Merely saying that there is a case to be made for applying the PP to nanotechnology is not saying much that is useful. What constitutes action A and what constitutes effect E? Should A be taken as the research or as the development of products or even as the use of products? Should E be taken as the indefinitely self-replicating machines or as the harm caused by their escape? (*A causes S and S leads to E.*) This leads to the second problem: What is the cause–effect relationship here? The relationship might be clear if E is the machines with that property but rather murky if it is the harm caused by their escape. It is clear if there is scientific evidence that nanoparticles harm humans or animals but less clear in the case of nanoelectronic developments harming personal privacy. The third problem related to the probability of E occurring. If E is interpreted in the first way in example (c), then its probability is high, and if in the second, it really depends on the time frame considered. It might be extremely low within 100 or 1000 years but extremely high, given Murphy's law, if the time frame is long enough.

ANSWERING CRITICISMS

Making Predictions

"I think there is a world market for maybe five computers" (Thomas Watson, Chairman of IBM, 1943).
"640K ought to be enough for anybody" (Bill Gates, 1981).

Watson and Gates could vouch for the fact that predicting is perilous, and some use this fact as an argument against the PP (e.g., Morris, 2000). It is certainly true that the

PP is (or it is argued should be) used in situations in which harmful consequences of some action are predicted. If the whole undertaking of prediction is inherently flawed and predicting is always unreliable, then applying the PP would never be justified. But clearly this is wrong. Much of our everyday lives is based on implicitly making predictions and acting on them. I came into work this morning to work on this chapter, assuming (or implicitly predicting) that my computer would still be on the desk and that I could still use it. I am currently predicting that I will spend the coming weekend in the mountains. I may not, of course, but it is a reasonable prediction. I plan to do it, I have done it before, and there appear to be no overriding obstacles to me doing it. Perhaps what is meant by critics of PP is that predicting the effects of new scientific or technological developments is so unreliable that it should not be done. This has some initial plausibility, and the quotations from Watson and Gates attest to the dangers. But this cannot be quite right either. New drugs and vaccines are developed because it is predicted that they will save lives, for example, a new drug for malaria. Huge investments are made by both the public and private sectors in various scientific and technological fields on the grounds that benefits and profits will result. Nanotechnology is being promoted in many countries because of its predicted benefits to humanity (for some predicted benefits of artificial photosynthesis see Pace, 2005). So there cannot be anything wrong with predicting in itself, even making predictions about outcomes of scientific and technological developments. Science and technology depend on it. Perhaps predicting benefits is reasonable but predicting harms is not. This would solve the critics' problem, but there is no reason to accept it. Predictions must be made with care, but they must be made.

An argument against prediction, with a twist, comes from Brown (2001). He objects that people such as Joy predict the future of technology without taking into account the human and social factors and calls it "tunnel vision." "It excludes all the other factors that come into play as technologies develop. In particular, it excludes the social factors that always shape and redirect technology," and this, he says, makes prediction much more difficult (p. 30). This seems true, but the twist comes when it is realized that it is partly because of critics like Joy that the development is tempered by human concerns. Brown himself recognizes this and talks of self-*un*fulfilling prophecies (p. 30). Therefore, while people like Joy might be wrong in their predictions, if they are wrong, it is *because* they made them. There is of course another way of interpreting the predictions of Joy and others. Perhaps they are making conditional rather than categorical statements. If we do X, Y, and Z, then a catastrophe will occur. This prediction raises awareness of concerns and plays a role in perhaps fairly minor changes in behavior—we do not do all of X, Y, and Z—and these changes in turn help avoid the catastrophe. The conditional statement is still true if it ever was because the antecedent no longer holds.

A Paradox?

Does the precautionary principle entail a paradox? Manson (2002) thinks so, on one common formulation of the principle [see also Sunstein (2005) and Clarke (2005)]. The problem is that in those cases in which the principle should be applied, it should also be applied to the alternative that it proposes. In order to try to answer this criticism, we will examine more closely what it says. The problem can be set out as follows:

1. Action A1 might cause bad effect Eb1 (harm eventuates because of A1).
2. Remedy R1 (don't do A1) stops Eb1 (PP applied).
3. But suppose that A1 causes good effect Eg1 (Eg1 eliminates some harm).
4. Then R1 stops Eg1 (harm eventuates because of R1).
5. So, if PP should be applied to A1 (because A1 causes harm), it should also be applied to R1 (because R1 prevents an action that would eliminate some harm).

To explain this we will return to the three previous nanotechnology cases. First we consider the example of the self-assemblers as described by Drexler. Whether these are possible or not is a contentious issue, as we saw earlier, but suppose that they are, at least in the mid to long term. According to Drexler (1986):

Assemblers will be able to make virtually anything from common materials without labor, replacing smoking factories with systems as clean as forests. They will transform technology and the economy at their roots, opening a new world of possibilities.

Take action A1 to be research into and development of these self-assemblers. A1 will potentially have enormous benefits for humankind and for those who first develop the assemblers. However, suppose again that the gray goo problem is real if these assemblers are developed, that is, the problem that the assemblers could get out of control and keep self-replicating until they destroyed Earth. This undoubtedly is not so good; Call this gray goo disaster effect Eb1. Because of the potential harm of gray goo, it is decided to halt research of the self-assemblers; call this remedy R1. This remedy stops the potential gray goo disaster (Eb1). But self-assemblers also potentially have many good effects, as Drexler states above. Call these Eg1. Halting research on self-assemblers then stops these good effects as well. So this halting, remedy R1, potentially causes a great deal of harm. The question then is, should the precautionary principle be applied to R1? It appears that it should, given that the purpose of the PP is to block potential harm. The problem now is, of course, that the PP should be applied both to the research into self-assemblers and to the halting of that research.

Second, we take the case of nanoparticles, a much more likely scenario. Nanoparticles are already being manufactured and used in a variety of products, including sunscreens and coatings on bottles and other food containers. Other likely uses will be in paints, lubricants, batteries, electronics, and so on. This use will produce products that are better in various ways, for example, more effective sunscreens, food containers that better protect the food, and longer lasting batteries. The problem is that little is known about the effects of these nanoparticles on humans. There is some fear that they could behave like asbestos and cause serious health problems. To date there is scant evidence, apart from some research that seems to indicate that fish and rats have been harmed by these particles [but see Gatti and Montanari (2005) for some current research]. Here, too, while applying the PP would avoid the harm that might be caused by the particles, applying it would also deprive humans for a number of goods, which may in itself be a harm. So the PP should be applied to inaction with respect to research and development of nanoparticles.

Third, we consider the privacy scenario. Research in nanoscience and nanoelectronics leads to the development of extremely tiny and powerful computer processors and sensitive sensing devices. These, coupled with other devices such as global positioning systems (GPS), enable the easy, inexpensive, and efficient monitoring of individuals. Just about every move that they do can be recorded and assessed by intelligent computer systems. This research and development will quite likely have the effect that individual privacy is lost to a large extent, and this will pave the way for totalitarian governments, or at least governments that exercise a large degree of control over their citizens, and will enable corporations to maintain strict control over their employees. So should these developments be stopped? In this age of terrorism, these developments will also have the effect of making it more difficult for terrorists. If a potential terrorist can do little that is not monitored, it will be much more difficult for him or her to be an actual terrorist. And this is undoubtedly good. So if the PP is applied to the development of these technologies and they are stopped, the harmful effects of loss of privacy will be avoided, but if it is, the threat of terrorist harm is increased, so the principle should be applied to this stopping as well.

It should be noted that this problem is likely to arise in all cases in which the PP might be applied in nanotechnology (and in all cases more generally). This is so because it is difficult to imagine any research that will not potentially have both good and bad consequences.

Possible Solutions to Paradox

One way out of the paradox is to draw on the distinction between positive and negative duties. Positive duties, duties to do good, are commonly (though by no means universally) thought to be weaker than negative duties, duties not to do harm. The duty not to kill is stronger than the duty to save a life. Consider the gray goo example. Undertaking the research that will possibly lead to gray goo is an example of causing harm (albeit unintentionally), violating a negative duty, while not undertaking it is allowing harm to happen, violating a positive duty. Suppose that the only way to save the life of Tom is to kill Harry and transplant his heart into Tom. While saving the life of Tom is good, killing Harry to achieve it is not justifiable. Doing nothing will result in the death of Tom but Harry's death would be the result of an action. Letting Tom die is not good, but killing Harry is clearly worse. It would appear, then, that there is no paradox in applying the PP in the gray goo case. Doing nothing will result in harm, but the action in question will cause harm.

Unfortunately the situation is not quite so straightforward because many of the problems that research into nanotechnology is designed to solve have been caused by human actions. There is a duty therefore to attempt to solve them, so the situation is not like that of Tom and Harry. It is more like the case where Thomasina is injured by a careless action of Harriet. Harriet then does have a duty to do some good to Thomasina as a result of the action that caused the harm in the first place. These kinds of duties are what Pogge calls *intermediate* duties and while stronger than positive duties are weaker that negative duties (Pogge, 2005, p. 34). So even if there is an intermediate duty to find a solution to some problem, that duty does not override the negative duty not to cause harm.

If this argument concerning duties is correct, then there is no paradox involved in applying the PP in the gray goo case or in any other. Still, this solution might be thought to be too easy so we will look more closely at our three examples in order to see if and where the paradox might arise.

Now consider this case. It is hinted at by Posner (2004) that perhaps the only way to avoid a catastrophe caused by global warming is by developments in nanotechnology. Posner also argues that the gray goo problem should be taken seriously. On these assumptions the following is the situation:

(a) Global warming will cause a catastrophe.
(b) The catastrophe can only be avoided through developments in nanotechnology.
(c) Nanotechnology will lead to gray goo, which itself will be a catastrophe.

This appears to be a perfect example of a situation in which the paradox arises for the PP. If the PP is applied to the nanotechnology research, then it allows a catastrophe, while if it is applied to the remedy (halting the research into nanotechnology), then it causes a catastrophe (gray goo). Attempting to solve the problem by invoking the distinction between intermediate (assuming that the global warming is caused by human activity) and negative duties seems to be disingenuous. If both doing A and not doing A result in a catastrophe, more seems to be required. If there is a way of solving the problem, it would have to be based on which catastrophe was the most likely (or least unlikely) or likely to happen sooner, assuming that they are equally catastrophic. The most sensible approach would be to try to work out which is likely to happen sooner. If the catastrophe caused by global warming is likely to happen sooner than that caused by gray goo, then there is a strong argument for the development of nanotechnology *if* that is the only way of avoiding the catastrophe.

If doing A and not doing A both result in credible threats, then of course the PP does not help much, but neither does any principle where there is nothing to choose between the alternatives. In this case it is still plausible to say that it is better not to do A simply because the duty not to cause harm is greater than that to prevent harm. Neither alternative might produce what we desire, but when taken together with the doctrine of positive, intermediate, and negative duties, the PP involves no paradox here.

If, however, there is reason to believe that the global warming catastrophe is likely to occur before that caused by gray goo, then the PP would not prescribe A, and so would not block preventing the harm caused by global warming and the problem reemerges. This leads us to consider a second way of avoiding the paradox, that of credible threats. We will look more closely in a moment at ways of cashing "credible," but for the moment accept that it can be done. In the gray goo example the PP should not be applied, simply because there is no credible threat, many would say. On current evidence it appears that the scientific problems in making the self-replicating robots are significant. At best (or worst) the ability to make them is far into the future (but perhaps we should not begin the quest), and at worst (or best) it would be physically impossible to ever make them, given the laws of physics. Posner, however, believes that the threat should be taken seriously because if it did eventuate, even if this possibility is small and remote, the result would be catastrophic. So while for many, gray goo does not pose a credible threat, for him it does, so there still appears to be a problem for the PP in the situation where gray goo is more remote than global warming. But if both threats are highly likely given enough time, and in the case of global warming, without any human intervention, then clearly the gray goo problem is not credible. The human race will be wiped out by global warming before gray goo has its chance. The threat of dying from a heart attack is not credible if I am to be executed tomorrow. So, again, the PP should not be applied.

In the second case, that of nanoparticles, there is a case to make that the PP could be applied but with no paradoxical consequences. Given what is known about asbestos, there is a credible threat of free nanoparticles causing health problems, even though there is currently scant evidence for it. However, halting the development of nanoparticles poses no credible threat. These particles, and the products in which they are being used and will be used in the future, are not being produced to prevent any great harm. Certainly these products can make life better, but they tend to make a good life better rather than alleviating any suffering.

The third case is different again. Developments in sensing devices and in nano-electronics will almost certainly lead to devices that make monitoring and surveillance and data mining much more available and efficient. This does pose a credible threat to personal privacy. This threat can easily be assessed given our experiences with current technology. But it is not obvious that the PP should be applied for several reasons. First, this new technology could help protect against very real threats, for example, from terrorists. Second, the technology itself does not encroach on personal privacy; certain uses of it do. And, again, these uses do not necessarily cause any harm. What others know about me is not so much the problem; what is the problem is what they do with that knowledge. So here it could be argued that regulations should be used to protect the individual's personal privacy, rather than applying the PP to the research and development.

Credible Threats[†]

A threat will be called credible if an hypothesis that that threat is caused by a particular action is a reasonable hypothesis, even if there is little actual evidence to support the causal link. There must of course be evidence that that sort of hypothesis is a reasonable one in the circumstances. The hypothesis that nanoparticles cause harm to humans is reasonable given what is known about asbestos and deserves further testing (it must be noted of course that we regularly breathe in nanoparticles without any apparent harm). It is plausible to believe that they might be harmful even though there is not enough evidence to even say that this is probable. It is less clear that gray goo presents a credible threat. For reasons mentioned earlier, there are serious doubts about whether self-replication of the required type is possible. If this is so, then an hypothesis such as "the development of self-replicating robots will lead to the gray goo problem," while

---

[†] This section draws heavily on Resnik, (2003).

perhaps true, is practically pointless given that the development of these robots is such a remote possibility. But even if they could be developed, the hypothesis has a difficulty. Self-replication itself is not a problem; it is uncontrolled self-replication that is or might be. If they are developed with in-built controls, then if there are no accidents and no malicious use, they are no threat. In a sense, then, there is no credible threat if a credible threat is one for which there is purely scientific evidence, as opposed to evidence of the manner in which something will be used, or of human frailty with respect to making mistakes. The privacy case highlights this too. A reasonable hypothesis is that developments in nanoelectronics will threaten personal privacy. But this is not purely a scientific hypothesis in the way that the one concerning nanoparticles is, although it is a social science hypothesis. It involves human behavior as well as the physical or biological sciences. Perhaps a better way of putting it is this: In cases like gray goo and privacy, a credible threat, in the sense required for the PP, must be spelled out using two hypotheses: one from the physical or biological sciences, linking the action with some intermediary state, and the second from the social sciences, linking that state with the harm.

Possible Remedies

At least in popular discussions, the remedy proposed by the PP to remove some danger is usually halting the research or development or some other particular action. This is certainly one remedy, but not necessarily the only one. Another might be to do A2, which is A1 with certain safeguards in place, or to simultaneously do A3, which might be research into overcoming the harm that A1 might cause. Yet another might be to develop policies that could be put in place if or when certain products are developed. This could be a sensible remedy in the nanoelectronics case and even perhaps the gray goo case. Perhaps this should normally be the remedy in cases where a credible harm is based partly on a social science.

PLAUSIBLE VERSION OF PRECAUTIONARY PRINCIPLE

We can summarize now by restating the general structure of the PP given at the beginning of the chapter:

> If an action A poses a credible threat P of causing some serious harm E, then apply an appropriate remedy R to reduce the possibility of E.

This formulation is plausible and its application is not trivial; it does make a difference. As we argued, the action must pose a credible threat and not just be a logical possibility. First, the hypothesis that the threat exists must be a plausible one given current scientific knowledge, even if no probability can be given. Second, the appropriate remedy can be a variety of things. It might be stopping the research altogether, halting or slowing it for a time to determine the seriousness of the threat or to allow time to develop measures to overcome or mitigate it, or looking for alternatives to the initial action. While this is weaker than many formulations and will not apply to as many cases, it is not without teeth. For example, if applied to the nanoparticles case, it will require at least a concerted attempt at establishing the risks to health and the environment and perhaps slowing the development of products until the threats have been properly assessed. In the privacy case its application will mandate the development of appropriate laws and regulations to protect privacy while the research and development are still being undertaken so that they are in place before the potentially privacy destroying technologies are widely available.

CONCLUSION

An attempt has been made here to show that sense can be made of the PP. It is a principle with content that is reasonable to apply to certain research, development, or actions, but even just within nanotechnology itself, different contexts will require different analyses of credible threats and different remedies.

REFERENCES

Ackerman, F., and Heinzerling, L. 2004. *Priceless: On Knowing the Price of Everything and the Value of Nothing*. New York: New Press.

Arnall, A. H. 2003. *Future Technologies, Today's Choices*, Report for the Greenpeace Environmental Trust, Imperial College, University of London, July.

Brown, J. S. 2001. Don't count society out: A response to Bill Joy. In M.C. Roco and W.S. Bainbridge (Eds.) *Societal Implications of Nanoscience and Nanotechnology*. National Science Foundation, pp. 30–36.

Clarke, S. 2005. Future technologies, dystopic futures and the precautionary principle. In P. Brey, F. Grodzinsky, and L. Introna (Eds.), *Ethics of New Information Technology: Proceedings of the Sixth International Conference of Computer Ethics: Philosophical Inquiry*. The Netherlands: University of Twente, pp. 121–125.

Drexler, K. E. 1986. *Engines of Creation: The Coming Era of Nanotechnology*. New York: Anchor Books.

Drexler, K. E. 2001. Machine-phase nanotechnology. *Scientific American* 285: 66–67.

Gatti, A. M., and Montanari, S. 2005. Nanosafty in nanotechnology. Paper presented at the International Congress of Nanotechnology, Building Infrastructures for the Next Frontier, CD.

Joy, B. 2000. Why the future doesn't need us. *Wired* 8.04: 238–262.

Manson, N. A. 2002. Formulating the precautionary principle. *Environmental Ethics* 24: 263–274.

Morris, J. 2000. Defining the precautionary principle. In J. Morris (Ed), *Rethinking Risk and the Precautionary Principle*. Oxford: Butterworth Heinman.

Pace, R. J. 2005. An integrated artificial photosynthesis model. In A. Collings and C. Critchley (Eds.), *Artificial Photosynthesis*. Weinheim: Wiley.

Phoenix, C., and Treder, M. 2004. Applying the precautionary principle to nanotechnology. Available: http://www.crnano/precautionary.htm.

Pogge, T. 2005. Real world justice. *Journal of Ethics* 9: 29–53.

Posner, R. 2004. *Catastrophe: Risk and Response.* Oxford: Oxford Unversity Press.

Resnik, D. B. 2003. Is the precautionary principle unscientific? *Studies in the History and Philosophy of Biological and Biomedical Sciences* 34: 329–344.

Smalley, R. 2001. Of chemistry, love and nanobots. *Scientific American* 285: 76–77.

Sunstein, C. R. 2005. Cost-benefit analysis and the environment. *Ethics* 115: 351–385.

UNESCO. 2005. United Nations Educational, Scientific and Cultural Organization, World Commission on the Ethics of Scientific Knowledge and Technology. *The Precautionary Principle.* Available: http://unesdoc.unesco.org/images/0013/001395/139578e.pdf.

Volkman, R. 2001. Playing God: Technical hubris in literature and philosophy. In *Proceedings of the Fifth International Conference on The Social and Ethical Impacts of Information and Communication Technologies*, Gdansk, June 18–20, Vol. 1, pp. 350–361.

Weed, D. L. 2003. Is the precautionary principle a principle? *IEEE Technology and Society Magazine*, Winter 2002/2003.

White, M. 2000. *Leonardo: The First Scientist.* London: Abacus.

Wingspread Statement on the Precautionary Principle. 1998. Available: www.gdrc.org/u-gov/precaution-3.html.

PART IV

ISSUES: HEALTH AND ENVIRONMENT

James Moor

Perhaps the most significant and highly anticipated contributions that nanotechnology will make to the world are in the areas of health and environment. Because the frailty of our bodies is a persistent liability of the human condition, it is no surprise that much funding and focus are currently directed to the field of nanomedicine. For instance, nanotechnology will allow us to create treatments that will better target and destroy unwanted cells (e.g., cancer cells) and will likely allow us to add years to our lives as well as keep us looking and feeling younger.

Significant nanotechnological work in the area of environmental applications is underway because enormous commercial opportunities are available and because the quality of our lives depends so essentially on the quality of our environment and ecosystem. For instance, nanotechnology likely will produce filters to purify water, clean up oil spills, and provide nontoxic coatings that protect objects from the environment. Nanotechnology may offer a path to develop processes of artificial photosynthesis (e.g., solar-powered paints may be able to remove carbon dioxide from the atmosphere and to convert sunlight into clean, usable energy).

However, even nanotechnology's most positive contributions may also lead to unintended consequences that we should consider. Nanoparticles in the lungs of some mice have resulted in their death, and the presence of some nanostructures in water has caused brain damage in fish. These studies are preliminary, but they suggest that we must be cautious in the application and disposal of nanoparticles. In the long term, nanotechnology offers us the possibility of radically changing the kinds of creatures we are and the kinds of environments in which we live. In Chapter 11, Anne Ingeborg Myhr and Roy Dalmo, leading scientists in their field from Norway, discuss the risks that new nanomaterials seem to pose to the environment, animals, and human health. Understanding and establishing these risks are critical to resolving the debate over whether stronger laws and regulations are needed to account for such risks, to the extent that existing measures were not designed with nanotechnology in mind.

In Chapter 12, pioneering researcher Robert Freitas offers a bold vision of the coming era of nanomedicine. He believes that the development of molecular machines, or nanorobots, will allow us to inspect, repair, and reconstruct elements of our cells. He imagines that artificial phagocytes—"microbivores"—will seek out and digest unwanted pathogens in our bodies and that defective chromosomes can be replaced. If nanomedicine is truly successful, then aging and death might be delayed for a long time or even indefinitely. Freitas argues such advances may render our current concept of disease confused and archaic, forcing us to evolve the concept in that patients may have a right to define what is "sick" or "well" from their own perspective. This discussion helps set the stage to investigate related ethical issues, such as the degree to which patients should be allowed to participate in deciding what happens to their bodies, when a patient might be deemed competent or incompetent to make these decisions, and whether society will or should allow patients to choose either an "illness" (e.g., blindness) or an "augmentation" (e.g., absence of aging) as their personal medical norm.

Beyond therapy, medical advances are often a double-edged sword in that they can also be used or misused by otherwise healthy individuals for personal advantage, such as steroid use by athletes. So one person's "therapy" may be another person's "enhancement." For instance, if nanotechnology enables an implantable computer chip to help Alzheimer's patients to improve their mental capacity, then the same device might also boost mental performance (such as information processing, recollection, etc.) in a healthy person. In Chapter 13, prominent theologian Ted Peters raises the question whether we are "playing God" by using nanotechnology to enhance ourselves. He considers three interpretations of the concept: to learn God's awesome secrets, to obtain the power of life and death, and to alter life and influence human evolution. Peters argues that to put the question of the limits of human enhancement in terms of "playing God" is not an illuminating way of posing the ethical question, and he surprisingly rejects the usual religious argument against nano-enabled enhancements.

Finally, in Chapter 14, David Guston, John Parsi, and Justin Tosi of Arizona State University continue the discussion but offer a unique reframing of the debate away from its contentious roots of religion versus science. Instead, the authors shift the focus to the broader, more foundational context, looking now at the debate not so much as a clash between religious values and scientific values but as a development that will challenge our democratic values such as personal choice, autonomy, and political pluralism. Will human enhancements help the least capable or will we use it as a way to further separate the haves from the have-nots? Might some enhancements incline us to make only certain kinds of choices (e.g., make us unswervingly patriotic)? Enhancements, they point out, might lead not to the maximization of human freedom but rather to its minimization. As many believe on both sides of the controversy, the ethics of human enhancement may be the single most important debate of this new century.

11

NANOTECHNOLOGY AND RISK: WHAT ARE THE ISSUES?*

Anne Ingeborg Myhr and Roy Ambli Dalmo

INTRODUCTION

Developments in nanoscience and nanotechnology (NT) include highly functional molecular systems, alternative manufacturing processes, molecular computing, brain–machine interfaces, tissue engineering, and recombinant genetic alterations of viral, plant, and animal systems [European Commission (EC), 2004]. These developments may have a tremendous impact on fields such as materials, electronics, and medicine, which may have many health and environmental benefits. With NT, it could be possible to design and synthesize pharmaceuticals, perform target anticancer therapies, better monitor the life signs of a patient, and make advanced microscopic repairs. In the environmental field, nanomachines could be used to clean up toxins or oil spills, recycle garbage, and eliminate landfills, thus reducing the present use of natural resources.

Technological progress may enhance the quality of life, but NT also raises health, environmental, and socioeconomic concerns that could count against the proposed benefits. These concerns must be addressed proactively, involving not only scientists but also other parties such as citizens and politicians. Hence, how to handle lack of scientific information and scientific disagreement are core issues together with the problem of how to increase transparency and participation. In this chapter, we will give some suggestion

* This work is funded by the Norwegian Research Council (Project No. 157157/150).

in how information about risk and uncertainty may help to direct further research, increase flexibility in decision making, and give guidance into how to take precautionary measures concerning development and use of NT.

POTENTIAL RISK ASPECTS

Concerns about adverse effects by nanoparticles and nanomaterials are primarily related to (Nanoforum, 2004; EC Sanco, 2004; Royal Society & Royal Academy of Engineering, 2004):

- Their large surface area, crystalline structure, and reactivity, which can facilitate transport in the environment. Upon entering living systems, nanoparticles may be difficult to control or they can lead to harm by interfering with other processes. Some manufactured nanoparticles may be more toxic per unit of mass than larger particles of the same chemical.
- Ultrafine particles that have a different biological behavior and mobility than the larger particles, and there is no linear relationship between mass and effect. *Prima facie*, it is likely that nanoparticles will be absorbed and taken up by cells more readily than larger particles.
- The "invisible" size of the particles being developed. Such particles could accidentally be distributed to living systems through air, soil, and water, initially causing damage to plants and animals while eventually becoming a hazard to humans. The expected wide-ranging use of nanomaterials in products may make it difficult to contain nanoparticles and control spread to the environment.

The evaluation of the risks related to nanoparticles is complicated by the fact that they already exist in the natural world (e.g., particles resulting from photochemical and volcanic activity). Some of these are highly toxic. For thousands of years, human activities such as mining, cooking, and combustion (e.g., more recently, vehicle exhaust gases) have led to the emission of nanoparticles to the environment. Since exposure to nanoparticles is not a new phenomenon, the question is then whether manufacturing and using nanoparticles present new risks?

Within the past three years, an increasing number of ecotoxicity studies have provided empirical evidence that occupational and environmental exposure to nanoparticles can lead to adverse health effects in living organisms. In 2004, Lam et al. reported that a suspension of carbon nanotubes, one of the most used types of engineered nanoparticles, caused unusual lesions in the lungs of mice, interfering with oxygen absorption. These findings were confirmed by Warheit et al. 2004, who discovered that immune cells gathered around nanotube assemblies, thereby blocking the bronchial passages in the rodent's lungs and causing them to suffocate. In mid-2004, Oberdörster et al. (2004) found that nanoparticles accumulated in the nasal passages, lungs, and brains of rats. Oberdörster (2004) documented oxidative stress in the brains of fish exposed to nanoparticles for 48 hours.

Potential Cellular Mechanisms of Nanoparticle Uptake

Nanoparticles can enter the body via the digestive tract by ingestion and drinking, the lungs via the respiratory tract, and possibly the skin through direct dermal exposure. Injection of nanoparticles in the body for medical purposes could constitute another (chosen) exposure route. Once in the body, nanoparticles may be redistributed to distant organs or tissues through blood circulation or by cell migration. Notably, under certain conditions, some nanoparticles may cross the blood–brain barrier (cf. Kreuter et al., 2002); this offers new therapeutic possibilities as well as new health concerns.

The key cells involved in uptake of small particulate matter including nanoparticles are macrophages and endothelial cells covering venous blood. Macrophages are often termed professional phagocytes due to their capability to engulf particles. Such cells are located in most tissues and organs in any vertebrate species. Macrophages in various organs and tissues have acquired different names and functions. (For example, liver macrophages are called Kuppfer cells, skin equivalents Langerhan's cells, and bone macrophages osteoclasts.) The cells are importantly located in tissues such as skin, lungs, and intestine often exposed to pathogens. Depending on their localization and level of differentiation, they may engulf mucosally penetrated or blood-borne particles (e.g., virus particles) with subsequent degradation before the cells may migrate to lymphoid follicles (e.g., lymph nodes) where active antigen presentation occurs. Inflammatory responses may even start during the initial phase of uptake of particles (Cruz et al., 1997) and indeed during the process where antigen degradation, processing, and major histocompatibility complex (MHC) presentation occur when applying antigen-loaded nanoparticles as, for example, vaccines. Interestingly, macrophages are widely distributed in nearly all organisms of the animal kingdom (Dalmo et al., 1997) and serve as scavengers of particulate matter such as nano- and microparticles present in the body. There is a great need of more exposure data to understand *in vivo* transfer, the mechanisms of toxicity and processes of elimination (e.g., the role of macrophages), and accumulation *in vivo* of nanoparticles.

Nanoparticle-Based Medicine: Benefits and Risks

Substrate and surface modifications are important elements when manufacturing nanoparticles for drug administration for medicinal applications. The rate of phagocytosis is largely determined by the physiochemical properties of polymeric substrate and increases upon particularization (Van Oss et al., 1975). The surface property of nanoparticles is a crucial issue in terms of their uptake by cells and targeted tissue (Labhasetwar et al., 1998; Chellat et al., 2005). Certain polymer-based nanoparticles may induce direct cytotoxic (cell death) responses on macrophages when administered. If no direct cytotoxic response occurs, nanoparticulates may induce a host response such as secretion of inflammatory cytokines and metalloproteinases that play a major role in both tissue destruction and homeostasis (Chellat et al., 2005). Some of the secretion may contain deleterious substances that may cause tissue damage. However, macrophages are often the desired cells of drug targeting because of their central role in the immune system. Furthermore, some bacteria and parasites may have macrophages as host cells, and to direct nanoparticles containing antibacterial and antiparasitic drugs to these cells hold promises to control disease outbreaks. As such, the systemic concentration of a given anti-infectious agent may decrease, and thus undesired effects on other cells and tissues may be prevented when applying nanoparticles containing drugs. In addition, antiviral effects of a nanoparticle-based vehicle system for nucleoside analogues (e.g., anti-HIV agents) have been reviewed (Chellat et al., 2005). Biocompatible and biodegradable polymer-based particles may be advantageous for drug delivery purposes. Of these polymers, polylactides (PLAs) and polylactide-*co*-glycolide (PLGA) have been the most extensively investigated for drug delivery. As polyesters in nature, these polymers undergo hydrolysis upon administration, forming biologically compatible and metabolizable moieties (lactic acid and glycolic acid) that are eventually removed from the body by the citric acid cycle. Drug nanocarriers may also be based on albumin, gelatin, alginate, collagen, and chitosan, which also are biocompatible and are biodegraded at different rates.

In conclusion, as different biological and physiological effects may occur after administration of various nanoparticles containing drugs or vaccines, a stringent assessment of nanoparticle-induced health effects should be done on each product in question. Application of in vitro and in vivo system studies combined with, for example, microarray technology and real-time polymerase chain reaction (PCR) should be a part of a risk assessment to elucidate any wanted or unwanted gene expression following administration of nanoparticle-based pharmaceutics and vaccines.

Environmental Stability of Nanomaterial and Nanoparticles

One of the great advantages of some nanomaterials is that they may be designed and built to last. However, this also makes them very persistent if they are released into the environment, something that is bound to happen considering the fact that nanoparticles are extremely mobile. Once in the environment, natural enzymes can change the surface properties of nanoparticles such as fullerenes—the C_{60} molecule consisting of 60 carbon atoms bonded in a nearly spherical configuration. Fullerenes can form aqueous colloids (from the Greek *collodion*, "resembling glue or jelly") termed nC_{60} and become resuspended after evaporation. In their native form, the small size, colloidal characteristics, and reactive surfaces of colloidal fullerenes make them ideally suited to carry toxic material over long distances. Thus, potentially, colloidal fullerenes could pollute aquifers and have adverse effects on terrestrial and aquatic organisms. Furthermore, there is a lack of knowledge regarding what affects the persistence and distribution of nanoparticles in living systems and in the environment and whether the physical properties of nanoparticles change between manufacture and disposal. For instance, Wiesner and Lecoaret (2004) revealed that fullerenes and oxide nanomaterials exhibited different transport properties. Nanoparticles and nanotubes in water have a tendency to aggregate, which may decrease environmental distribution but enhance adsorption of contaminants (Cheng et al., 2004). The concern about environmental effects is compounded by the fact that nanostructures and nanosystems can exhibit properties quite different from those of the corresponding bulk materials. Such properties include enhanced reactivity and greater ability to penetrate tissues and cell membranes. This means that even chemicals that are considered safe in bulk need to be tested for their effects as nanostructures.

Organisms may be exposed to different nanomaterials included in products like sunscreens, toothpastes, sanitary-ware coatings, and even food (Hoet et al., 2004) or after accidental release. Those particles may be taken not only by human macrophages but also by macrophages of all organisms (see above) after exposure. As such, a high number of animal species, being invertebrates and vertebrates, are potential receivers of released synthetic nanosized particulate matter.

The most prevailing questions that need to be answered in relation to the environmental and health implications of nanomaterials are (Hull, 2004): What are the fate and transport mechanisms of nanoparticles? Which exposure routes are relevant? How do nanoparticles impact the natural environment, including animal and human health? Experimental testing of carefully elaborated risk hypotheses may result in a solid basis for avoidance of potentially harmful use of NT.

RISK AND UNCERTAINTY

Research developments from "simple science" towards "systems science" have obvious potential applications to the study of the risks posed by NT. However, not all NTs should be considered complex problems. For instance, it is important to distinguish between free and fixed nanoparticles, the latter being much less likely to raise concerns because of their immobilization (European Commission, Sanco, 2005). However, the present lack of knowledge with regard to unexpected effects by the use and release of nanomaterials and nanoparticles entails the need for a precautionary approach.

Precautionary Principle

The precautionary principle (PP) is a normative principle for making practical decisions under conditions of scientific uncertainty. It has four central components: to initiate preventive action as a response to scientific uncertainty, to shift the burden of proof to the proponents of a potentially harmful activity, to explore alternative means to achieve the same goal, and to involve stakeholders in the decision-making process (Kriebel et al., 2001). The actual content of the PP, however, and the practical implications of its implementation in policy issues are controversial (Morris, 2002; Myhr and Traavik, 2003; Raffensperger and Tickner, 1999).

Several formulations of the principle, ranging from ecocentric to anthropocentric and from risk-adverse to risk-taking positions, have been put forward. Whichever formulation one uses, the implementation of the PP presupposes that:

- Some threat of harm must have been identified.
- Scientific uncertainty exists with regard to the potential harm.
- There are criteria to guide proactive and precautionary measures.

Implementation of the PP requires that indications of adverse impacts are being documented in some way and that risk-associated research is initiated. Such precautionary motivated research might initiate debates concerning the quality of risk-related scientific advice and identify areas where scientific understanding is lacking by investigating various models of risk and initiating basic research that concedes or rules out risks of ecological harm. An example of how precautionary motivated science may be beneficial is the study by Oberdörster (2004), which documented oxidative stress in the brains of fish exposed to nanoparticles and which can be used to investigate whether the changing chemical structure of the nanoparticles reduces toxicity.

The purpose of precautionary motivated research is to decrease uncertainty and initiate research on both short- and long-term unexpected effects. Hence, precautionary motivated science needs to be building on a basic research agenda; it involves broadening the scientific focus and reflexivity as well as opening up interdisciplinary approaches. However, at present, scientific information on environmental and health effects is limited, from both industry and public research institutions, due to lack of nanosafety-related research.

Raising Awareness of Uncertainty

Making decisions within the context of scientific uncertainty complicates the traditional weighting of benefits against costs. Technological and economical approaches, such as risk–cost–benefit analyses, may be used to specify the uncertainties within a reduced scientific framework. However, such approaches cannot cope with complex biological and ecological processes that, for instance, NT are going to be used in and released into. The decision-makers might be prone to rely on short-term considerations of risk and thereby not include adverse effects with a low probability or long-term hypotheses of risk in the decision (Scott et al., 1999). Hence, both technological and economical approaches tend to function as less restrictive standards of safety, insofar as risk and uncertainty are being permitted as long as there are benefits. In this context, uncertainty is often defined simply as lack of knowledge that can be reduced by further research. More comprehensive definitions of risk and uncertainty imply that uncertainty may be irreducible as well as, the existence of uncertainty and that underlying assumptions and framing of hypotheses might create uncertainty. For instance, important observations about uncertainty include (Funtowicz and Ravetz, 1990; Stirling, 2001; Wynne, 1992):

- Uncertainty is more than statistical error or inexactness of numbers; rather, it is increasingly understood as a multidimensional concept involving quantitative and qualitative dimensions. Uncertainty can manifest itself in different parts of the risk assessments (as system boundaries, model structure, parameters, and data).
- Most present-day uncertainty methodologies and practices focus only on quantitative uncertainty in model parameters and input data. Methods to address qualitative dimensions of uncertainty are absent or in an early stage of development. Further research does not necessarily reduce uncertainty. It may often reveal unforeseen complexities and irreducible uncertainty.
- In problems that are characterized by high system uncertainties, knowledge gaps, and high decision stakes, unquantifiable dimensions of uncertainty may well dominate the quantifiable dimensions.

Recognizing that uncertainty is more than unknown probabilities or insufficient data, different taxonomies of uncertainty have been developed (Stirling, 2001; Wynne, 1992):

- Hazard can be related to a specific adverse event. Risk represents the relationship between probability and consequences, hence a condition where the possible outcomes are identified and the relative likelihood of the outcomes is expressed in probabilities.
- Uncertainty refers to situations where we do not know or cannot estimate the probability of hazard, but the hazards to be considered are known. The uncertainty may be due to the novelty of the activity or to the variability or complexity involved.
- Ignorance represents situations where the kind of hazard to be measured is unknown (i.e., completely unexpected hazards may emerge). This has historically been experienced with BSE (or mad cow disease), dioxins, and pesticides, among others. With regard to NT, for instance, unprecedented and unintended nontarget effects may emerge by either passive inhalation or direct exposure. Furthermore, almost all present studies on potential adverse effects of NT have been health related, while almost no studies have been initiated on nanoparticle mobility within air, water, and sediments; bioavailability and transfer between organisms; and ecotoxicology on organisms of nanomaterials and fixed nanoparticles—areas where unexpected effects may arise over either the short or long term.
- Indeterminacy, or "great uncertainty," describes the inevitable gap between limited experimental conditions and reality, where the consequences of an activity can never be fully predicted. For instance, nanomaterials may have interactions with organisms in the environment which are difficult to reveal in laboratory studies. Use of nanoparticles and nanomaterials may cause accumulation within contained environments. Furthermore, there is a growing awareness that the behavior of many natural and social systems is more complex than scientists had previously believed. In particular, the dynamics of these systems may not be regular but may be characterized by thresholds or nonlinear behavior.
- Ambiguity arises where there are different frames of meaning and various interpretations about what the risks involved are. Nanotechnology is the result of interdisciplinary cooperation between physics, chemistry, biotechnology, material sciences, and engineering; how may these different disciplines approach the different aspects of risk? What will they consider are appropriate methods and models to apply to identify and reduce the risk involved?

Identification and Systematization of Uncertainty

Employment of model-based decision support—as for instance the Walker and Harremöes (W&H) framework (Walker et al, 2003)—may help to identify the types and levels of the uncertainty involved. The W&H framework has been developed by an international group of scientists with the purpose of providing a state-of-the-art conceptual basis for the systematic evaluation of uncertainty in environmental decision making.

One of the main goals of the W&H framework is to stimulate better communication between the various actors in the identification of areas for further research and in decision processes. In this framework, uncertainty is recognized at three dimensions:

1. Location—where the uncertainty manifests itself (e.g., distinguish between contexts such as ecological, technological, economic, social, and political), expert judgment and considerations, and models (e.g., model structure, model implementation, data, and outputs).
2. Nature—degree of variability which can express whether uncertainty primarily stems from inherent system variability/complexity or from lack of knowledge and information.
3. Level—the severity of uncertainty that can be classified on a gradual scale from "knowing for certain" to "complete ignorance."

For instance, Krayer von Krauss et al. (2004) have demonstrated and tested the W&H framework with the purpose of identifying scientists' and other stakeholders' judgment of uncertainty in risk assessment of genetically modified (GM) crops. In these studies the focus was on potential adverse effects on agriculture and cultivation processes by release of herbicide-resistant oilseed crops. Krayer von Krauss et al. interviewed seven experts in Canada and Denmark. To identify the experts' view on location uncertainty, the authors presented a diagram showing causal relationships and key parameters to the experts. With the purpose of identifying the level and nature of uncertainty, the experts had to quantify the level and describe the nature of uncertainty on the key parameters in the diagram. By asking the experts to identify the nature of uncertainty, it was possible to distinguish between uncertainties that may be reduced by doing more research and ignorance that stems from systems variability or complexity.

Approaches that define and systematize the uncertainty involved, such as the W&H framework, may help in using scientific knowledge more efficiently, in directing further research and in guiding risk assessment and management processes of NT.

UNPREDICTABILITY OF COMPLEX SYSTEMS

The study of complex systems is about understanding indirect effects and problems that are difficult to solve because the causes and effects are not obviously related (Chu et al., 2003; Gundersen and Holling, 2002; Scheffer, 2002). Thus, random variation in baseline data in conjunction with complex network interactions leads to futile numeric approaches and hence indeterminacy. Precise numbers can be obtained within various model systems; their quantitative mean and range as variables in changing geographical and environmental contexts rarely have the same level of precision.

Under such circumstances, the normal scientific approach of trying to produce a best estimate or final answer will not be useful since it may not necessarily reduce uncertainty. This is because uncertainties regarding the behavior of complex systems have nothing to do with a temporary insufficiency of our knowledge; everything has to do with objective, structural properties of complex systems. Putting pressure on a complex system at one place can often have effects on another place because the parts are interdependent. Hence, one needs to be aware that there will always be an inevitable gap between limited experimental conditions and reality, where the consequences of an activity can never be fully predicted. For instance, in observational studies of complex, poorly understood systems, errors in the independent variables, errors arising from choosing the wrong model to analyze and interpret of the data, and biases from the conduct of the study may arise (Kriebel et al., 2001).

An awareness of the uncertainties surrounding the complexity of systems entails employment of a precautionary approach that involves initiation of research which focuses on risk-associated aspects with NT. However, designing adequate human and environmental models for determination of risks and identification of unpredictable effects is indeed a difficult task. Present approaches need to be supplemented with methods that study whole systems with or without interaction with different organisms under various conditions. Modern analytic tools such as gene expression analysis technologies using microarray combined with proteomics on central organisms should be included in health-related NT studies. Analytic methods for studying systems in depth need to be employed together with toxicogenomic computer-based approaches for describing, modeling, and simulating the biological systems. In addition, it is crucial that methods for detection and monitoring are initiated with the purpose of following up the performed risk assessment, mapping the actual health and environmental effects, and identifying unanticipated effects. Long-term monitoring provides baselines against which to compare future changes and gives input data to improve future decisions.

ETHICS AND PUBLIC PARTICIPATION

Measures aimed at opening a dialogue with the public on NT must be taken as early as possible, as learned from other introduced technologies, in the development process of NT. The reasons for doing so are many:

- It may enhance transparency and promote informed judgment on NT.
- It may help to engage the public in the design of nanotechnologies (e.g., by identification of NT that is socially relevant).
- It may assist in harvesting the wealth of lay knowledge and the variety of different ethical perspectives embodied by the public.
- It may account for these in the risk assessment and management process.

Research needs to be conducted in such a way that the benefits and unintended adverse consequences are fairly distributed throughout society. Examples include equitable access to advanced medicine and other NT services and products.

The knowledge and perspectives of stakeholders can bring in valuable new views on local conditions which may help determine which data are relevant or which response options are feasible (Funtowicz and Ravetz, 1990, 1994; Wynne, 1992). Making full use of this reservoir of knowledge requires the establishment of an extended peer community, not only in the phase where response options are debated, but also in the problem framing and risk assessment processes that precede it. New platforms need to be established that bring together stakeholders, scientists working on evaluating risks, and scientists working on options for risk reduction and sustainable ways for NT to be developed (Renn and Roco, 2006).

REFERENCES

Chellat, F., Merhi, Y., Moreau, A., and Yahia, L. 2005. Therapeutic potential of nanoparticulate systems for macrophage targeting. *Biomaterials* 26: 7260–7275.

Cheng, X., et al. 2004. Naphthalene adsorption and desorption from aqueous C_{60} fullerene. *Journal of Chemical & Engineering Data* 49: 657–658.

Chu, D., Strand, R., and Fjelland, R. 2003. Theories of complexity: Common denominators of complex systems. *Complexity* 8: 19–30.

Cruz, T., Gaspar, R., Donato, A., and Lopes, C. 1997. Interaction between polyalkylcyanoacrylate nanoparticles and peritoneal macrophages: MTT metabolism, NBT reduction, and NO production. *Pharmaceutical Research* 14: 73–79.

Dalmo, R. A., Ingebrigtsen, K., and Bøgwald, J. 1997. Non-specific defence mechanism in fish, with particular reference to the reticuloendothelial system (RES). *Journal of Fish Diseases* 20: 241–273.

European Commission (EC). 2004. *Nanotechnology, Innovation for Tomorrow's World*. Brussels: Research Directorate-General, European Commission.

European Commission (EC) Sanco. 2004. Nanotechnologies: A preliminary risk Analysis on the basis of a workshop organized in Brussels on March 1–2, 2004, by the Health and Consumer Protection Directorate General of the European Commission. European Commission Community Health and Consumer Protection.

Funtowicz, S. O., and Ravetz, J. R. 1990. *Uncertainty and Quality in Science for Policy*. Dordrecht: Kluwer, pp. 7–16.

Funtowicz, S.O., and Ravetz, J.R. 1994. The worth of a songbird: Ecological economics as a post-normal science. *Ecological Economics* 10, 197–207.

Gundersen, C., and Holling, C. S. 2002. *Panarchy: Understanding Transformations in Human and Natural Systems*. Washington, DC: Island Press.

Hoet, P. H. M., Brüske-Hohlfeld, I., and Salata, O. V. 2004. Nanoparticles—known and unknown health risks. *Journal of Nanobiotehnology* 2: 12–26.

Hull, M. S. 2004. Nanomaterials and the environment: A call for research. In: *25 Years of Interdisciplinary Science Serving Global Society*. Abstract book p. 134. Fourth SETAC World Congress, November 14–18, 2004, Portland, OR: SETAC.

Krayer von Krauss, M., Casman, E., and Small, M. 2004. Elicitation of expert judgments of uncertainty in the risk assessment of herbicide tolerant oilseed crops. *Journal of Risk Analysis* 24: 1515–1527.

Kreuter, J., Shamenkov, D., Petrov, V., Ramge, P., Cychutek, K., Koch-Brandt, C., and Alyautdin, R. 2002. Apolipoprotein-mediated transport of nanoparticle-bound drugs across the blood-brain barrier. *Journal of Drug Targeting* 10 (4): 317–325.

Kriebel, D., Tickner, J., Epstein, P., Lemons, J., Levins, R., Loechler, E. L., Quinn, M., Rudel, R., Schettler, T., and Stoto, M. 2001. The precautionary principle in environmental science. *Environmental Health Perspectives* 109: 871–876.

Labhasetwar, V., Song, C., Humphrey, W., Shebuski, R., and Levy, R. J. 1998. Arterial uptake of biodegradable nanoparticles: Effects of surface modifications. *Journal of Pharmaceutical Sciences* 87: 1229–1234.

Lam, C. W., James, J. T., McCluskey, R., and Hunter, R. L. 2004. Pulmonary toxicity of single-wall carbon nanotubes in mice 7 and 90 days after intratracheal instillation. *Toxicological Sciences* 77: 126–134.

Morris, J. 2002. The relationships between risk analysis and the precautionary principle. *Toxicology* 181/182: 127–130.

Myhr, A. I., and Traavik, T. 2003. Genetically modified crops: Precautionary science and conflicts of interests. *Journal of Agricultural and Environmental Ethics* 16: 227–247.

Nanoforum. 2004. Benefits, risks, ethical, legal and social aspects of nanotechnology. European Nanotechnology Gateway. Available: www.nanoforum.org, accessed September 5, 2005.

Oberdörster, E. 2004. Manufactured nanomaterials (fullerenes, C_{60}) induce oxidative stress in juvenile largemouth bass. *Environmental Health Perspectives* 112: 1058–1062.

Oberdörster, G., Sharp, Z., Atudorei, V., Elder, A., Gelein, R., Kreyling, W., and Cox, C. 2004. Translocation of inhaled ultrafine particles to the brain. *Inhalation Toxicology* 16: 437–446.

Raffensperger, C., and Tickner, J. 1999. *Protecting Public Health and the Environment: Implementing the Precautionary Principle*. Washington, DC: Island Press.

Renn, O., and Roco, M. C. 2006. Nanotechnology and the need for risk governance. *Journal of Nanoparticle Research* 8: 153–191.

Royal Society & the Royal Academy of Engineering. 2004. Nanoscience and nanotechnologies: Opportunities and uncertainties. Available: http://www.nanotec.org.uk/, accessed July 5, 2005.

Scheffer, M. 2002. Catastrophic shifts in ecosystems. *Nature* 413: 591–596.

Scott, A., Stirling, A., Mabey, N., Berkhout, F., Williams, C., Rose, C., Jacobs, M., Grove-White, R., Scoones, I., and Leach, M. 1990. Precautionary approach to risk assessment. *Nature* 402:348.

Stirling, A. 2001. On science and precaution on risk management of technological risk. Available: http://ftp.jrc.es/pub/EURdoc/eur19056en.pdf, accessed July 5, 2005.

Van Oss, C. J., Gillman, C. F., and Newmann, A. W. 1975. *Phagocytic Engulfment and Cell Adhesiveness*. New York: Marcel Decker.

Walker, W. E., Harremoeës P., Rotmans, J., Van Der Sluijs, J. P., van Asselt, M. B. A., Janssen, P., and Kraye von Krauss, M. P. 2003. Defining uncertainty; a conceptual basis for uncertainty management in model based decision support. *Journal of Integrated Assessment* 4: 5–17.

Warheit, D. B., Laurence, B. R., Reed, K. L., Roach, D. H., Reynolds, G. A. M., and Webb, T. R. 2004. Comparative pulmonary toxicity assessment of single-wall carbon nanotubes in rats. *Toxicological Sciences* 77: 117–125

Wiesner, M., and Lecoanet, H. 2004. Motion of nanomaterials in water depends on type. Available: http://www.nanotechweb.org, accessed September 15, 2006.

Wynne, B. 1992. Uncertainty and environmental learning: Reconciving science and policy in the preventive paradigm. *Global Environmental Change* 2: 111–127.

12

PERSONAL CHOICE IN THE COMING ERA OF NANOMEDICINE*

Robert A. Freitas, Jr.

NANOMEDICINE: THE ROAD AHEAD

It is always somewhat presumptuous to attempt to predict the future, but in this case we are on solid ground because most of the prerequisite historical processes are already in motion and all of them appear to be clearly pointing in the same direction. Medical historian Roy Porter (1997a,b) notes that the nineteenth century saw the establishment of what we think of as scientific medicine. From about the middle of that century, the textbooks and the attitudes they reveal are recognizable as not being very different from modern ones. Before that, medical books were clearly written to address a different mindset.

But human health is fundamentally biological, and biology is fundamentally molecular. As a result, throughout the twentieth century, scientific medicine began its transformation from a merely rational basis to a fully molecular basis. First, antibiotics that interfered with pathogens at the molecular level were introduced. Next, the ongoing revolutions in genomics, proteomics, and bioinformatics (Baxevanis and Oullette, 1998) provided detailed and precise knowledge of the workings of the human body at the molecular level. Our understanding of life advanced from organs, to tissues, to cells,

* This chapter is based on materials previously published as Robert A. Freitas, Jr., *Nanomedicine*, Volume I: *Basic Capabilities*, Landes Bioscience, Georgetown, TX, 1999. Reprinted with permission.

Nanoethics: The Ethical and Social Implications of Nanotechnology. Edited by Allhoff, Lin, Moor, Weckert and finally to molecules in the twentieth century. By the turn of the century, the entire human genome had been mapped, inferentially incorporating a complete catalog of all human proteins, lipids, carbohydrates, nucleoproteins, and other molecules.

This deep molecular familiarity with the human body, along with simultaneous nanotechnological engineering advances (Freitas, 1998, 1999, 2000, 2003, 2005a), will set the stage for a shift from today's molecular scientific medicine in which fundamental new discoveries are constantly being made to a molecular technologic medicine in which the molecular basis of life, by then well known, is manipulated to produce specific desired results. The comprehensive knowledge of human molecular structure so painstakingly acquired during the twentieth and early twenty-first centuries will be used in the twenty-first century to design medically active microscopic machines. These machines, rather than being tasked primarily with voyages of pure discovery, will instead most often be sent on missions of cellular inspection, repair, and reconstruction. In the early decades of this century, the principal focus will shift from medical science to medical engineering. Nanomedicine (Freitas, 1999, 2003, 2005b,c,d) will involve designing and building a vast proliferation of incredibly efficacious molecular devices, including medical nanorobots, and then deploying these devices in patients to establish and maintain a continuous state of human healthiness.

The very earliest nanotechnology-based biomedical systems may be used to help resolve many difficult scientific questions that remain. These relatively primitive systems may also be employed to assist in the brute-force analysis of the most difficult three-dimensional structures among the 30,000 to 100,000 distinct proteins of which the human body is comprised or to help ascertain the precise function of each such protein. But much of this effort should be complete within the next 10 to 30 years because the reference human body has a finite parts list, and these parts are already being sequenced, geometered, and archived at an ever-increasing pace. Once these parts are known and understood, then the reference human being as a biological system is at least physically specified to completeness at the molecular level. Thereafter, nanomedical-based discovery will consist principally of examining a particular sick or injured patient to determine how he or she deviates from molecular reference structures, with the physician then interpreting these deviations in light of their possible contribution to or detraction from the general health and the explicit preferences of the patient.

In brief, nanomedicine will employ molecular machine systems to address medical problems and use molecular knowledge to maintain human health at the molecular scale.

The greatest power of nanomedicine (Freitas, 1999, 2003) will emerge, perhaps starting in the 2020s, when we can design and construct complete artificial nanorobots using rigid diamondoid nanometer-scale parts like molecular gears and bearings (Drexler, 1992). These medical nanorobots will possess a full panoply of autonomous subsystems, including onboard sensors, motors, manipulators, power supplies, and molecular computers. But getting all these nanoscale components to spontaneously self-assemble in the right sequence will prove increasingly difficult as machine structures become more complex. Making complex nanorobotic mechanical systems requires manufacturing techniques that can build a molecular structure by what is called positional assembly. This will involve picking and placing molecular parts one by one and moving them along controlled trajectories much like the robot arms that manufacture cars on automobile assembly lines. The procedure is then repeated over and over with all the different parts until the final product, such as a medical nanorobot, is fully assembled.

The positional assembly of diamondoid structures, some almost atom by atom, using molecular feedstock has been examined theoretically (Drexler, 1992; Merkle and Freitas, 2003) via computational models of diamond mechanosynthesis (DMS)—the controlled addition of carbon atoms to the growth surface of a diamond crystal lattice in a vacuum manufacturing environment. Covalent chemical bonds are formed one by one as the result of positionally constrained mechanical forces applied at the tip of a scanning probe microscope apparatus following a programmed sequence. Mechanosynthesis using silicon atoms was first achieved experimentally in 2003 (Oyabu et al., 2003). Carbon atoms should not be far behind (Freitas, 2004, 2005e).

To be practical, molecular manufacturing must also be able to assemble very large numbers of medical nanorobots very quickly. Approaches under consideration include using replicative manufacturing systems or massively parallel fabrication, employing large arrays of scanning probe tips all building similar diamondoid product structures in unison, as in nanofactories (Freitas and Merkle, 2004).

NANOMEDICAL TREATMENTS FOR MOST HUMAN DISEASES

The ability to build complex diamondoid medical nanorobots to molecular precision, and then to build them cheaply enough in sufficiently large numbers to be useful therapeutically, will revolutionize the practice of medicine and surgery (Freitas, 1999). The first theoretical design study of a complete medical nanorobot ever published in a peer-reviewed journal described a hypothetical artificial mechanical red blood cell or "respirocyte" made of 18 billion precisely arranged structural atoms (Freitas, 1998). The respirocyte is a blood-borne spherical 1-micrometer diamondoid 1000-atmosphere pressure vessel with reversible molecule-selective surface pumps powered by endogenous serum glucose. This nanorobot would deliver 236 times more oxygen to body tissues per unit volume than natural red cells and would manage carbonic acidity, controlled by gas concentration sensors and an onboard nanocomputer. A 5-milliliter therapeutic dose of 50 percent respirocyte saline suspension containing 5 trillion nanorobots could exactly replace the gas-carrying capacity of the patient's entire 5.4 liters of blood.

Nanorobotic artificial phagocytes called "microbivores" could patrol the bloodstream, seeking out and digesting unwanted pathogens, including bacteria, viruses, or fungi (Freitas, 2005a). Microbivores would achieve complete clearance of even the most severe septicemic infections in hours or less. This is far better than the weeks or months needed for antibiotic-assisted natural phagocytic defenses. The nanorobots do not increase the risk of sepsis or septic shock because the pathogens are completely digested into harmless sugars, amino acids, and the like, which are the only effluents from the nanorobot. Similar nanorobots can digest cancer cells and vascular blockages that produce heart disease and stroke. Biocompatibility issues related to diamondoid medical nanorobots have been examined elsewhere at length (Freitas, 2003).

Even more powerful applications—most importantly involving cellular replacement or repair—are possible with medical nanorobotics. For example, most diseases involve a molecular malfunction at the cellular level, and cell function is significantly controlled by gene expression of proteins. As a result, many disease processes are driven either by defective chromosomes or by defective gene expression. So in many cases it may be most efficient to extract the existing chromosomes from a diseased cell and insert fresh new ones in their place. This procedure is called *chromosome replacement therapy* (Freitas, 2007).

During this procedure, your replacement chromosomes are first manufactured to order, outside of your body, in a clinical benchtop production device that includes a molecular assembly line. Your individual genome is used as the blueprint. If the patient wants, acquired or inherited defective genes could be replaced with nondefective base-pair sequences during the chromosome manufacturing process, thus permanently eliminating any genetic disease. Nanorobots called chromallocytes (Freitas, 2007), each carrying a single copy of the revised chromosomes, are injected into the body and travel to the target tissue cells. Following powered cytopenetration and intracellular transit to the nucleus, the chromallocytes remove the existing chromosomes and then install the properly methylated replacement chromosomes in every tissue cell of your body (requiring a total dose of several trillion nanorobots), then exit the cell and its embedding tissue, reenter the bloodstream, and finally eliminate themselves from the body either through the kidneys or via intravenous collection ports.

The net effect of these nanomedical interventions will be to enable a process I call "dechronification" —or, more colloquially, "rolling back the clock." With regular checkups, cellular chromosomes and other parts of cells will be maintained in optimum condition with long-term degradation virtually eliminated. The end result will be the continuing arrest of all biological aging along with the reduction of current biological age to whatever new biological age is deemed desirable by the patient, severing forever the link between calendar time and biological health. These interventions may become almost commonplace several decades from today. Are there any serious ethical problems with this? According to the *volitional normative model of disease* (Section 4) that seems most appropriate for nanomedicine, if you are physiologically old and do not want to be, then for you oldness and aging—indeed, involuntary natural death itself—are a disease, and you deserve to be cured.

WHAT IS DISEASE?

Can aging and involuntary natural death really be considered a disease? "Disease" is a complex term whose meaning is still hotly debated among medical academics (Albert et al., 1988; Bradley, 1993; Cassell and Siegler, 1979; Faber, 1930; Murphy, 1997; Sheldon, 1992). But there is evidence that the more medical knowledge a practitioner possesses and the more he or she must interact with real patients in a clinical context, the more likely the practitioner will be to expand the interpretation of what constitutes disease. For example, in one survey (Campbell et al., 1979), four different groups of people—secondary school students, nonmedical academics, medical academics, and general practitioners—were read a list of common diagnostic terms and then asked if they would rate the condition as a disease. Illnesses due to microorganisms, or conditions in which the doctor's contribution to the diagnosis was important, were almost always considered a disease by everyone, but if the cause was a known physical or chemical agent, the condition was less likely to be regarded as disease. However, the closer the respondent was to the day-to-day treatment of real patients, the more likely he or she was to apply liberal standards in answering the question. General practitioners were most likely to call almost any unwanted condition—including depression, senility, tennis elbow, or malnutrition—a disease.

No less than eight different types of disease concepts are held by at least some people currently engaging in clinical reasoning and practice, including (Bradley, 1993; Daniel et al., 1988):

1. *Disease Nominalism.* A disease is whatever physicians say is a disease. This approach avoids understanding and forestalls inquiry, rather than furthering it.

2. *Disease Relativism.* A disease is identified or labeled in accordance with explicit or implicit social norms and values at a particular time. In nineteenth-century Japan, for example, armpit odor was considered a disease and its treatment constituted a medical specialty. Similarly, nineteenth-century Western culture regarded masturbation as a disease, and in the eighteenth century, some conveniently identified a mental disease called drapetomania, the "abnormally strong and irrational desire of a slave to be free" (Porter, 1997a,b). Various non-Western cultures having widespread parasitic infection may consider the lack of infection to be abnormal, thus not regarding those who are infected as suffering from disease.

3. *Sociocultural Disease.* Societies may possess a concept of disease that differs from the concepts of other societies, but the concept may also differ from that held by medical practitioners within the society itself. For instance, hypercholesterolemia is regarded as a disease condition by doctors but not by the lay public; medical treatment may be justified, but persons with hypercholesterolemia may not seek treatment, even when told of the condition. Conversely, there may be sociocultural pressure to recognize a particular condition as a disease requiring treatment, such as alcoholism and gambling.

4. *Statistical Disease.* A condition is a disease when it is abnormal, where abnormal is defined as a specific deviation from a statistically defined norm. This approach has many flaws. For example, a statistical concept makes it impossible to regard an entire population as having a disease. Thus tooth decay, which is virtually universal in humans, is not abnormal; those lacking it are abnormal, thus are "diseased" by this definition. More reasonably, a future highly aseptic society might regard bacterium-infested twentieth-century humans [who contain in their bodies more foreign microbes than native cells (Freitas, 1999)] as massively infected. Another flaw is that many statistical measurables such as body temperature and blood pressure are continuous variables with bell-shaped distributions, so cutoff thresholds between "normal" and "abnormal" seem highly arbitrary.

5. *Infectious Agency.*   Disease is caused by a microbial infectious agent. Besides excluding systemic failures of bodily systems, this view is unsatisfactory because the same agent can produce very different illnesses. For instance, infection with hemolytic *Streptococcus* can produce diseases as different as erysipelas and puerperal fever, and Epstein-Barr virus is implicated in diseases as varied as Burkitt's lymphoma, glandular fever, and nasopharyngeal carcinoma (Bradley, 1993).

6. *Disease Realism.*   Diseases have a real, substantial existence regardless of social norms and values and exist independent of whether they are discovered, named, recognized, classified, or diagnosed. Diseases are not inventions and may be identified with the operations of biological systems, providing a reductionistic account of diseases in terms of system components and subprocesses, even down to the molecular level. One major problem with this view is that theories may change over time—almost every nineteenth-century scientific theory was either rejected or highly modified in the twentieth century. If the identification of disease is connected with theories, then a change in theories may alter what is viewed as a disease. For example, the nineteenth-century obsession with constipation was reflected in the disease labeled "autointoxication," in which the contents of the large bowel were believed to poison the body. Consequently much unnecessary attention was paid to laxatives and purgatives and, when surgery of the abdomen became possible toward the end of the century, operations to remove the colon became fashionable in both England and America (Porter, 1997a,b).

7. *Disease Idealism.*   Disease is the lack of health, where health is characterized as the optimum functioning of biological systems. Every real system inevitably falls short of the optimum in its actual functioning. But by comparing large numbers of systems, we can formulate standards that a particular system ought to satisfy in order to be the best of its kind. Thus "health" becomes a kind of Platonic ideal that real organisms approximate, and everyone is a less than perfect physical specimen. Since we are all flawed to some extent, disease is a matter of degree, a more or less extreme variation from the normative ideal of perfect functioning. This could be combined with the statistical approach, thus characterizing disease as a statistical variation from the ideal. But this view, like the statistical, suffers from arbitrary thresholds that must be drawn to qualify a measurable function as representing a diseased condition.

8. *Functional Failure.*   Organisms and the cells that constitute them are complex organized systems that display phenomena (e.g., homeostasis) resulting from acting upon a program of information. Programs acquired and developed during evolution, encoded in DNA, control the processes of the system. Through biomedical research, we write out the program of a process as an explicit set (or network) of instructions. There are completely self-contained "closed" genetic programs, and there are "open" genetic programs that require an interaction between the programmed system and the environment (e.g., learning or conditioning). Normal functioning is thus the operation of biologically programmed processes (e.g., natural functioning), and disease may be characterized as the

failure of normal functioning. One difficulty with this view is that it enshrines the natural as the benchmark of health, but it is difficult to regard as diseased a natural brunette who has dyed her hair blonde in contravention of the natural program, and it is quite reasonable to regard the mere possession of an appendix as a disease condition, even though the natural program operates so as to perpetuate this troublesome organ.[1] A second weakness of this view is that disease is still defined against population norms of functionality, ignoring individual differences. As a perhaps overly simplistic example, 65 percent of all patients employ a cisterna chyli in their lower thoracic lymph duct, while 35 percent have no cisterna chyli—which group has a healthy natural program and which group is diseased?

VOLITIONAL NORMATIVE MODEL OF DISEASE

The author has proposed (Freitas, 1999) a new alternative view of disease which seems most suitable for the nanomedical paradigm, called the *volitional normative model of disease*. As in the "disease idealism" view, the volitional normative model accepts the premise that health is the optimal functioning of biological systems. Like the "functional failure" view, the volitional normative model assumes that optimal functioning involves the operation of biologically programmed processes.

However, two important distinctions from these previous views must be made. First, in the volitional normative model, normal functioning is defined as the optimal operation of biologically programmed processes as reflected in the patient's own individual genetic instructions, rather than of those processes which might be reflected in a generalized population average or "Platonic ideal" of such instructions; the relative function of other members of the human population is no longer determinative. Second, physical condition is regarded as a volitional state in which the patient's desires are a crucial element in the definition of health. This is a continuation of the current trend in which patients frequently see themselves as active partners in their own care.

In the volitional normative model, disease is characterized not just as the failure of "optimal" functioning, but rather as the failure of either optimal functioning or "desired" functioning. Thus disease may result from a failure to correctly specify desired bodily function (specification error by the patient), a flawed biological program design that does not meet the specifications (programming design error), flawed execution of the biological program (execution error), external interference by disease agents with the design or execution of the biological program (exogenous error), or traumatic injury or accident (structural failure). Note the presence of the word *or*, not *and*, in regard to the optimal or desired function mentioned above. If your biological function is not optimal (e.g., not executing as designed), then you are diseased. If your biological function is not desired, then you are also diseased. If both situations obtain simultaneously, disease is present. Only if neither condition applies is the patient disease free.

In the early years of nanomedicine, volitional physical states will customarily reflect "default" values which may differ only insignificantly from the patient's original or natural biological programming. With a more mature nanomedicine, the patient may gain the ability to substitute alternative natural programs for many of his or her original natural programs. For example, the genes responsible for appendix morphology or for sickle cell expression might be replaced with genes that encode other phenotypes, such as the phenotype of an appendix-free cecum or a phenotype for statistically typical human erythrocytes.[2] Many persons will go further, electing an artificial genetic structure which, say, eliminates age-related diminution of the secretion of human growth hormone and other essential endocrines. By the early twenty-first century, many members of the medical research community were already starting to talk about aging as a treatable condition (Aubrey et al., 2002; Finch, 1990; Nesse and Williams, 1998; Rudman, 1990; Schwartz, 1998; Stock and Campbell, 2000).

On the other hand, a congenitally blind patient might desire, for whatever personal reasons, to retain his or her blindness. Hence, for this person, the genetic programs that result in the blindness phenotype would not constitute disease as long as he or she fully understands the options and outcomes that are available.[3] (Retaining the blindness while lacking such understanding might constitute a specification error, and such a patient might then be considered diseased.) Whether the broad pool of volitional human phenotypes will tend to converge or diverge is unknown, although the most likely outcome is probably a population distribution (of human biological programs) with a tall, narrow central peak (e.g., a smaller standard deviation) but with longer tails (e.g., exhibiting a small number of more extreme outliers).

One minor flaw in the volitional normative model of disease is that it relies upon the ability of patients to make fully informed decisions concerning their own physical state. The model crucially involves desires and beliefs, which can be irrational, especially during mental illness, and people normally vary in their ability to acquire and digest information. Patients also may be unconscious or too young, whereupon default standards might be substituted in some instances.

Regarding such irrational desires, an interesting special case is the negating self-referential situation: What if a person desires that his function is not optimal? As a fanciful example, let us assume our patient is at a party, is not intoxicated or otherwise mentally impaired, and has purposely infected himself with a fast-acting strain of plague in order to compete with his friends to see who can suffer the unpleasant symptoms the longest before crying out for the antidote to be administered. Clearly, during the time he is infected and experiencing painful symptoms, our patient's body is performing as he informedly desires—he desires to feel sick. But what about the other half of the definition: Is his body performing optimally?

If his purpose was to commit suicide, then his biology is performing optimally (as programmed) and he is not diseased. The patient has informedly chosen a lethal degenerative state, and it is playing out perfectly according to plan with flawless execution. Committing suicide is not a disease condition if the act is fully informed and voluntarily chosen. However, because the patient's expressed intent is to call for an antidote at the last possible moment, this is clear evidence of a recognition on his part that his body is not performing optimally, because some therapeutic agent is required to restore the previous (preinfection) functioning and avoid the otherwise inevitable result of failing to administer the antidote (unwanted death). In this latter case, then, function is not optimal, and the patient is considered voluntarily diseased until he takes the antidote.

The volitional normative view of disease seems most appropriate for nanomedicine because it recognizes that the era of molecular control of biology could bring considerable molecular diversity among the human population. Conditions representing a diseased state must of necessity become more idiosyncratic and may progressively vary as personal preferences evolve over time. Some patients will be more venturesome than others—"to each his own." As an imperfect analogy, consider a group of individuals who each take their automobile to a mechanic. One driver insists on having the carburetion and timing adjusted for maximum performance (the "racer"); another driver prefers optimum gas mileage (the "cheapskate"); still another prefers minimizing tailpipe emissions (the "environmentalist"); and yet another requires only that the engine be painted blue (the "aesthete"). In like manner, different people will choose different personal specifications. One can only hope that the physician will never become a mere mechanic even in an era of near-perfect human structural and functional information; an automobile conveys a body, but the human body conveys the soul. Agrees theorist Otto Guttentag (1979): "The physician-patient relationship is ontologically different from that of a maintenance engineer to a machine or a veterinarian to an animal."

Nick Bostrom (personal communication, 2002) notes that the intuition underlying the volitional normative model is that disease is a systems failure, meaning a failure of a system to perform in the mode that is one of the systems' operating modes, and the particular mode that the subject informedly prefers: "Thus, it would not be a disease for my biceps to fail to be as strong as a bulldozer (because that's not one of the system's operating modes), and it is not a disease of my skin to lack tattoos (because although my skin system could operate in that mode, I do not desire it to do so). Of course, this results in a very permissive disease concept, according to which, for example, my biceps would be diseased if they are slightly smaller and less strong than they could be and I would want them to be." In response to this "small biceps" disease, the nanomedical doctor might enlarge the biceps to the size desired, provided this does not exceed the physically possible limits of the human anatomical/genetic system. If still larger biceps are desired and even a genetically altered human frame is insufficient to accommodate them, then a new nonbiological platform may need to be substituted or implemented. In that case we have moved beyond nanomedicine into the realm of transhuman engineering where a proper definition of disease would have to incorporate an assessment of alternative physical platforms and numerous additional factors.

The natural end result of nanomedicine is fully permissive medicine. Thus it will be absolutely essential to make sure that consent and desire are always as informed as possible. Medical simulations must be perfected into a rigorous engineering discipline. Perhaps from a public policy standpoint, we should increasingly raise the bar on patient educational and consent requirements before allowing the choice of increasingly "unnatural" elective nanomedical interventions. As a general public policy, some effort should be made to require greater informedness when greater interventions are desired. Another interesting question is the relationship between the desires of the individual and the need for public safety. As a policy matter, we might decide that an individual's desire to grow diamond-coated fingernails that are 10 inches long and as sharp as razors or to see only things that are red in color or to possess a psychopathic personality may be contravened by society's need to be safe from people with such modifications. The new disease model, if applied to nanomedicine, might make it easier for one person's desired functioning to come into conflict with another person's desired functioning. Societal conflict resolution laws, institutions, and traditions will need beefing up.

NOTES

1. The vermiform appendix may have some minor immune function, but it is clearly nonessential and can kill when infected. Yet natural selection has not eliminated it. Indeed, there is evidence for positive selection due to the following accident of physiological evolution. Appendicitis results when inflammation causes swelling, compressing the artery supplying blood to the appendix. High blood flow protects against bacterial growth, so any reduction aids infection, creating more swelling; if flow is completely cut off, bacteria multiply rapidly until the organ bursts. A slender appendix is especially susceptible, so untreated appendicitis applies positive selective pressure to maintain a larger appendix (Nesse and Williams, 1998).

2. It is often pointed out that sickle cell is advantageous in malaria-infested countries because the trait confers resistance to malaria. This flaw-tolerant view makes a virtue of necessity—a direct cure for malaria will undoubtedly be more efficient. Sickle cell is disadvantageous in hypoxic conditions, which is why no one with this trait can hold a civil airline pilot's license (Bradley, 1993).

3. Consider the situation in which a person's visual system genes code for total darkness, but over time as the person ages, some genetic defects creep in, and the person starts to be able to visually perceive the difference between lightness and darkness (e.g., day and night), where before all was darkness. If personal preferences have not changed, then according to the volitional normative model, the person now has a disease state which should be cured. Why? Because she specified and informedly selected genes that would produce a visual system that would allow no perception of light whatsoever, but now her eyes are malfunctioning and somehow generating some perception of light. This malfunction indicates nonoptimal function of the specified genetic instructions. To restore optimal function, the woman must be "re-blinded" by correcting her malfunctioning genes so that she will once again see only darkness.

REFERENCES

Albert, D. A., Munson, R., and Resnik, M. D. 1988. *Reasoning in Medicine: An Introduction to Clinical Inference*. Baltimore, MD: Johns Hopkins University Press.

De Grey, A. D. N. J., Ames, B. N., Andersen, J. K., Bartke, A., Campisi, J., Heward, C. B., McCarter, R. J. M., and Stock, G. 2002. Time to talk SENS: Critiquing the immutability of human aging. *Annals of New York Academy of Science* 959: 452–462. Available: http://research.mednet.ucla.edu/pmts/sens/article.htm.

Baxevanis, A. D., and Ouellette, B. F. F. (Eds.). 1998. *Bioinformatics: A Practical Guide to the Analysis of Genes and Proteins*. New York: Wiley-Interscience.

Bradley, G. W. 1993. *Disease, Diagnosis and Decisions*. New York: Wiley.

Campbell, E. J. M., Scadding, J. G., and Roberts, R. S. 1979. The concept of disease. *British Medical Journal* 2: 757–762.

Cassell, E. J., and Siegler, M. (Eds.) 1979. *Changing Values in Medicine*. Bethesda, MD: University Publications of America.

Drexler, K. E. 1992. *Nanosystems: Molecular Machinery, Manufacturing, and Computation*. New York: Wiley.

Faber, K. 1930. *Nosography: The Evolution of Clinical Medicine in Modern Times*, 2nd ed. New York: Paul Hoeber.

Finch, C. E. 1990. *Longevity, Senescence and the Genome*. Chicago, IL: University of Chicago Press.

Freitas, R. A., Jr. 1998. Exploratory design in medical nanotechnology: A mechanical artificial red cell. *Artificial Cells, Blood Substitutes, and Immobilization Biotechnology* 26: 411–430. Avialable: http://www.foresight.org/Nanomedicine/Respirocytes.html.

Freitas, R. A., Jr. 1999. *Nanomedicine*, Volume I: *Basic Capabilities*. Georgetown, TX: Landes Bioscience. Available: http://www.nanomedicine.com/NMI.htm.

Freitas, R. A., Jr. 2000. *Nanodentistry*. *Journal of the American Dental Association* 131: 1559–1566.

Freitas, R. A., Jr. 2003. *Nanomedicine*, Volume IIA: *Biocompatibility*. Georgetown, TX: Landes Bioscience. Available: http://www.nanomedicine.com/NMIIA.htm.

Freitas, R. A., Jr. 2004. Pathway to diamond-based molecular manufacturing. Invited lecture at the First Symposium on Molecular Machine Systems at the First Foresight Conference on Advanced Nanotechnology, October 22, 2004, Washington, DC. Avialable: http://www.MolecularAssembler.com/Papers/PathDiamMolMfg.htm. See also: http://www.MolecularAssembler.com/Nanofactory/DMS.htm.

Freitas, R. A., Jr. 2005a. Microbivores: Artificial mechanical phagocytes using digest and discharge protocol. *Journal of Evolution and Technology* 14: 1–52. Available: http://jetpress.org/volume14/Microbivores.pdf.

Freitas, R. A., Jr. 2005b. What is nanomedicine? *Nanomedicine: Nanotechnology, Biology, and Medicine*. 1: 2–9. Available: http://www.nanomedicine.com/Papers/WhatIsNMMar05.pdf.

Freitas, R. A., Jr. 2005c. Current status of nanomedicine and medical nanorobotics (invited survey). *Journal of Computational and Theoretical Nanoscience* 2: 1–25. Available: http://www.nanomedicine.com/Papers/NMRevMar05.pdf.

Freitas, R. A., Jr. 2005d. Nanotechnology, nanomedicine and nanosurgery. *International Journal of Surgery* 3: 1–4. Available: http://www.nanomedicine.com/Papers/IntlJSurgDec05.pdf.

Freitas, R. A., Jr. 2005e. A simple tool for positional diamond mechanosynthesis, and its method of manufacture. U.S. provisional patent application no. 60/543,802, filed February 11, 2004; U.S. patent pending, February 11, 2005. Available: http://www.MolecularAssembler.com/Papers/DMSToolbuildProvPat.htm.

Freitas, R. A., Jr. 2007. Chromallocytes: Cell repair nanorobots for chromosome replacement therapy. *Journal of Evolution and Technology*, in preparation.

Freitas, R. A., Jr., and Merkle, R. C. 2004. *Kinematic Self-Replicating Machines*. Georgetown, TX: Landes Bioscience. Available: http://www.MolecularAssembler.com/KSRM.htm. See also Nanofactory Collaboration website, http://www.MolecularAssembler.com/Nanofactory.

Guttentag, O. E. 1979. The attending physician as a central figure. In E. J. Cassell and M. Siegler. (Eds.), *Changing Values in Medicine.* Bethesda, MD: University Publications of America, pp. 107–126.

Merkle, R. C., and Freitas, R. A., Jr. 2003. Theoretical analysis of a carbon-carbon dimer placement tool for diamond mechanosynthesis. *Journal of Nanoscience and Nanotechnology* 3: 319–324. Available: http://www.rfreitas.com/Nano/JNNDimerTool.pdf.

Murphy, E. A. 1997. *The Logic of Medicine*, 2nd ed. Balitmore, MD: Johns Hopkins University Press.

Nesse, R. M., and Williams, G. C. 1998. Evolution and the origins of disease. *Scientific American* 279: 86–93.

Oyabu, N., Custance, O., Yi, I., Sugawara, Y., and Morita, S. 2003. Mechanical vertical manipulation of selected single atoms by soft nanoindentation using near contact atomic force microscopy. *Physical Review Letters* 90: 176102.

Porter, R. 1997a. *The Greatest Benefit to Mankind: A Medical History of Humanity.* New York: W. W. Norton & Company.

Porter, R. (Ed.). 1997b. *Medicine: A History of Healing, Ancient Traditions to Modern Practices.* New York: Barnes & Noble Books.

Rudman, D., et al. 1990. Effects of human growth hormone in men over 60 years old. *New. England Journal of Medicine* 323: 1–6.

Schwartz, W. B. 1998. *Life Without Disease: The Pursuit of Medical Utopia.* Berkeley, CA: University of California Press.

Sheldon, H. (Ed.) 1992. *Boyd's Introduction to the Study of Disease*, 11th ed., Philadelphia, PA: Lea & Febiger.

Stock, G., and Campbell, J. (Eds.) 2000. *Engineering the Human Germline: An Exploration of the Science and Ethics of Altering the Genes We Pass to Our Children.* Oxford: Oxford University Press.

13

ARE WE PLAYING GOD WITH NANOENHANCEMENT?

Ted Peters

Is nanoenhancement playing God? Is any form of human enhancement playing God? By "playing God," we mean manipulating the intricacies of human nature so that human nature becomes something other than what it is. We mean changing nature. And, if we change nature without permission, will we violate something sacred? Will nature strike back in vengeance and punish us? In order to avoid reprisal, should we avoid progress in nanotechnology?

The question of whether or not we should play God with human nature became the central ethical question during the Human Genome Project of the 1990s. This ethical question is being asked once again in our era of nanotechnology. Nanotechnology deals with the manipulation of matter at the level of atoms and molecules. Futurists project that nanotechnology combined with genetic advances could lead to dramatic breakthroughs in medical therapy and, of course, in enhancing human capabilities. Chief on the list of human enhancements is neurocognitive augmentation and intelligence expansion.

Nanoethics constitutes a form of analysis, assessment, evaluation, and recommendation regarding alternative scenarios which nanotechnology developments might follow. In this chapter we will look briefly at intelligence enhancement, identify scenarios with ethical valences, and then raise the question: Are nanotechnology innovators playing God?

We will show that the concept of playing God derives from the ancient Greek myth of Prometheus. The myth lives on in modern culture disguised as the figure

Nanoethics: The Ethical and Social Implications of Nanotechnology. Edited by Allhoff, Lin, Moor, Weckert
Copyright © 2007 John Wiley & Sons, Inc.

of Frankenstein. Today, we fear a Frankenstein scientist might violate nature through technological intervention and this will let loose the powers of chaos and destruction. In contrast, an ethical vision grounded in Christian theology does not operate out of this fear of violating nature. Rather, a biblically based theology affirms change and transformation rather than trying to retard scientific and technological advance. The Christian approach to ethics orients itself toward loving God and loving neighbor. The ethical question here would be: How can nanotechnology enhance the human capacity for loving God and neighbor?

WOULD WE CHANGE THE NATURE OF OUR HUMAN NATURE?

When we extrapolate present trends to project future scenarios, some nanotechnology futurists anticipate changes in human functioning so radical that we must ask the question: Will we alter human nature so that something posthuman or transhuman will result? If today's human beings are capable of giving technological birth to a new and superior species, is it ethical to pursue this? Would such a goal violate something intrinsically valuable or even sacred lying within our biologically inherited natural state? Does nanotechnology put human identity at risk?[1]

What about using nanotechnology to make ourselves smarter? Let us look briefly at what is being projected for human intelligence augmentation, most frequently referred to as neurocognitive enhancement. Sometimes it is named "intelligence amplification" (IA) or "cognitive augmentation" and even "machine-augmented intelligence." We are projecting the possible use of information technology and even genetic technology to augment or expand the range of human intelligence. What the next decades could bring is a new advance in the cybernetic revolution already begun in the 1950s and 1960s. Here is a scenario put forth by the Enhancement Technologies Group (ETG, 2006) that wants to increase the capability of a person to approach a complex problem and solve it: "Increased capability in this respect is taken to mean a mixture of the following: more-rapid comprehension, better comprehension, the possibility of gaining a useful degree of comprehension in a situation that previously was too complex, speedier solutions, better solutions, and the possibility of finding solutions to problems that before seemed insolvable."

Is this sufficiently radical to be considered a change in human nature? No. Yet, still more dramatic changes can be projected. Suppose smaller incremental enhancements are introduced but then amplified and reamplified until they grow exponentially? These new levels of intelligence could transfer themselves to accelerated computing platforms, such as optical nanocomputers or quantum nanocomputers. This would allow them to accelerate the brain's thinking speed significantly. Futurists have called the possibility of such an event the "Singularity." The idea of this singularity implies an impact upon our world that could "exceed that of any other foreseeable technological advance," says the Accelerating Futures group. "A Singularity, if successful, would create a massive upward spike in the quantity of intelligence here on Earth, a persistent positive-feedback process, continuously enhancing itself. In a favorable scenario, our freedom and potential could be maximized, opening up astonishing new possibilities that might have taken trillions of years for unaided humans to create alone." (Accelerating Future, 2006) Might this scenario count as an alteration of our human nature? Well, we are getting closer.

One of the assumptions frequently made in the contemporary neurosciences is that our minds or even our souls are reducible to the physical operations of our brains. Eugene d'Aquili and Andrew Newberg (1999, p. 75), for example, write: "In our model, the mind and the brain are essentially two different ways of looking at the same thing, the brain representing the structural aspects of the mind, and the mind representing the functional aspects of the brain. They each affect the other and are affected by the other in the rhythmic process of the empiric modification cycle." As long as this assumption holds and nanotechnology or nanobiotechnology enhances the brain, which in turn enhances the mind, we will not be able to say that human nature has been altered. Our identities will remain stable. Who we presently are will simply enjoy physical and mental enhancement.

If we operate with the assumption that brains and minds and hence souls are virtually isomorphic—" brains" and "minds" are different ways of looking at the same thing—then this implies that any form of mind enhancement will necessarily take the form of brain enhancement. To get to our mind, we must go through the body.

However, if we make a different assumption, then the scenario looks different. Suppose we assume that a person's mind or even soul consists of an information pattern or package. Suppose we assume that our mind is like software and our body is like hardware. Could the software be transferred to different hardware? Could we move our mind from our body into a computer? If this information pattern could be comprehensively removed from our physical body and placed in a computer, then the computer rather than our brain would be in a position to enhance us.

If we transfer our mind to a computer and if we keep backing it up, might we attain cybernetic immortality? Ray Kurzweil (1999, Chapter 6) says yes. In the past, he says, our mortality has been tied to the longevity of our bodies, to our hardware. So, when our bodies die, our hardware crashes, and our mental processes crash with it. When we instantiate ourselves in our computational technology, our software and hence our immortality will no longer be dependent on the survival of our physical brain. Our immortality will be contingent on our being careful to make frequent backups.[2] Would a disembodied mind located in a mechanical device such as a computer count as a change in human nature?

While we are on the subject of immortality, I might say in passing that what is proposed here has nothing to do with what Christian theology means by salvation. What Christians affirm is resurrection of the whole person—body, soul, spirit, communal relations—concomitant with God's renewal of the creation, the advent of the new creation. What Christian theologians reject is the idea that the soul—here in the form of the mind—extricated from the body constitutes salvation. Munich theologian Wolfhart Pannenberg (1991–1998, p. 572) writes, "The soul is not on its own the true person as though the body were simply a burdensome appendage or a prison to which the soul is tied so long as it has its being on earth. Instead, the person is a unity of body and soul, so that we can think of a future after death only as bodily renewal as well."

In short, a plan to extricate the human mind from the human body—what we might call a *soulechtomy*—assumes substance dualism; it assumes that the body and mind or soul are separate substances or separate realities. It assumes that who we are in essence is determined primarily if not exclusively by our mind and not our body. This is a highly questionable assumption in our era when many in both philosophy and theology affirm holism—that is, the integration of body, soul, and spirit. Nevertheless, some in the field of cybernetic technology will proceed with experiments based upon this dualistic assumption. The results may be quite interesting.

Just how interesting? Despite the observation that cybernetic immortality would have no impact on the Christian concept of resurrection, it would still be a marvelous—though not obviously advantageous—achievement. Perhaps disembodied consciousness will turn out to be impossible. Even short of disembodied consciousness, however, some alterations being projected by nanotechies could result in significant changes in how we human beings might live. How should we embrace such changes? Bioethicist Paul Wolpe (2002, p. 164) cautiously welcomes even the most radical changes: "We really are becoming some kind of cyborg, some kind of posthuman in the sense that for the first time in history we really are going to incorporate our synthetic technologies into the very physiology of our being—with major, though not necessarily entirely undesirable, consequences."

RELATIONAL INTELLIGENCE

We have just looked at two scenarios: one based on the assumption that minds are exhaustively dependent on brains and one based on the assumption that minds can be separated from brains. Now, let us take a look at a third assumption: Minds are inextricably embodied and our intelligence necessarily includes a relational component. What kind of scenario results from this assumption?

Theologian and computer scientist Noreen Herzfeld (2002) makes this third assumption. She says we should view intelligence as something more than merely the physical processes of the brain, yet it is inextricably tied to brain and even whole-body function. Mind is more than merely genetic and neuronal activity. Intelligence is a relational phenomenon.

Herzfeld uses the Turing test as an illustrative example. In order to answer the question, "can computers think?" British mathematician Alan Turing provided the now widely accepted answer, namely, simply ask them. Because it is impossible to observe thought processes in someone other than ourselves, we ascertain that he or she is intelligent through interaction, usually conversation. To date no computer built is intelligent. When a computer becomes intelligent, we will know it when we interact with it intelligently: "If we accept the Turing Test ... as the ultimate arbiter of intelligence, then we have defined intelligence relationally" (Herzfeld, 2002, p. 46) As a theologian, Herzfeld (p. 87) proceeds to affirm "a relational understanding of the *imago Dei,* one that sees the image of God as emergent only when and insofar as we are in relationship with God and with others"

Gregory Peterson (2003) would agree with Herzfeld: "We are not simply disembodied reasoning machines but persons in a bodily and communal context," he writes

(p. 218). This implies that simple nanoaugmentation of brain function may enhance a limited portion of the thought process of an individual, but it is not likely in itself to produce an advance in intelligence. The ethical implication is that we must take into account the relational dimension of human persons if we are to enhance the intelligence of human persons. Peterson by no means calls us to stop playing God; he only opens us to pursue possibilities with relational responsibility in mind (p. 219): "A truly Christian view of the future is not simply individualistic but communal, and it is difficult to see how such technologies will be used both fairly and equitably. At the same time, it is important to keep in mind how open the future is."

If we wish to answer a question asked earlier regarding the degree of identity change that would result from cybernetic immortality, perhaps the Turing test—now a relationality test—might be employed profitably. Suppose we take the information pattern that constitutes the mind of a person we know as Patrick. Suppose we remove it from his body and dispose of his body. Then we place his mind like software into a computer and boot it. Our question would be: Have we changed the nature—the essential nature or identity—of Patrick? To find out, we would step up to the computer and ask, "Patrick, is that you?"

On the one hand, we might receive no answer at all or a quizzical "no." We would then conclude that Patrick's essential nature had been altered and his identity lost. We might regret having tried to play God. On the other hand, the computer might answer back, "Yes, it's me. Patrick!" We would then ask, "Howya doin?"

If Patrick answers "fine" and proceeds to converse with us intelligently, recalling his past personal history, looking forward gleefully at his future adventures in his disembodied state, then we might conclude, "yes, it is Patrick." We will not have changed his essential nature. Rather, this technology will have extended into the future a nature that had previously been inherited.

When searching for an essential human nature in an antiessentialist postmodern culture that denies such a thing, philosophical theologian Robert Cummings Neville (1997) offers a relational definition. It includes the sense of obligation to those with whom one is in relation and it includes continuity of history: "The normative identity of each one of us is partly defined by what is normative for the communities of human beings in historical connection. ... The closest thing to an essence of human nature is having the obligation to take responsibility for being part of the history in which we ourselves are engaged." If we apply the Neville criterion, then Patrick will be Patrick even if his mind carries out social obligations from within a computer.

Such future projections lead to a number of questions. Will the changes envisioned here lead to the emergence of a new species, a transhuman or a posthuman being? If nanotechnology and nanobiotechnology are capable of producing a change so radical that human nature might undergo modification or alteration, would this violate a commandment such as: Thou shalt not play God? These are questions for nanoethicists to ask.

NANOETHICS

Nanotechnology along with bionanotechnology belong squarely within the field of futurology, the study of the future concomitant with unavoidable ethical deliberation.

Techno futurists operate according to what I call the *understanding–decision–control* (u-d-c) formula. The first task is to understand the direction current trends are taking us. In this case, we need to project the possible future scenarios nanoresearch will bring about. Such understanding includes distinguishing between desirable and undesirable futures, and this is where ethical deliberation helps us distinguish what we should pursue and what we should avoid. The second task is decision—that is, we make the decision now to pursue the technological scenario most likely leading to the desirable future. The third task is to take control of what is projected to happen in order to aid and abet a positive future becoming actualized.[3] Now, we know from experience what a will-o-the-wisp the desire for control can be, yet control is an objective in futuristic thinking.

Ethical deliberation belongs at stage one, envisioning a better future and setting the moral criteria for determining what counts as a better future. Nanospeculation is rife with wild-eyed and enticing scenarios for medical therapy and human enhancement. So we need to ask: What counts ethically as we compare various scenarios? The field of nanoethics today is shouldering moral responsibility for what should happen tomorrow. (Lin and Allhoff, 2006).

How should the ethical issue be formulated? It might appear that the ethical issue is this: Just how much change can we morally allow? Are we morally obligated to protect our inherited human nature? Such a formulation of the moral challenge is theologically misleading, however. What concerns the theologian is this: How can we envision a future with enhanced inclination to love God and love our neighbor? Unfortunately, the question of whether or not we should play God obscures this central concern. Let us pose the question of playing God and see where it leads us.

SHOULD WE PLAY GOD WITH OUR BRAINS?

This question may seem to have a double meaning. First, it asks whether we should physically modify our brains. Second, it asks whether we should employ our brains in deciding whether or not to play God. Perhaps it implies that only one without brains would play God. Be that as it may, it is the first of these meanings that will occupy us here.

What does the phrase "play God" mean? In recent decades it has come to refer to three things. First, to play God is to *learn God's awesome secrets*. When scientists study the inner workings of nature, especially the inner workings of living things, previous mysteries become revealed. What was dark and secretive now comes to light. If the natural world is God's creation and if God's mind is written into the blueprint of this creation, then scientists are gaining the ability to read the divine mind. This could be inspiring. Or, it could be frightening. For the most part, we presume that it is inspiring. No inhibition or restriction on the pursuits of science follows from this first understanding of playing God.

The second meaning is associated with the *power of life and death*. The context for this meaning of "playing God" is the clinic or hospital. It refers to the skill and training and dedication of the doctor or surgeon in whose hands your or my life has been placed. When feeling helpless due to disease or infirmity, the physician appears to us as "godlike" in power. Nurses may joke that the doctors' lounge is "where the gods dwell," but no one would prohibit physicians from employing their godlike powers to save human life.

Sometimes medical doctors are criticized for their pride, their hubris for thinking they know more than they do. This brings us to the third meaning of the phrase playing God. It is associated more with medical researchers than clinical physicians. To play God is to *alter life and influence human evolution.* Our society and our culture is ridden with fear that laboratory scientists will be so overfilled with pride—with *hubris*—that they may create new life forms that will violate something sacred in nature and cause a backlash in the form of uncontrollable disease or related calamity. The only way to prevent such a calamity is to restrain medical researchers, to cut their pride off at the knees, and prevent them from making fatal mistakes that could endanger all of us.

To play God is to make the mistake made by the mythical figure Prometheus. Prometheus, recall, stole fire from the sun to bring heat and light to the damp and dark earth. The god Zeus, the sky god who claimed provenance over the sun, felt violated by Prometheus' intrusion into the divine realm where he did not belong. So, Zeus punished Prometheus severely, chaining the Titan to a rock where an eagle could daily eat his liver. The repeated telling of this Greek myth carries a message: Do not let human pride or hubris so inflate your confidence in what you believe you can accomplish in the future that you anger the gods. In our modern world, no longer do we believe in the Greek gods. Yet, nature has replaced those Olympian gods. It is now nature who plays the role of Zeus. If our promethean scientists violate nature, we fear, then we may all suffer the consequences of nature's revenge.

The ancient myth of Prometheus lives on in our culture. Scientists like Frankenstein have replaced Prometheus, and nature has replaced the Olympian gods. Yet, the plot is the same. In the Frankenstein legends, the mad scientist oversteps the boundary between death and life. The result is the creation of a monster of chaos, who wreaks havoc and death on the community. In the novel and movie *Jurassic Park*, the mad geneticist oversteps the boundary of DNA and lets loose the monsters of chaos in the form of man-eating dinosaurs. These plots tantalize modern audiences because they twang a string deep within our cultural soul, the myth of Prometheus (Peters, 2003, pp. 9–15).

This is a pagan myth. It is not a biblical myth. Even so, the wisdom is not lost on the Bible. The story of the Tower of Babel in Genesis 11 makes a similar point: When we try to storm the gates of heaven by human artifice, we are destined for a big fall. "Pride goes before destruction" (Proverbs 16:18). Having said this, however, it is important to recognize that the phrase "playing God" as used today derives from the resilience of the Promethean myth within western culture, not from Jewish or Christian theology.

The force this myth exerts is to stimulate fear of scientific and technological progress, even to the point of prohibiting some forms of laboratory research. What fits here is the widespread general criticism of nanoenhancement—a criticism which is also voiced by some of its supporters–that enhancement is or will often be practiced with a reckless and selfish short-term perspective that is ignorant of the long-term consequences on individuals and the rest of society. This implies that the hubris of the scientists will blind them to long-term consequences, leading to foolish laboratory recklessness. Those who say we should not play God want to prevent this from happening by erecting a no-trespassing sign on human nature as we know it.

As I have said, this modern myth has replaced the ancient Greek gods with nature, especially human nature. To understand just what playing God could mean in light of projections of nano- or nanobioenhancement, we need to ask whether or not the human nature we have inherited is sacred or unchangeable. On the one hand, if for moral reasons our nature ought not to be changed, then we should put up a no-trespassing sign on our genetic code and brain physiology to keep scientific researchers out. On the other hand, if we observe that human nature is changing naturally, and if we think such a thing as transformation can be a good, then we might look forward to nanotechnology changes as a form of human improvement and an advance toward human well-being.

How should we formulate the ethical issue posed by the transforming potential of nanotechnology and related fields? Should we pose the issue this way: Just how far can we go with our technology before we become guilty of playing God? No. I do not believe this is an illuminating way to pose the ethical issue. Rather, we should ask: How can nanotechnology as well as every other technology enhance our sensitivity and ability to love God and neighbor.

PLAYING GOD WITH HUMAN NATURE

On what grounds should we hold up an ethical vision of loving God and neighbor? Does nature itself tell us such love is what we should value? No. A moral code drawn from naturalistic ethics is not likely to teach us to love. Nature is not likely to teach us that, in order to love, we may need to overcome the limits of nature. An ethics based upon love might lead us to transform what we have inherited in light of a vision of something better. Our high regard for loving comes from theological reflection on God's love, not from nature.

We have noted that the myth of Prometheus or Frankenstein does not derive from theology, either Jewish or Christian theology. At the heart of this myth in its modern form is reverence for nature. Nature, not God, appears to provide the grounding for what is sacred, whether the sacred is given religious labels or not. The commandment against playing God is grounded in a tacit or overt commitment to naturalistic ethics.

The various schools of *naturalistic ethics* theorize that we can reduce all moral concepts to concepts of natural science, usually biology. What is good for the human person or the human race can be reduced to what is "desired" or "satisfying" or "right." (Ewing, 1967, pp. 415–417). Frequently, naturalistic ethicists simply assume that the human nature we have inherited from our long evolutionary ancestry has established what is good for us. The corollary is this: We should not change ourselves any further. What nature has blessed us with is good enough; in fact, it has established what is good for us.

Nature in this case picks up equivocal meaning. On the one hand, nature is what is natural over against what is technological. Nature is what we discover before we alter it through science and technology. On the other hand, nature defines our essence. This natural essence picks up semireligious valence as something almost sacred, inviolable. When the two different meanings are combined, then technological intervention looks like a violation of the sacred. Technology becomes a way of playing God, which is a sin in the eyes of naturalistic ethics.

How do we know what human nature is? How might we know when we have changed it or violated it? The answer most frequently offered is this: intuition. We intuit what is natural. Now, this intuited knowledge could be either rational or emotional. Thomas Aquinas claims it is rational. He said we intuit natural law with our reason through *synderesis*, "the law of our intellect" (*Summa Theologica*, II.i.Q.94, Art. 1). Leon Kass (2002), former chair of President George W. Bush's Council on Bioethics, on the other hand, bypasses reason and goes straight to the emotions, to repugnance (p. 150): "Repugnance is the emotional expression of deep wisdom, beyond reason's power completely to articulate it." What the emotion of repugnance tells us, Kass states, is that we have a nature that is about to be violated by biotechnological alteration. This violation of nature is due to human pride, to hubris, to Prometheus playing God. What we learn from the feeling of repugnance is that genetic technologies such as cloning constitute "the Frankensteinian hubris to create a human life and increasingly to control its destiny: men playing at being God" (Kass, 2002, p. 149).

Whether we appeal to reason or to emotion to discern what nature teaches us, we can learn only what has been the case. We can learn only what we have inherited from the past, from the history of nature. What nature cannot provide is a vision of the transformation of nature, a vision of a future characterized by love. To envision transformation, we must be invited to move toward the future by a transcendent lure. For Christian theologians, the transcendent lure is the love of God imagined as the peaceable kingdom (Isaiah 11) or the city of God (Revelation 24–25) where every creature lives in harmony.

The problem with naturalistic ethics is that, on its own, it cannot justify a vision of the end toward which we should orient our technological development. Nature cannot produce its own ethical vision, its own criterion of what is good. A *description of what is* the case in nature cannot become a *prescription of what ought to be*. What we have learned scientifically about human nature can establish neither a fence against change nor a vision of what the good is that will orient our plan to change. "The criteria for an agent acting for the good cannot come simply from consideration of animal behaviour," writes Celia E. Deane-Drummond (2004). No amount of intuition—either rational or emotional—is sufficient to provide a guiding principle for the human good.

THE ORIENTING GOOD

Philosophers Plato and Aristotle accompanied by theologians Augustine and Thomas Aquinas view *the good* as an end to be pursued, not as a present possession. The good is that for which we aim. It is not something we have inherited. Further, the good toward which we aim transcends who we are as human beings. The good centers in our relationship with God (the God of Israel, not Zeus). Once our relationship with God is secure and profound, then other lesser or mundane goods find their proper orientation and can be appreciated for what they are. Ethics when pursued by Christian theologians begins with our relationship to God and then expands on Jesus' commandment to love God and love neighbor.

The goods toward which nanotechnology and nanobiotechnology are aimed belong in the category of lesser values, proffered by visions that leave God out of the picture.

Yes, indeed, visions of improved neurocognitive abilities are enticing. In themselves, they draw us toward improved human well-being. Yet, it must be observed, none of the nanotechnology scenarios to date have oriented themselves around a vision of our relationship to God or the aim of enhancing our ability to love our neighbor. We even notice that some nanotechnology scenarios assume that the individual person and individual intelligence can be considered apart from relationships with those whom we are obligated to love.

Note what is being said here. We are not basing these ethical deliberations on the naturalist's commandment to avoid playing God. Theologically speaking, the issue is not whether or not we have an inherited human nature that needs to be protected from change. We do not need to protect a mythological human essence. We do not need to fear the advance of scientific research. Rather, what is at stake ethically for the theologian is whether or not a given technology will respond to a transcendent ground for goodness and will enhance our capacity to love.

The Christian faith is not averse to change. In fact, the Christian faith looks forward to transformation. The God of the Bible is a transforming God, one who does new things: "I am about to do a new thing" (NRS Isaiah 43:19). This makes Christian theology quite compatible with envisioned transformations through science and technology. Ian G. Barbour (2002) puts it in terms of continued evolution (p. 70): "Our future is a continuation of evolutionary history and also a continuation of God's project, in which human beings now have a crucial role because of the new powers acquired through science and technology."

Relevant here is the school of *eschatological ethics* within Christian theology. Based upon Jesus' promise of a coming kingdom of God and the New Testament vision of a future new creation, an eschatological orientation toward ethics celebrates transformatory change while trying to guide such change toward wholesome and loving ends. Beyond the "gosh" and "gee whiz" glee of technological advance, the ethicist seeks the betterment of humankind (Gardner, 1986, p. 204): "A social ethic based upon the NT must be built first of all upon the eschatological promise of the coming kingdom rather than on creation or preservation. The relationship of the coming kingdom to creation is dialectical and to a certain extent transformationist"

The future of nanoethics from the point of view of the Christian theologian will ask the question: Can nanotechnology or nanobiotechnology enhance our ability to love God and love our neighbor?

NOTES

1. It is difficult scientifically to posit something like an essential human nature. To believe in "an ideal human type ... makes little sense," says Robert Pollack of Columbia University. It flies "in the face of the first tenet of natural selection, that the survival of a species over the long term will depend above all on the existence of a maximum of variation from individual to individual" (Pollack, 2006, p. 8)

2. The cybernetic immortality described here has nothing whatsoever to do with what Christians understand as "resurrection of the body." What Christians look forward

to (1 Corinthians 15:42–44) is a new creation that includes resurrection of the body in a spiritualized form. It also includes healing. Those who advocate cybernetic immortality assume substance dualism—the split between body and soul—and then seek immortality for the soul (or mind) apart from the body. Christian eschatology is holistic, including body, soul, and spirit.

3. My original analysis of future consciousness in terms of understanding—decision–control was worked out in *Futures—Human and Divine* (Louisville, KY: Westminster John Knox Press, 1978) and *Fear, Faith, and the Future* (Minneapolis, MN: Augsburg Press, 1980).

REFERENCES

Accelerating Future. 2006. Welcome to Accelerating Future. http://www.acceleratingfuture.com

Barbour, I. G. 2002. *Nature, Human Nature, and God*. Minneapolis, MN: Fortress Press.

d'Aquili, E., and Newberg, A. B. 1999. *The Mystical Mind: Probing the Biology of Religious Experience*. Minneapolis, MN: Fortress Press.

Deane-Drummond, C.E. 2004. *The Ethics of Nature: New Dimensions to Religious Ethics*. Malden, MA: Blackwell.

Enhancement Technologies Group. 2006. The Aims of the Group. http://www.ucl.ac.uk/~ucbtdag/bioethics/layintro.html

Ewing, A. C. 1967. Naturalistic ethics. In J. F. Childress and J. Macquarrie (Eds.), *The Westminster Dictionary of Christian Ethics* (1986). Louisville KY: Westminster John Knox Press.

Gardner, E. C. 1986. Eschatological ethics. In J. F. Childress and J. Macquarrie (Eds.), *Westminster Dictionary of Christian Ethics*. Louisuille, KY: Westminister John Knox Press.

Herzfeld, N. 2002. *In Our Image: Artificial Intelligence and the Human Spirit*. Minneapolis, MN: Fortress Press.

Kass, L. 2002. *Life, Liberty, and the Defense of Dignity*. San Francisco: Encounter Books.

Kurzweil, R. 1999. *The Age of Spiritual Machines*. New York: Viking.

Lin, P., and Allhoff, F. 2006. Nanoethics and human enhancement: A critical evaluation of recent arguments. Available: http://www.nanoethics.org/paper032706.html, accessed June 1, 2006.

Neville, R. C. 1997. Is there an essence of human nature? In L. S. Rouner (Ed.), *Is There A Human Nature?* Notre Dame IN: University of Notre Dame Press, pp. 107–108.

Pannenberg, W. 1991–1998. *Systematic Theology*, translated by G. Bromiley, 3 volumes. Grand Rapids, MI: William B. Eerdmans.

Peters, T. 2003. *Playing God? Genetic Determinism and Human Freedom*, 2nd ed. London and New York: Routledge.

Peterson, G. R. 2003. *Minding God: Theology and the Cognitive Sciences*. Minneapolis, MN: Fortress Press.

Pollack, R. E. 2006. "The Price of Science without Moral Constraints," *Cross Currents*, 56: 1 (Spring 2006).

Wolpe, P. R. 2002. Neurotechnology, cyborgs, and the sense of self. In S. J. Marcus (Ed.), *Neuroethics: Mapping the Field*. New York: Dana Press.

14

ANTICIPATING THE ETHICAL AND POLITICAL CHALLENGES OF HUMAN NANOTECHNOLOGIES*

David H. Guston, John Parsi, and Justin Tosi

INTRODUCTION

Nanotechnologies, as part of a set of converging technologies including biotechnology, information technology, and cognitive science (NBIC), are strongly implicated in expectations of the physical and cognitive enhancements of human beings (Roco and Bainbridge, 2002). Through a variety of plausible mechanisms including pharmaceuticals, nano-enabled neural implants, and brain stimulation, the NBIC enhancement of human beings may allow for the greater exercise of human freedoms, but it holds potential for undermining liberal democratic values as well. In this fundamental ambiguity, such technologies require a significant degree of scrutiny—part of a process that we call "anticipatory governance."

This chapter will challenge an emergent but common framing of such issues as a clash between religious values that would constrain human enhancement technologies and scientific values that would promote them. Instead, we shift the terrain to an explicitly political framing in which both these sets of values are important but are subordinate to concerns about democracy itself. We then examine what integrated human nanotechnologies might mean for the boundaries of some important democratic values, including

*The authors would like to thank Sean Hays, Jason Robert, Ben Thelen, and Jamey Wetmore, as well as the editors, for their helpful comments. Any remaining oversights or errors are, of course, our own.

Nanoethics: The Ethical and Social Implications of Nanotechnology. Edited by Allhoff, Lin, Moor, Weckert
Copyright © 2007 John Wiley & Sons, Inc.

personal choice, autonomy, and political pluralism. The chapter will also categorize a variety of plausible concerns regarding human enhancements, for example, challenging some of the conditions of free will that are also necessary for political freedom; undermining freedom of choice or conscience; eroding freedom of action by leaving individuals to make poor short-term choices or rendering them merely bystanders to, rather than participants in, their own behavior; and undercutting pluralism by delegitimating multiple perspectives of human good, ability, and achievement. The purpose of these explorations is not to argue against human enhancement per se but rather to provide an ethical and political assessment of its challenges that some current perspectives elide.

Because of the brief space allotted, we dispense with an extended discussion of the kinds of nanotechnologies implicated in human enhancement. It should suffice to make several brief observations:

1. There are many extant technologies, external to the human body, that enhance its capabilities, and trends in NBIC to reduce their size and power requirements and to improve human–machine interfaces mean that many of them will end up internal to the human body.
2. Society has experience with other human technologies, including transgender technologies, steroids and other drugs, and prosthetics and biomechanical devices, all of which provide helpful if not dispositive evidence to how individuals and society will behave with NBIC-related human enhancements.
3. The debate about such human enhancements has already been joined, regardless of the specific nature of the technologies at issue; it is our purpose to attend to that debate rather than to the ethical or political status of any particular technological enhancement that may or may not develop.

RELIGION VERSUS SCIENCE FRAME

A major and highly public facet of discussions about the ethics of advances in and applications of NBIC-related human enhancement can loosely be categorized as a debate between condemnation from a religious or quasi-religious perspective and unreflective endorsement of scientific and technical change. Lin and Allhoff (2006, p. 47) explain this schism: "For some, nanotechnology holds the promise of making us superhuman; for others, it offers a darker path toward becoming Frankenstein's monster." This more than vaguely Manichean discourse limits ethical exploration of and deliberation on human enhancement and, indeed, is part of the inspiration for this volume.

Examples of religiously inspired opposition to human enhancement are rife, but none is of higher profile than *Beyond Therapy*, a report drafted by the President's Council on Bioethics 2003 chaired by Leon Kass. The report, critical of human technologies that go "beyond therapy," deploys language with overt religious symbolism to criticize enhancements (p. 7): "Not everyone cheers a summons to a 'post-human' future. Not everyone likes the idea of 'remaking Eden' or 'man playing God.' Not everyone agrees that this prophesied new world will be better than our own." Both by utilizing a religious discourse and framing the opposition as centering on religious concerns, the council's discourse polarizes discussion about ethical approaches to human enhancement and limits the scope of critical engagement to religious aversion to changing human beings.

Beyond Therapy extends its framing by questioning the ends of human advancement through technology, but it again focuses on premises related to religious values because such advancement undermines "excellent activity" and "hard work." This argument, strongly linked to the Protestant ethic (Weber, 2002), holds that hard work is necessary and that such excellent activity is a sign of personal moral resolve or favor of the deity. Human technologies undermine both the necessity of hard work and its connection to the appearance of grace. Moreover, the moral advantages of such pursuits are lost with human enhancement for, according to *Beyond Therapy*, "character is not only the source of our deeds, but also their product" (Weber, 2002) NBIC-related human technologies may not merely be immoral in themselves, but they will lead individuals to be immoral because the intrinsic benefits (and external appearances) of doing work vanish with such easy and materialistic transformation.[1]

Advocates of human enhancement also pursue a framework that traps discussion between dire religious warnings and unbridled scientific acceptance. In contrast to the Kass report, and in fact a response to it, Ramez Naam (2005) argues that advancing human technology is natural and ought not to be obstructed (p. 9): "Far from being unnatural, the drive to alter and improve ourselves is a fundamental part of who we as humans are." Naam's argument also focuses on an alleged continuity between previous and current beneficial advances from medical technology and the promise of NBIC human technologies (p. 9): "Many past enhancements that we now take for granted—from blood transfusions to vaccinations to birth control—were called unnatural or immoral when they were first introduced." These comparisons intend to illustrate that criticism of the new is unjustified because scientific progress inevitably leads to benefits that are easily integrated into and do not undermine society.[2]

Many advocates of human technological enhancement embrace a rhetorical frame that places religion in opposition to science, because they then only need to limit their responses to this field which, they believe, is tilted in their favor. By emphasizing a history of the emergence of contemporary medical practice from an earlier, darker era of religious taboos to medical inquiry and interventions, they establish their version of the dichotomy between enlightened scientific progress and dogmatic religious opposition.

Both sides thus provide a vision of human technological enhancement that overdraws a conflict between religious and scientific values and, consequently, evades discussion of broader ethical and political dimensions. The necessity of such a broader discussion is particularly evident when advocates of technological enhancement make carte blanche claims to autonomy, as expressed though technological enhancement; James Hughes (O'Connell, 2006), executive director of the World Transhumanist Association—a leading advocacy group for human enhancement—argues that "cultural anxieties and religious or moral objections [are] illegitimate reasons for stripping individuals of control over their bodies and minds." While Hughes may or may not be correct about the legitimacy of religious-based restrictions on individual autonomy, his framing of the debate in sympathy with those who would claim religious framings undermines more complex examination of questions of autonomy. Reduced to religious opposition versus scientific endorsement, the debate becomes less compelling and lacks philosophical and ethical rigor.

POLITICAL FRAME FOR DEBATE

We wish not only to avoid the religious-versus-scientific framing of the human enhancement debate but also to offer an alternative. We are, in fact, sympathetic with Hughes's attempt to create a more political framing of these issues in his book *Citizen Cyborg* (Hughes, 2004). But whereas Hughes sees a seamless alliance of scientific inquiry and liberal democracy in opposition to religious values, we take a different perspective: Liberal democratic values are core, and science and religion are each in potential cooperation or potential conflict with them. We are thus skeptical of Hughes's unequivocal call to "embrace the transhuman technologies" as part of our right to control our bodies even "while proposing democratic ways to manage them and reduce their risks." Hughes's emphasis misses the lexical priority of democratic values that we propose. This is not to say that we believe that liberal democracies ought to treat science and religion the same. But it is rather to recognize that there are limits to the compatibility of liberal democratic thought and practice with either science or religion.

Our intent here is to examine three sets of values in regard to human technological enhancement: political–economic issues, questions of autonomy and freedom, and questions of pluralism. As political scientists, we have some stake in this shift, to be sure, but we believe it will bring more productive inquiry and dialogue around important questions obscured by the dichotomy of science versus religion. The reader will have to decide whether to acknowledge this pragmatism more than any disciplinary chauvinism.

Our brief list of issues is meant to be neither an exhaustive enumeration nor a complete examination but rather an initial foray into some areas in which politics, autonomy, and pluralism ought to be considered in conjunction with human enhancement technologies. Furthermore, we should note that one determination of our contribution is that it is necessary to explore such positions even prior to the manifestation of any particular technology that might concern us (Berne, 2005). There are at least three interrelated rationales for this necessity: First, as the transhumanist advocates point out, current or anticipated enhancement technologies are not unprecedented. But the lack of complete novelty on the part of such technologies does not render them ethically simple, and anticipating them may invite us to reexamine the ethical aspects of those precedents. Second, such human enhancement technologies are liable to influence the lives of virtually all of us—whether, as the transhumanists envision by continuing the trajectory of eyeglasses, heart valves, and hip replacements or as the religious-based opponents envision by transgressing communal values. Thus, all of us, scientists and nonscientists alike, share responsibility for these developments. Third—and here we offer what might be a novel but controversial insight—scientific researchers and technologists become engaged in dialogue with the social system much sooner when the repercussions of their work are conceived as not merely material but political and ethical. Well before knowledge-based innovation may have an actual impact on the ability of human beings to overcome accidental or inherent limitations to their cognitive, emotional, or physical abilities, the reality of those explorations as an agenda—an embodiment of social priorities, values, and aspirations—will influence how members of society conceive of their identities and their prospects within a society that has such an agenda. To the extent, then, that researchers set their own agendas, they bear responsibility for the impacts of not just their work but their intentions, and they are therefore obliged to a more engaged and productive role than benign neglect.

This frame that emphasizes both the ethical and the political pushes responsibility "upstream" into earlier explorations of knowledge-based technologies (Wilsdon and Willis, 2004). We call this process of prior exploration "anticipatory governance," and it refers not just to attempts at the anticipation or foresight of societal issues related to knowledge-based technologies but also to their governance or management by society broadly. Because of the wide distribution of expertise and practice in society, anticipatory governance perforce commences with exploration, participation, and deliberation.[3] It ends with a wide array of potential actions by governments, private-sector (for-profit and not-for-profit) groups, and third-sector organizations directed at rendering the knowledge-based technology subject to explicit, deliberate, and democratic choice and not to the whim of a narrow set of elites or a series of accidental pathways. Our attention to political–economic considerations, autonomy and freedom, and pluralism is a beginning of anticipatory governance and leads to a conclusion that discusses some governing activities based on our analysis.

POLITICAL–ECONOMIC CONSIDERATIONS

Here we discuss three important propositions relevant to the role of technological advance and considerations of distributional politics. The prospect that human enhancement through NBIC technologies will abide by these propositions is a potentially disturbing one for the democratic values we take as prior to scientific or religious ones.

First, the distribution of new technologies often follows the current pattern of the distribution of wealth in society. There has been a growing gap between the rich and poor both within the United States and between the developed and the developing world. There is no particular reason to believe that human technological enhancements will be distributed by any other means than the ability to pay and, in an economy that already has a highly skewed distribution of wealth, the initial distribution of enhancements among successful individuals raises the prospect of a cumulative and permanent advantage that could be hostile to democratic values. Such technologies may well be used to help individuals overcome the effects of initial genetic and social endowments that currently contribute to this skewing; indeed, a great portion of the relevant research is directed at rendering those with profound cognitive disabilities capable of functioning well and independently in society and thus better off both absolutely and relatively. But we also know that the recreational and cosmetic uses—as opposed to therapeutic uses—of psychoactive or performance-enhancing drugs and plastic surgery are a significant part of their political economies, and we know that the demarcation between therapeutic use and enhancement is a subtle and often troubling one. Even if such new technologies are targeted well at therapeutic uses, they will likely be targeted at therapies important for and functional in the social systems of the developed world, rather than in the social systems of the developing world. In many instances, "our" therapy may still be "their" enhancement. The current context thus combines a known and troubling set of political issues: the distribution of income and access, the regular pursuit of nontherapeutic uses, an indistinct boundary between therapy and enhancement, and mismatches between the priorities of the developed and developing world.

Second, new technologies tend to benefit the "haves" in society prior to benefiting the "have-nots." This temporal staging of benefits is conceptually distinct from the more general distribution issues above and particularly troubling with respect to enhancements. A tight correlation between specific enhancements, for example, intelligence and social skills like communication and persuasion, and specific capacities that society rewards highly raises the possibility of first-mover advantages that would be hard to overcome and hostile to democratic politics. Imagine an NBIC enhancement that would allow humans to download information directly into their brains through implanted biochips. The market value for such enhanced lawyers, lobbyists, CEOs, financial analysts, professors (!), and other such professionals would be extremely high, rendering the current "star system" of highly paid white collar workers pale by comparison and competition between enhanced and unenhanced job candidates in such fields meaningless. Imagine an NBIC enhancement that would extend quality years of human life spans. Beyond questions of whose life would be extended and what the social costs of having more elderly, even if healthy, people might be, there are questions that sound almost trivial but have real political import: In the U.S. Congress, where incumbency renders a huge advantage, life-span-enhanced politicians might become nearly invincible incumbents. In the private sector, although the corporation is a legal person that can live forever if well governed, life-span-enhanced CEOs could lord over their financial empires for generations. In either case, the greater identification of the office with the individual inhabiting it—rather than, say, with the political constituency or with the firm's shareholders or employees—is easily foreseen as detrimental to the spirit of democratic politics. The wealthy and powerful in society may have early access to enhancement technologies that can be easily anticipated to make them more wealthy and powerful prior to a broader distribution that might be hoped to help level the playing field.

Third, when technologies fail, they tend to reveal the ways that they have interacted with and reinforced social difference even more starkly. The failure of the technological system of levees in Louisiana after hurricane Katrina, which left victims dead and neighborhoods demolished along class and racial lines, demonstrated this principle plainly. While it is harder to envision how not-yet-extant technologies will fail than it is to envision how they will succeed, we might learn again from current enhancement technologies. For example, performance-enhancing drugs fail or, rather, contribute to a failed system around them by perverting fair competition—in school testing, in amateur and professional sports, and who knows where else. As with our current enhancement technologies, will we know in the future which students are enhanced and which are not? Which athletes? Which candidates for political office? A minor scandal flared in the United States in 2004 when a photograph appeared to show what might have been a radio receiver beneath President George W. Bush's jacket during one of that campaign's debates with Senator John Kerry. The soon-to-arrive capability to easily implant such a receiver severely tries many of our presumptions about debate, deliberation, and the power of reason in the public sphere. What will we think of the concept of fair competition—in academics, athletics, or politics—when the very qualities we judge and are judged by are the ones that privileged, unscrupulous, or simply highly competitive people can add to their portfolio of talents on a whim and a credit card?

Note that these brief arguments do not appeal to religious values on the one hand or vague notions of the progress of science on the other. They appeal to concepts like transparency, fairness in competition, and the distinction between economic worth and social value. These are notions that, we argue, are more important to democracy than either religious values or scientific freedom and, likely, more widely shared.

Such considerations regarding the use and distribution of human enhancement technologies give renewed importance to Rawls's (1999) ideas of "justice as fairness" and, in particular, the "maximin" principle, which holds that the basic structure of society should be organized to provide the maximum benefit to the most disadvantaged. Indeed, Rawls anticipated the debate over the use of human enhancement to effect a more equitable distribution of natural assets (by which he means abilities, intelligence, strength, etc.).[4] He noted that his maximin principle defends the greater natural assets of some as "a social asset to be used for the common advantage" (Rawls, 1999, p. 92) rather than unfair individual advantages to be reduced. The maximin principle also suggests that the least advantaged members of society deserve greater natural assets, as these provide them with greater capacity to pursue their chosen plan of life. Rawls even speculates that "if there is an upper bound on ability, we would eventually reach a society with the greatest equal liberty the members of which enjoy the greatest equal talent" (pp. 92–93). From a Rawlsian perspective, a just society not only would endorse therapeutic NBIC technologies but also might endorse enhancing ones as long as they are aimed at improving the lot of the least well-off either directly through enhancement or indirectly through benefits from enhancing others. But as we have yet to achieve such a goal for life-saving medicines, or food, or shelter, it seems a more than plausible irony that—using the promise of accessible medical benefits of enhancement technologies as an inducement for public support—transhumanists may very well establish the basis of a sociopolitical system that would increasingly skew the benefits to the few.[5]

AUTONOMY AND FREEDOM

Despite the framing of human technological enhancement as a manifestation of autonomy and freedom, its portrayal as in tension only with religious strictures obscures its more critical tension with different, and more democratic, senses of freedom. If human enhancements include cognitive ones, then the freedom at stake includes not only political freedom but also freedom of the will. Following Philip Pettit's (2001) theory of free subjects, which covers both the psychological and political conditions of freedom, we hold that in order to be free, agents must: (1) be able to choose their actions and beliefs guided by reason and their values, (2) identify with their actions as a participant rather than as a bystander, and (3) have security against domination from others who would exert pressure on them to influence their choice. While human enhancement could be a valuable tool for ensuring these conditions, it could also undermine them.

Human technological enhancements could improve or degrade the psychological ability to choose one's actions and beliefs. Enhancements could improve this capacity in persons with depression, for example, by directly regulating their serotonin levels to combat the muddled thought that often interferes with rational decision making in depression sufferers. Or, in a current example, sexual reassignment surgery can render one's self-perception more congruent with social perceptions and thus create a greater array of real-life options. Other enhancements might frustrate one's ability to make such choices freely. These might include enhancements that lead people to hold certain values or have certain desires, for example, the current "war on terror" could inspire the development of a citizen chip to facilitate an unswerving patriotism.[6] Behavior-altering enhancements also interfere with the free choice of actions. For someone to make a free choice of a belief or action, they must be fit to be held responsible for each step in the cognitive process leading to their final choice. But if, first, an enhancement interferes with, alters, or takes control of a step in one's deliberative process, the status of the resulting choice as "free" is brought into question. These examples also raise serious questions about symmetry and reversibility of enhancements: Will such enhancements be technically reversible? Will they leave residual habits of mind attuned to the enhancements, even if the enhancements are removed? Will enhanced individuals fully understand the differences in their lives and selves created by the enhancements?

Much the same is true of the challenge human enhancement presents to the second condition of being a participant in choosing one's actions rather than a bystander to those choices. Traditionally, humans can claim authorship of their own actions, seeing themselves as participants in the way the action unfolds. But enhanced humans may not be able to make such a claim, because even the possibility that an enhancement was responsible for their action turns them into bystanders contemplating that possibility rather than participants who enact it. One might never be sure that one has eliminated the influence of an enhancement from one's deliberations, for each impulse to accept or reject some reason could come from an effect of the enhancement. Consider the case of a steroid user who is enraged by a slight wrong. How much of a reaction is prompted by a rationally defensible sense of self-respect and indignation at being wronged and how much by the side effects of the enhancement? While it may or may not be the case that the ability to claim authorship of one's actions is an "all-or-nothing" proposition, the question of authorship—especially given unintended consequences and a legal system that emphasizes the role of intent and premeditation—is an important challenge.

Human enhancement could also present problems for the third condition of freedom, nondomination. The ability of individuals to select their own technological enhancements, absent external pressures, could be a great boon to individual liberty. But direct and even indirect exercises of power could render such enhancements tools of domination. On one hand, individuals making free choices about their own technological enhancements might be subject to social scorn or even state sanctions as deviants. This possibility is suggested, for example, by social and legal challenges that individuals who pursue sexual reassignment surgery face.[7]

On the other hand, one can imagine any number of situations in which individuals or groups might be pressed, overtly or subtly, into accepting enhancements. Market forces might make job-specific enhancements de facto compulsory, the way many athletes feel pressed into the use of steroids, human growth hormone, and blood doping. Governments might demand certain enhancements as requirements for citizenship, for example, national identity cards or passports could be nano-enabled in-body/on-body sensors. Similarly the exercise of certain liberties could be limited by governments, as public schools require vaccinations on the one hand or the purchase of technologies like laptop computers on the other. Private associations might demand enhancements as conditions of membership or recognition, for example, universities requiring students to have enhancements (like the implanted identity card) that made cheating less possible. It is even possible for individuals to interfere with their own freedom by accepting enhancements that have side effects that undermine their capacity for free thought and free choice of action, as discussed earlier in this section. Both the high stakes and the breadth of contexts in which domination by the more powerful might occur call for the cautious and anticipatory governance of enhancement technologies.

PLURALISM AND HUMAN *TELOS*

Pluralism is the idea that a good human life need not consist of any particular set of goods, practices, or values. Rather, the contents of a good life will differ across cultures, and even individuals within cultures, and it is up to each culture or individual to determine and pursue a conception of the good for itself. Pluralism is centrally important to the liberal tradition in political thought because of its connection to human autonomy and a free and robust civil society and its implicit limits on the power of the state. Pluralism also denies the existence of a definitive human *telos*, or purpose—either for an individual or for humanity as a whole. Pluralists hold, however, that persons individually or in groups voluntarily define their own *telos*.

Claims about the *telos* of human life conflict with pluralism in two ways: First, such claims propose an exclusive set of goods that a good human life must include. Second, these goods are supposed to be part of the purpose of a human life, they are given rather than chosen. Whereas a pluralistic understanding of the human good allows cultures or individuals to choose their own goods, a teleological understanding insists that such goods exist prior to anyone's preferences.

While it is not necessary to delve very deep into this debate, it is helpful to examine briefly the kinds of reasons one might give for rejecting the idea of a human *telos*. First, in recognizing our epistemic limitations, one might argue that even if there is a single human good, we could not possibly identify it. And we certainly could not be so confident in our estimation of the human good that we would feel comfortable imposing it on everyone. Given these limits, it seems reasonable to defer to each person's individual judgment of what is best for him or her. Second, we in fact observe pervasive cultural and biological differences among persons that do not seem compatible with one essential human purpose. It is plausible that a single person could take any one of several vastly different paths and be said to have led a good life. Individual persons and cultures are most closely acquainted with themselves and what is most conducive to their own well-being, and so they are in the best position to identify their own good.[8]

While human technological enhancements promise to enhance pluralism by multiplying the ways that humans may interact with their instruments and with the environment, there are also clearly developments that would challenge pluralist conceptions. For example, human technological enhancements may very well severely narrow the scope of what's held as good. Current therapies for cognitive or behavioral conditions (e.g., attention deficit disorder, social anxiety disorder) promote convergence on a single model of human cognition or behavior. We have no reason to expect that human technological enhancements would not force that convergence more narrowly still, focusing on a single good way to think or be.

A second example is human enhancement in the realm of sex and gender. *The International Statistical Classification of Diseases and Related Health Problems* identifies gender identity disorder, suggesting that sex, as a biological condition, is congruent with gender, a social construct. The medically prescribed treatment for gender identity disorder, sexual reassignment surgery, further enforces the notion that gender and sex are tied to one another, reducing what might be a more pluralistic set of options to those two in which sex and gender correspond. Moreover, sexual reassignment surgery may create limits in the patient's ability to choose how to act after making their gender and sex congruous, in turn feeding social pressures and reifying the correspondence of gender and sex.

But the problem may be deeper than any small set of examples. As we pointed out above, the central premise of arguments against a human *telos*, and thus for pluralism, will be an appeal to either (1) the impossibility of knowing the purpose of a human life or (2) the implausibility of the notion that there is a single good or purpose for an individual. Human technological enhancements carry the possibility of creating a more knowable end for humans that would undermine these premises. When one applies a human enhancement, one does so in order to make the person receiving the enhancement better suited to a specific kind of activity. Given the purposive nature of such enhancements, it seems that one who receives enough or very precise enhancements could be said to have an identifiable *telos*. More specifically, those responsible for enhancing that person will have a special perspective from which to make claims about that *telos*. Thus, human enhancements could lend credence to the paternalistic and antipluralist claim that some people know what is best for others.

The force of these examples seems to rely on the worry that human technological enhancements would change a person's capacities, which the value of self-realization would then demand that they develop. It is true that such changes in individual capacities do not require technological interventions—education and other common cultural practices involving habituation also change the way individuals' brains develop, with consequences for their capacities and, plausibly, subsequent self-realization. But it is also true that we, first, have vastly more experience with these more social interventions; second, rarely think about education and training from this particular political and ethical perspective; and third, when we do, we are able identify techniques like propaganda, indoctrination, and so forth that raise similar problems.

CONCLUSION

We have attempted to offer in this chapter a reframing of the discussion of human technological enhancement as a political discussion focused on democratic values rather than as a conflict between religious and scientific values. We have highlighted three general areas of the political economy of enhancements, issues of freedom and autonomy, and issues of pluralism that emerge from this more political framing. Each of these areas demonstrates the subtlety and ambiguity of human technological enhancements—that while it may offer benefits that correspond with democratic values, many problems from this same perspective are apparent. The framing of the debate over human technological enhancement as a battle between scientific values and religious ones prevents the more nuanced exploration of these subtle and ambiguous consequences. It also prevents using the possibility of technological change to reexamine contemporary arrangements of values and technological capabilities. That is, when we look at current practices of human cognitive or behavioral interventions through the lens of what future capacities might mean for democratic values, we may value them differently than we would by looking at them either as part of an ongoing conflict between science and religion or as merely incremental extensions of earlier technologies.

In this effort at reframing, we hope that the chapter has provided a provocative sense of the "anticipation" of anticipatory governance—that is, a slice of the forethought and deliberation that must serve as a background for decision making and institutional design. It is exactly these provocative complications that demand a more subtle and political framing than "religion versus science" admits as well as the kind of robust investigation and deliberation that anticipatory governance calls for.

The "governance" aspect must await a new forum for a similar explication, but one could imagine from the discussion what kinds of mechanisms might be explored: research-based mechanisms to investigate the reversibility of human technological enhancements, in terms of removable implants but also reversible habits of mind; technology-based governance mechanisms to cause significant enhancements to expire occasionally and offer the opportunity for reflective renewal; and social-based governance mechanisms to provide guidelines for use, prescriptions, age requirements, mental and psychological preparations, or time off for reflective renewal.

We hope that future discussions would begin from the premise that nanotechnology-enabled human technological enhancements are ethically and politically challenging from a democratic perspective and would begin to elaborate in detail some of these governance mechanisms.

NOTES

1. There are nonreligious perspectives on the problem of work, activity, and striving, e.g., Nozick's (1977) discussion of the "transformation machine." The problem may perhaps best be appreciated by the example of "Calvinball" —the game played by cartoon characters Calvin and Hobbes in which the players can change the rules of the

game at any time. If the limitations of life were like the rules in Calvinball, someone like Nozick might ask if there would be anything left for people to do.

2. Ironically, The President's Council on Bioethics examines the widespread use of birth control and other medical advancements as signs of the deleterious, although at times unintended, consequences of advancing human technology.

3. These functions are represented in what Guston and Sarewitz 2002 call "real-time technology assessment," an approach embodied in the NSF-funded Center for Nanotechnology in Society at ASU with which the authors are affiliated.

4. It should be noted, however, that Rawls confines his remarks to ensuring the best possible genetic endowment for descendents—a topic in intergenerational justice.

5. Indeed, some observers see exactly this injustice in the California stem cell initiative. See Sarewitz (2004).

6. These examples are overt actions with specific goals that provide such challenges to individuals and societies. Contemporary examples suggest that unintended consequences may raise challenges for organizations as well; e.g., the provision by the Naval Academy of cost-free corrective eye surgery has increased the number of potentially qualified pilots but decreased the number of qualified sailors interested in submarine duty.

7. For example, in many jurisdictions, individuals are allowed to undergo sexual reassignment surgery, but they are not then entitled to all the rights and privileges of their newly acquired gender, including, in some instances, marrying as a person of their acquired gender.

8. Less optimistically, one might claim that there is no human good or purpose at all and each person is left in existential struggle with his or her own life's project.

REFERENCES

Berne, R. W. 2005. *Nanotalk: Conversations with Scientists and Engineers About Ethics, Meaning, and Belief in the Development of Nanotechnology*. Mahwah, NJ: Lawrence Erlbaum.

Guston, D., and Sarewitz, D. 2002. Real-time technology assessment. *Technology in Society* 24(1/2): 93–109.

Hughes, J. 2004. *Citizen Cyborg: Why Democratic Societies Must Respond to the Redesigned Human of the Future*. Boulder, CO: Westview Press.

Lin, P., and Allhoff, F. 2006. Nanoethics and human enhancement: A critical evaluation of recent arguments. *Nanotechnology Perceptions* 2 (1): 47–52.

Naam, R. 2005. *More Than Human: Embracing the Promise of Biological Enhancement*. New York: Broadway Books.

Nozick, R. 1977. *Anarchy, State, and Utopia*. New York: Basic Books.

O'Connell, M. A. (2006). Human enhancement: Problem or solution? Available: http://news.monstersandcritics.com/lifestyle/consumerhealth, accessed June 7, 2006.

Pettit, P. 2001. *A Theory of Freedom: From the Psychology to the Politics of Agency*. Oxford: Oxford University Press.

President's Council on Bioethics. 2003. *Beyond Therapy: Biotechnology and the Pursuit of Happiness*. PR 43.8B 52/T 34.

Rawls, J. A. 1999. *A Theory of Justice*. Cambridge: Harvard University Press.

Roco, M. C., and Bainbridge, W. S. 2002. *Converging Technologies for Improving Human Performance: Nanotechnology, Biotechnology, Information Technology and Cognitive Science*. Arlington, VA: National Science Foundation/Department of Commerce.

Sarewitz, D. 2004. Stepping out of line in stem cell research. *Los Angeles Times*, October 25, p. B11.

Weber, M. (2002). *The Protestant Ethic and the Spirit of Capitalism*, 3rd ed., S. Kalberg, trans. Los Angeles: Roxbury.

Wilsdon, J., and Willis, R. 2004. *See-Through Science*. London: Demos.

PART V

ISSUES: DEMOCRACY AND POLICY

James Moor

Whatever problem in nanotechnology concerns us—be it damage to health or threat to privacy from nanoscale electronics or runaway nanobots—we will likely need to develop some kind of policy as a society to deal with it. In the context of a democracy, what kind of policies should we select and how should we select them?

One of the most frightening scenarios of the nanotechnological future is the creation of robots at the nanoscale that can self-replicate and pursue some courses of action that are destructive to human beings; this is the so-called gray goo threat. Bill Joy (Chapter 2) offers such an apocalyptic vision of our scientific future. In Chapter 15, bioethicist and sociologist James Hughes agrees with Joy that the threat is real, discussing cases of bioweapons, nanogoos, and killer robots as examples. However, Hughes disagrees that relinquishment is the answer; rather, he argues that these technologies can be regulated through transnational regulations and agencies empowered to verify and enforce these regulations. He suggests that we will need a surveillance regimen to do this that is even more invasive than the one attempted for the surveillance of nuclear power under the International Atomic Energy Agency (IAEA)—a proposal that understandably faces significant challenges related to such broad interests from commercial advantages to military secrecy.

In Chapter 16, political philosopher Colin Farrelly suggests that the regulation mechanism for controlling nanotechnology should come out of "deliberative democracy" : A deliberative democratic debate seeks a reasonable balance among conflicting

Nanoethics: The Ethical and Social Implications of Nanotechnology. Edited by Allhoff, Lin, Moor, Weckert
Copyright © 2007 John Wiley & Sons, Inc.

fundamental values. In order to keep nanotechnology in check, responsible legislative activism is required. This in turn will require a well-informed and reflective citizenry. Deliberative democracy is not simply a show of hands but rather a decision that results from careful, rational debate that is sensitive to a range of values and approaches. Further, the decisions and policies arising from deliberative democracy are treated as provisional outcomes, subject to reconsideration and revision at a later time.

Deliberative democracy hits upon the core of the democracy, namely participation by citizens. Nanotechnology is already acutely aware of lessons learned from biotechnology: By not engaging the public earlier, biotechnology invited and suffered an enormous public backlash over genetically modified foods, which stalled progress and suggested the lesson that technology might best—or most efficiently or responsibly—proceed tightly in step with public education and feedback rather than in a vacuum without or prior to it.

These events explain why there is such a strong focus today on public engagement as a way to help guide nanotechnology. But what does "public engagement" really mean and hope to accomplish? In Chapter 17, University of South Carolina's David Berube examines the widely used but arguably ambiguous concepts of a "stakeholder" and "the public." He argues that there are many senses of public that need to be considered. Moreover, distinctions among stakeholders are needed because some stakeholders are more involved than others. He believes that, contrary to initial appearances, these concepts are used often as rhetorical hammers to prevent criticism and to avoid real debate.

In Chapter 18, from U.K. think-tank Demos, Jack Stilgoe and James Wilsdon offer a specific case study of public engagement, exploring the particular issue of whether the government should allow the use of nanoparticles as a method of cleaning up contaminated land. They describe some encouraging results of scientists and the public meeting to discuss emerging technologies. The differences in knowledge did not prevent the free flow of conversation in these public meetings, yet Stilgoe and Wilsdon emphasize that more thought needs to be given to the why, who, how, what, and when of public engagement as well as their importance with regard to nanotechnology as opposed to other technologies. Given the prominent role of the public in democracy, these challenges to the enterprise of public engagement are also challenges to the democratic process itself.

15

GLOBAL TECHNOLOGY REGULATION AND POTENTIALLY APOCALYPTIC TECHNOLOGICAL THREATS

James J. Hughes

"Dad, what if there is no future?"

—Tristan Bock-Hughes, age 6

THREAT OF SELF-REPLICATING TECHNOLOGIES

In April 2000, Bill Joy, the chief technologist and cofounder of Sun Microsystems and inventor of the computer language Java, published a Luddite jeremiad in the unlikeliest of places, the militantly protechnology *Wired* magazine. Joy had developed a serious case of anticipatory doom as he contemplated the potentially apocalyptic consequences of three technologies: genetic engineering, nanotechnology, and robots imbued with artificial intelligence (AI). The key and qualitatively different threat that Joy saw in these technologies was that they all can potentially self-replicate. While guns don't breed other guns and go on killing sprees, gene-tailored plagues, future robots, and nanophages can theoretically do just that.

Joy concluded that we need to return to the peace movement's effort to have all nations renounce the development of weapons of mass destruction and apply it now to genetic, molecular, and AI research: "These technologies are too powerful to be

Nanoethics: The Ethical and Social Implications of Nanotechnology. Edited by Allhoff, Lin, Moor, Weckert
Copyright © 2007 John Wiley & Sons, Inc.

shielded against in the time frame of interest.... The only realistic alternative I see is relinquishment: to limit development of the technologies that are too dangerous, by limiting our pursuit of certain kinds of knowledge" (Joy, 2000; Chapter 2). Joy's call for relinquishment has had little effect on policy deliberation but has added weight to the growing neo-Luddite movement against nano- and biotechnology. In this chapter, I want to both endorse Joy's concern over the potentially apocalyptic consequences of these emerging technologies and explain why Joy's proposal for global relinquishment of these technologies is not a useful proposal and suggest a global regulatory alternative.

Threat Is Real

First, however, it is important to acknowledge that these technologies do pose potentially apocalyptic threats.

Bioweapons. The intentional design of bacterial and viral weapons began in a large way in the 1960s in the United States and the Soviet Union. In the 1980s the techniques for recombinant redesign of viruses and bacteria became available, and those techniques were applied to smallpox and other vectors before the collapse of the Soviet scientific infrastructure. Today, many nations and organizations have access to the technical knowledge and tools necessary to begin a program of bioweapons research, in particular experiments with genetic manipulation of biological agents (Williams, 2006; Chyba, 2006).

The genomes of influenza, plague, anthrax, SARS, pneumonia, and other pathogens have been sequenced and are in the public domain. Using this information, novel organisms could be designed to combine the virulence, latency, and lethality of previous pathogens, to only attack specific races or body parts, or to be resistant to antibiotics and antiseptic methods. The Soviet bioweapons program explored combinations of strains of anthrax, smallpox, plague, and Ebola (Williams, 2006). Warnings about gene-tailored bioweapons generated a biodefense program under U.S. President Clinton's administration, and after the terrorist attacks of September 11, 2001, and the 2001 anthrax attacks, the bioterrorism threat galvanized expanded biosurveillance and biodefense initiatives from U.S. President Bush's administration.

However, Joy is concerned not only with the intentional release of gene-tailored infectious agents designed as tools of mass destruction but also with the accidental release of genetically engineered microorganisms designed for benign purposes that might have similar catastrophic effects in our bodies or ecosystems. The key to effective gene therapy has been to find viral vectors sufficiently virulent that they would spread beneficial genes throughout the patient. Researchers have explored everything from the common cold to HIV as vehicles of gene transfer. Therapeutic success carries the risk that a gene vector could spread, mutate, and have unintended consequences. For instance, Australian researchers discovered that they had created a mousepox virus with 100 percent lethality (for mice) while trying to create a viral contraceptive (Nowak, 2001). Bacteria engineered to clean up oil spills could mutate to eat plastic. Biotechnology crops could slip out of their farms and wreak havoc on local ecosystems.

Nanogoos. While the threat of nanomaterial pollution has already inspired calls for a moratorium on nanotechnological innovation (ETC Group, 2005), threats from self-replicating nanorobots are more speculative and farther in the future. Although this holy grail of a programmable nanoreplicator is estimated to be several decades away, their eventual likelihood has generated much discussion of the apocalyptic scenario of "gray goo," in which a set of replicators escape their programmed constraints and begin eating everything, destroying all life on Earth. According to one estimate (Freitas, 2000), nanobots could eat Earth's biomass in about one week.

However, nanotechnologists have also demonstrated that rogue "ecophagous" nanorobots would likely starve, burn themselves up, or grow slowly enough to permit countermeasures (Freitas, 2000). Nanoengineers have proposed industry standards for making nanomachines dependent on specific resources, or self-limiting in their replication, to prevent outbreaks of nanoplagues (Foresight Institute, 2000). Blue goo, that is, nanoimmune systems, could be deployed to detect and destroy gray goo. Nonetheless, the threats of widespread destruction through the intentional or accidental release of destructive nanomachines will eventually be real.

Killer Robots. Finally, and most speculatively, Joy waxes eloquent about one of the oldest tropes of science fiction, that machine minds or robots might take over the world and destroy humanity: "Superior robots would surely affect humans as North American placentals affected South American marsupials (and as humans have affected countless species) ... biological humans would be squeezed out of existence" (Joy, 2000; Chapter 2).

Joy's concern about self-willed, self-replicating robots is tied up with the extrapolations of Hans Moravec, Ray Kurzweil, and others about the eventual emergence of machine minds. Computing power has doubled every 18 months for the last century, an observation dubbed Moore's law. Maintaining that exponential growth rate, personal desktop computers will match the neural complexity of the human brain in the next decade. If self-awareness and other features of living minds are emergent properties of complex information processing, then there is already today a possibility of the spontaneous emergence of self-willed intelligence in machines since the complexity of all the information technology connected through the Internet has already reached human brain levels. While some assume that this will herald a new golden age, Joy is certainly not alone is assuming that the consequences of such an event would range from severely disruptive to apocalyptic.

Many critics have dismissed Joy's concerns as "science fiction," meaning they do not believe in the possibility of superplagues, nanorobots, and self-willed AI. But even if these threats are low probability, we have to take seriously even the slightest threat of so huge a catastrophic effect. I agree with Bill Joy, the ETC Group, and the other advocates of technology bans that the apocalyptic threats from these technologies are very real and warrant dramatic action. But I disagree that technology moratoria are a practical proposal to address the risks of emerging technologies, since they cannot and will not be implemented. Apocalyptic technological risks can only effectively be reduced and prepared through effective transnational regulation, regulation which the Luddite critics do not believe would be adequate and which the industrial and military sponsors of emerging technologies see as threats to their corporate and national security interests. In fact, as Joy points out, this dilemma has been with us since the advent of nuclear weapons: Can we build an effective global infrastructure to ensure that we can accrue the benefits of dual-use technologies, such as nuclear power, without seeing a proliferation of their risks, that is, nuclear weapons?

GOVERNING PROLIFERATION OF DUAL-USE TECHNOLOGIES

If we accept that the threats from emerging technologies are in fact potentially apocalyptic and relinquishment a quixotic proposal, it should be clear that advocacy of either voluntary scientific and industry self-regulation, or self-regulation by nation states, is also an inadequate response. In the absence of effective global regulation, codes of ethics and professional self-regulation are welcome first steps and can provide crucial time for the formulation of global regulatory responses before the technologies proliferate, especially when the nations in the technological lead establish strict limits on the export of technologies of potential military significance as the United States does. But in the end, as with the regulation of nuclear, chemical, and biological weapons, these threats require the creation of transnational regulations and agencies empowered to verify and enforce those regulations. A brief examination of the history of arms control agreements and enforcement therefore is in order to underline the difficulties that such transnational regulation faces when the technologies are "dual use," having both beneficial and destructive uses, and when corporations and nation states are unwilling to compromise proprietary secrecy and national autonomy.

Lessons from Arms Control Regimens

Before the first atomic weapon was tested at the Trinity site in Nevada, Edward Teller announced calculations showing that the test could ignite Earth's atmosphere in an uncontrolled chain reaction. Robert Oppenheimer was so troubled that he consulted his mentor, Arthur Compton, who suggested a risk–benefit calculation that losing the war to the Nazis would be the better bet if the risk of destroying Earth's atmosphere was three in a million or more. By the time of the test, the Trinity team had proven that igniting the atmosphere was a theoretical impossibility. But how much of an unlikely possibility is still too possible? How do we know when we have passed the three-in-a-million chance, and is this even the appropriate level of risk to take with the future of life on the planet? How large must the potential rewards of some line of research be to gamble with human existence?

After World War II, many scientists and peace activists proposed a global renunciation of nuclear weapons. There was not then, nor has there been since, sufficient political support for disarmament to enforce such a ban given the perceived national security interests of the nuclear powers and the lack of an effective global body for enforcing treaties. The growth of the nuclear power industry, which produces fissile materials which can be used in bombs by states or terrorists, also made clear that the regulation of nuclear proliferation would need to permit beneficial uses of the technology while discouraging nuclear weapons proliferation. In 1957, the United Nations responded to the dilemma by creating the International Atomic Energy Agency (IAEA).

The IAEA's principal charge has been to ensure the safety of nuclear power. Since the Nuclear Non-Proliferation Treaty (NPT) entered into force in 1970, however, the IAEA has increasingly been called on to investigate states which are using nuclear power generation as a cover for nuclear weapons programs. The IAEA investigated allegations of an Iraqi nuclear weapons program before and after the U.S. invasion in 2003 and is currently involved in investigating nuclear programs in Iran and North Korea. However, again, the weakness of transnational governance, in particular the inability of the United Nations to muster sufficient military and economic coercion to force Iraq, Iran, or North Korea to cooperate with arms inspectors and obey international prohibitions on weapons-capable nuclear programs, contributed to the Bush administration's multi-factored rationales for the disastrous invasion of Iraq and the on-going brinksmanship with Iran and North Korea.

The difficulty of regulating weapons of mass destruction has by no means been limited to these "rogue states," however. Neither the United States nor Russia were ever willing to agree to "anytime, anywhere" inspections of nuclear facilities in the Strategic Arms Reduction Treaties of 1992 and 1993 and instead relied on other, far less certain forms of monitoring and verification. Similarly the United States and the Soviet Union refused to give international agencies a free hand to monitor and investigate labs with biodefense capabilities under the Biological Weapons Convention (BWC) which entered into force in 1975. Since the BWC had no investigatory or enforcement mechanisms, discussions began in the 1990s to strengthen the treaty to allow spot inspections of biodefense facilities, among other measures. In 2001 the Bush administration, responding to concerns about the protection of proprietary biotechnological information and the secrecy of U.S. biodefense research, withdrew the United States from the BWC. The BWC negotiations were also stymied by the insistence of developing countries that the regimen facilitate their acquisition of biotechnology for peaceful purposes (Marchant and Sylvester, 2006).

These efforts to regulate nuclear, biological, and chemical technologies to prevent their use as weapons of mass destruction show that complete prohibition of the technologies has never been politically feasible because of their dual, beneficial uses. The only progress, and that slight, has been with efforts to create agencies like the IAEA that monitor the safety of peaceful uses of the technologies while investigating and discouraging their weaponization. This is the same situation we face with the proliferation of nanotechnology, genetic engineering, and AI, which could cure diseases, provide new sources of energy, make cleaner and more efficient industrial processes, and generally provide a more prosperous future. Global bans on these technologies are as unlikely as they were with the nuclear and biological technologies.

Technology relinquishment is also impossible because of the need to pursue effective prophylactic and defensive measures to the use of emerging technologies by rogue states and terrorist groups. After the United States signed the BWC in 1972 and Richard Nixon dismantled the U.S. chemical weapons program, the Soviet Union and a number of other signatories secretly expanded their bioweapons programs. Yet with subsequent emergence of a robust biomedical infrastructure in the United States, we have the capacity to respond to potential bioweapons through initiatives like the U.S. Bioshield initiative enacted in 2004. A complete ban on work with pathogens like smallpox, anthrax, and Ebola would also inhibit research on development of effective biomonitors, vaccines, and antibiotics for those pathogens, as is being promoted through the Bioshield program. In fact, the need to conduct biodefense research was cited by the Bush administration in its withdrawal from the BWC in 2001. Similarly any comprehensive ban on nanotechnology or robotics would inhibit the ability of signatories to conduct defensive research on these technologies in anticipation of nano- and bioweapons deployed by nonsignatory and noncompliant states and non–state groups.

Relinquishment is also unattractive because the apocalyptic risks we face are not just from these technologies but also from nature itself. In the calculation of the risks and benefits from emerging technologies, there are apocalyptic risks on both sides. Biodefense research has application not just to potential bioweapons but also to emerging infectious diseases such as SARS and avian flu. New bio- and nanotechnologies may reduce the human burden on the ecosystem by growing more food on less land with fewer resources, creating new and more efficient energy sources and industrial processes, as well as making human beings less vulnerable to the consequences of rapid climate change and natural catastrophes such as earthquakes, floods, hurricanes, and asteroid impacts. Antiaging research, based on the convergence of accelerating bio-, nano-, and information technologies, offers the promise of saving billions of lives that would be lost this century to aging-related diseases. At the margins of prediction, and over the course of decades, technological renunciation may be *more* existentially risky than technological progress. Nonetheless, with appropriate regulation we can reduce the risks and substantially improve the likelihood of the benefits.

Transnational and National Regulation

Emerging technologies must therefore be included in the existing regimen of international arms control as well as environmental and product regulation, and that regimen must itself be strengthened. Trade in genetically modified plants and animals is subject to review by the Codex Alimentarius, a joint venture of the Food and Agriculture Organization of the United Nations and the World Health Organization, which establishes voluntary safety guidelines for trade in food and agricultural products. As potentially toxic substances, international trade in nanomaterials is subject to regulation under the World Trade Organization's Agreement on Sanitary and Phytosanitary Measures (Thayer, 2005). The agreement *encourages* nations to base domestic regulation on the international standards developed by the Codex Alimentarius but has no enforcement mechanism.

The sale of computing systems with the potential for self-willed intelligence are not currently subject to any international regulation other than intellectual property protection, although systems deemed to be of military significance, such as encryption algorithms, are barred for export by the U.S. Commerce Department. Insofar as technologies can be used to produce weapons, U.N. Security Council Resolutions 1540 and 1673 require all states to adopt measures to stop non–state actors from gaining access to them and to report on their steps to identify and prevent non–state actors' uses of these technologies.

Although some countries faithfully ensure that their domestic regulations are in compliance with these international agreements, most do not. Since the U.S. invasion of Iraq, which the Bush administration justified in part by the Hussein regime's non-cooperation with arms control inspections and the inability of the United Nations to compel Hussein's cooperation, this issue of strengthening the compliance mechanisms of international arms control agreements has become central in international diplomacy. In 2006 the issue is central to conflicts between Iran and North Korea on the one hand and the IAEA and world community on the other. The inability of the United Nations to mobilize force against Sudan permits Khartoum to obstruct international investigation of genocide in Darfur and the insertion of peacekeeping troops to protect the Darfuri. Despite the United Nations having more troops deployed under blue helmets than ever before, more than 100,000 personnel deployed in 18 different areas, the U.N. peacekeepers remain ad hoc and underfunded. There has been little success in convincing the U.N. member states to permit the creation of a supranational force capable of enforcing world law.

Even though they are only sporadically complied with, international regulations themselves are also often weakened by the disproportionate influence of corporate and nation state interests. The food safety regulations of the Codex Alimentarius are seen as inadequate by many nongovernmental organizations (NGOs), which point out that the body invites far more consultation from corporate spokespersons than from public health advocates and NGOs. More charitably, negotiating international regulations is difficult, contentious, and costly and therefore often forced to a minimal level. Also the goal of protecting free trade from capricious and protectionist trade barriers is often in conflict with the "precautionary principle" demands of NGOs and some European nations. For instance, in 2006 the World Trade Organization is finalizing a ruling that the European Union (EU) has no grounds to restrict import of genetically modified crops since it has no proof that such crops are unsafe. This sets a precedent for a similarly high bar for any national or regional efforts to restrict the proliferation of nanomaterials.

So the regimen of technology regulation required for preventing the proliferation of technologies of mass destruction must go well beyond the existing, voluntary regulation of trade and arms control to create international mechanisms to verify that nation states implement international agreements or else face compelling sanctions. An example of this level of world law and enforcement would be agreement under the Genocide Convention that countries permit international investigation of charges of genocide and that the U.N. Security Council will take action to prevent genocide. (Again, however, we have seen with the case of Darfur and the inability of the United Nations to go to war with Sudan how ineffective that agreement has been.) There are also the global intellectual protection agreements, monitored by the World Intellectual Property Organization and the General Agreement on Tariffs and Trade (GATT), which oblige nation states to investigate and stop domestic firms that violate global copyrights and patents or else be subject to international sanctions.

The regulation of the threats of potentially apocalyptic technologies thus requires not only that the safety of emerging technologies be addressed by transnational agreements but also that these agreements create and support agencies capable of engaging in surveillance and verification at both the national and transnational level, with triggers for compelling enforcement mechanisms, from economic sanctions to military force.

Global Surveillance Mechanisms

The principal obstacle to the building of an infrastructure of global technology regulation, after unwillingness to forego the potential benefits of the technologies, has been, as noted above, the unwillingness of nation-states and firms to open their military and private labs to a robust regimen of inspection and verification. With the even greater invasiveness required for effective monitoring of emerging technologies, the threats to corporate and national sovereignty are compounded. Given the rapid escalation in the level of threat, however, transnational agreements to monitor and control dangerous technology will soon be on the international agenda again.

The level of monitoring for potential apocalyptic nanotechnology, biotechnology, and AI will need to be even more invasive than the surveillance regimen attempted for nuclear power under the IAEA. Amy Stimson of the Center for Strategic and International Studies has argued that it would be possible to build systems for monitoring biotechnological facilities that would permit verification of the BWC without divulging proprietary or national security information (Stimson, 2004). Unfortunately such monitoring systems can inevitably be deceived, and even "anytime, anywhere" inspection has quickly become irrelevant as the size of the facilities necessary to conduct research and development has shrunk. Dangerous nanotechnology and biological research can be conducted in very small facilities, an order of magnitude less easily detected than the facilities necessary to build a nuclear weapon. The mobile, trailer-based Iraqi bioweapons labs turned out to have been a Bush administration fabrication, but they were nonetheless a possibility. In the case of AI research the idea of a "facility" is completely irrelevant, and the surveillance of dangerous AI would need to be distributed throughout the global information infrastructure.

Global surveillance for the signs of dangerous and aberrant technology will thus require the creation of novel and highly automated systems with global reach. An example would be the system of satellite monitoring for the heat signatures of rogue nanotechnology in the wild proposed by Robert Freitas (2000). Another would be the World Health Organization's Global Outbreak Alert and Response Network, which aims to rapidly identify new epidemic diseases, genotype the pathogens, and develop and deploy vaccines. The existing global network of public and private groups that monitor and fight computer viruses could similarly be coordinated with law enforcement and cyberwarfare agencies to monitor for the emergence of self-willed information architectures.

Another area for a global technology control regimen would be the standardizing and monitoring of good laboratory practices and safety standards. Materials and specimens need to be tracked and accounted for, laboratory records maintained, and laboratory workers properly trained and vetted. Harvard biologist George Church has proposed, for instance, that all DNA-synthesizing devices capable of rapidly "printing" novel DNA of novel microorganisms be tagged with electronic locators, programmed to forbid the synthesis of dangerous pathogens, sold only to approved laboratories, and registered with an international authority (Church, 2005; Wade, 2005; Chyba, 2006). Global intelligence monitoring of scientific publications would permit the identification of researchers and lines of research that may yield potential threats.

In 2004, in response to a National Academy of Science report on the regulation of biotechnology to prevent bioterrorism, the Bush administration created the National Science Advisory Board for Biosecurity to advise federal departments and agencies that conduct or support research that could be used by terrorists on ways of reducing the risk of diffusion of dangerous materials and scientific knowledge. However, these measures apply only to federally funded facilities in the United States. Transnational regulations that apply to private, academic, and government researchers need to be devised to identify the specific kinds of scientific research which should be subject to prepublication review and redaction by national and transnational authorities, and researchers and journals need to be educated about these guidelines (Purkitt and Wells, 2006).

It is interesting to note that the militant defender of emerging technologies, Ray Kurzweil, found a rare point of agreement with Bill Joy in 2005 when they published a joint statement in *The New York Times* condemning the publication online of the sequenced genome of the 1918 influenza virus, which they considered a recipe for bioterrorism. They wrote, "We urgently need international agreements by scientific organizations to limit such publications and an international dialogue on the best approach to preventing recipes for weapons of mass destruction from falling into the wrong hands" (Kurzweil and Joy, 2005).

Open and Democratic Societies

All these surveillance activities, and especially any restrictions on scientific research and publication, raise grave questions about the balance of safety with freedom. However, although there will be trade-offs between safety and freedom, as there has always been, another way to frame the issue is to emphasize the importance of open and democratic societies as a precondition for effective transnational threat identification and control. The principal global threats are not from scientific activities that are public and known, but from secretive military research programs and non–state actors hidden in closed regimes. The freer and more transparent the society, the more likely that regulators will be able to identify emerging technological threats.

Trade unions and NGOs in liberal democratic societies complement and support the regulatory apparatus. Citizens of authoritarian regimes are unable to organize or express concerns about environmental toxins or suspicious patterns of disease. In open societies, unions and civic organizations can assist in monitoring scientific research and raising the alarm when the public's interests are at risk. While citizen groups and diligent regulators in democratic societies are still often at a disadvantage in relation to the influence of corporate power and the military–industrial complex, they are at least still permitted to investigate, mobilize, and publicize. Democratic societies also can create and tolerate relatively independent government technology advisory bodies, such as the former Office of Technology Assessment which advised the U.S. Congress until dismantled in 1995.

More Science, Not Less

To many defenders of scientific progress, a global technology regulatory regimen like the one I have described will seem little better than a blanket ban on research. This "technolibertarian" perspective sees an unfettered marketplace as the best and safest guarantor of rapid scientific development. However, the bulk of technological innovation in the twentieth century has occurred in large academic, corporate, and military laboratories, within the constraints of regulation, and not in unregulated entrepreneurs' garages. By establishing national and international funds to develop safe, prophylactic, and remediative technologies, an effective regimen of technology regulation can stimulate innovation more than it slows it.

More science will be needed to create the information technologies for the regimen of surveillance of the computers, laboratories, industrial facilities, and the global ecosystem. Alongside our global immune system for computer viruses, we need active immune system defenses and rapidly deployable counter measures for dangerous nanotechnology, robots, and machine intelligence. The rapid convergence of the emerging technologies will bring with it novel solutions, such as the use of carbon nanotubes and sugar by a Clemson University team to coat and neutralize weaponized anthrax (Polowczuk, 2006).

Research should be devoted to engineering safety into the design of the technologies themselves. When Monsanto explored selling only sterile genetically engineered seed in order to protect its intellectual property rights, it was condemned by environmentalists, even though these "Terminator" seed lines were precisely the best way to prevent genetic pollution. Self-replicating nanomachines can be designed to minimize the risk of mutation and to require specific materials for reproduction (Foresight Institute, 2000). Nanofactories can be built with encrypted blackbox software that forbids tampering, reverse engineering, or the manufacture of dangerous substances and devices (Treder and Phoenix, 2003). Access to nanofactory source code would be restricted to engineers with proper vetting and oversight.

In the more difficult case of self-willed machine intelligence, 50 years ago Isaac Asimov proposed programming all AI with an unalterable moral code, the "three laws of robotics," which required that a robot put the welfare of humans and obedience to humans above its own interests. But the messiness of self-reflexive minds capable of learning and changing and the messiness of interpretability of specific moral dilemmas mean that efforts to encode these constraints into AI will probably only be as successful as moral education is for human beings. Nonetheless, information architectures with the capacity for self-awareness may be able to be designed with secure constraints and fail-safes that can be used in the event of self-willed behavior.

Developing prophylactic and defensive technologies will, however, require a level of industrial policy and state subsidy that is currently out of favor in the United States, at least outside the military–industrial complex. Private industry cannot be relied on to participate in the necessary research and development (R&D) without large public investments, because the market for preventing a hypothetical apocalypse is not an attractive investment risk. With the exception of antivirus software, which may offer a private-sector-based model for AI preparedness, there is no private market foreseeable for anti-nanotechnology measures or even pandemic vaccines and treatments. Indeed, two-thirds of the deaths in the developing world are due to about a dozen infectious diseases—malaria, dengue, and so on—few of which receive research attention from the pharmaceutical industry since they would not be able to recover their investments by selling a vaccine or treatment in sub-Saharan Africa. It was the market failure in antiretroviral drugs, which were far too expensive for the majority of the world's poor with HIV, that led to the creation of the reasonably successful Global Fund for HIV, Malaria and Tuberculosis to subsidize treatment in the developing world and price reductions in the face of threatened abrogation of the intellectual property agreements.

Even the Bush administration's multibillion dollar Bioshield program, initiated in 2004 to entice pharmaceutical companies to develop vaccines and treatments for potential bioweapons, has been unable to attract pharmaceutical firms, because they do not believe the products will be profitable enough since their principal market will be to governments for stockpiles. As a way around this dilemma, Bioshield will be creating a Biodefense Advanced Research and Development Agency (BARDA) to institutionalize the relationship between biotechnology firms and the defense establishment in the way that the Defense Advanced Research and Development Agency (DARPA) does (Mackenzie, 2006), with incremental payments for reaching R&D goals.

In fact, private firms, which both have benefited from decades of public investment in basic science and profit from these technologies with potentially catastrophic risks, should be asked to internalize the costs of new research into prophylactic measures through a targeted tax to support research into safe design and prophylaxis. We do not want to repeat the mistake of the 1980s Superfund, which used tax dollars to clean up closed factories' toxic sites, or the Price-Anderson Act, which gave a green light to nuclear power in the 1950s by providing a half billion dollars of public insurance for nuclear accidents without ensuring that the plants developed safe long-term nuclear waste management.

CONCLUSION

In 1947 Albert Einstein, sure that the advent of nuclear weapons had made the need for global governance inescapably obvious, addressed the new United Nations saying, "The final goal ... is the establishment of a supranational authority vested with sufficient legislative and executive powers to keep the peace. The present impasse lies in the fact that there is no sufficient, reliable supra-national authority. ... There can never be complete agreement on international control and the administration of atomic energy or on general disarmament until there is a modification of the traditional concept of national sovereignty."

In 2006 calls for the creation of powerful transnational agencies may sound as quixotic as calls for the complete abolition of emerging technologies through voluntary acts of conscience. However, the only way forward is the same way that we have addressed all previous technological threats, from toxic chemicals to dangerous cars: Investigate, educate the public, create political pressure for new laws and regulatory agencies to enforce the laws, spend public dollars on research into safer technologies, and keep popular pressure on those agencies to prevent their weakening and cooptation. The qualitative difference with these emerging apocalyptic threats, as compared to unsafe drugs, cars, and toasters, is that the regulation must be global and prophylactic. We cannot allow a potentially apocalyptic event to spur us into action. We must create this regimen before the threats emerge.

Seventeen years ago, the common wisdom was that we would have continued the Cold War well into the twenty-first century. Then the Soviet Union collapsed. Ten years ago, the common wisdom was that capitalism would be unchallenged in the twenty-first century. Then a global anticapitalist movement rose in city after city to protest the unaccountability of global financial institutions. Five years ago, many pundits considered Islamic fundamentalism to be waning and terrorist attacks to be the fundamentalists' last protest against the end of ideology. Since 9/11 and the Iraq War, there is no end in sight for Islamist insurgent violence and terrorism around the world.

So I do not think it utopian today to echo Einstein's calls for the creation of empowered supranational agencies capable of enforcing regulations on emerging supertechnologies. Creating these institutions will require a global movement powerful enough to force reluctant corporations and nationstates to put global survival ahead of private and national interests. It will be as difficult as it has been since 1947. But we really have no other choice.

REFERENCES

Associated Press. 2001. Physicist warns humans about A.I. *Seattle Times*, September 2. Available: http://archives.seattletimes.nwsource.com/cgi-bin/texis/web/vortex/display?slug=hawking02&date=20010902.

Bailey, R. 2001. Rage against the machines: Witnessing the birth of the neo-Luddite movement. *Reason*, July. Available: http://www.reason.com/0107/fe.rb.rage.html.

Bostrom, N. 2001. Existential risks: Analyzing human extinction scenarios and related hazards. Yale University Philosophy Department. Available: http://www.nickbostrom.com/existential/risks.html.

Church, G. M. 2005. A synthetic biohazard non-proliferation proposal. May 21. Available: http://arep.med.harvard.edu/SBP/Church_Biohazard04c.htm.

Chyba, C. 2006. Biotechnology and the challenge to arms control. *Arms Control Today*, October.

Dann, J., and Gardner, D. (Eds.) 1988. *Nanotech*. New York: Ace Books.

Dertouzos, M. 2006. Not by reason alone. *Technology Review* 103(5): 26.

Drexler, K. E. 1986. *Engines of Creation: The Coming Era of Nanotechnology*. New York: Anchor Books.

Drexler, M. 2001a. Undermining international bioweapons controls. *The American Prospect* 12(19) Oct. 12.

Drexler, M. 2001b. The invisible enemy. *The American Prospect* 12(19) Nov. 5.

ETC Group. 2005. A tiny primer on nano-scale technologies ... and the little BANG theory. Available: http://www.etcgroup.org/upload/publication/55/01/tinyprimer_english.pdf.

Einstein, A. 1947. An open letter: to the General Assembly of the United Nations. *United Nations world*. New York: October 1947, pp. 13–14.

Foresight Institute. 2000. *Foresight Guidelines on Molecular Nanotechnology, version 3.7.* Available: http://www.foresight.org/guidelines/current.html.

Forrest, D. 1989. *Regulating nanotechnology development.* Foresight Institute. Available: http://www.foresight.org/NanoRev/Forrest1989.html.

Freitas, R. A. 1999. Nanomedicine, Volume I: *Basic Capabilities.* Austin, TX: Landes Bioscience.

Freitas, R. A. 2000. Some limits to global ecophagy by biovorous nanoreplicators, with public policy recommendations. Foresight Institute. Available: http://www.foresight.org/NanoRev/Ecophagy.html.

Garrett, L. 1995. *The Coming Plague: Newly Emerging Diseases in a World out of Balance.* Pittsburgh: Penguin.

Garrett, L. 2001. *Betrayal of Trust: The Collapse of Global Public Health.* New York: Hyperion.

Guillemin, J. 2001. *Anthrax: The Investigation of a Deadly Outbreak.* Berkeley: University of California Press.

Joy, B. 2000. Why the future doesn't need us. *Wired,* April. Available: http://www.wired.com/wired/archive/8.04/joy.html.

Kantrowitz, A. 1992. The weapon of openness. In B. C. Crandall and J. Lewis. (Eds.), *Nanotechnology Research and Perspectives.* Cambridge, MA: MIT Press, pp. 303–311.

Kurzweil, R., and Joy, B. 2005. Recipe for destruction. *New York Times,* October 17.

Mackenzie, D. 2006. Biodefence special: Fortress America? *New Scientist,* October 7, pp. 18–21.

McMahon, S. 1996. Unconventional nuclear, biological and chemical weapons delivery methods: Wither the "smuggled bomb." *Comparative Strategy* 15: 123–134.

Marchant, G., and Sylvester, D. 2006. Transnational models for regulation of nanotechnology. *Journal of Law, Medicine and Ethics,* Fall. Available: http://papers.ssrn.com/sol3/papers.cfm?abstract_id=907161.

Miller, J. 2001. U.S. seeks changes in germ war pact. *New York Times,* November 1.

Miller, J., Engelberg, S., and Broad, W. J. 2001. U.S. germ warfare research pushes treaty limits. *New York Times,* September 4. Available: http://www.nytimes.com/2001/09/04/international/04GERM.html.

Morris, J. (Ed.). 2000. *Rethinking Risk and the Precautionary Principle.* Boston: Butterworth-Heinemann.

National Institutes of Health. 2001. NIH guidelines for research involving recombinant DNA molecules. Available: http://grants.nih.gov/grants/policy/recombinentdnaguidelines.htm.

National Science Foundation. 2001. *Societal Implications of Nanoscience and Nanotechnology.* Available: http://itri.loyola.edu/nano/NSET.Societal.Implications/.

Nowak, R. 2001. Disaster in the making. *New Scientist,* January 13.

Osterholm, M., and Schwartz, J. 2000. *Living Terrors: What America Needs to Know to Survive the Coming Bioterrorist Catastrophe.* New York: Random House.

Polowczuk, S. 2006. Clemson researchers develop nanotechnology to stop weaponized anthrax in its tracks. *Clemson News,* October 2. Available: http://clemsonews.clemson.edu/WWW_releases/2006/October/anthrax.html.

Preston, R. 1998a. Statement for the record by Richard Preston before the Senate Judiciary Subcommittee on Technology, Terrorism & Government Information and the Senate Select Committee on Intelligence on "Chemical and Biological Weapons Threats to America: Are We Prepared?" April 22, 1998. Available: http://www.senate.gov/~judiciary/preston.htm.

Preston, R. 1998b. The bioweaponeers. *The New Yorker*, March 9, pp. 52–65. Available: http://cryptome.org/bioweap.htm.

Pueschel, M. 2001. DARPA system tracked inauguration for attack. *U.S. Medicine*, April. Available: http://www.usmedicine.com/article.cfm?articleID=172&issueID=25.

Purkitt, H., and Wells, V. 2006. Evolving bioweapon threats require new countermeasures. *The Chronicle of Higher Education* 53(7): B18. Available: http://chronicle.com/weekly/v53/i07/07b01801.htm.

Reynolds, G. H. 2002. Forward to the future: Nanotechnology and regulatory policy. Pacific Research Institute. Available: http://www.pacificresearch.org/pub/sab/techno/forward_to_nanotech.pdf.

Rifkin, J. 1999. *The Biotech Century: Harnessing the Gene and Remaking the World*. New York: Jeremy Tarcher.

Roco, M. C. 2006. Survey on nanotechnology governance. Paper presented at the IRGC Working Group on Nanotechnology, Geneva.

Rosenberg, B. H. 2001. A way to prevent bioterrorism. *San Francisco Chronicle*, September 18, 2001.

Sale, K. 1995. *Rebels Against the Future: The Luddites and Their War on the Industrial Revolution: Lessons for the Computer Age*. Reading, MA: Addison-Wesley.

Selden, Z. 1997. Assessing the biological weapons threat. Business Executives for National Security. Available: http://www.bens.org/pubs_0297.html.

Stimson, A. 2004. Resuscitating the bioweapons ban: U.S. industry experts' plans for treaty monitoring. Washington, DC: Center for Strategic and International Studies, November.

Sunshine Project. 2001. The Biological Weapons Convention and the negotiations for a verification protocol, April. Available: http://www.sunshine-project.org/publications/bk2en.html.

Thayer, J. 2005. The SPS agreement: Can it regulate trade in nanotechnology? *Duke Law and Technology Review*, 0015. Available: http://www.law.duke.edu/journals/dltr/articles/2005dltr0015.html.

Treder, M., and Phoenix, C. 2003. The safe utilization of nanotechnology. Center for Responsible Nanotechnology. Available: http://www.crnano.org/safe.htm.

Twibell, T. S. 2001. Nano law: The legal implications of self-replicating nanotechnology. Available: http://www.nanozine.com/nanolaw.htm.

Wade, N. 2005. A DNA success raises bioterror concern. *New York Times*, January 12. Available: http://www.nytimes.com/2005/01/12/national/nationalspecial3/12gene.html.

Wejnert, J. 2004. Regulatory mechanisms for molecular nanotechnology. *Journal of Jurimetrics* 44: 1–29.

Williams, M. 2006. The knowledge. *Technology Review*. March/April. Available: http://www.technologyreview.com/printer_friendly_article.aspx?id=16485.

Zelicoff, A. P. 2001. An impractical protocol. *Arms Control Today*, May 2001. Available: http://www.armscontrol.org/act/2001_05/zelicoff.asp.

16

DELIBERATIVE DEMOCRACY AND NANOTECHNOLOGY

Colin Farrelly

INTRODUCTION

Two recent reports concerning nanotechnology illustrate both its potential promise and its potential peril. The first report is the encouraging news that nanotechnology might help in the delivery of gene therapy (Dodson, 2006). Worldwide, there are over 1000 clinical trials for gene therapy. There are currently 797 clinical trials for cancer, 102 trials for monogenetic diseases, and 106 for vascular diseases (*Journal of Gene Medicine*, 2006). Gene therapy involves switching off defective genes or inserting desirable genes into the cells to prevent or cure disease. One of the major obstacles facing gene therapy has been gene delivery, that is, ensuring that the desired genes get into the correct cells.

Nanotechnology might provide a solution to this problem. The efficacy of magnetic nanoparticle-based gene delivery has been demonstrated most clearly *in vitro* (Dodson, 2006, p. 286). This technique involves coupling genetic material to magnetic nanoparticles. "The particle/DNA complex (normally in suspension) is introduced into the cell culture where the field gradient produced by rare earth magnets (or electromagnets) placed below the cell culture increases sedimentation of the complex and increases the speed of transfection" (Dodson, 2006, p. 283).

The optimism one takes from the encouraging news about utilizing nanoparticle-based gene delivery is often tempered by news reports concerning the potential dangers of nanotechnology. The April 15, 2006, issue of the *Economist* reported the story about

Nanoethics: The Ethical and Social Implications of Nanotechnology. Edited by Allhoff, Lin, Moor, Weckert
Copyright © 2007 John Wiley & Sons, Inc.

Magic Nano, a bathroom cleaner that contains tiny silicate particles that reduce the scope for dirt and bacteria to cling to surfaces. Magic Nano went on sale in Germany in March 2006. Three days after it went on sale, it "was withdrawn from the market after nearly 80 people reported severe respiratory problems and six were admitted to hospital with fluid in their lungs" (*Economist*, 2006, p. 80). The Magic Nano incident led critics of nanotechnology, like Action Group on Erosion, Technology and Concentration (ETC Group), to call for a global moratorium on nanotechnology research (ETC Group, 2006). The concern (whether just perceived or real) that nanomaterials pose serious environmental, health, and safety risks is one of the major obstacles facing these new technologies.

The contrasting stories we hear concerning the potential pros and cons of nanotechnology illustrate the importance of taking seriously the question of what would constitute an *ethical* regulation of nanotechnology. Nanotechnology covers such a diverse spectrum of technologies (e.g., therapeutic) that different values and principles are appropriate for regulating different kinds of nanotechnologies. Those who feel that both sides of the pro- and anti-nanotechnology debate have valid concerns might feel that the real challenge we face is finding a reasonable *compromise* between these different values rather than crowning any one value (e.g., efficiency) or principle (the precautionary principle[1]) as "supreme."

One social theory that offers us a pluralistic and contextual ethical analysis of nanotechnology is deliberative democracy. Instead of trying to win a philosophical argument concerning the viability of first-order principles (e.g., efficiency, safety), deliberative democrats are more concerned with determining what would constitute a *reasonable balance* between conflicting fundamental values. In this chapter, I will examine what deliberative democracy can prescribe in terms of addressing the ethical and social concerns raised by nanotechnology. By examining how deliberative democracy applies to nanotechnology, we see that an ethical regulation of nanotechnologies requires a division of labor between many different institutions and individuals.

I argue that deliberative democracy prescribes that an ethical regulation of nanotechnologies requires *responsible* legislative activism which in turn requires accurate scientific information as well as an informed and reflective citizenry. Thus the ethical obligations of deliberative democracy extend to the way scientists conduct and communicate their research as well as to the way the media reports about nanoscience. The actions of scientists and journalists play a vital role in the formation of the reflective preferences of the larger citizenry. Thus deliberative democrats believe that informed, reasoned debate on accommodating the different stakes involved with regulating different kinds of nanotechnologies is essential if we hope to implement a fair and humane regulation of these new technologies.

DELIBERATIVE DEMOCRACY AS A "SECOND-ORDER" SOCIAL THEORY

What would constitute an ethical regulation of nanotechnology? What values and principles should regulate these new and potentially risky technologies? To answer these moral questions, one could turn to a diverse range of moral theories. Consequentialists, for example, believe that the right action or policy is that which produces the best consequences. But then of course one will ask: What constitutes the "best" consequences? Is the most ethical regulatory framework that which *maximizes* efficiency? Or it is that which *minimizes* the risk of harm? And *who*—legislatures, policy analysts, the general public, and so on–should be the judge of what constitutes the best consequences? These are tough questions we face with every new technology and they are sure to remain at the forefront of ethical debates concerning the regulation of nanotechnologies.

Most philosophical debates in ethics are debates among what Amy Gutmann and Dennis Thompson (2004) call "first-order" theories. First-order theories "seek to resolve moral disagreement by demonstrating that alternative theories and principles should be rejected" (Gutmann and Thompson, 2004, p. 13). Applied to the topic of nanotechnology, first-order theories might emphasize the expected utility such innovations could bring. Supporters of nanotechnology might argue that the great benefits nanotechnology offers, through applications in biology, physics, chemistry, engineering, and so on, demonstrate that we are morally obligated to opt for a regulatory framework that does not unduly restrain innovation in nanoscience. Alternatively, first-order theories that are premised on a precautionary principle might argue that these novel technologies should be subject to rigorous regulation, or possibly be prohibited, because of the potential risks of harm (e.g. to human health, the environment) they could bring.

The potential pros and cons of nanotechnology are likely to be both global in scope and temporal in reach. These benefits might be more valuable to those who live in parts of the world where they lack access to, for example, clean drinking water. Nanotechnology might have applications in water treatment and remediation. Or the potential costs of experimental nanotechnologies might be that it imposes burdens on those who might not exist for another generation, possibly longer, for example, if such technologies have dire consequences for the environment. So the stakes involved in the ethical regulation of nanotechnology will be diverse, and this raises a number of complex challenges for policymakers.

Nanotechnology covers such a diverse spectrum of technologies that different values and principles will be appropriate for regulating different kinds of technologies. Those who feel that both sides of the pro- and anti-nanotechnology debate have some valid concerns will believe that the real challenge is finding a reasonable compromise between these different values, rather than championing one value as supreme. This is prudent given that the stakes involved in different nanotechnologies can vary drastically. The stakes involved in a therapeutic innovation, like the delivery of gene therapy, are very different than those involved in a new cleaning technology. The safety standards we put in place for regulating these different technologies should be informed by the proposed benefits of their application and the expected harms of their nonapplication. So in the case of the delivery of gene therapy for fatal diseases, it is important to point out that nonintervention also has expected harms (e.g., premature death from the disease). And thus the reasons we invoke supporting or opposing a particular technology will need to be sensitive to the diverse range of substantive and procedural values that arise in negotiating a fair compromise between the different stakeholders involved in nanotechnologies.

It is important to note that the model of deliberative democracy is distinct from the popular "show of hands" (or aggregative) model of democracy. According to the latter, decision-making processes ought simply to aggregate the preferences of citizens in choosing public officials and parties. An outcome is thus just, according to this account of democracy, if it mirrors the preferences of the majority of people. Iris Marion Young (2000, p. 19) describes how the aggregative model conceives of democratic processes of policy formation:

> Individuals in the polity have varying preferences about what they want govern- ment institutions to do. They know that other individuals also have preferences, which may or may not match their own. Democracy is a competitive process in which political parties and candidates offer their platforms and attempt to sat- isfy the largest number of people's preferences. Citizens with similar preferences often organize interest groups in order to try to influence the actions of parties and policy-makers once they are elected. Individuals, interest groups, and public officials each may behave strategically, adjusting the orientation of their pres- sure tactics or coalition-building according to their perceptions of the activities of competing preferences.

Proponents of the aggregative model might invoke popular opposition against or popular support for nanotechnology as an important legitimizing justification for their position. But deliberative democrats believe such legitimacy is only warranted when this opposition or support results from deliberation rather than ignorance or knee-jerk reactions. So the process of having an informed, reasoned debate on nanotechnology is vital for deliberative democrats. The initial perceptions an ignorant citizenry have of new and novel technologies should not be the driving force behind the policies regulating nanotechnology. But the general public does have an important role to play in the formation of such policies. For deliberative democrats like Young (2000, p. 5), legitimacy depends "on the degree to which those affected by it have been included in the decision-making processes and have had the opportunity to influence the outcomes."

This participatory dimension is an integral part of deliberative democracy, but it is important to emphasize that this is an ongoing transformative process: "Through the process of public discussion with a plurality of differently opinioned and situated others, people often gain new information, learn of different experiences of their collective problems, or find that their own initial opinions are founded on prejudice or ignorance, or that they have misunderstood the relation of their own interests to others" (Young, 2000, p. 26). By collectively pursuing a second-order analysis of nanotechnology we are more likely to engage in this inclusive, transformative process. And this will better ensure that we implement an ethical regulation of nanotechnologies.

In addition to the moral considerations that arise from a principle of inclusion, there are several prudent reasons for taking seriously the requirement that we engage in a second-order analysis of nanotechnology. These pragmatic concerns might be ignored by analyses that focus on trying to win a first-order ethical argument or simply invoke a participatory model of democracy that equates legitimacy with the aggregation of existing (e.g., unreflective) preferences. By striving to engage in the transformative process of deliberative democracy, we can better ensure that the public policies we implement to regulate nanotechnologies are not unnecessarily inefficient (e.g., overtly risk adverse), irresponsible (e.g., empowering individuals to make decisions they are not well positioned to make decisions about), or informed by extremism. The latter concern, for example, is addressed by Cass Sunstein (2000) in "Deliberative Trouble: Why Groups Go to Extremes." Sunstein argues that most of the literature on deliberative democracy is not empirically informed. As such, deliberative democrats fail to recognize the potentially negative real-world consequences of deliberation. These include the social phenomenon of "group polarization" : "Group polarization means that members of a deliberating group predictably move toward a more extreme point in the direction indicated by the members' predeliberation tendencies" (Sunstein, 2000, p. 74).

As social beings, we place significant weight on reputational considerations. And such considerations could lead individuals to make mistakes. The power of group influences is effectively illustrated in the experiments of the social psychologist Solomon Asch (1998). Asch conducted a number of experiments that showed that intelligent people were willing to abandon the direct evidence of their own senses so they would conform to the reports of others. The dominance of conformity is an excellent example of an empirical consideration that must be incorporated into a social theory like deliberative democracy. If a group of like-minded individuals (e.g., environmentalists, conservatives) get together to deliberate, they are likely to become more extreme in the position. This results, argues Sunstein, from social influences on behavior (e.g., our desire to maintain our reputation, pressures to conform) and the effect of limited "argument pools."

Suppose, for example, you believe that all nanotechnologies are simply too risky and thus should be prohibited. Perhaps you believe that such interventions might have disastrous unforeseen consequences and thus we should not pursue such interventions. If you only discuss and debate nanotechnology with like-minded people, you are likely to become *more extreme* in your conviction that such technologies should be prohibited. Why? It's likely that the pool of arguments you have entertained will be narrower than the pool of arguments you might have entertained if you deliberated with a group of people who support such interventions. Supporters of nanotechnology might bring different information to the debate; they might invoke different principles or concerns (e.g., global justice) than those who oppose such technologies.

For example, proponents of magnetic nanoparticle-based gene delivery might point out that nonintervention also has expected harms. And in some cases, the expected harms of nonintervention could be certain (100 percent) and disastrous for the patient (e.g., premature death from disease). Furthermore, supporters of nanotechnology might also emphasize the great benefits such technologies could bring the developing world, for example, to help with water treatment or enhance agricultural productivity. These applications of nanotechnology could have enormous benefits to the most impoverished humans. By engaging in serious deliberation and dialogue with those with whom we disagree, we are more likely to avoid the extremism that can occur when the deliberative process is limited to homogeneous groups.

The concerns I raised against the critics of nanotechnology also equally apply to those who support these technologies. Deliberative democracy requires us to also be critical of an overtly romanticized account of the progress of science. Such an account might envision science being driven purely by the novel quest for truth, rather than fallible scientists or commercial interests. A healthy political polity must cultivate a culture of candor and disclosure so that we avoid the potential dangers that might arise from an overtly romanticized account of democracy and science. In his book on the importance of dissent, Cass Sunstein (2003) points out that the pressure to conform can often stifle dissent and that this can even occur in associations where members are connected by bonds of affection, friendship, and solidarity: "In such groups, members are often less willing, or even unwilling, to state objections and counterarguments for fear that these will prove disruptive and violate the group's internal norms. Families sometimes work this way" (p. 79). Virtuous families, workplaces, laboratories, scientific associations, legislatures, and so on, will recognize that dissenters often benefit others. And an application of deliberative democracy to nanotechnology should recognize that conformity does not necessarily promote societal interests. This means that a second-order analysis of nanotechnology should also take seriously what Gutmann and Thompson (2004) call "provisionality."

TAKING PROVISIONALITY SERIOUSLY

Deliberative democracy, argue Gutmann and Thompson (2004), is both morally and politically provisional. Deliberative democracy is morally provisional because "its principles invite revision in response to new moral insights or empirical discoveries" (Gutmann and Thompson, 2004, p. 57). The prescription for moral provisionality requires us to resist the tendency to treat "nanotechnology" as if it were one entity in need of regulation. It is imperative that we recognize that there are many distinct nanotechnologies. This is important because the stakes involved in regulating these distinct technologies will often be different and thus warrant different attention and consideration.

Consider, for example, the stakes involved in the regulation of magnetic nanoparticle-based gene delivery and Magic Nano. The values promoted by these two technologies are very different. One intervention is therapeutic, while the other is a cleaning product. Calls for a global moratorium on nanotechnology, like that made by the ETC Group, fail to recognize the importance of giving due consideration to the different values promoted by different applications of nanoscience. Perhaps there should be a moratorium on certain kinds of nanotechnology, and a deliberative debate would make explicit why such applications should be prohibited. But a provisionalist stance will not invoke one supreme value (e.g., safety) that trumps all other values. No society adopts such an attitude toward risk. Many existing technologies have some risk of harm and uncertainty associated with them. We permit our citizens to drive automobiles despite the fact that thousands of people are killed in accidents every year. We permit doctors to prescribe medications that might have serious, even fatal, side effects for some patients. But in such cases, responsible lawmakers weigh up the pros and cons of more restrictive policies rather than completely ignoring considerations of efficiency or the expected harms of nonintervention. Such a balanced, reasoned approach to policymaking should be extended to nanotechnologies. This requires credible information concerning both the potential pros and potential cons of different applications of nanoscience. We should not assume that the benefits of nanotechnology could not outweigh any degree of risk of harm, nor should we assume that the potential harm of such innovations is negligible or nonexistent. By prescribing we adopt a morally provisional attitude, deliberative democracy provides us with a useful social theory that instructs us to remain open minded and aware of the different stakes involved in ethically regulating nanotechnologies.

Deliberative democracy "affirms the need to justify decisions made by citizens and their representatives" (Gutmann and Thompson, 2004, p. 3). For Gutmann and Thompson, normative legitimacy rests upon a principle of reciprocity which accords weight to both procedural and substantive principles. To respect the different stakes involved in regulating nanotechnologies, it is important to also pursue *political* provisionality. Gutmann and Thompson (2004, p. 16) elaborate on this requirement and how it promotes the value of reciprocity:

> Political provisionality means that deliberative principles and the laws they justify must not only be subject to actual deliberation at some time, but also be open to actual reconsideration and revision at a future time. Like the rationale for treating principles as morally provisional, the justification for regarding principles as politically provisional rests on the value of reciprocity. From the perspective of reciprocity, persons should be treated not merely as objects of legislation or as passive subjects to be ruled. They should be treated as agents who take part in governance, directly or through their accountable representatives, by presenting and responding to reasons that would justify the laws under which they must live.

Nanotechnology has the potential to greatly influence, in a variety of ways, our life prospects. Whether it is DNA-computing devices, diagnostic machines, or cleaning products, citizens of the current generation (as well as future generations) are stakeholders and thus should be included in political processes that determine which policies we implement for different nanotechnologies. As a transformative ideal, deliberative democracy conceives of this participation as going beyond the simple aggregation of preferences. Indeed, reflective citizens will develop their preferences concerning nanotechnology in light of the input they receive from both the proponents and critics of nanotechnology.

For deliberative democrats, a responsible and ethical regulation of nanotechnologies is one in which public policy is shaped, in part, by the *reflective* preferences of the public. The qualification that preferences should be "reflective" is, of course, very important. Deliberative democrats do not endorse the view that science and public policy should simply cater to the knee-jerk reactions of the general public.

The cultivation of reflective preferences imposes diverse responsibilities not only on scientists but also on the media and government officials. Scientists need to win and retain the trust of the general public. Therefore, researchers must be forthcoming with respect to the potential pros and cons of these novel technologies. Overexaggerated claims concerning the potential benefits or harms of nanotechnology will only stifle a fair and responsible resolution of the complex values and interests at stake with these new technologies. The media must also be sure to accurately report the stakes involved in these advances. Due care must be taken to place these issues in a proper context, so that the potential harms involved in particular applications of nanotechnology are considered against the wider context of the potential harms of nonintervention.

The media play an important role in communicating the findings of scientists to the general public. But such communication goes beyond simply the "relaying of facts." Journalists also report on scientific advances or setbacks in a value-laden narrative. Such narratives, when informed and reflective, can help enhance public debate by inspiring a more inclusive or informed debate on regulating nanotechnologies. But such narratives can also obstruct the progression of science when such narratives trivialize the potential benefits of nanotechnologies or raise unfounded and disproportionate fear about its misapplication. So the quality of the media is vital to the health of a deliberative polity. And finally, the media also play an important role in ensuring that scientists have undergone responsible and credible research.

The choices we currently face with respect to regulating nanotechnologies are much more complex than the simplistic choice between a harm-free status quo and the potentially harmful situation that could result from the manipulation of material at the nanoscale. As the two examples of magnetic nanoparticle-based gene therapy and Magic Nano effectively illustrate, the stakes involved with regulating different types of nanotechnologies can differ drastically. In order to give adequate attention to these nuanced differences, scientists, journalists, legislatures, the media, and the general public should reject a generalized discourse that seeks to treat all nanotechnologies the same. Instead, we should aspire to engage in a second-order analysis that recognizes the different values at stake with different forms of nanoscale manipulation.

CONCLUSION

Deliberative democrats endorse a principle of *inclusion* which maintains that legitimacy depends "on the degree to which those affected by it have been included in the decision-making processes and have had the opportunity to influence the outcomes" (Young, 2000, p. 5). The principle of inclusion might sound like an attractive normative principle, but how this principle could be applied to something as novel and complex as the regulation of nanotechnology is something which moral and political philosophers need to seriously consider. A moralized conception of democracy must be informed by the empirical complexities of both collective decision making and scientific innovations. Collective decision making is subject to group polarization, and novel scientific advances often involve complexities too specialized and detailed to make any direct participatory regulation of nanotechnology viable or morally attractive. But this does not mean that an ethical regulation of nanotechnology requires us to defer to the judgment of elites. The public should have the opportunity to participate in the larger deliberation concerning the regulation of nanotechnology. Furthermore, those who have specialized knowledge concerning the likely benefits and costs of nanotechnologies have a moral responsibility to inform the public about these. So responsible law making requires the input of various deliberative bodies, including the general public, legislatures, policy experts, scientific associations, and so on, each of which plays an important role in helping us find a reasoned negotiated compromise when finessing the competing values often at stake with regulating nanotechnology.

As a second-order analysis, deliberative democracy prescribes that we avoid focusing exclusively on winning a debate concerning first-order principles of ethics. Critics might charge that a second-order analysis of nanotechnology yields prescriptions that are more indeterminate than first-order theories might yield. This may be true. But given the novelty of nanotechnology and the different potential applications of these technologies, this indeterminacy is not surprising. What would be truly surprising is if, after engaging in the procedural requirements of deliberative law making, we found that that we could justify an overarching policy recommendation for all nanotechnologies (e.g., a complete prohibition) by simply appealing to one particular moral, social, or economic value.

Any serious attempt to implement an ethical regulation of nanotechnology must address (rather than bracket or ignore) the fact of disagreement. Jeremy Waldron (1999) argues that disagreement is one of the "circumstances of politics." Paralleling David Hume's famous discussion of the circumstances of justice, Waldron (1999, pp. 153–154) argues:

> The prospect of persisting disagreement must be regarded, I think, as one of the elementary conditions of modern politics. Nothing we can say about politics makes much sense if we proceed without taking this condition into account (which is why so much that is said under the heading of "deliberative democracy" seems like dreaming). We may say ... that disagreement among citizens as to what they should do, as a political body, is one of the *circumstances of politics*. It is not all there is to the circumstances of politics, of course: there is also the need to act together, even though we disagree about what we do ... the circumstances of politics are a coupled pair: disagreement wouldn't matter if people didn't prefer a common decision; and the need for a common decision would not give rise to politics as we know it if there wasn't at least the potential for disagreement about what the common decision would be.

A second-order analysis takes seriously the question of the *means* we can use to pursue defensible ends. This is useful because it transcends the tendency, rampant in many debates in ethics, to focus exclusively on championing first-order principles. Once we take the issue of the means by which we can best promote efficiency, safety, inclusion, utility, and so on, seriously, we recognize that a division of labor is required. Liberal democracies contain numerous and diverse deliberative bodies. An inclusive reasoned debate between these diverse participants is more likely to lead us in the direction of an ethical regulation of nanotechnology than one that privileges the direct participation of the general public and their unreflective preferences concerning nanotechnology, or one that places the responsibility solely with policy analysts who might invoke a crude cost–benefit analysis irrespective of the input of others. Scientists, legislatures, activists, the media, and the general public all have a role to play in the new debates concerning nanotechnology. But such a moralized vision of democracy faces numerous challenges. I have not sought, in this chapter, to resolve these challenges; rather I have tried to bring the complexities of these challenges to the fore. By doing so, I hope I have made a compelling case that deliberative democracy is a normative ideal worth taking seriously if we hope to be prepared to meet the challenges that lie ahead as nanoscience progresses.

NOTE

1. Different variants of this principle are endorsed by different philosophers and policy analysts. A standard definition of the principle, principle 15 of the United Nations Rio Declaration on Environment and Development, states:

   In order to protect the environment, the precautionary approach shall be widely applied by States according to their capabilities. Where there are threats of serious or irreversible damage, lack of full scientific certainty shall not be used as a reason for postponing cost-effective measures to prevent environmental degradation.

   See http://www.unep.org/Documents.multilingual/Default.asp?
   DocumentID=78&ArticleID=1163.

REFERENCES

Asch, S. 1998. Opinions and social pressure. In E. Aronson (Ed.), *Readings about the Social Animal*, 8th edition. New York: Worth Publishers.

Dodson, J. 2006. Gene therapy progress and prospects: Magnetic nanoparticle-based gene delivery. *Gene Therapy* 13: 283–287.

Economist 2006. Has all the magic gone? *Economist* 378 (8473): 80–81

ETC Group 2006. http://www.etcgroup.org/upload/publication/14/01/nrnanorecallfinal.pdf

Gutmann, A., and Thompson, D. 1996. *Democracy and Disagreement*. Cambridge, MA: Harvard University Press.

Gutmann, A., and Thompson, D. 2004. *Why Deliberative Democracy?* Princeton, NJ: Princeton University Press.

Journal of Gene Medicine 2007. Gene therapy clinical trials worldwide, as of Jan. 2007. http://www.wiley.co.uk/genmed.clinical/

Sunstein, C. 2000. Deliberative trouble: Why groups go to extremes. *The Yale Law Review* 110 (1): 72–119.

Sunstein, C. 2003. *Why Societies Need Dissent*. Cambridge, MA: Harvard University Press.

Waldron, J. 1999. *Dignity of Legislation*. Cambridge: Cambridge University Press.

Young, I. M. 2000. *Inclusion and Democracy*. Oxford: Oxford University Press.

17

RHETORIC OF "STAKEHOLDING"*

David M. Berube

Stakeholder has become the word *du jour* in the world of nanotechnology policymaking. From government legislation to communiqués by nongovernmental organizations (NGOs), all pledge to have the concerns of all relevant stakeholders at heart, mostly without taking steps to define who composes these groups and what can be done to involve them. An analysis into the history and subtext of the term may be useful in shedding some light on this murky concept.

ORIGINS

Historically, the word stakeholder has been used to refer to someone entrusted to hold the stakes for two or more persons betting against one another such that he or she must deliver the stakes to the winner. Some groups want to make arguments that policymakers are gambling with our future when it comes to applied nanoscience; hence this term serves as a rhetorical tag for a host of associated meanings.

* I would like to thank law student Chris Dickson for his assistance on this chapter. All opinions expressed within are ours and do not necessarily reflect those of the National Science Foundation, the University of South Carolina, or the New York University Law School.

The term may have had its origins in gambling, but it has transcended into the legal sphere. Law defines a stakeholder as "a person holding property or owing an obligation that is claimed by two or more adverse claimants and who has no claim to or interest in the property or obligation" (Merriam-Webster, 1996). This appears to be a more appropriate application of the term for our purposes, especially when associated with the nanorealm. In this instance, "stakeholder" has been appropriated to discuss the concerns of people who, while owning no physical share in the company producing or using nanoparticles, may function as participants.

As the discussion moved from law to corporate governance, the appropriation of the term became more applicable to the typical policymaking process. This transition occurred in the 1930s and was initiated by Adlof Berle and Merrick Dodd, who were arguing about the social responsibilities of businesses. Specifically, "Berle and Dodd debated one of the great legal questions of their time as well as our own: should those who provide the capital for a business and assume its risk be required to accommodate those who have made no investment but who nevertheless seem to sincerely desire constraints on corporate activity?" (Jennings, 2006). A 1963 Stanford Research Institute research memo defined stakeholders as "those groups without whose support the organization would cease to exist" (Jennings, 2006). This seems to be the first appearance of the term in academic literature concerning strategic management. As more scholars became involved in the field, the context and meaning of the term became more polluted. Unfortunately, attempts to define what constitutes a stakeholder have been overly ambitious and mostly unsuccessful.

ROLE

To what degree must stakeholders be relevant to the survival of the organization for them to constitute a stakeholder? For example, stakeholders include terrorists, competitors, vegetation, nameless sea creatures, and generations yet unborn. Many additional groups of individuals have been added to the listing, such as clubs and organizations, societies, movements, clans, and so on.

With so many competing claims on the interests of a business, how can they all be adequately balanced? Surely stakeholders have some degree of vested interest in corporate behavior, and businesses should consider the effect on their corporate reputation if their performance is unfair and inequitable. But to what degree should they listen to the stakeholders versus the shareholders? "The most effective functionalist approach may be the one that highlights the probabilities of combinations between shareholders and stakeholders: the director is a shareholder; the shareholder is a director; the shareholder is a direct stakeholder (as a shareholder) and an indirect stakeholder (as a consumer and a citizen), etc. As well as the production of these probabilities, the functionalist approach may have to develop not only a convergent theory of the interests of stakeholders, but also a convergent theory of the interests of shareholders and stakeholders" (Bonnafous-Boucher, 2005). While this functionalist approach might rationalize shares and stakes in the corporate world, how readily it transfers to the public policy world is less clear.

Claims of stakeholder involvement and recruitment become particularly challenging when made in public policy forums. With its origins in strategic governance for business, stakeholder theory has unique implications when used in policymaking. For example, some of the strategic interests in undertaking stakeholder involvement are based on the ability to generate profit from them. How does this interaction work in regulation and governance? Is the interaction affected when government grants develop technologies the applications of which benefit business? These are intriguing questions that have not been addressed satisfactorily.

Stakeholder involvement in government initiatives is not a new development; U.S. Environmental Protection Agency (EPA, 2001) initiatives have tried to embrace stakeholder models for years: "In the early 1980s through its regulatory negotiation efforts, EPA began moving beyond traditional rulemaking to a collaborative process. Although these regulatory negotiation efforts were few, the framework used in these multi-stakeholder, consensus-based processes helped lay the groundwork for expanded public participation initiatives in the 1990s." The EPA attempted to overcome the definitional hurdles that arise with stakeholders by clarifying what was meant by its stakeholder initiatives: "Stakeholder involvement activities imply activities where EPA engages a select set of individuals, groups, or representatives of those individuals and groups to work directly on specific issues. Stakeholders are individuals and organizations or their representatives who work with EPA primarily because they have an interest in the Agency's work and policies or seek to influence the Agency's future direction." This definitional exercise while interesting seemed again to contribute little to stakeholder theory as it moved into the nanorealm.

NANOSTAKES

Supporters of the National Nanotechnology Initiative (NNI) have employed similar rhetoric under the guise of stakeholder involvement. There has been much discussion about getting the public involved. In the NNI Strategic Plan (2004) there is ample talk of public engagement. Goals listed include "creating a variety of opportunities for a broadly inclusive interdisciplinary dialogue on nanotechnology" ; "assessing and analyzing public understanding of, and attitudes toward, nanotechnology. A component of this is research on effective means to raise awareness of nanotechnology and obtain input from the general public" ; "fostering and encouraging forums for dialogue with the public and other stakeholders" ; and "distributing new informational materials about nanoscience and nanotechnology to better communicate with the broad public" —all read as stakeholder participation.

The rhetoric describing the intent of the Center for Nanotechnology in Society is particularly telling. The 2003 21st Century Nanotechnology Research and Development Act "specifies that the chosen center is to formulate a long-term vision for addressing societal, ethical, environmental, and education concerns; involve partners or affiliates to collaborate on topics related to responsible development of nanotechnology; include plans to involve a wide range of stakeholders; and develop a clearinghouse for information on communicating about nanoscience and nanotechnology and engaging the public in meaningful dialogue" (NNI, 2004).

Finally, claims of stakeholder engagement and outreach are not just limited to government. Nongovernmental organizations, academics, and many third-party groups such as the International Risk Governance Council and the International Council on Nanotechnology claim to involve stakeholder interests as well.

RATIONALE FOR STAKEHOLDER PARTICIPATION

Why include stakeholder rhetoric in the nanodebate? Why is it when a government-funded program associated with nanotechnology is announced, it seems to always include language about stakeholders? And how, if at all, does the reference to stakeholder participation differ from public outreach and participation? Simply put, there is no difference. The reference to stakeholders, by and large, is bureaucratese for public participation or at least public inclusion.

There are at least three reasons why it seems important to have the public on board for nanotechnology policy. While these rationales are not beyond rebuttal, they reappear regularly in policy dialogues.

First, nanoscience is expensive and returns on investment are mostly a decade or more after the initial investment. This means there are limited opportunities for the research agenda in this field to attract venture capital (VC) investment. Though there have been some exceptions, VC money is usually invested in later rounds in a company's history, usually after a demonstration of value beyond intellectual property has occurred. This means some, if not most, funding for nanoscience will need to be publicly funded. If citizens fail to support nano-related research, there might be problems in maintaining a sufficient research budget.

Second, advocates and detractors like to reference the European boycotts associated with American exports of genetically engineered foods when discussing nanoprod-ucts. Though it seems highly unlikely a viable boycott against nanoproducts can be mounted, the fear is repeated *ad nauseum*, mostly to consume as much rhetorical space as possible.

Nanoscience-enhanced products are pervasive and cover many different product lines; hence a boycott of sorts is difficult to mount. While a consumer may forgo buying nanowhicker pants, the calculus associated with buying nanomedicines is completely different. Labeling nanoproducts might take the steam out of a boycott movement. In addition, boycotts are less and less effective with increasing globalization. And the list of responses goes on *ad nauseum* again.

A variation on this theme involves a protest movement, but evidence to date suggests there is little to fear from the THONG folks (Laumer, 2005) and the students in the streets of Grenoble (Earth First, 2006) and elsewhere. There is no evidence a movement is fermenting and neither of the two most critical NGOs—the ETC Group from Canada and the Friends of the Earth—has been encouraging the development of one. Engendering fears of boycotts and protests seems to have convinced at least some that the public needs to function as a holder of stakes in the nanodebate.

Third, the public acts as consumers. Here we have a very controversial bit of political theory. While traditional views of *the* public sphere generally refer to citizens as political participants in an open democracy, there is the view that citizens in the twenty-first century function as consumers. This perspective has been drawn from media studies and refers to the public, especially women as consumers, as passive participants in contemporary consumer culture. This debate needs to occur elsewhere; nevertheless the concerns expressed in the nanodebate relate to whether the public will purchase consumer goods produced and/or including nanoparticles.

Somewhat related to the boycott issues above, this argument starts with two caveats: First, products involving nanotechnology may initially be more expensive than competing products irrespective of other variables, such as quality, and second, new nanoproducts may compete with current brands and will need to break brand loyalty. Of course (and regardless of the reason), should the public elect not to buy nano-related products, business and industry will cease to support its development.

In the corporate governance field, another reason stakeholders are considered relevant is they have the potential to become shareholders (Bonnafous-Boucher et al., 2005): "Stakeholder theory in corporate governance corresponds to a proprietorialist conception for which the virtual future of a stakeholder is to become a shareholder. This means that a certain amount of pressure is exerted on stakeholders to acquire shares in a company.... [T]heir behavior is analyzed hypothetically, 'as if' they were going to become shareholders."

Finally, one can argue consumers purchasing products participate in the economy much the same way as shareholders. This occurs on a few levels. For example, the rise of small investors and mutual funds now implicates citizen/consumers as shareholders. In addition, without the consumption of products by a consuming public, shares of a company are worthless.

ON SPHERES AND PUBLICS

Much of the rhetoric on stakeholders devolves into diatribes over the public sphere. This term, learned in introduction to political science classes while first-year college students, is used willy-nilly by stakeholder advocates as if it has some unique providence or imprimatur. To begin, it may be important to distinguish between *the* public sphere versus *a* public sphere. Not all references to public sphere and to publics have the same meaning. People can be the public sphere, a public sphere, a public, a counterpublic, and so on.

Here's the breakdown. There is *the public sphere* (see Habermas, 1992; Dewey, 1916; Lippman, 1999). Then, there is *the public*. Finally, there are many publics and even counter publics. So when someone makes the claim "we need public involvement," the first thing we should do is determine what that really means.

The public sphere is an entity that has comprehensive understanding and purvey over the broad range of public issues. Its titular function is in electing representatives to governance structures of all sorts. Traditionally, it was composed of white male landowners. When groups of people found this composition unacceptable, they organized into multiple separate public spheres—hence we get a public sphere to describe these groups. These latter are often reported as social movements—such as the Women's Movement—but, unlike single-issue movements, they advance a more comprehensive agenda.

Now we get to a public and a counterpublic. A public and a counterpublic are spaces of discourse and they are self-creating and self-organized though affected by preexisting forms and channels of communication. They must be more than a list of one's friends. They must include strangers though selected by shared social space. Consider, as an example, a National Rifle Association meeting.

DEFINING THE PUBLIC

Most of the time when someone uses apostrophe to call out to the public, they are not using the word "public" in its formal sense; they are talking about Mom and Pop, Joe "Six-pack," and the folks shopping at Wal-Mart.

It is important to note that the public as an entity is not overly concerned about nanotechnology and many studies support that conclusion. Here's some data: An American ISTPP National Nanotechnology Survey (2003; $n = 928$) found 65 percent of respondents had no subjective knowledge on nanotechnology with only 15 percent reporting that bad things might happen from its use. A study from North Carolina State (Cobb and Macoubrie, 2004; $n = 1536$) reported 52 percent had no familiarity with nanotechnology and 83 percent heard little to nothing. Even more interesting is an online survey ($n = 400$) conducted by *GolinHarris* in late 2004 (U.S. Leadership in nanoscience, 2004). Likely voters placed a high priority on U.S. leadership in technology. Even though 80 percent could not name a single company that is a leader in nanotechnology, 60 percent felt it was important for state governments to get involved in nanoscience research funding and 60 percent said the government should increase funding levels for nanotechnology research.

European data are similar. The 2001 European Commission (EC) *Eurobarometer 55.2* (Europeans, Science and Technology, 2001) released findings ($n = 16,029$) indicating that European Union (EU) respondents were uninterested in scientific and technical developments associated with nanotechnology with over 65 percent indicating they felt they did not understand the "topic" of nanotechnologies. A more recent British study reported "29 percent of respondents from both the workshops and the survey said they were aware of the term 'nanotechnology'" and "68 percent ... of those who were able to give a definition ... felt it would improve life.... Only 4 percent thought it would make things worse.... 13 percent of the workshop respondents said that nanotechnology would make things better or worse depended on how it was used" (BMRB Social Research, 2004). A late 2004 EC online study ($n = 749$) reported that 80 percent expect nanotechnology to play a role in their lives by 2015 and 75 percent of respondents believed Europe should embark on studies on the risks and societal implications of nanotechnology (Outcome of the Open Consultation, 2004). Finally, *Eurobarometer 64.3* (Gaskell et al., 2006; $n = 25,000$) reported the ratio of optimists to pessimists increased to 8:1 since 2001. Unsurprisingly, the percentage of "don't know" responses remained above 40 percent.

In Japan, the data set is similar as well. In study conducted by Fujita Yokoyama, and Abe (2006; $n = 1011$), 34.1 percent claimed that they knew about the word "nanotechnology" and 20.3 percent replied that they knew its simple explanation, whereas 55.2 percent claimed that they have heard about nanotechnology frequently or from time to time. Finally 88 percent thought positively about nanotechnology's benefit on society while 54.5 percent felt worried one way or another about the advancement of nanotechnology.

Reading these data remains problematic. Foremost, there is no evidence out there indicating how much of the public has any interest whatsoever in science and technology policymaking and how strong the opinion may be and whether it becomes an attitude. Additionally, most families are much too busy trying to pay their bills and raise their children to be concerned about a subject as esoteric as nanotechnology. Undoubtedly the price tag on science projects does not seem to be counterbalanced by the benefits, at least as the public reads it.

Remember the Supercollider. While the Supercollider was closed down for a host of potential reasons, the number 1 cause seems to be linked back to budgetary concerns. Scientists had a difficult time explaining why the public should be forced to pay for a multi-billion-dollar project designed to find Higgs boson and supersymmetric particles. Representative Sherwood Boehlert (Republican, New York), now chair of the House Science Committee, said, "There was a lot of arrogance in how this project was presented to Congress. They assumed that it couldn't be shut down" (Mervis and Seife, 2003, p. 39). Boehlert, a supporter of federal funding of nanotechnology, is concerned weak public support might damage the NNI; hence we have a preoccupation with stakes and stakeholding.

The data out there suggest the public has a low familiarity with nanotechnology and some of those studies are suspect. Indeed, anyone with a rudimentary understanding in statistical sampling and associated methodologies will tell you that a good amount of the public opining about nanotechnology might provoke expressing an opinion for the very first time in response to the question. When you ask for an opinion, you get one regardless whether the respondent had one in the first place. Absent the question, no opinion may have existed at all.

If there is a public that needs to participate, then we need to understand the demographics of that public so the message can be focused rather than the current efforts to outreach, most of which are insufficient and misdirected. It would make much more sense to determine who needs and wants to know and address their concerns in a convenient manner to ensure their participation.

THE ORGANIZED PUBLIC

Who are the highly relevant people? Let us start with representatives of the public, often self-proclaimed NGOs. To begin this discussion, here is a thought experiment. Consider the roles embraced by NGOs. They are both private interest (they exist to perpetuate their existence) and public interest (they exist to represent the public). When they function in the latter role, we must ask ourselves which public or how much of the public.

Here is some grist. For the purposes of this discussion, consider the Center for Responsible Nanotechnology (CRN) and the Foresight Nanotechnology Institute (FNI). While I may not agree with all their positions, they have contributed new concerns and ideas to the debate over nanotechnology and the people involved are quite pleasant. These two groups have found new capital in the work of the International Risk Governance Council, which has written a compelling document on risk over the two frames of development in applied nanoscience. Frame 1 involves passive nanostructures, such as nanoparticles of magnesium oxide to fight chemical accidents. Frame 2 involves active structures which in the long term could include molecular manufacturing. As such, we can expect to hear more from them in the years ahead.

Primarily, CRN involves two researchers, Mike Treder and Chris Phoenix, and they have a membership and some colleagues. FNI includes many more main researchers and spokespersons, such as Christine Peterson and Scott Mize, and has partnerships and a much more extensive membership base. When both CRN and FNI participate in debates over nanotechnology, is it legitimate they should be given equal attention as stakeholders? Do they represent the public as a NGO? If so, are they functioning within or as the public sphere or a public sphere? Or are they the public or a public or even a counterpublic?

Consider a second set of NGOs: Environmental Defense (ED) and Friends of the Earth (FOE). Environmental Defense has a long history of interest in environmental issues and a large membership with a highly professional and technically savvy international team of experts. Friends of the Earth has a large membership and a strong leadership team as well. While ED has made extensive efforts to participate in developing the knowledge base for debates over nanotechnology by participating in international and national forums, such as National Pollution Prevention and Toxic Advisory Committee of the EPA and the International Council on Nanotechnology, FOE has not. Indeed, but for the cosigning of the International Center for Technology Assessment's petition to the Food and Drug Administration (FDA; Kimbrell, 2006), an online publication on sunscreens and cosmetics (Friends of the Earth, 2006), a dedicated issue of *Chain Reaction* (Friends of the Earth Australia, 2006), and recycling of previous work by other groups, most of interest seems to be from its Australian team and their concerns are mostly about the inequities of globalization. Friends of the Earth represents a network with more members, but one has to question both its commitment and expertise in debates over issues related to nanotechnology since its agenda seems more concerned with antiglobalization than it does with nanotechnology. In this instance, how should its public capital be assessed?

THE VERNACULAR PUBLIC

Let us look at a class of the current efforts to reach out to the people as individuals: consensus conferences, juries, science cafes, and citizen schools. All four of these can generate useful information for stakeholders though their linkage to public participation as a concept is tenable. Fundamentally, all of these have problems of priming (think of the public as a pump). Their successes and failures are directly linked to how people are prepared for the experiment. Materials which are selected to be read by or orally delivered to the participants often reflect the ideological interests of those doing the selecting. While there may be roughly a balance between materials favorable and unfavorable to the subject, decisions to include some critics and not others or some criticisms and not others impacts the range of conclusions participants may draw.

This is not meant to support a case against these projects. If expenses are controlled, these experiments can provide the type of information which can be tested in other ways, such as broad-based surveys. As long as expectations and results are reported conservatively, these programs, especially cafes and citizen schools, offer excellent opportunities for local entities to include the public. Cafes are civic experiments and citizen schools are a unique form of continuing education, however both these experiments by involving self-selected populations which may not include the target demographic.

Some good news may be found in efforts to improve science education in elementary and secondary schools though results have been mixed. A new project offers hope. Recently, the National Science Foundation (NSF) has begun to support a national Nanoscale Informal Science Education Network (NISE Network). The NISE Network is supposed to collaboratively develop and distribute innovative approaches to engaging Americans in nanoscale science and engineering education, research, and technology. The Museum of Science, Boston (MoS) announced a partnership with the Science Museum of Minnesota and the Exploratorium in San Francisco. The $20 million award to the Museum of Science (2006) and its partners for the five-year effort is the largest award NSF has ever given to the science museum community.

While efforts in the classroom are affected by curriculum restrictions set by local school boards, the museum system offers a special means to reaching school-aged children. There have already been a series of museum exhibitions, both here (Steele, 2006) and abroad (Science Museum, 2006), that have examined nanothings for children; NISE is a much more directed effort and we wait to see the effect.

PRAYING OVER *PREY*

Broad public outreach in terms of popular culture remains completely underexplored. Elsewhere, I have argued that popular culture can set important benchmarks in science education (Berube, 2006). In addition, I drew the conclusion that blockbuster summer films are not something about which we need to concern ourselves. Nonetheless, colleagues of mine seem to raise the *Prey* flag warning of some impending overthrow of the NNI following its release.

In 2002, Michael Crichton wrote *Prey*. In the book, he described how biologically synthesized nanorobots wreak havoc in the United States. David Rejeski, director of the Foresight and Governance program at the Woodrow Wilson International Center for Scholars in Washington, D.C., not unknown for his hyperbole, has logged this warning (Brumfield, 2003): "The book is being made into a film. Within weeks of its release, tens of millions will know something about nanotechnology." First, the film does not seem to be in preproduction, and second, the informational impact remains asserted.

Internationally renowned toxicologist Vicki Colvin from Rice University's Center for Biological and Environmental Nanotechnology added her admonition (Brown, 2003): "This is science fiction, not science fact, however, the public relations nightmare it could spawn is just as frightening to me, a nanotechnology researcher, as nanorobots might be to some people." See criticism above.

As I explained in my book, *Prey* was on the best seller's list for only eight weeks and never reached number 1; Twentieth Century Fox has yet to find a director, a producer, or any actors for the movie (ETC Group, 2004). The only force that seems to be keeping the production likeliness of this "B" movie alive may be the nanotechnology community. How ironic if our rhetorical misgivings about *Prey* actually increases its visibility and pertinence, especially since *Prey* is no *Silent Spring*.

I am not advocating that we ignore the prospects of a movie being released that might impact public sentiment. Though when the SciFi Channel released *Path of Destruction* in which nanobots eat a hunk of Seattle (probably accelerated by the high level of caffeine in the city), no one seemed to notice.

As such, we find ourselves in agreement with Kelly Kordzik of Winstead and head of the Texas Nanotechnology Initiative. He believes an aggressive response might be prudent but he dampens the alarmist rhetoric (Kordzik, 2003, p. 8): "I would like to encourage those of us involved in the development of this emerging science to take responsibility for defining what nanotechnology is and not rely on Hollywood or the news media to do so."

POPULAR CULTURE AND PUBLIC ANCHORING

Communicating to lay audiences is challenging. Perception and risk communication research indicates that lay audiences do not rank order risks objectively. There are factors like dread, outrage, and stigma. There are biases associated with affect, affiliation, and availability. There are complicating heuristics of alarm, proportionality, and anecdotal evidence. For illustrative purposes and continuing on the thread of popular culture, one of the most interesting complicating biases has to do with anchoring and adjustment.

Anchoring and adjustment refer to two analytic procedures that the human mind undertakes when asked to process information and make estimates. They function as shortcuts or heuristics. According to Chapman and Johnson (2002, p. 121), "we define an *anchoring procedure* as one in which a salient but uninformative number is presented to subjects before they make a numeric judgment." This way, if an irrelevant number has a statistically significant effect on an estimation, there is no logical reason for its effect, only that some natural reaction in information processing must have occurred. A number of studies have been done using anchoring procedures to determine whether or not this can significantly alter our heuristic processes.

One study found correlation is often seen with anchors that are uninformative. Russo and Shoemaker (1989) asked participants to estimate the year Attila the Hun was defeated after considering an anchor constructed from their phone numbers. Since there is no logical relationship between the two, we would expect no correlation but that was not the case. The researchers asked subjects to think of the last three digits of their phone number; to add 400 to that number; to think of the resulting number as a date; and to consider whether Attila the Hun was defeated in Europe before or after that date. After that, they were asked to guess the date when he was actually defeated. They found that the answer to the last question positively depends on the date that people calculated from their home phone numbers, demonstrating the power of the heuristic.

Furthermore, there are also a few factors that can amplify the anchoring effect. Anchoring is more likely to occur if the anchor and response are on the same scale. Kahneman and Knetsch (1993) asked if people would pay $25 (low anchor) or $200 (high anchor) to clean up Toronto lakes and then estimate an average contribution for Torontonians. There was a noticeable anchoring effect resulting in mean estimates of $36 for the high anchor and $14 for the low anchor. Others were then asked to estimate the percentage of Torontonians that would contribute $100 and there was no significant anchoring effect.

The anchoring and adjustment effect as a heuristic bias is so strong that it occurs even when the anchors are extremely implausible results for the target question. Strack and Mussweiler asked for estimates of Einstein's first visit to the United States after considering anchors of 1215 and 1992, which produced significant effects similar to more plausible anchors such as 1905 and 1939. Finally, both Wilson et al. (1996) and Quattrone et al. (1981) found that warning participants that an anchoring effect may occur did little to deter its influence.

There are two major decision points during the cognitive process where the anchoring effect may take place. First, information regarding the target question is retrieved from memory. Consequently, the anchor could influence what information is retrieved or information compatible with the anchor may be selectively retrieved. Next, the information has to be integrated to make a judgment. The anchor could affect the integration by giving greater weight to information compatible with the anchor.

As such, when people reason, they use variables experts do not. This is a nonrational system. The many biases and heuristics functioning to complicate communication between experts and lay people are significant. This does not make the layperson irrational per se, it simply complicates involving them in rational decision-making situations, like policy in debates about science.

GEOGRAPHICAL ANOMALIES

Involving stakeholders, meaning the layperson, does not guarantee their voices will be heard. There remains quite a bit of tension between the public as stakeholders and experts in the field. Some scientists do not want to have to dumb down their ideas for the lay public. For example, this appeared in an email I received (Berube, 2005): "To those of us who are faced with the challenge of actually communicating this information, instead of the luxury of communicating about it, professional language is a necessity. Some ideas can only be expressed pragmatically in equation form; and if a person doesn't understand the basics of a sp3 carbon bond, or he isn't familiar with kt as a concept, it would take tens, if not hundreds, of hours to bring him/her up to speed. Why penalize the many thousands who took their chemistry courses in high school and did their homework? I reject the notion that either you or I, with our advanced degrees, can truly judge what is 'accessible' to the lay public."

These attitudes are not limited to scientists and technologists. Even some elected representatives question the wisdom of public engagement. In response to a proposal to solicit research on societal interest, Dana Rohrbacher, a Representative from California, offered this lament (Berube, 2005): "It sounds like to me you are putting all of the sociology and literature majors in charge of defining the goals of the engineering and science majors. Am I the only one who is skeptical of the social sciences here? We're injecting bureaucracies into the sciences and bureaucracies are good at transforming pure energy into solid waste. You'll be giving a forum to the very nuts you are trying to overcome."

As a result, valiant efforts at stakeholding represent an incredible challenge. We probably need a roadmap to help in composing a risk dialogue with laypersons on nanotechnology. While we wait for that to be designed, here are some ideas.

RECOMMENDATIONS

What follows are three general recommendations. They represent observations made about the state of nanotechnology policymaking and public engagement by us. They include finding ways to make sense from the clamor of voices, ways to make information available to people, and ways to address their needs within the comfortable popular culture venue.

When people speak, they do not speak with equal stakes. Empowering one group of the people with a louder voice than another is really not that new. Whether we make the determination on the basis of physical wealth or intellectual wealth, it happens inevitably sometimes before engagement when deciding who to invite among the many possible participants, other times during engagement as voices jockey for attention, and even after engagement in media coverage.

As people seem unconcerned about science policy, it is probably inappropriate for groups, like NGOs, to assert they represent their interests. Defending interests that are unexpressed is incredibly patronizing and no less elitist in construction than any other form of representation such as by elected officials and government bureaucrats.

Accordingly, stakeholders hold different levels of stakes in the debate over nanotechnology. Those with the most to lose or to win would hold quantitatively more stakes than others who mostly remain unaffected.

The general public will function primarily as consumers. If they choose to buy nanoproducts, they indicate approval. If they elect to act otherwise, much like Western Europeans did with genetically modified foods, they express their disapproval. Deciding who is a stakeholder may be challenging. However, once nearly everyone becomes a stakeholder, it is time to weigh the stakes with the primary stakeholders being the regulatory, business, and public interest communities.

Next we need a functioning clearinghouse. To date, we have been involved in two grant proposals both of which were supposed to create national clearinghouses. While my teams were not selected for either of these grants and you can label the following sour grapes, hear me out. We have been trying to involve people in the policymaking process of the NNI for at least six years. To date, the public has few coordinated resources at their disposal. While the National Nanotechnology Coordinating Office does its best, it is clearly understaffed and overcommitted. The National Nanotechnology Infrastructure Network was supposed to develop a comprehensive public portal and has not. The Center for Nanotechnology in Society network has been up less than a year, but in discussions with the principals from the different colleges and universities in the network, a clearinghouse is hardly likely anytime soon.

What we have been seeing is a broad distributed network of clearinghouses. For example, the Woodrow Wilson-Pew Emerging Technologies team has a product listing on its site, and the International Council on Nanotechnology has a toxicology database and a best practices database forthcoming. Nearly every government regulatory organization, department, and agency has some information on its website on nanotechnology. Almost every site has some media reporting whereby articles relevant to some aspect of nanotechnology are listed. Three strong sources for this information are the Meridian Nano and Development News, Nanotechweb, and mailings from Julia Moore at Woodrow Wilson.

What is missing is a national public clearinghouse where interested parties can find links and context for the material on nanotechnology scattered all over the nanolandscape. Simply put, we need some nanocartography because the geography on the nanolandscape is both immense and confusing. The public will feel more empowered if they can one-stop shop for information in a user-friendly format.

Though it might be overestimating the role of popular culture in answering questions about science, there is some weak anecdotal evidence and a few studies suggesting laypersons are affected by popular depictions of science. However, those studies link information to the mass media and not specifically to fictionalized portrayal of science and scientific events. As written elsewhere, while the release of the book *Prey* seemed to have left nanoscience and nanotechnology relatively unscathed, "we can only hope the movie will do for nanotechnology what *The Day After Tomorrow* did for global warming: very little" (Berube, 2006, p. 43).

However, if an artifact in popular culture, such as a film, might affect public support, then a documentary could easily function as an anchoring device for a balanced informational meme on nanotechnology. First, the documentary could address the target questions of promises and perils so the target questions or events are contextualized against the data from the documentary. The anchor could help influence what information is retrieved and, even if information compatible with the anchor is selectively retrieved, it allows us to position the heuristic to favor a balanced evaluation and a reasoned response. Next, we know the information has to be integrated to make a judgment. Almost by its very nature, the documentary format functions as an integrator. The documentary as anchor could affect the integration of the information about nanotechnology by giving greater weight to information compatible with the anchor. If the anchor is positive, then the weight should be positive as well. Finally, the documentary as anchor may affect how the judgment is translated to an expression, In turn establishing a powerful context the individual will turn to again and again in forming opinions and judgments, even attitudes.

Hence, maybe a well-produced documentary would establish a balanced anchor point for the public. If and when the "public" learns about a nanotechnology-related incident, especially an environmental health and safety problem, they will contextualize the event against the anchor point. Furthermore, with correct marketing, the documentary could be provided via a distributor so the content would be available to school-aged children. For example, Channel One News reaches 8 million children each day. Another distributor is First Edition and another is CNN's Classroom Edition.

PURPOSE OF STAKEHOLDER PARTICIPATION

So what do the government and other public entities, including trade organizations and research foundations, want with stakeholder involvement? Foremost, they want the public to buy into the proposition that nanotechnology is a wise investment for the reasons outlined above. However, there can be little doubt that the inclusion of the public as stakeholders is symbolic on many levels, especially in terms of sating their concerns (Berube, 2006, pp. 335–360).

Some people have convinced themselves that public involvement in nano-policymaking serves some greater goal of democratic participation. However, there is little evidence to suggest that there are any compelling trends to increase participatory democracy beyond the foreign policy rhetoric on democratizing the Middle East from the Bush administration. In addition, there is no reason to believe that science and technology policymaking is the linchpin to a movement toward more participation or that public participation in science and policy decision making is sufficient to contribute to a trend toward more participation.

On a different level, it is important to consider that some stakeholders may have more at stake than other stakeholders. Defining the stakeholders in debates over nanotechnology is incredibly difficult to do. To include everyone for any correlative interest completely guts the concept. For there to be stakeholders there need to be nonstakeholders. For the purposes of this essay, stakeholders could include promoters (e.g., government and private financing entities), regulators (e.g., environmental and securities), industry (especially insurance), some NGOs (e.g., health and safety groups, and the public (either represented by others or representing themselves). So, there is the rub: Once the public is included, no one is excluded. As noted above, we need to redefine the public for this purpose.

With a concerted effort to engage the general public, we can provide input without playing into the calculating hands of those who would stall the development of nanotechnology for reasons of their own, like antiglobalization "spin doctors," with positions having little if anything to do with the technology instant. At the same time, the concept of the public and stakeholder needs to be reexamined if we want to provide true meaning to these concepts instead of using them as rhetorical hammers to beat the audience into accepting a fait accompli by sating their criticisms through false participation.

REFERENCES

Berube, D. 2005. Stakeholders in the National Nanotechnology Initiative. PowerPoint presentation, at the 2005 NCA Preconference Rhetoric and the Politicization of Science, Boston, November 16, 2005. Boston: National Communication Association.

Berube, D. 2006. *NanoHype: The Truth behind the Nanotechnology Buzz.* Amherst, NY: Prometheus Books.

BMRB Social Research. 2004. Nanotechnology: Views of the general public, quantitative and qualitative research carried out as part of the nanotechnology study. BMRB International Report 45101666. Available: http://www.nanotec.org.uk/Market%20Research.pdf, accessed June 25, 2004.

Bonnafous-Boucher, M. 2005. Some philosophical issues in corporate governance: The role of property in stakeholder theory. *Corporate Governance* 5(2): 34–47.

Brown, D. 2003. Perception may be nano's biggest enemy, leaders tell Congress. *Small Times.* Available: http://www.smalltimes.com/print_doc.cfm?doc_id=5809, accessed April 24, 2003.

Brumfield, G. 2003. A little knowledge. *Nature* 424(6946): 248.

Chapman, G., and Johnson, E. 2002. Incorporating the irrelevant: Anchors in judgments of belief and value. In T. Gilovich, D. Griffin, and D. Kahneman (Eds.). *Heuristics and Biases: The Psychology of Intuitive Judgment* Cambridge: Cambridge University Press.

Cobb, M., and Macoubrie, J. 2004. Public perceptions about nanotechnology: Risks, benefits and trust. *Journal of Nanoparticle Research* 6(4): 395–405.

Dewey, J. 1916. *Democracy and Education.* New York: Macmillan.

Earth First! 2006. Action Reports: Grenoble, France: Actions against nanotechnologies on May 30th–June 2nd. Available: http://earthfirst.org.uk/actionreports/?q=node/1333, accessed July 19, 2006.

ETC Group. 2004. Nanotech news in living colour: An update on white papers, red flags, green goo, grey goo (and red herrings). *Communiqué* 85 (May/June): 7.

Europeans, Science and Technology. 2001. Eurobarometer 55.2. Available: http://ec.europa.eu/research/press/2001/pr0612en-report.pdf, accessed July 24, 2006.

Friends of the Earth. 2006. Nanomaterials, sunscreens and cosmetics: Small ingredients, big risks. Available: http://nano.foe.org.au/node/125, accessed July 20, 2006.

Friends of the Earth Australia. 2006. Size does matter: Nanotechnology—small sciences, big questions. Chain reaction. Available: http://www.foe.org.au/download/CR97.pdf, accessed July 20, 2006.

Fujita, Y., Yokoyama, H., and Abe, S. 2006. Perception of nanotechnology among the general public in Japan—of the NRI Nanotechnology and Society Survey Project. *Asia Pacific Nanotech Weekly* 4(6).

Gaskell, G., et al. 2006. Europeans and biotechnology in 2005: Patterns and trends, Eurobarometer 64.3: A report to the European Commission's Directorate-General for Research. Available: www.ec.europa.eu/research/press/2006/pdf/pr1906_eb_64_3_final_report-may2006_en.pdf, accessed July 24, 2006.

Habermas, J. 1992. *Habermas and the Public Sphere.* Cambridge, MA: MIT Press.

ISTPP National Nanotechnology Survey. 2003. College Station, Texas: Institute for Science, Technology and Public Policy, George Bush School and Government and Public Service, Texas A & M University, unpublished, June 16, 2004.

Jennings, M. 2006. University of St. Thomas, Houston: Stakeholder theory: Letting anyone who's Interested run the business—No investment required. Available: http://www.stthom.edu/academics/centers/cbes/marianne_jennings.html, accessed May 19, 2006.

Kahneman, D., and Knetsch, J. 1993. Anchoring or shallow inferences: The effect of format, unpublished manuscript. University of California, Berkeley.

Kimbrell, G. 2006. Consumer, health, and environmental groups launch first-ever legal challenge on risks of nanotechnlogy. International Center for Technology Assessment. Available: http://www.icta.org/press/release.cfm?news_id=19, accessed July 20, 2006.

Kordzik, K. 2003. Prey tell what nano is? Nope.... *Small Times*, January/February, p. 8.

Laumer, J. 2005. Treehugger.com: Nano-tech street protest on Chicago's Magnificent Mile. Available: http://www.treehugger.com/files/2005/05/nanotech_street_1.php, accessed July 19, 2006.

Lippman, W. 1999 (1927) *The Phantom Public*. New Brunswick, NJ: Transaction Press.

Merriam-Webster. 1996. *Dictionary of Law*. Springfield, MA: Merriam-Webster.

Mervis, J., and Seife, C. 2003. Lots of reasons, but few lessons. *Science* 302 (5642): 39.

Museum of Science. 2006. Museum of Science receives nanotechnology grant. Available: http://www.mos.org/doc/1892, accessed July 20, 2006.

National Nanotechnology Initiative: Strategic Plan. 2004. Nanoscale Science, Engineering, and Technology Subcommittee, Committee on Technology, National Science and Technology Council. Washington, DC.

Outcome of the Open Consultation on the European Strategy for Nanotechnology. 2004. Nanoforum. Available: http://www.nanoforum.org/dateien/temp/nanosurvey6.pdf?20122004094532, accessed July 18, 2005.

Quattrone, G. A., Lawrence, C. P., Finkel, S. E., and Andrus, D. C. 1981. Explorations in anchoring: The effects of prior range, anchor extremity, and suggestive hints. Stanford, CA: Stanford University.

Russo, J. E., and Shoemaker, P. J. H. 1989. *Decision Traps*. New York: Simon & Schuster.

Science Museum. 2006. Nanotechnology: small science, big deal http://www.sciencemuseum.org.uk/antenna/nano/, accessed July 20, 2006.

Steele, B. 2006. Cornell museum exhibits allow children to enter world of the very, very small. Chronicle Online. Available: http://www.news.cornell.edu/stories/Feb06/AAAS.Waldron.ws.html, accessed July 20, 2006.

U.S. Environmental Protection Agency, Office of Policy, Economics, and Innovation. 2001. Stakeholder involvement & public participation at the U.S. E.P.A.: Lessons learned, barriers, & innovative approaches. Available: http://www.epa.gov/stakeholders, accessed May 21, 2006.

U.S. leadership in nanoscience should be a government priority, says survey respondents. 2004. NewsNanoApex. Available: http://news.nanoapex.com/modules.php?name=News&fule=print&sid=5010, accessed September 22, 2004.

Wilson, T. D., Houston, C., Etling, K. M., and Brekke, N. 1996. A new look at anchoring effects: Basic anchoring and its antecedents. *Journal of Experimental Psychology* 4: 387–402.

18

RULES OF ENGAGEMENT: DEMOCRACY AND DIALOGUE IN CREATING NANOTECHNOLOGY FUTURES

Jack Stilgoe and James Wilsdon

Within an hour of arriving, the participants in our People's Inquiry into Nanotechnologies were in the thick of a debate. It didn't start well. The conversation moved from Mork and Mindy ("nanoo, nanoo") to the Teletubbies' vacuum-cleaning pet (NooNoo) before one person admitted, "I don't know. I don't do science." Yet just four weeks later, after 15 hours of discussion and deliberation and input from a range of expert witnesses, this group of 13 ordinary Londoners had produced a thoughtful set of recommendations.

At first, their task had seemed rather esoteric: to consider whether government should allow the use of nanoparticles as a method of cleaning up contaminated land. But for the Environment Agency, the United Kingdom's environmental regulator, this was a pressing question. A number of companies had applied to use nanoparticles in this way. To do so would require the release of novel nanoparticles into the environment. This was potentially controversial as an influential 2004 report from The Royal Society and Royal Academy of Engineering had cautioned against any such releases. In this context, the aim of our People's Inquiry was to expand the boundaries of societal discussion so that new regulations for the use of nanoparticles could better reflect the values and interests of the wider public.

Nanoethics: The Ethical and Social Implications of Nanotechnology. Edited by Allhoff, Lin, Moor, Weckert
Copyright © 2007 John Wiley & Sons, Inc.

PADDLING UPSTREAM

Despite the waves of expectation surrounding nanotechnologies that have excited scientists, policymakers, and investors over the past decade, the potential for a nanorevolution barely registers on most people's list of priorities or concerns. One opinion poll found that only 29 percent of the British public had heard of nanotechnologies, and only 19 percent had any idea what they are (Nanotec, 2004). Many of the nano-related products that are now available remain fairly prosaic: clothes, sports equipment, sunscreen. Yet if even a fraction of the transformative potential of these technologies is fulfilled, over time the public will start to learn, and care, far more about them. They will relate to nano both as citizens and as consumers.

Exercises in public participation, such as our People's Inquiry, reflect a wider shift in the culture and practice of science. Across Europe, after a decade punctuated by controversies over BSE (mad cow disease), genetically modified crops, and mobile phone masts, the science community has started to adopt a more conversational tone in its dealings with the public, if not always with enthusiasm, then out of a recognition that such controversies have made public engagement a nonnegotiable clause of their license to operate.

More recently, there has been growing interest in the potential to move public engagement "upstream" —to an earlier stage in processes of research and development. For example, the U.K. government's 2004 strategy for science and innovation includes a commitment "to enable debate to take place 'upstream' in the scientific and technological development process, and not 'downstream' where technologies are waiting to be exploited but may be held back by public skepticism brought about through poor engagement and dialogue on issues of concern" (Her Majesty's Treasury, 2004, p. 105).

We have also seen the increased use of new methods for engagement, such as citizens' juries, focus groups, consensus conferences, and deliberative polls. The intricacies of these techniques are less important than their motivations. At some level, they all invite broader consideration of issues that may otherwise have been discussed only by select groups. The new light they can shed on issues is particularly important for science and technology, where discussions have traditionally involved only experts.

EXPERIMENTS IN DEMOCRACY

The emergence of nanotechnologies at this point in a broader cycle of debate about science, technology, and society means that they have become a particular focus for democratic innovation and experimentation. In the United Kingdom, the first such process was NanoJury (www.nanojury.org), initiated by Greenpeace, the *Guardian* newspaper, and researchers at the University of Newcastle. This involved a group of 20 people from Halifax in West Yorkshire who met regularly over a four-month period in 2005 to discuss the social implications of nanotechnology.

NanoJury made recommendations about the use of nanotechnologies in health care and renewable energy, where it saw potential benefits. But it also called for better labeling and safety testing of manufactured nanoparticles, which some scientists regard as potentially toxic. Above all, it wanted the public to have a greater say in the direction of research. Richard Jackson, a Halifax businessman and one of the jurors, explained why: "I got the impression that even the scientists don't know where we're going with this technology. This isn't necessarily a bad thing, but we should be having a public debate about some of these questions."

Elsewhere, experiments with nanoengagement have taken different forms. In Wisconsin, a panel of 13 people emerged from their three-day "consensus conference" with experts recommending, among other things, that the burden of proof of nanotechnology safety should rest with the producer. In New Zealand, a project aiming to feed public views into nanopolicy revealed particular concerns about nanoparticles in the environment (Cook et al., 2005; Lafollette, 2005).

Such projects demonstrate that, with the right encouragement and support, the public are willing and even enthusiastic to enter into discussions of nanotechnology futures. Our work at Demos has taken some of these methods and applied them in new contexts, connecting them to a range of policy agendas. Below we summarize three recent experiments.

EXPERIMENT 1: BEHIND THE SCENES AT THE MUSEUM

The neogothic façade of the Natural History Museum dominates one of the busiest roads in Kensington, south London. The museum is full of dinosaur skeletons and artifacts of Victorian taxonomy and taxidermy. Increasingly, it is also the location for public conversations about science. In the autumn of 2005, we convened a meeting there of 12 nanoscientists and 12 nonscientists. We set out to demonstrate that a productive exchange is possible on "upstream" questions and uncertainties. In this respect, the meeting was a success. Our lay participants left feeling empowered by their encounter with the scientists, and our scientists were grateful for the opportunity to reflect on the social dimensions of their research. As one nanoscientist remarked at the end of the day:

> I was interested to see the things that people kept coming back to ... were the whole issue of responsibility and how we actually use technology. These are the same sort of issues we don't know anything about and have no control over. We possibly ought to. It's the same things I worry about when I'm not being a scientist. So in a way it's quite nice ... I'm not as detached from the real world as I thought I was.

This experiment revealed a deep public ambivalence, laden with hope of enormous benefits and fear that the myriad technologies would be unmanageable. The notion of responsibility was central. Before these things get discussed, it is all too easy to assume that responsibility is *something that someone has*. The more we talked about the issue that afternoon, the more we all realized that responsibility is something that emerges and is distributed. One scientist who took part acknowledged: "Scientists are in the same boat as everyone else I think. We have no power to make these big choices."

Woven into this conversation about responsibility, which is often expressed in terms of what happens when something goes wrong, was the question of directing nanotechnology to the most productive social ends. Richard Jones, professor of physics at Sheffield University, put it like this:

> I think what's important is not the narrow issue of "Do you do this piece of science and don't you do this piece of science?" Rather it's "What kind of world do you want to live in?" The things that worried the people in my focus group were the things that worried me. I am uncertain about how lots of this stuff will turn out. I have a positive view of how I would like it to turn out but there are people who have opinions about how it ought to turn out that I really don't like at all. It's quite reassuring to think that I am not alone in worrying about the things I worry about."

For more on this experiment, see Kearnes et al. 2006.

EXPERIMENT 2: A PEOPLE'S INQUIRY

Nanoparticles have been tested in a number of countries to clean up pollution, particularly from chlorinated hydrocarbons (Zhang, 2003). For a given mass, nanoparticles are more reactive than their bigger equivalents, and their size allows them to reach the parts of contaminated land that bigger particles cannot. Yet tests so far have analyzed the extent to which the nanoparticles are doing their job, rather than any unintended environmental effects they may have.

This was the focus of our People's Inquiry conducted in 2005 in partnership with the U.K. Environment Agency. The discussion took place in an interesting context: a technology on the horizon with suggested environmental benefits; expert advice that suggested we should prevent release until we knew more; a small group of experts around the world, most of whom openly acknowledged the inherent uncertainties; and virtually nonexistent public knowledge about the technology, let alone its potential benefits and hazards.

Over three days of deliberation, the participants in the People's Inquiry generated countless questions, which they were able to pose to the expert witnesses they interrogated. Some of these were factual:

> "How do things actually stick to these nanoparticles? Is it that it's actually physically sticky or has it got little things like Velcro on it, or has it got sucky things that suck the contaminant out? Or is it a gluey thing?"

> "Is the process of using nanoparticles for land remediation a quicker process than other methods?"

Other questions echoed those of current scientific and regulatory concern:

> "How far can the nanoparticles travel?"

> "Presumably nobody's actually looked at whether the things could be made to break down in cells?"

But most were open questions with no easy answers. They highlighted the areas of concern that were likely to define the future public context of nanotechnologies:

"Will there be any unanticipated effects?"

"Who has a say?"

"Would the fact that it's a quicker process mean that the safety issues may be overlooked?"

"What's the rush?"

"What about irresponsible companies?"

"Is information sharing too informal?"

The conclusions of the People's Inquiry could be grouped into two areas. First, uncertainty was seen as a defining feature of this emerging regulatory debate. Broadly speaking, the participants agreed with the Royal Society's recommendation that nanoparticle release be prevented. In line with the precautionary principle, uncertainty was seen as sufficient to justify action.

A second theme was openness. Our participants, realizing that they would never be experts in the various areas required to grapple fully with the issue, demanded that any steps taken should be more accountable. They were supportive of plans by the U.K. government to develop a notification scheme for nanotechnology companies but were skeptical of companies' willingness to declare data. Realizing that the most important challenges lay in the future, they demanded a more open approach to the application and governance of technology. They argued that regulation should be proactive but also responsive to the changing social and economic context of technology, including the emergence of new concerns and uncertainties.

A few months after the inquiry was complete, four of the participants visited the U.K. Department for Environment, Food and Rural Affairs for a meeting with the team of civil servants managing nanotechnology policy. The meeting involved a robust but constructive exchange of views, and both sides left feeling impressed by what they had heard. One of the public participants concluded that it had convinced her of the value of such exercises. "We can help policymakers," she said. "I feel like we have made some nanoscule contribution to society."

EXPERIMENT 3: NANOKUTAURIRANA: A DIALOGUE IN ZIMBABWE[1]

The Royal Society/Royal Academy of Engineering report spoke of the possibility of a "nanodivide." It pointed to (Her Majesty's Treasury, 2004, Chapter 6.3):

repeated claims about the major long-term impacts of nanotechnologies upon global society: for example, that it will provide cheap sustainable energy, environmental remediation, radical advances in medical diagnosis and treatment, more powerful IT capabilities, and improved consumer products.. . . Concerns have been raised over the potential for nanotechnologies to intensify the gap between rich and poor countries because of their different capacities to develop and exploit nanotechnologies, leading to a so-called "nano-divide."

Communities in the developing world rarely have much of a voice in debates about innovation. They are less likely to see the benefits of new technologies and are more likely to have risks imposed upon them. Nonetheless, there have been a number of efforts to keep the developing world voice alive. The Meridian Institute has facilitated a global dialogue on nanotechnology and the poor. And at Toronto University, a group has explored the potential for nanotechnology to tackle the Millennium Development Goals (Salamanca-Buentello et al., 2005).

Our contribution was in the form of an experiment conducted in July 2006 in partnership with the development NGO Practical Action. For several decades, Practical Action has been putting into practice the message of appropriate and participatory technologies for developing countries. We chose the potential contribution of nanotechnologies to water purification as the focus of our three-day workshop. Our dialogue aimed to bring the views and values of people for whom clean water is an everyday problem into debates about possible technical solutions.

Zimbabwe is a country with numerous problems. Its inflation and unemployment are higher than anywhere else in the world, and its government has recently tried to move the problem off its doorstep by clearing out slums. In Epworth, a suburb of Harare, these problems only exacerbate an issue that for many is an everyday struggle—the search for clean water. Technology may be able to play a role in this, but not without an understanding of this context. The first day of our workshop heard people's views. Water was unaffordable, it was scarce, it was a long way away, and it was normally collected by women and girls. Where wells exist, they are crammed next to latrines and difficult to seal off from contamination. In addition to a recent cholera outbreak, there is chemical pollution from factories downstream.

At the same time, the community in Epworth is skeptical of well-intentioned technological schemes. Too often in the past, they have been let down by treatment techniques that have failed to do their job or have broken and proved impossible to fix. Technology for these communities is as much about human capacity as it is about new widgets. As one participant put it: "When the NGO goes away, who has the knowledge to run and maintain it?"

For our participants, "technology" in general and "nanotechnology" in particular were understood as the system of which the thing—the filter, the treatment plant, or whatever—was a part. Skeptical of the West's assumed desire to impose technologies, they demanded some level of participation in the process. Features such as sustainability, maintenance, adaptability, and extension into communities were seen as vital. One of the Zimbabwean scientists who took part told us the difference between technology and traditional aid: "Technology can't be handed over to a community like a sack of mealy-meal."

The experiment in Zimbabwe revealed the gulf between understandings of the benefits of nanotechnology in the rich North and the poor South. No one should bemoan the growing interest in technologies with potential benefits for the developing world. But promises should be more measured. We need to ask, "What makes science and technology work for the poor?" (Leach and Scoones, 2006). Conversations about technology need to include the voices of real human needs. But there is a lot of work to do before nanotechnology can break the mold of other technological pathways and benefit the poor.

WHERE NEXT?

The experiments that we have described here represent part of the *hardware* of public engagement. They should be seen as a means to an end—improved innovation and governance of new technologies that reflect broad social values. At the same time, there is a need to focus on the *software* of public engagement, the cultures and practices that underpin much of science's relationship with society.

In several ways, our experiments paint a positive picture of the value of engagement. There is a willingness among scientists and members of the public to get together and talk about emerging technologies, even if many applications are not yet available. These conversations can flow freely; they are not necessarily compromised by differences in knowledge or understanding. And the results of these experiments are often useful to scientists and policymakers as a means of generating new questions and exploring assumptions. However, a number of important questions remain:

- The *Why* of Public Engagement. For all the talk of public engagement, there is still a lack of clarity about why it is taking place. Some still view conversations about science as primarily a way of persuading people to think scientifically and trust science. Others see public engagement as important for normative democratic reasons. But there is a third, more complicated rationale. Public engagement opens up firmly held assumptions about science, about benefits, about people, about the limits of knowledge which may otherwise have been left unexplored. Institutions and individuals need to reflect on these assumptions if they are to make good decisions. For nanotechnology, the question is therefore how the messages that emerge from public engagement begin to permeate science and policy.
- The *Who* of Public Engagement. Until very recently, public engagement consisted of conversations with the usual suspects—people with resources and loud voices. In some cases, such as specific areas of medical research, patients groups and other stakeholders may be relatively well defined. But in others we must engage with people who might not immediately recognize the value of being engaged. By the time the general public becomes an interested public, the opportunity for constructive engagement has often passed. Public engagement is easy if scientists choose to talk just to the people who come forward.
- The *How* of Public Engagement. Our experiments in engagement have tried to generate social intelligence by opening up the way the nanotechnology gets talked about. Such experiments might be seen as a starter motor, generating

enough momentum to lead to further, more natural conversations about new technologies. As these conversations grow, it is important that they connect to real decisions. Increasingly with science and technology, these decisions are made through complex global innovation networks. Finding ways to influence and shape these global processes will be a major governance challenge for the next decade and beyond.

- The *What* of Public Engagement. One of the experiments we describe focused on technologies that were available in the marketplace. The others focused on the visions and values of scientists. But for all of these experiments, in one sense the topic of engagement is the future and the place of technologies and people in it. Public engagement that seems to focus on technological products also needs to discuss wider social processes of innovation and governance. There is a need to distinguish between public engagement as a research exercise—providing a mechanism for evaluating the emergence of public opinion—and engagement that is intended to inform political, institutional, and cultural change.

- The *When* of Public Engagement. The strength of upstream engagement is that it takes place early, at a time when new questions can be asked. But it is sometimes misconstrued as a way of anticipating the *impacts* of technology—be they health, social, environmental, or ethical—rather than an opportunity for the public to help shape the trajectory of technological development. The hope is that engagement can be used to head off controversy—a prophylactic that we swallow early on and then stop worrying about. There is no recognition that the social intelligence which engagement generates might become outdated or irrelevant as technologies twist their way through the choices and commitments that make up the innovation process.

SCIENTISM RESURGENT

And despite the progress in this agenda, there are still those who maintain that the public is too ignorant to contribute anything useful to scientific decision making. In the United Kingdom, one vocal critic is Lord Taverne, founder of the pressure group Sense about Science. In a letter to *Nature*, Taverne (2004, p. 271) rejects "the fashionable demand by a group of sociologists for more democratic science." He goes on: "The fact is that science, like art, is not a democratic activity. You do not decide by referendum whether the earth goes round the sun."

But Taverne is setting up a straw man. Upstream engagement is not about members of the public standing over the shoulder of scientists in the laboratory, taking votes or holding referenda on what they should or should not be doing. Nor does it require us to impose cumbersome bureaucratic structures on science or force laypeople to be included on every research funding committee. Questions about structures do need to be considered but are a sideshow compared to the far more important—and exciting—challenge of building more reflective capacity into the *practice* of science. As well as bringing the public into new conversations with science, we need to bring out the public *within* the scientist—by enabling scientists to reflect on the social and ethical dimensions of their work.

We are still at an early stage in developing an understanding of the relationship between nanoscience, innovation, and democracy. But each of these experiments, in its own way, provides a glimpse of a more accountable model of science and innovation. Ultimately, the challenge of upstream public engagement extends across the overlapping and intermingled domains of nanotech, biotech, infotech, and neuroscience. Nanotechnologies are slowly being dragged into the public domain, but it is yet not clear whether they will become an iconic environmental and social issue in the way that genetic modification (GM) did in Europe in the 1990s. The GM example reminds us how particular technologies can become condensation points for new forms of political argument around issues of corporate power, the ownership of knowledge, and conflicting interpretations of sustainable development. Such processes of condensation are inherently unpredictable. But if nanotechnologies live up to even a fraction of the hype that is currently exciting scientists, policymakers, and business leaders, then perhaps the only certainty in this debate is that it has some distance to run.

NOTE

1. Nanokutaurirana is the Shona word, invented at our workshop, for "Nanodialogue."

REFERENCES

Cook, A. J., and Fairweather, J. R. 2005. Nanotechnology—Ethical and social issues: Results from New Zealand focus groups, December 2005. Available: http://www.lincoln.ac. nz/story_images/1330_RR281_s4140.pdf.

Her Majesty's Treasury/DTI/DfES. 2004. *Science and Innovation Investment Framework 2004–2014*. London: Her Majesty's Treasury.

Kearnes, M., Macnaghten, P., and Wilsdon, J. 2006. Governing at the nanoscale. Demos. Available: www.demos.co.uk.

Lafollette. 2005. Report of the Madison Area Citizen Conference on Nanotechnology. Available: http://www.lafollette.wisc.edu/research/Nano/nanoreport42805.pdf.

Leach, M., and Scoones, I. 2006. The slow race, making technology work for the poor. Demos. Available: www.demos.co.uk.

Nanotec. 2004. Nanotechnology: Views of the general public. Prepared for The Royal Society and Royal Academy of Engineering Nanotechnology Working Group by BMRB social research, January 2004. Available: http://www.nanotec.org.uk/Market%20Research.pdf.

Salamanca-Buentello, F., Persad, D. L., Court, E. B., Martin, D. K., Daar, A. S., and Singer, P. A. 2005. Nanotechnology and the developing world. *PLoS Medicine* 2(4): 300–303.

Taverne, D. 2004. Let's be sensible about public participation. *Nature* 432: 271.

Zhang. 2003. Nanoscale iron particles for environmental remediation: An overview. *Journal of Nanoparticle Research* 5: 323–332.

PART VI

ISSUES: BROADER SOCIETAL IMPACT

John Weckert

In this part, the policy focus of the previous one is sharpened to examine specific societal changes that may arise from nanotechnology's developments—the first of which is the likely impact to personal privacy, which is an issue often at the forefront for policymakers and the broader public. This is one area in which we can be fairly certain of the direction in which the development is heading given current technology and the way that it is used.

In Chapter 19, Jeroen van den Hoven, professor at Delft University of Technology in The Netherlands, explores some privacy issues as they are likely to arise with nanoelectronics facilitating ever more pervasive, ubiquitous computing and, just as importantly, inconspicuous or even invisible (because of size) computing. As a precursory lesson for nanotechnology, the use of radio frequency identification (RFID) chips is already widespread, and as these become smaller and cheaper, they could conceivably be implanted into almost any of the objects that we use, including our pets, children, and ourselves. This could, according to van den Hoven, create problems for privacy in the areas of information-based harm, equality, and justice as well as for personal autonomy and identity.

The technology by itself, of course, will not harm us; its use will. We can be fairly certain that it will be used not only for commercial reasons but also for what, in the United States, is called "homeland security." In recent years, there has been pressure exerted by governments on citizens to sacrifice some personal rights, including privacy, for the sake of greater security in the face of terrorism. Obviously, all available technologies that can aid security will be used, and nanotechnology is no exception.

In Chapter 20, Daniel Moore at Georgia Tech explores the use of nanotechnology in the military and, particularly, its defensive role in security. Sensing technologies are of particular importance for the early and quick detection of chemical and biological attacks, and perhaps there might be "swarms" of nanosized robots that could destroy biological, chemical, and other weapons. Other potential uses of nanotechnology in the military currently being researched include lighter and more robust equipment for soldiers as well as more offensive weapons, such as self-guided bullets and new laser weapons. Many of the technologies developed will, Moore argues, also have civilian uses.

In order to develop new technologies, a highly educated population is needed, particularly a highly educated scientific population, and this is an area in which there is some worry that nations, particularly the United States, are deficient. In Chapter 21, SRI researcher Patricia Schank and University of Michigan's Joe Krajcik and Molly Yunker consider this problem and suggest that nanoscience could assist in the reform of scientific education. The United States is injecting funds into nanotechnology through the National Nanotechnology Initiative (NNI), and university-level courses have begun to be introduced. They argue that there should also be courses in nanotechnology developed for secondary schools to help ensure an adequate number of future scientists to satisfy the needs of the United States for nanotechnology development and to present some suggestions on how the curriculum for such courses could be developed.

Finally, Chapter 22 takes a more global view and looks at how the developing world might be helped by nanotechnology. While it is often claimed that nanotechnology will have considerable benefits for developing countries (see Chapter 4), Joachim Schummer at the University of Darmstadt in Germany is not so sure. There is certainly some potential—for example in areas such as water purification, solar energy, and AIDS prevention—but, at least in the shorter term, nanotechnology solutions will be too expensive. Furthermore and in any case, many of the problems are due more to lack of education and information than to any deficiency in technology. Another reason why benefits to developing countries might not be so great is that those that currently supply raw materials to the developed world could be disadvantaged as new nanotechnology products require less of those materials. Finally, there are issues with the current intellectual property rights. These rights tend to favor the developed, mainly Western countries and hinder development in the poorer countries. Intellectual property rights will need to be reexamined if developing countries are to benefit to a greater extent from nanotechnology.

19

NANOTECHNOLOGY AND PRIVACY: INSTRUCTIVE CASE OF RFID

Jeroen van den Hoven

One of the problems with nanoethics is that it addresses problems of applications of nanoscience which are yet to come. In the first decade of the twenty-first century, we still have very few examples of widely used nanotechnology. It is advisable to start thinking about ethical implications of new technology at the early stages of its development, but it does not make reflection and analysis particularly easy. This predicament is a version of the Collingridge dilemma: In the first stages of the development of a new technology, it is still possible to influence the development of the technology, although there is little information about its effects. When the technology is entrenched and widely used, there is information about its effects, but there is little room to change the course of the development of the technology.

One of the areas where we have already a relatively clear picture of the impact of nanotechnology at this stage is the area of the privacy implications of submicrometer and nanoelectronics. This is an area where we can move beyond mere anticipation, speculation, and science fiction. Practically invisible badges, integrated circuits, tags, minute sensors or "smart dust," and wearable electronics are gradually finding their

* This chapter was originally published as Jeroen van den Hoven, "Nanotechnology and Privacy: The Instructive Case of RFID," *International Journal of Applied Philosophy*, vol. 2, no. 2: 215–228. Reprinted with permission.

way to the world of retail, supply chains, logistics, shops and warehouses, workplace, criminal justice, and homeland security.[1] New sensor and surveillance technology is the result of the rapid development of submicrometer and nanotechnology—in accordance with Moore's law, which states that the number of transistors on a chip doubles every 18 months. When combined with middleware and back-end databases, as well as a range of wireless and mobile communication modalities, such as Wi-Fi, ultrawide band, and Bluetooth, and connections to computer networks and the Internet, the technology will give rise to a panoply of privacy issues.

People will knowingly or unknowingly carry around tagged items ranging from clothing to watches, mobile phones, chip cards, identity documents, bank notes, or jewelry. These can all be read and uniquely identified from a distance (ranging from centimeters to hundreds of meters) by readers which may be hidden or not in the line of sight. This will make objects, and the people carrying or accompanying them, traceable wherever they go. They may be followed from shelf to shelf or from shop to shop and identified as the buyer, carrier, or user of an item, which can lead to further identifications and knowledge discovery in the associated databases.

Kris Pister (2001), one of the leading researchers in the field, sketches the following picture on the basis of current research:

> In 2010 your house and office will be aware of your presence, and even orientation, in a given room. In 2010 everything you own that is worth more than a few dollars will know that it's yours, and you'll be able to find it whenever you want it. Stealing cars, furniture, stereos, or other valuables will be unusual, because any of your valuables that leave your house will check in on their way out the door, and scream like a troll's magic purse if removed without permission (they may scream at 2.4 GHz rather than in audio). . . . In 2010 a speck of dust on each of your fingernails will continuously transmit fingertip motion to your computer. Your computer will understand when you type, point, click, gesture, sculpt, or play air guitar.

RADIO FREQUENCY IDENTITY CHIP

The core technology of this type of tracking and tracing is the widely used radio frequency identity (RFID) chip. An RFID chip or tag consists of a small integrated circuit attached to a tiny radio antenna which can receive and transmit a radio signal. The storage capacity of the chip can be up to 128 bits. The chip can either supply its own energy (active tag) from a battery or get its energy input from a radio signal from the antenna of the reader (passive tag). As for bar codes, there is an international number organization which provides and registers the unique ID numbers of RFID chips (EPC global, www.epcglobalinc.org). The RFID chip is ideally suited for the tracking and tracing of objects such as boxes, containers, and vehicles in logistic chains. The RFID tags are now also being used to trace and track consumer products and everyday objects on the item level as a replacement of barcodes. Governments and the global business world are preparing for a large-scale implementation of RFID technology in the first decades of the twenty-first century for these purposes.

Apart from a race to the bottom and the aim of making RFID chips smaller, one of the research challenges is to make them self-sufficient and energy saving, or even energy "scavenging," in which case they will get energy from their environment in the form of heat, light, or movement. The other challenge is to make them cheaper. One way to lower the unit cost of RFID chips is to find mass applications such as chipping bank notes, which the European Union (EU) is considering (Yoshida, 2001).

With RFID each object has its own unique identifier, and individuals will—apart from being walking repositories of biometric data—also show up in databases as clouds of tagged objects and become entangled in an "internet of things." [2] The RFID technology foreshadows what nanoelectronics has in store for our privacy: invisible surveillance.

The RFID chips are also referred to as "contactless technology," "contactless chips," or "proximity chips." Many authors on RFID have argued that there are privacy threats associated with the introduction of millions or even billions of smart tags and labels and RFIDs in health care, retail, travel, and law enforcement. As a result of opposition and critique of consumer organizations such as NOTAGS (2006) and CASPIAN, RFID has received serious negative moral connotations. Benetton planned to put RFIDs in all of its clothing with the help of Philips. This gave rise to vehement consumer protest and tainted the reputation of both Benetton and Philips. Tesco in the United Kingdom experimented with a photocamera in the store which was activated when consumers took a packet of Gillette razors of the shelf. The picture taken was then added to a consumer database. This also gave rise to intense public debate, for understandable reasons. Terms with a more neutral meaning are therefore welcomed by the industry and governments, since there are many advantages to be had from RFID technology in health care, safety, security, and industry that may go unnoticed because of bad publicity and bad reputation of a few relatively frivolous first applications.

The following examples give further evidence of a development toward tracking and tracing, monitoring, and surveillance. Precise real-time location systems using RFID tags have gone commercial (see www.ubisense.com). They use ultrawide-band communication to help locate tagged persons and objects in buildings with a precision of 30 cm. Several hospitals around the world monitor the location and movement of equipment and persons in the hospital with the help of RFID. The U.S. Department of Agriculture conducts experiments with smart dust and nanosensors which register properties of the environment and may help to detect the use of forbidden chemicals. The project is called "little brother" (http://www.qzonano.com/Details.asp?ArticleID=1318). A strategic U.S. defense initiative, *Camouflaged Long Endurance Nano Sensors* CLENS; (www.defensetech.org/archives/002275.html) allows precise location and tracking of soldiers during missions. Kris Pisters' group in California has many fascinating MEMSs (microelectronic mechanical systems) applications on display, microphones of 500 micrometers in diameter, and research on cameras of 1 millimeter. Extreme miniaturization in sensor technology and location-based services is clearly well underway.[3]

Not only objects and artifacts may be tagged on the item level, but also living creatures, animals, and human beings may be tagged. The U.S. Food and Drug Administration has decided to make chip implants in humans legal in the case of medical records (http://www.himss.org/asp/ContentRedirector.asp?ContentID=58984). The company Applied Digital Solutions introduces, as mentioned above, the Verichip for subcutaneous implantation in humans, and there are more examples (Weinberg, 2005):

1. In Japan, school children are chipped subcutaneously and are traced by a computer at school and to and from school.
2. The Baya Beach Club in Rotterdam and Barcelona offers people the possibility of having a chip for payments in the club to be placed under their skin by a doctor who is present in the club.
3. At the Ministry of Justice in Mexico 160 people received a chip under their skin to make it easier to trace them in case of kidnapping.
4. Millions of pets in the United States have implanted chips to make it easier to find them when they run away.

The U.S. federal government has recently experimented with RFID cards in immigration documents for foreign visitors in the context of the U.S. Visit Program, but the CEO of Digital Applications has taken this idea one step further; stating on national television that the chip could be used to tag immigrants and monitor their movements (http://biz.yahoo.com/bw/060515/2006051500598.html?.v=1).

PRIVACY

Privacy is one of the major moral issues that is discussed in connection with the development and applications of nanotechnology (Gutierrez, 2004; Mehta, 2003).
In this section, I present a framework for structuring debates on privacy in the context of nanotechnology. This framework provides a taxonomy of moral reasons for data protection. It also provides us with suggestions for the value-sensitive design of RFID and nanosurveillance technology.

Importance of Privacy

Laws and regulations to protect the personal sphere and the privacy of persons have been formulated and implemented in the last 100 years around the world, but not without debate and controversy. A good deal of practical and legal consensus has emerged. Data protection laws and regulations define constraints on the processing of personal information which function as de facto norms. These norms were already articulated in the Organisation for Economic Co-operation and Development (OECD) principles for data protection of 1980.[4] The main idea here—familiar in medicine and medical ethics—is informed consent, which forms the moral core of the European data protection laws (1995) and has started to influence thinking about privacy in the rest of the world. It states that, before personal data can be processed, informed consent of the data subject is required, the person has to be notified, he or she must be offered the opportunity to correct the data if they are wrong, the use is limited to the purpose for which the data were collected, and those who process data must guarantee accuracy, integrity, and security and for doing so and for acting in compliance with the requirements of data protection laws.

The requirements of security and accuracy are problematic in the case of RFID, since radio signals can in principle be sent and read by anyone. Even if individuals are aware of the tracking and tracing of objects and people as described above, there still would be problems with the technology from a data protection point of view: There could be cases of "sniffing, skimming, and spoofing" when unauthorized readers are trying to get hold of the information stored on RFID chips in one's possession. A group at Johns Hopkins University demonstrated that the minimal cryptographic on RFID chips can be cracked. A low-cost spoofing and cloning attack has been demonstrated on some RFID tags used for transport road tolling and the purchase of fuel at gas stations. The researchers created a cheap code-cracking device for a brute-force attack on the 40-bit cryptographic key space on the tag. A group from the free university of Amsterdam led by Andy Tanenbaum (2006) has shown that RFID chips can be infected by viruses that can spread via middleware into databases and propagate.

Why should we have such a stringent regimen for data protection at the level of the principles of the OECD and the EU Directive of 1995? Why make the requirement of informed consent by individuals a necessary condition for the processing of their information? This is often not spelled out in full detail, but if privacy and data protection are important, it is important to know exactly why they are important.

Privacy has been the subject of much philosophical discussion (Nissenbaum, 2004; Roessler 2005; Decew, 1997; Van den Hoven, 2007) and different authors have presented different accounts of privacy. Although there are many different accounts, I think the following taxonomy of moral reasons is useful for justifying the protection of personal information and constraints on the design and use of a new generation of nanosurveillance devices. The taxonomy has the advantage of turning the privacy discussion into a more or less tractable problem where moral reasons for data protection in a specific area or in a particular case can be spelled out and confronted with moral reasons of the same type which would seem to support arguments against data protection.

The following moral reasons can account for the importance given to individual control over personal data: (1) prevention of information-based harm, (2) prevention of informational inequalities, (3) prevention of informational injustice and discrimination, and (4) respect for moral autonomy and identity. In claiming privacy, we do not simply and nondescriptly want to be "left alone" or to be "private," but more concretely we want to prevent others from harming us, wronging us by making use of knowledge about us, or we want fair treatment and equality of opportunity and do not want to be discriminated against.

Information-Based Harm

The first type of moral reason for data protection is concerned with the prevention of harm, more specifically harm that is done to persons by making use of personal information about them. Criminals are known to have used databases and the Internet to get information on their victims in order to prepare and stage their crimes. The most important moral problem with "identity theft," for example, is the risk of financial and physical damages. One's bank account may get plundered and one's credit reports may be irreversibly tainted so as to exclude one from future financial benefits and services.

Stalkers and rapists have used the Internet and online databases to track down their victims. They could not have done what they did without tapping into these resources. In an information society there is a new vulnerability to information-based harm. The prevention of information-based harm provides government with the strongest possible justification for limiting the freedom of individual citizens and to constrain access to personal data.

The RFID information could be sniffed, people could be monitored, accurate pictures could be made of what they carry with them, and their identity could be stolen. We would also like to prevent people from deceiving others by stealing someone else's identity in order to manipulate the information about the nature of objects and present goods as new when they are old, as edible when they are poisonous, as legitimate when they are stolen, or as having cleared customs when they were in fact smuggled.

No other moral principle than John Stuart Mill's harm principle is needed to justify limitations of the freedom of persons who cause, threaten to cause, or are likely to cause, information-based harms to people. Protecting personal information, instead of leaving it in the open, diminishes the likelihood that people will come to harm, analogous to the way in which restricting the access to firearms diminishes the likelihood that people will get shot in the street. We know that if we do not establish a legal regimen that somehow constrains citizens' access to weapons, the likelihood that innocent people will get shot increases.

Informational Equality

The second type of moral reason to justify data protection is concerned with equality and fairness. More and more people are keenly aware of the benefits that a market for personal data can provide. If a consumer buys coffee at the shopping mall, information about that transaction can be generated and stored. Many consumers have come to realize that every time they come to the counter to buy something, they can also sell something, namely, information about their purchase or transaction (transactional data). Likewise, sharing information about ourselves—on the Internet with websites or through sensor technology—may pay off in terms of more and more adequate information (or discounts and convenience) later. Many privacy concerns have been and will be resolved in *quid pro quo* practices and private contracts about the use and secondary use of personal data. The RFID sensor would turn our environment into a transaction space, where information is generated constantly and systematically. But although a market mechanism for trading personal data seems to be kicking in on a global scale, not all individual consumers are aware of this economic opportunity, and if they do, they are not always trading their data in a transparent and fair market environment.

Moreover they do not always know what the implications are of what they are consenting to when they sign a contract or agree to be monitored. We simply cannot assume that the conditions of the developing market for personal data guarantee fair transactions by independent standards. Data protection laws can help to guarantee equality and a fair market for personal data. Data protection laws in these types of cases protect individual citizens by requiring openness, transparency, participation, and notification on the part of business firms and direct marketers to secure fair contracts.

For example, Amazon.com has already been accused of price targeting. In general, if a retailer knows that I like product X, bought lots of it, irrespective of its price, then they may charge me more for X than someone who does not know the product and needs to be enticed by means of low prices and discounts.

Informational Injustice

A third and important moral reason to justify the protection of personal data is concerned with justice in a sense which is associated with the work of the political philosopher Michael Walzer (1983). Walzer has objected to the simplicity of John Rawls's conception of primary goods and universal rules of distributive justice by pointing out that "there is no set of basic goods across all moral and material worlds, or they would have to be so abstract that they would be of little use in thinking about particular distributions" (p. 8). Goods have no natural meaning; their meaning is the result of sociocultural construction and interpretation. In order to determine what a just distribution of the good is, we have to determine what it means to those for whom it is a good. In the medical, political, and commercial spheres, there are different goods (medical treatment, political office, money) which are allocated by means of different allocation or distributive practices: medical treatment on the basis of need, political office on the basis of desert, and money on the basis of free exchange. What ought to be prevented, and often is prevented as a matter of fact, is dominance of particular goods. Walzer calls a good *dominant* if the individuals that have it, because they have it, can command a wide range of other goods. A monopoly is a way of controlling certain social goods in order to exploit their dominance. In that case advantages in one sphere can be converted as a matter of course to advantages in other spheres. This happens when money (commercial sphere) could buy you a vote (political sphere) and would give you preferential treatment in health care (medical), would get you a university degree (educational), and so on. We resist the dominance of money—and other social goods for that matter (property, physical strength)—and think that political arrangements are unjust. No social good X should be distributed to men and women who possess some other good Y merely because they possess Y and without regard to the meaning of X.

What is especially offensive to our sense of justice, Walzer argues, is first, the allocation of goods internal to sphere A on the basis of the distributive logic or the allocation scheme associated with sphere B; second, the transfer of goods across the boundaries of separate spheres; and third, the dominance and tyranny of some goods over others. In order to prevent this, the "art of separation" of spheres has to be practiced and "blocked exchanges" between them have to be put in place. If the art of separation is effectively practiced and the autonomy of the spheres of justice is guaranteed, then "complex equality" is established. One's status in terms of the holdings and properties in one sphere are irrelevant, *ceteris paribus*, to the distribution of the goods internal to another sphere.

Walzer's analysis also applies to information (Van den Hoven, 1999). The meaning and value of information is local, and allocation schemes and local practices that distribute access to information should accommodate local meaning and should therefore be associated with specific spheres. Many people do not object to the use of their personal medical data for *medical* purposes, whether these are directly related to their own personal health affairs, to those of their family, perhaps even to their community or the world population at large, as long as they can be absolutely certain that the only use that is made of it is to cure people from diseases. They do object, however, to their medical data being used to disadvantage them socioeconomically, to discriminate against them in the workplace, to refuse them commercial services, to deny them social benefits, or to turn them down for mortgages or political office. They do not mind if their library search data are used to provide them or others with better *library* services, but they do mind if these data are used to criticize their tastes and character.[5] They would also object to these informational cross-contaminations when they would benefit from them, as when the librarian advises them on a book on low-fat meals on the basis of knowledge of their medical record and cholesterol values or a doctor poses questions on the basis of the information that one has borrowed a book from the public library about AIDS.

We may thus distinguish another form of informational wrongdoing: "informational injustice," that is, disrespect for the boundaries of what we may refer to as "spheres of access." I think that what is often seen as a violation of privacy is often more adequately construed as the morally inappropriate transfer of data across the boundaries of what we intuitively think of as separate "spheres of access."

The RFID chips allow for a wide range of cross-domain profiling and information-processing practices which do not respect the boundaries of these spheres of access unless they are explicitly designed to do so.

Respect for Moral Autonomy and Identity

Some philosophical theories of privacy account for its importance in terms of *moral* autonomy (Van den Hoven, 1999, 2005, 2007) (i.e., the capacity to shape our own moral biographies, to reflect on our moral careers) in order to evaluate and identify with our own moral choices, without the critical gaze and interference of others and a pressure to conform to the "normal" or socially desired identities. Privacy, conceived along these lines, would only provide protection to the individual in his or her quality of a *moral* person engaged in self-definition, self-presentation, and self-improvement against the normative pressures which public opinions and moral judgments exert on the person to conform to a socially desired identity. Information about some individual, whether fully accurate or not, facilitates the formation of beliefs and judgments about that individual. Judgments and beliefs of others about that individual, when he or she learns about them or suspects that they are made or fears that they are made, may bring about a change in one's view of self, may induce him or her to behave or think differently than one would have otherwise done. They preempt acts and choices of self-determination and compromise one's status as a self-presenter. When individuals fail in this respect, that is a source of shame; it reveals that one cannot manage the way one presents oneself.

To modern individuals who have cast aside the ideas of historical and religious necessity, living in a highly volatile socioeconomic environment and with a great diversity of audiences and settings before which they make their appearance, the *fixation* of one's moral identity by means of the judgments of others is felt as an obstacle to "experiments in living," as Mill called them. Modern liberal individuals want to be able to determine themselves morally or to undo their previous determinations on the basis of more profuse experiences in life or additional factual information. Data protection laws provide individuals with the leeway to do just that.

This conception of the person as being morally autonomous—as being the author and experimenter of his or her own moral career—provides a justification for protecting personal data. Data protection laws thus provide protection against the freezing of one's moral identity by others than one's self and convey to citizens that they are morally autonomous.

A further explanation for the importance of respect for moral autonomy may be provided along the following lines. Factual knowledge of another person is always knowledge by description. The person, however, not only knows the facts of his or her biography but also is the only person *acquainted* with the associated thoughts, desires, and aspirations. However detailed and elaborate our files and profiles on a person may be, we are never able to refer to the data subject as he or she is able to do. We may only approximate his or her knowledge and self-understanding. Bernard Williams has pointed out that respecting a person involves "identification" in a very special sense, which could be referred to as "moral identification" (Van den Hoven, 1999):

In professional relations and the world of work, a man operates, and his activities come up for criticism, under a variety of professional or technical titles, such as "miner" or "agricultural labourer" or "junior executive." The technical or professional attitude is that which regards the man solely under that title, the human approach that which regards him as a man who has that title (among others), willingly, unwillingly, through lack of alternatives, with pride, etc. . . . . [E]ach man is owed an effort at identification: that he should not be regarded as the surface to which a certain label can be applied, but one should try to see the world (including the label) from his point of view.

Moral identification thus presupposes knowledge of the point of view of the data subject and a concern with what it is for a person to live that life. Persons have aspirations, higher order evaluations, and attitudes and they see the things they do in a certain light. Representation of this aspect of persons seems exactly what is missing when personal data are piled up in our databases and persons are represented in administrative procedures. The identifications made on the basis of our data fall short of respecting the individual person, because they will never match the identity as it is experienced by the data subject. It fails because it does not conceive of the other on his or her terms. Respect for privacy of persons can thus be seen to have a distinctly epistemic dimension. It represents an acknowledgment of the fact that it is impossible to really know other persons as they know and experience themselves.

Ubiquitous and pervasive computing with surveillance and monitoring as a permanent but invisible feature may change our conception of ourselves as self-presenters. Under such a technological regimen the notion of "self-presentation" and the associated forms of autonomy may disappear and become obsolete. The dominant view which is associated with the use of profiles and databases fails to *morally identify* individuals in Williams's sense. Only if citizens can have a warranted belief that those who process their data adopt a moral stance toward them and are genuinely concerned with moral identification next to other forms of identification can a universal surveillance and an entanglement of individuals in "an internet of things" be construed as morally acceptable.

CHALLENGE OF INVISIBILITY

Privacy was construed above in terms of moral reasons for protecting personal information (i.e., moral reasons for putting constraints on the acquisition, processing, and dissemination of personal information). The central constraint was *informed consent*; personal information can only be processed if the data subject has provided informed consent. Four moral reasons for making informed consent a necessary condition were discussed above. This indicates that the core problem concerning privacy with nanotechnology is epistemic in nature: It is the fact that we do not know that we are monitored, tracked, and traced. Stanley Benn (Schoeman, 1984, p. 230) already clearly stated what the problem with this epistemic condition is. We need to distinguish between two cases. First, if the information processing is covert, then it is clear that this interferes with our autonomy, because our thinking and choices are tainted by our false assumption (i.e., that we assume we are unobserved). Many of our assumptions and reasoning can be defeated just by adding the information that we are observed. Second, if the information processing is overt, we can adjust to being observed, but we no longer have the prior choice to be unobserved. In both ways our autonomy is compromised.

A related but slightly different aspect of invisibility and lack of relevant knowledge was articulated by Jeffrey Reiman (1996) in his essay on automated vehicle registration systems. If unbeknownst to me, my passage from A to B is registered, something strange happens. If asked what I did, I will respond that I drove from A to B. But this is only part of the story. My action could be more adequately described as "I drove from A to B and thereby created a record in the database of the system."

In the same way people will have to become aware of the fact that when they buy clothing they could be buying invisible transponders and memory sticks as well. It changes the conditions under which people consent to actions and intend things. Actions like "trying on a coat," "carrying a gift out of a shop," or "driving from A to B" are no longer what they appear to be to the agent. What actually happens is that one buys a gift *and* lets the store know which route one follows through the shop.

A sociotechnological system which obfuscates these mechanisms robs individuals of chances to describe their actions more adequately. Moreover it seems to violate a requirement of publicity or transparency, as articulated by both Rawls and Williams among others. The functioning of social institutions should not depend on a wrong understanding of how they work by those who are subject to them (Williams, 1985). Suppose that ubiquitous and covert surveillance arrangements work well and to the satisfaction of a majority; then they seem to work because those affected by them have a false understanding of why and how they work. This seems to violate a reasonable requirement of transparency.

A further fundamental problem needs to be discussed which is relevant to nanotechnology and ubiquitous surveillance by means of RFID and functionally equivalent technology. Is the information concerned *personal information* and does the data protection laws by implication apply?

The answer is affirmative. Although an RFID tag does not necessarily contain personal information, if it does and it is likely and that information can be linked without too much trouble and cost in a back-end database to a file which does contain data about a natural person, it counts as personal data.

VALUE-SENSITIVE DESIGN

Ed Felten, a Professor of Security and Computer Science at Princeton, has observed (http://michaelzimmer.blogspot.com/2005/04/rfid-passports-need-for-values-in.html):

> It seems that the decision to use contactless technology was made without fully understanding its consequences, relying on technical assurances from people who had products to sell. Now that the problems with that decision have become obvious, it's late in the process and would be expensive and embarrassing to back out. In short, this looks like another flawed technology procurement program.

Value-sensitive design is a way of doing ethics that aims at making moral values part of technological design, research, and development (http://www.ischool.washington.edu/vsd/outreach.html;http://www.nyu.edu/projects/valuesindesign/). It works with the assumption that human values and norms, our ethics for short, can be imparted to the things we make and use. It construes technology as a formidable force which can be used to make the world a better place, especially when we take the trouble of reflecting on its ethical aspects in advance.

Information technology has become a constitutive technology; it partly constitutes the things to which it is applied. It shapes our practices and institutions in important ways. What health care, public administration, politics, education, science, transport, and logistics will be in 20 years from now will in important ways be determined by the information and communication technology applications we decide to use in these domains:

- If our moral talk about the user's autonomy and talk of patient centredness and citizen centredness, privacy, are security is to be more than an empty promise, these values will have to be expressed in the (chip) design, systems architecture, and standards and specifications.

- If our laws, politics, and public policy about corporate governance, accountability, and transparency are to be more than just cheap talk, we have to make sure that they are incorporated in the systems we need to support the relevant policies in a global business environment.

- If we want our nanotechnology—and the use that is made of it—to be just, fair, safe, environmentally friendly, and transparent, we must see to it that our technology inherits our good intentions. Moreover, we want them to be seen to have those properties, and we want to be able to demonstrate that they possess these morally desirable features. We want to be able to compare different architectures from these value perspectives and motivate political choices and justify investments from this perspective.

Nanotechnology will take privacy discussions to the level of the design of materials, surfaces, and properties of artifacts and fabrics. This will require an adjustment in our thinking about legal and moral constraints on their development and use in addition to thinking about constraints on the use of the personal information they help to generate, store, and distribute. Avoine and Oechslin (2003) have already argued that it is not sufficient to discuss data protection at the level of the application or communication. They argue that also the physical level needs to be looked at.

There are various ways in which we could start to incorporate our values in our designs. IBM work on antennae of RFID chips shows, for example, that they can be easily torn off a label on a product to limit the range at which they can be read. The tag has a couple of indentations; the more you tear off, the more you limit the range at which the tag can be read. There are several ways by which the tags could be protected by means of encryption, made visible, comparable to the way we notify people that they are on a closed-captioned TV camera and the way we warn people that there are additives in food. In the same way we could notify people, empower them, and give them means of controlling the flow of their information.[6] The ideal of restoring a power balance regarding the use of one's personal data is sometimes referred to as *sousveillance*. We can think about simple measures which create a Faraday cage (e.g., wrapping your passport in aluminum foil) by introducing ways in which sensors can be "killed" or put in "privacy mode," or signals are jammed, or tags get blocked by blocker tags.

Customers have good moral reasons to want to control how they are perceived, in stores, in hospitals, and in the street, for moral reasons outlined above. They may fear harm, unfair treatment, or discrimination or may start not to feel free to be the person they want to be. This breach may be made explicit by means of the two ideas about privacy—data protection or control over information and constant observation. The focus of attention would seem to be the information that is generated and stored and reused and the fact that we may feel perceived and monitored from all sides.

CONCLUSION

Typically privacy is about information, and in a normative sense it refers to a non-absolute moral right of persons to have direct or indirect control over access to (1) information about oneself, (2) situations where others could acquire information about oneself, and (3) technology and/or artifacts that can be used to support the processing of personal data. Not only database specialists, ICT professionals, and security and cryptographers should think about privacy in the future, but also nanotechnologists and designers of material, fabrics, and sensors and sensor networks, supply chain managers, and retail people should think in terms of privacy designs. They will have to worry about how existing nanotechnology can be made visible, detected and neutralized, or be read and how the information it helps to generate and store can be protected by design.

NOTES

1. See EU paper for an overview of the legal issues (Kardasiadou and Talidou, 2006).
2. This is the title of a study of the International Telecom Union, www.itu.int/internetofthings.
3. See the project Smart Dust, autonomous sensing and communication in a cubic millimeter, http://robotics.eecs.berkeley.edu/~pister/SmartDust/.
4. The OECD identified eight basic principles: collection limitation principle, data quality principle, purpose specification principle, the use limitation principle, security safeguards principle, openness principle, individual participation principle, and accountability principle.
5. The world of books and libraries is one of the most likely candidates for complete item level tagging RFID.
6. See, e.g., the work of Juels et al. (2005), Garfinket et al., (2005), and Gao et al. (2004), who have studied cryptography for RFID.

REFERENCES

Avoine, G., and Oechslin, P. H. 2003. RFID traceability: A multilayer problem. Available: lasecwww.epfl.ch/pub/lasec/doc/AO05b.pdf.

DeCew, J. 1997. *In Pursuit of Privacy: Law, Ethics, and the Rise of Technology.* Ithaca, NY: Cornell University Press.

European Union (EU). 1995. EU data protection laws. EU Directive 95. Available: http://europa.eu.int/comm/internal_market/privacy/index_en.htm.

Garfinkel, S. L., Juels, A. and Pappu, R. 2005. RFID privacy: An overview of problems and proposed solutions. *IEEE Security and Privacy*, p. 34–43.

Gao, X., et al. 2004. An approach to security and privacy of RFID system for supply chain. In *Proceedings of the IEEE International Conference on E-commerce Technology for Dynamic E-Business* (CEC-East '04).

Gutierrez, E. 2004. Privacy implications of nanotechnology. EPIC. Available: www.epic.org/privacy/nano, last updated April 26, 2004, accessed June 28, 2004.

Juels, A., Syverson, P., and Bailey, D. 2005. High-power proxies for enhancing RFID privacy and utility. Available: www.rsasecurity.com/rsalabs/node.asp?id=2948.

Kardasiadou, Z., and Talidou, Z. 2006. Legal issues of RFID technology, http:/www.rfidconsultation.eu/docs/ficheiros/legal_issues_of_RFID_technology_LEGAL_IST.pdf

Mehta, M. D. 2003. On nano-panopticism: A sociological pespective. Available: http://chem4823.usask.ca/cassidyr/OnNano-Panopticism-ASociologicalPerspective.htm.

Nissenbaum, H. 2004. Privacy as contextual integrity. *Washington Law Review* 79: 101–139.

NOTAGS. 2007. CASPIAN: Consumers against supermarket privacy invasion and numbering. Available: www.nocards.org, www.notags.co.uk.

Pister, K. 2001. My view of sensor networks in 2010 http://robotics.eecs.berkeley.edu/~pister/ SmartDust/in2010.

Reiman J. 1996. Driving to the panopticon. In *Critical Moral Liberalism*, Lanham, CT: Rowman and Littlefield, pp. 169–188.

Roessler, B. 2005. *The Value of Privacy*. Oxford: Polity Press.

Schoeman, F. (Ed.). 1984. *Philosophical Dimensions of Privacy: An Anthology*. Cambridge: Cambridge University Press.

Tanenbaum A. et al. 2006. Is your cat infected with a computer virus. Available: www.rfidvirus.org/ papers/percom.06.pdf.

Van den Hoven, M. J. 1999. Privacy and the varieties of informational wrongdoing. *Australian Journal of Professional and Applied Ethics* 1(1): 30–44.

Van den Hoven, M. J. 2005. Privacy. In C. Mitcham and D. Johnson (Eds.), *MacMillan Encyclopedia for Ethics and Technology*. New York: MacMillan.

Van den Hoven, M. J. 2007. Privacy and dataprotection. In M. J. Van den Hoven and J. Weckert (Eds.), *Information Technology and Moral Philosophy*. Cambridge: Cambridge University Press.

Walzer, M. 1983. *Spheres of Justice*. New York: Basic Books.

Wanczyk, S. D. 2004. The nano-threats to privacy: Sci-fi or Sci-fact? Culture, Communication & Technology Program, Georgetown University, Vol. 3, spring 2004. Available: www.gnovis.georgetown.edu/includes/ac.cfm?documentNum=31.

Weinberg, J. 2005. RFID and privacy. Available: www.law.wayne.edu/weinberg/rfid.paper.new.pdf.

Williams, B. 1985. *Ethics and the Limits of Philosophy*. New York: Fontana Press.

Yoshida. 2001. Euro bank notes to embed RFID chips by 2005, *EETimes*. Available: http://www.eetimes.com/story/OEG20011219S0016.

20

NANOTECHNOLOGY AND THE MILITARY

Daniel Moore

In looking at how paradigmatic shifts in technology such as the development of nanotechnology have the ability to change society in various ways, it is imperative to look at how it changes the military. Advancing technologies create new weapons and new defenses. New technologies also create new targets for attack (such as water wheels in the Middle Ages and power stations in the modern era)[1] and new methods of defending those targets. New technologies can render old systems obsolete and be the impetus for the development of new systems. The development of satellite surveillance forced many nations and militant groups to develop underground bunkers, hiding places, and even underground nuclear testing areas. New military technologies can even change the entire nature of the world system and by what rules states and other actors on the world stage act. There is no doubt that the development of nuclear weapons has fundamentally changed the nature of the international politics and warfare—for better and for worse. As such, it is important to consider the effects of technological shifts on the military.

Nanotechnology represents a paradigmatic shift in the way technology is made and is thought about. Many distinct definitions for "nanotechnology" exist. They all have in common that they are designed to make a sharp distinction between nanotechnology and "bulk technology." Bulk technology is how we have made things in the past. The basic methods have been around for centuries. Steel is made and formed in furnaces from a bulk material, rock is chiseled away at, cement is mixed together, and glass is blown. To

Nanoethics: The Ethical and Social Implications of Nanotechnology. Edited by Allhoff, Lin, Moor, Weckert
Copyright © 2007 John Wiley & Sons, Inc.

be sure, the "bulk" style of technology has led to many great accomplishments and has led to many potent military applications. Bulk technologies can also make exquisitely small devices and materials. However, cutting, chipping, pounding, extruding, and other such procedures are the trade in hand. These are designed at taking a larger material and breaking it down into smaller parts. These do not provide the level of precision and control the nanotechnology can. Nanotechnology begins on the atomic scale and by controlling atomic or molecular processes and placement it builds up new materials, unique structures, and potentially awe-inspiring devices. The development of nanotechnology promises to make material, structure, and device virtually indistinguishable from each other.

It is useful to note the importance of material in nanotechnologies. Materials have always been the enabling technology of any era. As a society, we recognize the importance of this by naming eras in history after the prevalent material of the time—the Stone Age, the Bronze Age, and so on. Even more recent periods that have been dubbed the industrial age and the information age have been enabled and are chiefly identifiable by the materials of the time—steel and silicon/semiconductors, respectively. However, because in nanotechnology the structure and device is wedded to the material used in such a strong way, nanomaterials development becomes central to all nanotechnology development.

Nanomaterials have been important for a long time now. Nano-sized black particles have been used to reinforce tires for nearly 100 years. Another example is in the precipitation hardening of materials. An accidental discovery in 1906, it allowed for significant improvements in the strength of metals such as aluminum. It was discovered only with the advent of the electron microscope that nanoscale precipitates were the source of this hardening.

For the purpose of examining their impact on society, we can tentatively divide military nanotechnologies into three basic categories. The first category is incremental in nature. It is nanotechnologies that are useful by the mere fact that they are smaller. They do not have many novel properties. These nanotechnologies are facsimiles of larger technologies on a smaller scale.

The second category contains nanotechnologies that benefit from the novel or enhanced properties of nanoscale materials. Here, controlling the atomic structure of materials leads to improvements and fundamental changes in material properties. For example, materials can be made defect free. The smaller size of materials leads to increased surface-to-volume ratio. This allows for surface-specific reactions to become more frequent. Some materials can be manufactured with different crystal structures. For example, ZnS has a cubic crystal structure in its bulk form—this is most energetically favorable. However, when formed in nanoscale materials, ZnS can very easily be formed with a hexagonal crystal structure (Ma et al., 2003). Other materials show other novel properties. These materials and devices also interact with their environment. Nanoscale chemical sensors, targeted drug delivery systems, quantum effects, and systems that have mechanical/electrical reactions to environmental parameters are all included in this category.

The third category consists of what has been named "molecular manufacturing." This consists of the idea that molecular objects could be positioned to atomic precision to build complex objects with atoms and molecules that can be placed together one by one in any arrangement that is stable.

Within military nanotechnology, we can divide nanotechnology into several other categories: first, by the use of the nanotechnology (offensive or defensive); second, by the point of use of the nanotechnology (soldier or larger); and, third, by the ability to transfer the nanotechnology from military use to the general society. This third category can offer a look at an interesting division in military technology.

In examining nanotechnology and the military, it is necessary to look at all three of these categories, the interplay between them, and what impacts they might have. To begin, it is useful to discuss what specific types of technology are possible/are being worked on within each field.

A NANO-ENABLED MILITARY

In 2002, the U.S. Army established an interdepartmental research center at the Massachusetts Institute of Technology called the Institute for Soldier Nanotechnologies (ISN, http://web.mit.edu/ISN/). The ISN was charged with developing ways to substantially improve the survival and performance of U.S. soldiers using nanotechnology. These nanotechnologies would have a point of use of an individual soldier. Many of them occur automatically, without any conscious input from the soldier at all.

So what are some aspects of a nano-enabled military? By looking at some of the technologies in development and that are being discussed, a good idea of what a nano-enabled military looks like can be achieved.

By simply making devices smaller and lighter, the soldier can be made more mobile and have a smaller logistical footprint. The average soldier carries in excess of 100 pounds of equipment while on assignment.[2] Much of this weight is due to the electronic equipment (including communication equipment) and the power supplies (usually batteries) used to power them. By making smaller, lighter equipment, this weight could be reduced dramatically without sacrificing functionality, and the individual soldier could move quicker with less sacrifice (the typical bellwether given is the 45 pounds that the average imperial Roman soldier carried).[3] Much of this weight reduction can be accomplished by reducing the scale of the power generators that the soldiers have to carry. For example, recently nanoscale power generation has been demonstrated by utilizing an array of piezoelectric nanowires (Wang and Song, 2006). By converting mechanical, vibrational, or hydraulic energy into electricity, these "nanogenerators" can be used to power the electrical systems carried by the soldiers.

Other nanosystems being developed for soldiers utilize some of the novel properties that nanomaterials can have when interacting with their environment. An example of this is mechanically active materials and devices. These nanomaterials are capable of dynamically changing their stiffness and mechanical actuation. Embedded in a soldier's battle suit, mechanical actuators can allow a transformation from a flexible material to a stiff armor nearly instantaneously. This can distribute an energetic impact, such as a nearby explosion. Further, such materials can be transformed into a cast that stabilizes broken bones. Contracting materials in the battle suit can apply direct pressure to a wound, serve as a tourniquet, or even perform CPR to the soldier. All of these can, in theory, be activated by chemical and/or mechanical sensors in the suit, as electronic polymers can be used to create sensitive detectors of explosives and nerve gas and even identify specific biological agencies.

Using the metric of transferability and usefulness to the nonmilitary population of society, many of these technologies can be of great use to society. Most law enforcement and emergency response teams would be able to use much of this same technology to protect police officers and first responders. Reducing the load weight of firefighters would allow them to move more quickly and agilely in rescue operations.

Seemingly, especially from the description above, soldier nanotechnologies are defensive in nature and aimed at saving and protecting the soldier's life. However, it would be a folly to imagine that nanotechnology is not being explored for use in weapons.

"Nanoweapons" have the potential to change the nature of warfare in very fundamental ways. Just as a modern, technologically enhanced military reveals very little resemblance to undeveloped militaries, so too a military with nanoweapons shows little resemblance to a conventional military. Nanoscale materials have the potential to create intense laser technologies for use in weapons. Self-guided antipersonnel bullets are also considered. Targeted strikes on buildings can become even more surgical. The possibility of unleashing a "swarm" of nanoscale robots programmed only to disrupt the electrical and chemical systems in a building is a far more militarily desirable solution than destroying the entire building (provided that total destruction is not the objective).

A very good, specific example of nanoscale materials showing their impact in weaponry is with nanoaluminum. Bulk-scale aluminum contains aluminum atoms that cover roughly one-tenth of 1 percent of the surface area. Nano-structured aluminum contains aluminum atoms that cover roughly 50 percent. More atoms on the surface creates more sites for chemical reactions to occur. This is used in conjunction with metal oxides such as iron oxide to create superthermites, which increase the chemical reaction time by three orders of magnitude (Military Reloads with Nanotech, 2006). Therefore, greater amounts of energy can be released, creating more powerful conventional explosives and faster moving missiles and torpedoes (so fast, in fact, that they can bypass evasive actions).

A NANO-ENABLED DEFENSE SYSTEM

Homeland defense is, ostensibly, the primary function of any military. Sensing technology is one of the more useful applications of nanotechnology that is being developed. The smaller size of nanomaterials allows for a faster response time and greater sensitivity to species for which they are tuned. The small unobtrusive size also allows for the placement of sensors virtually anywhere without significant disruption to the people. With the threat of biological, chemical, or "dirty" bomb attack, this type of technology can provide for quicker detection of harmful species and, therefore, quicker annihilation. A network of sensors could be placed relatively simply around major cities in order to monitor for harmful releases. Water treatment centers are another potential "weak link" in the homeland defense system. Nanoscale sensors and filters that allow only "desired" chemical and biological species through provide an easy solution to this problem. Furthermore, the same "swarms" of nanoscale robots that act as a weapon can act to destroy "undesirable" biological, chemical, or even nanotechnological weapons.

Nanotechnology also offers greater defense in the field of electronics. The danger of an electromagnetic pulse (EMP) is one that is very difficult to shield completely against. Most shielding that provides some protection for electronics requires significant loss in performance. However, there is reason to believe that optical computing, DNA computing, and other nanotechnology-based computing options are more naturally resistant to EMPs.[4] All-optical computing has the added benefit of being less sensitive to electronic eavesdropping. Because the optical signal is confined to a fiber more tightly than an electronic signal is truly confined to a wire, it is more difficult for an external piece of equipment to listen in.

ETHICAL CONCERNS

Warfare and military development have always been wrought with ethical concerns. As such, the technology of warfare has carried with it much of the weight of these concerns. The most recent and familiar example of this is the introduction of atomic weapons to the craft of war. The ethical debates over nuclear weapons and their development continue even now, more than 60 years after their advent. This debate does not limit itself to nuclear weapons but instead extends to all nuclear technology. In the United States, the concerns over nuclear energy have led to a very strong norm against building nuclear energy facilities.

From a historical look at military technology's impact on society and the debates that have surrounded these technologies, several major ethical concerns can be examined. All of these are broad enough to be divided into smaller concerns, but it is the intention here to draw light on the broader questions that are being addressed.

It might be useful to start with the most drastic consideration in nanotechnology. That is what the development of nanoassembler technology means for international security. One of the most extensive considerations of the effects of nanoassembler technology on international security has been given by Mark Gubrud (1997) in a talk before the Foresight Institute:

The greatest danger coincides with the emergence of these powerful technologies: A quickening succession of "revolutions" may spark a new arms race involving a number of potential competitors. Older systems, including nuclear weapons, would become vulnerable to novel forms of attack or neutralization. Rapidly evolving, untested, secret, and even "virtual" arsenals would undermine confidence in the ability to retaliate or resist aggression. Warning and decision times would shrink. Covert infiltration of intelligence and sabotage devices would blur the distinction between confrontation and war. Overt deployment of ultramodern weapons, perhaps on a massive scale, would alarm technological laggards. Actual and perceived power balances would shift dramatically and abruptly. Accompanied by economic upheaval, general uncertainty and disputes over the future of major resources and of humanity itself, such a runaway crisis would likely erupt into large-scale rearmament and warfare well before another technological plateau was reached.

International regimes combining arms control, verification and transparency, collective security and limited military capabilities, can be proposed in order to maintain stability. However, these would require unprecedented levels of cooperation and restraint, and would be prone to collapse if nations persist in challenging each other with threats of force. If we believe that assemblers are feasible, perhaps the most important implication is this: Ultimately, we will need an integrated international security system. For the present, failure to consider alternatives to unilateral "peace through strength" puts us on a course toward the next world war.

This type of analysis rests on the idea that the introduction of nanotechnology (more specifically, molecular assembly nanotechnology) will be revolutionary and not, as can be argued the other technology "revolutions" were, evolutionary in nature. If we can get beyond the initial skepticism of a "transparen[t], collective security" that would "require unprecedented levels of cooperation and restraint" coupled with the call for "an integrated international security system" (Gebrud, 1997) in the next paragraph, we can start to look at the meat of these types of analyses. This analysis is purely speculative. It rests on claiming that there is no history that we can look to in order to guess at what will happen and then goes on to do just that—guess at what will happen. This seems a little unfair and these types of analyses (those that claim there is no precedent, no prior history from which we can draw a lesson) are often wrought with gloom-and-doom scenarios. At the very least, they tend to foretell the radical and swift overthrow of whatever current system is in place.

These types of analyses are useful, however, in that they make more moderate predictions seem more mainstream and more investigative. They also provide a starting point from which it is possible to work back to a more reasonable middle. Looking back in the history of military technological introduction, it is clear that it has instead been a process that gradually changes the international system—and is changed by it in gradual ways. The Cold War bipolarity was no more a cause of the doctrine of mutually assured destruction and nuclear proliferation than nuclear proliferation and mutually assured destruction were a cause of the Cold War. In fact, though many claim that the American–Soviet bipolar world was unprecedented in its nature, there was history that suggests that such bipolarity was predictable. When two great nations of distinctly different ideologies join forces to defeat a common enemy, the result is such a bipolar world. This occurred with Athens and Sparta after the two city-states joined together to defeat an invading Persian empire. Immediately after the Greek victory over the Persians, Athens was, by far, the major power in the Greek world (according to the sources available to us, which are, admittedly, Athenian). However, this power led to a showdown with the Spartans, who by nature of their ideology were suspicious of Athenian intentions. Certainly, there were many aspects of the post–World War II era that make it distinctly different from the post–Persian war Greek world, from the existence of the United Nations to nuclear weapons. However, these distinctions and differences do not mean that history cannot be learned from and utilized to suggest what the future may bring.

It is possible to look at what effect the introduction of new technologies has had on warfare and the military and draw some lessons for what may come with the introduction of various nanotechnologies. The first lesson is that a sudden, complete overturning of the current world system of states (with several non–state actors) is unlikely. The other end of the spectrum is equally unlikely. This end of the spectrum says that nanotechnology will bring about an end to fights about resources, food, and other things that states and people go to war over and, thus, bring about peace. However, with this, it would be wise to remember the words of Hedley Bull (1977): "We are accustomed, in the modern world, to contrast war between states with peace between states; but the historical alternative to war between states was more ubiquitous violence." Bull's warning was written in 1977 and history before and since tends to confirm this statement. Ubiquitous violence, flare-ups, small wars, police actions, and whatever other name is conferred to these actions taken by states has been the order of the day. The non–state actors, too, tend to increase their violent actions during times of supposed peace between states. Terrorism, rebellion, and genocidal acts grow more frequent.

It is useful then to look at what impact new technologies tend to have on these acts of violence—whether by a state or not. Many of the technologies are protective in their nature, as outlined above; they cause less civilians and combatants to die. Other technologies make precision guidance of weapons more precise and cause a weapon to have a higher fatality and specificity rate. What these add up to is quite interesting. New technologies, nanotechnology included, make the craft of war and violence easier and less costly. On the attacking side, this is evident. Less soldiers die because of advance in protective and medical technologies. Less civilians are injured because of populationwide protection. Less citizens are involved in the military because more powerful and more precise weapons require less ground troops. Because of the higher precision of the weapons, the costs could possibly be less on the defending side as well. So-called collateral damage, from which the more westernized, liberal states tend to shy away, can be minimized. Weapons can be made that strike only one building and do it with accuracy and precision. Further, nanotechnology allows for the simple shutting down of vital systems to populations such as water, electricity, and energy, as opposed to the utter destruction of the facilities in which they are housed. So warlike acts are easier to inflict on enemies of a nanotechnologically enabled state. Acts that become easier typically become more ubiquitous in their nature.

However, it has also happened that democratic nations, in which the vast majority of nanotechnology research and development are being done, have a low tolerance for casualties in military actions. With nanotechnological developments making it easier to protect, defend, and otherwise shield soldiers and populations from taking casualties, this tolerance will probably become even lower. This lessens the likelihood that long, drawn-out, high-casualty military actions will be tolerable to the population of the technologically advanced nations and will probably decrease. Prognostication is, in its nature, imperfect, but combining these last two probabilities, it seems likely that "small wars" in which technologically advanced nations perform "police actions" on less developed regimes will become more and more frequent, in no small part because of nanotechnology.

The international stage is not the only arena in which a nanotechnological revolution in the military will have an impact. It seems likely that the amount of health and mental care needed to be provided to members of the armed services will increase. As nanotechnology allows for stark increases in the ability to save a life, injuries that once were life threatening or led to a certain death become treatable. Illnesses and chemical attacks become less threatening. Further, a much higher percentage of soldiers will live through military actions and will, as such, be in some need of psychiatric care. Furthermore, it seems likely that as medical nanotechnology is able to fix more problems, more, newer problems will be noticed and be in need of treatment. Tailoring each treatment to individual patients based on their DNA and their environment again increases the actual care (though perhaps not the time) that each patient needs. Another issue that needs to be considered is that of a population that has an increasing amount of members who volunteered to serve in the military. When the chances of death are lessened, the idea of military service becomes more attractive and a greater percentage of the population are trained in the military.

CONCLUSION

There are many aspects to nanotechnology in the military that have not been discussed in this consideration. Instead, several frameworks for considering the impact of nanotechnology have been given. The first of these frameworks is in the nature of the technology being used—is the nanotechnology incremental, imbued with novel properties, or molecular nanotechnology? The second framework is in the nature of the perceived use of the nanotechnology—is it offensive or defensive? The third framework proposed is structured by the point of use of the nanotechnology—is it used by an individual person, a small group, or the entire society? Finally, the fourth framework deals specifically with military nanotechnology—how transferable is the technology to nonmilitary applications? As a note on the fourth framework, it should be acknowledged that it is not necessarily true that technology that is easily transferred to nonmilitary applications will have a greater impact on society than other technologies. There are many other frameworks with which to consider nanotechnology—this is not meant to be exhaustive. Many of them imply their own metric in examining the ethical use of the nanotechnology.

Several of the many ethical considerations that the introduction of nanotechnology to society is wrought with have also been considered. These considerations are in no way meant to be comprehensive or even authoritative on the ethical issues concerning the development of nanotechnology for military purposes. Instead, they have been designed to introduce some of the issues and to encourage thinking and debate about these issues. On the whole, nanotechnology will most probably be transformative in its nature and will bring about a highly enabled military. The proper use of nanotechnology in the military can only be discovered through an interactive discourse with an informed base. Just as some semblance of an agreement has been achieved on the use of conventional technologies in the military (though it still is not stable; the Geneva Conventions are neither perfect nor universally followed), so too will some agreement of the humane and proper use of nanotechnology in the military be achieved.

Recently, a volume of work by Jürgen Altmann (2006) has been published examining the potential military applications of nanotechnology. The book, *Military Nanotechnology: New Technology and Arms Control*, assesses the potential applications from the viewpoint of international security, especially considering the impact nanotechnology will have on arms control and international law. Given Altmann's background as an expert in disarmament and arms control, there is no doubt that this volume provides a top-rate and extensive look into these issues.

NOTES

1. Though to be fair, the main target of medieval sieges was typically the castle—it being the center of the entire surrounding countryside. The castle technology was born out of the necessity of protection from invading armies.

2. "Dean's data bears out decades of anecdotal evidence that soldiers carry backbreaking loads, often well over 100 pounds. In addition to hampering mobility, carrying such a burden is physically exhausting, and "comfort" items—like cold-weather clothing or extra food—are often sacrificed." See http://web.mit.edu/newsoffice/2004/soldier.html, accessed July 31, 2006.

3. Every Roman soldier carried basic equipment. All clothing was standard, consisting of a tunic, a cloak, and heavy boots. All the equipment was carried in a pouch called a sacina. Offensive equipment included the javelin and the basic short sword. Defensive equipment included the breastplate, the helmet, and the shield.

4. However, DNA computing has been predicted to be much slower than electronic computing. See the JASON report for a good review, at http://www.fas.org/irp/agency/dod/jason/, accessed July 31, 2006.

REFERENCES

Altmann, J. 2006. *Military Nanotechnology: New Technology and Arms Control*. New York: Routledge.

Bull, H. 1977. *The Anarchical Society: A Study of Order in World Politics*. London: Macmillan.

Gubrud, M. A. 1997. Nanotechnology and international security. Paper presented at the Fifth Foresight Conference on Molecular Nanotechnology 1997, Palo Alto, CA. http://www.foresight.org/conference/MNT05/Papers/Gubrud/, accessed July 31, 2006.

Ma, C., Moore, D. F., Li, J., and Wang, Z. L. 2003. Nanobelts, nanocombs and nano-windmills of wurtzite ZnS. *Journal of Advanced Materials* 15: 228–231.

MIT Technology Review. 2006. Military reloads with nanotech. Available: http://www.technologyreview.com/read_article.aspx?id=14105, accessed July 31, 2006.

Wang, Z. L., and Song, J. H. 2006. Piezoelectric nanogenerators based on zinc oxide nanowire arrays. *Science* 14: 242–246.

21

CAN NANOSCIENCE BE A CATALYST FOR EDUCATIONAL REFORM?*

Patricia Schank, Joseph Krajcik, and Molly Yunker

THE NEED

We live in a time when new technological tools have significantly improved the ability of scientific researchers to develop new products that have wide-ranging impact on our lives, from diagnosing disease to applying paint to our cars. The impact of these scientific advances requires a commensurate response in the educational community to help students develop new frameworks for making sense of the world. The current education system is not only failing to produce a populace scientifically literate enough to understand these scientific advances but also failing to prepare a workforce for new jobs and professions that have emerged. Moreover, as science becomes more interdisciplinary (as we have seen in areas such as global climate change, ecology, and genetics), we can no longer rely on the traditional ways of teaching science as a set of well-understood, clearly depicted, stand-alone disciplines. Advances in science and technology are blurring the lines between the individual scientific disciplines. We need to start to develop and prepare

* We thank Alyssa Wise, Nick Giordano, and Nora Sabelli for their helpful input on this essay. This material is based on work supported by the National Science Foundation under grants ESI-0426319, ESI-0608936, and ESI-0426328. Any opinions, findings, and conclusions or recommendations expressed in this material are those of the authors and do not necessarily reflect the views of the National Science Foundation.

Nanoethics: The Ethical and Social Implications of Nanotechnology. Edited by Allhoff, Lin, Moor, Weckert
Copyright © 2007 John Wiley & Sons, Inc.

new approaches now in order to have well-understood materials and pedagogies ready when the need for them becomes critical.

An important interdisciplinary area enabled by new tools is the science and technology of the nanoscale. Perhaps the tools that have led to the biggest breakthroughs are scanning probe instruments such as atomic force microscopes and scanning tunneling microscopes. These tools allow scientists to view and manipulate particles at the nanoscale, such as atoms and small molecules, allowing images and manipulation of phenomena invisible to the naked eye. The manipulation of materials at the nanoscale will allow scientists and engineers to build materials and structures with novel properties. New information and technologies resulting from this research will continue to have broad societal implications that will be realized in many fields, including health care, agriculture, food, water, energy, and the environment.

New models and ways of thinking must be developed to understand the behavior of matter at this important scale. The nanoscale is small enough that many of our models for bulk substances do not accurately predict the properties of materials but large enough that quantum calculations are prohibitively complicated. Unfortunately, our middle and high schools fail to help students develop models of how to understand properties and phenomena at different scales. For instance, our textbooks fail to address how small the nanoscale is in comparison with the microscopic and macroscopic worlds. In fact, many middle and high school students, as well as adults, have fundamental confusions regarding scale. For instance, many students believe that a virus is smaller than an atom (Tretter et al., 2006)!

The revolution that nanoscience and nanotechnology bring to diverse areas of human endeavor requires a commensurate response in the educational community to increase students' understanding of core concepts in the field. Although there are a growing number of nanoscale science and engineering programs at the undergraduate and graduate levels, there is a strong need for nanoscience education in middle school and high school, both to increase students' scientific literacy and to prepare them for further study. It is estimated that 2 million people with knowledge of nanoscience will be needed to work in a variety of professions worldwide by the year 2015 (Roco, 2003). A major concern of the National Science Foundation (NSF) and the National Nanotechnology Initiative (NNI) is that the United States will not have the workforce or intellectual capacity to compete worldwide in nanoscience efforts. Other countries have similar concerns and are creating initiatives to develop human capacity in nanoscale science. For example, the European Commission (2005) has defined an action plan for Europe to promote growth and jobs in nanotechnology through interdisciplinary education and training; the German Federal Ministry of Education and Research (2006) has developed a national strategy to promote education, research, and innovation in nanotechnology; and the Nanotechnology Researchers Network Center of Japan (2006) has organized a number of nanotechnology schools to train young researchers.

It is the responsibility of national, state, and local education leadership in the United States to prepare a much larger cross section of the U.S. population with the science and engineering knowledge necessary to function in a highly technological society and to maintain the momentum of discovery and innovation that will sustain the nation's economic prosperity. But current science education in the United States is failing on many fronts. Students are not making critical gains in standardized test scores (Gonzales et al., 2004). Science education is not addressing the critical need to prepare scientists to expand U.S. scientific research efforts (Yager, 2003), and it is not making progress in creating a scientifically literate citizenry (National Science Board, 2002). U.S. students rank near the bottom on international studies of educational performance in science and mathematics. Their dismal performance is due partly to the science textbooks currently in use. A review of middle school curriculum materials by Kesidou and Roseman (2002) showed that none of the nine middle school programs they examined were likely to enable students to meet national science standards. Their critique claimed that the materials covered many topics at a superficial level and focused on technical vocabulary. In addition, the materials did not take advantage of what we know about student learning and did not allow students to experience phenomena or representations related to important learning goals. Moreover, U.S. textbooks fail to introduce students to emerging ideas in science. In short, "Our systems of basic scientific research and education are in serious crisis. . . . The quality of the U.S. education system . . . has fallen behind those of scores of other nations . . . at a time when vastly more Americans will have to understand and work competently with science and math on a daily basis" (U.S. Commission on National Security/21st Century, 2001).

On the basis of such findings, the NSF has funded various groups to develop materials that can inform students and the general public about nanoscience and change the way science is taught in this country. In this essay, we explore the educational implications of current initiatives and the need for new educational initiatives in nanoscience. We believe that nanoscience can serve as a catalyst to reconsider how to bring about deep reform of science education and public policy in support of science education goals.

NANOSCIENCE IN MIDDLE SCHOOL AND HIGH SCHOOL

Including nanoscience education in middle school and high school curricula would do more than bring nanoscience concepts "down" to this level; it would also introduce a much-needed interdisciplinary framework into highly disjointed curricula and help students build understanding of concepts and principles of nanoscale science. Nanoscience brings together concepts from physics, chemistry, and biology as well as related areas such as materials science, mathematics, medicine, and engineering. In contrast, science education at the high school level is conducted primarily in discipline-specific courses, with little interplay between the disciplines. High school students typically do not experience interdisciplinary science until they enter an undergraduate institution, if at all. However, we know that the study of science as disconnected disciplines does not produce strong student understanding of the core unifying scientific concepts set forth in the national standards (National Research Council, 1996) and there is an urgent need to revise the science curriculum to reflect this reality. Moreover, important ideas in nanoscience are not central to national standards and are only weakly (if at all) introduced in grades 7 to 12. Introducing nanoscience themes and applications in grades 7 to 12 would provide a way to both establish and later revisit core science concepts and view them through a different lens. Nanoscience education introduces students to emerging ideas of science and supports understanding of the interconnections between the traditional scientific domains—reflecting the "unity in nature" (Roco, 2003) and providing compelling, real-world examples of science in action. Unfortunately, attempts to revise the science curriculum usually involve simply rearranging the sequence of topics without changing the actual content. This kind of reordering will not significantly improve the science curriculum. Another common approach is to insert examples and sidebars in science textbooks. This textbook "vignette" model often leaves these topics out of chapter summaries or assessments, leading instructors to ignore them or assign them as optional topics only, which is unlikely to provide students with a coherent understanding of science. Instead, strong connections that exist between the disciplines need to be more strongly reflected in national standards and benchmarks, and courses that have students use science concepts and principles in an interdisciplinary fashion need to be developed.

Two areas are likely to pose the greatest conceptual challenges to student understanding of core nanoscience concepts at the high school level. The first of these arises because nanoscale entities are generally difficult to both see and visualize. A large number of studies, mostly focused on learning in chemistry, document the problems students have understanding the behavior and nature of atoms and molecules (e.g., Bunce and Gabel, 2002; Nakhleh, 1992; Wu et al., 2001). We believe that understanding processes that involve creating and using nanoscale entities will pose similar difficulties for students. However, if curriculum developers make use of some of the new tools (such as scanning probe instruments) that have emerged from nanoscience, we may be able to make progress. Currently, however, these emerging technologies are not a central focus in science textbooks.

A second challenge to student understanding results from the concepts and physical laws that govern the behavior of particles at the nanoscale. Everyday, "macro level" experiences of how physical objects move and interact can be accurately described by Newtonian physics. However, at the nanoscale, different rules predominate. Gravity becomes negligible, while coulombic forces, quantum mechanics, and the random thermal motion of particles become central considerations. Generally, there is little in students' experience of the physical world and their intuitive conceptions regarding aggregate matter that can apply directly to conceptualizing nanoscale phenomena. In addition, the concept that dominant forces change with scale is not in science curricula because it is not yet addressed in national standards and benchmarks, although the American Association for the Advancement of Science is planning to include ideas related to nanoscience in the next revision of the *Atlas of Scientific Literacy*.

INITIATIVES IN NANOSCIENCE EDUCATION

Various groups have received funding to promote the learning of nanoscience concepts and to advance initiatives in the field. Many of these groups are addressing the challenges the United States is facing to remain competitive with other nations. They are dealing with these issues by developing curriculum materials that deal with emerging science concepts, influencing policy to modify existing national standards and benchmarks, and targeting the general public. Below we describe a few examples of innovative initiatives that are addressing these challenges.

The first National Center for Learning and Teaching in Nanoscale Science and Engineering (NCLT, www.nclt.us) in the United States is exploring ways to build national capacity in nanoscience by focusing on and exploring questions in the learning and teaching of nanoscale science through inquiry and design of materials. The mission of the center is to produce the next generation of leaders and researchers in nanoscience to keep the United States globally competitive. In NCLT, a diverse group of scientists, science educators, and learning scientists from universities including Northwestern University, the University of Michigan, Purdue University, the University of Illinois at Urbana-Champaign, and the University of Illinois at Chicago are collaborating to bring about changes in science education, particularly in grades 7 to 16.

The NanoSense project (nanosense.org) seeks to bring nanoscale science to high school classrooms by way of curriculum units. The NanoSense team consists of an interdisciplinary group of chemists, physicists, nanoscientists, and educators from SRI International, San Jose State University, and San Francisco Bay Area high schools who are developing, testing, and disseminating a number of materials to help high school teachers and students understand science concepts relating to nanoscale phenomena and integrate these concepts with traditional curricula. Units available on the project website include *Size Matters*, which focuses on concepts of size and scale, unusual properties of the nanoscale, tools of the nanosciences, and example applications; and *Clear Sunscreen*, which focuses on interactions of light and matter and, in particular, why zinc oxide nanoparticles block ultraviolet light but are transparent to visible light. Units in development focus on how nanoscience could advance energy production (*Clean Energy*) and water treatment (*Fine Filters*).

Nanoscale Informal Science Education (NISE, www.nisenet.org) aims to bring the research and education communities together to develop new methods and approaches to engage the general public (including school-age children) with nanoscale science and engineering. To accomplish this mission, NISE has created a number of working groups that are developing and testing approaches for introducing the nanoscale world to the public. For example, one group aims to engage adults and older youth through dialogue and deliberation around societal implications of nanoscale science, engineering, and technology. Another group is creating packages of museum exhibits, demonstrations, immersive media experiences, multimedia, and other resources to allow informal educational institutions to create custom sets of experiences for their visitors.

A core mission of nanoscience education initiatives is to prepare individuals to function and work in our society in the future. According to the NNI (National Science and Technology Council, 2005), nationwide, nanotechnology may account for a trillion-dollar annual market and may employ 2 million people within 10 to 15 years. The limited numbers of U.S. students who choose technical careers has led to a concern about whether the United States will have a workforce that is educated enough to take full advantage of future career opportunities, particularly in nanoscience. The NNI aims to address such concerns by simultaneously supporting the development of world-class research and education programs and resources to achieve the full potential of nanotechnology, including a skilled workforce and the supporting infrastructure and tools to advance nanotechnology. The NNI highlights contributions to education made possible by advances in information technologies, such as the use of scientific visualizations that bridge the perceptual gaps between the nano-, micro-, and macroscales.

The preparation of these future nanotechnology workers will need to begin early in their schooling to provide a strong basis for future endeavors in science education. Students ideally should develop a strong conceptual understanding of biology, chemistry, and physics but also of the connections between the sciences. Because most science education programs do not have an interdisciplinary component, connections between the disciplines need to be made explicit. These connections could take on a variety of forms, including weaving of nanoscience concepts and applications into existing curricula, creating a capstone-type course in the senior year of high school, devoting time at the end of each year to making connections between disciplines, and identifying opportunities for high school students to take enrichment courses at a nearby university if such courses are not offered at the high school.

With the emergence of new fields of science and the movement of these emerging fields into the classroom, it may be time for the disciplinary model to change. The artificial barriers between the classrooms of biology, chemistry, and physics fragment students' conceptions of science and limit their ability to make scientific connections in terms of underlying commonalities, which for the most part derive from molecular or other small aggregate interactions. A single course that, for example, melds chemistry, biology, and physics into a comprehensive curriculum could be a significant step in preparing individuals for the future needs of the United States. However, measurable change will not be achieved one course at a time. Our challenge is to develop tools and strategies for integrating ideas, concepts, and practices from the learning sciences by using cross-discipline (chemistry, physics, biology, and mathematics) connections in the pedagogy. The benefits of such integration are many, but only if it is affordable in terms of instructor time and motivational in terms of value added (see, e.g., Werner, 1996). Achieving these benefits requires the development of tools and strategies that are accessible to teachers across science disciplines, allow for teacher control, and demonstrate learning advantages for students. In the long term, we as a society need to revamp the way science is taught in our schools by restructuring K through 12 science education and creating science curricula that focus on interdisciplinary approaches that help students build meaningful understandings of the big ideas in science—ideas that provide insight into the development of the field, explain a range of phenomena, and help them to make individual, social, and political decisions regarding science and technology.

Whatever the solution, one thing is clear: Educational reform is needed to incorporate emerging science into the curriculum at the middle and high school levels. Perhaps one way to start such educational reform is to gather together university faculty, those in the nanoscience workforce, middle and high school teachers, and policymakers to discuss and debate the various options. Coming to an informed decision about how emerging topics should be introduced into the classroom while keeping a solid foundation in the disciplines would be extremely constructive and would allow educators to move forward in a direction that has been carefully examined and discussed. In addition, the inclusion of those who currently work in the field of nanoscience would allow consideration of what is necessary in order to prepare individuals to enter the technology workforce.

KEY CHALLENGES TO EDUCATION REFORM

First, a consensus on the importance of the interdisciplinarity of science needs to come to the fore. Science and technology are constantly in a state of change, and the educational system needs to change continuously to keep abreast. The individual disciplines of science are changing and merging. Likewise, science education needs to prepare students to function in society and in a workforce that has a need for experts in interdisciplinary fields. Students who are expert in chemistry alone will not be able to make the cognitive leap that accompanies nanoscience, in which knowledge of biology and physics is also necessary. To prepare nearly 2 million workers to function in the field of nanoscience, it is crucial that we begin preparing students early, so that they can think and use knowledge in an interdisciplinary fashion.

We have discussed a few of the challenges of preparing students and the public to function in a highly technological society and to maintain the momentum of discovery and innovation. Many more challenges remain, such as the following, summarized from Sabelli et al. (2005):

- Representing interactions and behaviors of concepts difficult to understand (e.g., tunneling, thermal noise, quantum effects, emergent behaviors)
- Understanding how to teach nanoscience to different audiences, at what levels and depths, and when to teach concepts within or across disciplines
- Identifying the developmental sequence of concepts to learn in nanoscience
- Preparing teachers to address interdisciplinary and innovative science topics such as nanoscience
- Balancing the physical and virtual experiences and knowing when and how they work
- Addressing how learner intuitions can be misleading
- Resolving the tension between reality and fiction or hype
- Developing and integrating compelling new forms of assessment into new nanoscience activities
- Establishing quality control and criteria for good nanoscience educational experiences
- Understanding the ethical, social, technical, and educational context of nanoscience

Below, we explore in more detail four specific, recurring challenges from our work to design and disseminate nanoscience curriculum and offer some proposed approaches to address the challenges. We focus on the following challenges:

- Defining the curriculum for a new and evolving (i.e., not fully understood) area of scientific study
- Situating an inherently interdisciplinary science within a typical high school classroom that focuses on one discipline (i.e., chemistry)
- Developing teacher support materials for content that is novel for teachers (and, in fact, for many scientists)
- Preparing preservice teachers for teaching interdisciplinary science

Challenge 1: Defining the Curriculum

Agreeing on a few core concepts and principles, or big ideas, through discussion and debate is an important first step in making sure that curricula meet the needs of the many stakeholders involved. Groups of people who need to be involved in this discussion include nanoscientists (content experts), science education researchers, teachers, technology developers, and learning scientists. Some of the big ideas in nanoscience that have been identified include the following (Krajcik et al., 2006):

1. Under certain conditions, some materials can spontaneously assemble themselves into larger structures without external intervention. This process provides a means for manipulating material at the nanoscale.
2. Concepts of size and scale form the cognitive framework used to make sense of nanoscale phenomena.
3. All matter is composed of atoms.
4. Properties of matter change at the nanoscale.
5. Nanotechnology is driven by the processes of science and engineering to solve problems.
6. Models help us understand, visualize, predict, hypothesize, and interpret data about natural and manufactured nanoscale objects and phenomena, which are by their very nature too small to see.
7. Recently developed tools allow the investigation, measurement, and manipulation of nanoscale matter atom by atom, leading to new understandings of matter and development of new structures.

In addition, learning goals that fall under the headings of these central concepts need to be made explicit, since they are not yet included in national standards. Knowing, however, that not all students will choose to further their studies of nanoscience past high school, what are the ideas that we want students to leave with?

Another issue is how to organize the curriculum: Should it be topically based around applications, organized by underlying themes, or structured around learning goals within traditional scientific disciplines? Our work suggests that organizing units around learning goals helps to ensure that students learn what is intended, by connecting students' prior knowledge to new information (Krajcik and Blumenfeld, 2006). However, research clearly shows that we also need to consider students' motivation and the context when developing materials for students (Blumenfeld et al., 2006). It is useful for students to have an understanding of how applications of nanoscience relate to their everyday lives, thereby contextualizing the concepts and making them meaningful for society. Moreover, we have found it valuable in our work to focus students' attentions on a problem in the field. Such a focus gives students motivation for learning the new ideas (Krajcik and Blumenfeld, 2006).

A third issue is finding reliable and verifiable information in a rapidly evolving area and making it accessible to learners. For example, in the literature we found numerous terminology differences and explanations that contradicted each other on various fronts regarding whether nanoscale zinc oxide particles used in new sunscreens block ultraviolet radiation by absorbing or by scattering the radiation. As with any new science, our understanding is still evolving, and there are few common frameworks available—particularly ones that are understandable at a high school level.

In response to this group of challenges, we have begun moving toward an expert-collaborative model in which curriculum developers work in close partnership with nanoscientists and teachers to develop curricular units. To make this model work, we are identifying and developing units based on specific, engaging nanoscience applications that tie into core high school science concepts and for which we have readily available, deep scientific expertise from partner scientists.

Challenge 2: Situating the Science

Curriculum developers may create nanoscience materials targeted for high school chemistry, but knowledge of physics and biology is quite helpful for both teachers and students in understanding nanoscience and its applications. Leveraging student knowledge of other disciplines, particularly in advanced classes, could not only reduce some of the burden on teachers but also help students begin to integrate their knowledge from the different disciplines. Team teaching approaches could also be effective, although coordinating such efforts adds another layer of complexity.

Another issue is how to help teachers determine where the curriculum fits with what they currently teach. Does the new curriculum delve deep enough into core science concepts so that it can replace standard units? Can it tie in at the end of current units? How do we focus strongly on the core science involved while still showing what is new and different about nanoscience? We have found it useful to provide teachers with alignment charts of where the curriculum addresses core science topics. Providing teachers with multiple ways to use the materials and a "drill-down" structure for progressively greater depth of understanding enables adjustment for different levels of students. The materials could take the form of replacement units or small lessons that can be embedded into the traditional curriculum.

Such options might serve as short-term solutions, but they will not bring out the level of interdisciplinary thinking that is necessary. We agree with other science education reformers (e.g., Hurd, 1991; Tinker, 2006) that there is a larger need to restructure K through 12 science education and build science curricula that focus on an interdisciplinary approach to help students build meaningful understandings of the big ideas in science. For example, Robert Tinker (2006, p. 1) argues that "Introductory science education needs a radical revision and nanoscience is the new content that is needed" and that this goal "can be accomplished with integrated science courses that span two or more grades." Paul DeHart Hurd (1991, p. 33) writes that "There is little recognition that in recent years the boundaries between the various natural sciences have become more and more blurred and major concepts more unified" and urges science educators to integrate science curricula and use thematic science instruction. Indeed, leading experts and organizations around the world are beginning to embrace this perspective. For example, the United Nations Educational, Scientific and Cultural Organization (UNESCO) has created the Integrated Science and Technology Education program to increase student interest in science and help them relate to the subject matter. In the long term, we will succeed only by restructuring the K through 12 science curriculum to take on a more interdisciplinary approach.

Challenge 3: Developing Teacher Support Materials for Novel Content

Teaching nanoscience will pose challenges to most secondary science teachers who have majored in one discipline. For example, although physics teachers might feel comfortable teaching ideas related to the interaction of light with matter, few have understandings of biological processes. One solution is to develop teacher support materials for areas in which the content reaches outside teachers' expertise. Still, lack of familiarity with the content makes it difficult for teachers to stimulate discussion by asking follow-up questions and to identify and address student misconceptions. Developers must create educational materials for teachers that provide deep explanations, provide strong guidance for discussion topics and questions, and identify and highlight potential misconceptions (Davis and Krajcik, 2005). The novelty of the content, combined with the newness of the field, raises pedagogical and content demands that some teachers may not be prepared to deal with. Teachers are not able to know all the answers to students' (and their own) questions, and many questions go beyond our current understanding as a scientific community. To help teachers engage these challenges, we have recast them as opportunities to model the scientific process and provide concrete strategies for how to do so. In this way, we aim to have teachers and students experience science in action as an empowering and energizing experience rather than as an exercise in frustration.

Ongoing professional development experiences also can provide learning opportunities for teachers. Teachers could attend summer institutes or weekend workshops in which they are introduced to nanoscience concepts, tools, and phenomena. Such opportunities could include experiences with scientists (pairing up a scientist and a teacher) and team teaching in which novice teachers observe expert teachers enacting a nanoscience lesson. The NCLT program offers such summer institutes for teachers.

Research internships for teachers could help them "get up to speed" on current nanoscience concepts and technologies. Such internships could be modeled after the successful local industry–teaching partnership, Industry Initiatives for Science and Math Education (IISME, www.iisme.org). Teachers who receive IISME fellowships participate in a 6- to 8-week research project in a local industry, government, or university lab setting, with a stipend. Teachers network through weekly meetings, design and critique lessons developed from their research projects, and then present these lessons to others at their schools or districts during inservice training.

Challenge 4: Preparing Preservice Teachers

A final challenge, which goes hand in hand with challenge 3, is preparing preservice teachers for teaching nanoscience. Teacher preparation is already a complex situation in the United States. Requirements of No Child Left Behind (NCLB) for science testing at the elementary, middle, and secondary levels are renewing scrutiny of teacher qualifications in science. The difficulties associated with certification of teachers in an interdisciplinary field such as nanoscience are great. Teacher education programs would have to be expanded to provide interdisciplinary teaching certificates. Currently, teachers are able to gain certification in multiple disciplines, but the majority become certified in their (one) academic major alone. One near-term solution is to have science methods courses for preservice teachers address interdisciplinary, innovative, and emerging science topics such as nanotechnology, so that teachers can help students experience science in an interdisciplinary fashion.

FURTHER CHALLENGES AND IMPLICATIONS

Despite the considerable challenges, we believe it is possible and necessary to introduce new and evolving areas of science at the middle and high school levels. Cutting-edge science can be used to engage students, reinforce core science concepts, provide insight into job opportunities in the sciences, and give students a better idea of how the traditional disciplines tie together. Looking forward, nanoscale science further challenges the learning and science research community to explore new pedagogies and societal implications of this new technology.

Challenges to Conceptual Understanding of Nanoscience

The challenges to helping students develop an understanding of nanoscience are both conceptual and practical; objects and concepts at the nanoscale are hard to visualize and difficult to describe, and their relationships to the observable world can be counterintuitive. These difficulties suggest the need to conceptualize a continuum of scales that can represent the nonobservable phenomena in nature to help students integrate their views of matter at all scales. These scale issues must be addressed before students can be expected to gain an understanding of more complex phenomena and properties of matter at the nanoscale. New learning technologies hold promise for helping learners develop conceptual understanding. Science educators need to take advantage of existing technology that allows students to visualize and manipulate representations of materials at the nanoscale (e.g., Tinker, 2006), and the tools of nanoscientists need to be made available to learners. For example, multiscale modeling tools used by scientists could be adapted to allow students to simulate how specific properties change as the size scale changes and to explore, for example, the importance of ratios of surface area to volume in catalysis (Sabelli et al., 2005). In addition, a learning progression explicating the order of concepts and principles from middle school through high school needs to be developed to clarify what students need to know to master future concepts. A learning progression would allow students to build deeper and more meaningful understanding of big ideas of science and explore ideas through successively more complex ways of thinking and understanding.

Epistemological Concerns

Some central epistemological ideas can lead to better understanding of why science at the nanoscale requires a different educational approach. Two examples of such ideas are that (1) small quantitative changes in some property can aggregate toward large *qualitative* differences and (2) all matter can be considered as individual particles, as small groups of particles, or as large groups of particles, each entailing different scientific models and theories. Some educators may believe that these ideas make the nanoscale even less accessible to middle and high school students; however, with the right approach, students can gain some understanding of these complex ideas in middle and high school.

Social Implications

A discussion of the social implications of nanotechnology as part of nanoscience education is important to give students tools to help them put in perspective the significant hype, positive as well as negative, found in most public discussions of the topic. Limiting education to "show and tell" awareness demonstrations could build the hype without providing the underlying context, whether that hype extols nanotechnology's potential or decries its dangers. These discussions should take place in the context of possible future applications of nanotechnology. They would also provide a good opportunity for students to gain experience in debating important, controversial issues, a skill that is mentioned in the National Science Education Standards (National Research Council, 1996). Clearly, citizens of the United States must have the skills necessary to make informed decisions about possible implications of nanotechnology.

CONCLUDING COMMENT

To be successful, nanoscience education will need to make a sharp departure from traditional ways of teaching. As Hsi et al. (2006) suggest, "Addressing these challenges will hopefully lead to new thinking, techniques, and partnerships between learning scientists, educators, and scientists, just as the advancement of nanoscale science, engineering, and technology has led to new disciplines, technologies, and collaborations." The challenges are formidable, and it is only by having diverse experts work together that we will find solutions. The research community needs to carefully study this process of change and realize that some initial attempts will fail and that successful change will take years to accomplish. Such long-term, carefully studied change in science education will occur only with the collaboration and active support of all stakeholders, including policymakers and the federal government.

REFERENCES

Blumenfeld, P. C., Kempler, T. M., and Krajcik, J. S. 2006. Motivation and cognitive engagement in learning environments. In R. K. Sawyer (Ed.), *The Cambridge Handbook of the Learning Sciences*. New York: Cambridge University Press, pp. 475–488.

Bunce, D., and Gabel, D. 2002. Differential effects on the achievement of males and females of teaching the particulate nature of chemistry. *Journal of Research in Science Teaching* 39(10): 911–927.

Davis, E. A., and Krajcik, J. S. 2005. Designing educative curriculum materials to promote teacher learning. *Educational Researcher* 34(3): 3–14.

European Commission. 2005. *Nanosciences and Nanotechnologies: An Action Plan for Europe 2005–2009*. Available: http://cordis.europa.eu/nanotechnology/actionplan.htm, accessed October 11, 2006.

German Federal Ministry of Education and Research. 2006. *Nanotechnology: A Future Technology with Visions*. Available: http://www.bmbf.de/en/nanotechnologie.php, accessed October 11, 2006.

Gonzales, P., Guzman, J. C., Partelow, L., Pahlke, E., Jocelyn, L., Kastberg, D., et al. 2004. *Highlights from the Trends in International Mathematics and Science Study (TIMSS)* 2003 (NCES 2005—005). Washington, DC: U.S. Government Printing Office.

Hsi, S., Sabelli, N., Krajcik, J., Tinker, R., and Ellenbogen, K. 2006, June. Learning at the nanoscale: Research questions that the rapidly evolving interdisciplinarity of science poses for the learning sciences. Innovative Session, 7th International Conference of the Learning Sciences, Bloomington, IN. Available: http://nanosense.org/documents/papers/ICLS2006HsiSabelli.pdf, accessed August 22, 2006.

Hurd, P. D. 1991. Why we must transform science education. *Educational Leadership* 49(2): 33–35.

Kesidou, S., and Roseman, J. E. 2002. How well do middle school science programs measure up? Findings from Project 2061's curriculum review. *Journal of Research in Science Teaching* 39: 522–549.

Krajcik, J. S., and Blumenfeld, P. 2006. Project-based learning. In R. K. Sawyer (Ed.), *The Cambridge Handbook of the Learning Sciences*. New York: Cambridge University Press.

Krajcik, J., Schank, P., Stevens, S., and Sutherland, L. 2006. Report of the workshop to identify and clarify nanoscience learning goals, unpublished manuscript, University of Michigan.

Nakhleh, M. B. 1992. Why some students don't learn chemistry. *Journal of Chemical Education* 69(3): 191–196.

Nanotechnology Researchers Network Center of Japan. 2006. *Nanotech School*. Available: http://www.nanonet.go.jp/english/school/, accessed October 11, 2006.

National Research Council. 1996. *National Science Education Standards*. Washington, DC: National Academy Press.

National Science Board. 2002. Science and technology: Public attitudes and public understanding. In *Science and Engineering Indicators-2002*. Arlington, VA: National Science Foundation,

Chapter 7. Available: http://www.nsf.gov/statistics/seind02/c7/c7h.htm, accessed September 10, 2005.

National Science and Technology Council Committee on Technology and Subcommittee on Nanoscale Science, Engineering, and Technology. 2005, March. *The National Nanotechnology Initiative: Research and Development Leading to a Revolution in Technology and Industry.* Arlington, VA: National Nanotechnology Coordination Office.

Roco, M. C. 2003. Converging science and technology at the nanoscale: Opportunities for education and training. *Focus on Nanotechnology* 21(10): 1247–1249.

Sabelli, N., Schank, P., Rosenquist, A., Stanford, T., Patton, C., Cormia, R., et al. 2005. *Report of the Workshop on Science and Technology Education at the Nanoscale.* Menlo Park, CA: SRI International.

Tinker, R. 2006. Nanoscience and the new secondary science curriculum. Paper presented at the 2006 Workshop to Identify and Clarify Nanoscience Learning Goals. Boston, MA: The Concord Consortium.

Tretter, T. R., Jones, M. G., Andre, T., Negishi, A., and Minogue, J. 2006. Conceptual boundaries and distances: Students' and adults' concepts of the scale of scientific phenomena. *Journal of Research in Science Teaching* 43: 282–319.

U.S. Commission on National Security/21st Century. 2001. *Road Map for National Security: Imperative for Change.* Washington, DC: Author. Available: http://govinfo.library.unt.edu/nssg/PhaseIIIFR.pdf, accessed November 7, 2005.

Werner, M. 1996. Barriers to a collaborative, multidisciplinary pedagogy. In *Proceedings of the 1996 International Conference on Software Engineering: Education and Practice.* New York: IEEE, pp. 203–210.

Wu, H.-K., Krajcik, J. S., and Soloway, E. 2001. Promoting conceptual understanding of chemical representations: Students' use of a visualization tool in the classroom. *Journal of Research in Science Teaching* 38(7): 821–842.

Yager, R. E. 2003. Science education. In *The Encyclopedia of Education*, 2nd ed. New York: Macmillan References USA.

22

IMPACT OF NANOTECHNOLOGIES ON DEVELOPING COUNTRIES

Joachim Schummer

INTRODUCTION

Thanks to two Canadian groups, there has been a lively debate since 2003 on the possible impacts of nanotechnology on the developing world. A group from the Joint Centre for Bioethics at the University of Toronto has, besides addressing various other ethical issues, pointed out the opportunities of nanotechnology for developing countries, both by developing products that meet their specific needs and by providing a chance for their own industrial development (Court et al., 2004; Mnyusiwalla et al., 2003; Salamanca-Buentello et al., 2005). In contrast, the Action Group on Erosion, Technology and Concentration (ETC Group), a nongovernmental organization based in Winnipeg, has argued that nanotechnology will further increase the divide between rich and poor countries through political and socioeconomic conditions that favor multinational corporations.[1] Several other authors joined the debate—for example, by assessing the actual research and development (R&D) activities and potential of developing countries (Maclurcan, 2005) and by clarifying the socioeconomic context of specific needs (Invernizzi and Foladori, 2005). Moreover, in 2005, the United Nations Industrial Development Organization (UNIDO) convened an international conference, UNESCO established an expert group, and the Washington-based nongovernmental Meridian Institute started an

Nanoethics: The Ethical and Social Implications of Nanotechnology. Edited by Allhoff, Lin, Moor, Weckert
Copyright © 2007 John Wiley & Sons, Inc.

initiative to bring international stakeholders together for an ongoing dialogue (Meridian Institute, 2005; North-South dialogue, 2005; UNESCO, 2005).

Supplementing previous publications (Schummer, 2005, 2006, 2007), this chapter adds to the debate by two main contributions. First, I put some efforts on conceptual clarifications and systematical analyses. In particular, after discussing the meaning of "developing countries," I will point out the diversities of technologies that are nowadays called nanotechnology as well as the variety of possible impacts that these technologies can have on developing countries. That will span the scope for hundreds of case studies to be made and point to the problems of one-sided approaches. Second, I will use that framework for the analysis of a few selected issues that have previously not been addressed or, in my view, not carefully enough: whether nanotechnologies meet specific needs of the poor, how they can impact the economies by changing material demands, and how their impact is affected by changing intellectual property rights.

CLARIFICATIONS

What Are Developing Countries?

Both the term "developing countries" and its meaning are contentious. Most countries, including the richest ones, are developing according to some indices, whereas some of the poorest countries are actually stagnating or losing ground. The methods for measuring the state of a country's development range from simple per-capita gross domestic product (GDP) to complex indices which try to capture sustainable conditions of living, including political stability and equality among the population. For pragmatic reasons, I will use the term developing countries for countries with a low or medium state of development according to the most widely accepted human development index (HDI) by the United Nations Development Programme (UNDP).[2] The HDI is a composite index that combines per-capita GDP with life expectancy and educational standards. According to that index, the least developed countries are all in sub-Saharan Africa to be followed by South Asia, Arab states, East Asia, and Latin America.

Beyond these statistical and geographical features, most of the less developed countries share some characteristics. For instance, historically, they were former colonies and frequently still have some special ties (economical, political, or military) to their former colonial powers. Many happen to be rich in material resources for the long-term benefit of the colonial powers. Large parts of their populations suffer from very basic needs, like malnutrition and the lack of safe drinking water, sanitation, education, and health care, despite devastating epidemics like AIDS and malaria. Rural exodus has even increased these needs through exploding slums around big cities. They have only poor infrastructures of public and private R&D, including small public research budgets and virtually no venture capital. Even if they are currently developing such infrastructures—as in China—they have little experience in technology governance, including the launch and conduct of research programs, safety and environmental regulations, marketing and patenting strategies, and so on.

What Are Nanotechnologies?

Among definitions of "nanotechnology," three different approaches are currently in use and all are conspicuously vague.

The first approach, which philosophers call *nominal definition*, provides necessary and sufficient conditions that a technology must meet to be called a nanotechnology. Typical definitions require that the technology must investigate and manipulate material objects in the range 1 to 100 nanometers in order to explore novel properties and to develop new devices and functionalities that essentially depend on this range. Unfortunately, such a definition covers all the classical natural science and engineering disciplines that investigate and manipulate material objects, such as chemistry, materials science, solid-state physics, pharmacy, molecular biology, and chemical, mechanical, and electrical engineering. This is because almost any material is structured in the range 1 to 100 nanometers in such a way that its structure in this range determines their properties and (technologically speaking) their functionalities (Schummer, 2004a).

The second approach, called *teleological definition*, defines nanotechnology by its future goals. In order to be specific, one needs to provide more than just generic values, like health, wealth, security, and so on, and more than just relative attributes, like smaller, faster, harder, cheaper. Since its first introduction by Eric Drexler (1986) teleological definitions of nanotechnology have come in the particular form of visions about a futuristic technology to be developed that will radically change everything, from industrial production to the somatic, mental, and social conditions of human life. According to this approach, current research belongs to nanotechnology if it is guided by the vision of the future nanotechnology which in turn will achieve the prospective goals. Apart from the questionable feasibility of the futuristic visions, it is impracticable to identify current research as belonging to nanotechnology by the visions that researchers publicly propagate.

The third definitional approach, called *real definition*, refers to a list of specific research topics. Such lists, which vary from country to country and over time, typically include scanning probe microscopy, nanoparticle research, nanostructured materials, polymers and composites, ultrathin coating, heterogeneous catalysis, supramolecular chemistry, molecular electronics, molecular modeling, lithography for chip production, semiconductor research and quantum dots, quantum computing, microelectronic mechanical systems (MEMSs), liquid crystals, light-emitting diodes (LEDs), solar cells, fuel cells, biochemical sensors, targeted drug delivery, molecular biotechnology, genetic engineering, neurophysiology, tissue engineering, and so on. Unrelated as these topics are to each other apart from their common topicality, it is appropriate to speak of nanotechnologies (plural) rather than of one nanotechnology (singular), particularly because there is, in contrast to many claims and hopes, no particular interdisciplinary collaboration (Schummer, 2004b).

In the following, I will refer to the real definition, despite its substantial shortcoming of liberally attaching the nanolabel, because that is how scientists, science managers, business, and the media mostly use nanotechnology nowadays. From an ethical perspective, it is hard to identify any one possible issue that would equally apply to all these research fields. For discussing the impact on developing countries, I will therefore select only some specific fields as well as the general context in which they emerge. Before, however, I will provide a systematic survey of what the possible impacts can be, which might be used as a checklist for future scrutiny.

What Are Possible Impacts of Technologies on Developing Countries?

In order to analyze the impacts of nanotechnologies on developing countries, we need to consider the full life cycle of technologies in their socioeconomic contexts, from early R&D decisions and activities, to the manufacturing and use of products, to the dumping of waste, and the various roles that developing countries could play in each of these phases.

In the earliest state, when decisions about governmental R&D funding are made, negative impacts particularly result from wrong decisions that are misled, for instance, by unfounded hopes, hype, unclear concepts, or wrong information. While richer countries can afford the waste of research money to a certain degree, the effect of big and misguided projects on poorer countries with small research budgets can be disastrous, because their relative investments, for instance for new instrumentation, is much higher. It is particularly important, therefore, that they do not simply copy industrialized countries but instead focus their research efforts on well-defined projects tailored to specific needs rather than on such vague projects as nanotechnology overall. Informed science policy decisions would also be cautious about hype words such as "novel" and, instead, rely on careful patent researches that prove whether a research field is already claimed by patents or not. If such a new and promising field is identified and focused on, developing countries could benefit not only from meeting their specific needs but also from becoming leaders in a new technology.

In the actual R&D state, uncertainties remain, some of which require sensible decisions as to what directions of research and product development should be followed. Yet, since scientific research always explores the unknown, there are also uncertainties regarding the safety of researchers and their direct environment that can only be handled with caution. The lack of long-standing research experience in related fields and of strict safety regulations in many developing countries increase the risks of hazards there, for instance by unknown nanoparticle toxicities. Furthermore, if the product development includes test phases, people in developing countries could easily become the guinea pigs for risky technologies by other countries because of lower wages, poorer regulations of human experiments, and less public attention to hazards.

In the state of manufacturing and marketing technological products, countries can play different roles as producers, consumers, and providers or buyers of materials, know-how, and waste processing. Each role can be beneficial or harmful for a country. For instance, if a country hosts the manufacturing of products, it may economically benefit from revenues and employment but also carry the risks of environmental pollution, uncertain worker safety, and hazards. The consumption of a product may meet the specific need of the population, but the necessary imports could lead to trade deficit and the dependence on manufacturing countries. The materials demands by a new technology can be economically beneficial to a country that mines these materials, but also harmful, if the new technology replaces former technologies for which the country had previously provided the materials. A country can benefit from selling certain know-how, unless it is the primary importer of the products manufactured somewhere else. Waste processing has become an attractive global market, but if shortsightedly performed at low regulation standards and poor recycling rates, it goes at the expense of environmental resources and public health.

Whether a product is actually useful and its use is beneficial to a country are difficult to assess in advance. Scientists frequently jump from mere inventions to overly optimistic conclusions, ignoring the prevailing socioeconomic and cultural factors—such as social acceptance, customs, and specific needs; moral, legal, economic, and political barriers; and social and environmental costs—as well as unexpected negative side effects. Ultimately, the product's impact on the HDI seems to be a useful measure. However, the HDI is difficult to estimate in advance and ignores important value aspects. A technological product can increase the inequality within a country and thus induce the perception of injustice by its mere use. For instance, an expensive health product benefits only the economic elite and increases the health divide between poor and rich. Or, if the beneficial use of a product requires advanced education, the product benefits only the educational elite. Furthermore, any technological product made for the improvement of life is based on and confers an idea of what a good life is. Since countries differ to some degree in their ideas of a good life, the wide use of imported technological products can impact the cultural value system [See Schummer (2006) for some examples from nanotechnology].

Finally, technologies can impact countries also from a global economical perspective. The U.S. National Nanotechnology Initiative and others have propagated that nanotechnologies will bring about the "next industrial revolution." If that is more than a thoughtless marketing slogan, then it should alert welfare economists to the opportunities and risks of industrial revolutions. For developing countries, it might be a signal to embark on nanotechnologies as soon as possible, as a unique opportunity to quickly catch up with their economic development, achieving in a few years what industrialized countries have needed for centuries. However, such hopes rest on a simplistic understanding of the historical industrial revolution, according to which some technological innovations alone would have moved the economies of European countries in the nineteenth century. Many of today's historians of economy rather hold to the "dependency theory" according to which "one country's industrial revolution is another country's underdevelopment and these are two sides of the same coin of world capitalist development" (Hudson, 1992, p. 20). [For a review of various theories, see Shrum and Shenhav (1995)]. The dependency theory emphasizes other factors, such as international trade, property rights, economic infrastructure, human resources, and political power, that determine the relative developmental state of a country, which technological innovations can only reinforce. If nanotechnologies have a potential for an legitimate industrial revolution—which is doubtful because of their unclear identity—the dependency theory would predict that, all else equal, they would reinforce the divide between the rich and the poor.

Given the diversity of nanotechnologies and the many different factors through which they can impact developing countries, it is obvious that no simple answer can be provided. Indeed, we need hundreds of case studies that integrate all the available scientific, engineering, economic, political, legal, sociological, cultural, and ethical knowledge, which requires true interdisciplinary cooperation. In the following, therefore, I will discuss only a few selected issues that assess some of the previous suggestions and point to problems that have thus far been neglected.

ADDRESSING SPECIFIC NEEDS OF DEVELOPING COUNTRIES

Water Purification

Safe drinking water is arguably one of the most important needs in many developing countries; at least 1.1 billion people lack access to safe water, and this results in several million deaths per year, mostly children in poor Asian and African countries [UN Millennium Project, 2004; World Health Organization (WHO), 2005]. Many authors have suggested that nanotechnology will provide the crucial remedy. To assess that promise, we need to have a closer look at the pollutants that are particularly important for unsafe water in nonindustrialized areas, which are microbes that are usually from human sources due to insufficient sanitation and heavy metals dissolved from minerals.

Apart from some specific microbial diseases, like schistosomiasis, trachoma, and intestinal helminths, "approximately 4 billion cases of diarrhea each year cause 2.2 million deaths" (UN Millennium Project, 2004, p. 23), which is by far the biggest problem owing to unsafe water. According to the WHO (2005), the death toll of diarrheal diseases could be prevented by better sanitation (32 percent) and hygiene education (up to 45 percent) and by improved water supply (6 to 25 percent) or water treatment (35 to 39 percent). It is difficult to see where nanotechnologies could help here other than by competing with established and simple but efficient water treatments, like chlorination,[3] that are still lacking in many areas. The main problems are not of technological nature but a lack of basic infrastructure, facilities, and education.

It happened that many developing countries, by the help of development projects from rich countries since the 1970s, rather than providing better sanitation and hygiene education, focused on improved water supply by replacing surface water with underground water from wells. Unfortunately, in many regions (particularly in Bangladesh, Nepal, India, Taiwan, Thailand, Argentina, Chile, China, and Mexico), the switch to the allegedly safer underground water supplies has led to high concentrations of arsenic (and other heavy metals), which has become the number 1 poison in drinking water in rural areas.[4] Since arsenic, like other heavy metals, readily binds with iron hydroxide, a number of simple but highly efficient filters tailored to the needs and possibilities of poor rural areas have been developed, ranging from Susan Murcott's sand-plus-iron nails to Arup SenGupta's granular alumina or polymeric beads covered with iron hydroxide.[5]

Against the background of the real problems and their existent efficient solutions, one needs to be careful with media reports announcing nanotechnology's solution to the drinking water problems of the developing world. There is no doubt that micro- and nanoporous filter development can lead to improved removal of microbes and other pollutants from water and that desalination plants can open up new water sources. However, these filters and plants will hardly be affordable and manageable by the neediest in the foreseeable future. One should also note that filters based on zeolites and ceramics, which are nowadays subsumed under nanotechnology, have been produced for many decades (Sherman, 1999), without meeting the needs of developing countries. And the latest approach, the use of the extremely expensive carbon nanotubes in water filters, is a project by the U.S. military that, rather than helping developing countries, should provide "water pure enough to use for medical purposes right on the battlefield" (Kelly, 2004).

In sum, rather than having a significant positive or negative impact specifically on developing countries, nanotechnology-based water purification has largely failed to address the specific needs and problems.

Solar Energy

About 2 billion people worldwide have no access to electricity, and most of them live in rural areas of developing countries (World Energy Council, 1999). Although access to electricity is not essential for living, it is a major development step that replaces inefficient energy forms, as for instance in lighting, and enables and facilitates important processes and infrastructures like refrigeration, communication, education, and health clinics.

Unlike the latest water purification nanotechnologies, solar energy technologies seem to be much more promising for developing countries, particularly for those in geographical areas with high solar radiation. Of the three main technologies, photovoltaics, solar collectors, and solar thermal power plants, only the first one has thus far been related to nanotechnologies if one ignores the coatings of mirrors and other specialized materials. What makes photovoltaics (and solar collectors) particularly interesting for developing countries is their decentralized use in rural areas, that is, they do not depend on central power plants and grids, and their sustainability. Therefore many international organizations have promoted solar rural electrification since the 1980s, such as UNESCO's annual summer schools on Solar Electricity for Rural Areas and the Solar Village Programme.

However, the use of photovoltaics in rural areas of poor countries means that the technology must meet requirements that essentially differ from, say, their use in Southern California. When solar cells are the first ever electricity supply in a village, people at first need to accustom themselves to electricity. Apart from considerable cultural barriers, people need to build up and learn how to use basic electric facilities, including cables, switches, fuses, transformers, and rechargeable batteries, in addition to the electric devices for which the whole setting is built up. Nanotechnologies cannot contribute to that. They can perhaps improve the efficiency and price of solar cells by a few percentage points or make solar cells smaller, more flexible, and transportable, which are humble contributions to the real problems. As with water purification, the real challenges are very basic and largely of educational and cultural nature. However, technology can help develop integrated photovoltaic devices that are easy to handle, durable, and cheap. It is up to nanotechnologists to find out if they can assist here.

AIDS Prevention

AIDS/HIV is arguably the most devastating epidemic in the recorded history of humanity. In 2005, about 4.1 million people became newly infected with HIV and 2.8 million died from AIDS-related diseases, with an estimated 40 million people living with HIV infection. It happened that the least developed countries, particularly in sub-Saharan Africa, are mostly affected by the epidemic; for instance, Swaziland has an adult HIV prevalence as high as 33.4 percent (UNAIDS, 2006).

Against that background, a small Australian company has recently caught the attention of the nanomedia because one of its products, a dendrimer called SPL7013, might be used for a vaginal microbicide gel to prevent HIV infection of women during sexual intercourse. Dendrimers are treelike polymers that have been researched since the late 1970s. Because the nanolabel was attached to dendrimers in the early 2000s, the nanomedia could praise nanotechnology as a cure against AIDS.

The UNAIDS (2006) report claims that "[t]he steady growth of the AIDS epidemic stems not from the deficiencies of available prevention strategies but rather from the world's failure to use the highly effective tools at its disposal to slow the spread of HIV" (p. 124). Since vaccines will likely be unavailable for many years, the primary prevention tools against sexual transmission are condoms and safer sex education. Yet, from Catholic Church policy to male preference of condom-free intercourse, many social factors have prevented effective implementation. Therefore, many experts indeed advocate the development of vaginal microbicides, because it gives women control over their own protection.

Vaginal microbicides (i.e., antiviral agents against HIV to be inserted in the vagina shortly before sexual intercourse) have been developed since the early 1990s (Weber et al., 2005). At least 33 agents with 10 different inhibitor mechanisms are currently under development, of which 5 have reached clinical phase III trials (Lederman et al., 2006). SPL7013 has recently entered only phase I, and because of the typically high production costs of dendrimers, it is unlikely that it could ever be affordable in poor countries. Indeed, it would have to compete with cheap microbicidial substances like soap (sodium lauryl sulfate, also called the "invisible condom"), cellulose sulfate, and lemon juice (all currently in phases I to III), as well as with a bunch of other prevention methods specifically tailored to the needs and customs in poor countries (Short, 2006).

I do not want to diminish any R&D efforts on microbicide, because any possibility of AIDS prevention should be researched. However, the nanolabel, which could equally be attached to soap or cellulose, seems to be reserved for high-tech research that is, for economical reasons, very unlikely to benefit the neediest.

CHANGING MATERIALS DEMANDS

The impact of nanotechnologies on materials demands seems to be less obvious because we tend to associate nanotechnology with small things. On an industrial world market scale, however, small things easily sum up to hundreds or thousands of metric tons of materials per year that cost millions to billions of dollars. Since raw material resources that need to be mined, particularly metals, happened to be mostly in developing countries, any change of materials demand on the world market mostly affects the economies of these countries. Western countries have a long history in researching substitutes for expensive, natural, or foreign materials resources. For instance, synthetic dyes substituted for natural dyes from Asia in the late-nineteenth century, synthetic ammonia substituted for natural niter from Chile in the early twentieth century, and plastics have substituted for wood, natural rubber, and metals since the mid-twentieth century. All these substitution processes had drastic effects on local and national economies. Many of the research topics provided in the real definition of nanotechnology follow this long-term trend.*

Catalysis

Most of the catalysts used in oil refinement, chemical industry processes, and automobile air pollution abatement are based on precious metals that are largely mined in developing countries. For instance, rhenium, which is used in petroleum re-forming, has a world market of about $47 million and comes mainly from Chile[6] (44 percent), Kazakhstan (19 percent), and Peru (12 percent). The most widely used catalysts for pollution abatement and chemical processes are based on platinum and palladium, with world markets of $6.2 billion and $1.3 billion, respectively (ETC Group, 2005a). Both metals are mainly mined in South Africa (78 and 38 percent, respectively) and Russia (12 and 44 percent). The platinum production alone corresponds to about 2.5 percent of South Africa's GDP. One of the declared short-term goals of nanotechnology by science policymakers is the production of "improved catalysts with one or more orders of magnitude less precious metals" (President's Council, 2005, p. 22), which would dramatically affect the economy of the supplying countries. On the other hand, platinum and palladium are also the most promising catalysts for hydrogen fuel cells such that the negative effects of one nanotechnology could be compensated by another.

Electronics

The impact of the materials demand by the electronics industry is more complex. There are ambitious goals, following up the long-term substitution policy by industrialized countries, to replace semiconducting and metallic elements with carbon-based materials. For instance, organic semiconductors, including carbon nanotubes, are researched as possible substitutes for semiconductor elements, like gallium, germanium, indium, cadmium, selenium, arsenic, and antimony, for many of which China is the main supplier. In addition, carbon nanotubes, because of their extraordinary electrical and thermic properties, are expected to substitute for high-conductive metals in electronics, like copper, silver, and gold. Although the amount of these three metals used in electronics is relatively low compared to other uses (with a combined market of more than $100 billion), technological breakthroughs could affect their market prices and thus the economies, for instance, of Chile (36 percent of copper world production), Peru (15 percent of silver),

*The data in the rest of this section are from the U.S. Department of the Interior (2006).

and South Africa (12 percent of gold). A similar effect is expected from the ongoing shift in electronic signal transmission from cables to glass fibers and wireless connections.

Research and development of optoelectronic devices [e.g., LEDs, laser diodes, liquid crystal diodes (LCDs), photodetectors] and solar cells employ various semiconducting elements other than silicon, but it is difficult to see a general trend that would impact specifically developing countries. However, if quantum dots (i.e., materials with semiconducting properties varying by particle size rather than by elemental composition) become more advanced, they would make the industry more independent from specific semiconducting elements. The "hottest" element in optoelectronics is indium, the price of which has risen by a factor of 10 since 2002. The extraordinary combination of light transparency and electric conductivity makes nanolayers of indium–tin–oxide (ITO) an ideal choice for most optoelectronic devices, which sum up to several hundred metric tons of indium per year and a world market of $370 million. China has quickly responded to the new demand and almost tripled its indium mining production since 2002, with a global share in 2005 of 55 percent. But, again, the magic carbon nanotubes have been promised to be future substitutes for ITO.

Countries that have benefited from recent materials demands in electronics but are challenged by new nanotechnological developments include:

- Chile, which produces 39 percent of the global lithium for recharchable batteries, is challenged by the transportable fuel cells.
- Many African countries, including Mozambique, Congo, Rwanda, Ethiopia, Nigeria, Namibia, Burundi, Uganda, and Zimbabwe, which together produce about a third of the global tantalum for capacitors, are challenged by ceramics capacitors.

Materials

With more than a billion metric tons per year, steel is the most important industrial material and will certainly remain so for several decades. Yet, there are many different types of steel for specific purposes, depending on the alloying elements other than iron which are frequently mined in developing countries. Typical alloying elements, including their 2005 world markets and mining productions by developing countries, are:[7]

- Nickel ($22 billion; Indonesia, 9%; Cuba, 5%; Columbia, 5%; China, 5%; Dominican Republic, 3%; Botswana, 2.5%)
- Molybdenum ($11.7 billion; Chile, 28%; China, 17%, Peru, 6%)
- Manganese (approximately $5 billion; South Africa, 22%; Gabon, 13%; Brazil, 13%)
- Vanadium ($2.4 billion; South Africa, 42%; China, 34%)
- Chromium ($2.0 billion; South Africa, 44%; Kazakhstan, 18%; India, 17%)
- Cobalt ($1.8 billion; Congo, 31%; Zambia, 17%; Cuba, 7%)
- Niobium ($490 million; Brazil, 88%)

The market prices of these metals strongly fluctuate, depending on national stockpile policies, world politics, and economy. However, apart from short-term trends, materials research could have a long-term impact on the demand for metals that are used for specialized high-end steels and other alloys. Particularly the blossoming fields of (nanostructured) ceramics, composites, and aluminum alloys aim to develop substitutes, the prices of which depend less on raw materials and thus less on imports from developing countries, and more on the value added by domestic manufacturing.

The chemical element that seems to be mostly challenged by nanotechnological advances is tungsten, 90 percent of which is mined in China with a global market of $1.35 billion in 2005. Since many decades, its major uses have been the production of ultrahard materials (tungsten carbide and nitride) and filaments and electrodes in lighting applications, for both of which nanostructured ceramics have emerged as competing materials. In addition, LEDs (and perhaps filaments out of carbon nanotubes) are likely to conquer the lighting industry, leading to further reduced demands of tungsten.

Apart from becoming less dependent on raw materials, industrialized countries have pushed materials research toward more sophisticated manufacturing that produces the desired material properties through nanostructuring, nanocomposites, coating technologies, and so on. The value of the resulting materials thus depends less on the value of the raw materials and more on the added value by the manufacturing. In a global economy, that devalues the raw materials mined in and exported by developing countries, which, in order to be competitive in other areas, need to import the manufactured materials at much higher prices. In the twentieth century, many developing countries exported cheap ores, unrefined metals, crude oil, and so on, and imported expensive refined metals, alloys, petroleum, plastics, and so on, leading to increasing trade deficits and astronomic debts. Now that many developing countries can manage these older refinement industries that are no longer protected by patents, the recent boost in materials engineering is likely to renew the postcolonial pattern on another industrial level of more sophisticated materials engineering.

CHANGING INTELLECTUAL PROPERTY RIGHTS

Although that issue is not specific to nanotechnologies, these technologies are emerging when intellectual property rights (IPRs) and practices have been changed in Western countries and worldwide with negative side effects on developing countries. Three trends are particularly important in that regard (ETC Group, 2005b).

Changing IPR Criteria in Developed Countries

The subject matter eligible for IPRs has incrementally changed since the early 1980s, particularly in the United States and, more recently, in Europe (Sampat, 2003). Since 1980, genetically modified organisms and DNA sequences are patent eligible in the United States. Apart from ethical concerns about the patentability of living organisms, the move started an erosion of two previously upheld patent criteria. First, it undermined the distinction between material objects (here, the actual DNA molecules) and mere information (here, the DNA sequence codes) that might be used for further R&D

in, say, bioinformatics (Eisenberg, 2002). Second, with the introduction of automatic DNA sequencers, the production of patentable knowledge became routine work, which the original "nonobvious" clause had excluded to keep "obvious" know-how in the public domain. In the early 1980s, also software, which was previously treated like mathematical and scientific truths, became patent eligible, thereby further eroding the two mentioned patent criteria. Moreover, since the late 1990s also databases, including DNA sequence databases, are covered by IPRs (David, 2000). These legal changes, along with liberalizations in the actual patent granting practice, have moved types of knowledge that were formerly public domain into the realm of proprietary knowledge and commodities. It is far from clear whether that move has been beneficial, or even an incentive, for industrial research overall, and it is rather questionable if it has a net positive impact on national or global welfare.

Changing IPR Practice at Universities

The changes in patent legislation had an indirect impact also on publicly funded research. Starting with the Bayh-Dole Act of 1980 in the United States and more recently in some European countries, new regulations require that university employees must report their inventions of possible commercial value to their university administration in so-called disclosure reports prior to possible publication. The administration then decides on whether patents are filed in order to earn revenues from licenses. Based on these disclosure reports, the number of patent filings in the United States increased from 600 in 1991 to 17,000 in 2004, which increased the annual license revenues of universities from $200 million to $1.4 billion in that period (Association of University Technology Managers, 2006). While the policy has improved the income of universities and, evidently, the exclusive knowledge transfer to small local companies and start-ups, it is likely that it has directed publicly funded research to the needs of local business rather than to the specific needs of developing countries. Even if such needs are addressed, researchers can no longer decide themselves on the use of their results, and publications are much delayed through the patent filings. Most importantly, however, the policy has once more moved types of knowledge that were formerly public domain into the realm of proprietary knowledge and commodities.

Extension of IPRs to Developing Countries

Since 2000, the World Trade Organization (WTO) requires that all existing and aspiring member countries sign the Trade Related Intellectual Property Rights agreement (TRIPs), which, in essence, extends the intellectual property rights of developed countries (including much of the recent changes) to developing countries as a measure to prevent "product piracy." Since the early debates about that agreement, which was initiated by the U.S. government, welfare economists have shown that such an extension benefits research-innovative, industrialized countries only, though not always, while having a negative effect on both the welfare of less developed countries and the global welfare (Deardorff, 1992; Helpman, 1993). Historically, agreements such as TRIPs were less important as long as the know-how gap between rich and poor countries was big enough so that developing countries could neither imitate the products of developed countries nor compete with their own innovations. For quickly developing countries, the impact of TRIPs depends on their imitation–innovation ratio, while for the least developed countries with little innovation but some imitation potential the impact on welfare is clearly negative (Liebig, 2005).

Apart from their specific negative impacts on developing countries discussed above, all three trends move knowledge from the public to the private domain. Therefore, increasing amounts of know-how, which would formerly have been available for free for further innovation and product development, is either unavailable, if exclusive licenses were granted, or must be purchased. While R&D in all countries is affected by these changes, developing countries suffer most for four reasons. First, located in the periphery of R&D networks, their chance to obtain exclusive licenses first, say from a U.S. university, is very low. Second, global companies have long entered the so-called knowledge economy by creating huge patent portfolios for the sale and exchange of licenses and by creating knowledge monopolies and cross-licensing networks in which emerging industries in developing countries can hardly participate. Third, while identifying and purchasing the necessary licenses are difficult and costly for any industry, emerging industries in developing countries are particularly handicapped because they frequently have not the same informational and financial resources. Fourth, the increasing costs of patent filings and litigations required for new product developments pose a growing barrier to any R&D effort in poor countries.

In sum, the recent changes in IPRs have brought considerable disadvantages for developing countries such that the divide between poor and rich countries is likely to increase. Ironically, the more nanotechnologies produce commercial goods of broader interests, the more they will contribute to widening the gap.

CONCLUSION

The selected issues discussed in this chapter allow drawing mostly pessimistic conclusions on the impact of nanotechnology on developing countries. However, as outlined in Section 2, the overall situation is much more complex because of the diversities of both nanotechnologies and their possible impacts. Thus, I finally wish to balance the pessimistic conclusions by some more optimistic outlooks.

If developing countries are threatened by declining demands of their natural resources, they could initiate (collaborative) projects that are tailored to increase these demands by new useful products.

If existing nanotechnologies are less able to address the specific needs of developing countries, that is because the specific socioeconomic contexts have been ignored in framing the problems to which the technologies should be the solution. Smarter engineers would consider these contexts from the very beginning and develop their products accordingly without caring about the arbitrary nanolabel.

If changing IPRs hinder emerging industries in developing countries to imitate products for their local market and to develop new products for the global market, they could focus their innovation potential on products tailored to their local needs. After all, consumer saturation in rich countries has redirected many multinational companies toward the markets of developing countries. However, unlike local industries, they lack exactly the knowledge of the specific socioeconomic conditions, which is substantial to product development.

Finally, if nanotechnologies should increase the divide and thus contribute to further inequity, poor countries might more massively insist on their rights guaranteed by numerous international conventions, from the UN Millennium Goals to the UNESCO (2005) *Universal Declaration on Bioethics and Human Rights*, of which Article 15 states:

> Benefits resulting from any scientific research and its applications should be shared with society as a whole and within the international community, in particular with developing countries.

NOTES

1. See ETC Group (2003) as well as many other reports available from http://www. etcgroup.org/en/issues/nanotechnology.html.
2. Preface: Human Development Reports: http://hdr.undp.org, accessed September 9, 2006.
3. Another simple method is solar water disinfection, which exposes water filled in UV-transparent bottles for some hours to sunlight. See SODIS, www.sodis.ch, accessed September 9, 2006.
4. The other important nonbiological pollutant in drinking water is fluoride, leading to serious damages of teeth and bones (fluorosis) in many Asian and African countries. See http://www.who.int water_sanitation_health/diseases/fluorosis/en, accessed September 9, 2006. If no other water source is available, flouride ions need to be adsorbed by alumina or charcoal.
5. These filters are running already in several hundred villages. For the project websites, see http://web.mit.edu watsan/worldbank_summary.htm and http://www.lehigh.edu/ ~aks0/arsenic.html; see also the Grainger Prize by the U.S. National Academy of Engineering http://www.graingerchallenge.org, all accessed September 9, 2006.
6. According to the HDI, Chile is ranked among the countries with high human development, which has largely been owing to its rich material resources.
7. Other elements mined in developing countries and used for specialized steels include bismuth, tellurium, tungsten, tantalum, titanium, and boron, but their main uses are frequently in other applications and for some the exact data are withheld.

REFERENCES

Association of University Technology Managers (AUTM). 2006. *AUTM licensing survey: FY 2004*. Northbrook, IL: AUTM, pp. 18, 26.

Court, E., Daar, A. S., Martin, E., Acharya, T., and Singer, P. A. 2004. Will Prince Charles et al diminish the opportunities of developing countries in nanotechnology? Available: http://www.nanotechweb.org/articles/society/3/1/1, accessed September 9, 2006.

David, P. A. 2000. A tragedy of the public knowledge 'commons'? Global science, intellectual property and the digital technology boomerang. Oxford Intellectual Property Research Centre. Working paper. Available: http://www.oiprc.ox.ac.uk/EJWP0400.pdf, accessed September 9, 2006.

Deardorff, A. V. 1992. Welfare effects of global patent protection. *Economica* 59: 35–51.

Drexler, E. 1986. *Engines of Creation: The Coming Era of Nanotechnology.* New York: Anchor Books.

Eisenberg, R. 2002. How can you patent genes. *American Journal of Bioethics* 2: 3–11.

ETC-Group. 2003. The Big Down: Atomtech—Technologies converging at the nanoscale. Available: http://www.etcgroup.org/upload/publication/171/01/thebigdown.pdf, accessed September 9, 2006.

ETC-Group. 2005a. The potential impacts of nano-scale technologies on commodity markets: The implications for commodity dependent developing countries. Available: http://www.etcgroup.org/upload/publication/45/01/southcentre.commodities.pdf, accessed September 9, 2006.

ETC-Group. 2005b. Nanotech's 'second nature' patents: Implications for the global south. Available: http://www.etcgroup.org/documents/Com8788SpecialPNanoMar-Jun05ENG.pdf, accessed September 9, 2006.

Helpman, E. 1993. Innovation, imitation, and intellectual property rights. *Econometrica* 61: 1247–1280.

Hudson, P. 1992. *The Industrial Revolution.* London: Arnold.

Invernizzi, N., and Foladori, G. 2005. Nanotechnology and the developing world: Will nanotechnology overcome poverty or widen disparities? *Nanotechnology Law & Business* 2(3): 101–110.

Kelly, M. 2004. Vermont's Seldon Labs wants to keep soldier's water pure. *Small Times,* April 24, Available: http://www.smalltimes.com/document_display.cfm?section_id=97& document_id=7764, accessed September 9, 2006.

Lederman, M. M., Offord, R. E., and Hartley, O. 2006. Microbicides and other topical strategies to prevent vaginal transmission of HIV. *Nature Reviews Immunology* 6 (May): 371–382.

Liebig, K. 2005. Die internationale Regulierung geistiger Eigentumsrechte und ihr Einfluss auf den Wissenserwerb in Entwicklungsländern. PhD Dissertation, University of Göttingen.

Maclurcan, D. C. 2005. Nanotechnology and developing countries, Part 1: What possibilities? Part 2: What realities? AZoJono—Journal of Nantechnology Online. Available: http://www.azonano.com/details.asp?ArticleID=1428 and http://www.azonano.com/Details.asp?ArticleID=1429, accessed September 9, 2006.

Meridian Institute. 2005. Nanotechnology and the poor: Opportunities and risks. Available: http://www.meridian-nano.org/gdnp/, accessed September 9, 2006.

Mnyusiwalla, A., Daar, A. S., and Singer, P. A. 2003. Mind the gap: Science and ethics in nanotechnology. *Nanotechnology* 14: R9–13.

North-South dialogue on nanotechnology: Challenges and opportunities. 2005. Trieste, Italy, February 10–12, 2005. Available: http://www.ics.trieste.it/ActivityDetails.aspx? activity_id=387 accessed September 9, 2006.

President's Council of Advisors on Science and Technology. 2005. The National Nanotechnology Initiative at Five Years: Assessment and Recommendations of the National Nanotechnology Advisory Panel. Washington, DC, May 2005.

Salamanca-Buentello, F., Persad, D. L., Court, E. B., Martin, D. K., Daar, A. S., and Singer, P. A. 2005. Nanotechnology and the developing world. *PLoS Medicine* 2 (5): 100–103. Available: http://medicine.plosjournals.org/perlserv?request=get-document& doi=10.1371/journal.pmed.0020097, accessed September 9, 2006.

Sampat, B. N. 2003. Recent changes in patent policy and the 'privatization' of knowledge: Causes, consequences, and implications for developing countries. In *Knowledge Flows, Innovation, and Learning in Developing Countries*. Washington, DC: Center for Science, Policy, and Outcomes, pp. 39–81.

Schummer, J. 2004a. Interdisciplinary issues of nanoscale research. In D. Baird, A. Nordmann, and J. Schummer (Eds.), *Discovering the Nanoscale*. Amsterdam: IOS Press, pp. 9–20.

Schummer, J. 2004b. Multidisciplinarity, interdisciplinarity, and patterns of research collaboration in nanoscience and nanotechnology. *Scientometrics* 59: 425–465.

Schummer, J. 2005. Forschung für die Armen versus Forschung für die Reichen: Verteilungsgerechtigkeit als moralisches Kriterium zur Bewertung der angewandten Chemie. In C. Sedmak (Ed.), *Option für die Armen: Die Entmarginalisierung des Armutsbegriffs in den Wissenschaften*. Freiburg: Herder, pp. 605–626.

Schummer, J. 2006. Cultural diversity in nanotechnology ethics. *Interdisciplinary Science Reviews* 31(3): forthcoming.

Schummer, J. 2007. Identifying ethical issues of nanotechnologies amidst the nano hype. In H. ten Have (Ed.), *Nanotechnologies, Ethics, and Politics*. Paris: UNESCO, in press.

Sherman, J. D. 1999. Synthetic zeolites and other microporous oxide molecular sieves. *Proceedings of the National Academy of Science USA* 96: 3471–3478.

Short, R. V. 2006. New ways of preventing HIV infection: Thinking simply, simply thinking. *Philosophical Transaction of the Royal Society B* 361(1469): 811–820.

Shrum, W., and Shenhav, Y. 1995. Science and technology in less developed countries. In S. Jasanoff, et al. (Eds.), *Handbook of Science and Technology Studies*. Thousand Oaks: Sage, pp. 627–651.

UNAIDS. 2006. Report on the global AIDS epidemic. Available: http://www.unaids.org/en/ HIV_data/2006GlobalReport/default.asp, accessed September 9, 2006.

UNESCO. 2005. *Universal Declaration on Bioethics and Human Right*. Available: http:// portal.unesco.org/en/ev.php-URL_ID=31058&URL_DO=DO_TOPIC&URL_SECTION=201 .html, accessed September 9, 2006.

U.S. Department of the Interior & U.S. Geological Survey. 2006. Mineral Commodity Summaries 2006. Washington, DC.

UN Millennium Project. 2004. Interim full report of Task Force 7 on water and sanitation. Available: at http://www.unmillenniumproject.org/documents/tf7interim.pdf, accessed September 9, 2006.

Weber, J., Desai, K., and Darbyshire, J. 2005. The development of vaginal microbicides for the prevention of HIV transmission. *PLoS Medicine* 2(5): e142. Available: http:// medicine.plosjournals.org/perlserv?request=get-document&doi=10.1371/journal.pmed. 0020142, accessed September 9, 2006.

World Energy Council. 1999. The challenge of rural energy poverty in developing countries. London. Available: http://www.worldenergy.org/wec-geis/publications/reports/rural/download/download.asp, accessed September 9, 2006.

World Health Organization (WHO). 2005. Water, sanitation and hygiene links to health: Facts and figures. Available: http://www.who.int/entity/water_sanitation_health/factsfigures2005.pdf, accessed September 9, 2006.

PART VII

ISSUES: THE DISTANT FUTURE?

Fritz Allhoff

Undoubtedly, nanotechnology will have an effect on our future. Throughout this volume, we have tried to be cautious about such prognostications, paying particular attention to disentangling promise from hype. This goal has been especially important to us: A lot of the contemporary discussions regarding nanotechnology seem more aligned with science fiction than with actual applications of the science. To be sure, the science has tremendous potential, but it is important to recognize what it will *not* do as well as what it will. So, if you look back at this volume, you will notice that we have tried to focus on likely and near-term applications of the science rather than upon some of the more popular fantastic claims.

But what about these fantastic claims? Certainly, some of them will never be actualized, but maybe some will. And, while there are practical reasons to emphasize near-term applications of nanotechnology, there are imaginative and philosophical reasons to consider some potentially long-term applications as well. In this, our final part, we will consider some of these: molecular manufacturing, space exploration, artificial intelligence, and life extension.

Molecular manufacturing is, in some ways, the ultimate goal of nanotechnology: to be able to build things precisely, molecule by molecule. The success of nanotechnology, however, does not depend on the success of molecular manufacturing; nanotechnology is simply the manipulation of matter at the nanoscale in ways that take advantage of novel properties therein and need not employ molecule-by-molecule construction. But

Nanoethics: The Ethical and Social Implications of Nanotechnology. Edited by Allhoff, Lin, Moor, Weckert
Copyright © 2007 John Wiley & Sons, Inc.

what if molecular manufacturing becomes possible? Scientifically, at least, there seems no clearly fatal reason why it is not feasible, but the economics of it are certainly daunting. In Chapter 23 Mike Treder and Chris Phoenix, the two founders of the Center for Responsible Nanotechnology, explore the promise of molecular manufacturing as well as some of the economic dimensions.

Then we turn to space exploration, paying particular focus to the role that nanotechnology may play. Already, ethicists are showing some interest in space exploration, and the confluence of these general interests with those in nanotechnology form the basis of Chapter 24 by long-time space advocate Tihamer Toth-Fejel and University of Michigan's Chris Dodsworth. The most obvious contribution that nanotechnology will play in space exploration is through its contributions to materials science and to synthetic chemistry. In addition to the clear advantages of having stronger and more flexible products, nanotechnology also offers the potential to lower the weight of those products. Such benefits could have substantial benefits in terms of fuel load requirements (i.e., we would need less fuel to propel lighter things), which could then be manifested in extending our range of exploration. This chapter explores various ethical issues in this area.

Third, we consider applications of nanotechnology to artificial intelligence; this discussion is effected in Chapter 25 by J. Storrs Hall, a research fellow at the Institute of Molecular Manufacturing. Nanotechnology's contribution here will be in the improvements that it offers for computational hardware and, as such hardware improves, so do the prospects for artificial intelligence. And, of course, there are attendant ethical issues therein. Some of these can be esoteric and philosophical, such as questions about whether artificial intellects are deserving of moral status, can form intentions, and so on. Less abstractly, though, we might simply wonder whether society would be better off with artificial intelligence or whether there might be drawbacks given its effects on humans. Hall considers these and related questions.

Finally, nanotechnology might be able to extend our lives. Generally, nanotechnology could have applications in medicine; for example, there are potentially ways in which it could be used to destroy cancer cells in less invasive means than those offered by chemotherapy. If we are healthier, then we will live longer. But, more optimistically, nanotechnology might be used to effect cellular repair that could slow, halt, or reverse the effects of aging. In theory, this could be done indefinitely, thus making immortality a real possibility. But are longer life spans (whether marginally or dramatically) *good*? Should we pursue them? Certainly there seem to be some advantages, though we might also worry about problems that could therein arise, such as those that might be presented by overpopulation, economics strains, and so on. In the final chapter, Sebastian Sethe, researcher at the Sheffield Institute of Biotechnological Law and Ethics, addresses many of these issues.

23

CHALLENGES AND PITFALLS OF EXPONENTIAL MANUFACTURING

Mike Treder and Chris Phoenix

These early years of the twenty-first century already are a time of rapid advances in science and technology. Every day brings news of startling developments in fields such as genetic engineering, neuroscience, and nanotechnology. So what *will* the near future actually bring us? Human beings that glow in the dark, like our bioengineered pets? Robot servants? Flying cars? Genuine artificial intelligence (AI)? Or something even more exotic?

There is good reason to believe that within the next 10 to 20 years the most significant changes to society will go far beyond glowing people or flying cars. Many of them may result from the introduction of *personal nanofactories*, a powerful application of exponential general-purpose molecular manufacturing, made possible by advanced nanotechnology.

In this chapter, we will explain exponential general-purpose molecular manufacturing: the basic concepts behind it and why it will be a technological breakthrough of transformative power. We will show why preparing for it is vitally important—*and* will be very difficult. Along the way, we will explore how several types of social systems may respond to the changes that molecular manufacturing will bring, including unprecedented material abundance and other opportunities. We will take a brief look at the possible timeline (sooner than many people will expect), explore problems in familiar areas such as military conflict, and touch on new classes of problems that humanity will have to face.

Nanoethics: The Ethical and Social Implications of Nanotechnology. Edited by Allhoff, Lin, Moor, Weckert
Copyright © 2007 John Wiley & Sons, Inc.

By the time you finish the chapter, it should be clear that the challenges and opportunities created by molecular manufacturing cannot be addressed by any simple solution.

MOLECULAR MANUFACTURING

Exponential general-purpose molecular manufacturing—let's take this big phrase apart to see what it means and why it is so important.

- *Manufacturing*: The ability to make products, in this case ranging from clothing, to electronics, to medical devices, to books, to building materials, and much more.
- *Molecular* manufacturing: The automated building of products from the bottom up, molecule by molecule, with atomic precision, using molecular-scale tools. This will make products that are extremely lightweight, flexible, durable, and potentially very "smart."
- *General-purpose* molecular manufacturing: A manufacturing technology that will find many applications across many segments of society. Its extreme flexibility, precision, high capacity, and low cost will cause rapid adoption almost everywhere and therefore will have disruptive effects in many industries.
- *Exponential* general-purpose molecular manufacturing: The word exponential refers to the rapid pace—probably unprecedented—at which this technology may be deployed. A compact, automated molecular manufacturing system will be able to make *more* manufacturing systems; we are talking about factories that can build duplicate factories—and do it in less than a single day. The math is simple: If one factory makes two and two factories make four, then within 10 days you could have one thousand factories, in 10 more days a million factories, and 10 days after that a *billion* factories. Within the span of just a few weeks, in theory, every household in the world could have one of their own to make most of the products they need at just the cost of raw materials.

Exponential general-purpose molecular manufacturing means a manufacturing system—a personal nanofactory—capable of making a wide range of technologically advanced products far superior to what we have today, much cheaper, and much faster and able to multiply its own source of production exponentially.

The consequences of this are mind-boggling, to say the least. It could mean the drastic restructuring of whole industries, including mining, refining, transportation, storage, and wholesale and retail distribution. It could mean millions of jobs lost or shifted. It could represent a radical transformation of traditional power structures which may not come about easily or peacefully. It could also mean opportunities like we have never had before to relieve poverty, prevent illness, and offer education to millions of people in developing nations.

Imagine the economic value in possessing such a revolutionary technology. Imagine the military advantages it would offer. How much would a government or even a rich and powerful corporation pay to possess molecular manufacturing? We do not know for sure whether it would take US$10 billion, US$1 billion, or even less to begin developing it today, but by 2020 it may require as little as US$10 million. This is because many of the required capabilities are being developed rapidly in other technologies. And exponential general-purpose molecular manufacturing obviously would be worth at least hundreds of billions of dollars and perhaps hundreds of trillions. It is only a matter of time before the technology arrives, and when it does, the consequences could be staggering.

If made widely available at low cost (the raw materials should be very cheap), personal nanofactories could solve many of the world's problems. Simple products like plumbing, water filters, and mosquito nets—made on the spot—would greatly reduce the spread of infectious diseases. The efficient, inexpensive construction of strong and lightweight structures, electrical equipment, and power storage devices would allow the use of solar power as a primary and abundant energy source. Computers and display devices could become stunningly inexpensive and available to nearly everyone. Much social unrest can be traced directly to material poverty, ill health, and ignorance. Molecular manufacturing could greatly reduce these problems, but only if it is wisely administered.

If corporations or governments try too hard to restrict distribution and legitimate access is not provided, a black market will quickly develop. The risk here is that unauthorized nanofactories may not have the necessary safety measures built in. All sorts of dangerous products—from weapons to poisons to microscopic surveillance devices—could be made at low cost in mass quantities. To complicate matters, tiny manufacturing systems could be used to make bigger ones, and each large one could make thousands of duplicates. Smuggling of these systems would be impossible to prevent. Some solution will have to be found.

It is impossible to overestimate the effects these developments may have on society and on our individual lives. Informed preparation is essential.

EXPANDING RESOURCES

Now that we have introduced the concept of personal nanofactories, let's take a different approach to try and understand the implications and the challenges brought on by such a transformative technology.

Most people have certain possessions that could easily be sold if the price is right and others that would not be sold under any normal circumstances. For example, one's bookshelves may contain paperback fiction, photo albums, and old textbooks that haven't been opened in a decade or two. Photo albums are not normally sold—their sentimental value to the owner is far higher than their value to anyone else. Mass-market paperbacks, on the other hand, can easily be replaced and might be sold to any visitor who values them more than the current owner. A visitor who asked to buy one's personal photo albums would likely be met with suspicion and even hostility.

Sentimental value is not the only reason for keeping possessions off the market; things that are important to survival will not be sold except in very unusual circumstances. Also, individuals are not the only entities that recognize the distinction between saleable and protected items. Whereas people may cheerfully sell a plot of land, a nation will be very unlikely to permanently shrink its borders for mere money.

The goal of commerce is to help trades happen easily and efficiently, since every voluntary trade enriches both parties (at least according to economic theory). By contrast, for resources that must be protected, the goal is to prevent any transactions from taking place—to maintain the status quo. The reason is that any transaction will reduce the sum total value of the objects that change hands.

Achieving such different goals might be expected to require rather different types of institutional approaches. In fact, the author Jane Jacobs (1992) has observed exactly that. In *Systems of Survival*, she describes two different systems of institutional ethics, "Guardian" and "Commercial." Studying how these systems have developed, she describes a number of sharply contrasting rules. For example, Guardians traditionally shun trade, while Commercials of course exist for trade. Guardians are allowed to deceive, while Commercials should be honest.

Now think back to the bookshelf that provided our first example. There was a third kind of book on the shelf: a book containing useful information (a textbook) that the owner nevertheless did not need. In such a case, the owner could go to the bother of trying to sell the book, but there is another alternative. It may be preferable simply to give the book away—to donate it to some place where it will be found by someone who can use it.

A physical book can only be in one place at a time, but information has no such restriction. And although some information is most valuable when kept secret, a lot of information grows in total value as it is shared. All that remains is to make sharing easy and rewarding, and the information can spread from its originator almost indefinitely, providing benefit without any fixed limit.

Thanks to computers and the Internet, sharing information is far easier than it has ever been. In many parts of the world, information in gigabyte quantities is literally too cheap to meter—there is no incremental cost for sharing or receiving almost any data file. In the centuries before computers, great scientists and artists made their creations available to the world, and sufficiently valuable information was copied widely—by hand, if necessary. But today, it is not only the great information that is worth sharing. Near-trivial observations, computer programs, and works of art are shared over the Internet—and thanks to modern search engines, the valuable fraction can be found and used.

The ethic of sharing information, or the "Informational" system, is different again from the Guardian and Commercial systems. As in the Guardian system, financial compensation is discouraged; as in the Commercial system, the use of force is also discouraged. Whereas Guardians can lie to achieve their aims and Commercials can conceal information, the Informational system works best not just with honesty but also with openness.

The Guardian system is essential, obviously, to guarantee a group's survival, but it operates on a *zero-sum* basis, meaning that the assets of one group are not voluntarily traded with another group. Rather, they are protected, even hoarded. If one entity wants something another has, it must be taken by force. The total sum of what is available does not grow due to this style of exchange between groups: It remains static, or even decreases, as when a stolen automobile is broken up for spare parts. Hence, zero sum is a reasonable description of the (lack of) potential for expansion of assets.

By contrast, the Commercial system allows groups to increase the value of their possessions by augmenting them through trade. A tribe or corporation with a surplus of goods can exchange some of what they have with another tribe or company that has something the first group needs. As a result, both parties are better off than they were before. This system is therefore considered win–win, or *positive sum*, because the potential exists for everyone to gain.

Now that even modestly valuable things that can be duplicated at near-zero cost, the Informational system is becoming increasingly important. The open-source software movement has produced large, high-quality, valuable pieces of software, including an entire computer operating system—and given them away, simply because so many people found it worthwhile to work on the projects and then share their work to be used by whoever could benefit. One of the ethics of the Informational system is that the creator's name should accompany their creation, so that their reputation will be enhanced.

The Informational system is neither altruism, nor communism, nor charity. Creation and discovery are fun—just ask any child with finger paints or any backyard astronomer. Sharing one's creations is also fun, especially when the result is recognition and reputation. Whereas communism is an inefficient system for redistributing scarce resources, the Informational system is a very efficient system for distributing resources that are fundamentally nonscarce. There is no obligation to share any given piece of information, any more than a person is obliged to sell or give away any of their possessions. It is worth stressing this point, because those new to the Informational system frequently confuse it with coercive scarcity-based systems. The Informational system is not suitable for scarce physical goods, but when applied to information that can be shared to virtually unlimited extent at virtually no cost to anyone, the Informational system can lead to an *unlimited-sum* outcome.

Just as the Informational system is inappropriate in many situations, so too are the Guardian and Commercial systems. A retail store that viewed its customers with Guardian suspicion and its stock with Guardian possessiveness would waste so many opportunities that it would quickly go out of business. A person or other entity that was willing to sell its basis of survival for short-term financial gain would quickly cease to exist. Likewise, even though the free market is an excellent system for allocating naturally scarce resources, imposing artificial scarcity on information in order to treat it commercially can lead to massive and tragic loss of opportunity.

Applying the wrong system can cause either lost opportunities or wasteful dissipation, but mixing the systems incautiously is at least as bad. The ethics of each system are too dissimilar; an organization that tries to follow a combination of approaches will find itself led in opposite directions. The result will either be paralysis or excessive license. The results are so bad that Jane Jacobs (1992) calls such mixed systems "monstrous moral hybrids," giving examples of the Mafia, the Third Reich, and communism. [For a review see Phoenix and Treder (2003).]

How might we expect various organizations that follow one of these three systems of community action to respond to the transformative impacts of nanofactory technology? Before answering that, let's take a closer look at just how disruptive those effects could become.

EFFECTS: GOOD, BAD, AND UGLY

Molecular manufacturing will be an extremely powerful technology with a wide range of possible effects. Some of the effects are good, such as inexpensive local manufacture of humanitarian relief supplies. Many of the effects are bad, including the widespread availability of untraceable, highly advanced weapons. Some products of molecular manufacturing may be either good or bad, depending on how they are used; examples include surveillance equipment and space flight hardware. Any of several different competitions could have extremely negative effects, such as a rapid and unstable arms race leading to war.

Given a portable, self-contained, self-building factory system that can make a wide range of products directly from blueprints in essentially unlimited quantities, it should not be difficult to design and rapidly construct new products whenever and wherever desired. An explosion of creativity similar to the World Wide Web could develop quickly.

The good news is that general-purpose exponential manufacturing could create a level of low-cost abundance far beyond the capabilities of any present-day economy. If distributed wisely, this abundance and its accompanying security could reduce present-day sources of conflict. However, as we will see in the next section, wise distribution of resources is not easy. There are a number of reasons why the hoped-for abundance may not be developed or may not have the desired effects.

The bad news is that rapid development and availability of new products could include new kinds of weapons. Arms races could develop almost overnight, with each side (whether a nation or a smaller group) rapidly countering the other's previous advances. Due to several factors, such an arms race would likely be unstable and lead quickly to open conflict. On a large scale, such conflict could be devastating, perhaps even threatening the survival of civilization; even on a smaller scale, it could represent a terrible risk. There may even be a danger that a nihilistic or genocidal group or person could do irreparable damage on a global scale single handedly using only modest resources. It is too early to tell whether or not the capability to build tons of milligram-scale antipersonnel weapons will be widely available, but such discomforting scenarios must be taken seriously and carefully analyzed.

As we will see in the next section, the issues raised by molecular manufacturing include several extremes that appear to be opposites: oppressive control versus anarchic destruction, unbridled hedonistic consumption versus crushing scarcity. In fact, however, these are not mutually exclusive; they may be concurrent and may reinforce each other. Avoiding such an outcome will not be easy.

ORGANIZATIONAL RESPONSES

A technology that can be copied at will and that can produce a wide range of valuable products out of nothing but information, energy, and simple raw materials will naturally spread widely unless something or someone actively prevents it. A number of organizations will want to do just that.

Security/Guardian organizations will want to limit availability of destructive technology while preserving for themselves the means to damage their enemies. A manufacturing technology that could quickly produce any weapon downloaded from the Internet would be a major security threat, especially when the weapons could contain enough "smarts" to be used remotely in time and space from the attacker. Crime requires means, motive, and opportunity, all of which have imposed limits on criminality; however, possession of a nanofactory would provide the means and opportunity to do almost anything. Although new defenses would surely be developed, this would not be a lot of comfort to a Guardian contemplating a continuing stream of new weapon designs. Thus, it seems clear that Guardians will have a strong incentive to restrict private availability of the technology.

But even if private ownership of nanofactories were forbidden by law, this would not solve the security problems. Illegal ownership might develop—it only takes one nanofactory to make thousands more, and they could be made quite concealable. Either a stolen nanofactory or an independent development project (which will rapidly become easier to achieve) could put the first nanofactory into private hands. Finally, even if private ownership of nanofactories were made impossible (which almost certainly would require draconian levels of repression), arms races between national militaries would likely still lead to war.

Commercial groups also may have an incentive to limit the availability of nanofactories. If products of personal nanofactories are abundant and inexpensive, it may be difficult to make a large profit by selling stuff—or at least, this will be the fear of many existing Commercial interests. That this may not necessarily be the case is shown by examples from the entertainment and software industries. The movie industry fought against the introduction of VCRs, but as it turned out, video rentals form a major revenue stream today. And while patents are widely considered to be necessary to support innovation, software patents did not exist until the mid-1980s—years after the development of Unix, the IBM PC, the Apple Macintosh, and the Internet.

Extremes of communism and capitalism are both likely to be suboptimal. Although it may be tempting to think that such a radical shift in the economics of production could finally allow communism to work, the reasons why communism failed go beyond the economic context. Setting by fiat the resources allocated to a person—whether above or below what they have earned—turns out to be intensely demotivating, and the result is wasted opportunity and societal depression. On the other hand, with capitalism, the vast disparity between cost of production and value of product combined with the reduced value of labor would cause nearly instant and total concentration of wealth, impoverishing the vast majority of people.

The Informational system appears to be an excellent fit for some aspects of molecular manufacturing. Nanofactory blueprint files could be transferred and modified as easily as software programs or other types of information. The open-source software movement demonstrates that some people are eager to spend thousands of hours developing a product that they intend to give away without financial compensation; it seems likely that nanofactory product development could proceed successfully along similar lines. There is no obvious reason why an Informational approach would want to restrict nanofactories; on the contrary, that approach would work best if nanofactories were available to all without restriction.

A combination of Informational and Commercial options (though not necessarily combining both styles in any single organization) may turn out to be the optimal way to deliver the benefits of molecular manufacturing. To the extent that nanofactory blueprint development is similar to software development, history shows that this approach can work quite well for all concerned. Commercial software products tend to be more user friendly because money is invested in making what the customer wants, not what is fun for the programmers to write. As a result, even the free products of the open-source movement cannot outcompete commercial products. At the same time, free products are available for those who cannot afford commercial software. Meanwhile, the commercial software industry benefits from the creative ideas of the independent Informational creators who do not have to conform to business plans or conventional wisdom.

If a similar system were implemented for molecular manufacturing, it might look like this: Nanofactories are available for free or nearly free. Commercial designs are protected by a variety of legal and technical mechanisms. At the same time, the necessities of life are available to anyone, not by charity or by law, but simply because some hobbyist who wanted their designs widely used had made them available at no cost. In this scenario, no one has to be impoverished to the point of damaging their physical security; however, those who want luxury products would have to pay for them, thus maintaining a structure of commercial incentives. (It is not yet known whether this system would improve security due to distributed development of technologies of defense and accountability or damage security due to widespread availability of the means to do harm.)

WHERE, WHEN, WHAT, AND HOW?

Much will depend on how quickly and by whom molecular manufacturing is developed. If the technology matures slowly—and openly—over the next 15 or 20 years, there may be time to adjust with relatively little disruption. If it is developed many more years in the future, its effects may be muted by other technologies. However, if it is developed rapidly and soon, it could be quite disruptive, even dangerous.

Molecular manufacturing will work by a synergy of several technologies that are individually fairly mundane. It will require only a few different manufacturing operations that can be performed many times in programmed automated sequence. These operations will, bit by bit, build products out of atoms, just as your body builds proteins by fastening together one amino acid at a time. Mechanically guided chemistry has already been achieved, and even automated in some cases, using scanning probe microscopes as well as engineered molecules.[1] Automated manufacture is being developed today and will be aided by the complete uniformity of atoms. Several branches of nanotechnology are working to develop nanoscale devices.

When precise nanoscale machines are the fundamental components of both the manufacturing system and the product, several important benefits will arise. Certain carefully constructed surfaces can be virtually frictionless and wear free. Smaller machines operate more rapidly and at higher power density. Flawless structures can be far stronger than today's bulk-manufactured materials, especially when built of carbon—a very versatile atom that is an excellent candidate for molecular manufacturing processes. Systems built of these high-performance machines—including the manufacturing systems—should be many orders of magnitude more powerful than either biological organisms or today's machines. (For more information see http://www.e-drexler.com.)

Strong incentives exist for early and rapid development. The fact that molecular manufacturing can arise from mundane technologies implies that when molecular manufacturing becomes possible, its potential will be extreme by comparison with other contemporary technologies, including the technologies that combine to enable it. As a general-purpose manufacturing technology, it will be applicable in a wide range of contexts, potentially disrupting or replacing a number of industries and activities. Any person or group that has access to molecular manufacturing could outcompete those without access:

- Within a matter of months and possibly weeks any nation that possessed a monopoly on nanofactory technology could become the world's dominant military power.
- Any company that owned the exclusive rights to nanofactory technology would be worth trillions of dollars, no matter how small it started.
- On a less greedy or power-hungry note, any organization that had the awesome potential of nanofactory technology at its disposal could work miracles toward whatever humanitarian or other worthy goals it desired.

Despite the predicted large advantages, it is far from certain that today's centers of innovation and power will develop molecular manufacturing first or will retain control of it even if they do. In the United States, for example, opposition from several prominent scientists has reduced the near-term potential for a nanofactory development program. It may be that by the time a major effort is funded, the resources required will be small enough that multiple independent or competing efforts may be launched by diverse organizations.

A close race to develop nanofactory technology might have unpredictable effects. It could increase proliferation and reduce control. Conversely, it could increase the determination of whoever first achieves a major manufacturing capability to preemptively prevent others from finishing their development projects. In economic competition, this may be as simple as getting patents; in military competition, however, the methods could be far more destructive.

In addition to when it is developed and by whom, a lot depends on how rapidly the technology can be ramped up from the lab to a generally useful manufacturing system. In theory, the transition could be quite rapid. A well-planned program would involve preparatory development of powerful computer-aided design (CAD) software and early product designs and design skills, so that user-friendly nanofactories and their supporting machinery (e.g., feedstock and power supplies) would be ready to build as soon as the earliest hardware became available. A far-sighted program, in which only debugging would stand between the lab and widespread use, might complete the transition in a matter of months. An incremental program that took development one step at a time—which is the current trend of the U.S. National Nanotechnology Initiative—might easily require years to move from the lab to the user, giving other molecular manufacturing programs a chance to catch up.

NEW PROBLEMS

So far, we have talked about decisions made and problems confronted within the context of the world's major systems of action: Guardian, Commercial, and Informational. But we would be remiss not to mention other issues as well, including environmental implications and new applications of powerful computer technology.

Manufacturing on a massive scale inevitably will have some effects on the environment. These include waste byproducts such as heat (from running machines) and discarded products. (The manufacturing process itself is not expected to produce waste materials, since every atom will be held in a known position, and can be converted into a useful or at least harmless molecule.) Producing enough energy to supply a rapidly expanding manufacturing economy may also be environmentally problematic—even solar cells require land area.

There are two speculative problems that have been the focus of much controversy and little definitive study. Both involve self-perpetuating systems growing out of bounds destructively. One of these potential problems is mechanical self-replicators that are small enough yet full-featured enough to gather energy and materials from nature. Although such devices–commonly known as "gray goo" —would be very difficult to design and have no economic value, neither the laws of physics nor human nature appear to prevent them from being built. Opinions vary as to how dangerous and destructive such a device could be and how difficult it might be to clean up. Some experts, including the authors of this chapter, tentatively believe that this is not a primary or early risk of molecular manufacturing—unstable arms races appear a lot more serious—but it could be a problem eventually and certainly merits more study.

The other type of self-perpetuating system is AI. This is not a direct consequence of molecular manufacturing but may be strongly facilitated by it. A number of different scenarios have been proposed by which an AI, designed according to any of several approaches, might successfully usurp most or all resources needed by humans. Serious study and discussion of these issues are just beginning and should be diligently pursued.

Molecular manufacturing will raise or highlight a number of medical issues. Rapid prototyping of molecule- and cell-scale machine systems should greatly accelerate diagnosis of disease conditions. With good diagnostics, treatment can become more confident and can be developed more rapidly. Within a few years after nanofactory technology arrives in the hands of researchers, most medical problems should be treatable—unless the researchers are hamstrung by obsolete bureaucracy. This raises issues of excessive population, although the growth in resources and efficiency provided by molecular manufacturing should more than compensate for the foreseeable future. (Conversely, denying new and inexpensive medical treatments or deliberately failing to develop them would result in many millions of unnecessary deaths.) A more difficult issue is human enhancement. Potentially troubling issues include whether it is ethical to enhance only a subset of humanity and whether it is ethical (or wise) to enhance people to such an extent that they lose sympathy with unenhanced humans.

A final issue is the increasing integration of computers into human lives, especially in the case of surveillance. Security cameras are becoming a fact of life in public places. However, this is minor compared to the degree of surveillance that could be deployed—and likely will be—once molecular manufacturing makes supercomputers effectively free. It will become possible to monitor and record every volume of human-occupied space, full time, and then search the record with image recognition, object tracking, speech transcription, and data mining. Whoever has access to the surveillance network (or networks) will be able to see into the private lives and actions of anyone they choose. This could create a major shift in human lifestyle as well as giving unprecedented power to military and law enforcement.

CONCLUSION

Exponential general-purpose molecular manufacturing will create new and extreme opportunities in a number of areas, including personal freedom, concentration of wealth and power, surveillance, widespread abundance, human interactions, and human enhancement. Many of these opportunities will create opposing pressures. Negative consequences, including unstable arms races, massive oppression, and economic upheaval, may spiral out of control. Extreme solutions will act to perpetuate conflict and strengthen the opposing forces. Dealing constructively with these options and competitions will require massive applications of wisdom and creativity.

There may not be much time left to prepare. Already, programmable nanoscale machines have been built, and several different techniques exist for atomically precise fabrication. Several commercially viable technologies are converging toward the atomic scale. Once launched, a well-funded and well-managed development program might require less than a decade to succeed. The amount of funding required will decrease exponentially as time goes on and may already be under a billion U.S. dollars. The time required may diminish more slowly; thus, delay in starting a program could exponentially increase the potential number of competitors.

It should not be assumed that human nature, presented with an opportunity for unprecedented abundance, will naturally become more constructive. Billion-dollar frauds at a number of large U.S. institutions over the past few years show that even the richest and most powerful people can still be shortsighted and destructive. The governments of Pol Pot, Idi Amin, and Saddam Hussein further underscore the point that immense power over others frequently will not be used for good. (This should give pause to those who assume that AIs will automatically be benevolent.)

It will not be easy to find a course that minimizes both small-scale human destructiveness—crime, terrorism, and incivility—and large-scale oppression. It will not be easy to give greedy people the capitalist incentive to be productive while simultaneously preserving the unlimited-sum benefits that can arise from nonscarce unregulated information. Extreme policies will only make things worse—and those who profit from things going wrong may have a strong incentive to promote precisely those policies. The best we can recommend at this point is to increase awareness of the enormous potentials of molecular manufacturing and then promote intense research into how to avoid the worst problems while maximizing the benefits.

NOTE

1. Nadrian Seeman has built a machine out of molecules of DNA, programmed by other DNA molecules, that assembles DNA strands in programmable sequence. See http://www.trnmag.com/Stories/2005/061505/DNA_machine_links_molecules_061505.html. See http://www.foresight.org/stage2/mechsynthbib.html for some examples of scanning probe microscopes.

REFERENCES

Jacobs, J. 1992. *Systems of Survival: A Dialogue on the Moral Foundations of Commerce and Politics.* New York: Random House.

Phoenix, C., and Treder, M. 2003. Three systems of action. Available: http://crnano.org/systems.htm.

24

NANOETHICS AND THE HIGH FRONTIER*

Tihamer Toth-Fejel and Christopher Dodsworth

INTRODUCTION

The National Nanotechnology Initiative (NNI, 2001) defines nanotechnology as "the understanding and control of matter at dimensions of roughly 1 to 100 nanometers, where unique phenomena enable novel applications." This definition emphasizes the discovery of new science, but the original definition by Eric Drexler (1986, p. 288) emphasized molecular manufacturing, which involves building productive nanosystems—molecular machines that can rearrange individual atoms and molecules in bulk matter with atomic precision.[1] The applications covered by these definitions of nanotechnology will have a significant impact on our lives, especially with regard to the settlement of space.

In the near term, nanoparticles, carbon nanotubes, better synthetic chemistry, and improved materials will all lower the price to orbit while incrementally increasing capabilities and safety of space systems. As productive nanosystems produce diamondoid

* Many thanks for all the hard work of ideas and criticisms contributed by Fritz Allhoff, Janis Bunting, Robert Freitas, Michael Gleghorn, J. Storrs Hall, Jennifer Lahl, Tibor Pacher, Tom McKendree, Chris Phoenix, Ted Reynolds, and Thomas Toth-Fejel (and our apologies to them for sometimes ignoring their advice). All opinions expressed herein belong solely to the authors and not to any affiliated organizations.

in large quantities, the price to orbit will drop by two to four magnitudes (McKendree, 2001) because:

1. Molecularly precise diamondlike materials increase strength-to-weight ratios by a factor of 50. (Diamond also has a thermal conductivity four times greater than copper). This will reduce the size of single-stage-to-orbit rockets to the dry mass and cargo capacity of a large automobile and also enable the construction of launch systems such as rotating tethers (Cate, 2002) and space piers (Hall, 2005).
2. Productive nanosystems can assemble copies of themselves, allowing controlled exponential growth of manufacturing capability as rapidly as software distribution over the Internet.
3. Nanostructured materials will increase the efficiency and durability of photovoltaics while lowering their price. It will eventually be affordable to pave roads and roof houses with them as well as to build inexpensive solar power satellites. At the same time, they will significantly increase the efficiency and power density of fuel cells for transportation applications. These will lower the remaining cost component of getting to orbit: energy.

That, however, is just the beginning of nanotechnology applications.

Building extraterrestrial communities without nanotechnology is not much different from the colonization of dry land 400 million years ago by lungfish that were following the plants and insects. In both cases, organisms are simply moving to a new environment.

One way to settle space is to build city-sized sun-orbiting hollow toroids or cylinders from asteroidal resources, fill them with an atmosphere, spin them, and introduce a terran ecosystem into them. Gerard O'Neill (1974) launched the first serious scientific and engineering analysis of such habitats (now called O'Neill colonies) and concluded that they were feasible, though expensive. Another way to settle space is with terraforming: modifying a planet or moon so that it becomes more habitable to humans in terms of atmosphere, temperature, and/or ecosystem (Freitas, 1983). With only ordinary technology, building O'Neill colonies and terraforming planets would be huge undertakings, possible only with extended cooperation or bitter competition between many nations. In this sense, the settlement of space would be a high-technology copy of the initial European colonization of the Americas. With productive nanosystems, however, the situation will be changed significantly: Settlement on other planets and in free space becomes achievable by small groups of people and will be more similar to the American settlement of the West. In addition, it will enable us to multiply the amount of Earth-like living area (in the form of O'Neill colonies) by a factor of 3000 using the materials in the asteroid belt. If, on the other hand, we used advanced nanotechnology to build very large hydrogen-to-carbon fusion reactors and used replicating machines to take apart and harvest the gas giants (namely, Jupiter, Saturn, Uranus, Neptune), then we could multiply the effective living space of the terran ecosystem by a factor of 1.2 billion.

There is a price: Nanotechnology is so powerful and dangerous that it would probably be suicidal to achieve it *without* spreading out into space. Furthermore, the extraterrestrial environment will exert pressure on people to adapt, and nanotechnology will enable some surprising adaptations. These will, in turn, lead to even more ethical issues.

STANDARD ARGUMENTS FOR AND AGAINST SPACE

In this section, we shall briefly consider some of the standard arguments against the settling of space in order to provide some context for the issues that nanotechnology will raise in Sections 3 and 4.

Space Is Inhospitable

One of the arguments against space settlement is that space is a dead expanse, inhospitable to life, and not our natural habitat; therefore, we should not live in it.

Practically speaking, the hospitality of the frontier depends upon our level of technological sophistication: Space contains plenty of atoms to manipulate and large amounts of energy to harness. Almost a century ago Konstantin Tsiolkovsky (1911) wrote, "A planet is the cradle of mind, but one cannot live in a cradle forever." He outlined a 16-point plan for settling in space, and the first 9 points have already been achieved (the ninth one being the harvesting of crops; in this case, wheat grown on the Russian space station *Mir*) (Kusin and Lytkin, 1996).

At a more theoretical level, this argument against space settlement is specious because of David Hume's (1978) claim that there is no reason that nature and ethics go together. However, it depends which "nature" is being discussed here—Mother *Nature* or the essential *nature* of things?" Given the lack of philosophical sophistication of the "unnaturalness of space settlement" argument, the former is more likely, and therefore Hume's claim is correct.

Keep Space Pristine

Another argument is based on a revulsion against modifying an environment: Just as we keep national parks free of development, so we should not pollute the pure and pristine rocks of the Moon or Mars with our slime, germs, and biological waste—or ourselves.

This argument, too, has little going for it. There is no compelling reason to think that the entirety of the universe ought to be kept free from human development—unless rocks really do have rights and human beings are an inherently evil cancer growing on the face of the universe. It is true that we often value undisturbed wilderness and even take steps to preserve it through the creation of national parks or limits on the use of machinery. But such limits are usually justified through concerns over pollution—which would harm humans or other life—or through appeals to the esthetic value of the area. Given the vastness of space, there is little reason to think that whatever esthetic value it might have could not be preserved alongside vast human settlements.

American Indians[2] and Fermi Paradox

Another argument against spreading humanity into space is the problem of American Indians: What if some part of space is in the midst of developing an ecosystem with a life of its own? Are settlers required to respect this life, as European settlers ought to have respected the Americans who were there first? For the sake of argument, let's consider the most likely candidate for settlement in the near future, Mars (though in the future it could be any planetary body).

Suppose there were a primitive Martian ecosystem that, given time to evolve, might produce intelligent life. Does this produce a moral imperative not to settle Mars? It is hard to see why: We already have examples of ecosystems that can and do support life here on Earth, and we do not take that as a reason for us not to settle there; on the contrary, an unpopulated area that has useful natural resources capable of supporting life is a reason for us to expand into that area, not a reason for us to avoid it.

The argument from the possibility of future life on Mars becomes more relevant with the following thought experiment. Suppose that aliens settled on Earth millions of years ago, populating the planet. If that had happened, presumably humans would not have evolved and we would not exist. What if the aliens knew that human life would arise without their interference?

The answer is not obvious. This question is closely related to the problem of what, if anything, we owe to future generations of humans. Most people agree that we owe future generations a habitable Earth. Most people do not, however, think that we owe it to future generations to ensure that every possible potential descendant exists. Absent some rare religious convictions, almost no one thinks that we are under a constant obligation to have intentionally reproductive sex. The aliens are in a similar situation: If they do not settle Earth, humans will arise. But they are not clearly under any obligation to ensure that humans do evolve. Moreover, unlike our obligations to future generations, which might be grounded partially in the fact that we are causally responsible for producing future humans, any obligations that aliens might have to us cannot be so grounded.

Alternatively, from a moral viewpoint which takes the maximization of unique information as the highest good, there would be an obligation to let intelligent life evolve without interference, because then it will bring up something different (and thus valued). This view assumes that any instance of developing life would necessarily be unique; there may not be enough diversity to warrant noninterference.

Because there appears to be no life in our solar system, this argument is a nonissue. The Fermi paradox notes that at current rates of technological progress, humans will completely occupy every star in our galaxy within 250,000 years—an eyeblink in the lifetime of stars, much less a galaxy. Assuming that humans have evolved around a normal star and at a normal time, any aliens emerging anywhere in the Milky Way should have been here by now. Because they are not here, they do not exist anywhere. So, again, the problem of oppressing "Indians" disappears.

Protecting Ecosystem Through Redundancy

The preceding arguments against space settlement are weak, and there are some strong arguments in favor of settling space.

We have learned fairly recently that the extraterrestrial environment is not as friendly as it appears. Yes, we live in the "life belt" in our Milky Way, and Earth orbits between extremes of fire and ice in our own solar system. But every 30 million years or so, an asteroid comes smashing in, causing a mass extinction. A space-faring civilization could not only prevent that, it could expand the volume of Earth's biosphere by many magnitudes. And by doing so, it would provide redundancy in case something fast and deadly makes it though an asteroid interception network. A sufficiently long-range expansion would even provide insurance against a nearby supernova but would take many years to achieve.

Turner Thesis and Great Experiment

Frederick Jackson Turner's (1892) essay, "The Significance of the Frontier in American History," was one of the most influential explanations of the historical development of the United States, and it spawned a controversy that remains today (Lavender, 2000).

The question that Turner faced, as the frontier had just been closed three years before, was this: "What happens to a society without a frontier?" Turner's claim was that the frontier was the source of America's egalitarian democracy, individualism, and spirit of innovation. It turns out that there were actually more land grants after the frontier was officially closed than before that point, but Jackson's fear was that without a frontier, Western enlightenment values of humanism, reason, science, and progress would die (Zubrin, 1999). This worry is echoed today by social critics who point to the apparent loss of vigor of American society, including the impotence of governmental institutions such as the National Aeronautics and Space Administration (NASA) (David, 2006) and the Federal Emergency Management Agency (FEMA) (Garrett and Sobel, 2003), the spread of irrationality and risk adversity (Marchand and Mossman, 2005), popular culture's increased vulgarity (Bloom, 1987), and the rejection of the very idea of progress (Burch, 2001).

Many solutions have been proposed, but the chief one among them, social engineering, has always been an uncertain enterprise fraught with ethical problems as well as financial and political ones. The horrific social experiments of the twentieth century, such as Nazism and communism, should give us pause before we embark on such projects. Settling the frontier of space, while technically difficult, is *much* simpler than establishing social engineering projects in existing nations and expecting them to achieve working utopias. Moreover, space is to us what North America was to the original European colonists: an almost unlimited source of raw materials and room in which to expand. And just as these resources provided the opportunity for the colonists to experiment with different forms of government and social structures, so too could space provide for the possibility of communities centered on differing visions of society.

NANOTECH REVOLUTION REQUIRES SPACE SETTLEMENT

The advent of nanotechnology renders the colonization of space not merely important but absolutely necessary. The reason is simple: The kinds of technology that will render the settlement of space feasible can also be easily abused. The Berlin wall, which thousands of East European refugees risked their lives to cross, was made of wet Kleenex compared to the mind-numbing control that a nanotechnology-enabled dictator could exert (Freitas, 2006b). For example, a government monopoly on nanotechnology spy devices could usher in an Orwellian dictatorship in which no person could ever utter a dissenting opinion. In George Orwell's *1984*, television screens with built-in cameras dominated every room and public area (Orwell, 1981). Avoiding them was tricky but possible. Nanotechnology will make possible inexpensive, pervasive, and unobtrusive cameras of which James Bond could only dream. Even worse, nanotechnology could make functional magnetic resonance imaging (fMRI) systems so inexpensive that the secret police could have one permanently attached to each citizen to monitor brain patterns—ostensibly to prevent terrorism (Johnson, 2005). In general, once we are able to build electrical circuits (like video camera and fMRI machine circuits) on the molecular level, imagination will be the only limit to the ways that a government could produce easily concealable surveillance devices.

Totalitarian governments are not the only entities that might abuse nanotechnology. Consider natural and artificial zeolites, which offer present-day examples of how nanomaterials can be designed to extract specific heavy metals from the environment (Fryxell, 2006).[3] While these techniques are being used for remediation, they could also be used for concentration. The uranium concentration of seawater is only about 3.3 milligrams per cubic meter of seawater (Analytical Center for Non-Proliferation, 2004), but a nanotechnology-produced membrane operated by a single individual on the open ocean could easily get 15 pounds of uranium needed for an atomic bomb.[4]

The settlement of space actually provides a partial solution to these worries. Just as some of the first American colonists emigrated from their home countries in search of a place where they could have religious freedom, modern-day dissenters, or those worried about nuclear disasters,[5] could emigrate to space and form their own communities. The comparison here is particularly apt: The New World was a particularly good place to start a new insular community because it was relatively unpopulated and because it contained a virtually inexhaustible supply of natural resources. With the advent of mature nanotechnology, space is a similar environment: The Sun provides abundant free energy, and the copious supplies of carbon, silicon, oxygen, and other life-supporting elements throughout the solar system are the only raw material nanotechnology needs to support human life.

It is true that paranoid governments on Earth may consider independent space colonies a threat, especially if they have extradited all their dissenters there. And there is no guarantee that totalitarian governments will not form in space too. In fact, with all the room and opportunity for law breaking in the political power vacuum, it is almost certain that eventually some will arise. Yet in space there is a large amount of room in which to run, and there are theoretical limits to how quickly one can be chased.

Much turns upon the speed of technological development. If starship speed or weapon development proceeds according to Moore's law—doubling every 18 months—then running away from a sufficiently paranoid state may not be possible unless one's own technology advances at a similar rate.[6] Historically, however, free societies usually generate new knowledge better than controlled ones, so there is reason to think that a totalitarian society might never catch up with its dissidents. Space, then, provides a possible escape from any totalitarian regime that nanotechnology might enable.

HOW NANOTECH MODIFIES STANDARD ARGUMENTS

Because nanotechnology is so powerful, it has a heavy impact on the arguments for making the rest of the solar system part of our ecosystem.

In fact, productive nanosystems will be so powerful that it can be argued that space settlement cannot really occur without them. The International Space Station and the Space Shuttle were developed during the 1960s, and the new Crew Launch Vehicle (CLV) and the Crew Exploration Vehicle (CEV) are derivative of the Shuttle and the Apollo, respectively. Trying to explore and inhabit space in any significant way using pre-nanotechnology space hardware is subject to enormous and unnecessary risks of failure and loss of life. The argument is that we should not go to Mars or even return to the Moon until we can go there with nanotechnology-based space hardware that can virtually guarantee that the explorers will not die from medical causes (e.g., from running out of food, air, or water or radiation exposure), propulsion system malfunction, or other disasters. In addition, pouring billions of dollars into soon-to-be-obsolete space vehicles could be better spent on achieving productive nanosystems sooner—with all its attendant advantages in saving lives and lowering the cost to orbit.

The only caveat to this "nanotechnology-first" argument is the problem of social inertia. If people are not accustomed to thinking about the importance of space settlement, then they may turn back from space. This withdrawal from frontiers—as the Chinese abruptly did in 1436, only a few years after almost discovering Europe—would be disastrous.

Unnecessary Worries: Nanoparticle Toxicity and Evolving Nanobots

Some environmental and governmental organizations are worried about nanoparticle toxicity. But for a number of reasons, this is not something that needs any attention, especially in space:

- Space is dead. And it is so dangerous that even if we spread our deadliest toxins everywhere we went, it would barely alter our chances of dying in space.
- A mechanosynthetic nanofactory has as much chance of releasing unintended nanoparticles as an automobile assembly line has of accidentally letting a shipment of engines get misrouted and permanently lost.
- Productive nanosystems will be able to produce large, molecularly precise products using planar assembly directly, so there will be no reason for primitive nanoparticles to be produced in the first place.
- Internal life preservation systems, in terms of internal cellular repair nanobots, will make it very difficult to poison someone on purpose, much less accidentally.

Michael Crichton's (2002) portrayal in *Prey*—that nanobots will evolve hostile superintelligence—is unrealistic. It is true that macroscale self-replicating robots have been designed and built, but they depend on a complex and ordered substrate of feedstock parts. It is theoretically possible that nanobots might be designed to use the same feedstock molecules that life does, and they might be made more efficient than existing life forms. But that is a very difficult design problem.

Building robots that evolve is even more difficult. The only thing that researchers have been able to accomplish thus far in artificial intelligence (AI, Lenat and Brown, 1984) and robotics (Lipson and Pollack, 2000) is applying hill-climbing algorithms to find solutions to multidimensional problem spaces. The minor successes in these areas, combined with the perversity of humans like those who design computer viruses, suggest that we should be alert for targeted self-replicating nanomachines (Freitas, 2006a) but that we should not worry too much about them evolving into dangerous predators.

There are more important things to worry about. One of the most immediate worries, shared by advocates of both nanotechnology and space settlement, is the specter of the self-refuting precautionary principle. As Sam Kazman (2003) points out, "Technological advancement may well pose risks, but so does technological stagnation. In that sense, the Precautionary Principle itself is an incredibly risky proposition." The truth of this observation has been illustrated often in history (notably by the Chinese withdrawal from ocean-going ships in the 1400s and by the English attempts to ban technological advances in post–World War I Germany). There is nothing wrong with taking precautions, but there are serious dangers in extending a principle into a zero-tolerance policy with no allowance for counterbalancing principles.

Enhancement for Survival

Space is a dangerous place. Among cosmic radiation, hard vacuum, and micrometeorites traveling at 10 miles per second, it is a race to see what kills humans first. To counteract these dangers, people will be motivated to modify not only the environment outside the airlock but also their own bodies to defend against these dangers. Such modifications might range from the prosaic, such as healing broken bones or destroying cancer cells, to the more innovative, such as repairing radiation damage and tolerating zero gravity and hard vacuum. Other modifications may include subcutaneous pressure suits, superefficient artificial red blood cells (Freitas, 1998), radiation repair nanobots, and electric-powered mitochondria, obviating the necessity for space suits and other cumbersome equipment. These enhancements to the human body would make family-sized settlements possible in free space, whereas unimproved humans would need city-sized O'Neill colonies (Hall, 2005, pp. 171–183). The possibility of human enhancement, present on Earth, is a more important issue in space because a modification might be not just an enhancement but also a necessity for survival. Some people claim that in vivo technologies that allow one to endure high-energy cosmic radiation and hard vacuum are unnatural and therefore wrong. But they forget that nature is anything but static and that chaotic change is the norm, both on Earth and off it.

It may help to back up and gain some perspective. The "invention" of photosynthesis during the Archean eon about 3 billion years ago started spewing toxic (to the existing organisms) free oxygen into the atmosphere and started the predator–prey cycle of violence that has plagued this planet ever since. By the Proterozoic eon, just over 2 billion years ago, there was enough oxygen polluting the atmosphere that the ozone layer formed (San Diego Natural History Museum, geologic time line, http://www.sdnhm.org/fieldguide/fossils/timeline.html.), thereby cutting off the UV radiation that replenished the food supply of amino acids that the primitive microbes ingested to survive.

At the current rate of progress in nanotechnology, in two decades the work on diamond mechanosynthesis (Freitas, 2006c; Peng et al., 2006) will most likely result in machines that can pull carbon dioxide out of the air to make diamond. Keith Henson (personal communication, 1987) pointed out that because diamond is such a useful engineering material and air is free (unlike fossil fuels), this will cause so much carbon dioxide to be removed from the atmosphere that plants will not be able to survive (not to mention the global cooling that might result). If this scenario becomes true, then environmentalists will be forced to dig up and burn millions of tons of coal to keep enough carbon dioxide in the atmosphere.

It actually gets worse than that because around the same time we will undoubtedly find ways to enhance our bodies and our brains. For example, we might find ways to improve the efficiency and power density of our metabolism by using electricity to recharge the energy molecule ATP that powers our muscles and brains. The current mechanism, which metabolizes sugar in three steps (glycosis process, oxygen-dependent Krebs cycle, and cytochrome electron transport system), is only 39 percent efficient (Johnson, 2006). While this is almost 20 times better than fermentation, there is certainly room for improvement.

After nanobots enhance our bodies in such ways (possibly three decades from now), we will be faced with a really big question: Should we remake our environment as drastically as the early photosynthetic microbes did? This process will start fairly innocuously, with the semiautonomous repaving of roads and reroofing of homes with productive nanosystems. It is not clear how politics affect this scenario, but eventually these machines will be followed by general-purpose nanofactories that will collect and store solar energy more efficiently than plants. Some nanofactories might be made to be more autonomous and more intelligent than others, though it is not clear that this must be so; after all, we have no reason to make laser printers intelligent. However, if someone accidentally (like the Morris worm) or purposefully (like the computer virus writers) builds an evolving autonomous nanofactory, then it is likely to establish an evolving ecosystem that can compete with Earth's biosphere. But is this bad?

The development of photosynthesis by the first blue-green algae demonstrates that preserving the original environment as a static ideal may not be the best thing to do, even if it were possible. However, it is also difficult for us to envision how or why a nanotechnology-reworked world would be better. Given the radical improvements brought about by the development of photosynthesis—oxygen respiration, sexual reproduction, multicellularism, and intelligence—it is reasonable to believe that further radical changes in the environment might also be good, even though they seem as strange to us as ancient myths and mystical visions: One that comes to mind is the lamb lying down with the lion while a child plays in a nest of vipers. Another improvement might be the prevention of any extinction of plant or animal species. However, the method might seem disconcerting: Just as a given mechanical structure could be built using nanobots, so too could any living creature. Therefore we might preserve plants or animals by backing up the information needed to reconstruct them. But on what grounds would this be a real improvement?

One could ask the same question of the giant sequoias settling in Northern California about 2000 years ago. These majestic trees depend on forest fires to spread and were part of the many arboreal invasions that occurred after the glaciers retreated 20,000 years ago. What makes the largest sequoia, the 2100-year-old General Sherman tree, intrinsically more valuable than a dandelion in a lawn? Is there any objective value in that this particular tree has the highest volume of any tree in the world—other than the value that human beings have conferred on it? The problem is [as G. E. Moore (1998) claimed], that there seems to be no logical path from such naturalistic properties to ethical claims.

The final complication to human modifications is that some people will undoubtedly consider genetically passing their enhancements to their children. Given the political vacuum in space, this is likely to happen, despite ethical controversies. However, human genetic engineering will probably not happen in any significant way, essentially because human reproductive exponential growth (with a doubling time of about 25 years) is much slower than Moore's law (18 months).

Next Step in Gaian Philosophy

When the Apollo astronauts first began taking photographs of Earth, our perceptions of ourselves began to change; people began to identify with Earth as a single entity. Helped by the scientific theories of James Lovelock, this psychological process of "framing" has continued into a worldview of deep ecology centering on Gaia, the superorganism of Earth. This idea gave support to recycling, antidevelopment activities, vegetarianism, and energy conservation.

Currently, vegans oppose carnivorism because it kills animals (Hyland, 2003). With nanotechnology-enabled mitochondrial enhancements, however, vegans themselves may become open to a similar argument. Just as technology was improved to increase our agricultural ability to the point where we didn't need to hunt, we will eventually gain the ability to eat nothing but light or electricity, making vegetarianism unnecessary and possibly even morally suspect. After all, what could be better than avoiding the killing of plants by feeding on the pure light of the Sun? Currently, no philosophers have proposed that plants have rights, but what will happen when we no longer need to eat them?

So the photonians may feel superior to those who eat plants (or even worse, animals). How deep will these prejudices run? Will their enhancements make photonians significantly more powerful, either physically or economically? If so, will the prejudices be deep enough, and the sudden disparity be so large, as to lead to war?

Ultimate Enhancement?

All of the enhancements we have discussed so far have involved modifying either the external world so that it is made more congenial for us or ourselves so that we can survive in an otherwise hostile world. Rather than trying to cope with the real world, though, one might instead live in a simulated world. Science fiction is replete with such stories: The holodeck in *Star Trek*, brains in vats, and the *Matrix* readily come to mind. Nanotechnology will no doubt aid in the creation of ever more realistic virtual worlds (Baxter, 2001). By itself, of course, nanotechnology isn't sufficient; true virtual reality also requires sufficiently advanced software capable of simulating the environment, including interactions with artificial (and real) people.

Nanotechnology could, however, more directly enable a variant on this theme. Current medical technology already allows us to keep an otherwise healthy unconscious person alive somewhat indefinitely. Nanotechnology will only help. But it could also enable a person to stimulate the pleasure centers of his or her brain continuously, somewhat the way drugs do, albeit without any of the medically dangerous side effects. People could live in a semiconscious state their entire lives, experiencing nothing but physical pleasure of various sorts. Though this life does not offer all of the advantages of a virtual world, there is surely something alluring about living in such a pleasure machine.

However, it seems unlikely that many would choose to live in such a state. Such a life would be utterly deprived of many of the things we value in addition to (and often more highly than) simple physical pleasure. Sufficiently advanced nanotechnology and brain science would probably be able to simulate aesthetic and intellectual pleasure along with a sense of accomplishment. But such a life would contain no real accomplishment for one would never *do* anything. There would never be an opportunity to exercise one's own agency.

There are far too many things that people care about besides physical pleasure, and these other concerns make a nanotechnology-enabled pleasure machine seem almost worthless. To bring out this point fully, consider what life would be like in a utopia. In this utopia, which would be something like the Christian heaven, all technological problems would be solved; there would be no need of work to produce food, to sustain our bodies, or otherwise to survive. In such a world, would one want to be hooked up to a pleasure machine or live on a holodeck?

Shelly Kagan in "The Grasshopper, Aristotle, Bob Adams, and Me" (unpublished) argues that we would not. According to him, there are things that we value beyond physical pleasure and even any other pleasures that might be simulated. Chief among these are the value of having relationships with other people. Though one might simulate these things on a holodeck, that would not be enough; it matters too that the ones we care about actually exist and that we stand in the right sort of causal relationship to them. Consider Kagan's example of the love that a husband has for his wife (p. 10):

> What is of value in such a case isn't merely the state produced (that is, my wife's knowing of my love) but the [causal] *production* of such a state by me (my *telling* her). Something similar presumably holds true for a variety of personal relations . . . there is intrinsic value in relationships of the right sort, but the value to be had here is not nearly exhausted by the simple fact of *standing* in those relationships; there is also value in *relating*.

Another way to view this argument is by examining the four traditional models of a good life: the contemplative, the active, the stoic, and the hedonistic. Daniel Robinson (1997) asks, "Given the possibility of experiencing a life that conforms exactly to a person's desires, under what conditions would someone instead prefer a life full of suffering, moral failure, and disappointment only because it was real?"

After all the fear, loathing, and sloth are expunged, the answer is, "Under all conditions." But then how can we attain the good life? Looking at heroes and saints, we discover that a good life is one that is lived for the good of others. Such a life cannot be simulated because in a simulation there is there is nobody else for whom good can be done. This is not quite true in multiplayer games played over the Internet, but in those cases, how real is the good that is done to fellow player characters? It turns out that a life lived in service to others will subsume the traditional models of the good life: We must think about how to do good for the other, we must work hard to accomplish any results, we must be stoically prepared for a lack of results, and we will be joyful as a result of our service (Robinson, 1997).

Just because holodecks and other simulations are possible in a nanotechnology-enabled society, it does not follow that they are good for us. After sufficient reflection, one would not want to live only in a holodeck. It turns out that in space, as on Earth, nanotechnology will not change the two most important principles that define humanity: our orientation to understand and conform to the reality that surrounds us and our need to relate to the people around us.

CONCLUSION

The public at large is generally interested in space as a continuation of the colonization of the New World. There is less consensus about the desirability of nanotechnology, but unfortunately the synergistic interaction between the two areas is rarely even considered.

There are good arguments for settling space: Opportunities for creating real wealth, distributing and protecting the ecosystem of Earth, enjoying a political vacuum in which to experiment with new forms of government, and (according to the Turner thesis) preserving humanistic values of individuality, ingenuity, and egalitarianism.

Nanotechnology accentuates most of these arguments and generates a few ethical issues of its own, especially questions about the in vivo molecular enhancement of humans to adapt to space environments. The other major question revolves around the drastic reworking of the universe by humans. In both cases, the response is determined by assumptions about reality that have been addressed for ages by the world's religions. One answer is based on the assumption that we are made in the image and likeness of God and that as his stewards we have free rein to do as we wish in light of a coming judgment. A different view is that we are only accidental conglomerations of atoms, in which case it is capricious human whim and fallible human reason that control the destiny of the universe.

While settling space will probably ameliorate many problems and nanotechnology will probably ameliorate many more, neither will solve the perennial questions with which philosophy has struggled for millennia: What manner of creature are we and how ought we live? But with nanotechnology to increase our life span and intelligence and with the increased opportunities made possible by settling space, we might have a better chance of contemplating and perhaps even solving some of these questions.

NOTES

1. Actually, the word "nanotechnology" was first used by Tokyo Science University Professor Norio Taniguchi (1974) as follows: "'Nano-technology' mainly consists of the processing of, separation, consolidation, and deformation of materials by one atom or one molecule." But Taniguchi never did any further work in that direction.

2. The people whom these words are meant to represent have made their preference clear: The majority of American Indians/Native Americans believe it is acceptable to use either term or both. See http://www.infoplease.com/spot/aihmterms.html.

3. See especially "Actinide-Specific Interfacial Chemistry of Monolayer Coated Mesoporous Ceramics," http://samms.pnl.gov/EMSP.pdf.

4. Actually, they would need to collect 2083 pounds, since only 0.72 percent of it would be radioactive ^{235}U.

5. Worries about individuals gaining access to nuclear devices may be ameliorated by the kind of transparent society that nanotechnology could make possible. See D. Brin (1998).

6. At speeds approaching the speed of light, a dictator would need to expend the power of stars and galaxies to catch up with fleeing dissidents. The caveat is that if the dissidents are much fewer in number or are scattered by long distances, then their rate of technological progress will be slower.

REFERENCES

Analytical Center for Non-Proliferation. 2004. Nuclear technologies and non-proliferation policies—Issue 13: Evaluation of cost of seawater uranium recovery and technical problems toward implementation. Available: http://npc.sarov.ru/english/digest/132004/appendix8.html.

Baxter, S. 2001. The planetarium hypothesis: A resolution of the Fermi paradox. *Journal of the British Interplanetary Society* 54: 210–216.

Bloom, A. 1987. *The Closing of the American Mind.* New York: Simon & Schuster.

Brin, D. 1998. *The Transparent Society: Will Technology Force Us to Choose Between Freedom and Privacy?* Perseus Press. Available: http://www.davidbrin.com/privacyarticles.html.

Burch, G. 2001. Progress, counter-progress, and counter-counter-progress. Paper presented at Extro 5, June 16, 2001. Available: http://www.gregburch.net/progress.html.

Cate, V. 2002. SpaceTethers.com. Available: http://spacetethers.com/.

Crichton, M. 2002. *Prey.* New York: HarperCollins.

David, L. 2006. NASA vision plans doomed. Available: http://www.space.com/news/060724_cev_needsrevision.html.

Drexler, E. 1986. *Engines of Creation: The Coming Era of Nanotechnology.* New York: Anchor Books.

Freitas, R. A., Jr. 1983. Terraforming mars and venus using machine self-replicating systems. *Journal of the British Interplanetary Society*, 36: 139–142. Available: http://www.rfreitas.com/Astro/TerraformSRS1983.htm.

Freitas, R. 1998. Exploratory design in medical nanotechnology: A mechanical artificial red cell. *Artificial Cells, Blood Substitutes, and Immobilization Biotechnology*, 26: 411–430. Available: http://www.foresight.org/nanomedicine/Respirocytes.html.

Freitas, R. A., Jr. 2006a. Molecular manufacturing: Too dangerous to allow? *Nanotechnology Perceptions: A Review of Ultraprecision Engineering and Nanotechnology* 2: 15–24; Available: http://www.rfreitas.com/Nano/MMDangerous.pdf.

Freitas, R. A., Jr. 2006b. What price freedom? *Nanotechnology Perceptions: A Review of Ultraprecision Engineering and Nanotechnology* 2: 99–106; Available: http://www.rfreitas.com/Nano/WhatPriceFreedom.pdf.

Freitas, R., Jr. 2006c. Nanofactory collaboration. Available: http://www.molecularassembler.com/Nanofactory/.

Fryxell, G. 2006. Self-assembled monolayers on mesoporous supports. Available: http://samms.pnl.gov/. See also Actinide-specific interfacial chemistry of monolayer coated mesoporous ceramics. Available: http://samms.pnl.gov/EMSP.pdf.

Garrett, T., and Sobel, R. 2003. The political economy of FEMA disaster payments. *Economic Inquiry* 41(3): 496–509. Available: http://www.be.wvu.edu/divecon/econ/sobel/All%20Pubs%20PDF/The%20Political%20Economy%20of%20FEMA%20Disaster%20Payments.pdf.

Hall, J. 2005. A space pier. International Space Development Conference, Arlington, VA: May 19–22.

Hall, J. S. 2005. *Nanofuture: What's Next for Nanotechnology*. Buffalo, NY: Prometheus Books.

Hume, D. 1978. *A Treatise of Human Nature*. L. A. Selby-Bigge and P. H. Nidditch (Eds.). Oxford: Oxford University Press, pp. 469–470.

Hyland, J. R. 2003. Is vegetarianism a virtue? Is carnivorism a vice? *Human Religion*. Available: http://www.all-creatures.org/hr/hra-isveg.htm.

Johnson, J. G. 2006. Cellular respiration. In *Advanced Placement Biology*, Chapter 8. Available: http://www.sirinet.net/~jgjohnso/apbio8.html.

Johnson, K. 2005. Functional MRI could become lie detector. *Clinical Psychiatry News*, February 2005, 33(2): 59.

Kazman, S. 2003. Better never. *Navigator*, December. Available: http://www.theobjectivistcenter.org/showcontent.aspx?ct=765&h=53.

Kusin, E. N., Lytkin, V. V., and Madry, S. 1996. Did you know? Available: http://www.informatics.org/museum/diduno.html.

Lavender, C. 2000. Frederick Jackson Turner. The significance of the frontier in American history. Available: http://www.library.csi.cuny.edu/dept/history/lavender/frontier.html.

Lenat, D. B., and Brown, J. S. 1984. Why AM and EURISKO appear to work. *Artificial Intelligence* 23: 269–294.

Lipson, H., and Pollack, J. B. 2000. Automatic design and manufacture of robotic lifeforms. *Nature* 406: 974–978.

McKendree, T. 2001. A technical and operational assessment of molecular nanotechnology for space operations. Ph.D. Dissertation, University of South Carolina. Abstract. Available: http://www.foresight.org/Conferences/MNT9/Abstracts/McKendree/.

Marchant, G., and Mossman, K. 2005. Please be careful. *Legal Times* 28(33). Available: http://www.law.asu.edu/files/Programs/Sci-Tech/Commentaries/Marchant%20Mossman%208-15-05.pdf#search=%22spread%20of%20irrationality%22.

Moore, G. E. 1998 (1903). *Principia Ethica*. Amherst, NY: Prometheus Books.

National Nanotechnology Initiative. 2001. What is nanotechnology? Available: http://www.nano .gov/html/facts/whatIsNano.html.

O'Neill, G. 1974. The colonization of space. *Physics Today*, September 1974 pp. 32–40. Available: http://www.nas.nasa.gov/About/Education/SpaceSettlement/CoEvolutionBook/.

Orwell, G. 1981 (1984). New York: Signet New American Classics.

Peng, J., Freitas, R. A., Jr., Merkle, R. C., Von Ehr, J. R., Randall, J. N., and Skidmore, G. D. 2006. Theoretical analysis of diamond mechanosynthesis. Part III. Positional C2 deposition on diamond C(110) surface using Si/Ge/Sn-based dimer placement tools. *Journal of Computational and Theoretical Nanoscience* 3: 28–41. Available: http:// www.MolecularAssembler.com/Papers/JCTNPengFeb06.pdf.

Robinson, D. N. 1997. Lecture 50: Four theories of the good life: From saints to heroes to brains in vats. In *The Great Ideas of Philosophy*. Chantilly, VA: The Teaching Company.

Taniguchi, N. 1974. On the basic concept of "nano-technology." In *Proceedings of International Conference on Production Engineering in Tokyo*, Part II. Japan Society of Precision Engineering.

Tsiolkovsky, K. E. 1911. Personal letter. Available: www.uranos.eu.org/biogr/ciolke.html.

Turner, F. J. 1893. The significance of the frontier in American history. *Report of the American Historical Association*, pp. 199–227. Available: http://www.library.csi.cuny.edu/dept/history/ lavender/frontierthesis.html.

Zubrin, R. 1999. Mars: The frontier humanity need. *Space Visions*, November. Available: http://www.space.com/news/zubrin_visions_991116.html.

25

ETHICS FOR ARTIFICIAL INTELLECTS*

J. Storrs Hall

BACKGROUND

On April 13, 2029, the asteroid Apophis (2004 MN4) will pass within 22,000 miles of Earth. Our current knowledge of Apophis' position—we can place it with confidence within a region of space approximately the size of Earth itself—is enough to be reasonably certain that it will not strike Earth at that time. However, within that envelope of uncertainty, there is a window about the size of a city block, called a resonance keyhole. If Apophis is actually in the keyhole, the flyby with Earth in 2029 will alter its orbit such that it will return to strike Earth in 2036 with an energy of 870 megatons.[1]

Other events of 2029 cannot be predicted with such precision. However, we can predict with a fair confidence that two significant watersheds will have been passed in technological development: a molecular manufacturing nanotechnology which can produce a wide variety of mechanisms with atomic precision and the development of artificial intelligence (AI).

* This chapter was originally published as J. Storrs Hall, "Nano-Enabled AI: Some Philosophical Issues," *International Journal of Applied Philosophy*, vol. 2, no. 2: 247–261. Reprinted with permission. The author wishes gratefully to acknowledge the attention and insights of Robert A. Freitas, Jr., Douglas Hofstadter, Christopher Grau, David Brin, Chris Phoenix, John Smart, Ray Kurzweil, Eric Drexler, Eliezer Yudkowsky, and Robin Hanson.

Detailed arguments for the predictions of nanotechnology appear in Kurzweil (2005) and Hall (2005). Arguments for the advent of AI, given sufficient processing power, appear in those sources and Moravec (1999). We are concerned with a joint implication: If both of these technologies are present, greater-than-human intelligence will not only exist but will be ubiquitous.

The net present value of an intelligent, educated human being can be estimated at a million dollars; that is to say, a machine that could do such a human's job would be worth that much to buy. We will refer to three estimates of human-equivalent processing power (HEPP): Kurzweil at 10^{17} IPS (instructions per second), Moravec at 10^{14} IPS, and Minsky (personal communication)[2] at 10^{11} IPS. The author's own estimate agrees with Moravec's. The cost of a Minsky HEPP exceeded the value of an educated human in the 1990s; a Moravec HEPP is doing so this decade, and a Kurzweil HEPP will do so in the 2010s.

Moore's law, the historical trendline for cost of computers, predicts that by 2029 a Moravec HEPP—the best estimate of computer power we can reasonably equate to a human brain—will cost one dollar.

Note that we are intentionally ignoring the software side of the AI. While that is currently the most problematic aspect in a scientific sense, once AI is developed, the software—complete with education—can be copied with negligible cost.

The number of applications to which a human-level intelligence adds at least a dollar of value is staggering. Thus we can confidently predict that human-level AIs will be exceedingly numerous.

Artificial intelligences of greater-than-human intelligence are also likely. We know that humans with IQs of up to 200 or so can exist, and thus such levels of intelligence are possible. Less is known about the organization of complexity in intelligent systems than the generation of raw computational speed. Even mere speed can be useful, though. An AI operating at 1000 times human speed could read an average book in 1 second with full comprehension or take a college course, with plenty of homework and research, in 10 minutes. It could write a book in 2 or 3 hours and produce a human's lifetime intellectual output, complete with all the learning and experience that formed it, in a couple of weeks.

By 2036, as Apophis returns, the Earth it approaches may well be home to tens of billions of such superintelligent AIs.

LEIBNIZ VERSUS THE MARTIANS

It seems inescapable that an understanding of the moral character of the AIs is crucial in evaluating such a scenario. We will assume as a starting point that AIs can and will exist. That is, we will assume that machines can be built and programmed not only to converse in English and perform competently at any intellectual activity that humans can master but also that are mentally autogenous: They learn, have insights, and so forth, in the human manner, growing in wisdom as they gain experience.

Turing's (1950) test for machine intelligence is simply a game where the computer will be considered to think if it can simulate a human conversing via a text-only interface, well enough to fool a human judge some reasonable percentage of the time. There is an implicit assumption among AI practitioners that once an AI passes the Turing test intuitive doubts as to its qualities of mind will evaporate in the face of experience. Indeed, there is evidence that this happens well before it is ought to: Weizenbaum (1976) noted with alarm that people imputed humanlike qualities to his Eliza program, a pattern-matching conversationalist of nearly transparent simplicity. This phenomenon, now called the Eliza effect, and its turbocharged latter-day cognates involving robots with body language and facial expressions are strong warnings that our intuitions as to other minds are less reliable than we like to think.

However, this leaves us with a vexing open question as to the aspects of mind in machines. The seminal intuition is expressed by the philosopher Leibniz (in 1714) in his *Monadology* 17:

> Supposing that there were a machine whose structure produced thought, sensation, and perception, we could conceive of it as increased in size with the same proportions until one was able to enter into its interior, as he would into a mill. Now, on going into it he would find only pieces working upon one another, but never would he find anything to explain perception.

For perception we can substitute any subjective phenomenon, up to and including the experience of conscious will.[3]

The problem with this intuition as a guide to the realities of mind can be seen with a modern version of Leibniz' scenario:

> Suppose that you have been abducted by Martians and taken to their laboratory, where they put you into an super-nano-scope that allows them, and you, to observe any aspect of your body or brain at any scale down to the molecular. The Martians are able to discover, with you looking over their shoulders, that absolutely everything you do or feel can be explained by physics, chemistry, biology, and so forth; whatever decision you make, whatever action you take, is completely predictable by mechanistic scientific laws.

A human, too, is a "mere" machine; there is no more free will to be found in a molecular machinery of the cell than in a gear. Leibniz' insight holds, and the succeeding centuries of science have served only to fill in the details. Vitalism, the school of thought that there must be some special essence to life that operated under different laws than mere physics and chemistry, has retreated steadily since the Enlightenment, and the end is in sight.

This leaves us with a dilemma. It is essentially an extension of the one at the core of the mind–body issue as well as the freedom–determinism issue: What can the mentalistic terms like "intend," "believe," and "meaning" actually mean? It is invalid to reject them, as operationalists sometimes do, as illusions: Illusion is itself a mentalistic term.

The philosophical school of thought that, over the past few decades, has been taken to resolve this dilemma is the computational theory of mind (CTM). The basis of the CTM, its notion of what kinds of thing can rightly be said to exist, was originally stated by Putnam and essentially said that the brain is a computer and the mind is the process of its running its program. In rejecting vitalism, we are essentially forced to accept this, since in the broad sense "a computation" is synonymous with "the detailed working out, for a specific instance, of the formal rules of the description of a deterministic system (Putnam, 1960)."

The nuclei and electrons which make up a cell, such as a neuron, are governed by the laws of quantum mechanics. By empirical observation and extrapolation of the physics, however, we note certain regularities: Nuclei tend to trap electrons to form atoms, and atoms tend to share electrons in covalent bonds to form molecules. A cell contains thousands of molecular species which undergo various physical and chemical reactions with each other. The reactions proceed at rates determined by the concentrations. Thus in a computational model of the cell, the concentrations of these species can be represented by a numeric vector, specifying the concentrations, whose time behavior is governed by a system of differential equations which model the reactions. If the cell is a neuron, it can be modeled at a higher level of abstraction involving electronic circuit elements.

Each of these models, quantum mechanics, molecules, chemical concentrations, and so forth, forms a *level of abstraction*. We tend to think of the cell, for certain purposes, as a chemical reactor and ignore all the complexity of individual molecules that make it up. We just can't hold it all in our heads at once and have to break it down. But in going from each of these levels to the next higher one, phenomena are lost. For example, the typical models of molecules as atoms with bonds assumes a static distribution of charge, where the actually varying pattern can subtly affect the docking behavior of large molecules. The simple atoms-with-bonds model captures much, but not all, of the lower level's crucial phenomena.

The computational theory of mind we are forced to accept is like the quantum level of description of a cell. It seems risky to assume that there are fewer salient levels of abstraction in a useful theory of mind above, say, the neuron level than there are for a cell (or modern software). It is likely that the mental states of the standard CTM are near the top of a deep and as-yet dimly understood hierarchy of explanation. At every level, we're likely to see phenomena like the covalent approximation: exceptions to the (elegant forms of) the higher level theory, which can be explained (or computed) only by reference to the lower level, or by databases of special cases, which are essentially cached results of precomputed lower level cases.

Although we cannot offer any substantial detail, we can make the following predictions as to the ultimate shape of a mature CTM:

- It will be causal and mechanistic.
- It will involve multiple levels of abstraction, but higher levels may require reference to lower levels in exceptional cases.
- It will contain forms of computation like associative memory that are not part of standard algorithmic practice.
- At the higher levels, the architecture will be modular with definable information flows between modules. This does not preclude the possibility of various global communication channels, however.

- At intermediate levels, there will be information patterns recognizable as symbols, but these will be nonatomic with a wealth of implicit relationships implied by their structure.
- Beliefs, consciousness, free will, and the other aspects of mind which are of interest will be identified with various configurations and properties of the mental computational architecture in a satisfying way. The vast majority of perceptions, inferences, memory formation, and so forth, are heuristic in form, adaptive in the ancestral environment, but not general, sound, or complete in a mathematical sense.

To justify the use of "satisfying" in the above, we will attempt an example. The best developed theory of this form of which the author is aware is for free will.

First, a cognitive architecture from McDermott (2001): An AI contains a model of the world.[4] This is essentially a computational imagination, a subprogram similar in many ways to a computer game. In order to take choices between possible actions, it simulates the actions in the model to estimate their effect and applies a utility function to the resulting world states. The model must necessarily contain a model of the AI itself to perform the simulated actions; but just as necessarily, causality in the world model is broken at the point of the self-model, since the self-model is directed by the AI's own decision algorithm from outside the world model.

Thus, the AI's self-model is exempt from causal law in a way unique in its model, and thus in its understanding, of the world. It cannot be otherwise: Any attempt to model the actual decision-making mechanism within the self-model leads to an infinite regress and prevents the algorithm from terminating. If the AI's intuitions of causality are readouts of the model, it must conceive itself free.

Secondly, Wegener (2002) describes a strong basis for understanding the sensation of having acted with conscious will. While consciousness in general is beyond the scope of this example, suffice it to say that there appears to be a mechanism which produces a summary narrative from all the various information processed in the mind. Various acts in this trace record are tagged as having been willed. The trace, however, is a heuristic reconstruction (and vast simplification) of the actual decision process.

Lacking the Martians' super-nanoscope, Wegener convincingly makes his analysis based on boundary cases, where the subject believes he willed something he didn't or vice versa [and the remarkable delay between beginning to do an action and consciously deciding to do it in the Libet (2004) experiments]. Note that the heuristic reconstruction works properly in the vast majority of cases; the boundary cases are quite analogous to visual "optical illusions." Strong evidence for the heuristic and post hoc nature of the sensation of intention is found in the confabulations (unconsciously generated rationalizations) produced with such "will illusions."

The modeling–evaluation–acting–recording structure sketched above is a good one for rapid learning. The dynamics of the world model can be implemented as a database of causal pairs of the form "this happened and then (therefore) that happened." The most important of these will be the ones of the form "I did this, therefore that happened."

The conscious-will summarizer produces exactly this latter kind of record to augment the model continuously with experience.

Together, these analyses evoke a system that is satisfying, at least to this author, in the sense that it is exactly what we should expect. The mind is the operation of a machine formed by evolution to survive and reproduce on the savannas of Africa. Our self-image is exactly appropriate to creatures who can choose and plan by considering possibilities. Our sensation of will, like our vision, is heuristic, inexact, but usually right where it usually matters. Rapid learning of the consequences of our actions is invaluable.

Evolution had no charter to give us clear insight into the intricacies of cognitive data processing any more than it had for celestial mechanics or protein folding. Only the painstaking march of science has done that, and often against a strong inertia bolstered by intuitions of geocentrism or vitalism. A mature theory of mind, coherent with the evolutionary theory of our origins and the physical theory of our construction, must explain our intuitions on that basis, rather than taking them for granted.

MORAL MACHINERY

The nice thing about ethical theories, like standards, is that there are so many of them from which to choose. The major problem seems to be that there is no agreed-upon starting point:

- Divine revelation? If so, from which religion?
- Eudaimonia, Aristotle's ethics of personal virtue?
- Kant's categorical imperative or other "golden rule" ?
- Utilitarianism, maximizing the good over the whole population? If so, how are we to define the good, not to mention the population?

In the face of this, many modern commentators eschew a theoretical framework and appeal more or less directly to the moral intuitions of their readers. To some extent, although little acknowledged, this follows the "moral sense" theory propounded by Adam Smith (1759).

But such moral intuitions, of course, are modules in our mechanical minds formed by evolution in an environment of tribal foragers. They are as much contingent facts of evolutionary history as the shape of an oak leaf. Surely, we must not simply identify the good with some arbitrary property (such as evolutionary fitness). However, it seems perfectly defensible to base a study of the good on what our moral modules tell us and how they got to be that way. One can see little justification for moral inquiry otherwise.

We are forced to proceed essentially as with the mentalistic phenomena. We can gain some preliminary extensional definition of the good by reference to intuition, including the intuitions of the great moral philosophers. We can then regularize and abstract it and refer to cognitive architecture for its function and to the environment of evolutionary adaptation for its effect. After that, we will be on our own; our existing environment differs from the ancestral one significantly, and the environment we foresee as a result of superintelligent AI differs almost unrecognizably.

Internally, a particular ethic seems to resemble the grammar of a natural language. There are structures in our brains that predispose us to learn our native ethic, in that they determine within broad limits the kinds of ethics we can learn and that while the ethics of human cultures vary within those limits they have many structural features in common. [This notion is fairly widespread in latter twentieth-century moral philosophy, e.g., Rawls (1971) and Donagan (1977).] Our moral sense, like our competence at language, is as yet notably more sophisticated than any simple set of rules or other algorithmic formulation seen to date.

Ethics have much in common from culture to culture: structural similarities reminiscent of the deep structure of language syntax. One in particular is salient: Moral imperatives are associated with actions which contravene self-interest or common sense. Ethics are something more than arbitrary customs for interactions. There is no great difference made if we say "red" instead of "rouge," so long as everyone agrees on what to call that color; similarly, there could be many different basic forms of syntax that could express our ideas with similar efficiency.

But one of the points of an ethic is to make people do things they would not do otherwise. The reason is that, particularly for social animals, there are many kinds of interactions that have the character of a prisoner's dilemma game: a setup in which each player can do better by cheating the other one, but if instead they both cooperate, they'll both do better than if they both cheat. For example, any kind of trade requires finding a solution to the prisoner's dilemma.

Furthermore, and perhaps even more importantly, there were many actions whose long-term effects we simply don't understand. Thus, in many cases, the adoption of a rule that seemed to contravene common sense or one's own interest, if generally followed, can have a substantial beneficial effect on a human group.

Many animals—social insects are an extreme example—have evolved innate behaviors that model altruism or foresight beyond the individual's understanding. Some of these, such as altruism toward one's relatives, can clearly arise simply from selection for genes as opposed to individuals. However, there is reason to believe that there is much more going on and that humans have evolved an ability to be programmed with arbitrary (within certain limits) ethics.

The reason a human ethic is learned is the same as the reason that toolmaking is learned: The ancestral environment changed fast enough that a general capability for rapid adaptation was more adaptive than any specific innate capability. Hunting techniques had to change faster than we could evolve beaks or saberteeth; we learned to make and modify stone knives and spears appropriate to the game and clothing appropriate to the climate. The environment which would have made innate long-term or altruistic behaviors adaptive was unstable as well.

The ethics themselves are produced by cultural evolution, not individuals (usually). The individual must, for any of this to work, absorb the ethic, like language, from the culture as a natural part of maturation, and it must then occupy a place in the cognitive database that is authoritative and read only (or at least very difficult to change). In other words, the individual must sense the learned ethic as a universal absolute. Otherwise it would not be able to perform its function of modifying behavior against the strong motives of self-interest and common sense.

In sum, our argument is that there is a separate "ethic-learning" module, similar to the language-learning one, and it feeds into an action evaluation database. A fuller theory, beyond our present scope, would identify a plethora of subsidiary modules, including those producing and interpreting affective display.

This at first sounds like an error theory: Here's why we believe right and wrong exist, but it's only this gadget in our brains designed to fool us. But consider: The ethic we inherit is developed by cultural evolution, as is, say, science. Science may not be ultimate absolute truth—but it is the best we have and much better than any individual could invent alone. Our learned cultural ethic is similar. Its distilled wisdom is greater than our individual knowledge, since it was gathered over historical time and many people.

For most cultural knowledge, how to make a stone knife for, example, the individual's cognitive endowment—experience, inferential ability, and the results of immediate experiment—is an appropriate optimizer. Seeing a better way to make a stone knife, a person adopts it and contributes to the culture thereby. In contrast, the individual's intelligence is counterproductive in some cases: notably, participation in situations of the prisoner's dilemma variety, where the individual's interests conflict with the group's. These are the situations ethics addresses.

ETHICS FOR MACHINES

It is common for singulatarians, who study the possibilities of a particularly rapid increase in technology in the relatively near future, to worry about autogenous AIs. They might, it is reasoned, remove any conscience or other constraint we program into them or simply program their successors without them. But it is in fact we, the authors of the first AIs, who stand at the watershed. We cannot modify our brains (yet) to alter our own consciences, but we are faced with the choice of building our creatures with or without them.

An AI without a conscience, by which we mean both the innate moral paraphernalia in the mental architecture and a culturally inherited ethic, would be a superhuman psychopath. Prudence, indeed, will dictate that superhuman psychopaths should not be built; however, it seems almost certain that it will be done within the next two decades. Most existing AI research is completely pragmatic, without any reference to moral structures in cognitive architectures. Furthermore, much of the most advanced research is sponsored by the military, where the notion of an autonomous machine being able to question its orders on moral grounds is anathema. The other major venue where research seems likely to produce AI is corporate industry, where the top goal seems likely to be the fiduciary benefit of the company.

Some commentators have suggested that AIs should be designed with built-in rules that approximate what we would call ethics. For example, Bostrom's (2003) prescription of a "friendly" top-down motivational structure for an AI approximates what, on a close reading, Asimov's (1950) Three laws of robotics amount to. Asimov conceived an internal mental structure in a dynamical systems formulation (see "Runaround") and understood the problems inherent in reinterpretation of words and assumed that the laws can be built into the structure of the mind at a deeper level (see, among others, "Reason").

But Asimov's robots were not autogenous, and as noted above, the current probable sources of AI are not such as to admit of a generally adopted philanthropic formulation. The reasonable assumption, then, is that a wide variety of AIs with differing goal structures will appear in the coming decades.

A subtext of the singulatarian concern is that there may be the possibility of a sudden emergence of (a psychopathic) AI at a superhuman level due to a positive feedback in its autogenous capabilities. There are three reasons for a lack of alarm.

First, although hardware for running a human-level AI exists, only a handful of the top supercomputers qualify. These are multimillion-dollar installations and have strong previous calls on their time. Even if someone were to pay to dedicate a supercomputer to running an AI full time, it would only approximate a normal human intelligence. Ubiquitous superintelligence must wait for a decade or two of Moore's law, implying nanotechnology.

Second, even when the hardware is available, the software is not. Some of the fears of sudden superintelligence are based on the notion that an early superintelligence would make writing the smarter next one faster, and so forth. It does seem likely that a properly structured AI could be a better programmer than a human of otherwise comparable cognitive abilities. It is ironic to note, however, that automatic programming is currently one of the most poorly developed of AI's subfields. Any reasonable extrapolation of current practice predicts that early human-level AIs will be secretaries and truck drivers, not programmers.

Even when AI computer scientists are achieved, adding one more to the existing field, which is already bending its efforts to improving AI, will not materially affect progress. Only when the total AI which is in fact devoting its efforts to this project begins to rival the intellectual resources of the existing field of AI will significant acceleration occur.

Third, intelligence does not spring fully formed like Athena from the forehead of Zeus. Even we humans, with the processing power of a supercomputer at our disposal, take years to mature. A human requires about a decade to become really expert in any given field—including AI programming. More to the point, it takes the scientific community some extended period to develop a theory and the engineering community some further time to put it into practice. Even if we had a complete and valid theory of mind, which we do not, putting it into software would take years, and the early versions would be incomplete and full of bugs.

Human developers will need years of experience with early AIs before they get it right. Even then they will have systems that are the equivalent of slow, inexperienced humans. Software has a law of advance similar to Moore's law for hardware, less celebrated and less precisely measurable but nevertheless real. Advances in computer science tend to produce software speedups analogous to the hardware ones. The completely understood, tightly coded, highly optimized software of mature AI may run a human equivalent in real time on a machine of the Moravec HEPP class, but early versions will not.

There are two wild-card possibilities to consider. First is rogue AIs living on botnets—groups of hijacked PCs communicating via the Internet. It's unlikely, of course, that any one project could hijack a significant fraction of the Internet for very long! Furthermore, the extreme forms of parallelism needed to make use of this form of computing, along with the communication latency involved, will tend to require a more complex system design. That, together with the existing increasingly sophisticated security community, will make the development of AI software much harder in this mode than in a standard research setting. Thus, while we can expect botnet AI's in the long run, they are unlikely to be first.

The second possibility is that Minsky is right. Very few business or academic local area networks (LANs) currently offer less than a Minsky HEPP. If somehow an early AI were to find a "resonance keyhole" that allowed strong positive feedback into such a highly optimized form, it would find ample processing power available. And this could be aboveboard—a Minsky HEPP costs much less than a person is worth economically.

Let us, somewhat presumptuously, attempt to explain Minsky's intuition by an analogy: A bird is our natural example of the possibility of heavier-than-air flight. Birds are immensely complex: muscles, bones, feathers, nervous systems. But we can build working airplanes with tremendously fewer moving parts. Similarly, the brain can be greatly simplified, still leaving an engine capable of general conscious thought.

The author's intuition is that Minsky is closer to being right than is generally recognized in the AI community, but that computationally expensive heuristic search will turn out to be an unavoidable element of adaptability and autogeny—and thus of any AI capable of the runaway feedback loop singulatarians fear.

Almost certainly, then, at least a full decade will elapse between the appearance of the first genuinely general, autogenous AIs and the time that they become significantly more capable than humans. This will indeed be a crucial period in history, but no one person, group, or even school of thought will control it. The question instead is, what can be done to influence the process to put the AIs on the road to being a stable community of moral agents?

A possible path is shown in the experiments of Axelrod (1984). He ran a computer tournament in which various programs were forced to play the prisoner's dilemma with each other over and over again. Surprisingly, the programs which won out were cooperators: They prospered by helping each other, where the programs that were too shortsightedly self-interested knocked each other out. The original biological evolution of our own morality, as described by the field of evolutionary ethics, is thought to have happened in much the same way. Superintelligent AIs should be just as capable of understanding this as humans are.

The environment in which AI morality will evolve, however, will have some significant differences from the one in which ours did. The bad news:

- The disparities between the abilities of AIs could be significantly greater than those between humans and more correlated with an early "edge" in the race to acquire resources. This can negate the evolutionary pressure to reciprocal altruism.
- Corporate AIs will almost certainly start out self-interested, and evolution favors effective self-interest.

It has been suggested [e.g. by Pinker (1997), Yudkowski (2003), and Hawkins (2004)], that AIs would not have the "baser" human instincts built in and thus not need moral restraints. But it should be clear that they *could* be programmed with baser instincts, and it seems obvious to this author that corporate ones will be and that military ones will be programmed with different but equally disturbing motivational structures.

Furthermore, it should be noted that *any* goal implies self-interest. Consider two agents, either of whom might get the use of some given resource. Unless the agents' goals are identical, each will further its own goal more by using the resource for its own purposes and consider it at best suboptimal and possibly counterproductive for the resource to be controlled by the other agent and thus applied to some other goal.

It should go without saying how greatly goals can vary even if both agents are programmed to seek, say, "the good of humanity."

Back to human–AI differences—the good news:

- As a general rule, smart is good. As a matter of practical fact, criminality is strongly negatively correlated with IQ in humans.[5]
- Significantly greater and more detailed forms of memory transfer will be available than with humans. Thus, individual AIs are likely to have access to experience at the extrapersonal scales for which human morality is a heuristic.
- Intra- as well as inter-AI structure may well be designed on a economic as opposed to a dominance (pecking order) model, since this is in fact more efficient. Thus AI's could be without the mechanics we seem to have whereby authority can short-circuit morality, as in the Milgram (1963) experiments where people tortured others because a "scientist" told them to (or the Nazi experience, where much worse happened in the name of following orders).
- The economic law of comparative advantage implies that cooperation between individuals of greatly differing capabilities remains mutually beneficial.
- Individual lifetime is not arbitrarily limited, so an AI has the prospect of living into the far future in a world whose character its actions help create. Forever is a long time to try to hide an illicit deed.
- Artificial intelligences intending to alter their own morality modules could make the source code public and invite public scrutiny and revisions.
- Moral AIs would be able to track other AIs in much greater detail than humans do each other for vastly more individuals. This allows a more precise formation and variation of cooperating groups.
- Artificial intelligences will have considerably better insight into their own natures and motives than humans do. Thus an AI may have the ability to be more completely honest than humans, who believe their own confabulations. [It is worth noting that some commentators, such as Nadeau (2006), propose that *only* an AI could be a moral agent, because confabulation means that humans' reasons for acting differ from our perceived intentions!]

We can only at present theorize about the ultimate moral capacities of AIs, but this list strongly suggests that an AI with a moral character not only on par with but significantly better than that of humans is not only possible but perhaps even likely.

One obvious ethical innovation that will be needed is a sound treatment of the question of the ethical relationship of minds of vastly different capabilities. Another will be the question, all too soon to be a possibility, of direct manipulation and modification of the minds of others—with or without consent.

By the time Apophis returns in 2036, the technological means could exist not only to prevent its doing mischief but also, if desired, to capture it as a valuable material resource. Neglect of the appropriate advances in astronautics would clearly be a dereliction of duty. Similarly, research and development in the moral nature of mind is certainly a duty of the highest order, not only now and for us but also for the AIs themselves when they do arrive.

NOTES

1. See *Astronomy* 34(5), May 2006, pp. 46–51. An 870MT impact would leave a crater about 3 miles in diameter and destroy most buildings within 25 miles but would not cause damage on a global scale.
2. Note that the actual informal estimate was somewhat lower than the one used here.
3. I take Searle's famous Chinese Room to be essentially a reapplication of this same intuition (applied to a different end).
4. It is a Popperian creature, allowing its theories to die in its stead.
5. For example, see Herrnstein and Murray (1994, p. 246): In one major national study, among white males aged 15 to 23, the average IQ of those never arrested was 106, of those ever sentenced to a correctional facility 93.

REFERENCES

Asimov, I. 1950. *I, Robot*. New York: Doubleday.

Axelrod, R. 1984. *The Evolution of Cooperation*. New York: Basic Books.

Bostrom, N. 2003. Ethical issues in advanced artificial intelligence. In I. Smit et al. (Eds.), *Cognitive, Emotive and Ethical Aspects of Decision Making in Humans and in Artificial Intelligence*, Vol. 2. International Institute of Advanced Studies in Systems Research and Cybernetics, pp. 12–17.

Donagan, A. 1977. *The Theory of Morality*. Chicago, IL: University of Chicago Press.

Drexler, K. E. 1992. *Nanosystems: Molecular Machinery, Manufacturing, and Computation*. New York: Wiley.

Hall, J. S. 2005. *Nanofuture: What's Next for Nanotechnology*. Buffalo, NY: Prometheus.

Hawkins, J. 2004. *On Intelligence*. New York: Owl Books.

Herrnstein, R. and Murray, C. 1994. *The Bell Curve: Intelligence and Class Structure in American Life*. New York: Free Press.

Kurzweil, R. 2005. *The Singularity is Near*. New York: Viking.

Leibniz, G. W. 1714. *Monadology*. Originally written in French. Available: philosophy. eserver.org/leibniz-monadology.txt.

Libet, B. 2004. *Mind Time: The Temporal Factor in Consciousness*. Cambridge, MA: Harvard University Press.

McDermott, D. V. 2001. *Mind and Mechanism*. Cambridge, MA: MIT Press.

Milgram, S. 1963. Behavioral study of obedience. *Journal of Abnormal and Social Psychology* 67: 371–378.

Moore, G. E. 1903. *Principia Ethica*. West Nyack, NY: Cambridge University Press.

Moravec, H. 1999. *Robot: Mere Machine to Transcendent Mind*. New York: Oxford University Press.

Nadeau, J. E. 2006. Only androids can be ethical. In K. Ford, C. Glymour, and P. Hayes (Eds.), *Thinking about Android Epistemology*. Cambridge, MA: AAAI/MIT, pp. 241–248.

Pinker, S. 1997. *How the Mind Works*. New York: Norton.

Putnam, H. 1960. Minds and machines. In S. Hook (Ed.), *Dimensions of Mind*. New York: New York University Press.

Rawls, J. 1971. *A Theory of Justice*. Cambridge, MA: Harvard/Belknap.

Smith, A. 1759. *The Theory of Moral Sentiments*. West Nyack, NY: Cambridge University Press.

Turing, A. M. 1950. Computing machinery and intelligence. *Mind* 59: 433–460.

Yudkowski, E. 2003. *Creating Friendly AI*. Available: http://www.singinst.org/CFAI/index.html.

Wegener, D. M. 2002. *The Illusion of Conscious Will*. Cambridge, MA: MIT Press.

Weizenbaum, J. 1976. *Computer Power and Human Reason*. San Francisco: W.H. Freeman.

26

NANOTECHNOLOGY AND LIFE EXTENSION

Sebastian Sethe

INTRODUCTION

It is a very old story. In may be the oldest recorded tale there is: Gilgamesh embarks on a quest to find a certain herb that will restore his youth. Mankind was expelled from the garden lest "he take also of the Tree of Life, and eat, and live for ever" (Genesis 3:22–24). But alas, we had already eaten from the tree of knowledge and yearned for more of both fruit.

Ever since there was human scientific endeavor, people have sought to discover ways to ward off death (Gruman, 1966). But it was not until the advent of modern technology that advances in knowledge and technology doubled life expectancy in the developed world. Future technology may give us the ability to extend the human life span well beyond its current limits.

The prospect of life extension (LE) has been present since technology at the nanoscale was conceived. In his pioneering 1959 lecture, Richard Feynman (1960) theorized: "small machines might be permanently incorporated in the body to assist some inadequately-functioning organ." A significant proportion of Eric Drexler's (1986) visionary *Engines of Creation* is devoted to a discussion of how nanotechnology could assist medicine, including how "cell repair machines" could drastically extend our life span, and the prospect of reversible biostasis. Nanotechnology as a tool in LE also

---

Nanoethics: The Ethical and Social Implications of Nanotechnology. Edited by Allhoff, Lin, Moor, Weckert
Copyright © 2007 John Wiley & Sons, Inc.

featured prominently in the recently influential NIBC report (Connolly, 2002). Even the possibility to use nanoimaging to digitize and electronically express consciousness has emerged in the popular imagination (Wachowski and Wachowski, 1999). There are, in short, a variety of technological stories about nanotechnologically enabled life extension (NLE).

In considering *moral* aspects of NLE, one can differentiate between moral endorsements and criticisms. The critics can be further distinguished according to three main themes: virtue (NLE is not morally desirable for the individual), utility (NLE will create more unhappiness than happiness overall), and aesthetics (there is something unpalatable about NLE). Another common objection does not discuss the LE ethics directly but argues that the resources devoted to NLE would be more wisely invested into other moral projects. There are of course many variations and different points of emphasis within these general themes that cannot be addressed in this introductory overview. Instead, I will select a sample issue from each area.

DEATH, AGING, AND DISEASE

Death Is Bad

Anyone who does not contemplate suicide is likely to agree that life is valuable for some reason—but ideas about what makes a "good life" will vary a great deal. Happily, when considering the moral implications of *extending* life span, we do not have to tackle the "meaning of life" in the absolute. Considering that the debate takes place exclusively at the table of the living, one can sidestep the question of "why?" by asking "'why not?" When extending life one is, at least temporarily, denying death. From a moral perspective, why should we be concerned about death? In fact, as Lucretius (50 B.C.E) wonders: Is there a moral difference between death and prenatal nonexistence?

For most contractarian, rights-based, or consequentialist moral theories, the situation is rather straightforward: Moral relations (desires, promises, rights, duties, beauty, pleasure, etc.) are meaningful to the living. From a deontological perspective, death can be undesirable because it deprives a person of autonomy (O'Neil, 1993). A yet wider view need not even identify particular moral goods: "Death, *no matter how inevitable*, is an abrupt cancellation of indefinitely extensive possible goods" (Nagel, 1979, p. 10). As the possibility of death shapes the living person's outlook on life, some argue that death denial is the only psychological and philosophical recourse (Becker, 1973). Existentialism espoused this struggle with death as the hallmark of conscious existence (Heidegger, 2000). But this situation has also been described as an insult to the living, "not because there will be nothing in the future, [but] because there will be nothing of the future of what was in the past" (Kamm, 1993, p. 54). Alternatively, one might simply state that the reason why death is a bad is found in the reasons of why life is valuable (Blackford, 2004).

A combination of these arguments gives us a strong indication as to why death is reasonably regarded as intrinsically bad in most moral theories.

Death Is Good

Still, some would disagree with this conclusion. Controversially, Sigmund Freud postulated an indwelling death instinct (Levin, 1992). Spiritual perspectives would not view death as oblivion, postulating the existence of "afterlife." Such a story is undoubtedly a psychologically and socially appealing consolation. Indeed, some would endorse any method of (presumed) self-delusion as virtuous (Beyleveld and Brownsword, 2001). But the possible existence of an afterlife does not in itself provide an answer to the question of how long a good life would be (Mellon, 2004).

Others may want death as a tool. In some instances, the intrinsic badness of death has to be measured against the acute and prolonged badness of a life experience (such as torture or profound misery), to the point where the negative of death might be overridden by a predilection for nonliving. Here, discussants are reminded that even extreme LE scenarios do not deny the option of voluntary death.

Other proponents for "death as tool" would use death to make a point or to give meaning to their life (Jonas, 1992; Kass, 2001; Williams, 1973). According to this account, death is good precisely because it provides a counterpoint against which to perceive the goodness of life: "So long as there is any such thing as death, human beings can be great" (Goodman, 1981). Purely from an aesthetic point of view, one might have some sympathy with finding nobility in struggle. But the argument fails within its own aesthetics. "Death" can prevail Sartre's (1958/1989) "nothingness" —the cessation of possibility. Possibilities "die" even where life goes on. Extended life, even immortality, is not synonymous with omnipotence. If biological death were postponed and abolished, nothingness would still prevail. Hopes and expectations could still be crushed, and in the face of this, human beings could still be "great" within this theory of aesthetics.

Aging and Disease

"Age" as a cause of death will rarely be found in mortality statistics (Hayflick, 2002). Barring accidents, most people in developed nations currently die of vascular complications or cancer (National Vital Statistics Reports, 2006), conditions intricately linked with cellular aging (Fossel, 2004) that fit the common definition of disease. Still, some would object to classifying aging as disease, viewing aging as ubiquitous and natural. It has been argued in response that, since senescence is now thought of as an evolutionary by-product rather than an end it itself (Rose, 2004), the stochastic quality of death by aging defies its presumed "naturalness" (Caplan, 2005). For good reasons, gerontology is moving away from a juxtaposition of aging and disease toward a discussion of age-associated pathology (Blumenthal, 2003; Norm, 2004; Sames, 2005).

Moreover being a common occurrence or "naturalness" is difficult to take as a serious argument against treatment. A person who is dying of cancer might not care whether the malignancy was triggered, hastened, or caused by a genetic disposition, a mutation, infection, an aberrant stem cell, immune system failure, oxidative stress, pollutants, radiation, or any combination of age-related factors. The question of whether curing cancer in the young is morally desirable whereas curing cancer in the aged is inappropriate shifts the issue of whether aging is a disease from science to politics. In this arena, "Should we consider aging a disease?" is essentially asking "Should aging be cured?" (Murphy, 1986).

Immortality

Another question is whether aging is not inevitable. Does not the second law of thermodynamics dictate that everything must deteriorate (Berry, 1995)? Yet by healing a wound, shedding skin cells, sipping a drink, taking a breath, we are constantly denying organismal death. The second law only spells doom in a closed system. Those wishing to preserve life do not have to remove the subject from aging, not even to understand all reasons for the aging process: NLE can allow deterioration to occur as long as it can be reversed. This formulates the inevitability of aging not as a philosophical but as an engineering question (Aubrey et al., 2002).

Yet, surely, everything has to die? The invocation of "immortality" is controversial, even among proponents of NLE (Best, 2004). Even if aging and disease were eliminated, death would still be an option—not least considering the human tendency to desire the demise of others. But are moral implications of LE really contingent on such questions as whether the universe itself is "mortal" (Crane, 1994; Dyson, 1979; Tipler, 1995)? In the present context, we focus on NLE, not as potential immortality, but as the feasibility of nonmortality: the notion that death may lose its sting merely by losing its semblance of preordained, reasonably foreseeable imminence.

INDIVIDUAL CONCERNS

Frailty & Stagnation

Harking to stories like the classic Tithonus or Gulliver's Struldbruggs, some accounts imagine NLE as an extension of old age and increasing frailty. Francis Fukuyama (2002), for example, envisages a geriatric society occupied with the perpetuation of decrepitude. Many gerontologists would claim that "compression of morbidity" (Fries, 1983) rather than LE is the practical aim of their studies. Yet, at least in the context of NLE, those therapies which will have any noticeable effect on life span are very unlikely to act at the stage where system failure is imminent (DeGrey, 2005).

Other individualistic arguments draw on the (often implicit) hypothesis that the human brain is not equipped to deal with vastly extended life spans. At a more trivial level, this might be a fear of boredom, which assumes that patterns of experience will inevitably repeat *and* that there are no "repeatable pleasures" (Fischer, 1994) (i.e., that the human ability to derive satisfaction from experience always diminishes in repetition). This is speculation which those seeking an extended life are probably entitled to dismiss with some glee. In fact, it might well be the case that humanity will undergo a selection where those who can experience joy from ongoing discovery will choose to live substantially longer compared to other character types.

The somewhat cynical question of boredom alludes to a more serious issue in the longevity of the mind. It is common experience that personalities are essentially formed during childhood, whereas adults are often very set in their ways. This could mean that ubiquitous long life leads to an altogether less flexible and dynamic society, where the majority are less willing to change their outlook and convictions, new culture and technology stifled, and strife and inefficiency perpetuated. There are good reasons to believe that some, if not the majority, of our decreasing ability to learn and adapt as we age is an artefact of brain aging and will thus be subject to remedy of advanced NLE treatments. Still, those who have spent a lifetime developing a theory, following a creed, or hating an enemy are presumably less likely to change their mind than those younger and less encumbered by their past. Yet the problem of such ossification is not confined to future technology. Similar considerations have inspired legislators to limit the term any one individual can spend in a position of power. To fear, for example, that LE would benefit dictators (Ungar, 2000) is to take a very resigned view about our moral responsibility to effect social change proactively.

Identity

Interestingly, the other main sceptical argument from a psychophilosophical perspective relies on exactly the opposite hypothesis: According to this view, long life might be problematic, not because we change too little, but because we change too much and lose our identity in the process of getting older. A person might change so completely over time that this change would amount to the death of the original (Lewis, 1976; Perrett, 1986) and thus be ultimately undesirable or at least futile (Glannon, 2000a,b,c,). "Such a life would be like a book, where a later chapter is completely unrelated to an earlier one, which is contrary to the idea of a continuing narrative." This might be puzzling if one assumes that identity is a process, not a permanent fixture. To stick with the metaphor, the book may not be a disappointing narrative as long as it is read from beginning to end which is after all the fashion in which we experience life (Harris, 1987). Changing identity is not a process to which we usually object. On the contrary, we value such capacity for change, the ability to reconsider, broaden, and adjust knowledge, dispositions, and character traits.

SOCIAL CONCERNS

Overpopulation

In popular discourse, overpopulation is seen as the root of many environmental problems and societal ills (Ehrlich, 1968). But it can be observed that as a nation reaches a certain level of affluence, the population growth rate tends to slow to replacement level or even below. Contrary to popular belief, birth rates are indeed declining not only in the Western countries but worldwide (More, 2004).

It is also not always clear why a larger population is considered morally problematic. Most concerns seem to evolve around the assumption that a great population will not be sustainable. Since Thomas Malthus raised his concerns, population has increased manifold without any decline in living standards (Trewavas, 2002). The question of population pressure is obviously defined by other characteristics than just life expectancy: Birth rates, infrastructure, availability of resources, capacity to recycle waste, space management, land use, and concepts of privacy all play a role. Some of these issues need to be considered in the context of overall technological development. As we are focusing on nanotechnology with special emphasis on "extreme" projections, one can speculate that once nanotechnology is advanced enough to significantly retard or halt aging it will also enable much better resource management, production of organic resources from nonorganic matter, energy production entirely from renewable sources, fully effective recycling, and so on, and enable the claiming of living space. Where bio-nanotechnology permits not only NLE but expansive biological reconfiguration, adapting the human body to other environments or sizes will become possible, and the vision of mind digitization coupled with advanced virtual reality might obviate issues of room altogether.

All these considerations are clearly speculative on social, technical, economic, and ecological grounds. In many respects, moral issues in environmentalism are independent from future developments in NLE. If we are currently squandering resources in a nonsustainable manner, then this problem needs to be solved independently of how long people live. Relying on death is not a very creative way to tackle such problems (More, 2004), especially considering that population-linked doomsday scenarios have generally been dispelled by human ingenuity (Boserup, 1981).

In concentrating on the underlying *moral* issues at play, we are challenged to question the relevance that these differing visions might have in the first place. If one decided that the vision of a crowed planet is too terrible to permit, what type of intervention should be adopted? Would we decline to invest in medical innovation? Withhold its use? Encourage suicide or sanction killings? In population ethics, one is precariously balancing the real interest of existing people against the hypothetical interests of those projected to be born (Parfit, 1984) and potentially also balancing a hypothetical quality of life against the imposition of an early death (Davis, 2005).

The instinct and desire to procreate are strong in many. This may be due to evolutionary reasons but also to a conscious decision to defy death by trying to perpetuate something of oneself—which indicates that such desires might be less strong in "immortals" (Perry, 2000). Some suggest a scheme where those who have become "immortalized" could agree not to reproduce (Harris, 2000). Apart from enforceability, one could regard this arrangement as troubling where it might lead to social stagnation as discussed above, but this should be a problem which future societies can work out.

Such an array of uncertainties surrounds potential population pressures and NLE that it seems presumptuous to preclude today the moral decisions that are the concern, privilege, and responsibility only of future societies.

Social Justice

Another common ethical concern often is grounded in various concepts of social justice. At its most basic, the argument would not attack LE as such but would claim that we should not currently be researching such technology while resources could be used directly to extend life of the less fortunate. A broader discussion about spheres of responsibility is clearly beyond the scope of this essay. I may merely point out that even though we already live in a world where some are allotted almost twice the life expectancy of others, few would argue that the best reform could be found in a policy that would significantly reduce life expectancy in developed nations.

A related prevalent concern is that advanced NLE will only be available to the rich. Will NLE always remain the privilege of a select few or will the rising tide lift all boats? Some suggest that as nanotechnology is subject to "accelerating returns" (Kurzweil, 2005), potentially high prices for early adopters (Platt, 1998) will rapidly decline. If we assume for the sake of argument that NLE will always be costly, it still remains questionable whether the purported detriments to wider humanity (e.g., resource depletion, envy) will be so egregious as to require "collective suttee" (Davis, 2004). Also, "we do not normally think it an ethical requirement to prevent good being done to some unless and until it can be done to all" (Harris, 2002). In transplantation medicine, for example, the availability of organs is a very real factor of LE: Those lucky enough to be allotted an organ survive much longer. Generally, society has been able to agree on laws that regulate the allocation of these special resources. We have not chosen to destroy all organs as they become available in order to preserve equality in despair. Similarly, if LE treatments would turn out to be irrevocably scarce, this must not mean that only the ability to pay will be decisive. Treatment could be allotted randomly (Broome, 1984), as a social reward (Vance, 1956), according to imminent need (Harris, 1987), within a general utilitarian framework (Miller and Sethe, 2005), or even as "affirmative prolongevitism" (Overall, 2003). There is no intrinsic reason why such arrangements must be morally flawed if instituted in a society that can agree on an equitable system of apportionment.

NANOTECHNOLOGY AND LIFE EXTENSION

Medicine at Nanoscale

The most obvious link between nanotechnology and LE is its prospective use in the medical field. In a sense, modern medicine has operated at the nanoscale at least since Paul Ehrlich proposed his "magic bullet" of chemotherapy. Then, as now, the ability to perceive small structures has proven key. In this context, the current vogue of giving advanced chemistry the "nano-" label is not always helpful, but such semantics should not detract from the observation that an increasing ability to operate at the nanoscale will lead to more powerful tools to save and extend lives (Connolly, 2002).

As argued above, aging and death cannot be reduced to purely intrinsic biological processes. This highlights that LE interventions can be of nonmedical origin. As chemistry, nanoscience already contributed to the green revolution and to the invention of life-saving materials as mundane as seatbelts and hardhats. If nanotechnology lives up to its promise, we can anticipate methods to reduce and cleanse pollution, better forensics to deter violent crime, safer houses and vehicles, enhanced emergency response systems and security, and so on. Thus NLE may occur irrespective of nanomedicine.

Nanorobotics

The bolder projections of nanotechnology envisage nanorobotics: machines operating at a molecular level. In medicine, early versions of such machines could assist with more accurate diagnosis and consistent drug delivery. More advanced nanobots could be tasked with cell-like activities. The ultimate aim of medical nanorobotics, however, is to construct general-purpose cell repair machines (Freitas, 1999). Molecular machines holding onboard computers could be instructed to perform specific repair functions with great precision in complete synergy. Although such machines might also present a problem of waste heat (Phoenix, 2001), it is assumed that at this stage of technological accomplishment humans would be largely immune to disease and minor wear and tear, including aging (Freitas, 2004).

From a moral perspective, if we do reach the stage where sophisticated molecular machines regularly assist, repair, and maintain our system, how much will we come to depend on such machines and how much will their function change us? With such advanced technology, it will be very difficult to distinguish between medical assistance and superhuman enhancements. For example will a person taking nourishment directly from photosynthesis be *morally* changed? Medical nanomachines will presumably be in need of regular upgrades and maintenance: Will this involve greater dependency of consumers to a few powerful providers? Such communication systems could be susceptible to third-party signals. Will we all need to maintain "firewalls" to protect our inner software and how would that change us?

Cryonics

Probably the most efficient known way to ward off any deterioration of the body is studied and applied in cryonics: lowering the body temperature to a point where biological decay is no longer possible (Ettinger, 1964). The obvious problem is that no procedure is known for reversing the stasis and bringing the body back to personhood. Not only must future (Shermer, 2001) technology be capable of reversing the initial damage or illness, it must also repair the damage caused by the stasis procedure itself and restore consciousness to the patient. Views differ widely about how realistic it is that future nanotechnology will be able to perform these functions (Darwin, 1991; Merkle, 1992; Shermer, 2001). As an example, debates persisted for many years whether the damages caused by ice crystallization during the freezing process could ever be repaired (Drexler, 1981; Fahy, 1991). [Recent technological advances mean that ice crystal formation can now be largely eliminated with advanced procedures (Lemler et al., 2004; Pichugin et al., 2006).]

Cryonics is one prominent illustration of the moral difficulties in establishing protocols today that need to anticipate a nanotechnology of the future. Such is obviously a highly speculative enterprise, and thus cryonics is only applied where it is considered a method of last resort: as an alternative to burial for those declared legally dead. Nonetheless, a host of ethical challenges arise: For example, there is a clear moral obligation on those who stand to profit from cryonic arrangements not to misrepresent the (arguably) rather remote chance of success (a responsibility that, in this author's impression, the two primary cryonic providers currently appear to meet). In light of the above discussion, we can recall that death is a matter of technical capacity (Whetstine et al., 2005). Those placed in cryostasis are, by current standards of technology, irrevocably incapable of acting as autonomous persons. This does not, however, preclude a special moral status for these bodies in stasis, especially if the technology to revive them does indeed become available (Hughes, 2001).

In fact, if resuscitation by nanotechnological means becomes an imminent but not yet reliable possibility (analogous to the situation in current stem cell or gene therapy), will there be a moral obligation to cryopreserve the terminally ill or at least to maintain those already in stasis (Halperin, 1996)? Conversely, who will make the decision to give up the experiment or to attempt resuscitation? Should it ever succeed, will a nanotechnologically reconfigured being be considered the same as the cryopreserved body from which it was derived?

Conversion of Embodiment

This latter question is not confined to cryonics. Among the most radical scenarios for NLE is the conversion of a person's state of biological embodiment into a state that is entirely different in kind. The most popular projection in this context is that the core elements of what constitutes a person (e.g., personality, memory, thought patterns) can be abstracted from their biological basis and be expressed faithfully by other (probably digital) means, thereby transferring personhood to another expression substrate. In the context of nanotechnology, it is speculated that scanning a person's brain at the molecular or atomic level will enable construction of a digital model of that person's consciousness (Kurzweil, 2005). Such a model could be converted into a new physical embodiment or even function as a digital consciousness.

If we can simulate brain function to such a degree that the simulation claims to be self-aware, what moral and legal rights will this nanotechnologically derived entity have? Can we pause, alter, or delete it the way we do with other programs (Rothblatt et al., 2005)? Will it be entitled to other "natural" rights such as autonomy, dignity, privacy?

If we assume that the entity thus modeled is a valid continuation of the original, then such a process would be a drastic step in LE toward a semblance of immortality. Once it is possible to render a faithful copy of a person into information, it is also possible to distribute that information over networks or to keep multiple "backups." What will we make of those who will seek to gain immortality by producing vast numbers of themselves? More complex still, what is the moral status of nanotechnologically codependent, cosentient, and otherwise connected identities (Milburn, 2005; Sandberg, 2001)?

CONCLUSION

If this brief overview of issues in NLE can but convey one idea, it ought to be that the oldest story of humanity will be rewritten in a nanotechnology age. In moral philosophy, it can simply be a useful story to challenge assumptions and platitudes: What is it really that we fear when we talk about, for example, boredom or overpopulation? It is no less a challenge to the very foundations of philosophy: Why should we fear death? What do we mean by identity? What concept of justice are we operating?

It is also a challenge of asking the right scientific questions. We have looked at concepts of life, death, aging, and disease and concluded that drawing distinctions from commonplace assumptions does not help in identifying those points which are morally relevant. From a moral point of view, the questions of "is it alive?" and "is it dead?" are less interesting than "can it (ever) act as a person?" "Is aging a disease?" is morally less relevant than "does human flourishing require that we combat involuntary death?" For antiaging enthusiasts, the realization that there is no single driver of aging may come as a disappointment: Even with nanotechnology, there is unlikely to be an "immortality switch." It may also be viewed as a liberating—rather than to defeat aging at once, LE interventions can target deterioration at many different levels as long as they preserve the identity of the person.

Nanotechnology, by mere extrapolation of its potential abilities, presents us with deeply fundamental challenges. The practical relevance of many of these questions is rather within the realm of science fiction, but this does not mean that their contemplation is purely spurious. Epistemology, moral philosophy, and natural science have always benefited from thought experiments relying on future technology [e.g., Einstein's clock-in-the-box or the teleportation discussion on identity by Derek Parfit (1984)]. In any case, it is always the stories we tell now that shape our attitudes to the technology of the future.

If the hasty and ill-reasoned reaction to the cloning of Dolly is any guide (Wilkie and Graham, 1998), we would do well to think carefully about the implications of NLE so that when such technologies do arrive as forecast, we can refrain from reacting on instincts that were largely configured by bad science fiction storytelling.

Medical science is a story of curiosity and hope—in spite of moral confusions and anxieties, the curiosity of hope that will ultimately drive research in life extension nanotechnology.

REFERENCES

Becker, E. 1973. *The Denial of Death*. New York: Collier Macmillan.

Berry, A. 1995. *The Next 500 Years*. London: Headline Publishing.

Best, B. 2004. Some problems with immortalism. In B. J. Klein et al. (Eds.), *The Scientific Conquest of Death—Essays on Infinite Lifespans*. Argentina: LibrosEnRed, pp. 233–238.

Beyleveld, D., and Brownsword, R. 2001. *Human Dignity in Bioethics and Biolaw*. New York: Oxford University Press.

Blackford, R. 2004. Should we fear death? Epicurean and modern arguments. In B. J. Klein et al. (Eds.), *The Scientific Conquest of Death—Essays on Infinite Lifespans*. Argentina: LibrosEnRed, pp. 257–269.

Blumenthal, H. 2003. The aging–disease dichotomy: True or false? *Journal of Gerontology* 58A (2): 138–145.

Boserup, E. 1981. *Population and Technological Change: A Study of Long-Term Trends*. Chicago, IL: University of Chicago Press.

Broome, J. 1984. Selecting people randomly. *Ethics* 95: 38–55.

Caplan, A. 2005. Death as an unnatural process—Why is it wrong to seek a cure for ageing? *EMBO Reports* 6 (Special Issue): 72–75.

Connolly, P. 2002. Nanobiotechnology and life extension. In M. C. Roco and W. S. Bainbridge (Eds.), *Converging Technologies for Improving Human Performance*. Available: http://www.wtec.org/ConvergingTechnologies/, pp. 182–191.

Crane, L. 1994. Possible implications of the quantum theory of gravity. Eprint 17, February 1994. Available: http://arxiv.org/hep-th/9402104.

Darwin, M. 1991. Cold war: The conflict between cryonicists and cryobiologists. *Cryonics*, June 1991, pp. 2–8. Available: http://www.alcor.org/Library/html/coldwar.html.

Davis, J. K. 2004. Collective suttee: Is it unjust to develop life extension if it will not be possible to provide it to everyone? *Annals of the New York Academy of Sciences* 1019: 535–541.

Davis, J. K. 2005. Life-extension and the Malthusian objection. *Journal of Medicine and Philosophy* 30: 27–44.

DeGrey, A. D. N. J. 2005. Resistance to debate on how to postpone ageing is delaying progress and costing lives. *EMBO Reports* 6 (S1): S49–S53.

DeGrey, A., Ames, B., Anderson, J., Bartke, A., Campisi, J., Heward, C., McCarter, R., and Stock, G. 2002. Time to talk SENS–critiquing the immutability of human aging. In *Annals of the New York Academy of Sciences* 959: 452–462.

Drexler, K. E. 1981. Molecular engineering: An approach to the development of general capabilities for molecular manipulation. *Proceedings of the National Academy of Sciences* 78: 5275–5278.

Drexler, K. E. 1986. *Engines of Creation*. New York: Anchor.

Dyson, F. J. 1979. Time without end: Physics and biology in an open universe. *Reviews of Modern Physics* 51 (3): 447–460.

Ehrlich, P. R. 1968. *The Population Bomb*. New York: Ballantine.

Ettinger, R. C. W. 1964. *The Prospect of Immortality*. New York: Doubleday.

Fahy, G. M. 1991. Molecular repair of the brain—A scientific critique. *Cryonics* 12(2): 8–11, February.

Feynman, R. 1960. There's plenty of room at the bottom. *Engineering and Science*, February. Available: http://www.zyvex.com/nanotech/feynman.html.

Fischer, J. M. 1994. Why immortality is not so bad. *International Journal of Philosophical Studies* 2: 257–270.

Fossel, M. 2004. *Cells, Aging, and Human Disease*. New York: Oxford University Press.

Freitas, R. A. 1999. *Nanomedicine*, Volume I: *Basic Capabilities*. Landes Bioscience.

Freitas, R. A. 2004. Nanomedicine. In B. J. Klein et al. (Eds.), *The Scientific Conquest of Death—Essays on Infinite Lifespans*. Argentina: LibrosEnRed, pp. 77–91.

Fries, J. F. 1983. The compression of morbidity. *Milbank Memorial Fund Quarterly* 61: 397–419.

Fukuyama, F. 2002. *Our Posthuman Future*. New York: Farrar, Straus & Giroux.

Glannon, W. 2002a. Identity, prudential concern and extended lives. *Bioethics* 16(3): 266–283.

Glannon, W. 2002b. Reply to Harris. *Bioethics* 16(3): 292–297.

Glannon, W. 2002c. Extending human life span. *Journal of Medicine and Philosophy* 27(3): 339–354.

Goodman, L. M. 1981. *Death and the Creative Life—Conversations with Eminent Artists and Scientists as They Reflect on Life and Death*. New York: Springer Publishing, p. 81.

Gruman, G. J. 1966. A history of ideas about the prolongation of life: The evolution of prolongevity hypothesis to 1800. *Proceedings of the American Philosophical Society* 56(9): 1–102.

Halperin, J. L. 1996. *The First Immortal*. New York: Random House.

Harris, J. 1987. QALYfying the value of life. *Journal of Medical Ethics* 13: 117–123.

Harris, J. 2000. Intimations of Immortality. *Science* 288: 59.

Harris, J. 2002. Response to Glannon. *Bioethics* 16(3): 284–291.

Hayflick, L. 2002. Has anyone ever died of old age? Paper presented at the 55th Annual Scientific Meeting of the Gerontological Society of America, Boston, November 25, 2002.

Heidegger, M. 2000 (1926). *Being and Time*. Malden, MA: Blackwell.

Hughes, J. 2001. The future of death: Cryonics and the telos of liberal individualism. *Journal of Evolution and Technology* 6(1). Available: http://www.jetpress.org/volume6/death.htm.

Jonas, H. 1992. The burden and blessing of mortality. *Hastings Center Report* 22(1): 34–40.

Kamm, F. 1993. *Morality, Mortality*, Vol. I. New York: Oxford University Press.

Kass, L. 2001. L'Chaim and its limits: Why not immortality? *First Things* 113: 17–24.

Kurzweil, R. 2005. *The Singularity is Near—When Humans Transcend Biology*. London: Duckworth.

Lemler, J., Harris, S. B., Platt, C., and Huffman, T. M. 2004. The arrest of biological time as a bridge to engineered negligible senescence. *Annals of the New York Academy of Sciences* 1019: 559–563.

Levin, J. 1992. *Theories of the Self*. New York: Hemisphere.

Lewis, D. 1976. Survival and identity. In A. O. Rorty (Ed.), *The Identities of Persons*. Berkeley, CA: University of California Press, pp. 17–40.

Lucretius. 50 B.C.E. *On the Nature of Things (De Rerum Naturae)*, translated by W. E. Leonard. Available: http://classics.mit.edu/Carus/nature_things.html.

Merkle, R. C. 1992. The technical feasibility of cryonics. *Medical Hypotheses* 39(1): 6–16.

Mellon, B. F. 2004. Some ethical and theological considerations. In B. J. Klein et al. (Eds.), *The Scientific Conquest of Death—Essays on Infinite Lifespans*. Argentina: LibrosEnRed, pp. 157–167.

Milburn, C. 2005. Nano/splatter: Disintegrating the postbiological body. *New Literary History*, 36: 283–311.

Miller, J., and Sethe, S. 2005. Gods with a limited budget: Putting the utility back into utilitarian health politics. *Interdisciplinary Science Reviews* 30(3): 273–278.

More, M. 2004. Superlongevity without overpopulation. In B. J. Klein et al. (Eds.), *The Scientific Conquest of Death—Essays on Infinite Lifespans*. Argentina: LibrosEnRed, pp. 169–185.

Murphy, T. 1986. A cure for aging? *Journal of Medicine and Philosophy* 11: 237–255.

Nagel, T. 1979. *Mortal Questions*. New York: Cambridge University Press.

National Vital Statistics Reports. 2006. Vol. 54, No. 19, June 28. Available: http://www.cdc.gov/nchs/data/nvsr/nvsr54/nvsr54_19.pdf.

Norm, W. 2004. How does one define aging in relation to pathology? *Lifespan* 12: 1–9.

O'Neil, O. 1993. Ending world hunger. In T. Reagan (Ed.), *Matters of Life and Death—New Introductory Essays in Moral Philosophy*, 3rd ed. New York: McGraw-Hill, pp. 235–279.

Overall, C. 2003. *Aging, Death, and Human Longevity: A Philosophical Inquiry*. Berkeley: University of California Press.

Parfit, D. 1984. *Reasons and Persons*. New York: Clarendon.

Perrett, R. 1986. Regarding immortality. *Religious Studies* 22: 219–233.

Perry, M. 2000. *Forever For All: Moral Philosophy, Cryonics, and the Scientific Prospects for Immortality*. Boca Raton, FL: Universal Publishers.

Phoenix, C. J. 2001. Nanotechnology and life extension. In *Doctor Tandy's First Guide to Life Extension and Transhumanity*. Boca Raton, FL: Universal, pp. 75–108.

Pichugin, Y., Fahy, G. M., and Morina, R. 2006. Cryopreservation of rat hippocampal slices by vitrification. *Cryobiology* 52(2): 228–240.

Platt, C. 1998. Hamburger helpers. In *Cryonics*, pp. 13–16.

Rose, M. 2004. Biological immortality. In B. J. Klein et al. (Eds.), *The Scientific Conquest of Death—Essays on Infinite Lifespans*. Argentina: LibrosEnRed, pp. 17–28.

Rothblatt, M. et al. 2005. *Bina48 Vs. Exabit Corporation* (Fla. Md 2005). Available: http://terasemjournals.net/PC0102/bina48_01a.html.

Sames, K. 2005. Aging as consequence of organ differentiation. In K. Sames, S. Sethe, and A. Stolzing (Eds.), *Extending the Lifespan Biotechnical, Gerontological, and Social Problems*. LIT, pp. 63–80.

Sandberg, A. 2001. The Calculus of Identity. Available: http://www.aleph.se/Trans/Cultural/ Philosophy/identity.html.

Sartre, J. P. 1958/1989. *Being and Nothingness—An Essay on Phenomenological Ontology*. New York: Routledge.

Shermer, M. 2001. Nano nonsense and cryonics—True believers seek redemption from the sin of death. *Scientific American* 285(3): 29.

Tipler, F. J. 1995. *The Physics of Immortality: Modern Cosmology, God and the Resurrection of the Dead*. New York: Macmillan.

Trewavas, A. 2002. Malthus foiled again and again. *Nature* 418: 668–670.

Ungar, H. 2000. Political consequences. E-letter to *Science* in response to J. Harris, "Intimations of immortality. *Science* 288(5463): 59.

Vance, J. 1956. *To Live Forever*. New York: Ballantine.

Wachowski, A., and Wachowski, L. 1999. *The Matrix*. Groucho II Film Partnership, Silver Pictures, Village Roadshow Productions.

Whetstine, L., Streat, S., Darwin, M., and Crippen, D. 2005. Pro/con ethics debate: When is dead really dead? *Critical Care* 9: 538–542.

Wilkie, T., Graham, E. 1998. Power without responsibility: Media portrayals of Dolly and science. *Cambridge Quarterly of Healthcare Ethics* 7: 150–159.

Williams, B. 1973. The makropulos case. In B. Williams, *Problems of the Self: Philosophical Papers 1956–1972*. New York: Cambridge University Press, pp. 81–100.

INDEX

Abstraction, 342
Access to information, 32
Accountability, 318
Accuracy, in predictions, 106
Acheson-Lilienthal report, 30
Action Group on Erosion, Technology and
    Concentration (ETC), 216, 220, 228, 291
Activism, legislative, 216
Adenosine triphosphate (ATP) synthase, 74, 331
Advanced nanotechnology, 12, 109–110
Advisory bodies, 209
Advocacy, 80–81, 188, 229
Africa, 58
Age of Spiritual Machines, The (Kurzweil), 18–19,
    21, 25
Aging process, 355–356, 359, 362
Agony and the Ecstacy, The (Stone), 23
Agricultural biotechnology, 76–77
Agriculture, uncertainty and, 156
AIDS
    characterized, 62–63
    prevention strategies, 298
    treatments, 58
Air pollution, 299
Albumin, 152
Alginate, 152
Alivisatos, Paul, 81
Allhoff, Fritz, 5, 178, 186
All-optical networks, 83
Alternative fuels, 85
Altmann, Jürgen, 275
Aluminum, 270
Alvarez, Luis, 31
Amazon.com, 259
Ambient computing, 73
Ambiguity, 155, 185, 195
Ambivalence, 243–244
American Competitiveness Initiative, 84
American ISTPP National Nanotechnology Survey,
    230
Anchoring, 234–235
Anthrax, 202, 206
Antibiotics, 161

Anticapitalist movement, global, 212
Anticipatory self-defense, 128
Antidevelopment, 332
Antigens, nanoparticle exposure and, 151
Antiglobalization, 238
Antiviral medications, 52
Apocalyptic nanotechnology, 208
Apocalyptic risks, 203
Apocalyptic threats, 14, 212
Apophis, 339, 350
Applied Digital Solutions, 255
Applied (normative) epistemology, 112–113
Applied science, 77
Aquinas, St. Thomas, 181
Archimedes, 129
Arendt, Hannah, 120–121
Aristotle, 32, 181
Arms, *see* Military technology; Nuclear; Weaponry
    control, 204–207
    race, 30, 32, 110, 316
ARPANET, 102
Artificial intelligence (AI)
    background, 339–340
    characterized, 12, 14–15, 47, 72, 83, 102, 133,
        205, 210, 310, 320, 330
    corporate, 348–349
    ethics for, 346–350
    Leibniz *vs.* Martians, 340–344
    moral standards, 344–346
    research sources, 346
    rogue, 348
Artificial replicators, 53
Asbestos testing, 143
Asch, Solomon, 219
Asimov, Isaac, 210, 346–347
Assets, types of, 191
Assumptions, 112, 247, 262
Asteroids, 324, 339
Astronauts, safety equipment for, 67
Atoms
    manipulation of, 6
    -with-bonds model, 342
Attali, Jacques, 34–35

Nanoethics: The Ethical and Social Implications of Nanotechnology. Edited by Allhoff, Lin, Moor, and Weckert
Copyright © 2007 John Wiley & Sons, Inc.

Aufhebung, 126
Autointoxication, 166
Automated manufacturing, 318
Automated nanosystems, 63–64
Automated work spotting, 50
Autonomy, 187, 191–193, 260–262, 354
Aversion, 128
Avian flu, 206

Back-end databases, 254, 263
Bacteria
    genetically modified, 62
    nanomedical treatments, 163
Bacterial weapons, 202
Barbour, Ian G., 182
Baruch, Bernard, 30
Baruch Plan, 30
Base-pair sequences, 164
BASF, 6
Bayesianism, 122
Behavior-altering enhancements, 192
Behavioral therapy, 194–195
Belief system, 260, 343
Benetton, 255
Bergson, Henri, 126
Berle, Adlof, 226
Berube, David, 77, 233, 235–238
Best practices, 237
Bethe, Hans, 34
Beyond Therapy, 186–187
Biases, 113, 235
Biochemical
    markers, 73
    sensors, 293
Biocompatibility, in nanomedicine, 163
Biodefense Advanced Research and Development
        Agency (BARDA), 211
Biodefense research, 202, 206
Bioengineering, 43, 49
Bioethics, 7, 13
Bioinformatics, 161, 302
Bio-inspired nanosystems, 87
Biokleptic nanotechnology, 74
Biological, generally
    agents, 202
    evolution, 348
    health, 164
    intelligence, 46–47
    nanotechnology, 74
    sciences, 25, 144
    systems, 86–87
    weapons, 21, 33, 204, 270–271
Biological Weapons Convention (BWC), 33,
        205–206, 208

Biology, as discipline, 7
Biomarkers, 94
Biomechanical devices, 186
Biomedical
    research, funding for, 82
    systems, nanotechnology-based, 162
BioMEMs (biolgical micro-electronic mechanical
        systems), 44–45
Biomonitors, 206
Biosciences, advances in, 62
Bioshield, 211
Biosphere, 327
Biotechnological information, 205
Biotechnology
    abuse of, 51
    advances in, 47–48
    characterized, 74, 100, 200
    obstacles to, 58
    revolution, 95
    self-replicating, 43, 51
Bioterrorism, 42–43, 52
Bioweapons, 202, 205–206. *See also* Biological,
        weapons
Birth control, 187
Blackbox software, 210
Blindness, 168
Blocked exchanges, 259
Blood-brain barrier, 151
Blood transfusions, 187
Blue goo, 51
Bluetooth, 254
Bochlert, Sherwood, 231
Bombs
    atomic, 29–30, 111, 328
    dirty, 270
    hydrogen, 30
Borg (*Star Trek*), 21, 27
Bostrom, Nick, 169
Botnets, 348
Bottom-up approach, 120
Boycotts, 228–229
Brain, generally
    development, influential factors,
        194
    function, *see* Brain function
    implants, 45
    -machine interfaces, 149
    playing God with, 178–180
    science, 333
    stimulation, 185
Brain function
    blood-brain barrier, 151
    nanoaugmentation of, 177
Brand loyalty, 229

Brave New World totalitarianism, 41
Broadcast architecture, 50, 53–54
Bronze Age, 268
BSE, 155, 242
Buckminsterfullerene, 82
Budgets/budgeting, 228, 231, 294
Bulk technology, 73, 267–268
Bulletin of the Atomic Scientists, 30–31
Bureaucracy, 236, 248
Burkitt's lymphoma, 166
Bush, George W., 83
Bush Administration, 205, 207, 211, 238
Business trends, 98

Camouflaged Long Endurance Nano Sensors
    (CLENS), 255
Cancer, 62–63, 83, 94, 163, 166, 330, 355
Capitalism, 317
Carbon, generally
    characterized, 163, 319
    dioxide, 65, 331
    nanotubes, 11, 63, 65, 67–68, 81, 299, 301, 323
Career development, 281–282
Carnivore (FBI), 50–51
CASPIAN, 255
Catalysis, 293
Catastrophes, 128–129, 138, 142
Catastrophic risks, 211
Categorical statements, 139
Causal effects, 127
Causal production, 129
Cause-and-effect relationships, 135, 138
Celestial mechanics, 344
Cell phones, 60, 65
Cellular replacement, 163–164
Center for Nanotechnology in Society, 227, 237
Center for Responsible Nanotechnology (CRN), 232
Chaos theory, 24, 122–123
Chemical accidents, 232
Chemical industry, 77, 299
Chemical weapons, 21, 33, 204, 270–271
Chemical Weapons Convention (CWC), 33
Chemistry, as discipline, 7
China, 71, 86, 292, 299–301
Chip production, 293
Chitosan, 152
Chromallocytes, 164
Chromosome replacement therapy, 164
Church, George, 208
Cisco, 98
Citizen Cyborg (Hughes), 188
Clarke, Arthur C., 31
Clean energy, 58–61, 85–86
Clean water, 58, 61–62, 83

Clearinghouses, 236
Climate changes, impact of, 59, 76, 86, 206
Clinton, President Bill, 8, 80–82
Clinton Administration, 202
Cloning
    attack, 247
    impact of, 25, 33, 362
Closed innovation, 98
Closure condition, 127–128, 130
Coal, 331
Coatings, 140, 153, 293, 297, 301
Code of ethical conduct, 34
Codex Alimentarius, 206–207
Cognition, 113
Cognitive, generally
    architecture, 343–346
    augmentation, 174
    disabilities, 189
    enhancement, 113
    therapy, 194–195
Cold War, 33, 212, 272
Collagen, 152
Collingridge dilemma, 253
Colloid science, 73
Colvin, Vicki, 234
Commercialism, 28
Commercialization, 58
Commercial system, institutional ethics, 314–315,
    317–318
Communication networks, 65–66
Communications technologies, 85
Communism, 315, 317, 327
Comparative advantage, 349
Compassion, 35
Competition, fairness in, 190–191
Competitiveness
    economic, 109
    national, 107–108, 111
Complex systems, unpredictability and, 156–157
Complexity
    impact of, 14, 19, 24, 35, 107
    self-organization and, 119–120
    unchaining, 120–121
Compliance, 34
Comprehensive Test Ban Treaty, 33
Compton, Arthur, 204
Computational theory of mind (CTM), 341–342
Computer(s), generally
    ethics, 7
    networks, 254
    scientists, functions of, 18
    technology, benefits of, 314
    viruses, 42, 51, 330
Conditional statements, 139

Conditioning, 166
Confabulation, 349
Conflict resolution, 170
Conformity, 219–220
Consciousness, 175, 186, 343, 361
Consensus conference, 243
Consequentialism, 124, 217
Conservation, environmental, 64
Conservatism, 111–112
Consumer culture, 229
Contactless technology, 255
Contamination
    adsorption of, 152
    cross-, 260
    detection, 65
Control, significance of, 32–33
Copyrights, 207
Corporate governance, stakeholder theory, 229
Cost-benefit analysis, 12, 122, 133, 137, 223
Counterfactual propositions, 126
Counterpublic, 230
Critiques, radical, 112
Cross-contamination, informational, 260
Crow, Michael, 103–105
Cryonics, 360–361
Cultivation processes, 107, 156
Cultural evolution, 345–346
Curie, Marie, 110–111
Cybernetics, 119, 121
Cytochromes, 331
Cytotoxicity, 151

d'Aquili, Eugene, 175
Dalmo, Roy, 151
Darwin Among the Machines (Dyson), 24–25
Data protection, 256, 258, 261
Day After Trinity, The, (Dyson), 30
Deane-Drummond, Celia E., 181
Death
    causes of, 164
    perceptions of, 354–355
    premature, 217
Debates
    anti-nanotechnology, 217
    on future, 17–36
    human enhancements, 186, 188, 195
    nanotechnology *vs.* nanoethics, 3–15
    nuclear technology, 271
    philosophy, 217
    societal implications, 40–54
    types of, 71–77
Decentralization, 10
Dechronification, 164

Decision-making process
    deliberative democracy, 218, 222
    influential factors, 153, 178, 192, 238
Decision theory, 122
Decision tree, 127
Decryption systems, 53
Defense Advanced Research Project Agency
    (DARPA)
    ARPANET, 102
    research and development (R&D), 211
    ULTRA Electronics Program, 81
Defensive technologies, 43, 47–48, 51–54
Deficit model, 76
Deliberations, 113–114
Deliberative democracy
    characterized, 200, 215–216, 222–223
    provisionality, 220–222
    reflective preferences, 221–222
    as second-order social theory, 216–220, 222–223
Democracy
    deliberative, *see* Deliberative democracy
    experiments in, *see* Experiments in democracy
    public engagement software, 247–249
Democratic societies, 209
Democratic values, 188–189
Dengue, 211
Deontology, 124
Department of Defense (DoD), 45
Dependency theory, 295
Depression, 165, 192
Desalination, 62, 86
Descriptive scientists, 87
Desertification, 59
Design, value-sensitive, 256, 263–264
Destructive nanotechnology, 51, 53
Deterministic
    chaos, 122–123
    view, 77
Developed countries, 76
Developed world
    characterized, 61, 64
    developing world *vs.*, 189–190
Developing countries
    AIDS prevention needs, 298
    characterized, 71, 86
    defined, 292
    dependency theory, 295
    intellectual property rights (IPR), 301–303
    materials demands, changes in, 298–301
    solar energy needs, 297
    technological advances, impact on, 294–296,
        303–304
    water purification needs, 296–297

Diagnostic devices, 73
Diamond, 324
Diamond Age, The (Stephenson), 94
Diamond mechanosynthesis (DMS), 163, 331
Diamondoid products, 163, 323–324
Digital Applications, 256
Dignity, 13
Direct stakeholder, 226
Disclosure legislation, 302
Disease(s)
  BSE, 155, 242
  defined, 164–167
  in developing countries, 86
  idealism, 166
  functional failure, 166–167
  infectious, 62–64, 206, 211, 313
  infectious agency, 166
  life extension and, 355–356, 362
  monogenetic, 215
  nominalism, 165
  outbreak controls, 152
  realism, 166
  relativism, 165
  sociocultural, 165
  statistical, 165
  treatment of, 163–164
  tropical, 59, 63, 139, 211
  vascular, 215
  volitional normal model of, 167–170
  water purification and, 296
Distributional politics, 189
DNA
  computing, 271
  sequences, 63, 73, 301–302
  synthesis, 208–209
Documentaries, 237–238
Dodd, Merrick, 226
Dominance, 259
Doomsday clock, 30–31
Downstream public engagement, 242
Drapetomania, 165
Drexler, Eric, 7, 11, 26–27, 31, 41, 50, 72–74,
    93–94, 140, 293, 323, 353
Drinking water, 217, 296. *See also* Clean water;
    Water
Drucker, Peter, 91–92, 94–95
Drug(s)
  delivery, 73, 152, 293
  discovery, 66, 139
  nanoparticle applications, 152
  performance-enhancing, 189–190
  psychoactive, 189
Dualism, 176

Duality, 42
Dual-use technologies, 204–211
Dupuy, Jean–Pierre, 125, 128, 130
Dysentery, 62
Dyson, Freeman, 29–30
Dyson, George, 24–25
Dystopia, 19–20

Easterbrook, Gregg, 25
Eavesdropping, electronic, 209
Ebola, 62, 202, 206
Economic
  disparities, 57
  worth, 191
Economics, human enhancement and, 188–191
Education, nanotechnology-related, 8. *See also*
    Educational reform
Educational institutions, research universities, 84
Educational reform
  challenges to, 283–288
  curriculum, 284–285
  epistemological concerns, 288
  high school level, 278–280, 288
  middle school level, 279–280, 288
  nanoscience education initiatives, 280–283
  need for, 277–279, 288–289
  teacher preparation, 287
  teacher support materials, 286–287
  team teaching, 285–286
EHS impacts, 11, 14
Einstein, Albert, 211–212
Electricity, 59–61, 269, 297, 331
Electrodes, 301
Electrodynamics, 92
Electromagentic pulse (EMP), 271
Electromagnets, 215
Electronics/electronic equipment, 60–61, 299–300
Eliza/Eliza effect, 341
Email, surveillance of, 50–51
Emergency response
  systems, 359
  teams, 270
Emerging industries, 303
Emerging supertechnologies, 212
Emerging technologies, 204, 206–208, 210, 280
Encryption, 53
Energy
  alternative sources of, 85, 102
  conservation, 332
  consumption, global, 64, 85
  conversion devices, 74
  sources, 205
Engines of Creation (Drexler), 26–27, 31, 72, 353

Enhancement Technologies Group, 174
Enlightened doomsaying, 130
Enlightenment model, 103, 111
Enough (McKibben), 76
Environmental, generally
  degradation, 64
  healing, 58, 64–65
  impact, 77
  movement, 75
  pollution, 294
  preservation, 58, 64–65
Environmental Defense (ED), 232
Environmental, health, and safety (EHS) risks, 9, 11, 14
Environmental Protection Agency (EPA)
  functions off, 85, 87, 227
  Toxic Advisory Committee, 232
Epistemic uncertainty, 122
Epistemological problems, 112–113
Epistemology, 362
Epstein-Barr virus, 166
Error theory, 346
Erysipelas, 166
Eschatological ethics, 182
Essential unpredictability, 123
Eternity, 35
Ethical, generally
  constraints, 114
  legal, and social implications (ELSIs), 43, 54, 102, 112
  legal, and societal issues related to nanotechnology (NELSIs), 102, 112
  standards, 52–53
Ethics
  Christian approach to, 174
  development of, 345–346
  of the future, 124–125, 130
  institutional, 314
  for machines, 346–350
  public participation, 157–158
  significance of, 32
Ethics for the New Millenium (Dalai Lama), 35
European Commission, 230, 278
European investment, 97
European Union (EU), 207, 230, 255, 257
Eutrophication, 76
Evolution/evolution theory, 24–25, 52, 344
Evolutionary nanotechnologies, 72–73, 75
Excessive scientific technologies, 72
Existentialism, 354
Expectation, self-fulfilling, 129
Experience beamers, 46
Experiments in democracy

Nanokutaurirana (Zimbabwe), 245–247
Natural History Museum, behind the scenes of, 243–244
People's Inquiry, 241, 244–245
Explosives, 270
Exponential manufacturing, *see* Molecular manufacturing

Fabric treatments, 73, 85
Faraday cage, 264
Farm industry/farmers, 65
Fear, sources of, 36, 228, 362
Federal Emergency Management Agency (FEMA), 327
Felten, Ed, 263
Fermi paradox, 326
Fertilizers, 76
Feynman, Richard, 7, 26, 72, 80–82, 119, 353
Filter(s)
  bacterial, 86
  clean water, 62
  polluted waters, 65
  viral, 86
  water purification systems, 296–297
Firefighting equipment, 270
First-order theories, 217, 223
Fixed point, 127
Food containers, 140
Forecasts, accuracy of, 12
Foreign government investments, 84–85
Foresight Guidelines for Responsible Nanotechnology Development, 58
Foresight Nanotechnology Institute (FNI), 27, 50, 53, 58, 68, 232
Forest degradation, 64
Fossil fuels, 76, 85, 331
Frailty, 356–357
Framing, 332
Fraternités (Attali), 34–35
Free market, 315
Freedom, 191–193
Free subjects theory, 191
Free will, 124–126, 343
Freitas, Robert, 44–45, 208
Frenzy phase, revolution patterns, 95
Friends of the Earth (FOE), 228, 232
Fuel cell technology, 60, 293
Fukuyama, Francis, 356
Fullerenes, 152
Full-immersion visual-auditory environments, 46
Functional magnetic resonance imaging (fMRI), 328
Funding
  allocation of, 106

impact of, 81, 84
importance of, 10
military, 96–97
need for, 75, 86
research and development (R&D), 294
sources of, 68, 81–82, 84–85, 95, 102, 228
Fungi, nanomedical treatments, 163
Future technology, perceptions of, 48
Futurists, 126

Gaia, 332
Galaxies, collision of, 31
Gas engines, efficiency of, 74
Gates, Bill, 138–139
Gelatin, 152
Gell-Mann, Murray, 24
Gene(s), *see* Genetic, generally
    coding, 74
    delivery, 215, 219
    encoding, 87
    expression analysis, 152, 157, 164
    sequences, 63
    therapy, 52, 202, 215, 217, 222, 361
Generalists, 35
General-purpose
    exponential molecular manufacturing, 312,
        316
    molecular manufacturing, generally, 312,
        319
    technologies, 81
Genetic(s), generally
    code, 180
    disorders, 63
    engineering, *see* Genetic engineering
    modification, 25, 43–44, 156, 236, 249, 301
    significance of, 47
Genetic engineering
    characterized, 18, 21, 25–26, 83, 149, 205, 210,
        293
    control of, 33
    self-replication, 33
    shields from, 31–32
Genetically modified (GM) crops/foods, 25, 156,
    236
Genetically modified organisms (GMOs), 43–44
Genetics, nanotechnology, and robotics (GNR)
    technologies, 21–22, 27–28, 32, 34
Geneva Conventions, 274–275
Genocide, 273
Genocide Convention, 207
Genomes, 164
Genomics, 161
Geocentrism, 344

Georgia Institute of Technology, Center for
    Biologically Inspired Designs (CBID), 7
German Federal Ministry of Education and
    Research, 278
Germany, educational reform, 278
Gillette, 255
Global, generally
    capitalism, 28
    energy crisis, 92
    energy needs, clean solutions for, *see* Clean
        energy
    governance, 108
    intelligence, 209
    positioning systems (GPSs), 141
    public good, 109
    trade, 12
    warming, 102, 142–143, 237
Globalization, 228, 232
God, in nanoethics, 173, 177–181
GolineHarris, 230
Good life models, 333–334
Governance, *see* Science and technology (S&T)
        governance
    anticipatory, 189, 195
    strategic, 227
Government
    interaction with science, 75–76
    research and funding, 68
    totalitarian, 141
Governmental organizations, 10
Grants, sources of, 87
Grassroots organizations, 102
Gray goo, 51, 75, 140–143, 199, 203, 320
Great revolutions, 92–93
Greenhouse gas pollution, 65
Greenpeace, 137, 242
Green revolution, 92
Groundwater, contaminated, 83
Group polarization, 219
Guardian system, institutional ethics, 314–315,
    317
Gubrud, Mark, 271–272
Guston, David, 196
Gutenberg, Johann, 101
Guttentag, Otto, 169

Hall, J. Storrs, 324, 330, 340
Happiness, perceptions of, 35
Harm
    information-based, 257–258
    precautionary principle, 134, 136–137, 144,
        153–154
    risk of, 220

Hasslacher, Brosl, 24, 26–27
Have Spacesuit Will Travel (Heinlein), 22
Hazard, uncertainty and, 155
Health/health care advances, 58, 62–64, 73, 85
Heart disease, 163
Herbert, Frank, 21
Herzfeld, Noreen, 176–177
Heuristics, 113, 234–235, 343–344, 348
Hillis, Danny, 20–21, 24
Hiroshima, 29–30, 111
HIV infection, 62–63, 202, 211, 298
Holism, 176
Holland, 256
Homeland defense, 270–271
Homeland security, 85, 254
Hughes, James, 187–188
Human development index (HDI), 292, 295
Human enhancement
  autonomy of freedom, 191–193, 195
  impact of, 8, 10–11, 13–14, 103, 320–321
  pluralism, 193–195
  political-economical considerations, 189–191
  political frame, 188–189, 195
  religion *vs.* science frame, 186–188, 195
  types of, 185
Human-equivalent processing power (HEPP), 340, 347
Human genome, 12–13, 164
Human Genome Project, 43, 102, 173
Humanitarianism, 11
Humanity's challenges, types of, 58
Human-made systems, 29
Human nature
  in antiessentialist postmodern culture, 177
  changing, 181
  nature of, 174–176
  playing God with, 180–181
Human-scale engineering, 74
Hume, David, 223, 325
Hunter-gatherers, 101
Hurd, Paul DeHart, 286
Hydrocarbon fuels, 59–60
Hydrogen
  economy, 77
  fuel, 299
  production, 60
Hydrolysis, 152
Hypercholesterolemia, 165
Hypothetical risk, 122

IBM, 81
Idea transportation, 98
Identification, moral, *see* Moral identification
Identity

cards, 193
  importance of, 13, 357
  theft, 257–258
Immigration, 256
Immortality, 8–9, 12, 18, 21, 25, 34–35, 175–177, 356, 361
Immune system, influential factors, 50, 52, 87, 151
Imperative of Responsibility, The (Jonas), 124
Incompressibility, 123
Indeterminacy, 155
India, 71
Indirect stakeholder, 226
Indoctrination, 194
Industrial Revolution, 23, 92, 96–98, 295
Industry Initiatives for Science and Math Education (IISME), 286–287
Infectious agency, 166
Influenza/influenza virus, 202, 209
Information, generally
  markets, 113
  processing, 52
  revolution, 95
  science, 99
  self-willed, 208
  sharing, 83, 314
  technologies, *see* Information technology
Informational system, 314–315, 317–318
Information technology
  accessibility of, 58, 65–66
  advances in, 23–24
  characterized, 85, 102, 113, 210, 263
Informed consent, 257
Initiatives, sources of, 103
Innovation
  artificial intelligence, 350
  impact of, 249, 303, 327
  institutional, 113
  knowledge-based, 188–189
  merging, 99
  types of, 23, 73, 98
Installation period, revolution patterns, 95
Institute of Molecular Manufacturing, 310
Institutional investors, 87
Intel, 86, 96, 98
Intellectual property, 11, 77, 210. *See also* Intellectual property rights (IPR)
Intellectual wealth, 236
Intelligence
  artificial, *see* Artificial intelligence
  expansion, 173–174
  self-willed, 203, 206, 210
Intelligent computer systems, 141
Interdependency, 35
Intermediate duties, 142

International Atomic Energy Agency (IAEA), 199,
205, 207–208
International Center for Technology Assessment,
232
International Council on Nanotechnology, 228, 232,
237
International Risk Governance Council, 228, 232
International Space Station, 329
*International Statistical Classification of Diseases
and Related Health Problems, The,* 194
Internet
access to, 65–66
historical perspectives, 102
impact of, 51, 92, 254
privacy issues, 258
Internships, 286
Intertwined technologies, 49
Intuition, 123, 169, 181, 344, 348
Invisibility, 262–263
Invisibility cloak, 13
Iran, 205, 207
Iraq War, 212
Irrationality, 327
Irreversibility, precautionary principle, 136
Irrigation revolution, 95
I, Robot (Asimov), 22
Islamic fundamentalists, 212

Jackson, Richard, 243
Jacobs, Jane, 314
Japan, 97, 256, 278
Java, 23, 26, 34
Jini, 23, 26, 34
Jonas, Hans, 124, 126
Jones, Richard, 7, 244
Jouvenel, Bertrand de, 125
Joy, Bill, 14, 17–38, 41, 46, 50–51, 82–83, 89, 137,
199, 201–203, 209
Judgment(s), 113, 157, 193, 222, 234–235, 237,
260
Justice as fairness, 191

Kaczynski, Theodore, (Unabomber), 19, 21, 49–50
Kagan, Shelly, 333
Kalil, Thomas, 82
Kass, Leon, 181
Kauffman, Stuart, 24, 27–28
Kazman, Sam, 330
Kelly, Kevin, 121
Keynes, John Maynard, 122
Khartoum, 207
Kirkpatrick, Kelly, 83
Knight, Frank, 122
Knowledge

access to, 32, 202
-based technologies, 188–189
economy, 303
-enabled mass destruction (KMD), 22
gaps, 86
production, 77
Known risk, 122
Konarka Technologies, 60–61
Kordzik, Kelly, 234
Kraj cik, Joseph, 284–286
Krebs cycle, 331
Kurzweil, Ray, 14, 17–18, 31, 35, 38–54, 203, 209,
340

Lab-on-a-chip, 62, 86
Land use, 358
Law enforcement, 270
Law making, deliberative democracy and, 216,
222–223. *See also* Legislation
Lawrence Livermore National Laboratories, 62
Learning, *see* Education; Educational reform
process, 166
sciences, 282
Legal standards, 52
Legislation
Bayh-Dole Act of 1980, 302
data protection, 256–258, 261
nanomedicine issues, 170
Nuclear Non-Proliferation Treaty (NPT),
205
Price-Anderson Act, 211
Toxic Substances Control Act, 84
21st Century Nanotechnology Research and
Development Act, 83, 227
Legislative activism, 200
Leslie, John, 31
Level uncertainty, 156
Life, generally
expectancy, 41
extension, *see* Life extension (LE)
preservation systems, 329
span, 8, 25, 72, 190, 334
Life extension (LE)
aging, 355–356, 359, 362
cryonics, 360–361
death, perceptions of, 354–355, 362
disease, 355–356, 362
embodiment, conversion of, 361
ethics, 354
immortality, 356, 361
implications of, 15, 353–354
individual concerns, 356–357
medicine, at nanoscale, 359
nanorobotics, 360

Life extension (*Continued*)
  nanotechnicalogically enabled (NLE), 354, 356–359, 361
  social concerns, 357–359
Lifestyle changes, 64, 321
LiftPort Group, 68
Light-emitting diodes (LEDs), 293, 301
Lighting, nanotechnology-based, 64
Lignes d'horizons (Attali), 34
Linn, Patrick, 5, 178, 186
Liquid crystal diodes (LCDs), 293, 300
Literature review, 22–23, 26
Lithography, 293
Local area networks (LANs), 51, 348
Location uncertainty, 156
Longevity, 12, 58, 62–64
Long Now Foundation, 20–21
Long-term nanotechnology, 58, 62, 66
Loop, 125, 127–128, 130
Los Alamos National Laboratory, 66
Lovelock, James, 332
Lovins, Amory, 25–26
Lovins, Hunter, 25
Luddite challenge, 18–20

Machine-phase nanotechnology, 94–95
McCulloch, Warren, 119–120
Machines, intelligent, 18, 24
McKibben, Bill, 49, 76
Macrophages, 151, 153
Mad cow disease, 155, 242
Magic Nano, 216, 220, 222
Magnetoresistance, 72
MAJC, 24
Major revolutions, 92–93, 95
Malaria, 58–59, 62–63, 139, 211
Malnutrition, 165
Malthus, Thomas, 358
Manhattan Project, 32–34, 111
Manipulation, 350
Manufacturing methods, positional assembly, 162–163
Manufacturing processes, 149
Many gods objection, 135
Margin of error, 130
Mars/martians, 326, 329, 340–344
Massachusetts Institute of Technology, Institute for Soldier Nanotechnologies (ISN), 95, 269
Mass destruction, knowledge-enabled, 35–36
Mass production, 87
Materials
  nanostructured, 324
  science, 73, 92–93, 99
Mathematical models, 41

Maurois, André, 125
Maximin principle, 191
Max Planck Institute, 45
Mechanical engineering, 72
Media, impact of, 221–222, 237
Medical, generally
  advances, 6, 14
  data, privacy issues, 260
  engineering, 162
  ethics, 75, 256–257
  field, 52
  nanotechnology, 274
  research, funding for, 102
  science, 48–49
  technology, space systems, 333
  therapy, 173
Medicine, *see* Medical
  access to, 157
  advances in, 62, 73
  nanoparticle-based, 151–152
  at nanoscale, 359
Merkle, Ralph, 50
Metaethical principles, 124
Metals
  alloys, 300–301
  demand for, 299–301
  heavy, 65, 328
  precious, 299
Metaphysics, 125–127, 130
Metaphysics (Aristotle), 32
Mexico, 256
Microarray technologies, 152, 157
Microbivores, 163
Microelectronic mechanical systems (MEMs), 255, 293
Microprocessors, development of, 24
Microrevolutions, 92–94
Middleware, 254
Military technology
  defense system, nano-enabled, 270–271
  ethical issues, 271–274
  types of, 6, 27, 267–269, 274–275
Military-industrial complex, 209
Military Nanotechnology: Potential Applications and Preventive Arms Control (Altmann), 275
Mill, John Stuart, 258
Mind enhancement, 17
Minor revolutions, 92–94
Mize, Scott, 232
Mobile communications, 254
Modeling-evaluation-acting-recording structure, 343–344
Molecular, generally

biotechnology, 293
computing, 149
diversity, 169
electronics, 24, 26–27, 72, 85, 293
manufacturing, *see* Molecular manufacturing
medical devices, 162
modeling, 293
nanomachine systems, 65
nanotechnology (MNT), 53
systems, 149
Molecular manufacturing
    artificial intelligence and, 339–340
    debate, 56
    defined, 312
    exponential, characterized, 312–313
    environmental effects, 320
    future directions for, 319–322
    human enhancement, 320–321
    impact of, 11–14, 53, 163, 232, 262–270,
        309–311, 316, 321
    information resources, 313–315
    materials, 318–319
    nanofactory technology, 318–319
    organizational responses, 316–318
    problems with, 320–321
    prototyping, 320
    regulation of, 321–322
Momentum, 248
Monadology (Leibniz), 341
Monopolies, 259, 303, 319, 328
Moore, Duncan, 82
Moore's law, 12, 24, 85, 94, 203, 254, 328, 340, 347
Moral(s), generally
    autonomy, 260–262
    identification, 261
    importance of, 32
    philosophy, 362
    provisionality, 220–222
    responsibility, 222
    standards, 344–346
    theories, 217, 354
Morality, standards, 344–346
Moral sense theory, 344–345
Moravec, Hans, 19–21, 24–25, 31, 203, 347
Mousepox virus, 202
Multilayer structures, 72
Multinational corporations, 291
Multiscale modeling, 287–288
Myhr, Anne Ingeborg, 153

Naam, Ramez, 187
Nagasaki, 29–30, 111
Nanoaluminum, 270
Nanobioenhancement, 180

Nanobiotechnology, 175, 177, 181–182
Nanobot(s)
    evolving, 329–334
    replication, 47
    technology, 3, 21, 45–47, 50
Nanobusiness, 75
Nano-cognoscenti, 110
Nanocomposites, 301
Nanodebate, 229. *See also* Debates
Nanodivide, 245–246
Nanoelectronics, 85, 138, 141, 143–144
Nano-enabled military, 269–270
Nanoengineered entities, replication of, 53
Nanoenhancement
    characterized, 173–174
    human nature, changes in/to, 174–176, 180–181
    nanoethics, 177–182
    playing God, 173, 177, 179–180
    relational intelligence, 176–177
    types of, 173
Nanoethics
    as distinct discipline, 9–12
    formulation of, 177–178
    issues in, 11–13, 57
    nanoenhancement, 179
    orienting good, 181–182
    playing God, 173, 177–181
    status of, 8–11
Nanofactory technology, 11–12, 210, 313, 316–319,
    329
Nanogenerators, 269
Nanogoos, 203
NanoJury, 242–243
Nanomachines, 62
Nanomachines, 99
Nanomachines
    characterized, 62, 99
    destructive, 203
    self-replicating, 210
Nanomaterials
    adverse effects of, 149
    effects of, generally, 86
    environmental stability of, 152–153
    types of, 6, 11, 13, 268–269
Nanomedicine
    development of, 161–162
    disease, defined, 164–167
    future directions of, 162–163
    human diseases, treatment of, 163–164
    importance of, 21
    volitional normative model of disease, 167–170
Nanoparticle(s)
    adverse effects of, 150–152
    cellular mechanisms of uptake, 151

Nanoparticle(s) (*Continued*)
  environmental stability of, 152–153
  mobility of, 155
  precautionary principle, 143–144
  research and development, 140–141
  revolution, 95
  significance of, 138, 323
  technology, 94
  toxicity, 75
Nanorevolution, 242
Nanorobots/nanorobotics
  medical, 162–164, 360
  self-replicating, 203
Nanorods, 83
Nanoscale
  devices, 41
  research, 10
  robots, 75
  techniques, 33
Nanoscale Informal Science Education (NISE), 281
Nanoscale science and engineering (S&E), 80–81, 83–86
Nanoscale Science and Engineering Centers, 83, 84
Nanoscience
  characterized, 74–75, 149
  conceptual understanding of, 287–288
  funding for, 228
  provisionality and, 220, 223
NanoSense project, 281
Nanospeculation, 178
Nanostructing, 301
Nanotech Schism, 3
Nanotechnologically enabled life extension (NLE), 354, 356–359, 361
Nanotechnologist, 97
Nanotechnology, generally
  advanced forms of, 12, 47–48
  characterized, 5–6
  defined, 293–294
  as distinct discipline, 6–11
  ethical and social issues, overview of, 13–15
  examples of, 44–47
  golden age of, 41
  influential factors, 68
  myths, 26, 72
  revolution, *see* Nanotechnology Revolution
Nanotechnology Researchers Network of Japan, 278
Nanotechnology revolution
  historical perspectives, 91–93
  military developments, 95–97
  nanotechnology defined, 93–94
  perceptions of, 94–95, 97–99
  technological developments, 95–97

Nanotubes, 9, 11, 63, 65, 67–68, 81, 84–85, 299, 301, 323
Nanoweapons, 270–271
Nanowires, 81, 85
National Academy of Science, 209
National Aeronautics and Space Administration (NASA), 59, 67, 327
National Cancer Institute, 87
National Center for Learning and Teaching in Nanoscale Science and Engineering (NCLT), 281
National Economic Council, 82
National Institute for Environmental Health Sciences, 86
National Institute for Occupational Safety and Health, 86
National Institute of Standards and Technology (NIST), 96
National Institutes of Health (NIH), 83, 87, 96
National Nanotechnology Coordination Office, 83, 237
National Nanotechnology Initiative (NNI)
  advocacy for, 80–81
  budget for, 84–86, 92
  development of, 81–84
  educational reform, 278, 281–282
  evolution of, 84
  functions of, 6–7, 14, 84, 85–87
  on industrial revolution, 295
  motivation of, 99, 104
  nanotechnology defined by, 323
  National Toxicology Program, 84
  progress since 2000, 83–84
  stakeholder involvement, 227, 231, 237
National Pollution Prevention, 232
National regulation, 206–208
National Science and Technology Council, 81
National Science Education Standards, 288
National Science Foundation (NSF)
  functions of, 81, 83–84, 92, 96, 278
  National Informal Science Education Network (NISE Network), 233
National security, 85. *See also* Homeland defense; Homeland security
National Space Society, 67
Natural assets, 191
Natural disasters, response to, 66
Naturalistic ethics, 180–181
Natural science, 362
Nature uncertainty, 156
Negative duty, 141–142
Negotiations, regulatory, 227
Neural implants, 46–47, 185

Neurobioinformation and cognitive sciences
  (NBICs), 102–103, 107, 120–121, 185–187,
  189–191
Neurocognitive
  abilities, 182
  augmentation, 173
Neurological disorders, 47
Neuron transistors, 45
Neurophysiology, 293
Neurotechnology, 102
Neville, Robert Cummings, 177
Newberg, Andrew, 175
Next Industrial Revolution, 3
Nietzsche, 32
Nitrogen, 76
Nixon, Richard, 205
Noble, David, 95–96
No Child Left Behind (NCLB) program, 287
Nominal definition, 293
Nonbiological
  intelligence, 47–48
  self-replicating entities, 51
Nongovernmental organizations (NGOs), 71–72, 76,
  207, 209, 228, 231–232, 236, 238, 246, 291
Nongovernment initiatives, 68
Nonlinear systems, 24
Normative dimension, 112–113
North Korea, 205, 207
NOTAGS, 255
Nuclear
  accidents, 211
  energy, 77
  power, 31, 199, 204
  technology, 271
  weapons, *see* Nuclear weapons
  waste management, 211
Nuclear Non-Proliferation Treaty (NPT), 205
Nuclear weapons
  arms race, 30, 32, 110, 316
  discussion of, 36
  nuclear, biological, and chemical (NBC)
    weapons, 21, 28, 32, 34
  threat from, 33
  types of, 82, 204–205
Nucleoside analogues, 152

Observational studies, 157
Observer-participant, 129
Occurring time, 125–128, 130
Office of Management and Budget (OMB), 81
Office of Science and Technology Policy (OSTP),
  82
Office of Technology Assessment, 102, 209

Oil
  consumption, 65
  dependency, 85
  refinement, 299
  spills cleanup, 65, 202
Ongoing normative assessment, 128–130
Ontology, 128
Open innovation, 98
Open societies, 209
Open-source software, 315, 317–318
Opinion, 113
Oppenheimer, J. Robert, 29–30, 111, 204
Optical computing, 271
Optical nanocomputers, 174
Optimism, 36, 71, 215
Optimistic predictions, 12
Optoelectronic devices, 300
Order of life, 29
Orders of magnitude, 270, 299, 319
Organisation for Economic Co-operation and
  Development (OECD), 256–257
Out-of-controlness, 121
Outreach activities, 87, 228
Outsourcing, 98
Overpopulation, 357–358

Pale Blue Dot (Sagan), 28
Pannenberg, Wolfhart, 175
Paradox, precautionary principle, 135, 139–143
Parasitic infections, 165
Parlour game, 126
Participatory democracy, 238
Passports, 193
Patents, 68, 97, 207, 301, 303, 317
Pathogens, bioengineering, 52–53
Pauling, Linus, 111
Peer community, 158
Peer review process, 85
People's Inquiry, 241–242, 244–245
Perez, Carlota, 91–92, 95
Permissive medicine, 169
Personality development, 357
Pervasive computing, 66
Pessimism, 47
Pessimistic predictions, 12
Pesticides, 25
Peterson, Christine, 232
Peterson, Gregory, 176–177
Pettit, Philip, 191
Phagocytes, nanorobotic artificial, 163
Pharmaceuticals, 149, 152, 185
Philips, 255
Philosophers, nanoethics, 181–182

Phoenix, Chris, 232
Photosynthesis
    artificial, 60, 139
    development of in space, 330–331
Photovoltaic (solar)
    cells, 59, 67
    devices, 85, 297
Physical sciences, 144
Physical scientists, functions of, 24
Physical wealth, 236
Physics, solid-state, 93
    picoJava, 24
Piezoelectric nanowires, 269
Pioneer Award, establishment of, 85–86
Pister, Kris, 254
Pitts, Walter, 119–120
Plague, 202
Plato, 181
Pluralism, 77, 188, 193–194
Pneumonia, 202
Policymaking process, 218, 220, 231, 238, 247. *See
    also* Public policy
Politics
    arguments, 249
    deliberative democracy, 223
    human enhancement perceptions, 188–191
    provisionality, 221
    science and technology (S&T) policy, 108
Pollution
    cleansing, 359
    impact of, 203, 294
    space, 325
    types of, 64–65
Polylactide-*co*-glycolide (PLGA), 152
Polylactides, 152
Polymerase chain reaction (PCR), 152
Polymer science, 73, 83
Porter, Roy, 161
Positional assembly, 162–163
Positive duty, 141–142
Poverty/impoverishment, 58, 63, 65, 247, 313
Precautionary principle (PP)
    applications in nanotechnology, 137–138
    benefits of, 133, 136
    characterized, 14, 121–124, 130
    clarification of, 134
    criticisms of, 135, 138–144
    formulations, 134, 136, 145, 153
    national/transnational regulation, 207
    plausible version of, 144–145
    space systems, 330
    uncertainty and, 153–154
Precious metals, 299
Predictability, 105–107, 110

Prediction(s)
    impact of, 86, 114, 340
    precautionary principle, 135, 138–139
Preemptive attack, 128
President's Council of Advisors on Science and
    Technology (PCAST), 82
Preventive war, 128
Prey (Crichton), 233–234, 237, 330
Primary goods, 259
Printing advances, 11–12
Privacy
    debate, 10
    importance of, 11, 14, 253–254, 256–257, 264
    information-based harm, 257–258
    informational equality, 258–259
    informational injustice, 259–260
    invisibility, 262–263
    issues of, generally, 13–14, 34
    legislative concerns, 145
    loss of, 141
    moral autonomy and identity, 260–262
    rights, 49
    threats to, 143–144
Private investments/investors, 84
Probability, 155
Processing chips, 6
Procter & Gamble, 6
Product
    development, 58, 145, 294, 304
    piracy, 302
Productive, generally
    nanosystems, 60–61, 67
    nanotechnology, 65
Profiling, 260
Prognostication, 273
Projected, generally
    equilibria, 128–130
    time, 125–130
Promethean myth, 179, 181
Propaganda, 194
Proprietary
    information, 34, 205, 208
    issues, 10
    knowledge, 302
Prosthetics, 186
Protein folding, 344
Proteomics, 157, 161
Protestant ethic, 187
Prototyping, 320
Public(s)
    anchoring, 234–235
    defined, 230–234
    deliberation, 113
    engagement, 242, 247–248

health issues, 295
organized, 231–232
spheres and, 229–230
vernacular, 232–233
Public policy, 14, 52–53
Public relations, 103
Puerperal fever, 166
Pure science, 77

Quality of life, 25, 64, 149, 358
Quantum computing, 66, 72–73, 85, 293
Quantum dot technology, 60, 73, 81, 83–84, 93–94, 293, 300
Quantum mechanics, 342
Quantum nanocomputers, 174
Quantum physics, 5, 92, 94
Quantum well structures, 73
Quickening technologies, 54

Radical nanotechnology, 73–74, 77
Radio frequency identity devices (RFID) chip technology, 14, 254–257, 260, 263–264
Rawls, John, 259
Real definition, 293
Reasoning skills, 114, 262
Reciprocity, 221
Recycling, 332, 358
Red herring, 126
Reductionism, 166
Reduction to practice, 87
Reed, Mark, 24
Refinement industries, 301
Regulation
    governance, 14, 50–53, 227
    impact of, 51–54
    proactive, 245
    transnational, 203–204
Regulatory agencies, 84
Reiman, Jeffrey, 262
Reinsurance, 86
Religion/religious beliefs, impact of, 186–188. *See also* Protestant ethic; Theology, Christian
Relinquishment, 32–35, 41–42, 49–52, 205–206
Replication/replication codes, 24, 53–54. *See also* Self-replication
Reprogramming, 52
Repugnance, 181
Research
    agenda/priority setting, 106–107
    awards and recognitions, 85–86
    biomedical, 166
    budget for, *see* Budgets/budgeting
    cultural barriers to, 87
    ethics, 89

funding, 84, 87
    halting, 140, 142
    high-risk, 85, 87
    long-term, 85
    moratorium on, 216
    nanosafety-related, 154
    scientific, 209
Research and development (R&D)
    developing countries, 302–303
    global technological regulation, 210
    programs, 103–104, 107
Resource management, 358
Respirocyte, 163
Responsibility, 243–244
Reverse engineering, 210
Reversibility, human enhancements, 195
Rhodes, Richard, 30
Risk(s)
    adversity, 327
    apocalyptic, 206
    assessment, 75, 86, 157–158
    aversion, 135, 137, 153
    balance of, 52
    hypothetical, 122
    management, 77
    perceptions of, 77
    potential, 122
    types of, 27–28, 32, 47, 58, 109, 122–123, 134–135, 145, 211
Risk-benefit calculation, 204
Risk-cost-benefit analysis, 154
Robinson, Daniel, 333–334
Robot: Mere Machine to Transcendent Mind, "The Short Run" (Moravec), 19–20
Robots/robotic technology, *see* Nanorobots
    characterized, 18, 21, 48, 99
    humans merging with, 18–20
    immortality through, 35
    intelligent, 17–18, 25
    killer, 203–204
    nanoscale, 271
    precautionary principle, 133
    research, 19
    self-replicating, 33, 75, 142–144
    shields from, 31–32
Roco, Mike, 81
Rogue states, 205
Rohrbacher, Dana, 236
Roukes, Michael, 87
Royal Academy of Engineering, 241, 245
Royal Society, 241, 245
Rules of engagement, 241, 247–248

Safety issues, 25, 243
Sagan, Carl, 28
St. Augustine, 181
Salvation, 175
Sanctions, international, 207
Sarewitz, Daniel, 103–105
SARS, 62, 202, 206
Sartre, Jean-Paul, 126
Satellites, 66
Savaage, Leonard, 122
Scanning probes, 163, 318
Scenario approach, 125–130
Schummer, Joachim, 292–293, 295
Science(s)
    of the future, 130
    global technology regulations, 210–211
Science and technology (S&T) governance
    characterized, 102–104
    deliberations, 110–113
    influences on, 108
    pragmatic synthesis, 113–114
    research investment, 109
    strategic dimension of, 107–110
Science fiction, nanotechnology compared with,
        13–14, 17, 22, 72, 93, 203
Scientific medicine, 161–162
Scientism, 248–249
Searle, John, 35
Secure information, 49
Security, see Surveillance
    development of, 359
    international, 271–272
    issues, 12–13
    molecular manufacturing and, 317
Self-assemblers, 121, 140
Self-contradiction, 129
Self-image, 344
Self-model of artificial intelligence, 343
Self-organization, 119–120
Self-perception, 192
Self-presentation, 261
Self-preservation, 32
Self-referentiality, 129
Self-refutation, 130
Self-regulation, 204
Self-replicating
    impact of, 21–22, 27–28, 33, 42–43, 47–51, 75,
        83, 121, 143–144
    manufacturing system, 52
    nanomachines, 137, 330
    nanotechnology entities, 54
    technologies, threat of, 201–204
"Self-Replication: Even Peptides Do It"
    (Kauffman), 27–28

Self-unfulfilling prophecies, 139
Semantics, 10
Semiconductors, 60, 293, 299
Senescence, 355
SenGupta, Arup, 296
Senility, 165
Sensing devices, 143
Sensors, types of, 193, 254, 270, 293
Sepsis/septic shock, 163
Serotonin levels, 192
Shared virtual-reality environment, 45
Shields, construction of, 31–32
Short-term nanotechnology, 58–59, 62
"Significance of the Frontier in American History"
    (Turner), 327
Silicon, 163
Simulations, 169, 334
Singularity, 174
Singulatarians, 347–348
Small Business Innovation Research (SBIR), 87
Small Business Technology Transfer Programs, 87
Smalley, Richard, 72, 82
Smallpox, 202, 206
Smart dust, 45
Social, generally
    assets, 191
    engineering, 327
    ethics, 182
    issues, 10
    justice, 358–359
    responsibility, 226
    sciences, 144
    systems, influential factors, 189–190
    theory, 216–220, 222–223
    value, 191
Socioeconomic conditions, impact of, 260–261,
        291, 313
Software
    computer-aided design (CAD), 319
    development, 23–24
    reliability of, 24, 36
    viruses, 41, 46, 50–52
Soil contamination, 65
Solar, generally
    cells, 293, 300
    energy, 59–60, 83, 94, 297
    panel technology, 60
Soulechtomy, 176
Sousveillance, 264
Soviet Union, see Communism
    bioweapons program, 202
    collapse of, 212
    nuclear arms race, 30
    nuclear attack by, 31

Space
  development, 58, 66–68
  elevator, 68
  ethics, 10
  exploration, 6, 14, 66, 68, 86
  management, 358
  systems/settlements, *see* Space
    systems/settlements
  travel, 22, 31
Spacecraft innovations, 67–68
Space Shuttle, 329
Space systems/settlements
  arguments against, 325–327
  characterized, 12–13, 68, 323–324, 334
  Crew Exploration Vehicle (CEV), 329
  Crew Launch Vechicle (CLV), 329
  ecosystem, 326–327
  enhancements for survival, 330–334
  extraterrestrial communities, 324
  Gaian philosophy, 332
  Mir space station, 325
  nanobots, evolving, 329–334
  nanoparticle toxicity, 329–330
  need for, 327–329
  orbit, price of, 323–324
Spain, 256
SPARC, 24
Spin doctors, 238
Spin-offs, 87
Spintronics, 85
SPL7013, 298
Spoofing, 247
Spy nanobots, 47
Stagnation, 356–357
Stakeholders/stakeholding
  geographical anomalies, 235–236
  nanostakes, 227–228
  origins, 225–226
  popular culture, 234–235
  Prey analogy, 233–234, 237
  publics, 229–233, 234–235
  purpose of participation, 238
  rationale for participation, 228–229
  recommendations, 236–238
  role of, 226–227
  spheres, 229–230
  support for, 289
Standard of living, 85, 102
Stanford Research Institute, 226
Start-up companies, 84, 87
Steam turbines, efficiency of, 74
Stem cell therapy, 361
Stephenson, Neal, 94
Steroids, 186, 192–193

Stimson, Amy, 208
Stone, Irving, 23
Stone Age, 268
Strategic Arms Reduction Treatises, 205
Strategic Defense Initiative, 31
Streptococcus, 166
Stroke, 163
Subjective probability, 122
Subsidies, 113
Sudan, 207
Suicide, 168
Sunscreens, 73, 140, 153, 285
Sunstein, Cass, 219–220
Supercollider, 231
Supercomputers, 321
Superfund, 211
Supramolecular chemistry, 293
Surgery
  nanomedical applications, 163
  sexual reassignment, 192–194
Surveillance
  computer-assisted, 50
  devices, 8
  global, 208–209
  invisible, 255
  network, 321
  technology, 10, 45, 57, 108, 199, 254
  universal, 262
Surveys, on stakeholding, 230–231, 233
Survival, global, 212
Synderesis, 181
Synthetic(s)
  chemistry, 323
  nanorobots, 75
  nanotechnology, 74
Systems of Survival (Jacobs), 314

Tahan, Charles, 91, 93, 94
Taniguchi, Norio, 7
Tautology, 130
Taverne, Lord, 248
Technoeconomic
  paradigms, 92
  revolution, 97
Technological advances
  benefits of, 149
  impact of, 3–5, 47–48, 83
  motivation for, 49
Technological development, global bans on, 108
Technological revolution
  characterized, 14, 58, 92, 101–102
  hierarchy of, 87, 92–93
Technological Revolutions and Financial Capital
    (Perez), 91

Technology regulation, global, 201–212
Telecosm, 17
Teleological definition, 293
Telephone conversations, surveillance of, 50
Teller, Edward, 29, 204
Telos, 193–194
Tennis elbow, 165
Terrorism/terrorist
  applications, 27, 273
  attacks (9/11), 50–51, 212
Tesco, 255
Textbooks, educational reform and, 278–280
"The Grasshopper, Aristotle, Bob Adams, and Me"
  (Kagan), 333
Theology, Christian, 175–176, 181–182
"There's Plenty of Room at the Bottom" (Feynman),
  26, 72, 80–81
Think tanks, 102
THONG, 228
Thoreau, 34
Thought experiments, 13
Threats
  precautionary principle, 134–136, 142–144
  seriousness of, 144
  types of, 201–204, 212
3-D printers, 11–12
Tinker, Robert, 286
Tipping points, 123
Tissue engineering, 149, 293
Titanium dioxide, 73, 84
Toothpastes, 153
Totalitarian governments, 328
Toxic gases, 65
Toxicity, 75, 84, 94, 151, 154
Toxicology, 77
Trade Related Intellectual Property Rights (TRIPs),
  302–303
Trade unions, 209
Transformative technology, 218, 313
Transgender technologies, 186
Transhumanism/transhumanist movement, 72, 76–77
Transhuman technologies, 169, 188
Transnational
  agencies, importance of, 211–212
  agreements, 205, 207
  regulation, 206–209
Transparency, 33, 157, 191, 262–263
Treder, Mike, 232
Trinity test, 29, 33, 111, 204
Truth-seeking, 32
Tsiolkovsky, Konstantin, 325
Tuberculosis, 63, 211
Tunnel vision, 139
Turing, Alan, 176

Turing Test, 176, 340–341
Turner, Frederick Jackson, 327, 334
Turning point, revolution patterns, 95
Tyranny, 259

UNAIDS, 298
*Unbounding the Future: The Nanotechnology
  Revolution* (Drexler), 26
Uncertainty
  identification and systematization of,
    155–156
  impact of, 14, 121–124, 130, 220, 272
  radical, 125
  raising awareness of, 154–156
  risk and, 153–156
Unchaining, 121
Understanding-decision-control (u-d-c) formula, 178
United Kingdom (U.K.)
  Department for Environment, Food and Rural
    Affairs, 245
  Environment Agency, 241, 244
United Nations (UN), *see* United Nations
    Educational, Scientific and Technology
    Education Organization (UNESCO)
  Baruch Plan, 30
  Development Program (UNDP), 292
  functions of, 64, 206–207, 211, 273
  Industrial Development Organization (UNIDO),
    291
  Millennium Goals, 304
  Security Council, 207
United Nations Educational, Scientific and
    Technology Education Organization
    (UNESCO)
  developing countries and, 291, 297
  Integrated Science and Technology Education
    program, 286
Solar Electricity for Rural Areas and the Solar
    Village Programme, 297
United States
  Bioshield initiative, 206
  Department of Agriculture, 26, 255
  Department of Defense (DOD), 83, 95
  Department of Health and Human Services
    (HHS), Cancer Nanotech Plan, 63
  government, spending in nanotechnology, 6–7
U.S. Congressional testimony on Societal
    Implications of Nanotechnology
  abridged written testimony, 44–54
  verbal testimony, 40–44
U.S. Department of Energy (DOE)
  functions of, 60
  Nanoscale Science Research Centers, 84
  Office of Science, 96

U.S. Food and Drug Administration (FDA), 255
U.S. National Cancer Institute, 63
Universal Declaration on Bioethics and Human Rights, 304
University centers, 102
University of California at Berkeley, Center for Interedisciplinary Bio-Inspiration in Education and Research (CIBER), 7
University of Toronto, Joint Centre for Bioethics, 291
Unix, 23
Unlimited sum, 315
Unpredictability, 104–107, 110, 123, 156–157
Upstream public engagement, 242, 248–249
Uranium, 328
Utopia/Utopian environment, 18, 26, 34–35, 333
UV radiation, 331

Vaccines
    development of, 58, 66
    global regulation, 206
    as human enhancement, 187
    nanoparticle-based, 152
    pandemics, 211
Value
    judgments, 114
    system, 32
Van den Hoven, Jeroen, 257, 259–261
Vegetarianism (vegans), 332
Venture capital (VC), 87, 98, 228
Verichip, 255–256
Vest, Chuck, 83
vi, 23
Viral weapons, 202
Virtual reality, 45–46, 333
Viruses
    detection of, 64
    genetically engineered, 83
    nanomedical treatments, 163
Visions of Technology (Rhodes), 30
Visual analogies, 119–120
Vitalism, 341, 344
von Neumann, John, 119–120, 123
von Neumann probes, 31

Walzer, Michael, 259
Warfare
    Ancient Greece, 272–273
    Cold War, 272
    Iraq War, 212
    military technology, 267–275
Waste processing, 295
W&H framework, 155–156

Water
    consumption, 61
    detoxification, 86
    purification, 62, 68, 86, 296–297
    shortage, 61
Water-borne illness, 61
Watson, Thomas, 138–139
Watson-Crick base-pairing, 28
Wealth
    accumulation, 92
    creation, 77
    distribution, 189
Weaponry, *see* development of, 57
    types of, 316
    weapons of mass destruction (WMDs), 21–22, 33–34, 45, 205
Well-being, influential factors, 180, 182, 194
Whistleblowing, 34
White Plague, The (Herbert), 21
"Why the Future Doesn't Need Us" (Joy), 41, 82–83
Wi-Fi, 254
Williams, Stan, 82
Wilsdon, James, 75, 76, 189
Wireless
    connections, 300
    local area networks, 46
Wolfram, Stephen, 24
Wolpe, Paul, 176
Women's health, AIDS prevention strategies, 298
Woodrow Wilson
    Center for International Scholars, 86
    -Pew Emerging Technologies, 237
World Health Organization
    functions of, 206
    Global Outbreak Alert and Response Network, 208
World Intellectual Property Organization and the General Agreement on Tariffs and Trade (GATT), 207
World Trade Organization (WTO)
    Agreement on Sanitary and Phytosanitary Measures, 206
    functions of, 207, 302
Worldview, influential factors, 112

Xenon, 81
X-ray diffraction spectrometer, 67

Young, Iris Marion, 218

Zeptogram, 83
Zerhouni, Elias, 85
ZnS, 268